EXPERIENCING
Race, Class, and Gender
in the United States

EXPERIENCING
Race, Class, and Gender
in the United States

VIRGINIA CYRUS
Rider College

MAYFIELD PUBLISHING COMPANY
Mountain View, California
London ✦ Toronto

Library of Congress Cataloging-in-Publication Data

Cyrus, Virginia
    Experiencing race, class, and gender in the United States /
    Virginia Cyrus.
      p. cm.
    Includes index.
    ISBN 1-55934-125-4
    1. United States—Social conditions—1980- 2. United States—Race
relations. 3. Social classes—United States. 4. Pluralism (Social
sciences)—United States. 5. Women—United States. 6. Gays—United
States. 7. Discrimination—United States. I. Title.
HN59.2.C97   1992
305'.0973—dc20   92-24205
                                            CIP

Manufactured in the United States of America

10 9 8 7 6 5 4 3 2 1

MAYFIELD PUBLISHING COMPANY
1240 Villa Street
Mountain View, California 94041

Sponsoring editor, Franklin C. Graham; *production editor,* Lynn Rabin Bauer;
manuscript editor, Betsy Dilernia; *text and cover designer,* Terri Wright; *cover
art,* Carlos Almaraz, *Love Makes the City Crumble,* 1983. Oil on canvas, 66 × 66".
Photo courtesy of the Jan Turner Gallery, © of the Almaraz Estate; *manufacturing
manager,* Martha Branch. The text was set in 10/11 Garamond by G&S Typesetters
and printed on 50# Finch Opaque by Banta Company.

Page 11, copyright © 1981 by Houghton Mifflin Co., adapted and reprinted by
permission from *The American Heritage Dictionary of the English Language.*

Acknowledgments and copyrights continue at the back of the book on pages 445–
450, which constitute an extension of the copyright page.

Contents

v

Power 185

PART X   *Change Makers*   418

PREFACE

A new awareness of our diversity as a people is the acknowledged reality of the United States in the 1990s. Students in college now will live and work in a society that is multicultural and global, and college must prepare them for this world. *Experiencing Race, Class, and Gender in the United States* provides an initial step toward that end, offering students the opportunity to explore the complexity of American society and its historic, social, and economic makeup. This book focuses on the United States because students need to have a better understanding of their own society before they can begin to understand and effectively interact with other cultures. The book also demonstrates that no single "norm" represents the American experience; instead, many points of view and wide varieties of experience exist, and always have existed, in this country. *Experiencing Race, Class, and Gender in the United States* introduces the basic issues of American multiculturalism and diversity and examines the many difficult and highly politicized questions posed by such complexity.

To wrestle with such questions, students first need to develop an enhanced sense of their own identities and life situations and a positive understanding of the experiences and values of the many different groups that make up contemporary American society. In order to experience differences among groups with understanding and appreciation, and not with fear and rancor, students need to be encouraged to foster empathy for the perspectives of those who seem different from themselves and to acknowledge the many similarities that are often overlooked.

This book is organized into three main divisions: "Identity" (Parts I–IV), "Power" (Parts V–VIII), and "Change" (Parts IX and X). The first division, "Identity," requires students to examine their own lives and those of others in order to understand how everyone's identity is shaped by the experience of race, ethnicity, gender, and socio-economic class and how group stereotypes affect individual identity.

The anthology moves from questions of individual identity to an exploration of the institutional forces that exert power over everyone. This second main division,

"Power," examines the important connections between social forces and individuals and groups to promote an understanding of the kinds of challenges and structural obstacles that prejudice and discrimination create. The readings probe the issues of structural discrimination and power—specifically the dynamics of racism, sexism, and heterosexism. The selections provide personal testimony, historical background, data from law and the social sciences, and analytical discussions of how power and discrimination operate in American life.

People who have not critically examined the inequities of American society previously may feel a combination of anger, frustration, and even despair when they first confront such knowledge. Thus, the third main division, "Change," shows students how they can direct this emotional energy to improving the social order by acting on their own new-found awareness. Part IX, "Taking Action," outlines concrete, step-by-step strategies for effecting personal change and initiating collective social action. Finally, the book closes as it began, with individual experiences: Part X, "Change Makers," introduces some very ordinary people who have succeeded, often at great personal cost, to effect real social change.

Experiencing Race, Class, and Gender in the United States grew out of a five-year effort at Rider College to respond to the demographic realities of this nation as we move into the twenty-first century. Starting in 1987, we evaluated our curriculum to determine its inclusiveness. Although we found that it addressed diversity more fully than we had anticipated, we also felt that much more work needed to be done. Thus, with funding from the New Jersey Department of Higher Education, we implemented a comprehensive faculty development program. In addition to the more conventional tactic of revising traditional courses, we formed an interdisciplinary faculty team to create a course on the diversity of American cultures for first-year and second-year students. This book is a direct outgrowth of that effort, and it has been tested in draft form in multiple sections of our course.

The team decided that understanding such complex concepts as power, racism, and sexual harassment required the insights of many disciplines. Accordingly, the interdisciplinary approach of this book provides a broad, integrative perspective on these issues. *Experiencing Race, Class, and Gender in the United States* incorporates three kinds of sources: individual stories, both literary and biographical; compilations of information and data from sociology, psychology, history, and communications; and analytical pieces from a number of disciplines. The readings range from straightforward journalistic articles to literary works to complex analyses of data. The authors represent both genders as well as the broad spectrum of ethnicities, cultures, and classes that make up the population in the United States. Their contributions appear throughout the book to demonstrate both that race and racism are not just "black and white" and that everyone has gender and class identities.

The introductions to the three main divisions and the ten parts provide a context for the readings, identifying the major concerns and issues and defining important theoretical terms (which are highlighted by bold-face type). Notes follow some of the readings to explain references that may be unfamiliar to students. Every selection is followed by a set of questions, "Understanding the Reading," to aid comprehension and to stimulate critical thinking about the issues the selection raises, and by "Suggestions for Responding," writing topics and activities to encourage personal exploration of the issues. Finally, each of the three main divisions and the ten parts ends with suggestions for additional activities such as field or library research, individual and group projects, and life-experience exercises.

The *Instructor's Resource Guide* will enable faculty from different disciplines to use this book. In addition to offering ideas about ways to approach the anthology, it suggests additional activities and provides a compilation of relevant audio-visual materials and recommendations for further reading.

Acknowledgments

I wish to acknowledge the assistance of many people in the creation and preparation of *Experiencing Race, Class, and Gender in the United States* and the instructor's manual. The book rests on the foundation of theory and analysis created by the pioneers in Women's Studies and Ethnic Studies, to whom I am profoundly beholden. I am equally indebted to the collaborative efforts of a number of my colleagues at Rider College. During the five years I worked on curriculum integration with Anne Law, Carol Nicholson, Mary Pinney, and Lise Vogel, I benefited from their insight, creativity, and good humor, which this book reflects in many ways.

I am deeply indebted to my collaborators, who invested hundreds of hours developing, teaching, and evaluating Rider College's interdisciplinary course on race, class, gender, and ethnicity in America. Many of the best reading selections and original and effective assignments come from these associates and dear friends—Bosah Ebo, Joseph Gowaskie, Anne Law, and Sandra Stein. I cannot thank them enough for their creative insights and thoughtful suggestions.

I give special thanks to the students who shared their responses to the course and the book; to Rider's associate provost, Phyllis Frakt, who provided continuing support for all phases of these projects; to Rider librarian Kathryn Holden, who could trace the most obscure source for me; to Arlene Wilner of Rider, Caryn McTighe Musil of the Association of American Colleges, and Paula Rothenberg of the New Jersey Project for their expert reviews of the manuscript and their invaluable suggestions for revision; and to Rider College for granting me a year-long sabbatical to prepare this book. Thanks also go to Katherine Anne Ackley, University of Wisconsin—Stevens Point; Robert Blair, The University of Wooster; Mary E. Galvin, State University of New York at Albany; Emma R. Gross, University of Utah; Michael P. Johnson, Pennsylvania State University; Keith M. Kilty, Ohio State University; Gail Thoen, University of Minnesota; and Shirley J. Yee, University of Washington, who provided the reviews for Mayfield.

My appreciation also goes to Mayfield Publishing Company for early encouragement of this project; to Franklin Graham, who shared my belief in the need for an interdisciplinary book like this; to Lynn Rabin Bauer for her invaluable guidance and support during production; to Pamela Trainer, permissions editor; and to my copy editor, Betsy Dilernia, whose empathy and perceptiveness have made this a better book.

Last, but far from least, I thank my family for their encouragement and active involvement in this project—Cynthia, who proofread the manuscript; Liesl, who spent a summer as my courier and library legs; and John, who shopped, cleaned, read and reread the manuscript, and in general served as my man Friday. Thank you all.

EXPERIENCING
Race, Class, and Gender
in the United States

The America* that existed at the time most of us were born is a far cry from the America in which we live today and will live in our future. Two generations ago, most people thought of the "typical" American as being white and middle-class, speaking English, and living in a nuclear family where father, the "head of the household," went off to the office every day, while mother shopped, cleaned, and made brownies. This image rested on some degree of truth: In 1950, white English speakers dominated all social institutions, and 78% of all households consisted of married-couple families. However, even then this country was more diverse than these facts would suggest.

Experiencing Race, Class, and Gender in the United States

Few of these characteristics represent American reality today. We are now conscious of the rainbow that tints the skins of typical Americans, if for no other reason than the fact that one out of every four of us now define ourselves as Hispanic or nonwhite. Moreover, the nuclear family is disappearing: One out of every two or three marriages ends in divorce, and more and more unmarried women who get pregnant keep their babies. As a result, more than one-quarter of all families with children under age 18 are headed by unmarried females, and married couples comprise little more than half of all households.

Gender roles, especially women's, also have changed during our lifetime, as women have streamed into the workplace. In the years following World War II, fewer than one-third of all women were in the labor force, but today more than half of all women and more than two-thirds of women between ages 25 and 54 work outside the home. In 1950, only 12% of women with children under age 6 were employed, but by 1985 more than half were.

As dramatic as these shifts seem, the future is likely to reflect even greater change. By the early part of the next century, it is projected that white males will account for fewer than 10% of new entrants into the workforce. Women starting or returning to work will account for two-thirds of the growth in employment, with

*"America" is used in this book in the vernacular sense, referring to the United States; it is not intended to detract from or dismiss the many other cultures and citizens of the Western Hemisphere.

minority and immigrant males accounting for most of the rest. Finally, by the middle of the next century, the average American will no longer be a non-Hispanic white.

This book is designed to both enhance our understanding of American society and American culture and help us prepare for life in our changing future. The book rests on several assumptions. First, an awareness of the diversity of our society is essential for all of us as we face the future; we can adapt better to what we know and understand than to the unfamiliar or unknown.

The second assumption is that there is no single American experience; America is composed of many subgroups. This is why we begin by examining our individual and shared identities. In the first division, "Identity," we look at racial and ethnic heritages, gender, socioeconomic class, and current cultural stereotypes as factors that directly affect identity.

Each of us has an individual identity, but we are also part of the larger community and are affected by the social attitudes and beliefs of that community, especially those relating to the various subgroups to which we belong. Because these various groups are thought of and treated differently, not everyone benefits equally from the privileges and advantages of society. In the second division, "Power," we examine how racist and sexist social convictions serve the interests of the powerful, and disadvantage and oppress the powerless.

Finally, we assume that an awareness of the social forces that influence all of us makes it possible to shape and control their effects. Anyone, acting individually or in a group, can bring about social change, as we see in the third division, "Change." Before we get to these major themes, let's consider several general issues.

Names and Labels

In order to talk about social subgroups, we need to be able to name them appropriately. For instance, at what age does a male become a "man" instead of a "boy," and when does a "woman" stop being a "girl"? When, if ever, is it appropriate to call her a "lady"? What is the correct title for the person who runs a meeting—chairman, chairwoman, chairperson, or just plain chair? Some people consider the issue of names and language trivial, but what we are called and what we call ourselves powerfully influence our sense of self and the way others view us.

"What's in a name?" Shakespeare asked, going on to assert that "a rose by any other name would smell as sweet." In the context of this book, however, one can scarcely underestimate the significance of group labels. For instance, how do we identify "nonwhite" people? That word itself is problematic in its implication that white is the standard one either meets or fails to meet. Similarly, "minority" gives "majority" status to whites, who, while making up the greater proportion of American society, actually are in the minority globally. The label "third world people" assumes that whites populate a "first world," which implies hierarchical superiority. However, the term does have the advantage of expressing a commonality of American minorities with the majority of all people in the world, and suggests the oppression they all have suffered at white people's hands. "People of color" seems to be the current preference, but it does imply that white is not a color. Moreover, it is a peculiarly western European and American term, since an Asian Indian and an African would not think of distinguishing themselves as "a person of color."

Specific names for people from Africa, Asia, and South and Central America are equally problematic. A century ago, Americans of African descent were casually referred to by an offensive, derogatory term; in more polite company, they were called "colored people" (as in the National Association for the Advancement of Colored People, founded in 1909) or "Negroes" (as in the National Negro Business League, founded in 1900). During the civil rights movement, they declared themselves to be "blacks" and asserted that "Black is beautiful." Since then they have called themselves first "Afro-American" and most recently "African-American." Each name change represents a shift in the way the group sees itself and is seen by others.

The same holds true for other American minority groups. The U.S. Census Bureau lumps together as "Hispanic" people from quite different backgrounds solely on the basis of the language they speak: Spanish. This label excludes many immigrants from Central and South America simply because they speak Portuguese, French, or indigenous or other languages; and it conceals the reality that one can be both a Hispanic and a person of color. Hispanic peoples may prefer to be known as Latins, Latinas/os, Spanish-Americans, Latin Americans, or *La Raza*. Some identify themselves by more specific labels, such as Mexican-American, Mex-American, or Chicana/o (an identity that grew out of the civil rights movement). Others consider themselves to be Cuban or Cuban-American; Puerto Rican, Puerto Rican-Americans or Newyorican; or Caribbean-, Dominican-, Haitian-American, and so on.

Similarly, the label "Asian-American," formerly "Oriental," includes peoples from at least nineteen distinct groups who actually represent very different cultures and social arrangements. Think about how much a Bengali has in common with a Mongolian, for example, or a Sri Lankan with a Japanese. The same is true of "Native Americans." (Or are they "American Indians"?) They see themselves as members of distinct nations and usually prefer to be called by those names, such as Shoshone, Kiowa, Apache, Chickasaw, Seminole, or Navajo.

How, then, do we know what to call one another? Probably the best rule is to call people what they want to be called, but even this is less than a perfect solution because preferences change, and even within a given group there is often disagreement rather than consensus about the implications of the alternative labels. In this book, we use the terms African-American and black interchangeably, and we do not capitalize color designations. In discussing the individual reading selections, we try to use the ethnic terminology that the author uses. Not everyone will agree with these language choices, however, and we acknowledge that they certainly are debatable.

Theories About Diversity and Group Interaction

In addition to considering appropriate labels for the various American subgroups, we need to explore how the groups interact with one another and how they fit into the totality of American culture. Whether our ancestors came across a land bridge 10,000 years ago, were on the Mayflower, survived the Middle Passage on a slave ship or endured steerage, or whether we just arrived, all Americans originated somewhere else. Where each of us or our ancestors came from affects not just who we are individually, but what America is.

Three theories have been proposed to explain the impact that heterogeneous immigrant cultures have had on one another and on the American way of life. The **assimilation theory** argues that American culture demands that new arrivals become absorbed into the dominant culture, that they assimilate. According to this theory, early European immigrants, in particular Protestants from England, created a society that reflected their roots. As new immigrants arrived or were transported here, as in the case of Africans, and as the native populations lost power and autonomy, all were forced to discard the unique features of their former cultures and adopt the values and norms of the European-American culture. Even today, many people believe that current immigrants must assimilate in order to survive here.

Another theory rejects the idea of British or even European supremacy and describes America as a melting pot. According to the **melting pot theory,** all the various heritages have influenced one another, blending together to create a unique American culture in which no group or single set of values is dominant. Everyone is equally American.

Today, many people consider America to be multicultural. The **multiculturalism theory** views American culture as a combination of many subsocieties. Multiculturalism claims that each group retains some of its customs and traditions, that these are accepted as valid and valuable, and that all groups coexist. This is obviously an overly optimistic picture of our society, but like the other two theories, it does contain elements of truth. We are *not* all alike or assimilated, and it is obvious that some groups and values dominate American culture while others are marginalized, devalued, or repressed. Nonetheless, we must learn to live with our differences.

Any theory is, of necessity, an abstraction. A **theory** is simply a systematic way of organizing knowledge so that it explains a variety of occurrences. However, no single theory can adequately account for all specific, real experiences. In general, a combination of the three theories is needed to describe American society realistically. Clearly, European-Americans played a central role in establishing American social institutions that did serve their interests. While other groups have been shaped and controlled by these institutions, we cannot ignore the ways in which these "others" have helped to shape social policies and practices as well. Although we all influence and are influenced by the larger society, we cannot fully escape our distinctive heritages either.

Sociopolitical Positions

Recently, some people have expressed the worry that recognition of the multicultural dimension of our society results in a devaluation or destruction of traditional values. According to these people, ethnic, racial, and gender perspectives distort and may even corrupt America's cultural and intellectual traditions. They are worried that advocates of the inclusion of these nontraditional perspectives are intolerant extremists advocating a radical program. They claim that supporters of diversity demand that everyone comply with their "politically correct" program. What is ironic about this position is that these people advocate a single perspective, the traditional one, while multiculturalists value diversity and feel that examining society and ideas from multiple perspectives, including the traditional one, enhances and enriches our lives, our society, and our understanding of the world.

There are less emotionally charged words than political "correctness" or "incorrectness" to describe the various positions people take on social issues. Political scientists see social views as running along a continuum between two extremes: reactionary, opposition to any change or progress, and radical, support of extreme change. In between are conservatives, who want to maintain the status quo, and liberals, who favor progress and reform. These positions are also more informally called right wing, the reactionaries and conservatives, and left wing, the liberals and radicals. Regardless of where we position ourselves on the political spectrum, this book raises issues that we need to consider and debate with an open mind.

Ideological Principles

Each position reflects a different response to the traditional ideology of our culture. An **ideology** is a system of assumptions, theories, and beliefs characterizing a particular group or culture; the system supports and reinforces political, social, and economic arrangements. Three ideological tenets of traditional American culture are relevant to our interests here, and all three have at one time or another been challenged by those who are disadvantaged by their consequent prejudices.

The first ideological principle is **Eurocentricity,** the assumption of the supremacy of European-Americans and their values and traditions. For example, like most Europeans, most Americans are Judeo-Christian monotheists (believers in one god). These people tend to belittle such Asian religions as Hinduism and Shinto that worship multiple gods or gods in many forms. Most Americans also value the European principles of objectivity and scientific methodology and believe that verifiable truth can be established by measurement of physical phenomena and confirmed by repeatable experiments. Many European-Americans also tend to devalue mysticism, like the beliefs of many Native Americans and several Asian cultures that unseen, intangible spiritual forces animate and influence the natural world and human interactions with it.

The second ideological principle is that traditional American culture is a **patriarchy,** a hierarchical system of social organization in which structures of power, value, and culture are male-dominated. Under patriarchy, men are seen as "natural" heads of households, Presidential candidates, corporate executives, college presidents, etc. Women, on the other hand, are men's subordinates, playing such supportive roles as housewife, mother, nurse, and secretary. As we all know, this position has been under serious attack during the past two decades.

The third important principle of American ideology is the belief in **capitalism,** the economic system characterized by private ownership of property and free enterprise, with its accompanying emphasis on profits and competition. An important feature of this system in the context of this book is that it results in an inequitable distribution of resources, and in times of economic downturn can lead to poverty in the midst of wealth. Our culture, which holds each individual responsible for his or her own welfare, contrasts with cultures that make priorities of cooperation and mutual responsibility, as some Native American communities do.

The unique multiple-dimensionality of America that gives our country its rich texture has also left us a heritage of divisiveness and inequity. All three ideological principles have been used to rationalize **prejudice,** negative attitudes about certain groups of people, and to justify **discrimination,** actions that flow from those prejudices and disadvantage members of "other" groups. Eurocentric prejudice and discrimination result in **racism,** the subordination of certain groups of people based on their origins and physical characteristics. Patriarchal values lead to **sexism,** the subordination of women and the assumption of the superiority of men solely on the basis of sex. The **classism** that our capitalist society fosters stigmatizes poor and working-class people and their cultures and assigns high status to the affluent and their culture solely because of their relative wealth.

As mentioned before, each of these ideological beliefs has been challenged by individuals acting alone or organized for united action. Racism has been under siege throughout much of our history, from the abolitionist crusade in the nineteenth century through the civil rights movement of the 1950s and 1960s, to current activism by such groups as the National Association for the Advancement of Colored People and the Southern Poverty Law Center. From suffragists to modern **feminists,** advocates of equality between the sexes and of the value of females, women and some men have struggled to combat the sexism in our society. Likewise, classism has been challenged by social reformers, labor unions, and Marxist socialists. Efforts by all these activists teach us that we don't have to resign ourselves to life in a society we think could be improved.

This book is intended to increase our awareness and understanding of the complexities of American society and culture. The readings have been selected to help us get inside the lives, minds, and hearts of the many peoples of America, so we can appreciate their interests, values, and concerns. The various authors speak in many distinctive voices, but despite their diversity they reveal common themes that connect us as members of American society. Some voices will sound familiar and speak to our background, values, and experiences. Others may seem alien and will challenge us, as the saying goes, to walk a mile in another's moccasins. Collectively they will help us gain insight into who we are and what has shaped our identity. The readings will also enhance both our understanding of some of our social problems and our appreciation of the rich diversity of American life.

Who are you? The way you answer this question depends on many factors, not the least of which is the context in which it is asked. Most frequently—meeting a professor, for instance—you give your full name, but when you arrive at your dorm, you might instead respond that you are the new roommate. At a big family reunion with lots of relatives you've never met, you might identify yourself as Stan and Ruth's daughter. Think about the many other ways you could respond. "I'm a college student." "I'm an economics major." "I'm a big fan of yours." "I'm your new neighbor." "I'm Tony's spouse." "I'm Puerto Rican." "I'm the place kicker." "I'm the baby-sitter." "I'm a New Yorker." "I'm an American." The list is almost endless.

Identity

In fact, you are all these things. Your individual identity is a unique blend of the many aspects of your life. These elements include your gender, your age, your placement in your family, your religion and your devotion to it, your race, your ethnic heritage and how (or even whether) your family has preserved it, your sexual orientation and experience, your education, your employment history, your socioeconomic background. What else would you add?

Identity incorporates both the set of personal characteristics by which an individual is recognizable and those that define one's affiliation with a group. American culture puts considerable emphasis on the former. From Daniel Boone to Rambo, we make heroes of the nonconforming loner who acts independently, often in opposition to or defiance of society. Advertisers suggest that using their products will set us apart from the crowd and demonstrate our unique individuality.

This view of identity seems to make some sense, in that some psychologists suggest that a personal sense of identity begins when a child first recognizes his or her mother as a separate being, who in turn recognizes the child as an individual. From there, however, we go through innumerable developmental stages, as we perceive and accept or reject the values and distinctions established by our particular lifestyle.

Despite the myth of American individualism, our identity—our self-definition or sense of selfhood—is actually shaped not by separation but by affiliation, by bonding and identifying with others. As children, we observe the people around us and learn the qualities associated with those who seem like us, especially in terms of such characteristics as gender, race, age, or religion. For example, we learn what it means to be female or male by our interactions with the women or men around us. Then we internalize the characteristics that we recognize as appropriate to womanliness or manliness.

Psychologists have differing theories about how this internalization takes place. Some see it as a cognitive process by which we learn how people are labeled and accept those labels for ourselves. Others think it is behavioral, that we learn how to act in response to rewards and punishments. Still others believe internalization to be the emotional desire to feel connected with others like us.

Whatever the process may be, all agree that what we learn about who we are in childhood is central to how we perceive ourselves and act as adults. Even though most of us continue throughout our lives to develop new and more inclusive identities, the "new me" is most accurately understood as an integration of some new or newly discovered facet of ourselves with our previous identifications and self-images. Our individuality—our identity—is actually a constellation of the various affiliations we accept and that are attributed to us.

In this division, "Identity," we look at how race and ethnicity, gender, economic status, and stereotypes influence identity formation in American culture. Part I, "Ethnic and Racial Identity," explores the nature of race and ethnicity by considering them from both theoretical and personal perspectives and in both historical and contemporary contexts. Part II, "Gender Identity," examines how we learn to be male and female in our society, and how gender roles affect the way we relate to and interact with one another. Part III, "Economics and the American Dream," shows that, despite the belief that America is a classless society or that everyone is middle-class, sharp disparities in the distribution of wealth determine individual and group values and access to opportunity. Finally, Part IV, "Stereotypes and Prejudice," examines how we create and learn the rigid, often negative, characterizations we attribute to certain groups—especially gender and racial groups.

The purpose of the "Identity" section is to help you consider your own identity in these contexts. Even though any single selection may not speak specifically to your personal experience, the themes the readings explore will help you recognize and evaluate your place in the overall mosaic. As we come to realize that we actually have a great deal in common with some people who initially seemed different from us, when we discover that they and their experiences are more like our own than we had thought, we are more capable of understanding and sympathizing with the discrimination to which some people are subjected.

I

Ethnic and Racial Identity

YOU MAY BE SURPRISED TO LEARN THAT RACE AND ethnicity are not as easily distinguished from each other as is commonly assumed. Even though we use these terms in everyday conversations, most of us don't have an accurate understanding of what they really mean and how imprecise they actually are.

When we identify someone as a member of an **ethnic group,** we mean that she or he belongs to some identifiable group within American society. This is the most important component of ethnicity: membership in a subgroup within an environment dominated by another culture.

Ethnic subgroups are defined by many complex, often variable traits, such as religion, language, culture, customs, traditions, physical characteristics, and, probably most important in this country, ancestral origin. Ancestral origin is the reason we often label ethnic groups as "hyphenated-Americans": African-Americans, German-Americans, Filipino-Americans, Chinese-Americans, and so on.

"Wait a minute," you are probably saying, "some of those groups are racial, not ethnic." Don't be so sure.

One definition of **race** in *The American Heritage Dictionary* is "any group of people united or classified together on the basis of common history, nationality, or geographical distribution." In

this sense, race does not differ substantially from ethnicity. Scientists identify race solely in terms of physical characteristics, such as skin color, texture and color of hair, and other attributes, especially facial features. However, these attributes are not as discrete or self-evident as it might seem at first. From earliest times, human populations have migrated and intermingled, mixing and blending their biological makeup. Precise lines of racial demarcation are blurred, so that, at best, systematic classifications of race are complex and must be carefully qualified.

For this reason, many people have come to believe that race is less a scientific actuality than it is a **social construct**—a classification based on social values. Consider, for example, a child whose mother is black and father is white or one whose mother is white and father Japanese. Even though both are half white, in America the first would be categorized as black and the other as Asian. This racial assignment reflects social assumptions rather than either child's genetic composition. In other words, each child's race is socially constructed. An even more glaring example of the absurdity of our racial classification is the U.S. Census Bureau's policy of assigning Native American status to anyone with as little as one-eighth native lineage.

Today many of us tend to think of African-Americans, Asian-Americans, and Native Americans as racial groups and Jewish-Americans, Italian-Americans, and Irish-Americans as ethnic groups. In the early part of this century, however, each of the latter three was called a race and was said to have distinctive physical features that marked group identity, a belief that now strikes us as quaintly absurd.

Although we tend to consider both ethnic and racial identity to be fixed and unalterable, in fact, they are fluid and quite subjective. You may call yourself German-American because your forebears came from Germany, but they may have seen themselves instead as Prussian or Bavarian, or members of one of the many other nation states that only later were united to form the Germany we know today.

Our current racial and ethnic groupings reflect another blind spot in social thought: our insensitivity to the realities of cultural heritage. The label European-American, for example, camouflages the differences between Scandinavians and the French and between those two groups and the Poles, the British, and the many other distinct European cultures. Most Native American Indians identify themselves as Sioux or even Lakota Sioux, Arapaho, Laguna, and so on, not as a categorical "Indian" or "Native American."

Similarly, when we classify all African-Americans as one homogeneous group, we ignore the extreme divergence of African cultures. Ethiopian Plains culture differs tremendously from that which developed in Morocco or West Africa; moreover, like Native Americans, Africans are more likely to consider themselves Zulu, Ibo, Hausa, or Yoruba than South African or Nigerian—or even African. Finally, today there are at least nineteen Asian and Pacific Island populations lumped together under the Asian-American label. These include the Hmong, Cambodians, Laosians, the Sikh, and Burmese in addition to the more widely recognized groups representing Japan, China, Korea, India, and the Philippines.

Finally, it is important to note that all these subgroups exist within the American context, and every subgroup has been transformed by the influences of this larger society. Nevertheless, even when many historical features of the subgroup have been lost or altered, members may continue to identify with the recreated group. These are the hyphenated-Americans.

The readings in Part I present a small sampling of the innumerable accounts that are part of this evolutionary process. Some of them and some of the themes they present may reflect your heritage; others may not. However, each of them is part of the American experience, and we need to understand them if we are to understand what it means to be American. This is where we are now, learning about and becoming sensitive to the multiplicity and complexity of the ethnic and racial cultures that have shaped the America we know today and that will mold our nation in the future.

The first two selections provide different perspectives on ethnic identity and explore several related issues. John Hope Franklin discusses historical changes in Americans' attitudes about and treatment of immigrants and ethnic groups, illuminating the distance between the American ideal that "all men are created equal" and the reality of exclusion. Arthur Mann both analyzes the varying degrees to which Americans feel ethnic identity and explains how the slavery system forced the slaves to abandon their African ways, making African-American ethnic culture unique.

The next two readings describe the effects of assimilation, the forcing of minority groups to abandon the unique features of their former cultures and to adapt to the values and norms of European-American culture, which was dominated by the English Protestant ethic. In Grace Paley's story, Jewish immigrant parents see that their daughter's selection as the narrator of her public school's Christmas play is a difficult but necessary part of assimilation into American society. Polingaysi Qoyawayma, renamed Elizabeth Q. White by white missionaries, tells of a similar conflict when she returns for a visit to her traditional Hopi parents after her conversion at the Christian mission; her rejection of her parents' beliefs about the spiritual power of nature is painful to all three.

Michael Novak finds his ethnic identity problematic for other reasons. He argues that many European-American ethnics like him, especially those he labels PIGS—Poles, Italians, Greeks, and Slavs in working-class America—are marginalized, unappreciated, and derided despite the economic contributions these groups have made.

Like Novak, many second-generation Americans struggle to understand their distinctive identity, achieving self-acceptance in different ways.

For Celia Alvarez, work on an oral history project clarified her connections with working-class Puerto Rican women in the United States and taught her that she can be part of the larger American society and still retain her connections to her community of birth. Shanlon Wu tells of his lifelong search for positive Asian-American role models, none of which really fit him until he realizes he must mold his own life.

On the other hand, Catherine Rocha, in an interview with Lester D. Langley, rejects the politicized Chicana label, feeling, like Hector Barreto, that she is part of mainstream middle-class America. Finally, in her interview with John Langston Gwaltney, Rosa Wakefield describes what being black means to her, but her contemplation of the differences between blacks and whites and among blacks exposes how complex and subjective ethnic identification is.

The last three selections explore the impact of recent population changes on American culture and society. According to Stephen Goode, recent Muslim immigrants are adding another ingredient to today's America, a theme Robbie Clipper Sethi also explores in her story about a Sikh ceremony, which, when executed in a modern suburb, is not American, but is not quite Sikh either. Sethi's story also shows that although it may be continually evolving, a distinctive American culture is identifiable when looked at from the perspective of an immigrant or "outsider." Finally, William A. Henry III reports on how contemporary changes in demography influence social, political, and economic realities in America today and into the next century.

By the time you have finished the readings in this part, you will have some sense of the elements most central to ethnic identity and may have thought about your family and your life in the light of those factors.

1

Ethnicity in American Life: The Historical Perspective

JOHN HOPE FRANKLIN

The United States is unique in the ethnic composition of its population. No other country in the world can point to such a variety of cultural, racial, religious, and national backgrounds in its population. It was one of the salient features in the early history of this country; and it would continue to be so down into the twentieth century. From virtually every corner of the globe they came—some enthusiastically and some quite reluctantly. Britain and every part of the continent of Europe provided prospective Americans by the millions. Africa and Asia gave up great throngs. Other areas of the New World saw inhabitants desert their own lands to seek their fortunes in the colossus to the North. Those who came voluntarily were attracted by the prospect of freedom of religion, freedom from want, and freedom from various forms of oppression. Those who were forced to come were offered the consolation that if they were white they would some day inherit the earth, and if they were black they would some day gather their reward in the Christian heaven.

One of the interesting and significant features of this coming together of peoples of many tongues and races and cultures was that the backgrounds out of which they came would soon be minimized and that the process by which they evolved into Americans would be of paramount importance. Hector St. Jean de Crevecoeur sought to describe this process in 1782 when he answered his own question, "What, then, is the American, this new man?" He said, "He is either an European, or the descendant of an European, hence that strange mixture of blood, which you will find in no other country. . . . He is an American, who, leaving behind him all his ancient prejudices and manners, receives new ones from the new mode of the life he has embraced, the new government he obeys, and the new rank he holds. He becomes an American by being received in the broad lap of our great *Alma Mater.* Here individuals of all nations are melted into a new race of men, whose labours and posterity will one day cause great changes in the world."

This was one of the earliest expressions of the notion that the process of Americanization involved the creation of an entirely new mode of life that would replace the ethnic backgrounds of those who were a part of the process. It contained some imprecisions and inaccuracies that would, in time, become a part of the lore or myth of the vaunted melting pot and would grossly misrepresent the crucial factor of ethnicity in American life. It ignored the tenacity with which the Pennsylvania Dutch held onto their language, religion, and way of life. It overlooked the way in which the Swedes of New Jersey remained Swedes and the manner in which the French Huguenots of New York and Charleston held onto their own past as though it was the source of all light and life. It described a process that in a distant day would gag at the notion that Irish Catholics could be assimilated on the broad lap of Alma Mater or that Asians could be seated on the basis of equality at the table of the Great American Feast.

By suggesting that only Europeans were involved in the process of becoming Americans, Crevecoeur pointedly ruled out three quarters of a million blacks already in the country who, along with their progeny, would be regarded as ineligible to become Americans for at least another two centuries. To be sure, the number of persons of African descent would increase enormously, but the view of their ineligibility for Americanization would be very slow to change. And when such a change occurred, even if it merely granted freedom from bondage, the change would be made most reluctantly and without any suggestion that freedom qualified one for equality on the broad lap of Alma Mater. It was beyond the conception of Crevecoeur, as it was indeed beyond the conception of the founding fathers, that Negroes, slave or free, could become true Americans, enjoying that fellowship in a common enterprise about which Crevecoeur spoke so warmly. It was as though Crevecoeur was arguing that ethnicity, where persons of African descent were concerned, was either so powerful or so unattractive as to make their assimilation entirely impossible or so insignificant as to make it entirely undesirable. In any case Americanization in the late eighteenth century was a precious commodity to be cherished and enjoyed only by a select group of persons of European descent.

One must admit, therefore, that at the time of the birth of the new nation there was no clear-cut disposition to welcome into the American family persons of any and all ethnic backgrounds. Only Europeans were invited to fight for independence. And when the patriots at long last relented and gave persons of African descent a chance to fight, the concession was made with great reluctance and after much equivocation and soul-searching. Only Europeans were regarded as full citizens in the new states and in the new nation. And when the founding fathers wrote the Constitution of the United States, they did not seem troubled by the distinctions on the basis of ethnic differences that the Constitution implied.

If the principle of ethnic exclusiveness was propounded so early and so successfully in the history of the United States, it is not surprising that it would, in time, become the basis for questioning the ethnic backgrounds of large numbers of prospective Americans, even Europeans. Thus, in 1819, a Jewish immigrant was chilled to hear a bystander refer to him and his companion as "more damned emigrants." A decade later there began a most scathing and multifaceted attack on the Catholic church. On two counts the church was a bad influence. First, its principal recruits were the Irish, the "very dregs" of the Old World social order; and secondly, its doctrine of papal supremacy ran counter to the idea of the political and religious independence of the United States. Roman Catholics, Protestant Americans warned, were engaged in a widespread conspiracy to subvert American institutions, through parochial schools, the Catholic press, immoral convents, and a sinister design to control the West by flooding it with Catholic settlers. The burning of convents and churches and the killing of Catholics themselves were indications of how deeply many Americans felt about religious and cultural differences for which they had a distaste and suspicion that bordered on paranoia.

Soon the distaste for the foreign-born became almost universal, with Roman Catholics themselves sharing in the hostility to those who followed them to the new Republic. Some expressed fear of the poverty and criminality that accompanied each wave of immigrants. Some felt that those newly arrived from abroad were a threat to republican freedom. Some saw in the ethnic differences of the newcomers an immediate danger to the moral standards of Puritan America. Some feared the competition that newcomers posed in the labor market. Some became convinced that the ideal of a national homogeneity would disappear with the influx of so many unassimilable elements. Soon, nativist societies sprang up all across the land, and they found national expression in 1850 in a new organization called the Order of the Star Spangled Banner. With its slogan, "America for Americans," the order, which became the organizational basis for the Know-Nothing party, engendered a fear through its preachments that caused many an American to conclude that his country was being hopelessly subverted by the radical un-Americanism of the great variety of ethnic strains that were present in the United States.

If there was some ambivalence regarding the ethnic diversity of white immigrants before the Civil War, it was dispelled by the view that prevailed regarding immigrants in the post–Civil War years. The "old" immigrants, so the argument went, were at least assimilable and had "entered practically every line of activity in nearly every part of the country." Even those who had been non-English speaking had mingled freely with native Americans and had therefore been quickly assimilated. Not so with the "new" immigrants who came after 1880. They "congregated together in sections apart from native Americans and the older immigrants to such an extent that assimilation had been slow." Small wonder that they were different. Small wonder that they were barely assimilable. They came from Austro-Hungary, Italy, Russia, Greece, Rumania, and Turkey. They dressed differently, spoke in unfamiliar tongues, and clung to strange, if not exotic customs. It did not matter that Bohemians, Moravians, and Finns had lower percentages of illiteracy than had the Irish and Germans or that Jews had a higher percentage of skilled laborers than any group except the Scots. Nor did it matter that, in fact, the process of assimilation for the so-called "new" group was about as rapid as that of the so-called "old" group.

What did matter was that the new nativism was stronger and more virulent than any anti-immigration forces or groups of the early nineteenth century and that these groups were determined either to drive from the shores those who were different or to isolate them so that they could not contaminate American society. Old-stock Americans began to organize to preserve American institutions and the American way of life. Those who had been here for five years or a decade designated themselves as old-stock Americans and joined in the attack on those recently arrived. If the cult of Anglo-Saxon superiority was all but pervasive, those who were not born into the cult regarded themselves as honorary members. Thus, they could celebrate with as much feeling as any the virtues of Anglo-Saxon institutions and could condemn as vehemently as any those ideas and practices that were not strictly Anglo-Saxon. Whenever possible they joined the American Protective Association and the Immigrant Restriction League; and in so doing they sold their own ethnicity for the obscurity that a pseudoassimilation brought. But in the end, they would be less than successful. The arrogance and presumption of the Anglo-Saxon complex was not broad enough to embrace the Jews of eastern Europe or the Bohemians of central Europe or the Turks of the Middle East. The power and drive of the Anglo-Saxon forces would prevail; and those who did not belong would be compelled to console themselves by extolling the virtues of cultural pluralism.

By that time—near the end of the nineteenth century—the United States had articulated quite clearly its exalted standards of ethnicity. They were standards that accepted Anglo-Saxons as the norm, placed other whites on what may be called "ethnic probation," and excluded from serious consideration the Japanese, Chinese, and Negroes. It was not difficult to deal harshly with the Chinese and Japanese when they began to enter the United States in considerable numbers in the post–Civil War years. They simply did not meet the standards that the arbiters of American ethnicity had promulgated. They were differ-ent in race, religion, language, and public and private morality. They had to be excluded; and eventually they were.

The presence of persons of African descent, almost from the beginning, had helped whites to define ethnicity and to establish and maintain the conditions by which it could be controlled. If their color and race, their condition of servitude, and their generally degraded position did not set them apart, the laws and customs surrounding them more than accomplished that feat. Whether in Puritan Massachusetts or cosmopolitan New York or Anglican South Carolina, the colonists declared that Negroes, slave or free, did not and could not belong to the society of equal human beings. Thus, the newly arrived Crevecoeur could be as blind to the essential humanity of Negroes as the patriots who tried to keep them out of the Continental Army. They were not a part of America, these new men. And in succeeding years their presence would do more to define ethnicity than the advent of several scores of millions of Europeans.

It was not enough for Americans, already somewhat guilt-ridden for maintaining slavery in a free society, to exclude blacks from American society on the basis of race and condition of servitude. They proceeded from that point to argue that Negroes were inferior morally, intellectually, and physically. Even as he reviewed the remarkable accomplishments of Benjamin Banneker, surveyor, almanacker, mathematician, and clockmaker, Thomas Jefferson had serious doubts about the mental capabilities of Africans, and he expressed these doubts to his European friends. What Jefferson speculated about at the end of the eighteenth century became indisputable dogma within a decade after his death.

In the South every intellectual, legal, and religious resource was employed in the task of describing the condition of Negroes in such a way as to make them the least attractive human beings on the face of the earth. Slavery was not only the natural lot of blacks, the slaveowners argued, but it was in accordance with God's will that they should be kept in slavery. As one sanctimonious divine put it, "We feel that the souls of our slaves are a solemn trust and we shall strive to present them faultless and complete before the presence of God. . . . However the world may judge us in connection with our institution of slavery, we conscientiously believe it to be a great missionary institution—one arranged by God, as He arranges all moral and religious influences of the world so that the good may be brought out of seeming evil, and a blessing wrung out of every form of the curse." It was a difficult task that the owners of slaves set for themselves. Slaves had brought with them only heathenism, immorality, profligacy, and irresponsibility. They possessed neither the mental capacity nor the moral impulse to improve themselves. Only if their sponsors—those to whom were entrusted not only their souls but their bodies—were fully committed to their improvement could they take even the slightest, halting steps toward civilization.

What began as a relatively moderate justification for slavery soon became a vigorous, aggressive defense of the institution. Slavery, to the latter-day defenders, was the cornerstone of the republican edifice. To a governor of South Carolina, it was the greatest of all the great blessings which a kind Providence had bestowed upon the glorious region of the South. It was, indeed, one of the remarkable coincidences of history that such a favored institution had found such a favored creature as the African to give slavery the high value that was placed on it. A childlike race, prone to docility and manageable in every respect, the African was the ideal subject for the slave role. Slaveholders had to work hard to be worthy of this great Providential blessing.

Nothing that Negroes could do or say could change or seriously affect this view. They might graduate from college, as John Russwurm did in 1826, or they might write a most scathing attack against slavery, as David Walker did in 1829. It made no difference. They might teach in an all-white college, as Charles B. Reason did in New York in the 1850s, or publish a newspaper, as Frederick Douglass did during that same decade. Their racial and cultural backgrounds disqualified them from becoming American citizens. They could even argue in favor of their capacities and potentialities, as Henry Highland Garnet did, or they might argue their right to fight for union and freedom, as 186,000 did in the Civil War. Still, it made no sense for white Americans to give serious consideration to their arguments and their actions. They were beyond the veil, as the Jews had been beyond the veil in the barbaric and bigoted communities of eastern Europe.

The views regarding Negroes that had been so carefully developed to justify and defend slavery would not disappear with emancipation. To those who had developed such views and to the vast numbers who subscribed to them, they were much too valid to be discarded simply because the institution of slavery had collapsed. In fact, if Negroes were heathens and barbarians and intellectual imbeciles in slavery, they were hardly qualified to function as equals in a free society. And any effort to impose them on a free society should be vigorously and relentlessly resisted, even if it meant that a new and subordinate place for them had to be created.

When Americans set out to create such a place for the four million freedmen after the Civil War, they found that it was convenient to put their formulation in the context of the ethnic factors that militated against complete assimilation. To do it this way seemed more fitting, perhaps even more palatable, for the white members of a so-called free society. And they had some experience on which to rely. In an earlier day it had been the Irish or the Germans or the free Negroes who presented problems of assimilation. They were different in various ways and did not seem to make desirable citizens. In time the Irish, Germans, and other Europeans made it and were accepted on the broad lap of Alma Mater. But not the free Negroes, who continued to suffer disabilities even in the North in the years just before the Civil War. Was this the key to the solution of the postwar problems? Perhaps it was. After all, Negroes had always been a group apart in Boston, New York, Philadelphia, and other northern cities. They all lived together in one part of the city—especially if they could find no other place to live. They had their own churches—after the whites drove them out of theirs. They had their own schools—after they were excluded from the schools attended by whites. They had their own social organizations—after the whites barred them from theirs.

If Negroes possessed so many ethnic characteristics such as living in the same community, having their own churches, schools, and social clubs, and perhaps other agencies of cohesion, that was all very well. They even seemed "happier with their own kind," some patronizing observers remarked. They were like the Germans or the Irish or the Italians or the Jews. They had so much in common and so much to preserve. There was one significant difference, however. For Europeans, the ethnic factors that brought a particular group together actually eased the task of assimilation and, in many ways, facilitated the process of assimilation, particularly as hostile elements sought to disorient them in their drive toward full citizenship. And, in time, they achieved it.

For Negroes, however, such was not the case. They had been huddled together in northern ghettoes since the eighteenth century. They had had their own churches since 1792 and their own schools since 1800. And this separateness, this ostracism, was supported and enforced by the full majesty of the law, state and federal, just to make certain that Negroes did, indeed, preserve their ethnicity! And as they preserved their ethnicity—all too frequently as they looked down the barrel of a policeman's pistol or a militiaman's shotgun—full citizenship seemed many light years away. They saw other ethnic groups pass them by, one by one, and take their places in the sacred Order of the Star Spangled Banner, the American Protective Association, the Knights of the Ku Klux Klan—not always fully assimilated but vehemently opposed to the assimilation of Negroes. The ethnic grouping that was a way station, a temporary resting place for Europeans as they became Americans, proved to be a terminal point for blacks who found it virtually impossible to become Americans in any real sense.

There was an explanation or at least a justification for this. The federal government and the state governments had tried to force Negroes into full citizenship and had tried to legislate them into equality with the whites. This was not natural and could not possibly succeed. Negroes had not made it because they were not fit, the social Darwinists[1] said. Negroes were beasts, Charles Carroll declared somewhat inelegantly. "Stateways cannot change folkways," William Graham Sumner, the distinguished scholar, philosophized. The first forty years of Negro freedom had been a failure, said John R. Commons, one of the nation's leading economists. This so-called failure was widely acknowledged in the country as northerners of every rank and description acquiesced, virtually without a murmur of objection, to the southern settlement of the race problem characterized by disfranchisement, segregation, and discrimination.

Here was a new and exotic form of ethnicity. It was to be seen in the badges of inferiority and the symbols of racial degradation that sprang up in every sector of American life—in the exclusion from the polling places with its specious justification that Negroes were unfit to participate in the sacred rite of voting; the back stairway or the freight elevator to public places; the separate, miserable railway car, the separate and hopelessly inferior school; and even the Jim Crow[2] cemetery. Ethnic considerations had never been so important in the shaping of public policy. They had never before been used by the American government to define the role and place of other groups in American society. The United States had labored hard to create order out of its chaotic and diverse ethnic backgrounds. Having begun by meekly suggesting the difficulty in assimilating all groups into one great society, it had acknowledged failure by ruling out one group altogether, quite categorically, and frequently by law, solely on the basis of race.

It could not achieve this without doing irreparable harm to the early notions of the essential unity of America and Americans. The sentiments that promoted the disfranchisement and segregation of Negroes also encouraged the infinite varieties of discrimination against Jews, Armenians, Turks, Japanese, and Chinese. The conscious effort to degrade a particular ethnic group reflects a corrosive quality that dulls the sensitivities of both the perpetrators and the victims. It calls forth venomous hatreds and crude distinctions in high places as well as low places. It can affect the quality of mind of even the most cultivated scholar and place him in a position scarcely distinguishable from the Klansman or worse. It was nothing out of the ordinary, therefore, that at a dinner in honor of the winner of one of Harvard's most coveted prizes, Professor Barrett Wendell warned that if a Negro or a Jew ever won the prize the dinner would have to be canceled.

By the time that the Statue of Liberty was dedicated in 1886 the words of Emma Lazarus on the base of it had a somewhat hollow ring. Could anyone seriously believe that the poor, tired, huddled masses "yearning to breathe free," were really welcome here? This was a land where millions of black human beings whose ancestors had been here for centuries were consistently treated as pariahs and untouchables! What interpretation could anyone place on the sentiments expressed on the statue except that the country had no real interest in or sympathy for the downtrodden unless they were white and preferably Anglo-Saxon? It was a disillusioning experience for some newcomers to discover that their own ethnic background was a barrier to success in their adopted land. It was a searing and shattering experience for Negroes to discover over and over again that three centuries of toil and loyalty were nullified by the misfortune of their own degraded ethnic background.

In the fullness of time—in the twentieth century—the nation would confront the moment of truth regarding ethnicity as a factor in its own historical development. Crevecoeur's words would have no real significance. The words of the Declaration of Independence would have no real meaning. The words of Emma Lazarus would not ring true. All such sentiments would be put to the severe test of public policy and private deeds and would be found wanting. The Ku Klux Klan would challenge the moral and human dignity of Jews, Catholics, and Negroes. The quotas of the new immigration laws would define ethnic values in terms of race and national origin. The restrictive covenants[3] would arrogate to a select group of bigots the power of determining what races or ethnic groups should live in certain houses or whether, indeed, they should have any houses at all in which to live. If some groups finally made it through the escape hatch and arrived at the point of acceptance, it was on the basis of race, now defined with sufficient breadth to include all or most peoples who were not of African descent.

By that time ethnicity in American life would come to have a special, clearly definable meaning. Its meaning would be descriptive of that group of people vaguely defined in the federal census returns as "others" or "non-whites." It would have something in common with that magnificent term "cultural pluralism," the consolation prize for those who were not and could not be assimilated. It would signify the same groping for respectability that describes that group of people

who live in what is euphemistically called "the inner city." It would represent a rather earnest search for a hidden meaning that would make it seem a bit more palatable and surely more sophisticated than something merely racial. But in 1969 even a little child would know what ethnicity had come to mean.

In its history, ethnicity, in its true sense, has extended and continues to extend beyond race. At times it has meant language, customs, religion, national origin. It has also meant race; and, to some, it has always meant only race. It had already begun to have a racial connotation in the eighteenth century. In the nineteenth century, it had a larger racial component, even as other factors continued to loom large. In the present century, as these other factors have receded in importance, racial considerations have come to have even greater significance. If the history of ethnicity has meant anything at all during the last three centuries, it has meant the gradual but steady retreat from the broad and healthy regard for cultural and racial differences to a narrow, counter-productive concept of differences in terms of whim, intolerance, and racial prejudice. We have come full circle. The really acceptable American is still that person whom Crevecoeur described almost two hundred years ago. But the true American, acceptable or not, is that person who seeks to act out his role in terms of his regard for human qualities irrespective of race. One of the great tragedies of American life at the beginning was that ethnicity was defined too narrowly. One of the great tragedies of today is that this continues to be the case. One can only hope that the nation and its people will all some day soon come to reassess ethnicity in terms of the integrity of the man rather than in terms of the integrity of the race.   [1989]

Notes

1. SOCIAL DARWINISM: The theory that applied Darwin's theory of evolution, "survival of the fittest," to society; it assumed that upper classes were naturally superior, and the failure of the lower classes was the result of their natural inferiority, not of social policies and practices.

2. JIM CROW: Laws and practices, especially in

the South, that separated blacks and whites and enforced the subordination of blacks.

3. RESTRICTIVE COVENANTS: Codes prohibiting members of some groups—often blacks, Jews, and Asians—from buying real estate in certain areas.

Understanding the Reading

1. Today, why do we today find de Crevecoeur's 1782 definition of "the American, this new man" inadequate or inappropriate?
2. How did the principle of ethnic exclusion that omitted people of African descent affect later immigrant groups in the nineteenth century?
3. What does nativism mean?
4. How was the exclusion of African-Americans from American society justified?
5. How was it maintained?
6. How did the treatment of African-Americans affect other groups in the twentieth century?

Suggestions for Responding

1. According to Franklin, America has not lived up to its ideals. Do you think his pessimistic views are justified? What arguments would you offer to support or refute his analysis?
2. Is the "really acceptable American" today still that person whom de Crevecoeur described, as Franklin claims? Why or why not? ✦

2

Liberty Means Choice

ARTHUR MANN

Within each of us there is a tugging and a pulling among the several things each of us is. No survey is likely to render that reality in human terms, a matter best left to both biographers and psychologists who credit every personality as unique. Yet, in the following words of an experienced people-watcher, we catch a glimpse of the ambiguities and ironies to which ethnics are subject:

> Minorities are in fact often divided as to what rights they really want, or think they want. Even indi-

vidual members of minorities are often divided within themselves, and change in mood from year to year or month to month, or even at different times of the day. A partly integrated society forces versatility in role-playing in an unusual degree on minority members. I have observed both in faraway countries and nearer at home certain minority people playing one role in the presence of local majority people, a second role, equally artificial, in the presence of more militant members of their own minority, and a third role, more natural, with their own friends, all minority people but none of them aggressively minoritarian. (That is a point too: minorities are not being minorities, or thinking of themselves as minorities, all the time.) In the first context these people may sound like social integrationists; in the second they may behave as if they were at heart secessionists; and in the third they may show themselves to be on the whole economic integrationists, with not much more taste for social integration in the full sense than for secession. But the conviction with which they adopt these roles will vary according to mood, the previous day's news, or even the rumors of the day itself.[1]

The obstacles to classifying Americans are such that one is tempted not to try. Still, with respect to scale of ethnic identification among individuals, there is now as in the past a configuration. Beyond the affiliation that others might ascribe to them, immigrants and their descendants fall into one of four categories:

Total identifiers live out their lives entirely within the ethnic group. They reside with their own kind, go to school with their own kind, work with their own kind, pray with their own kind, eat the food of their own kind, relax with their own kind, marry their own kind, and vote and campaign for their own kind. But the persons who do so willingly constitute a tiny fraction of the population. More commonly, total identifiers are recent immigrants who, for reasons of poverty and prejudice, have no choice but to live completely by themselves.

Partial identifiers take their ethnicity in measured and selective doses. It is usually most important to them in primary associations, but they are apt to define themselves in non-ethnic terms at work, in the community, or at college. The more such individuals play autonomous roles, the more they see themselves as being more than solely ethnic. They constitute a majority of Americans who retain ties to their ancestry.

Disaffiliates grew up in ethnic or ethno-religious neighborhoods but cannot go home again because they have chosen not to. They are most often found in the worlds of academia, the media, and show business. They are intellectuals, in a word. In a witty and combative article Andrew Greeley wrote that they are the same as ethnic groups. That they constitute a tribe of their own is true. They have their own values, rituals, heroes, ways of bringing up children, and so on. Yet, unlike members of ethnic groups, disaffiliates are not tied together by a common ancestry. They number in the many millions and are likely to remain numerous when one considers the extraordinarily high percentage of Americans who go to college.

Hybrids cannot identify themselves through a single stock. They are of mixed ancestry and come from families that, for a long time, have intermarried. In a course at the University of Chicago on ethnicity in American history, there are students in whom the ethnicity has been so completely washed out that they have a hard time getting hold of the concept. Some of them even resent it, thinking that it is a mark of bigotry to sort out people according to their origins. Often these students are westerners, particularly from California, where it is usual to describe one's self as originating from Iowa, Pennsylvania, or some other eastern state. Such Americans are, in literal fact, products of the melting pot.

Each of these categories calls for refinements. It is extremely hard to place people in a fluid society and for people to place themselves in it. Perhaps that is why America engenders more alienation than societies where everyone knows exactly where he or she fits. But such were the places from which masses of immigrants were uprooted and set in motion. In adjusting to America they, and later their progeny, fashioned ties of belonging appropriate to changing conditions. The process is likely to go on, for where boundaries are loose there is freedom to choose.

Persisting Dilemma

It is now a given that blacks form one of many groups in America, yet bitter memories prevent them from viewing themselves as comparable to others in a pluralist democracy. None but their kind was brought to the New World in chains; defined as things in the national compact; fought over in the country's only civil war; needful of special Constitutional amendments; or set apart from everyone else by the supreme tribunal of the land. Throughout their history in America others have told blacks who they were.

Forced bondage destroyed ties to what they had been. Men and women did not arrive from the dark continent in the seventeenth and eighteenth centuries as undifferentiated Africans. They came as Ashanti, Ibo, Yoruba, Wolof, or members of still other tribes, with cultural and linguistic differences that were as significant as those that marked off incoming groups from Europe. The latter were each free, however, to nourish their distinctive ways. Slavery stripped Africans of most of theirs, and before long they came to know themselves only by common color and inferior status.

In the two centuries after the first emancipations of the Revolutionary era, free blacks struggled to fashion a new identity. Not the least of the difficulties was the choice of an appropriate name for their kind. It shifted from African in the eighteenth century to colored and Afro-American in the nineteenth, back to colored early in the twentieth and then to Negro and most recently to black. No immigrant group experienced the same confusion or designated itself by so gross a category as race or continent.

The name mattered less, W. E. B. Du Bois noted, than the place blacks occupied in America. Although like Horace Kallen a Harvard Ph.D. (1895) and a student of William James, Du Bois did not define the position in pluralist terms. A few years after leaving Harvard he wrote: "One ever feels his twoness—an American, a Negro; two souls, two thoughts, two unreconciled strivings; two warring ideals in one dark body." Unable to resolve those dualisms during his long life, Du Bois died in 1963 both a Communist and a Ghanaian citizen. "I was not an American," he said before leaving the United States, but "a colored man in a white world."

In the 1920s some writers and artists of the Harlem Renaissance[2] glimpsed the possibility that Negroes might become equal participants in multiethnic America. Deriving the hope from the writings of Charles William Eliot and from the still popular credo of self-determination, such intellectuals traveled the full distance to pluralism. They numbered few among the educated classes, whose quest for integration precluded the cultural distinctiveness of American blacks. Meanwhile, millions of persons rallied to Marcus Garvey's black nationalist movement. It was not to be the last mass separatist expression.

The anomalous position of blacks is reflected in the literature on ethnicity. An occasional Ralph Waldo Emerson welcomed people of color to his smelting pot, but Israel Zangwill was less sanguine that racial intermarriage would be common. Frederick Jackson Turner and Theodore Roosevelt, like Crevecoeur in the eighteenth century, made no room at all for blacks in the American crucible. Even the father of cultural pluralism left them out of his plan for transethnic America. The new pluralists of our day also drew a color line in their ancestral mosaic.

But if exceptional in vital respects, the black experience intersects the immigrant experience at two critical points. The black identity is also an American artifact; and they have a vital stake in making the national creed a reality. Indeed, as the excluded outsiders for so long, they have been the persistent reminder of the liberties that are supposed to include all American citizens.

The right to affiliate as one chooses is basic. There is considerable disagreement about where blacks now stand in that respect in comparison to when Martin Luther King, Jr., dramatized the openness of the American dream. Many whites believe that blacks have achieved parity, while a number of blacks insist that nothing has changed. The truth lies in neither extreme, because neither considers the same persons and both refer to "the black" as if that term were the singular.

No trend of the past two decades is more striking than the upward mobility of millions of blacks. To a sizable body of individuals who remain trapped in the pathologies of the underclass, freedom of affiliation seems light years away from realization. But for young educated men and women of a growing middle class, options have opened as perhaps never before. The big question is whether the movement will not only continue but also broaden to take in people still outside it.

Forecasting the future of the most persistent dilemma in American history is risky, but recent experience suggests lines of direction. Improving conditions have not only raised expectations for fuller participation but actually brought increasing numbers of blacks closer to the goal of deciding for themselves how they will affiliate and in what degree. And that blacks desire this long deferred quest is apparent. Even Marxians among them concede: "Liberalism, if it amounts to anything, must mean the freedom of the individual to choose his or her allegiances."

GUIDES FROM THE PAST

Ethnic diversity has been a persistent factor in American history, but it has defied rigid categorization. Significantly, attempts to reduce it to a pat formula have risen in troubled times. Israel Zangwill's melting-pot model, Madison Grant's Anglo-Saxon racism, and Horace Kallen's grand design for a federation of nationalities were single-minded prescriptions for the immigrant problem. Today few persons seriously think that any of the three comprehends the American mix as it actually is or was in all its variety.

An assessment of the new pluralism proposed by the white-ethnic revival must also begin with historical context. There was no sign of a revival when the 1960s opened with the election of the nation's first Catholic President. Kennedy's victory laid to rest an issue that previously divided the old and newer stocks, and the reconciliation moved on to near unanimous approval of repealing the immigration-quota laws. For a brief moment, multiethnic America was at ease with itself.

The decade closed to the tumult of Vietnam and other divisive discontents. Separatist factions, themselves symptoms of a fragmenting society, also contributed to the ungluing process. Normally sanguine persons feared that America would come fully apart. It did not, but the post–World War II era consensuses washed away. Neither the 1972 presidential landslide nor the end of the war in Southeast Asia, nor the resolution of the Constitutional emergency caused by Watergate[3] brought the American people together again.

Begotten and sustained by the national identity crisis, the new pluralism called for a renewal of traditional ties. Although purporting to describe America as it was and had been, the new pluralism was really a proposal for things as they ought to be. In that respect it stood in a direct line from earlier blueprints. Like Horace Kallen and his followers, the new pluralists wanted to remake the United States into a commonwealth of ethnic groups. Conversely, the advocates of both the melting pot and Anglo-Saxonism hoped, although for different reasons and in different ways, to collapse varied ancestral groups into a uniform American type and culture.

Like many another extreme expression engendered by the troubled 1960s, the revival petered out by the Bicentennial year. Government did not stay permanently interested; the media discovered other newsmaking subjects; foundations addressed themselves to new problems; and academia tamed the movement by conceding ethnic-studies programs to it. Meanwhile, various group leaders turned into themselves, tired, gave up, dropped out, joined the mainstream, or found alternative causes in, among other things, women's liberation and the exhilaration of American sports.

It is next to impossible for the United States to avoid prescriptions. Theories may come and go, but ethnic diversity remains a condition of American life, and the question persists: What is one to make of that condition? Despite the popularity of *Roots* and *Holocaust,* TV will not do as a guide. The nostalgia and *angst* of the 1970s, as in the previous decade, draw attention away from the character of group life in America, the relation of individuals to it, and the common nationality that has historically held together the multiplicity of peoples assembled on this continent-sized country of ours.

Notwithstanding the certitudes of ethnic ideologues, America is not merely a collection of ethnic groups. Nor was it so in the past. There exists now as previously a complex of political, occupational, religious, civic, and neighborhood associations. They sometimes overlap with the ethnic, but the boundaries for the most part are fluid rather than fixed. Neither in practice nor in theory has America's *historic* pluralism consisted of isolated fortresses.

America is home for individuals as well as for groups, and no more than the latter do the former care to be boxed in. For many persons ethnic affiliation strengthens sense of self. Not only life-giving under normal circumstances, that identity provides psychic protection when an encroaching state reduces Americans to categories that are meaningful only to bureaucrats. Most prized when voluntary instead of ascribed, ethnic affiliation leaves room for additional identities appropriate to one's position in life.

Both individual and group rights inhere in America's concept of nationality. Formulated during the Revolution for a people whose development denied them the bond of common origins, it stated that Americans were unique in the liberties they enjoyed as citizens in a free society. Nothing better illustrates that enduring character of the national identity than the now close to 200-year-old naturalization procedure. Upon identifying with the Constitutional principles of the Republic, a candidate becomes a citizen of the United States and therefore an American in nationality. Legally, he shares the new status with all Americans of no matter what descent.

It is easy enough to cite the occasions when that inclusiveness collapsed under one form of bigotry or another. From the Alien and Sedition Acts[4] of the 1790s through the Know-Nothing[5] eruptions of the 1850s through the triumph of Anglo-Saxonist proscriptions in the 1920s through the internment of Japanese-Americans[6] in the 1940s, there is an ugly legacy of hatred, violence, and dangerous and foolish thinking. But the prescriptive part of the national creed, in every instance thus far, provided a resilient and therefore self-correcting mechanism. Without that eighteenth-century given of the liberties which America was supposed to represent, there could have been no basis for saying that the people of this country were Americans all.

Other multiethnic countries make finer distinctions. In the USSR a person takes at age sixteen one of the officially recognized Soviet nationalities by which he will be known on his passport until he dies. Even democratic Canada requires in its census that individuals state their "original" nationality on the father's side, no matter how many generations ago the first paternal ancestor arrived in Canada. When a citizen of Fiji returns from a trip abroad he must declare on his landing permit whether he is by nationality Fijian, Indian, or European.

Should any of those regulations come to be imposed on Americans, the United States will cease to be what it has been. It was the first country in modern history to take the position that expatriation is a basic human right. It thereby served its own interest as the world's leading receiver of immigrants, but it also released a liberating idea for mankind: the idea that nationalities are changeable rather than irrevocable. As with so much else in America, the welcome to newcomers symbolized a fresh start, the chance to begin anew, an opportunity to choose.

At the same time, the terms for becoming a naturalized citizen did not require immigrants to give up their religions, languages, memories, customs, music, foods, or whatever else they cared to preserve in the folk culture. Unlike such countries as Brazil or France, America's definition of nationality was civic rather than cultural. It therefore left space for different ethnic affiliations while upholding to a diverse people the unifying values of the nation's democratic polity and society.

That American conception of self was severely battered in the late 1960s and early 1970s, and though the crisis has receded, the country still has to regain the former sense of wholeness and pride and confidence. Much of the world, meanwhile, remains organized against liberty. America's place in the conflict should be obvious. For two centuries the national identity has rested on the peculiar faith that the One and the Many are not only mutually compatible but essential to freedom. Few other multiethnic countries live by a transcending creed that the members of their constituent tribes or nationalities have willingly chosen.   [1979]

Notes

1. Conor Cruise O'Brien, "On the Rights of Minorities," *Commentary,* June 1973, p. 48.
2. HARLEM RENAISSANCE: The flowering of black culture—music, literature, and art—centered in Harlem in the 1920s.
3. CONSTITUTIONAL EMERGENCY CAUSED BY WATERGATE: Charges of a political cover-up

eventually forced President Richard Nixon to resign from office.
4. ALIEN AND SEDITION ACTS: Federal laws that, among other things, outlawed "false, scandalous, and malicious" statements against the government, Congress, or the President.
5. KNOW-NOTHING: A mid-nineteenth-century political movement that was hostile to immigrants and Catholics.
6. INTERNMENT OF JAPANESE-AMERICANS: The removal during World War II of all people of Japanese descent from the West Coast states to inland camps.

Understanding the Reading

1. Explain what Mann means by "total identifiers," "partial identifiers," "disaffiliates," and "hybrids."
2. Why does Mann think that "America engenders more alienation" than other societies?
3. Why is the African-American experience unique?
4. How is it similar to the experiences of other immigrants?
5. Why is "the right to affiliate as one chooses" basic to liberty?
6. What does Mann mean by "the new pluralism"?
7. Why does Mann feel "America is not merely a collection of ethnic groups"?
8. Why is naturalization important to America's concept of nationality?
9. How does the United States differ from other multiethnic countries?

Suggestions for Responding

1. Mann quotes O'Brien as saying that "a partly integrated society forces versatility in role playing." Think of an occasion when you were a racial or ethnic minority in a group. Describe how you felt and how you adjusted your behavior to the circumstance.
2. What kind of affiliation—total, partial, disaffiliated, or hybrid—do you have with your ethnic roots? What influences created your attitude?
3. Using the introduction to Part I and the selections by Franklin and Mann, write your

own definition of ethnic group or ethnicity. Be sure to clarify and explain each characteristic. ✦

 3

The Loudest Voice

GRACE PALEY

There is a certain place where dumb-waiters boom, doors slam, dishes crash; every window is a mother's mouth bidding the street shut up, go skate somewhere else, come home. My voice is the loudest.

There, my own mother is still as full of breathing as me and the grocer stands up to speak to her. "Mrs. Abramowitz," he says, "people should not be afraid of their children."

"Ah, Mr. Bialik," my mother replies, "if you say to her or her father 'Ssh,' they say, 'In the grave it will be quiet.'"

"From Coney Island to the cemetery," says my papa. "It's the same subway; it's the same fare."

I am right next to the pickle barrel. My pinky is making tiny whirlpools in the brine. I stop a moment to announce: "Campbell's Tomato Soup. Campbell's Vegetable Beef Soup. Campbell's S-c-otch Broth . . ."

"Be quiet," the grocer says, "the labels are coming off."

"Please, Shirley, be a little quiet," my mother begs me.

In that place the whole street groans: Be quiet! Be quiet! but steals from the happy chorus of my inside self not a tittle or a jot.

There, too, but just around the corner, is a red brick building that has been old for many years. Every morning the children stand before it in double lines which must be straight. They are not insulted. They are waiting anyway.

I am usually among them. I am, in fact, the first, since I begin with "A."

One cold morning the monitor tapped me on the shoulder. "Go to Room 409, Shirley Abramowitz," he said. I did as I was told. I went in a hurry up a down staircase to Room 409, which contained sixth-graders. I had to wait at the desk without wiggling until Mr. Hilton, their teacher, had time to speak.

After five minutes he said, "Shirley?"

"What?" I whispered.

He said, "My! My! Shirley Abramowitz! They told me you had a particularly loud, clear voice and read with lots of expression. Could that be true?"

"Oh yes," I whispered.

"In that case, don't be silly; I might very well be your teacher someday. Speak up, speak up."

"Yes," I shouted.

"More like it," he said. "Now, Shirley, can you put a ribbon in your hair or a bobby pin? It's too messy."

"Yes!" I bawled.

"Now, now, calm down." He turned to the class. "Children, not a sound. Open at page 39. Read till 52. When you finish, start again." He looked me over once more. "Now, Shirley, you know, I suppose, that Christmas is coming. We are preparing a beautiful play. Most of the parts have been given out. But I still need a child with a strong voice, lots of stamina. Do you know what stamina is? You do? Smart kid. You know, I heard you read 'The Lord is my shepherd' in Assembly yesterday. I was very impressed. Wonderful delivery. Mrs. Jordan, your teacher, speaks highly of you. Now listen to me, Shirley Abramowitz, if you want to take the part and be in the play, repeat after me, 'I swear to work harder than I ever did before.'"

I looked to heaven and said at once, "Oh, I swear." I kissed my pinky and looked at God.

"That is an actor's life, my dear," he explained. "Like a soldier's, never tardy or disobedient to his general, the director. Everything," he said, "absolutely everything will depend on you."

That afternoon, all over the building, children scraped and scrubbed the turkeys and the sheaves of corn off the schoolroom windows. Goodbye Thanksgiving. The next morning a monitor brought red paper and green paper from the office. We made new shapes and hung them on the walls and glued them to the doors.

The teachers became happier and happier. Their heads were ringing like the bells of childhood. My best friend Evie was prone to evil, but she did not get a single demerit for whispering. We learned "Holy Night" without an error. "How wonderful!" said Miss Glacé, the student teacher. "To think that some of you don't even speak the language!" We learned "Deck the Halls" and "Hark! The Herald Angels". . . . They weren't ashamed and we weren't embarrassed.

Oh, but when my mother heard about it all, she said to my father: "Misha, you don't know what's going on there. Cramer is the head of the Tickets Committee."

"Who?" asked my father. "Cramer? Oh yes, an active woman."

"Active? Active has to have a reason. Listen," she said sadly, "I'm surprised to see my neighbors making tra-la-la for Christmas."

My father couldn't think of what to say to that. Then he decided: "You're in America! Clara, you wanted to come here. In Palestine the Arabs would be eating you alive. Europe you had pogroms. Argentina is full of Indians. Here you got Christmas. . . . Some joke, ha?"

"Very funny, Misha. What is becoming of you? If we came to a new country a long time ago to run away from tyrants, and instead we fall into a creeping pogrom, that our children learn a lot of lies, so what's the joke? Ach, Misha, your idealism is going away."

"So is your sense of humor."

"That I never had, but idealism you had a lot of."

"I'm the same Misha Abramovitch, I didn't change an iota. Ask anyone."

"Only ask me," says my mama, may she rest in peace. "I got the answer."

Meanwhile the neighbors had to think of what to say too.

Marty's father said: "You know, he has a very important part, my boy."

"Mine also," said Mr. Sauerfeld.

"Not my boy!" said Mrs. Klieg. "I said to him no. The answer is no. When I say no! I mean no!"

The rabbi's wife said, "It's disgusting!" But no one listened to her. Under the narrow sky of God's great wisdom she wore a strawberry-blond wig.

Every day was noisy and full of experience. I was Right-hand Man. Mr. Hilton said: "How could I get along without you, Shirley?"

He said: "Your mother and father ought to get

down on their knees every night and thank God for giving them a child like you."

He also said: "You're absolutely a pleasure to work with, my dear, dear child."

Sometimes he said: "For God's sakes, what did I do with the script? Shirley! Shirley! Find it."

Then I answered quietly: "Here it is, Mr. Hilton."

Once in a while, when he was very tired, he would cry out: "Shirley, I'm just tired of screaming at those kids. Will you tell Ira Pushkov not to come in till Lester points to that star the second time?"

Then I roared: "Ira Pushkov, what's the matter with you? Dope! Mr. Hilton told you five times already, don't come in till Lester points to that star the second time."

"Ach, Clara," my father asked, "what does she do there till six o'clock she can't even put the plates on the table?"

"Christmas," said my mother coldly.

"Ho! Ho!" my father said. "Christmas. What's the harm? After all, history teaches everyone. We learn from reading this is a holiday from pagan times also, candles, lights, even Chanukah. So we learn it's not altogether Christian. So if they think it's a private holiday, they're only ignorant, not patriotic. What belongs to history, belongs to all men. You want to go back to the Middle Ages? Is it better to shave your head with a secondhand razor? Does it hurt Shirley to learn to speak up? It does not. So maybe someday she won't live between the kitchen and the shop. She's not a fool."

I thank you, Papa, for your kindness. It is true about me to this day. I am foolish but I am not a fool.

That night my father kissed me and said with great interest in my career, "Shirley, tomorrow's your big day. Congrats."

"Save it," my mother said. Then she shut all the windows in order to prevent tonsillitis.

In the morning it snowed. On the street corner a tree had been decorated for us by a kind city administration. In order to miss its chilly shadow our neighbors walked three blocks east to buy a loaf of bread. The butcher pulled down black window shades to keep the colored lights from shining on his chickens. Oh, not me. On the way to school, with both my hands I tossed it a kiss of tolerance. Poor thing, it was a stranger in Egypt.

I walked straight into the auditorium past the staring children. "Go ahead, Shirley!" said the monitors. Four boys, big for their age, had already started work as propmen and stagehands.

Mr. Hilton was very nervous. He was not even happy. Whatever he started to say ended in a sideward look of sadness. He sat slumped in the middle of the first row and asked me to help Miss Glacé. I did this, although she thought my voice too resonant and said, "Show-off!"

Parents began to arrive long before we were ready. They wanted to make a good impression. From among the yards of drapes I peeked out at the audience. I saw my embarrassed mother.

Ira, Lester, and Meyer were pasted to their beards by Miss Glacé. She almost forgot to thread the star on its wire, but I reminded her. I coughed a few times to clear my throat. Miss Glacé looked around and saw that everyone was in costume and on line waiting to play his part. She whispered, "All right. . . ." Then:

Jackie Sauerfeld, the prettiest boy in first grade, parted the curtains with his skinny elbow and in a high voice sang out:

"Parents dear
We are here
To make a Christmas play in time.
It we give
In narrative
And illustrate with pantomime."

He disappeared.

My voice burst immediately from the wings to the great shock of Ira, Lester, and Meyer, who were waiting for it but were surprised all the same.

"I remember, I remember, the house where I was born. . . ."

Miss Glacé yanked the curtain open and there it was, the house—an old hayloft, where Celia Kornbluh lay in the straw with Cindy Lou, her favorite doll. Ira, Lester, and Meyer moved slowly from the wings toward her, sometimes pointing to a moving star and sometimes ahead to Cindy Lou.

It was a long story and it was a sad story. I carefully pronounced all the words about my lonesome childhood, while little Eddie Braunstein wandered upstage and down with his shepherd's stick, looking for sheep. I brought up

lonesomeness again, and not being understood at all except by some women everybody hated. Eddie was too small for that and Marty Groff took his place, wearing his father's prayer shawl. I announced twelve friends, and half the boys in the fourth grade gathered round Marty, who stood on an orange crate while my voice harangued. Sorrowful and loud, I declaimed about love and God and Man, but because of the terrible deceit of Abie Stock we came suddenly to a famous moment. Marty, whose remembering tongue I was, waited at the foot of the cross. He stared desperately at the audience. I groaned, "My God, my God, why hast thou forsaken me?" The soldiers who were sheiks grabbed poor Marty to pin him up to die, but he wrenched free, turned again to the audience, and spread his arms aloft to show despair and the end. I murmured at the top of my voice, "The rest is silence, but as everyone in this room, in this city—in this world—now knows, I shall have life eternal."

That night Mrs. Kornbluh visited our kitchen for a glass of tea.

"How's the virgin?" asked my father with a look of concern.

"For a man with a daughter, you got a fresh mouth, Abramovitch."

"Here," said my father kindly, "have some lemon, it'll sweeten your disposition."

They debated a little in Yiddish, then fell in a puddle of Russian and Polish. What I understood next was my father, who said, "Still and all, it was certainly a beautiful affair, you have to admit, introducing us to the beliefs of a different culture."

"Well, yes," said Mrs. Kornbluh. "The only thing . . . you know, Charlie Turner—that cute boy in Celia's class—a couple others? They got very small parts or no part at all. In very bad taste, it seemed to me. After all, it's their religion."

"Ach," explained my mother, "what could Mr. Hilton do? They got very small voices; after all, why should they holler? The English language they know from the beginning by heart. They're blond like angels. You think it's so important they should get in the play? Christmas . . . the whole piece of goods . . . they own it."

I listened and listened until I couldn't listen any more. Too sleepy, I climbed out of bed and kneeled. I made a little church of my hands and said, "Hear, O Israel . . ." Then I called out in Yiddish, "Please, good night, good night. Ssh."

My father said, "Ssh yourself," and slammed the kitchen door.

I was happy. I fell asleep at once. I had prayed for everybody: my talking family, cousins far away, passersby, and all the lonesome Christians. I expected to be heard. My voice was certainly the loudest.   [1956]

Understanding the Reading

1. Characterize Shirley's family and neighbors.
2. What objections do the adults have to her part in the Christmas play?
3. Why do her parents allow her to participate?
4. What does she learn from this experience, and how does it change her?

Suggestions for Responding

1. Describe a situation when you have had to participate in or at least confront a cultural activity that conflicted with or was alien to your own beliefs or values?
2. What does this story reveal about the lives and values of Jewish immigrants? ✦

4

To Be Hopi or American

Polingaysi Qoyawayma
(Elizabeth Q. White)

Like many converts to a new religion, Polingaysi was overly zealous. She was young, she was courageous, she was brash—brash enough to challenge her Hopi elders and the whole beautifully interwoven cultural pattern of Hopi life. Had she at that time been able to do so, she would have abolished all the age-old rites, the kiva[1] rituals, the sprinkling of sacred cornmeal, and especially the making of *pahos,* or prayer sticks.

At the same time, tempering her radical approach, she had a deep and unsatisfied curiosity concerning the very things that aroused in her the strongest resentment. As she walked across the field one day after visiting her family at New Oraibi, she saw a *paho* thrust into the sand on a

little hillock, its single eagle feather fluttering at the end of a short length of white cotton string.

Prayer sticks, either the long, wandlike ones with many feathers tied to them, or the short, sharpened sticks called *pahos,* are held in reverence by the Hopi people. For four days after the "planting" of a prayer, these sticks are thought to possess the essence of the offered prayer and to be very powerful and sacred. To disturb one before it has lost its power is to court disaster. Accident, even death, Polingaysi had been taught, might result.

Well known to her was the story of the white woman who took prayer sticks from a shrine, then fell and broke her leg. Behind this accident the Hopi people saw the work of the invisible forces. The spirits had resented her action and had tripped her, they were convinced.

As she bent to pull the *paho* from the sand, Polingaysi felt a wave of superstitious fear sweep over her. But she was a Christian now, she reminded herself, and need not fear the magic in a stick with a feather on it. Defiantly, she carried it home and challenged her father with it.

"What does this stick mean to you and to the Hopi people?" she asked with more arrogance than she realized. "To me, pah! It means nothing. It has no power. It's just a stick with a bit of cornhusk and a feather attached to it. Why do you, in this day and age, when you can have the message of the Bible, still have faith in sticks and feathers?"

Her father, true Hopi that he was, recoiled from the proffered *paho,* refusing to touch it. There was a worried look in his eyes.

"Must you know?" he asked.

"Of course, I must know," Polingaysi declared. "Why shouldn't I know?"

"Lay it on the table," her father said, "and I will tell you."

She placed the stick on the rough board table which she had goaded the little man into making, and the two of them bent over it.

"Do you see that blue-green, chipped-off place here at the top?" her father asked, pointing. "That is the face of the prayer stick. It represents mossy places, moisture. Now this below is the body of the prayer stick. A red color, as you can see, like our colored sand. That represents the earth. Moisture to the earth, then, is what the *paho* is for."

"A prayer for rain?"

"That, yes, and more. The stick carries a bundle on its back."

"The bit of cornhusk, bound with string? What is it for? What does it mean?"

"I don't know what is bound up in the cornhusk," her father said, "and I won't open it to find out. However, I think you might find there some grass seeds, a pinch of cornmeal, a pinch of pollen, and a drop of honey."

"But, why, why?" Polingaysi demanded impatiently. "What good does it do?"

The little Hopi man had been carving a Kachina doll[2] from the dried root of a cottonwood. He turned away and went back to his work, sitting down crosslegged on the floor and picking up his knife and the unfinished doll. Polingaysi stood looking down at him, waiting for his answer. He thought before he began to speak.

"The good it does depends on many things, my daughter. It depends most of all on the faith of the one who made the *paho*. If all those things I mentioned are inside the little bundle that it carries on its back, it would mean that the one making the *paho* planted it in Mother Earth as a prayer for a plentiful harvest, with moisture enough to help Earth produce full ears of corn, plump beans, sweet melons." He looked up at her and his small face was worried. "Surely you have not forgotten the meaning of the feather? Feathers represent the spirits that are in all things. This one represents the spirit that is in the prayer the *paho* offers up."

Polingaysi turned away and took the *paho* in her hands. About to tear open the cornhusk, she looked down to see her father's hands stilled and horror in his expression. Suddenly she could not open the *paho*'s treasure without his permission. She could not fly in the face of tradition to that extent, knowing it would offend his spirit, however silent he remained, however little he reproached her openly.

"May I open it?"

Her father bent his head, possibly questioning the propriety of such an action and fearing the harm it might do him and his daughter. After a moment of hesitation, he sighed, saying, "It seems well weathered. I think it is more than four days old. If so, its purpose has been served and the power has left it. Use your left hand."

Gently, in spite of her pretended scorn, Polin-gaysi opened the bit of wrapped cornhusk. It had been folded while still green into a tiny triangle. In this little pouch there was a bit of material about the size of a pea. Seeds, cornmeal, pollen, held together with honey, as her father had predicted.

"Can't you see there's nothing of value in here?" Polingaysi cried.

"Not to you," her father agreed. "Not to me. But to the one who made it in prayer."

She would have questioned him further, but he took his work and went outside, his face enigmatic.

"For pity's sake, Mother," Polingaysi burst out, turning to Sevenka who had been working quietly on a basket during the discussion, "does everything in the life of a Hopi have a hidden meaning? Why, for instance, should I use my left hand to open that thing?"

"It seems foolish to you because you are young and do not understand everything," her mother said patiently. "Perhaps you are foolish because you do not understand Hopi ways, though you are a Hopi. I will tell you about the left hand.

"The left hand is on the heart side of the body. It is the hand that moves most slowly. It selects, instead of grabbing as the right hand does. It is cleaner. It does not touch the mouth during the eating of food, nor does it clean the body after release of waste materials.

"Do you remember watching our medicine man—the Man With Eyes—at his work? In his healing rites and also in his religious ceremonies he uses the left hand, for those reasons I have just given you. The left hand, then, is the hand that is of the heart and the spirit, not of nature and the earth."

Polingaysi struggled to deny the beauty of the words her mother had spoken. She sought a scoffing answer, but found none. After a moment the older woman continued.

"One more thing I will tell you about the *pahos*. They must be kept free of the white man's ways if they are to have the full power of old times. That is why Hopi people do not sharpen them to a point with white man's steel blades, but grind them to sharpness on sandstone."

At that moment Polingaysi saw one of her mother's brothers passing the window. He knew nothing of the discussion and she had no desire to reopen it. With her left hand she placed the *paho* on the window sill.

"Polingaysi!" the old man cried, his face crinkling into a big smile of welcome. "It is a great treat to my spirit to see you after so long a time. We are always happy to see our child come home, even if she does make us sit at a wooden platform when we eat."

Polingaysi lost some of her contentiousness and laughed. He had always complained about sitting at the table, insisting that he could not keep his feet warm while he was eating unless he sat on them, Hopi-fashion. Her little grandmother had been completely mystified by the table, and though Polingaysi had patiently explained its use, the old lady had laboriously climbed up onto it, instead of seating herself on the wooden bench that served as a chair.

She looked at her uncle and thought of all the new ideas she had gleaned during her life among white people. The old man had no desire to share her knowledge. To him the old way was best. He asked little of life: enough food to keep the breath in his thin, worn old body, a little heat in the fireplace, a drink of water when he was dry.

It was she who was forever holding out her cup to be filled with knowledge.   [1964]

Notes

1. KIVA: An underground room used by Hopi men for ceremonies or councils.
2. KACHINA DOLL: A doll made of wood and decorated with paint, feathers, and so on that represents various spirits to Native Americans in the Southwest.

Understanding the Reading

1. Why does Polingaysi respond to the *paho* with both fear and arrogance?
2. Explain what Polingaysi means when she complains that "everything in the life of a Hopi has hidden meaning"?
3. What does this selection tell you about "Hopi ways"?
4. Why would it be important that *pahos* "be kept free from white man's ways"?
5. What does the closing sentence mean?

Suggestions for Responding

1. Describe a generational conflict, especially one based on some ethnic tradition, between you and an older family member. What were the immediate and the long-term outcomes?
2. Both Paley and Qoyawayma describe the experience of assimilation. Some people feel this process was essential to creating a unified American society, while others believe the costs, both the loss of cultural variety and the pain to individuals and families, were too high. Which position do you support? Why? ✦

5

Neither WASP nor Jew nor Black

MICHAEL NOVAK

Growing up in America has been an assault upon my sense of worthiness. It has also been a kind of liberation and delight.

There must be countless women in America who have known for years that something is peculiarly unfair, yet who only recently have found it possible, because of Women's Liberation, to give tongue to their pain. In recent months I have experienced a similar inner thaw, a gradual relaxation, a willingness to think about feelings heretofore shepherded out of sight.

I am born of PIGS—those Poles, Italians, Greeks, and Slavs, those non-English-speaking immigrants numbered so heavily among the workingmen of this nation. Not particularly liberal or radical; born into a history not white Anglo-Saxon and not Jewish; born outside what, in America, is considered the intellectual mainstream—and thus privy to neither power nor status nor intellectual voice.

Those Poles of Buffalo and Milwaukee—so notoriously taciturn, sullen, nearly speechless. Who has ever understood them? It is not that Poles do not feel emotion—what is their history if not dark passion, romanticism, betrayal, courage, blood? But where in America is there anywhere a language for voicing what a Christian

Pole in this nation feels? He has no Polish culture left him, no Polish tongue. Yet Polish feelings do not go easily into the idiom of happy America, the America of the Anglo-Saxons and yes, in the arts, the Jews. (The Jews have long been a culture of the word, accustomed to exile, skilled in scholarship and in reflection. The Christian Poles are largely of peasant origin, free men for hardly more than a hundred years.) Of what shall the young man of Lackawanna think on his way to work in the mills, departing his relatively dreary home and street? What roots does he have? What language of the heart is available to him?

The PIGS are not silent willingly. The silence burns like hidden coals in the chest.

All four of my grandparents, unknown to one another, arrived in America from the same county in Slovakia. My grandfather had a small farm in Pennsylvania; his wife died in a wagon accident. Meanwhile, Johanna, fifteen, arrived on Ellis Island, dizzy from witnessing births and deaths and illnesses aboard the crowded ship. She had a sign around her neck lettered PASSAIC. There an aunt told her of a man who had lost his wife in Pennsylvania. She went. They were married. She inherited his three children.

Each year for five years Grandma had a child of her own. She was among the lucky; only one died. When she was twenty-two and the mother of seven (my father was the last), her husband died. "Grandma Novak," as I came to know her many years later, resumed the work she had begun in Slovakia at the town home of a man known to my father only as "the Professor"; she housecleaned and she laundered.

I heard this story only weeks ago. Strange that I had not asked insistently before. Odd that I should have such shallow knowledge of my roots. Amazing to me that I do not know what my family suffered, endured, learned, and hoped these last six or seven generations. It is as if there were no project in which we all have been involved, as if history in some way began with my father and with me.

The estrangement I have come to feel derives not only from lack of family history. Early in life, I was made to feel a slight uneasiness when I said my name.

Later "Kim" helped. So did Robert.[1] And "Mister Novak" on TV. The name must be one of the most Anglo-Saxon of the Slavic names. Nevertheless, when I was very young, the "American" kids still made something out of names unlike their own, and their earnest, ambitious mothers thought long thoughts when I introduced myself.

Under challenge in grammar school concerning my nationality, I had been instructed by my father to announce proudly: "American." When my family moved from the Slovak ghetto of Johnstown to the WASP suburb on the hill, my mother impressed upon us how well we must be dressed, and show good manners, and behave —people think of us as "different" and we mustn't give them any cause. "Whatever you do, marry a Slovak girl," was other advice to a similar end: "They cook. They clean. They take good care of you. For your own good." I was taught to be proud of being Slovak, but to recognize that others wouldn't know what it meant, or care.

When I had at last pierced the deception— that most movie stars and many other professionals had abandoned their European names in order to feed American fantasies—I felt only a little sadness. One of my uncles, for business reasons and rather late in life, changed his name, too, to a simple German variant—not long, either, after World War II.

Nowhere in my schooling do I recall any attempt to put me in touch with my own history. The strategy was clearly to make an American of me. English literature, American literature, and even the history books, as I recall them, were peopled mainly by Anglo-Saxons from Boston (where most historians seemed to live). Not even my native Pennsylvania, let alone my Slovak forebears, counted for very many paragraphs. (We did have something called "Pennsylvania History" somewhere; I seem to remember its puffs for industry. It could have been written by a Mellon.[2]) I don't remember feeling envy or regret: a feeling, perhaps, of unimportance, of remoteness, of not having heft enough to count.

The fact that I was born a Catholic also complicated life. What is a Catholic but what everybody else is in reaction against? Protestants reformed "the whore of Babylon." Others were "enlightened" from it, and Jews had reason to help Catholicism and the social structure it was rooted in fall apart. The history books and the whole of education hummed in upon that point (for during crucial years I attended a public school): to be modern is decidedly not to be medieval; to be reasonable is not to be dogmatic; to be free is clearly not to live under ecclesiastical authority; to be scientific is not to attend ancient rituals, cherish irrational symbols, indulge in mythic practices. It is hard to grow up Catholic in America without becoming defensive, perhaps a little paranoid, feeling forced to divide the world between "us" and "them."

English Catholics have little of the sense of inferiority in which many other Catholic groups tend to share—Irish Catholics, Polish Catholics, Lithuanians, Germans, Italians, Lebanese, and others. Daniel Callahan (*The Mind of the Catholic Layman, Generation of the Third Eye*) and Garry Wills ("Memories of a Catholic Boyhood," in *Esquire*) both identify, in part, with the more secure Catholicism of an Anglo-Catholic parent. The French around New Orleans have a social ease different from the French Catholics of Massachusetts. Still, as Catholics, especially vis-à-vis the national liberal culture, nearly all have felt a certain involuntary defensiveness. Granted our diverse ethnic circumstances, we share a certain communion of memories.

We had a special language all our own, our own pronunciation for words we shared in common with others (Augústine, contémplative), sights and sounds and smells in which few others participated (incense at Benediction of the Most Blessed Sacrament, Forty Hours, wakes, and altar bells at the silent consecration of the Host); and we had our own politics and slant on world affairs. Since earliest childhood, I have known about a "power elite" that runs America: the boys from the Ivy League in the State Department as opposed to the Catholic boys in Hoover's FBI who (as Daniel Moynihan once put it), keep watch on them. And on a whole host of issues, my people have been, though largely Democratic, conservative: on censorship, on communism, on abortion, on religious schools, etc. "Harvard" and "Yale" long meant "them" to us.

The language of Spiro Agnew, the language of George Wallace, excepting its idiom, awakens childhood memories in me: of men arguing in the barbershop, of my uncle drinking so much beer he threatened to lay his dick upon the porch rail and wash the whole damn street with steaming piss—while cursing the niggers in the mill below,

and the Yankees in the mill above—millstones he felt pressing him. Other relatives were duly shocked, but everybody loved Uncle George; he said what he thought.

We did not feel this country belonged to us. We felt fierce pride in it, more loyalty than anyone could know. But we felt blocked at every turn. There were not many intellectuals among us, not even very many professional men. Laborers mostly. Small businessmen, agents for corporations perhaps. Content with a little, yes, modest in expectation, and content. But somehow feeling cheated. For a thousand years the Slovaks survived Hungarian hegemony and our strategy here remained the same: endurance and steady work. Slowly, one day, we would overcome.

A special word is required about a complicated symbol: sex. To this day my mother finds it hard to spell the word intact, preferring to write "s—." Not that much was made of sex in our environment. And that's the point: silence. Demonstrative affection, emotive dances, an exuberance Anglo-Saxons seldom seem to share; but on the realities of sex, discretion. Reverence, perhaps; seriousness, surely. On intimacies, it was as though our tongues had been stolen, as though in peasant life for a thousand years—as in the novels of Tolstoi, Sholokhov, and even Kosinski—the context had been otherwise. Passion, certainly; romance, yes; family and children, certainly; but sex rather a minor if explosive part of life.

Imagine, then, the conflict in the generation of my brothers, sister, and myself. (The reviewer for the *New York Times* reviews on the same day two new novels of fantasy—one a pornographic fantasy to end all such fantasies [he writes], the other in some comic way representing the redemption wrought by Jesus Christ. In language and verve, the books are rated evenly. In theme, the reviewer notes his embarrassment in even reporting a religious fantasy, but no embarrassment at all about preposterous pornography.) Suddenly, what for a thousand years was minor becomes an all-absorbing investigation. Some view it as a drama of "liberation" when the ruling classes (subscribers to the *New Yorker*, I suppose) move progressively, generation by generation since Sigmund Freud, toward concentration upon genital stimulation, and latterly toward consciousness-raising sessions in Clit. Lib.[3] But it is rather a different drama when we stumble suddenly upon mores staggering any expectation our grandparents ever cherished. Fear of becoming "sexual objects" is an ancient fear that appears in many shapes. The emotional reaction of Maria Wyeth in Joan Didion's *Play It as It Lays* is exactly what the ancient morality would have predicted.

Yet more significant in the ethnic experience in America is the intellectual world one meets: the definition of values, ideas, and purposes emanating from universities, books, magazines, radio, and television. One hears one's own voice echoed back neither by spokesmen of "middle America" (so complacent, smug, nativist, and Protestant), nor by the "intellectuals." Almost unavoidably, perhaps, education in America leads the student who entrusts his soul to it in a direction which, lacking a better word, we might call liberal: respect for individual conscience, a sense of social responsibility, trust in the free exchange of ideas and procedures of dissent, a certain confidence in the ability of men to "reason together" and adjudicate their differences, a frank recognition of the vitality of the unconscious, a willingness to protect workers and the poor against the vast economic power of industrial corporations, and the like.

On the other hand, the liberal imagination has appeared to be astonishingly universalist and relentlessly missionary. Perhaps the metaphor "enlightenment" offers a key. One is *initiated into light*. Liberal education tends to separate children from their parents, from their roots, from their history, in the cause of a universal and superior religion. One is taught regarding the unenlightened (even if they be one's uncles George and Peter, one's parents, one's brothers, perhaps) what can only be called a modern equivalent of *odium theologicum*.[4] Richard Hofstadter described anti-intellectualism in America (more accurately, in nativist America rather than in ethnic America), but I have yet to encounter a comparable treatment of anti-unenlightenment among our educated classes.

In particular, I have regretted and keenly felt the absence of that sympathy for PIGS which simple human feeling might have prodded intelligence to muster, that same sympathy which the educated find so easy to conjure up for black culture, Chicano culture, Indian culture, and other cultures of the poor. In such cases one finds the universalist pretensions of liberal culture suspended; some groups, at least, are entitled to be both different and respected. Why do the educated classes find it so difficult to want to understand the man who drives a beer truck, or the fellow with a helmet working on a site across the street with plumbers and electricians, while their sensitivities race easily to Mississippi or even Bedford-Stuyvesant?

There are deep secrets here, no doubt, unvoiced fantasies and scarcely admitted historical resentments. Few persons in describing "middle Americans," "the silent majority," or [authors Richard] Scammon and [Ben] Wattenberg's "typical American voter" distinguish clearly enough between the nativist American and the ethnic American. The first is likely to be Protestant, the second Catholic. Both may be, in various ways, conservative, loyalist, and unenlightened. Each has his own agonies, fears, betrayed expectations. Neither is ready, quite, to become an ally of the other. Neither has the same history behind him here. Neither has the same hopes. Neither lives out the same psychic voyage, shares the same symbols, has the same sense of reality. The rhetoric and metaphors proper to each differ from those of the other.

There is overlap, of course. But country music is not a polka; a successful politician in a Chicago ward needs a very different "common touch" from the one needed by the county clerk in Normal. The urban experience of immigration lacks that mellifluous, optimistic, biblical vision of the good America which springs naturally to the lips of politicians from the Bible Belt. The nativist tends to believe with Richard Nixon that he "knows America, and the American heart is good." The ethnic tends to believe that every American who preceded him has an angle, and that he, by God, will some day find one, too. (Often, ethnics complain that by working hard, obeying the law, trusting their political leaders, and relying upon the American dream, they now have only their own naiveté to blame for rising no higher than they have.)

It goes without saying that the intellectuals do not love "middle America," and that for all the good, warm discovery of America that preoccupied them during the 1950s no strong tide of respect accumulated in their hearts for the Yahoos,

Babbitts, Agnews, and Nixons of the land. Willie Morris in *North Toward Home* writes poignantly of the chill, parochial outreach of the liberal sensibility, its failure to engage the humanity of the modest, ordinary little man west of the Hudson. The Intellectual's Map of the United States is succinct: "Two coasts connected by United Airlines."

Unfortunately, it seems, the ethnics erred in attempting to Americanize themselves before clearing the project with the educated classes. They learned to wave the flag and to send their sons to war. They learned to support their President—an easy task, after all, for those accustomed to obeying authority. And where would they have been if Franklin Roosevelt had not sided with them against established interests? They knew a little about communism—the radicals among them in one way, and by far the larger number of conservatives in another. To this day not a few exchange letters with cousins and uncles who did not leave for America when they might have, whose lot is demonstrably harder than their own and less than free.

Finally, the ethnics do not like, or trust, or even understand the intellectuals. It is not easy to feel uncomplicated affection for those who call you "pig," "fascist," "racist." One had not yet grown accustomed to not hearing "hunkie," "Polack," "spic," "mick," "dago," and the rest. A worker in Chicago told reporter Lois Wille in a vividly home-centered outburst:

> The liberals always have despised us. We've got these mostly little jobs, and we drink beer and, my God, we bowl and watch television and we don't read. It's goddamn vicious snobbery. We're sick of all these phoney integrated TV commercials with these upper-class Negroes. We know they're phoney.
>
> The only time a Pole is mentioned it's to make fun of him. He's Ignatz Dumbrowski, 274 pounds and 5-foot-4, and he got his education by writing in to a firm on a matchbook cover. But what will we do about it? Nothing, because we're the new invisible man, the new whipping boy, and we still think the measure of a man's what he does and how he takes care of his children and what he's doing in his own home, not what he thinks about Vietnam.

At no little sacrifice, one had apologized for foods that smelled too strong for Anglo-Saxon noses; moderated the wide swings of Slavic and Italian emotion; learned decorum; given oneself to education, American style; tried to learn tolerance and assimilation. Each generation criticized the earlier for its authoritarian and European and old-fashioned ways. "Up-to-date" was a moral lever. And now when the process nears completion, when a generation appears that speaks without accent and goes to college, still you are considered "pigs," "fascists," and "racists."

Racists? Our ancestors owned no slaves. Most of us ceased being serfs only in the last two hundred years—the Russians in 1861. Italians, Lithuanians, Slovaks, Poles are not, in principle, against "community control" or even against ghettoes of our own.

Whereas the Anglo-Saxon model appears to be a system of atomic individuals and high mobility, our model has tended to stress communities of our own, attachment to family and relatives, stability, and roots. Ethnics tend to have a fierce sense of attachment to their homes, having been homeowners for less than three generations: a home is almost fulfillment enough for one man's life. Some groups save arduously in a passion to *own;* others rent. We have most ambivalent feelings about suburban assimilation and mobility. The melting pot is a kind of homogenized soup, and its mores only partly appeal to ethnics: to some, yes, and to others, no.

It must be said that ethnics think they are better people than the blacks. Smarter, tougher, harder working, stronger in their families. But maybe many are not sure. Maybe many are uneasy. Emotions here are delicate; one can understand the immensely more difficult circumstances under which the blacks have suffered; and one is not unaware of peculiar forms of fear, envy, and suspicion across color lines. How much of this we learned in America by being made conscious of our olive skin, brawny backs, accents, names, and cultural quirks is not plain to us. Racism is not our invention; we did not bring it with us; we had prejudices enough and would gladly have been spared new ones. Especially regarding people who suffer more than we.

When television commentators and professors say "humanism" or "progress," it seems to ethnics like moral pressure to abandon their own traditions, their faith, their associations, in order to reap higher rewards in the culture of the national corporations. Ethnic neighborhoods usually do not like interviewers, consultants, government agents, organizers, sociologists. Usually they resent the media. Almost all spokesmen they meet from the world of intellect have disdain for them. It shows. Do museums, along with "Black art" and "Indian art," have "Italo-American" exhibitions or "Lithuanian-American" days? Dvorak wrote the *New World Symphony* in a tiny community of Bohemian craftsmen in Iowa. All over the nation in print studios and metal foundries when the craftsmen immigrants from Europe die, their crafts will die with them. Who here supports such skills? [1971]

Notes

1. KIM AND ROBERT [NOVAK]: A movie star and a television news broadcaster.
2. MELLON: Andrew Mellon, an American industrialist and financier.
3. CLIT. LIB.: A derogatory label for sexual liberation.
4. *ODIUM THEOLOGICUM:* Mutual hatred among theologians, the result of differences in doctrinal interpretation.

Understanding the Reading

1. Why does Novak say that Poles lack language?
2. Why did many people in public life abandon their eastern European names?
3. What is the "power elite"?
4. What does Novak mean when he says, "We did not feel this country belonged to us. We felt fierce pride in it"?
5. What does "anti-unenlightenment" mean?
6. What does Novak mean by "the universalist pretensions of liberal culture"?
7. What distinctions does Novak make between a "nativist America" and an "ethnic America"?
8. What evidence does Novak provide to challenge the notion that ethnic Americans are racist?

Suggestions for Responding

1. Like Novak, most of us have felt alienated, outside the cultural mainstream, in one way or another. Describe a time or a circumstance when you felt different and your belief system or "natural" behavior was devalued. What was your reaction? Did you try to "adjust" to the expectations and values of others, or did the experience strengthen your allegiance to your ways?
2. What can we learn about the values of the dominant American culture from the experiences described by Paley, Qoyawayma, and Novak? ◆

6

El Hilo Que Nos Une/*The Thread That Binds Us: Becoming a Puerto Rican Woman*[1]

CELIA ALVAREZ

My mother migrated to New York in the early 1950s during the period of rapid urbanization and industrialization concomitant with Operation Bootstrap[2] on the Island. She was also a seamstress. She married soon after her arrival and subsequently had the three of us, one right after the other.

Raised in the projects of downtown Brooklyn near the Brooklyn Navy Yard I often wondered: What were we doing here? How did we get here? And why? Nobody said too much, however; no one wanted to talk about the poverty and pain, the family truces and secrets which clouded the tremendous upheaval from Ponce[3] to San Juan to New York.

I grew up speaking Spanish, dancing *la pachanga, merengue,* and *mambo,* eating *arroz con habichuelas* and drinking *malta y café.* I was smart, and learned to play the chords of the bureaucratic machinery of housing, education, and welfare very well at a very young age. I translated for everyone—my mother, her friends, our neighbors, as well as my teachers. My parents kept us close to home and it was my responsibility to keep my brother and sister in tow.

It was hard to understand it all, to try to make sense of who I was as a Puerto Rican in New York, so I read everything I could get my hands on; watched the games the government would play between Afro-Americans and Puerto Ricans with social service monies; heard the poverty pimps tell their lies; watched the kids die of dope or heard about them getting killed down elevator chutes in the middle of a burglary; noted the high over-priced tags on old food being sold in the only supermarket in the neighborhood; knew of kids being raped and thrown off the roof. And I asked, "Why?"

The socially active local parish church became my refuge. It was there that I began to make connections with the poor whites, Afro-Americans, and Asians in my community, and said there had to be a better way for us all. I participated in a variety of activities including youth programs, the local food coop, and newsletter, which basically involved me in community organizing, although I didn't know you called it grass-roots work then. I got swept up by the energy of the civil rights movement and wanted to go to the march on Washington[4] but my mother said, "No!" She worried about me—didn't like me wearing my Martin Luther King button or getting involved in politics. She was afraid I would get hurt. I always liked being out on the street talking to people, however, and she knew from way back that I was not destined to stay inside.

Tensions flourished when I turned fourteen and told my parents I was going out with a Puerto Rican boy in the neighborhood. Unfortunately, "boyfriend" in America and *novio* in Puerto Rico did not translate to mean the same thing. In 1968 I was chaperoned and followed by my father wherever I went because of that grave mistake. Their biggest fear? That I would get pregnant. They even threatened to send me to Puerto Rico. I had it all planned out that I would run away and stay with my cousin. She was the first to move out and get her own place. At least we could keep each other company. It never happened but we've been close ever since.

During this same period I started high school in a predominantly white school in the heart of Flatbush.[5] I found myself desegregating the Catholic school system, one of five or six *latinas* and Afro-Americans in my class. I was known as one of the girls from the ghetto downtown and was constantly called upon to defend my race. One day it went too far. Someone said my father didn't work and that their parents supported my coming to their school. I "went off"! You just didn't talk about my family!

I never told my parents about the racist slurs—never had the heart. They were breaking their backs to send me to school; my father kept his job at a city hospital for thirty years and took on a second job at the docks. We would all go to help him clean offices at night and on weekends after our day outings together. My mother went back to work in a paper factory down the street. Prior to that, she had taken care of the children of women in the neighborhood who worked. I've also worked since about the time I was fourteen.

Anyway, I graduated high school with honors. I had every intention of going to college—I thought it would give me the credentials to be in a position to act on the miseducation that I saw we were getting. Of course I needed money to go, so I went to talk to my guidance counselor. She always prided herself in being able to say a few words in Spanish . . . her way of "relating." I inquired about government grants programs as well as anything else that she could tell me about. All she could say to me was, "Well, you're not the only one who needs money to go to school, dear."

No thanks to her, I managed to get to college with the help of ASPIRA.[6] I marched over to their office on 14th Street—we didn't have a club in our school, there were too few of us—and presented myself to one of the counselors there. I'll always be grateful that he took me under his wing despite the fact he had an overbooked case load. I applied to about ten schools, got into most of them and decided to go to a new institution in New England that broke away from the traditional, predetermined academic program and was primarily based on a mentoring system between student and teacher.

So I left home and landed in a progressive liberal arts college which looked more like a country club than anything else. It was so quiet I had to study with my radio blasting to concentrate. Ironically, it was there that I found my first Afro-American and Puerto Rican teachers. I was relieved to know someone who understood the reference points in my life without my having to explain. After pursuing some studies on Puerto Rico and the Caribbean—for the only formal mention of Puerto Rico in all my schooling up to that point had been in a geography class in which we had discussed its mineral resources—I studied questions of language planning, bilingualism and education, language, culture, and identity. I thought that knowledge of these areas would be useful to the Puerto Rican community. I always made it a point to keep my foot in both the community and academe. I have struggled to stay integrated as a human being despite the efforts of academic institutions to make me over or deny my existence.

To make a long story short, I went on to graduate school where I fought to keep my sanity and sense of self-worth in the midst of the racist sentiment that permeated my department, telling me in a variety of ways that I should not be there, let alone survive my course of study. If one were to look at their track record with regard to women of color one would see how they manage to justify their own position; for to survive requires that we deny who we are, from where we come, and where we are going as a people. I was told that because I had "made it" to such an elitist institution, I obviously was no longer a member of my community. I was admonished not to study the reality of Puerto Ricans because somehow I would be "getting over" and not doing valid research. Ironically, given my gender, class background, nationality, and race, I was as marginalized as ever in that setting.

Which brings me back to our oral history project. Listening to these women's stories has served as a tremendous source of inspiration and validation of my own experience as a Puerto Rican woman. They captured and brought back to life the struggles of my own socialization during the 1960s. Though born in New York, I grappled with many of the same social issues and problems as Flor, Lucila, and Eulalia. However, it was within the context of the educational opportunities historically afforded me through the civil rights movement, in conjunction with my own parents' determination, that I was able to actualize myself in higher education and be in a position to help define this project. This oral history project enabled me to integrate all the different parts of myself—my skills as an intellectual, organizer, and nurturer, as well as my experience as a working-class Puerto Rican woman.

Through the public events linked to our research, I have been able to bring this experience back home: *to my own neighborhood* in Brooklyn, which I came to find out was one of the earlier Puerto Rican settlements in New York; and *to my mother* who came to our event on Puerto Rican garment workers and finally understood what it was I did at the university and how it was not a rejection but a continuation of her legacy to me. Our relationship qualitatively changed after that event: there was more honesty between us; we spoke woman to woman. And it is because of this convergence of historical and personal circumstances that I am sharing this collective experience with you, the reader.

Beyond its impact on me individually, I believe the oral history process in which we have been engaged has provided a space for the collective experience and voice of Puerto Rican working women to be heard. For this oral history project was a process of "coming out"—not just for women of our mothers' or grandmothers' generations but for ourselves as well. For how do we see ourselves if we are invisible, if our most courageous acts as a people go unrecognized? In order to create an authentic connection with others we must first deal with the sources of our own oppression; we must break the silence of our invisibility; but we must speak in our own voice, first to ourselves and then to each other. For in moving beyond our own individual lives we can come to appreciate the connections between us, the continuity and the change, and dispel the fears which keep us apart.

This is from where we come. We respect the dignity of our people despite the devastation of economic deprivation, racial hostility, and sexual repression. We respect the struggles of the women who have preceded us for they set the groundwork upon which we will define our own destinies, for ourselves, on our own terms, in our collective struggle to be free from economic, racial and national oppression.   [1988]

Notes

1. As a graduate student, Alvarez collected oral histories of Puerto Rican women who worked in the New York garment industry. In this selection, she reflects on what this work meant to her personally.
2. OPERATION BOOTSTRAP: A program of tax credits and other incentives designed to encourage Puerto Rican economic development.
3. PONCE: A city in Puerto Rico; San Juan is the capital of Puerto Rico.
4. MARCH ON WASHINGTON: A 1963 civil rights demonstration in Washington, D.C.

5. FLATBUSH: A neighborhood in Brooklyn.
6. ASPIRA: An organization that encourages and assists minority students to obtain a college education.

Understanding the Reading

1. What difficulties did Alvarez have fitting into college?
2. What benefits did she get from her college studies?
3. What does Alvarez mean when she says that "to survive requires that we deny who we are"? Why is it required?
4. How does she feel she was "marginalized"?
5. What does she bring together as a result of her graduate work?

Suggestions for Responding

1. What have you done, or what would you like to do, to come to a fuller understanding and appreciation of one of your parents? What difference did/would it make in your relationship?
2. Both Alvarez and Novak are trying to answer the question, as Alvarez puts it, "How do we see ourselves if we are invisible?" What might or should be done to eliminate this sense of invisibility experienced by members of some groups, or is it a societal problem at all? ✦

7

In Search of Bruce Lee's Grave

SHANLON WU

It's Saturday morning in Seattle, and I am driving to visit Bruce Lee's grave.[1] I have been in the city for only a couple of weeks and so drive two blocks past the cemetery before realizing that I've passed it. I double back and turn through the large wrought-iron gate, past a sign that reads: "Open to 9 P.M. or dusk, whichever comes first."

It's a sprawling cemetery, with winding roads leading in all directions. I feel silly trying to find his grave with no guidance. I think that my search for his grave is similar to my search for Asian heroes in America.

I was born in 1959, an Asian-American in Westchester County, N.Y. During my childhood there were no Asian sports stars. On television, I can recall only that most pathetic of Asian characters, Hop Sing, the Cartwright family houseboy on "Bonanza."[2] But in my adolescence there was Bruce.

I was 14 years old when I first saw "Enter the Dragon," the granddaddy of martial-arts movies. Bruce had died suddenly at the age of 32 of cerebral edema, an excess of fluid in the brain, just weeks before the release of the film. Between the ages of 14 and 17, I saw "Enter the Dragon" 22 times before I stopped counting. During those years I collected Bruce Lee posters, putting them up at all angles in my bedroom. I took up Chinese martial arts and spent hours comparing my physique with his.

I learned all I could about Bruce: that he had married a Caucasian, Linda; that he had sparred with Kareem Abdul-Jabbar;[3] that he was a buddy of Steve McQueen and James Coburn, both of whom were his pallbearers.

My parents, who immigrated to America and had become professors at Hunter College, tolerated my behavior, but seemed puzzled at my admiration of an "entertainer." My father jokingly tried to compare my obsession with Bruce to his boyhood worship of Chinese folk-tale heroes.

"I read them just like you read American comic books," he said.

But my father's heroes could not be mine; they came from an ancient literary tradition, not comic books. He and my mother had grown up in a land where they belonged to the majority. I could not adopt their childhood and they were wise enough not to impose it upon me.

Although I never again experienced the kind of blind hero worship I felt for Bruce, my need to find heroes remained strong.

In college, I discovered the men of the 442d Regimental Combat Team, a United States Army all-Japanese unit in World War II. Allowed to fight only against Europeans, they suffered heavy casualties while their families were put in internment camps. Their motto was "Go for Broke."

I saw them as Asians in a Homeric epic, the protagonists of a Shakespearean tragedy; I knew no Eastern myths to infuse them with. They embodied my own need to prove myself in the Caucasian world. I imagined how their American-born flesh and muscle must have resembled mine: epicanthic folds[4] set in strong faces nourished on milk and beef. I thought how much they had proved where there was so little to prove.

After college, I competed as an amateur boxer in an attempt to find my self-image in the ring. It didn't work. My fighting was only an attempt to copy Bruce's movies. What I needed was instruction on how to live. I quit boxing after a year and went to law school.

I was an anomaly there: a would-be Asian litigator. I had always liked to argue and found I liked doing it in front of people even more. When I won the first-year moot court competition in law school, I asked an Asian classmate if he thought I was the first Asian to win. He laughed and told me I was probably the only Asian to even compete.

The law-firm interviewers always seemed surprised that I wanted to litigate.

"Aren't you interested in Pacific Rim trade?" they asked.

"My Chinese isn't good enough," I quipped.

My pat response seemed to please them. It certainly pleased me. I thought I'd found a place of my own—a place where the law would insulate me from the pressure of defining my Asian maleness. I sensed the possibility of merely being myself.

But the pressure reasserted itself. One morning, the year after graduating from law school, I read the obituary of Gen. Minoru Genda—the man who planned the Pearl Harbor attack. I'd never heard of him and had assumed that whoever did that planning was long since dead. But the general had been alive all those years—rising at 4 every morning to do his exercises and retiring every night by 8. An advocate of animal rights, the obituary said.

I found myself drawn to the general's life despite his association with the Axis powers. He seemed a forthright, graceful man who died unhumbled. The same paper carried a front-page story about Congress's failure to pay the Japanese-American internees their promised reparation[5] money. The general, at least, had not died waiting for reparations.

I was surprised and frightened by my admiration for General Genda, by my still-strong hunger for images of powerful Asian men. That hunger was my vulnerability manifested, a reminder of my lack of place.

The hunger is eased this gray morning in Seattle. After asking directions from a policeman—Japanese—I easily locate Bruce's grave. The headstone is red granite with a small picture etched into it. The picture is very Hollywood—Bruce wears dark glasses—and I think the calligraphy looks a bit sloppy. Two tourists stop but leave quickly after glancing at me.

I realize I am crying. Bruce's grave seems very small in comparison to his place in my boyhood. So small in comparison to my need for heroes. Seeing his grave, I understand how large the hole in my life has been, and how desperately I'd sought to fill it.

I had sought an Asian hero to emulate. But none of my choices quite fit me. Their lives were defined through heroic tasks—they had villains to defeat and wars to fight—while my life seemed merely a struggle to define myself.

But now I see how that very struggle has defined me. I must be my own hero even as I learn to treasure those who have gone before.

I have had my powerful Asian male images: Bruce, the men of the 442d and General Genda; I may yet discover others. Their lives beckon like fireflies on a moonless night, and I know that they—like me—may have been flawed by foolhardiness and even cruelty. Still, their lives were real. They were not houseboys on "Bonanza."

[1990]

Notes

1. BRUCE LEE: A Chinese-American movie star skilled in the martial arts.
2. "BONANZA": A television series about a family of ranchers.
3. KAREEM ABDUL JABBAR: A professional basketball star; Steve McQueen and James Coburn are white movie stars who played very physical roles.
4. EPICANTHIC FOLD: A fold of skin on the upper eyelid that tends to cover the inner corner of the eye.
5. REPARATION: Payment to Japanese-Americans to compensate them for internment during World War II.

Understanding the Reading

1. Why couldn't Wu identify with his father's heroes?
2. What did the heroes Wu identified with have in common?
3. What does Wu mean when he says that the struggle for heroes "defined me"?

Suggestions for Responding

1. What "heroes" did you identify with as you grew up? Did they in any way influence your sense of your ethnic identity? If so, how? If not, why not?
2. Both Wu and Alvarez come to grips with their identity. Explain the similarities and differences in their experiences. ✦

8

"I'm Just as White as You"

LESTER D. LANGLEY

In Kansas City I encountered yet another variation of the midwestern Hispanic American—antichicano and feminist. Catherine Rocha, as director of records in the Jackson County, Missouri, Courthouse, is the highest-ranking appointed Mexican American in Kansas City, which is geographically and culturally the center of the American heartland. We spoke above the chatter of daily business penetrating her office door. On the desk were piles of records, copies of real estate documents, and the like.

Given her youthful vigor and attractiveness, I was incredulous when she told me of her three grown children, two away at college. There seemed little of the presumably typical matronly Hispanic woman, save for a few reminders about the centrality of the family in her life. Her husband is the first Hispanic judge in Kansas City, so the entire clan had obviously latched onto the American mainstream. With her traditional values coupled with a noticeable strain of feminism, Catherine Rocha struck me as a cross between Phyllis Schlafley[1] and Gloria Steinem, an improbable and potentially explosive combination.

For one thing she cares little for the term "chicano," which becomes standard terminology once you hit the southwest, where more radical Mexican Americans launched the movement of *la raza*.[2] "I prefer Mexican American," she said rather bluntly, not telling me if retaining the hyphen indicated ethnic insensitivity. César Chávez, the militant organizer of the Delano, California, grape boycott of the late sixties, had appeared in Kansas City a year or so before and had received (to her obvious satisfaction) a lukewarm reception.

Kansas City has a small Hispanic community—blacks are thought of as *the* minority—but hereabouts in the middle-class heartland they avidly pursue the American dream. "Equality of opportunity" is a phrase the upwardly bound Mexican American uses unhesitatingly. But, as in Chicago, cultural pride, which often stems as much from country of origin as language, has had to accommodate political reality. "We got here first," she said, referring to the Mexican migration into the midwest, but in the Hispanic Chamber of Commerce the Mexican Americans have brought in the Cubans and Puerto Ricans "because it gives us strength."

When I raised the issue of minority politics and equality of opportunity I obviously struck a raw nerve. Like most ambitious middle-class Mexican Americans, Catherine Rocha has some rueful memories of other days, especially the early 1960s, when the Hispanic vote went solidly for Democrats. In Texas it probably guaranteed Kennedy's victory. But when the big federal programs began rolling out from Democratic-controlled Washington, she reminded me, the blacks got most of the largess—not just civil rights, which they deserved, but here in Kansas City they pocketed most of the money filtering into small business and community redevelopment.

Very few of her views, it seemed to me, varied much from those of a staunchly Republican small-town Kansan. With her (and surprisingly large numbers of middle-class Hispanics) the Republican presidents after LBJ rate highly—even Nixon merits a few kind words—because they alertly responded to latent Hispanic resentment by channeling more federal money to the small but rapidly growing Hispanic business community. Black leaders argue, of course, that the Republicans gave the support to Hispanics because they wanted to punish an overwhelmingly

Democratic black constituency. (Some readers may recall Dick Gregory's[3] quip in the 1964 campaign: "I know the blacks for Goldwater, and they're both nice guys.")

Her chosen candidate is Henry Cisneros, the nationally known mayor of San Antonio. The reason lies only partly in their cultural bond. Language and skin color often provide strong links in the political world, but for her and other Hispanics Cisneros is an appealing candidate not so much because he is another Hispanic political hopeful but because he has managed to cultivate the all-American image and still retain his cultural identity. "He's educated and not an embarrassment for us," she said proudly. I sensed that she believes her own career in some respects paralleled Cisneros' and that Hispanics have been ignored because they didn't fit any stereotype of the "typical" Hispanic. "I grew up in a Mexican neighborhood. I come from the same background, but I have aspirations." Then with a reminder that education is vital for fulfilling the (Hispanic-and-all-other-ethnic-categories) American dream, she said, a bit haughtily, "I'm just as white as you."

She shares a conviction of "equality of opportunity" with another Kansas City Mexican American, Hector Barreto, a founder and former head of the U.S. Hispanic American Chamber of Commerce. Over the years the chamber has quietly expanded across the country, promoting the interests of Hispanic-owned business. Barreto was not born American but represents that go-getter enthusiasm in business Americans are fond of attributing to themselves but persist in denying to the Mexican. Back in Guadalajara, he plunged into the cattle business at age sixteen. By twenty-one he was broke, but in the financial disaster had learned the proverbial economic lesson that keeping money is a great deal more difficult than making it. That persistent Hispanic trait of pride meant he couldn't stay in Mexico and embarrass his *familia,* so he headed north, believing, as many Mexicans still do, that the American economy generates endless wealth and unparalleled opportunity. His first job was grubbing for potatoes. No *campesino* (farm worker) accustomed to the backbreaking work of the fields (as were my fellow cotton pickers in the Panhandle), he stayed at it only to get enough money to go into something else—and because he could not return home a failure. Then, following the migra-

tory trail deep into the heartland, the Mexican variation of the cattle drive of the nineteenth century, he hired on as a railroader, driving spikes, and from there moved to toting two-hundred-pound slabs of meat from packing houses into boxcars.

He wound up a restaurateur; he knew nothing of haute cuisine or, frankly, how to cook hamburgers. But the tacos he carried in his lunch pail fascinated the tough Yankees he worked with, so he opened a taco stand to satisfy the presumably endless demand of two thousand packing-house laborers for what must have been for them an exotic dish. When the packing house closed, his customers vanished. Barreto got a job as a janitor and, on the side, started another restaurant, turning it into a family affair. A few years later he had $5,000 in the bank and connections with another businessman who imported from Mexico. Barreto began selling the distinctive Mexican tile to shopping centers across the country. Kansas City newspapers began to print stories about "potato picker makes good."

But his success—and that of other Hispanics in business—did little to alter the American image of the Spanish-speaking. Though there already existed Hispanic chambers of commerce in San Antonio and Miami and elsewhere, they had done little more than promote local Hispanic causes or sponsor traditional Mexican celebrations like the Cinco de Mayo, which commemorates the famous Mexican victory over an invading French army in 1862. Media scenes of indolent *campesinos* propped up against a cactus sleeping away the afternoon so infuriated Barreto he was determined to change things.

In 1979 at a White House Conference on Small Business he discovered another barrier— blacks had twice the number of delegates as the Hispanics. Few wanted to join forces because, as Barreto learned, the Hispanics had too little to offer. More bluntly, the black delegates made it clear their goal was the promotion of *black* minority business. Through this experience Barreto realized the agenda Hispanic entrepreneurs had to chart if they were to enter the mainstream of American business. With a blistering denunciation of the unfairness of government toward Hispanic business, which he attributed mostly to Hispanics' failures to organize and use their economic clout, he transformed the U.S. Hispanic Chamber of Commerce into a truly national pressure group. After that he began meeting with hemispheric leaders. He had joined that proverbial American elite known as "movers and shakers." In a more meaningful way (at least for Barreto) he had fought his way into the American middle class.

In the past decade or so the social science literature dealing with Mexican Americans and other Hispanics has begun to address the question: what is a middle-class Hispanic and what does he stand for? It is not a simple question, because for Hispanics, more so than for blacks, crossing that economic line dividing the working from the middle class can often demand rejection of one's cultural heritage or ethnic identity. Those academics continually befuddled by the twin forces playing on the Hispanic American conscience—the one a determination to "make it" in WASP society,[4] the other a desire to preserve one's cultural heritage, which may mean staying in the barrio[5] or taking a firmer stand for, or even against, bilingualism—are often guilt-ridden products of a privileged social class.

Mexican Americans like Catherine Rocha, who was born an American citizen, and Hector Barreto, who became one through naturalization, know about the pitfalls confronting the Hispanic middle class without, as blacks used to say, "wise white guidance." Middle-class Hispanics are greater believers in those vaunted American values of education, hard work, persistence, and, above all, equality of opportunity than the most devoted WASP. But the middle-class Mexican American often feels a suppressed need to show he is 110 percent American. Much like the southerner of an earlier era who boasted his loyalty to the country in one breath and his affection for "Dixie" in the second, the middle-class Hispanic American, especially those of Mexican heritage, often laud solid middle-class values yet speak fondly of *la cultura* or the barrio. These seemingly contradictory worlds pose less a dilemma for them than for their mainstream American observers who persist in believing that the middle class constitutes a culture.   [1988]

Notes

1. PHYLLIS SCHLAFLEY: An outspoken opponent of the Equal Rights Amendment; Gloria Steinem is the feminist founder of *Ms.* magazine.

2. *LA RAZA:* A political organization whose purpose is to elect Mexican-Americans to public office.
3. DICK GREGORY: A black comedian and political activist.
4. WASP SOCIETY: White, Anglo-Saxon Protestant society.
5. BARRIO: A Latino neighborhood, sometimes considered a ghetto.

Understanding the Reading

1. What are the distinctions suggested by the labels "chicano," "Mexican American," and "Mexican-American"? What about other labels, such as "Hispanic" and "Latino"?
2. Why was Rocha pleased that César Chávez was not warmly received in Kansas City?
3. What does Rocha mean when she says, "I'm just as white as you"?
4. What does Barreto's story show?
5. What is the dilemma of middle-class American Hispanics?

Suggestions for Responding

1. What has influenced you or some member of your family to move away from an ethnic affiliation?
2. Discuss why you think Catherine Rocha rejects a hyphenated-American identity while Alvarez and Wu find it desirable? ✦

9

Rosa Wakefield

JOHN LANGSTON GWALTNEY

Florida-born, Miss Rosa Wakefield has known me practically all my life, and I have always thought of her as a worthy senior with so much dignity that the last thing she needs to think about is standing upon it. She is seventy-eight and hale and preeminently sound-minded. Her buttermilk pies and watermelon pork are as fine as they were when I was a fifth-grader puzzling with her over a text which asserted confidently that the Nigerian Hausa[1] were not black. I do not know anyone who has done more people more good with less noise than Miz Wakefield.

You understand that I am not an educated person. I was born with good sense and I read everything I can get to read. At least I know that I don't know very much. Now, if you still think I can help you, I'll be very glad to answer any question I can for you.[2] I can't answer for nobody but myself. I will tell you what I think and why I happen to think that way. I was never the first person you heard when you came to my father's house or a party, but that never meant that I wasn't thinking as fast as some of these loud folks was talking.

Now, this first question is something I have thought about a great deal ever since I was a little girl. I think that I think more about anything I might think about than most people. That's because I was my father's oldest daughter and my mother died early, so I always had to think for more than one person. And that is a responsibility. It's bad enough when you make a mistake for one person, but when you make a mistake for more than one person—you know, when you make a mistake that's going to hurt somebody who can't think for herself or hisself—then you really feel that more than you would if you had just hurt yourself. I always thought about that. My father and I sort of brought the others up. Now, I don't want to brag on myself, but I guess we didn't do but so bad. Now, the truth is that I think we did a good job.

But now, right there you have one of the big differences between blackfolks, or colored folks, or whatsoever you might call us, and whitefolks. We don't like to spell things out but so much. We know what we mean, like you knew what I meant. You know that I don't really mean that I think we did a pretty good job in raising all those children. You know that I mean that it was very hard to do so and we did it right.

White people are some writing folks! They will write! They write everything. Now, they do that because they don't trust each other. Also, they are the kind of people who think that you can think about everything, about whatever you are going to do, before you do that thing. Now, that's bad for them because you cannot do that without wings. I think that maybe you can't even do that *with* wings. They say that God's brightest angel fell. Now, ask yourself! Do you think God would have made this brightest angel if He knew that this angel was going to turn against Him? Now, it don't make one bit of sense to think that He would have done that. If He knew this brightest angel was going to ape up, what would He want to go and make this angel for? Now, if the Lord can be surprised, who are we to think that we can think about everything before it happens? All you can do is do what you know has got to be done as right as you know how to do that thing. Now, white people don't seem to know that.

I worked hard to put the others through school, and now they help me so the old lady can stir up a little sweet bread and talk to nice people like you. But, you see, there is hard work behind everything we do. You know that this sweet bread didn't make itself. I was telling you about my trips. You know that trip to Africa and that trip to Norway didn't pay for themselves! But, you see, if you eats these dinners and don't cook 'em, if you wears these clothes and don't buy or iron them, then you might start thinking that the good fairy or some spirit did all that. They asked a little white girl in this family I used to work for who made her cake at one of her little tea parties. She said she made it and then she hid her face and said the good fairies made it. Well, you are looking at that good fairy.

Blackfolks don't have no time to be thinking like that. If I thought like that, I'd burn cakes and scorch skirts. But when you don't have anything else to do, you can think like that. It's bad for your mind, though. See, if you think about what is really happening, you will know why these things are happening. When I get these cards on my birthday or Easter, I know that's because I sent my younger brother to school as clean as I could send him and made him get some sense into his head by seeing that he did what that teacher told him to do. They all send me a card on Mother's Day because they say that I was a mother to them. Now, they know that I am living all these other days, too, and they see to it that I don't want for anything I really need and a lot of things the old lady might just want. Rosa has washed her dishes and a lot of other folks' dishes for a long time, so she doesn't really need any machine to wash dishes, but she got one sitting right there in that kitchen! Now, Rosa didn't buy it and she didn't tell anybody to buy it, but it was bought. Now, my youngest brother is a professor too, but if he comes in here and sees something that has to be done, from washing dishes to scrubbing that floor, the next thing you know he just goes on and does it like anybody else. I never married, but any niece or nephew I got will come here if they *think* I need something and go wherever I want to send them.

Now, our children are more mannerable, but now so many of our children are trying to act like white children that it's hard to tell the difference just by the way they act these days. Some of these sorry things passing for young men and ladies that you see in the streets these days are enough to make you hang your head in shame! But so far, praise God, all our children have kept level heads and are doing just fine. In the summer we get together more and they tell me some things that are really hard to believe. I tell them to be nice to everybody that is nice to them and not to do every fool thing that they see being done. Little Rosa, my niece, brought a girl from Nigeria and a girl from Sweden. Now, that pleased me because I have read about those places and I have seen those countries and people there were nice to me, so I was glad to be nice to one of their girls.

We are revern' colored folks! We don't all have the same color skin, but we all have a strong family resemblance. My niece's mother is a German woman, and a finer lady you will never meet. But all you have to do is take one look at my niece and you will know that she is my niece. We all have a very strong family resemblance and we are a family that helps each other. If you know one of us, you know us all. We try to look out for each other. I told my brother about you and those mules and he said you looked just like a Wakefield. All you got to do to look just like a Wakefield is be black and do something good. But he's right this time—you do look a lot like us. You're quiet like we are, too. I guess in your work you have to be quiet because once you get us blackfolks talking, you won't get much of a chance to make much noise! But once a lady was out here, and she couldn't pay for her taxi because that driver had charged her way too much. We helped her and she swore that I looked just like her. Now, I'm a brown woman and this lady I'm telling you about looked as white as any white woman you will ever see. People like to claim kin with people they like. White people do that much more than we do, though. They can' stand the idea of anything good being black. If a black person does something good, they say he did that because of the white in him.

My father was sickly, but he worked hard all his life. He taught me and I tried to help teach the others. People have to go to school now, but they wouldn't have to do that if they would take up time with one another. I went to one college course to learn about the Negro. I'm sorry I did that now because all they did was to sit there and tell each other how they felt—I mean, how it felt to be black. Shoot! I have been feeling black all my life because I am not white! Now, what I wanted to know was not how they felt, because I already knew that; I wanted to know something about our great people and where we came from and how we kept on being folks all through slavery time.

My church and my folks got together and sent the old lady to Spain and Morocco. Everywhere I went I saw some of us. There was colored everywhere I set my foot. Now, I couldn't understand them, but I was looking at them and if I'm black, and we both know I am, there is nothing else in God's world for them to be but black too. There was all kinds of colors! Some of them were white like the people that call themselves white over here. Some of them looked mighty Wakefield. Now, I saw that in Spain and I saw that in Africa. In Morocco some of those people could have been your brother or mine. Some of them had kinky hair and some of them had straight hair and some had wavy hair. Some of them looked like Jews and Italians, but there was all kinds of folks, Most of those people looked like what we used to call munglas. I have read that the Moroccans are white and I know that Americans are supposed to be white, but it looks to me like they are just as mixed up as we are over here. Half of these whitefolks I see out here look like they are passing[3] to me. That's the same way it is in Cuba and Puerto Rico. I have seen those countries and I know that most of those people are colored, just like most of those people in Morocco. I'm telling you what I saw, not what somebody told me. A lot of these people from those foreign countries may not speak English, but you can look at them and see that they are Aun' Hagi's[4] children. A lot of them don't want to admit their color because they are afraid that these whitefolks over here would give them a hard time. Now, they are right about that.

I have been a cook and a maid and a housekeeper, and I have worked in hospitals. I still do every now and then, but I was in the hospital not long ago and I met this doctor that they said was an Arab. Well, he was darker than many people in my own family. I was proud to see one of the race better hisself. But, you know, that devil didn't want to hear a thing about his color! They had a lot of doctors from India and Jordan working there too. Now, a lot of the colored people didn't want to have anything to do with them because they said if they will pass like that, maybe they are not really doctors, either. I know folks that pass, but these doctors were just plain fools about it! I know people who pass to get a job that they should be able to get anyway, but they don't try to act like them all the time. There was this young Iraqian doctor there and he was darker than me, but he sure did everything he could think of and then some to show how white he was supposed to be. I don't trust anybody who would deny their color like that. And if Rosa Wakefield can't put her trust in you, you will never get your hands on her blood pressure or her diabetis or anything else! [1980]

Notes

1. NIGERIAN HAUSA: Negroid people of Niger and northern Nigeria.
2. This interview is one of the oral histories black anthropologist Gwaltney recorded in an effort to preserve the values and diversity of black culture in the South.
3. PASSING: A reference to light-skinned blacks trying to "pass" as whites.
4. AUNT HAGI: A reference to the biblical figure Hagar, the servant of Sarah and Abraham and mother of Abraham's son, Ishmael.

Understanding the Reading

1. What values does Rosa Wakefield hold?
2. What characteristics does she think differentiate "blackfolks" and "whitefolks"?
3. Explain her beliefs about racial identity.
4. What questions do you think Gwaltney posed to elicit Wakefield's responses?

Suggestions for Responding

1. What advice do you think Rosa Wakefield might give to any one of the preceding six writers?

2. If you were collecting oral histories from your family or your community, what kinds of information would you want to focus on? In other words, what characteristics and values do you expect to identify? What questions would you ask to obtain that information? ◆

10

More Minarets Among the Steeples

STEPHEN GOODE

When Nazir Khaja came to the United States in 1970 to study medicine, he had two things on his mind. First was to obtain a highly coveted American medical degree. Second, he says, was to assure himself "socioeconomic viability," the opportunity to live well.

That done, Khaja, who was born in Hyderabad, India, says something happened that he had not anticipated at all: He got interested in his religious roots.

"I knew I was a born Muslim," he says. "But I began to wonder what it meant to be a member of this faith." Then he began to realize that he wanted to stay.

A bit later, a Pakistani friend who made frequent business trips to the United States confessed that he planned to relocate his family here. Another Muslim acquaintance, a Pakistani teacher who won a scholarship to study in the States, decided the same thing. Their reasons were similar, according to Khaja: "We realized our Islamic identity could be preserved in the United States" and combined with what the country had to offer: jobs and a high standard of living.

Rapidly increasing numbers of their fellow believers are reaching the same conclusion. Khaja, who heads the Islamic Information Service, which he founded in 1985 in Los Angeles, estimates that there are 4 million Muslims living in the United States. That makes for roughly twice as many Muslims as Episcopalians.

More than 650 mosques (a number that is rapidly increasing, says Khaja), many of them with schools for the young, can be found across the country in cities as diverse as Hattiesburg, Miss., Dearborn, Mich., and Tempe, Ariz. Muslims elsewhere meet regularly in hundreds of Islamic centers and in the homes of the faithful.

Many are descendants of Muslims who left the Ottoman Empire and arrived on American shores around 1900. Most are more recent arrivals, like Khaja, men and women who came to study in the 1960s and later and remained.

They are a highly educated group. Yvonne Haddad, professor of history at the University of Massachusetts at Amherst and author of books and articles on Muslims in America, investigated six mosques and found that three of every four members had college degrees. Also, she says, many Muslims have advanced degrees in such fields as medicine and engineering.

Muslim magazines in English such as The Minaret, published by the Islamic Center of Southern California in Los Angeles, run ads for videotapes of "Adam, the Muslim Moppet" and for Muslim real estate agents. Another ad suggests a call to travel agents Iqbal and Nahid Mirza to arrange "Your Florida Fantasy in Orlando," probably about as American as one can get.

More significantly, though, after decades of quiescence, some U.S. Muslims have become politically active. After Iraq's invasion of Kuwait, for example, the Public Affairs Council at the Islamic Center in Los Angeles issued a strong condemnation but asked that U.S. troops not become involved. The council was deeply involved in local politics in the past year, too, taking positions on propositions on the ballot and inviting politicians such as the Rev. Jesse Jackson to speak at the center.

At its 27th annual Labor Day meeting in Dayton, Ohio, the Islamic Society of North America, a group based in Plainfield, Ind., took up such issues as educating public officials about Muslim concerns. And shortly after that, the Council of Masajid of the United States, an umbrella group of 195 U.S. mosques, signed an agreement to become involved with Religion in American Life, an organization formerly made up of only Christians and Jews.

Religion in American Life, which advertises church and synagogue schedules in such places as hotels, now also publicizes mosque activities. "Before, we were cautious about joining any Christian and Jewish groups, because we felt we'd be drowned in the greater numbers," says Dawud Assad, head of the Council of Masajid in New York. "Things have changed."

Assad, an American-educated mechanical engineer born in Jerusalem, thinks U.S. Muslims share two goals equally hard to achieve. One is to counter the negative image of Muslims as terrorists and fanatics that he claims is purveyed by television, movies and the media in general. The second is to supplant that with a positive image that he says is more in keeping with reality.

In the past year, for example, the Islamic Center in Los Angeles became embroiled in a controversy after members discovered that a new history text adopted for the California public schools carried a description of Islam as the "religion of sword-carrying bedouins." That image, notes Khaja, hardly fits the 750,000 people of the faith who live in California.

The members lodged protests, and Muslims across the state testified at public hearings, and the offending material was removed. Khaja says the event ushered in a new level of involvement in state affairs.

Muslim leaders find it much more comfortable to deal with the positive image that they want Americans to have. In part, they think this will come if U.S. Christians and Jews recognize the similarities Judaism and Christianity share with Islam: their monotheism, for example, and their reverence for the prophet Abraham.

But mostly, Khaja and Assad think that once Americans have a clearer idea about the way Muslims live and worship, misunderstanding will clear up quickly. Khaja's information service produces nationally viewed TV programs hosted by young, very Americanized moderators whose guests—experts from other faiths, prominent Muslims—talk about Muslim piety and the reverence the faithful show God.

The programs also stress Islam's commitment to the poor, its requirement to give alms and its prohibition of such things as alcohol, drugs and sexual promiscuity—a complete way of life that gives direction to the lives of the faithful and offers a way to overcome, in Khaja's words, "those problems that so trouble us in America today: the breakup of the family, drug addiction and homosexuality."

That picture appeals to many. More than 1 million U.S. Muslims are black, many of them converts from Christianity. Increasingly, too, mosques are seeing conversions among whites and other races, though that is difficult to trace because no one has collected overall records on Islam's growth.

Still, there are problems whose solutions will take time. Immigrants often come from countries ruled by tyrants, and they are mistrustful of government and deeply reluctant to get involved politically, notes Haddad, who is from Syria.

When President Bush on his Thanksgiving visit to Saudi Arabia said he was sickened by photographs of children taken in Kuwait after the Iraqi invasion, the reaction among many American Muslims was cynicism. Haddad says, "Muslims wondered why the president had 'selective nausea,' when there are photographs of Palestinian children and their suffering that would be equally sickening."

And the Democrats, Haddad says, are perceived equally negatively, particularly after 1984 presidential candidate Walter F. Mondale made much of returning money received from Christian Arabs. "The feeling," according to Haddad, "was that if money from Christian Arabs was regarded as polluted, how would Islamic Arab money be regarded?"

But these are attitudes Khaja thinks can be overcome. Islam has a process called *ijma* in which solutions to new problems not directly addressed in the Koran (such as surrogate parenting) are reached through consensus among Islamic scholars. That tradition is not unlike American democracy, according to Khaja, which he describes as "a kind of reaching a consensus among the masses of people."

He does present one caveat: American Muslims "have entered American democracy at a time in its evolution when it rules God out" and has moved "to the extremes of church-state separation." This, he says, "is something Islam will not allow." The consensus the Islamic faithful must work in "is one that accepts God and then works from there," a position he describes as very close to that of the Founding Fathers, "who had definite religious values."

Interestingly, the Salman Rushdie affair[1] gave Islam a big boost in the United States. Assad says that sales of Muslim holy books grew considerably, and Haddad found that attendance at mosques jumped by 50 percent. The reason, says Assad, is that "parents did not want their children to become alienated from their faith, as Rushdie had."

Haddad thinks that Southern California Muslims will continue to be the most politically and socially active in the United States, with other mosques following the example, some more than others.

Still, she adds, most U.S. Muslims will not escape American influence. Mosques long have been paralleling the roles of churches and synagogues as community centers, with bake sales, potluck dinners and groups for women and the young. These are not mosque activities in traditionally Muslim societies, she notes.

Khaja, with his Southern California perspective, finds that assimilation, once begun, proceeds rapidly. The children of the Pakistani businessman, he says, are members of the local Young Republican club.

And there are political successes. Recently, when it approved the building of a new mosque, the Los Angeles City Council forbade the addition of a minaret and dome. Mayor Tom Bradley, says Khaja, let it be known "through the pipeline" that he might be willing to overrule this order. Muslims organized and protested the restriction, and it was overturned.

For Assad, the increasing visibility of Islam in the United States—from the dedication of a new mosque in South Brunswick, N.J., in December to the construction of Islamic centers all across the country—is most encouraging.

Optimistically, he predicts the bad image the faith has among many Americans will be largely a thing of the past in "five or six years." Finally, he says, "we have only ourselves to blame for America's ignorance about Islam. We've been silent when we should have been talking." [1991]

Note

1. SALMAN RUSHDIE AFFAIR: In 1989, Rushdie's book, *The Satanic Verses,* was declared blasphemous by Iran's Ayatollah Khomeini, causing riots in some Muslim countries and forcing Rushdie into protective hiding in response to the Ayatollah's order for his execution.

Understanding the Reading

1. Characterize Muslims in the United States.
2. What have these Muslims done to organize themselves, and why?

3. What negative images do they want to correct?
4. What Muslim religious beliefs are described in the article?
5. Explain *ijma*.
6. How has American culture begun to influence Muslims in the United States?

Suggestion for Responding

Speculate about how the growing Muslim presence will affect life in the United States. ◆

11

The House Warming

ROBBIE CLIPPER SETHI

The thing is, you have to bless everything big you get—a house, a husband, a male child. Fundamentally you have nothing against counting your blessings, privately, like when you lay down to sleep, but you'd rather not have to go through a public religious ceremony in your own house. You figure you've avoided that with Christianity; it didn't occur to you ten years ago, when you married a decadent member of a devout Indian sect, that you'd ever do anything to warrant participation in a Sikh[1] service again.

You give the priest a couple hundred dollars, and he promises to read the book,[2] start to finish, only getting up when an assistant or an interested Sikh agrees to spell him for a few pages. In an ideal world, you would volunteer your father, brothers, or lesser male relations for an hour, the way you'd volunteer your friends to give their blood after the hospital has given you a number of transfusions you would otherwise have had to pay for. But your father and brothers are WASP Americans, and they wouldn't come anyway. You've lost contact with the rest of your family. And even your husband and his cousins can't read their mother tongue. Your husband's father tries to read for an hour, but he breaks into a fit of coughing so bad that your mother-in-law has to run into the kitchen and tell the priest to put

down his glass of Coke without ice and spring her husband before the house-blessing prayer turns into a dirge.

They started reading in the Gurudwara,[3] a split level that the local Sikh association has converted into a temple. On Saturday morning, coincidentally Halloween, they drive the book twenty miles past the K-Mart and the 7-11 to your house, where they set up a little sanctuary in your living room. You don't have to worry about moving furniture; you haven't had the money for furniture since you moved in three months ago. You did have to drag your mother-in-law from store to store looking for a white sheet that did not come prepackaged with a fitted bottom sheet, edged with polyester lace or dotted with little white on white fleurs-de-lis, designer signed. They've spread the sheet on the floor. They've taped a canopy to your ceiling. When you take it down, it will pull off four little one-inch squares of brand-new paint, but for now it makes the room look exotic, like a tent in the desert, shiny and gold.

Under that they put the book—the size of a library dictionary—on a pedestal a foot off the floor; they cover the binding with another cloth of gold. The priest sits behind it, cross-legged, his white beard flowing like a spray of Spanish moss on an old, gnarled stump. Next to him another old man in a beard and white turban sits behind an Indian squeeze-box: an accordion that sits like a child's piano on the floor. With one hand he plays a Ravi Shankar medley while he opens and closes a bellows in the back of the wheezing contraption with the other.

Beside him sits a third man, young, his black beard just as long and lush as the other's, moving his lips and staring at the sheet on the floor.

People come in and out, their feet bare, their heads covered, out of respect for the book, with scarfs, handkerchiefs, veils, the ends of their saris, an occasional turban. Your husband's cousins are there, and so are their blond wives. The eldest, Claire, a pure-bred English Texan, has had her hair frosted so frequently that her bangs have turned completely blond; darker roots reveal her darker origins. She hasn't been the same since a pedophile cruising the malls praised her children for their big eyes, chocolate hair, and permanent, healthy tans. "How did you get them?" the woman asked.

"The usual way," Claire said. "The eldest was a breach."

Claire likes to tell this story, every time the family has a function, her pink face growing pinker as she builds up to the indignant punchline: "My children don't even look like me; everyone thinks they're adopted!"

The younger sister-in-law, of Scandinavian extraction, has never even had to use Sun-in to get the platinum look that has earned her entire family, unbeknownst to them, your in-laws' epithet, "the white-haired people." When he married her, her husband said he wanted to follow in his brother's footsteps, with a blond, two kids, an Oldsmobile, and a house in the country. Her kids are hardly brown at all, except for their eyes. Their light brown hair will turn as they get older. Hopefully by then they'll learn to respect your property, too, but for now they'd just as soon empty all the ground-level cabinets in your kitchen while their mother looks on, smiling.

The cousins are both wearing turbans over their original uncut hair, but their kids have all had haircuts. Even the pure-blooded little Sikhs in the room have escaped having their hair pulled into tight little braids and pinned on top of their heads where it won't get into their eyes, cake up with chewing gum, or tempt some little under-aged heathen to cut off a hunk. You once asked their parents about this. You know it's a personal question, but you only pulled it out after they'd started the conversation by asking you why you haven't had any children. "In America they will be teased," the parents say. "Americans will call them hippie, Charles Manson, and the Fairy Queen."

You know all this without even walking in the door. You've seen it all before—at weddings, turban-tyings, any context that the older generation can dream up for recalling the India they don't have the stamina to live in anymore. In fact, you've actually managed to miss half the ceremonies, having spent the morning with your husband's sullen thirteen-year-old Americanized niece sixty miles to the east, where your father-in-law prides himself on getting a deal on two twenty-five-pound trays of fried farmer's cheese floating in a sea of briny peas, obscure, subcontinent curried pulse beans, deep-fried dumplings in yoghurt and rice. You pulled up to the repast seething in three aluminum caldrons in the

parking lot behind the tiny strip-mall restaurant that made you wait half an hour while the cook deep-fried a stack of greasy pancakes.

You and the niece unload the first rack of the yellow liquid that has been smelling up your car all the way from Edison, and you notice a pool of grease escaping into the carpet on the floor of the back seat. "Oo, yucky," she says. The trunk is also drenched. You realize for the next six months you will be driving U.S. 80 in a Toyota that smells, as your paternal grandmother would have said, "like a Chinese laundry or something."

You kick your way through a shoe-store full of wing tips, Reeboks, sandals, and little patent leather mary janes in your garage, and you fear they've turned your entire house into a temple, but you don't take off your shoes. You figure that until you get the food out of your car, you can't possibly pay your respects to the other world.

In the house the scent of incense takes over where your curried car left off. You can never smell incense without remembering the taste of marijuana, an unfortunate association in your current state of mind. People you don't know, drinking Coke and orange juice in your kitchen, turn their eyes on your feet when they hear your heels clicking on your own kitchen tiles.

Eventually you locate your husband, standing in the back yard with a glass of scotch, giggling with a group of other forty-year-old boys, more bloated with responsibility and the years, thank God, than he is. "I refuse to have any more to do with the food," you tell him, smelling your hands to locate the exact source of the turmeric you know that even incense will never quite get rid of. You fight a blasphemous urge to sneak out of the house and choke down a steak, raw.

"Go make an appearance at the prayer," your husband says. "It's almost over. Please."

You catch a vision of a child of your own flesh and blood, your brother's daughter, yellow-haired, like you when you were two. She runs across the yard and grabs the spangled scarf your mother-in-law selected to go with the traditional Punjabi[4] tunic and baggy pants you had a tailor make in India five years ago for occasions just like this. At the time, your husband said, "I don't much like *chunis*." He never likes anything that casts a sheen. But you are like your brother's child: anything pretty is worth wrapping around your head. Later you discovered that the long, translucent scarfs Indian women match so carefully with their clothes are necessary not just for covering their heads in the presence of God, but for hiding their faces when an older male walks into the room.

You throw the *chuni* to your niece, and she squeals and covers her translucent face with it. "Weird shit," her mother says. She brought your blood to this thing out of curiosity, perhaps, or out of a nostalgia for the flaky religions and exotic rituals she was mature enough to leave behind when the sixties turned into the seventies. You'd like to think she came with the intention of springing you from this unfortunate function, or at least to lend you a little moral support. Your brother didn't make it. "He would never be able to take this," his wife says, and you almost wish you'd played it safe like him and married a lapsed Protestant.

You have to retrieve the *chuni* in order to pay your respects to the book. You know you have to be seen doing that once, or the priest will tell your mother-in-law that one of the white girls didn't stick her head into the room, and, knowing instinctively which one, she'll grumble about your obvious damnation, if the Sikhs have such a thing, as long as she can retain her memory in the face of Alzheimer's, stroke, hardening of the arteries, and all the day-time television she watches for want of a car, a reading knowledge of English, or a craft suitable to her age and abilities. Besides, it's your house they're blessing.

You know that it's the custom to prostrate yourself in front of the book while one priest is reading, one priest is praying, and the other priest is singing—the best part of the service, like the Methodism you grew up with. You know you have to throw at least one dollar bill in front of the book, where a pile of paper money has already mounted up like the leaves your father-in-law rakes into neat little piles in the front yard. But, having tried it once or twice, you can no longer bring yourself to throw money at a book. It's American money, after all, and somehow it doesn't look authentic lying there recalling Mammon in front of someone's holy scriptures. Besides, when you used to go to church, all your mother ever gave you was a quarter, and if a special holiday, like Christmas or Easter, required any larger denomination, she would seal it up in an envelope you brought home expressly for that purpose, with a full-color picture of Jesus on

it, so that everyone would know you put something in the basket, but nobody would know how much.

Your husband's niece is worse than you are. Her mother pushes her into the room, head covered with the muffler someone pilfered from your closet. "Mom!" the kid says, and she runs at full tilt out into the yard.

Your brother's child won't relinquish the *chuni,* so you pick her up, spread an end of it over both your heads, and carry her into the prayer room. She sits on your lap on the floor, next to your husband's friend's wife, Sheela, who has poured herself into a street-length dress. You wonder what the priest thinks of this nice Hindu girl, her full-caste child in her lap, baring her legs like a go-go dancer. Your feeling of superiority lasts until the squeeze-box wheezes shut and the priest starts talking. You don't understand this stuff. You think you recognize a few words— God, house, your husband's father's name—but you have never quite been able to convince yourself, as soon as they break into their native language, that they're not talking about you, so you hug your niece, the whitest child in the room, and she plays with your bangles for a while, wrapping her little pink fingers around them on your wrist; then she gets up and runs to the other room, where her mother has been watching from what any Christian woman might consider a safe distance.

The youngest priest, his beard flowing like the beard of a black-and-white Jesus, stands up and presses his palms together. You should have snuck out during the change of ministers. Now you're going to have to pray. He starts talking. You think you recognize the words husband, wife, children, especially wife, which he repeats over and over again, as if he thinks he has to remind you and every other woman in the room what you are expected to be, and you know he's talking about you; it's no longer just paranoia, not even a healthy, sneaking suspicion. You get up on your knees and crawl out of the room.

Your husband's cousin's wife, the natural white-haired one, is in the kitchen, drinking beer and interrogating your brother's wife about the rest of your delinquent family. "Keep it down," you say. "I mean, it is a prayer."

Her youngest slides a glass off the counter. It shatters on the floor. He looks at his mother for approval. "Oh, bad, Hergobinder," she sighs, and he breaks into a wail. She picks him up to comfort him while you pick up the larger pieces of glass, dying to tell her it was bad enough she had to give her kid an Indian name without raising him like a wild Indian, too. "Take him trick-or-treating," you mutter to your thirteen-year-old niece.

"We're not wearing costumes," she says.

He's wearing a pair of white leggings, tight on his doll-like calves, and a miniature Nehru jacket.[5] Hang one of your old peace signs around his neck, and he'll be wearing a costume in the same meager spirit as the one you wore the year you went out as a beatnik. Your husband's niece is wearing a pair of skin-tight orange-and-blue Day-Glo pants and a long T-shirt with Mickey Mouse on the front, his ears hanging from her breasts, which are already larger than yours will ever be, and the logo, "Mickey died for our sins."

"Take him out in the yard," you say.

"I'm going to miss the party I'm supposed to go to," she says, "if we don't eat soon."

The doorbell rings. Your father-in-law opens the door on a man his age, American, in khakis and a shirt, and a four-year-old, her baby hair pulled into a teased pony tail, in a tutu and a pair of black tights. "I'll handle this," you say.

The little girl holds out a plastic pumpkin basket and you drop a Milky Way into it. In the room adjoining the hall, the priest is still going on about houses, wives, and children. He's beginning to sound like an American politician. You almost long to go trick-or-treating with this unlikely couple. "What are you?" you ask the little girl.

"Can't you guess?" she says. "Where have you been?"

"Madonna," her grandfather says.

You wonder if he's listened to the lyrics of "Like a Virgin." He's more concerned about the Babel[6] in the other room. "House blessing prayer," you say.

"What does that old man keep under his turban?" the little girl says.

You say, "Hair."

"He looks like Santa Claus," she says.

You think about that: pressed white beard, belly, red silk shirt.

"It's not Christmas," she says. "It's Halloween!"

You know. You want to tell her.

"I think it's a good costume anyway," she

says, as her grandfather smiles good-bye, sorry, and guides her away.

You drag the vacuum out of the closet and go after Hergobinder's glass, drowning out the rest of the young priest's syllables—wife, children, God—in Punjabi, of course, a language you tactically decided not to learn when you begged your husband to translate a forty-five-minute conversation between your mother-in-law and her daughter, only to discover they were caught up in comparing the price and quality of various Japanese polyesters.

When the sermon stops, your husband rushes in. "Serve!" he says. "The priests have to go to another party."

Everybody eats but your Indo-American niece, who wrinkles up her nose at the mere thought of her ancestral food. You'd give her a piece of candy, but then everyone would want a piece of candy, and there wouldn't be enough for all the trick-or-treaters you're expecting in this suburban breeding ground. Your car is already defaced; you don't think it could stand the trick of a rotten pumpkin on the hood, though soaped windows, mixed with a steady, autumn rain, would at least go part-way toward restoring it to its original, pre-turmeric condition.

Your husband and his father drive the priests back to the temple, leaving you to bid their guests good-bye. They stand so long at the door that your feet hurt, your back is aching. The sun goes down. They pat you on the shoulder, tell you that you must come see them in Hoboken, Jersey City, Jackson Heights. You make a lot of promises you know you will be too sick to honor. A band of kids dressed up as bums, nurses, skeletons, and super-heroes stares down the hill at this departing horde of men and women in turbans, pajamas, leisure suits, and saris; they turn back toward the main road, as if they thought your house might be the kind that gives out razor blades.

Your husband's cousins' wives stand around the kitchen while you wash the dishes. "Another splendid family reunion," they say. You wish you could relate to them as partners in the same mistake, but one of them still teases her hair, and the younger one will never understand the difference between Joe and Eugene McCarthy.

Your brother's wife left, taking your blood with her. You wanted to go too, back to your hometown where your psychedelic friends used to talk about Eastern religions as if they knew what they were talking about. When your husband comes back, even the cousins are gone. The house is clean, with no help from his arthritic mother. You tell your father-in-law he might as well go to bed too, but he wants to sit around in the prayer room a little longer, though it is stripped down to an unfurnished living room again.

It's early, but to be alone, you climb upstairs to the bedroom. You leave your Halloween costume on the floor and crawl between the sheets on your antique brass bed. Your husband comes in. "Did you meet the priest?" he says.

"I couldn't exactly miss him."

"I thought you'd introduce yourself. First thing he said when we got into the car: 'You didn't introduce me to your wife.'"

You think your husband must have mistranslated; it wouldn't be the first time. You say, "'Which one was your wife?' might be a little more like it." You hope he'll have better luck with the gist of the sermon. "What did he say? The young one, when the music stopped and he got started talking."

"You don't want to hear it!" He laughs. He puts his arms around you. He smells like incense, scotch.

"Good night," you say. You close your eyes.

"The poor guy hasn't been here very long," your husband says, "one or two weeks."

"Out of India?" And you thought *you* had culture shock.

"The other priests thought it would be a good experience for him to give the sermon. He didn't want to. He didn't know what to say. They told him anything he said would be more authentic, coming direct from the Punjab, that is."

"What was it all about?" you ask. "Politics?" Coming straight from the Punjab, you suspect it had something to do with Khalistan—the independent state Sikhs have been demanding to save themselves from absorption by the Hindu majority.

"Something like: in a Sikh house the children must learn their religion; the husband doesn't have the time to teach them; maintaining the tradition must be the job of the wife."

"With all those half-breeds running around? All us white women?"

The poor man must have spoken the first thing that popped into his head. Divine inspiration. Though you consider yourself a heathen, you flash back on your belief in the last book of the Bible, an unshakable paranoia that has effectively prevented you from having children. You're not sure whether to feel guilty or not, whether to give in to the urge to get onto the next plane, so your husband might have half a chance of marrying into the house of his god. "Are you trying to say we need a Sikh woman?" you ask.

"I'm not saying anything," he answers.

He takes off his clothes and turns out the light. A harvest moon shines through the few remaining leaves of the oak outside your window. You hope by now that all the trick-or-treaters have gone home. You don't want to have to get up to remind your father-in-law that all he has to do is give each kid a piece of candy. Soon he'll stop praying and go to bed, and the dead will walk the earth. Your husband tightens his arms around you and sweeps one last vision of little hybrid monsters out of your head. You will never know, in this life, whether you've been cursed or blessed.   [1992]

Notes

1. SIKH: Sikhism is a 500-year-old religion that arose from an attempt to reform and reconcile Hinduism and Islam. It is monotheistic and rejects both the Hindu caste system and the oppression of women. Many Sikhs, however, recognize Hindu gods and observe Hindu holidays. Orthodox Sikhs never cut their hair, and males wrap theirs in turbans. The traditional dress for a Sikh woman is a tunic, long pants, and a *chuni,* a chiffon scarf dyed to match her outfit and sometimes decorated with embroidery and spangles, which is used to cover her face in public.

2. THE BOOK: The Sikh holy scripture, called the Adi Granth, the Sikh equivalent of the Christian Bible, the Jewish Torah, and the Muslim Koran.

3. GURUDWARA: A Sikh temple.

4. PUNJABI: Characteristic of the Punjab, the northwest part of the Indian subcontinent; most Sikhs come from this region.

5. NEHRU JACKET: A squarish jacket with a narrow, stand-up collar, worn buttoned from throat to waist.

6. BABEL: Noise and confusion; a reference to the biblical story that God punished people for trying to build a tower to heaven by giving them different languages.

Understanding the Reading

1. What Sikh traditions and values are described in the story?
2. In what ways have American customs and habits influenced this Sikh family?
3. How does the fact that the house blessing occurs on Halloween provide a commentary on both Sikh and American cultures?

Suggestions for Responding

1. Describe a strange or foreign tradition or ceremony you have witnessed or in which you have participated. Explain how you responded, and consider what it revealed to you about what you had accepted as "normal."
2. Goode and Sethi both describe how a recent immigrant group attempts to maintain religious traditions within the context of middle-class America. Speculate on the effects this practice will have on American culture. ✦

12

Beyond the Melting Pot

WILLIAM A. HENRY III

Someday soon, surely much sooner than most people who filled out their Census forms last week realize, white Americans will become a minority group. Long before that day arrives, the presumption that the "typical" U.S. citizen is someone who traces his or her descent in a direct line to Europe will be part of the past. By the time . . . elementary students . . . reach midlife, their diverse ethnic experience in the classroom will be echoed in neighborhoods and workplaces throughout the U.S.

Already 1 American in 4 defines himself or herself as Hispanic or nonwhite. If current trends in immigration and birth rates persist, the Hispanic population will have further increased an estimated 21%, the Asian presence about 22%, blacks almost 12% and whites a little more than 2% when the 20th century ends. By 2020, a date no further into the future than John F. Kennedy's election is in the past, the number of U.S. residents who are Hispanic or nonwhite will have more than doubled, to nearly 115 million, while the white population will not be increasing at all. By 2056, when someone born today will be 66 years old, the "average" U.S. resident, as defined by Census statistics, will trace his or her descent to Africa, Asia, the Hispanic world, the Pacific Islands, Arabia—almost anywhere but white Europe.

While there may remain towns or outposts where even a black family will be something of an oddity, where English and Irish and German surnames will predominate, where a traditional (some will wistfully say "real") America will still be seen on almost every street corner, they will be only the vestiges of an earlier nation. The former majority will learn, as a normal part of everyday life, the meaning of the Latin slogan engraved on U.S. coins—E PLURIBUS UNUM, one formed from many.

Among the younger populations that go to school and provide new entrants to the work force, the change will happen sooner. In some places an America beyond the melting pot has already arrived. In New York State some 40% of elementary- and secondary-school children belong to an ethnic minority. Within a decade, the proportion is expected to approach 50%. In California white pupils are already a minority. Hispanics (who, regardless of their complexion, generally distinguish themselves from both blacks and whites) account for 31.4% of public school enrollment, blacks add 8.9%, and Asians and others amount to 11%—for a nonwhite total of 51.3%. This finding is not only a reflection of white flight from desegregated public schools. Whites of all ages account for just 58% of California's population. In San Jose bearers of the Vietnamese surname Nguyen outnumber the Joneses in the telephone directory 14 columns to eight.

Nor is the change confined to the coasts. Some 12,000 Hmong refugees from Laos have settled in St. Paul. At some Atlanta low-rent apartment complexes that used to be virtually all black, social workers today need to speak Spanish. At the Sesame Hut restaurant in Houston, a Korean immigrant owner trains Hispanic immigrant workers to prepare Chinese-style food for a largely black clientele. The Detroit area has 200,000 people of Middle Eastern descent; some 1,500 small grocery and convenience stores in the vicinity are owned by a whole subculture of Chaldean Christians with roots in Iraq. "Once America was a microcosm of European nationalities," says Molefi Asante, chairman of the department of African-American studies at Temple University in Philadelphia. "Today America is a microcosm of the world."

History suggests that sustaining a truly multiracial society is difficult, or at least unusual. Only a handful of great powers of the distant past—Pharaonic Egypt and Imperial Rome, most notably—managed to maintain a distinct national identity while embracing, and being ruled by, an ethnic mélange. The most ethnically diverse contemporary power, the Soviet Union,[1] is beset with secessionist demands and near tribal conflicts. But such comparisons are flawed, because those empires were launched by conquest and maintained through an aggressive military presence. The U.S. was created, and continues to be redefined, primarily by voluntary immigration. This process has been one of the country's great strengths, infusing it with talent and energy. The "browning of America" offers tremendous opportunity for capitalizing anew on the merits of many peoples from many lands. Yet this fundamental change in the ethnic makeup of the U.S. also poses risks. The American character is resilient and thrives on change. But past periods of rapid evolution have also, alas, brought out deeper, more fearful aspects of the national soul.

POLITICS: NEW AND SHIFTING ALLIANCES

A truly multiracial society will undoubtedly prove much harder to govern. Even seemingly race-free conflicts will be increasingly complicated by an overlay of ethnic tension. For example, the expected showdown in the early 21st century between the rising number of retirees and the dwindling number of workers who must be taxed to pay for the elders' Social Security benefits will probably be compounded by the fact that

a large majority of recipients will be white, whereas a majority of workers paying for them will be nonwhite.

While prior generations of immigrants believed they had to learn English quickly to survive, many Hispanics now maintain that the Spanish language is inseparable from their ethnic and cultural identity, and seek to remain bilingual, if not primarily Spanish-speaking, for life. They see legislative drives to make English the sole official language, which have prevailed in some fashion in at least 16 states, as a political backlash. Says Arturo Vargas of the Mexican American Legal Defense and Educational Fund: "That's what English-only has been all about—a reaction to the growing population and influence of Hispanics. It's human nature to be uncomfortable with change. That's what the Census is all about, documenting changes and making sure the country keeps up."

Racial and ethnic conflict remains an ugly fact of American life everywhere, from working-class ghettos to college campuses, and those who do not raise their fists often raise their voices over affirmative action and other power sharing. When Florida Atlantic University, a state-funded institution under pressure to increase its low black enrollment, offered last month to give free tuition to every qualified black freshman who enrolled, the school was flooded with calls of complaint, some protesting that nothing was being done for "real" Americans. As the numbers of minorities increase, their demands for a share of the national bounty are bound to intensify, while whites are certain to feel ever more embattled. Businesses often feel whipsawed between immigration laws that punish them for hiring illegal aliens and anti-discrimination laws that penalize them for demanding excessive documentation from foreign-seeming job applicants. Even companies that consistently seek to do the right thing may be overwhelmed by the problems of diversifying a primarily white managerial corps fast enough to direct a work force that will be increasingly nonwhite and, potentially, resentful.

Nor will tensions be limited to the polar simplicity of white vs. nonwhite. For all Jesse Jackson's rallying cries about shared goals, minority groups often feel keenly competitive. Chicago's Hispanic leaders have leapfrogged between white and black factions, offering support wherever there seemed to be the most to gain for their own community. Says Dan Solis of the Hispanic-oriented United Neighborhood Organization: "If you're thinking power, you don't put your eggs in one basket."

Blacks, who feel they waited longest and endured most in the fight for equal opportunity, are uneasy about being supplanted by Hispanics or, in some areas, by Asians as the numerically largest and most influential minority—and even more, about being outstripped in wealth and status by these newer groups. Because Hispanics are so numerous and Asians such a fast-growing group, they have become the "hot" minorities, and blacks feel their needs are getting lower priority. As affirmative action has broadened to include other groups—and to benefit white women perhaps most of all—blacks perceive it as having waned in value for them.

THE CLASSROOM: WHOSE HISTORY COUNTS?

Political pressure has already brought about sweeping change in public school textbooks over the past couple of decades and has begun to affect the core humanities curriculum at such élite universities as Stanford. At stake at the college level is whether the traditional "canon" of Greek, Latin and West European humanities study should be expanded to reflect the cultures of Africa, Asia and other parts of the world. Many books treasured as classics by prior generations are now seen as tools of cultural imperialism. In the extreme form, this thinking rises to a value-deprived neutralism that views all cultures, regardless of the grandeur or paucity of their attainments, as essentially equal.

Even more troubling is a revisionist approach to history in which groups that have gained power in the present turn to remaking the past in the image of their desires. If 18th, 19th and earlier 20th century society should not have been so dominated by white Christian men of West European ancestry, they reason, then that past society should be reinvented as pluralist and democratic. Alternatively, the racism and sexism of the past are treated as inextricable from—and therefore irremediably tainting—traditional learning and values.

While debates over college curriculum get the most attention, professors generally can resist or subvert the most wrong-headed changes and students generally have mature enough judgment to sort out the arguments. Elementary- and secondary-school curriculums reach a far broader segment at a far more impressionable age, and political expediency more often wins over intellectual honesty. Exchanges have been vituperative in New York, where a state task force concluded that "African-Americans, Asian-Americans, Puerto Ricans and Native Americans have all been victims of an intellectual and educational oppression. . . . Negative characterizations, or the absence of positive references, have had a terribly damaging effect on the psyche of young people." In urging a revised syllabus, the task force argued, "Children from European culture will have a less arrogant perspective of being part of a group that has 'done it all.'" Many intellectuals are outraged. Political scientist Andrew Hacker of Queens College lambastes a task-force suggestion that children be taught how "Native Americans were here to welcome new settlers from Holland, Senegal, England, Indonesia, France, the Congo, Italy, China, Iberia." Asks Hacker: "Did the Indians really welcome all those groups? Were they at Ellis Island when the Italians started to arrive? This is not history but a myth intended to bolster the self-esteem of certain children and, just possibly, a platform for advocates of various ethnic interests."

VALUES: SOMETHING IN COMMON

Economic and political issues, however much emotion they arouse, are fundamentally open to practical solution. The deeper significance of America's becoming a majority nonwhite society is what it means to the national psyche, to individuals' sense of themselves and their nation—their idea of what it is to be American. People of color have often felt that whites treated equality as a benevolence granted to minorities rather than as an inherent natural right. Surely that condescension will wither.

Rather than accepting U.S. history and its meaning as settled, citizens will feel ever more free to debate where the nation's successes sprang from and what its unalterable beliefs are. They will clash over which myths and icons to invoke in education, in popular culture, in ceremonial speechmaking from political campaigns to the State of the Union address. Which is the more admirable heroism: the courageous holdout by a few conquest-minded whites over Hispanics at the Alamo, or the anonymous expression of hope by millions who fled through Ellis Island? Was the subduing of the West a daring feat of bravery and ingenuity, or a wretched example of white imperialism? Symbols deeply meaningful to one group can be a matter of indifference to another. Says University of Wisconsin chancellor Donna Shalala: "My grandparents came from Lebanon. I don't identify with the Pilgrims on a personal level." Christopher Jencks, professor of sociology at Northwestern, asks: "Is anything more basic about turkeys and Pilgrims than about Martin Luther King and Selma? To me, it's six of one and half a dozen of the other, if children understand what it's like to be a dissident minority. Because the civil rights struggle is closer chronologically, it's likelier to be taught by someone who really cares."

Traditionalists increasingly distinguish between a "multiracial" society, which they say would be fine, and a "multicultural" society, which they deplore. They argue that every society needs a universally accepted set of values and that new arrivals should therefore be pressured to conform to the mentality on which U.S. prosperity and freedom were built. Says Allan Bloom, author of the best-selling *The Closing of the American Mind:* "Obviously, the future of America can't be sustained if people keep only to their own ways and remain perpetual outsiders. The society has got to turn them into Americans. There are natural fears that today's immigrants may be too much of a cultural stretch for a nation based on Western values."

The counterargument, made by such scholars as historian Thomas Bender of New York University, is that if the center cannot hold, then one must redefine the center. It should be, he says, "the ever changing outcome of a continuing contest among social groups and ideas for the power to define public culture." Besides, he adds, many immigrants arrive committed to U.S. values; that is part of what attracted them. Says Julian Simon, professor of business administration at the University of Maryland: "The life and institutions here shape immigrants and not vice versa. This business about immigrants changing our institutions and our basic ways of life is hogwash. It's nativist[2] scare talk."

CITIZENSHIP: FORGING A NEW IDENTITY

Historians note that Americans have felt before that their historical culture was being overwhelmed by immigrants, but conflicts between earlier-arriving English, Germans and Irish and later-arriving Italians and Jews did not have the obvious and enduring element of racial skin color. And there was never a time when the non-mainstream elements could claim, through sheer numbers, the potential to unite and exert political dominance. Says Bender: "The real question is whether or not our notion of diversity can successfully negotiate the color line."

For whites, especially those who trace their ancestry back to the early years of the Republic, the American heritage is a source of pride. For people of color, it is more likely to evoke anger and sometimes shame. The place where hope is shared is in the future. Demographer Ben Wattenberg, formerly perceived as a resister to social change, says, "There's a nice chance that the American myth in the 1990s and beyond is going to ratchet another step toward this idea that we are the universal nation. That rings the bell of manifest destiny.[3] We're a people with a mission and a sense of purpose, and we believe we have something to offer the world."

Not every erstwhile alarmist can bring himself to such optimism. Says Norman Podhoretz, editor of *Commentary:* "A lot of people are trying to undermine the foundations of the American experience and are pushing toward a more Balkanized[4] society. I think that would be a disaster, not only because it would destroy a precious social inheritance but also because it would lead to enormous unrest, even violence."

While know-nothingism[5] is generally confined to the more dismal corners of the American psyche, it seems all too predictable that during the next decades many more mainstream white Americans will begin to speak openly about the nation they feel they are losing. There are not, after all, many nonwhite faces depicted in Norman Rockwell's paintings. White Americans are accustomed to thinking of themselves as the very picture of their nation. Inspiring as it may be to the U.S. role in global politics, world trade and the pursuit of peace, becoming a conspicuously multiracial society is bound to be a somewhat bumpy experience for many ordinary citizens. For older Americans, raised in a world where the numbers of whites were greater and the visibility of nonwhites was carefully restrained, the new world will seem even stranger. But as the children . . . in classrooms across the nation are coming to realize, the new world is here. It is now. And it is irreversibly the America to come.

[1990]

Notes

1. SOVIET UNION: A former Euro-Asian nation that dissolved in 1991; many of its republics now form the Commonwealth of Independent States.
2. NATIVIST: A policy of favoring native inhabitants over immigrants.
3. MANIFEST DESTINY: A nineteenth-century belief that the white people had the duty and right to control and develop the entire North American continent.
4. BALKANIZED: Divided into small, hostile groups.
5. KNOW-NOTHINGISM: A mid-nineteenth-century political movement that was hostile to immigrants and Catholics.

Understanding the Reading

1. What problems does Henry see that make it difficult to sustain "a truly multiracial society"?
2. What does "cultural imperialism" mean?
3. According to Henry, what is wrong with "a revisionist approach to history"? Why do some people advocate it?
4. What distinction do traditionalists make between a "multiracial" society and a "multicultural" one?

Suggestions for Responding

1. Do you think that, as Professor Bender asks, "our notion of diversity can successfully negotiate the color line"?
2. What does Wattenberg mean when he suggests that America is "the universal nation"? What does Podhoretz mean when he warns against America becoming "a more Balkanized society"? Which view do you support? Why?
3. What will living in a "conspicuously multiracial society" mean to your personal future? ◆

SUGGESTIONS FOR RESPONDING TO PART I

1. Write a paper analyzing the racial and ethnic features of your identity. Consider your ancestral origins and how your heritage has influenced who you are today. Reflect on such factors as physical characteristics, language, religion, and family customs and traditions. Also, think about such expressive behaviors as dress, music, dance, family stories, holidays, and celebrations. These all may be markers of your ethnic heritage.

   If you think you have nothing to write about, remember that in the United States everyone has a racial and ethnic heritage. While it is central to some people's identity, others may not be conscious of it at all. This is often because they are members of the dominant racial and ethnic culture, which assumes its values and traditions are "universal" or at least most significant or appropriate. If you belong to this group, look at yourself from the outside, from the perspective of another cultural system, several of which have been represented in these readings.

2. In response to the Gwaltney selection, you

wrote questions you would ask if you were conducting an oral history interview. Singly or as a member of a group, evaluate those questions again. Then use them to interview an older person in your family or community.

Many people find it helpful to write the questions on file cards so they can be reorganized to adjust to the direction the interview takes. You may find some questions no longer relevant once the interview is underway; also, more important questions may occur to you on the spot. A tape recorder is useful, especially if you plan to prepare a word-for-word transcript, but always ask your informant for permission before you switch it on. Either with or without a recorder, it is important to take written notes (unless it makes your informant uncomfortable); in this way you can highlight key pieces of information.

Your final report could resemble Gwaltney (a verbatim transcription of the words of your informant), or it may be more interpretive (like Langley's piece). In either case, lis-ten to the tape and reread your notes *several* times before you begin to write, and refer to them after you have completed your report to confirm its accuracy.

3. Your instructor may want you to make an oral presentation of your ethnicity analysis or your oral history. In this case, prepare *brief* notes, again on file cards. Try to talk naturally and not read word for word. Rehearse your presentation several times to be sure you stay within the required time limit. You will feel more comfortable in front of your class if you have rehearsed at least once before an audience (a friend or roommate, for example). If this isn't possible, try speaking to a wall mirror. Above all, relax. Try to look at your audience, even if it seems difficult, because their reactions will be encouraging. Remember, you are talking to friends.

4. After completing Part I, how would you answer the questions, "Who is an American?" and "Is there an American culture?" Support your responses with evidence from the readings.

II
Gender Identity

"IS IT A GIRL OR A BOY?" THIS IS INEVITABLY THE FIRST question asked about a new baby. As we grow older, we identify ourselves and each other as boys or girls, as women or men. In American culture, gender is the most salient feature of one's identity. It shapes our attitudes, our behavior, our experiences, our beliefs about ourselves and about others. Gender is so central to our perception of social reality that we often are not even conscious of how it shapes our behavior and our social interactions.

We all know the traditional definitions of masculinity and femininity. A "real man" should be **masculine**—that is, he should be strong and mechanically oriented, ambitious and assertive, in control of his emotions, knowledgeable about the world, a good provider. A "real woman" should be **feminine**—that is, passive and domestic, nurturing and dependent, emotional, preoccupied with her appearance, and maternal. These gender-appropriate characteristics and behaviors affect many areas of our lives: physical and psychological aspects, occupational choices, interpersonal relations, and so on.

The basis for gender distinctions is not wholly clear yet, and the "nature/nurture" debate—whether or to what degree gendered behavior is controlled by biology or by socialization—continues. Scientists are investigating the roles that hormones, genes, chromosomes, and other

physical features play in women's and men's psychological development, but these issues are complex and beyond the scope of this book.

We will concentrate on the view of many social scientists who study the diversity of appropriate or "natural" male and female behaviors in different cultures and other times. They see in this diversity strong evidence of the central role that culture plays in creating gender roles. As a result, they distinguish between **sex,** the biological "fact" of one's physiological and hormonal characteristics, and **gender,** the social categories that ascribe roles, appropriate behaviors, and personality traits to women and men. In this sense, male and female **sex roles** refer to differences in reproductive traits. The masculine and feminine behaviors described above are features of **gender roles.**

Social scientists believe that we learn our appropriate gender roles by a process called socialization. Gender roles are only one kind of role we learn. A **role** is any socially or culturally defined behavioral expectation that is presumed to apply to all individuals in the category. **Socialization,** the process by which we learn those roles, includes the many pressures, rewards, and punishments that compel us to conform to social expectations. These are deeply embedded in every aspect of our culture. Our treatment of infants and children, our language, educational system, mass media, religion, laws, medical institutions and mental health systems, occupational environments, intimate relationships—all teach and reinforce appropriate gender behavior.

In the first selection, Carol Gilligan reviews psychological theories and the studies on which they are based, showing the biases inherent in many of them. She outlines her own theory that boys learn and practice competitive behaviors and girls learn and practice cooperative ones. Gilligan theorizes that these different experiences result in different value systems in adult women and men.

The next two selections challenge the assumptions that underlie the mainstream, middle-class cultural conception of male privilege and masculine identity. Scott Russell Sanders recalls the lives of the working-class men and women he grew up around and reminds us that not all men, especially not those laborers, enjoy the kind of masculine supremacy and privilege ascribed to middle-class, white-collar males. Dennis Altman briefly analyzes how male bonding and forced masculinity reinforce and are reinforced by **homophobia**—fear, dislike, or hatred of gay men and lesbians.

The options the traditional role makes available to women are no better than those made available to men. In her short piece, Jamaica Kincaid puts us into the head of a young woman receiving rather unsympathetic instruction on appropriate and inappropriate gender behavior. (Doesn't each of us, regardless of age, carry in our head a variation of this voice?) Most of us would find the generally negative message proclaimed by Kincaid's speaker psychologically damaging. It is interesting to consider how mes-

sages like this might contribute to the loss of self-esteem in adolescent girls, which Bruce Bower documents in his review of recent research studies.

Problems created by the feminine gender role continue to plague women in their adult years. In her humorous explanation of why she, too, would like a wife, Judy Syfers exposes the many inequities built into the traditional woman's role. Casey Miller and Kate Swift consider the importance of names in establishing one's identity; although their analysis is almost two decades old, women continue to experience many of the disadvantages of our patriarchal naming system.

The last two selections examine the impact of gender roles on male-female relationships. Aaron T. Beck presents five differences in the communication patterns of women and men and explains how these disrupt male-female relationships. Although gender roles are currently undergoing a transformation, such traditional patterns still survive. In the closing piece, Anthony Astrachan explains how men's responses to greater equality for women are influenced by their socioeconomic class, race, and age.

The readings in Part II should help you assess your own gender identity and give you fuller insight into the experiences of those of the opposite sex. A clearer sense of some of the realities that are the consequence of traditional gender roles and gender expectations may encourage you to question just how "natural" traditional gender roles are. It will also help you consider whether or not you want to see changes in gender roles and sexual relationships, and how to act on that decision.

13

*Woman's Place in Man's Life Cycle**

CAROL GILLIGAN

The penchant of developmental theorists to project a masculine image, and one that appears frightening to women, goes back at least to Freud, who built his theory of psychosexual development around the experiences of the male child that culminate in the Oedipus complex.[1] In the 1920s, Freud struggled to resolve the contradictions posed for his theory by the differences in female anatomy and the different configuration of the young girl's early family relationships. After trying to fit women into his masculine conception, seeing them as envying that which they missed, he came instead to acknowledge, in the strength and persistence of women's pre-Oedipal attachments to their mothers, a developmental difference. He considered this difference in women's development to be responsible for what he saw as women's developmental failure.

Having tied the formation of the superego or conscience to castration anxiety, Freud considered women to be deprived by nature of the impetus for a clear-cut Oedipal resolution. Consequently, women's superego—the heir to the Oedipus complex—was compromised: it was never "so inexorable, so impersonal, so independent of its emotional origins as we require it to be in men." From this observation of difference, that "for women the level of what is ethically normal is different from what it is in men," Freud concluded that women "show less sense of justice than men, that they are less ready to submit to the great exigencies of life, that they are more often influenced in their judgements by feelings of affection or hostility."

Thus a problem in theory became cast as a problem in women's development, and the problem in women's development was located in their experience of relationships. Nancy Chodorow, attempting to account for "the reproduction within each generation of certain general and nearly universal differences that characterize masculine and feminine personality and roles," attributes these differences between the sexes not to anatomy but rather to "the fact that women, universally, are largely responsible for early child care." Because this early social environment differs for and is experienced differently by male and female children, basic sex differences recur in personality development. As a result, "in any given society, feminine personality comes to define itself in relation and connection to other people more than masculine personality does."

In her analysis, Chodorow relies primarily on Robert Stoller's studies which indicate that gender identity, the unchanging core of personality formation, is "with rare exception firmly and irreversibly established for both sexes by the time a child is around three." Given that for both sexes the primary caretaker in the first three years of life is typically female, the interpersonal dynamics of gender identity formation are different for boys and girls. Female identity formation takes place in a context of ongoing relationship since "mothers tend to experience their daughters as more like, and continuous with, themselves." Correspondingly, girls, in identifying themselves as female, experience themselves as like their mothers, thus fusing the experience of attachment with the process of identity formation. In contrast, "mothers experience their sons as a male opposite," and boys, in defining themselves as masculine, separate their mothers from themselves, thus curtailing "their primary love and sense of empathic tie." Consequently, male development entails a "more emphatic individuation and a more defensive firming of experienced ego boundaries." For boys, but not girls, "issues of differentiation have become intertwined with sexual issues."

Writing against the masculine bias of psychoanalytic theory, Chodorow argues that the existence of sex differences in the early experiences of individuation and relationship "does not mean that women have 'weaker' ego boundaries than men or are more prone to psychosis." It means instead that "girls emerge from this period with a basis for 'empathy' built into their primary definition of self in a way that boys do not." Chodorow thus replaces Freud's negative and derivative description of female psychology with a positive

---

* For permission to photocopy this selection please contact Harvard University Press. See the Credits section, page 447, for the complete credit.

and direct account of her own: "Girls emerge with a stronger basis for experiencing another's needs or feelings as one's own (or of thinking that one is so experiencing another's needs and feelings). Furthermore, girls do not define themselves in terms of the denial of preoedipal relational modes to the same extent as do boys. Therefore, regression to these modes tends not to feel as much a basic threat to their ego. From very early, then, because they are parented by a person of the same gender . . . girls come to experience themselves as less differentiated than boys, as more continuous with and related to the external object-world, and as differently oriented to their inner object-world as well."

Consequently, relationships, and particularly issues of dependency, are experienced differently by women and men. For boys and men, separation and individuation are critically tied to gender identity since separation from the mother is essential for the development of masculinity. For girls and women, issues of femininity or feminine identity do not depend on the achievement of separation from the mother or on the progress of individuation. Since masculinity is defined through separation while femininity is defined through attachment, male gender identity is threatened by intimacy while female gender identity is threatened by separation. Thus males tend to have difficulty with relationships, while females tend to have problems with individuation. The quality of embeddedness in social interaction and personal relationships that characterizes women's lives in contrast to men's, however, becomes not only a descriptive difference but also a developmental liability when the milestones of childhood and adolescent development in the psychological literature are markers of increasing separation. Women's failure to separate then becomes by definition a failure to develop.

The sex differences in personality formation that Chodorow describes in early childhood appear during the middle childhood years in studies of children's games. Children's games are considered by George Herbert Mead[2] and Jean Piaget as the crucible of social development during the school years. In games, children learn to take the role of the other and come to see themselves through another's eyes. In games, they learn respect for rules and come to understand the ways rules can be made and changed.

Janet Lever, considering the peer group to be the agent of socialization during the elementary school years and play to be a major activity of socialization at that time, set out to discover whether there are sex differences in the games that children play. Studying 181 fifth-grade, white, middle-class children, ages ten and eleven, she observed the organization and structure of their play-time activities. She watched the children as they played at school during recess and in physical education class, and in addition kept diaries of their accounts as to how they spent their out-of-school time. From this study, Lever reports sex differences: boys play out of doors more often than girls do; boys play more often in large and age-heterogeneous groups; they play competitive games more often, and their games last longer than girls' games. The last is in some ways the most interesting finding. Boys' games appeared to last longer not only because they required a higher level of skill and were thus less likely to become boring, but also because, when disputes arose in the course of a game, boys were able to resolve the disputes more effectively than girls: "During the course of this study, boys were seen quarrelling all the time, but not once was a game terminated because of a quarrel and no game was interrupted for more than seven minutes. In the gravest debates, the final word was always, to 'repeat the play,' generally followed by a chorus of 'cheater's proof.'" In fact, it seemed that the boys enjoyed the legal debates as much as they did the game itself, and even marginal players of lesser size or skill participated equally in these recurrent squabbles. In contrast, the eruption of disputes among girls tended to end the game.

Thus Lever extends and corroborates the observations of Piaget in his study of the rules of the game, where he finds boys becoming through childhood increasingly fascinated with the legal elaboration of rules and the development of fair procedures for adjudicating conflicts, a fascination that, he notes, does not hold for girls. Girls, Piaget observes, have a more "pragmatic" attitude toward rules, "regarding a rule as good as long as the game repaid it." Girls are more tolerant in their attitudes toward rules, more willing to make exceptions, and more easily reconciled to innovations. As a result, the legal sense, which Piaget considers essential to moral development, "is far less developed in little girls than in boys."

The bias that leads Piaget to equate male development with child development also colors Lever's work. The assumption that shapes her discussion of results is that the male model is the better one since it fits the requirements for modern corporate success. In contrast, the sensitivity and care for the feelings of others that girls develop through their play have little market value and can even impede professional success. Lever implies that, given the realities of adult life, if a girl does not want to be left dependent on men, she will have to learn to play like a boy.

To Piaget's argument that children learn the respect for rules necessary for moral development by playing rule-bound games, Lawrence Kohlberg adds that these lessons are most effectively learned through the opportunities for role-taking that arise in the course of resolving disputes. Consequently, the moral lessons inherent in girls' play appear to be fewer than in boys'. Traditional girls' games like jump rope and hopscotch are turn-taking games, where competition is indirect since one person's success does not necessarily signify another's failure. Consequently, disputes requiring adjudication are less likely to occur. In fact, most of the girls whom Lever interviewed claimed that when a quarrel broke out, they ended the game. Rather than elaborating a system of rules for resolving disputes, girls subordinated the continuation of the game to the continuation of relationships.

Lever concludes that from the games they play, boys learn both the independence and the organizational skills necessary for coordinating the activities of large and diverse groups of people. By participating in controlled and socially approved competitive situations, they learn to deal with competition in a relatively forthright manner—to play with their enemies and to compete with their friends—all in accordance with the rules of the game. In contrast, girls' play tends to occur in smaller, more intimate groups, often the best-friend dyad, and in private places. This play replicates the social pattern of primary human relationships in that its organization is more cooperative. Thus, it points less, in Mead's terms, toward learning to take the role of "the generalized other," less toward the abstraction of human relationships. But it fosters the development of the empathy and sensitivity necessary for taking the role of "the particular other" and points more toward knowing the other as different from the self.

The sex differences in personality formation in early childhood that Chodorow derives from her analysis of the mother-child relationship are thus extended by Lever's observations of sex differences in the play activities of middle childhood. Together these accounts suggest that boys and girls arrive at puberty with a different interpersonal orientation and a different range of social experiences. Yet, since adolescence is considered a crucial time for separation, the period of "the second individuation process," female development has appeared most divergent and thus most problematic at this time.

"Puberty," Freud says, "which brings about so great an accession of libido[3] in boys, is marked in girls by a fresh wave of *repression,*" necessary for the transformation of the young girl's "masculine sexuality" into the specifically feminine sexuality of her adulthood. Freud posits this transformation on the girl's acknowledgment and acceptance of "the fact of her castration." To the girl, Freud explains, puberty brings a new awareness of "the wound to her narcissism" and leads her to develop, "like a scar, a sense of inferiority." Since in Erik Erikson's expansion of Freud's psychoanalytic account, adolescence is the time when development hinges on identity, the girl arrives at this juncture either psychologically at risk or with a different agenda.

The problem that female adolescence presents for theorists of human development is apparent in Erikson's scheme. Erikson charts eight stages of psychosocial development, of which adolescence is the fifth. The task at this stage is to forge a coherent sense of self, to verify an identity that can span the discontinuity of puberty and make possible the adult capacity to love and work. The preparation for the successful resolution of the adolescent identity crisis is delineated in Erikson's description of the crises that characterize the preceding four stages. Although the initial crisis in infancy of "trust versus mistrust" anchors development in the experience of relationship, the task then clearly becomes one of individuation. Erikson's second stage centers on the crisis of "autonomy versus shame and doubt," which marks the walking child's emerging sense of separateness and agency. From there, development goes on through the crisis of "initiative versus guilt," successful resolution of which represents a further move in the direction

of autonomy. Next, following the inevitable disappointment of the magical wishes of the Oedipal period, children realize that to compete with
their parents, they must first join them and learn
to do what they do so well. Thus in the middle
childhood years, development turns on the crisis
of "industry versus inferiority," as the demonstration of competence becomes critical to the child's
developing self-esteem. This is the time when
children strive to learn and master the technology
of their culture, in order to recognize themselves
and to be recognized by others as capable of becoming adults. Next comes adolescence, the
celebration of the autonomous, initiating, industrious self through the forging of an identity
based on an ideology that can support and justify
adult commitments. But about whom is Erikson
talking?

Once again it turns out to be the male child.
For the female, Erikson says, the sequence is a bit
different. She holds her identity in abeyance as
she prepares to attract the man by whose name
she will be known, by whose status she will be
defined, the man who will rescue her from emp-
tiness and loneliness by filling "the inner space."
While for men, identity precedes intimacy and
generativity[4] in the optimal cycle of human separation and attachment, for women these tasks
seem instead to be fused. Intimacy goes along
with identity, as the female comes to know herself as she is known, through her relationships
with others.

Yet despite Erikson's observation of sex differences, his chart of life-cycle stages remains unchanged: identity continues to precede intimacy
as male experience continues to define his life-
cycle conception. But in this male life cycle there
is little preparation for the intimacy of the first
adult stage. Only the initial stage of trust versus
mistrust suggests the type of mutuality that Erikson means by intimacy and generativity and
Freud means by genitality. The rest is separateness, with the result that development itself
comes to be identified with separation, and attachments appear to be developmental impedi-
ments, as is repeatedly the case in the assessment
of women.

Erikson's description of male identity as
forged in relation to the world and of female
identity as awakened in a relationship of intimacy
with another person is hardly new. In the fairy
tales that Bruno Bettelheim describes an identical

portrayal appears. The dynamics of male adolescence are illustrated archetypically by the conflict
between father and son in "The Three Languages." Here a son, considered hopelessly stupid by his father, is given one last chance at
education and sent for a year to study with a master. But when he returns, all he has learned is
"what the dogs bark." After two further attempts
of this sort, the father gives up in disgust and orders his servants to take the child into the forest
and kill him. But the servants, those perpetual
rescuers of disowned and abandoned children,
take pity on the child and decide simply to leave
him in the forest. From there, his wanderings take
him to a land beset by furious dogs whose bark-
ing permits nobody to rest and who periodically
devour one of the inhabitants. Now it turns out
that our hero has learned just the right thing: he
can talk with the dogs and is able to quiet them,
thus restoring peace to the land. Since the other
knowledge he acquires serves him equally well,
he emerges triumphant from his adolescent confrontation with his father, a giant of the life-cycle
conception.

In contrast, the dynamics of female adolescence are depicted through the telling of a very
different story. In the world of the fairy tale, the
girl's first bleeding is followed by a period of intense passivity in which nothing seems to be
happening. Yet in the deep sleeps of Snow White
and Sleeping Beauty, Bettelheim sees that inner
concentration which he considers to be the necessary counterpart to the activity of adventure.
Since the adolescent heroines awake from their
sleep, not to conquer the world, but to marry the
prince, their identity is inwardly and interperson-
ally defined. For women, in Bettelheim's as in
Erikson's account, identity and intimacy are intricately conjoined. The sex differences depicted in
the world of fairy tales, like the fantasy of the
woman warrior in Maxine Hong Kingston's recent autobiographical novel which echoes the
old stories of Troilus and Cressida and Tancred
and Chlorinda, indicate repeatedly that active adventure is a male activity, and that if a woman is
to embark on such endeavors, she must at least
dress like a man.

These observations about sex difference support the conclusion reached by David McClelland
that "sex role turns out to be one of the most important determinants of human behavior; psychologists have found sex differences in their

studies from the moment they started doing empirical research." But since it is difficult to say "different" without saying "better" or "worse," since there is a tendency to construct a single scale of measurement, and since that scale has generally been derived from and standardized on the basis of men's interpretations of research data drawn predominantly or exclusively from studies of males, psychologists "have tended to regard male behavior as the 'norm' and female behavior as some kind of deviation from that norm." Thus, when women do not conform to the standards of psychological expectation, the conclusion has generally been that something is wrong with the women.

What Matina Horner found to be wrong with women was the anxiety they showed about competitive achievement. From the beginning, research on human motivation using the Thematic Apperception Test (TAT) was plagued by evidence of sex differences which appeared to confuse and complicate data analysis. The TAT presents for interpretation an ambiguous cue—a picture about which a story is to be written or a segment of a story that is to be completed. Such stories, in reflecting projective imagination, are considered by psychologists to reveal the ways in which people construe what they perceive, that is, the concepts and interpretations they bring to their experience and thus presumably the kind of sense that they make of their lives. Prior to Horner's work it was clear that women made a different kind of sense than men of situations of competitive achievement, that in some way they saw the situations differently or the situations aroused in them some different response.

On the basis of his studies of men, McClelland divided the concept of achievement motivation into what appeared to be its two logical components, a motive to approach success ("hope success") and a motive to avoid failure ("fear failure"). From her studies of women, Horner identified as a third category the unlikely motivation to avoid success ("fear success"). Women appeared to have a problem with competitive achievement, and that problem seemed to emanate from a perceived conflict between femininity and success, the dilemma of the female adolescent who struggles to integrate her feminine aspirations and the identifications of her early childhood with the more masculine competence she has acquired at school. From her

analysis of women's completions of a story that began, "after first term finals, Anne finds herself at the top of her medical school class," and from her observation of women's performance in competitive achievement situations, Horner reports that, "when success is likely or possible, threatened by the negative consequences they expect to follow success, young women become anxious and their positive achievement strivings become thwarted." She concludes that this fear "exists because for most women, the anticipation of success in competitive achievement activity, especially against men, produces anticipation of certain negative consequences, for example, threat of social rejection and loss of femininity."

Such conflicts about success, however, may be viewed in a different light. Georgia Sassen suggests that the conflicts expressed by the women might instead indicate "a heightened perception of the 'other side' of competitive success, that is, the great emotional costs at which success achieved through competition is often gained—an understanding which, though confused, indicates some underlying sense that something is rotten in the state in which success is defined as having better grades than everyone else." Sassen points out that Horner found success anxiety to be present in women only when achievement was directly competitive, that is, when one person's success was at the expense of another's failure.

In his elaboration of the identity crisis, Erikson cites the life of George Bernard Shaw[5] to illustrate the young person's sense of being coopted prematurely by success in a career he cannot wholeheartedly endorse. Shaw at seventy, reflecting upon his life, described his crisis at the age of twenty as having been caused not by the lack of success or the absence of recognition, but by too much of both: "I made good in spite of myself, and found, to my dismay, that Business, instead of expelling me as the worthless imposter I was, was fastening upon me with no intention of letting me go. Behold me, therefore, in my twentieth year, with a business training, in an occupation which I detested as cordially as any sane person lets himself detest anything he cannot escape from. In March 1876 I broke loose." At this point Shaw settled down to study and write as he pleased. Hardly interpreted as evidence of neurotic anxiety about achievement and competition, Shaw's refusal suggests to Erikson "the extraordinary workings of an extraordinary personality [coming] to the fore."

We might on these grounds begin to ask, not why women have conflicts about competitive success, but why men show such readiness to adopt and celebrate a rather narrow vision of success. Remembering Piaget's observation, corroborated by Lever, that boys in their games are more concerned with rules while girls are more concerned with relationships, often at the expense of the game itself—and given Chodorow's conclusion that men's social orientation is positional while women's is personal—we begin to understand why, when "Anne" becomes "John" in Horner's tale of competitive success and the story is completed by men, fear of success tends to disappear. John is considered to have played by the rules and won. He has the *right* to feel good about his success. Confirmed in the sense of his own identity as separate from those who, compared to him, are less competent, his positional sense of self is affirmed. For Anne, it is possible that the position she could obtain by being at the top of her medical school class may not, in fact, be what she wants.

"It is obvious," Virginia Woolf says, "that the values of women differ very often from the values which have been made by the other sex." Yet, she adds, "it is the masculine values that prevail." As a result, women come to question the normality of their feelings and to alter their judgments in deference to the opinion of others. In the nineteenth century novels written by women, Woolf sees at work "a mind which was slightly pulled from the straight and made to alter its clear vision in deference to external authority." The same deference to the values and opinions of others can be seen in the judgments of twentieth century women. The difficulty women experience in finding or speaking publicly in their own voices emerges repeatedly in the form of qualification and self-doubt, but also in intimations of a divided judgment, a public assessment and private assessment which are fundamentally at odds.

Yet the deference and confusion that Woolf criticizes in women derive from the values she sees as their strength. Women's deference is rooted not only in their social subordination but also in the substance of their moral concern. Sensitivity to the needs of others and the assumption of responsibility for taking care lead women to attend to voices other than their own and to include in their judgment other points of view. Women's moral weakness, manifest in an apparent diffusion and confusion of judgment, is thus inseparable from woman's moral strength, an overriding concern with relationships and responsibilities. The reluctance to judge may itself be indicative of the care and concern for others that infuse the psychology of women's development and are responsible for what is generally seen as problematic in its nature.

Thus women not only define themselves in a context of human relationship but also judge themselves in terms of their ability to care. Women's place in man's life cycle has been that of nurturer, caretaker, and helpmate, the weaver of those networks of relationships on which she in turn relies. But while women have thus taken care of men, men have, in their theories of psychological development, as in their economic arrangements, tended to assume or devalue that care. When the focus on individuation and individual achievement extends into adulthood and maturity is equated with personal autonomy, concern with relationships appears as a weakness of women rather than as a human strength.

[1982]

Notes

1. OEDIPUS COMPLEX: Freud's theory that as they mature, children develop sexual desire for the opposite-sex parent and hostility to the same-sex parent and that girls experience penis envy.
2. GEORGE HERBERT MEAD: An early American sociologist.
3. LIBIDO: Sexual drive.
4. GENERATIVITY: The adult stage of development, characterized by concern for raising the next generation.
5. GEORGE BERNARD SHAW: A British dramatist and writer.

Understanding the Reading

1. Explain how Chodorow's theory of women's development differs from Freud's theory.
2. What does Chodorow mean when she says that for boys, but not for girls, "issues of dif-

ferentiation have become intertwined with sexual issues"?

3. Why does Chodorow think males have difficulty with relationships and females have problems with individuation?

4. What differences did Lever find in boys' play and girls' play, especially in their attitudes toward rules?

5. Why does Gilligan find Erikson's theory about adolescent development problematic?

6. According to Bettelheim's analysis, what do fairy tales teach about male and female development?

7. What did Horner's study show about women's attitudes toward competition, and how does it differ from McClelland's theory?

Suggestion for Responding

Explain Gilligan's general theory about female and male development. ✦

14

The Men We Carry in Our Minds

SCOTT RUSSELL SANDERS

"This must be a hard time for women," I say to my friend Anneke. "They have so many paths to choose from, and so many voices calling them."

"I think it's a lot harder for men," she replies.

"How do you figure that?"

"The women I know feel excited, innocent, like crusaders in a just cause. The men I know are eaten up with guilt."

"Women feel such pressure to be everything, do everything," I say. "Career, kids, art, politics. Have their babies and get back to the office a week later. It's as if they're trying to overcome a million years' worth of evolution in one lifetime."

"But we help one another. And we have this deep-down sense that we're in the *right*—we've been held back, passed over, used—while men feel they're in the wrong. Men are the ones who've been discredited, who have to search their souls."

I search my soul. I discover guilty feelings

aplenty—toward the poor, the Vietnamese, Native Americans, the whales, an endless list of debts. But toward women I feel something more confused, a snarl of shame, envy, wary tenderness, and amazement. This muddle troubles me. To hide my unease I say, "You're right, it's tough being a man these days."

"Don't laugh," Anneke frowns at me. "I wouldn't be a man for anything. It's much easier being the victim. All the victim has to do is break free. The persecutor has to live with his past."

How deep is that past? I find myself wondering. How much of an inheritance do I have to throw off?

When I was a boy growing up on the back roads of Tennessee and Ohio, the men I knew labored with their bodies. They were marginal farmers, just scraping by, or welders, steelworkers, carpenters; they swept floors, dug ditches, mined coal, or drove trucks, their forearms ropy with muscle; they trained horses, stoked furnaces, made tires, stood on assembly lines wrestling parts onto cars and refrigerators. They got up before light, worked all day long whatever the weather, and when they came home at night they looked as though somebody had been whipping them. In the evenings and on weekends they worked on their own places, tilling gardens that were lumpy with clay, fixing broken-down cars, hammering on houses that were always too drafty, too leaky, too small.

The bodies of the men I knew were twisted and maimed in ways visible and invisible. The nails of their hands were black and split, the hands tattooed with scars. Some had lost fingers. Heavy lifting had given many of them finicky backs and guts weak from hernias. Racing against conveyor belts had given them ulcers. Their ankles and knees ached from years of standing on concrete. Anyone who had worked for long around machines was hard of hearing. They squinted, and the skin of their faces was creased like the leather of old work gloves. There were times, studying them, when I dreaded growing up. Most of them coughed, from dust or cigarettes, and most of them drank cheap wine or whiskey, so their eyes looked bloodshot and bruised. The fathers of my friends always seemed older than the mothers. Men wore out sooner. Only women lived into old age.

As a boy I also knew another sort of men, who did not sweat and break down like mules. They were soldiers, and so far as I could tell they scarcely worked at all. But when the shooting started, many of them would die. That was what soldiers were *for,* just as a hammer was for driving nails.

Warriors and toilers: those seemed, in my boyhood vision, to be the chief destinies for men. They weren't the only destinies, as I learned from having a few male teachers, from reading books, and from watching television. But the men on television—the politicians, the astronauts, the generals, the savvy lawyers, the philosophical doctors, the bosses who gave orders to both soldiers and laborers—seemed as remote and unreal to me as the figures in Renaissance tapestries. I could no more imagine growing up to become one of these cool, potent creatures than I could imagine becoming a prince.

A nearer and more hopeful example was that of my father, who had escaped from a red-dirt farm to a tire factory, and from the assembly line to the front office. Eventually he dressed in a white shirt and tie. He carried himself as if he had been born to work with his mind. But his body, remembering the earlier years of slogging work, began to give out on him in his fifties, and it quit on him entirely before he turned 65.

A scholarship enabled me not only to attend college, a rare enough feat in my circle, but even to study in a university meant for the children of the rich. Here I met for the first time young men who had assumed from birth that they would lead lives of comfort and power. And for the first time I met women who told me that men were guilty of having kept all the joys and privileges of the earth for themselves. I was baffled. What privileges? What joys? I thought about the maimed, dismal lives of most of the men back home. What had they stolen from their wives and daughters? The right to go five days a week, 12 months a year, for 30 or 40 years to a steel mill or a coal mine? The right to drop bombs and die in war? The right to feel every leak in the roof, every gap in the fence, every cough in the engine as a wound they must mend? The right to feel, when the layoff comes or the plant shuts down, not only afraid but ashamed?

I was slow to understand the deep grievances of women. This was because, as a boy, I had en-

vied them. Before college, the only people I had ever known who were interested in art or music or literature, the only ones who read books, the only ones who ever seemed to enjoy a sense of ease and grace were the mothers and daughters. Like the menfolk, they fretted about money, they scrimped and made do. But, when the pay stopped coming in, they were not the ones who had failed. Nor did they have to go to war, and that seemed to me a blessed fact. By comparison with the narrow, ironclad days of fathers, there was an expansiveness, I thought, in the days of mothers. They went to see neighbors, to shop in town, to run errands at school, at the library, at church. No doubt, had I looked harder at their lives, I would have envied them less. It was not my fate to become a woman, so it was easier for me to see the graces. I didn't see, then, what a prison a house could be, since houses seemed to me brighter, handsomer places than any factory. I did not realize—because such things were never spoken of—how often women suffered from men's bullying. Even then I could see how exhausting it was for a mother to cater all day to the needs of young children. But if I had been asked, as a boy, to choose between tending a baby and tending a machine, I think I would have chosen the baby. (Having now tended both, I know I would choose the baby.)

So I was baffled when the women at college accused me and my sex of having cornered the world's pleasures. I think something like my bafflement has been felt by other boys (and by girls as well) who grew up in dirt-poor farm country, in mining country, in black ghettos, in Hispanic barrios, in the shadows of factories, in Third World nations—any place where the fate of men is just as grim and bleak as the fate of women.

When the women I met at college thought about the joys and privileges of men, they did not carry in their minds the sort of men I had known in my childhood. They thought of their fathers, who were bankers, physicians, architects, stockbrokers, the big wheels of the big cities. They were never laid off, never short of cash at month's end, never lined up for welfare. These fathers made decisions that mattered. They ran the world.

The daughters of such men wanted to share in this power, this glory. So did I. They yearned for a say over their future, for jobs worthy of their abilities, for the right to live at peace, unmolested, whole. Yes, I thought, yes yes. The difference between me and these daughters was that they saw me, because of my sex, as destined from birth to become like their fathers, and therefore as an enemy to their desires. But I knew better. I wasn't an enemy, in fact or in feeling. I was an ally. If I had known, then, how to tell them so, would they have believed me? Would they now?

[1984]

Understanding the Reading

1. Why do Sanders and his friend Anneke think it is harder today to be a man than a woman?
2. Describe the two kinds of men Sanders knew when he was growing up.
3. Why was he "baffled" by the women he met in college?
4. Compare the lives led by women he knew when he was growing up with the lives of their men.
5. Why does he think he should be considered women's ally?

Suggestions for Responding

1. Write an essay describing and comparing the lives of the men and women you knew when you were growing up.
2. Analyze how your gender identity was influenced by your socioeconomic class. ✦

15

Why Are Gay Men So Feared?

DENNIS ALTMAN

Gay men are the victims of insults, prejudice, abuse, violence, sometimes murder. Why are gay men hated by so many other men? Some maintain that homosexuality is unnatural or a threat to the family. But celibacy is also unnatural, yet nuns and priests are not regularly attacked. And there is also a good case to be made that homosexuality actually *strengthens* the family by liberating some adults from childbearing duties and so increasing the pool of adults available to look after children.

But the real objection to homosexuality (and lesbianism) is undoubtedly more deep-seated: It is threatening because it seems to challenge the conventional roles governing a person's sex, and the female and male roles in society. The assertion of homosexual identity clearly challenges the apparent naturalness of gender roles.

Men are particularly prone to use anger and violence against those they think are undermining their masculinity. And it is here that we can find at least some of the roots of homophobia and gay-bashing.

As Freud understood, most societies are built upon a set of relationships between men: Most powerful institutions like parliaments and business corporations are male-dominated. And this "male bonding" demands a certain degree of sexual sublimation.

In many societies, the links between men are much stronger than the relations that link them to women. But these bonds are social rather than individual, and for this reason need to be strictly governed. Armies, for example, depend upon a very strong sense of male solidarity, though this does not allow for too close an emotional tie between any *specific* pair of men.

Thus the most extreme homophobia is often found among tightly knit groups of men, who need to deny any sexual component to their bonding as well as boost their group solidarity by turning violently on "fags" or "queers," who are defined as completely alien. This is a phenomenon found among teenage gangs, policemen, and soldiers. A particularly prominent example of this was Germany's Nazi Party, which shortly after coming to power purged those of its members who were tempted to turn the hypermasculinity of Nazism into an excuse for overt homosexual behavior.

Many observers of sexual violence have argued that the most virulent queer-basher is attacking the homosexual potential in himself—a potential that he has learned to suppress. Because homosexuality is "un-masculine," those who struggle with feelings of homosexuality (often unacknowledged) will be particularly tempted to resolve them through "masculine" expressions of violence. In court cases involving violence against gay men, the idea of preserving one's male honor is often pleaded as a defense.

Homophobia has effects that go far beyond those individuals against whom it is directed. Like racism and sexism, it is an expression of hatred that harms the perpetrator as well as the victim; the insecurities, fears, and sexual hang-ups that lead young men to go out looking for "fags" to beat up are dangerous to the entire society.

Those societies that are best able to accept homosexuals are also societies that are able to accept assertive women and gentle men, and they tend to be less prone to the violence produced by hypermasculinity.   [1989]

Understanding the Reading

1. According to Altman, what is the relationship between male bonding and homophobia?
2. In what ways can violence against gay men be seen as "preserving one's male honor"?

Suggestion for Responding

Explain how Altman's analysis of men's homophobia relates to the male stereotype. ◆

16

Girl

Jamaica Kincaid

Wash the white clothes on Monday and put them on the stone heap; wash the color clothes on Tuesday and put them on the clothesline to dry; don't walk barehead in the hot sun; cook pumpkin fritters in very hot sweet oil; soak your little clothes right after you take them off; when buying cotton to make yourself a nice blouse, be sure that it doesn't have gum on it, because that way it won't hold up well after a wash; soak salt fish overnight before you cook it; is it true that you sing benna[1] in Sunday School?; always eat your food in such a way that it won't turn someone else's stomach; on Sundays try to walk like a lady and not like the slut you are so bent on becoming; don't sing benna in Sunday School; you mustn't speak to wharf-rat boys, not even to give directions; don't eat fruits on the street—flies will follow you; *but I don't sing benna on Sundays at all and never in Sunday school;* this is how to sew on a button; this is how to make a buttonhole for the button you have just sewed on; this is how to hem a dress when you see the hem coming down and so to prevent yourself from looking like the slut I know you are so bent on becoming; this is how you iron your father's khaki shirt so that it doesn't have a crease; this is how you iron your father's khaki pants so that they don't have a crease; this is how you grow okra—far from the house, because okra tree harbors red ants; when you are growing dasheen,[2] make sure it gets plenty of water or else it makes your throat itch when you are eating it; this is how you sweep a corner; this is how you sweep a whole house; this is how you sweep a yard; this is how you smile to someone you don't like too much; this is how you smile to someone you don't like at all; this is how you smile to someone you like completely; this is how you set a table for tea; this is how you set a table for dinner; this is how you set a table for dinner with an important guest; this is how you set a table for lunch; this is how you set a table for breakfast; this is how to behave in the presence of men who don't know you very well, and this way they won't recognize immediately the slut I have warned you against becoming; be sure to wash every day, even if it is with your own spit; don't squat down to play marbles—you are not a boy, you know; don't pick people's flowers—you might catch something; don't throw stones at blackbirds, because it might not be a blackbird at all; this is how to make a bread pudding; this is how to make doukona;[3] this is how to make pepper pot; this is how to make a good medicine for a cold; this is how to make a good medicine to throw away a child before it even becomes a child; this is how to catch a fish; this is how to throw back a fish you don't like, and that way something bad won't fall on you; this is how to bully a man; this is how a man bullies you; this is how to love a man, and if this doesn't work there are other ways, and if they don't work don't feel too bad about giving up; this is how to spit up in the air if you feel like it, and this is how to move quick so that it doesn't fall on you; this is how to make ends meet; always squeeze bread to make sure it's fresh; *but what if the baker won't let me feel the bread?*; you mean to say that after all you are really going to be the kind of woman who the baker won't let near the bread?   [1983]

Notes

1. BENNA: Calypso music.
2. DASHEEN: A tropical plant with a starchy, edible root.
3. DOUKONA: A spicy pudding.

Understanding the Reading

1. What kinds of activities and behaviors most concern the mother?
2. What do they reveal about the role she wishes her daughter to fulfill?
3. How does the daughter feel about the instruction?
4. What is the relationship between mother and daughter?

Suggestions for Responding

1. We all have "voices" in our heads from childhood telling us how we must or must not behave if we are to become appropriately masculine or feminine. Record your version of Kincaid's story.
2. Describe the kind of society in which this story is set, especially in terms of its attitude toward women. In what ways is it similar to and different from your world today? ✦

17

Teenage Turning Point

BRUCE BOWER

Youngsters often experience a decline in self-esteem as they enter their adolescent years, a time marked by the abrupt move from the relatively cloistered confines of elementary school to the more complex social and academic demands of junior high. Social scientists have documented this trend—often more pronounced among girls—over the past 20 years through questionnaires and interviews aimed at gauging how adolescents feel about themselves.

But a new survey of U.S. elementary and secondary students bears the worst news yet about plummeting self-esteem among teenage girls. The controversial findings, released in January [1991] by the American Association of University Women (AAUW), have refocused researchers' attention on long-standing questions about the meaning of such studies and their implications, if any, for educational reform and for male and female psychological development.

The concept of self-esteem itself remains vague, contends psychiatrist Philip Robson in the June 1990 *Harvard Medical School Mental Health Letter.* Some researchers assess a person's "global" self-esteem with questions about general feelings of worth, goodness, health, attractiveness and social competence. Others focus on people's evaluations of themselves in specific situations. Robson, of Oxford University in England, notes that an individual might score high on one type of test but not on another, presumably because the measures reflect different aspects of self-esteem.

Moreover, he argues, high test scores may sometimes indicate conceit, narcissism or rigidity rather than healthy feelings of self-worth.

Despite the complexities involved in determining how people truly regard themselves, the AAUW survey suggests that adolescent girls experience genuine, substantial drops in self-esteem that far outpace those reported by boys. Girls also reported much less enthusiasm for math and science, less confidence in their academic abilities and fewer aspirations to professional careers.

The survey, conducted last fall by a private polling firm commissioned by AAUW, involved 2,400 girls and 600 boys from 36 public schools throughout the United States. Black and Hispanic students made up almost one-quarter of the sample. Participants, whose ages ranged from 9 to 16 (fourth through tenth grades), responded to written statements probing global self-esteem, such as "I like the way I look" and "I'm happy the way I am."

In a typical response pattern, 67 percent of the elementary school boys reported "always" feeling "happy the way I am," and 46 percent still felt that way by tenth grade. For girls, the figures dropped from 60 percent to 29 percent.

For both sexes, the sharpest declines in self-esteem occurred at the beginning of junior high.

Compared with the rest of the study sample, students with higher self-esteem liked math and science more, felt better about their schoolwork and grades, considered themselves more important and felt better about their family relationships, according to the survey.

Boys who reported doing poorly in math and science usually ascribed their performance to the topics' lack of usefulness, whereas girls who reported a lack of success in these areas often attributed the problem to personal failure.

Although the survey included too few boys to allow a racial breakdown for males, race did appear to play an important role in the strength of self-esteem among girls. White and Hispanic girls displayed sharp drops in all the measured areas of self-esteem—appearance, confidence, family relationships, school, talents and personal importance—as they grew older. In contrast, more than half the black girls reported high levels of self-confidence and personal importance in both elementary and high school, and most attributed this to strong family and community support, says psychologist Janie Victoria Ward of the University of Pennsylvania in Philadelphia, an adviser to the study. Their confidence in their academic abilities, however, dropped substantially as they passed through the school system, Ward says.

"Something is going on in the schools that threatens the self-esteem of girls in general," asserts psychologist Nancy Goldberger, another adviser to the survey. "A lot of girls come to doubt their own intelligence in school."

Goldberger, who teaches psychology at the Fielding Institute in Santa Barbara, Calif., calls for intensive, long-term studies to address how schools short-change female students.

An AAUW pamphlet published last August argues that school-age girls represent the proverbial square peg attempting to fit into the round hole of most educational programs.

Starting early in life, societal pressures urge girls and boys to think and behave in contrasting ways that create gender-specific learning styles, according to the AAUW pamphlet. Schools, how-

ever, generally tailor instructional techniques to the learning style of boys, leaving girls with a tattered education and doubts about their academic abilities, the pamphlet contends.

This argument rests heavily on research directed by Harvard University psychologist Carol Gilligan. In her much-praised and much-criticized book, *In a Different Voice* (1982, Harvard University Press), Gilligan asserted that girls and boys generally follow divergent paths of moral development. She based her contention on several studies of Harvard undergraduates, men and women at different points in the life cycle, and women considering abortion.

In Gilligan's view, females respond to an inner moral voice emphasizing human connections and care, and they attempt to solve moral dilemmas by responding to the needs and situations of those affected by the problem. Males, on the other hand, focus on abstract principles such as justice and follow a moral code centered on the impartial application of rules of right and wrong.

Gilligan's most recent research, described in *Making Connections: The Relational Worlds of Adolescent Girls at Emma Willard School* (1990, Harvard University Press), draws on findings collected over a three-year period among 34 students at a private girls' school in Troy, N.Y. Gilligan and her co-workers argue that many girls, at least in this predominantly white, privileged sample, show an aggressive confidence in their identities and ideas around age 11, only to find their self-assurance withering by age 15 or 16.

During this period of increasing separation from parents, marked by a search for an independent identity and future career possibilities, girls feel torn between responding to others and caring for themselves, the Harvard researchers maintain. In addition, they say, adolescent girls encounter more pressure from parents and teachers to keep quiet and not make a fuss than do adolescent boys or younger girls.

The gender gap seen in academic achievement during early adolescence arises largely because a social and educational emphasis on career development and personal advancement clashes with girls' distinctive sense of connection to others, Gilligan's team asserts. The researchers maintain that girls often learn best and gain increased self-confidence through collaboration with other students and faculty, not through competition among individuals as practiced in most schools.

Boys, in contrast, often perform best on competitive tasks or in games with a strict set of prescribed rules, the investigators contend.

Some adolescence researchers argue that Gilligan paints too stark a contrast between the moral development of boys and girls. Others say Gilligan's ideas have an intuitive appeal, but her small studies lack a sound empirical foundation on which to build educational reforms. These researchers see Gilligan's work as a preliminary corrective for previous studies, based largely on male participants, that suggested the ability to reason from abstract principles represented the pinnacle of moral development.

Similarly, social scientists differ over the extent to which self-esteem dips during adolescence and the meaning of the AAUW survey data. In fact, some investigators question whether a significant gender gap in self-esteem exists at all.

Most surveys of teenagers' self-esteem, including the AAUW project, focus on students and neglect school dropouts. This approach may lead to overestimates of self-esteem among boys, argues sociologist Naomi Gerstel of the University of Massachusetts in Amherst. More boys than girls drop out of school, and male dropouts may regard themselves in an especially poor light, Gerstel points out.

Furthermore, she says, since no one has examined the moral "voice" of boys in the intensive way Gilligan studied her group of girls, Gilligan's theory has yet to meet a scientifically rigorous test. Gilligan's ideas prove "problematic" when educators attempt to use them to formulate specific educational reforms, Gerstel writes in the Jan. 4 [1991] *Science*.

The self-esteem reports gathered in the AAUW survey fail to provide evidence for any particular need to change school instruction, contends psychologist Joseph Adelson of the University of Michigan in Ann Arbor. "It's been known for some time that girls report greater self-esteem declines in adolescence, but the reasons for those declines are unclear," he says. "It's inappropriate to take the correlations in this survey to politicized conclusions about educational reform."

In his view, gender differences in mathematics achievement remain particularly mysterious and probably stem from a number of as-yet-unspecified social or family influences. Preliminary studies directed by Carol S. Dweck, a psychologist at Columbia University in New York City, suggest that bright girls show a stronger tendency than bright boys to attribute their difficulty or confusion with a new concept—such as mathematics—to a lack of intelligence. Thus, when bright girls confront mathematics, initial confusion may trigger a feeling of helplessness, Dweck writes in *At The Threshold* (1990, S. Shirley Feldman and Glen R. Elliot, editors, Harvard University Press).

Many girls with considerable potential in mathematics may deal with this sense of helplessness by throwing their energies into already mastered verbal skills, Dweck suggests. Rather than indict their intelligence, both boys and girls who shrink from challenging new subjects may need to learn how to channel initial failures into a redoubled effort to master the material, she says.

Gender differences in reported well-being—an aspect of personal experience closely related to self-esteem—also prove tricky to study, Adelson observes. A statistical comparison of 93 independent studies, directed by psychologist Wendy Wood of Texas A&M University in College Station, serves as a case in point. In examining these studies, which focused on well-being and life satisfaction among adult men and women, Wood and her colleagues found that women reported both greater happiness *and* more dissatisfaction and depression than men. Wood contends that societal influences groom women for an acute emotional responsiveness, especially with regard to intimate relationships, and that this helps explain why women report more intense emotional highs and lows than men.

"No clear advantage can be identified in the adaptiveness and desirability of [men's and women's] styles of emotional life," she and her colleagues write in the March 1989 *Psychological Bulletin*.

Researchers have yet to conduct a similar statistical comparison of the literature on adolescent self-esteem and well-being. But according to Adelson, a persistent problem plagues the interpretation of all such studies. If females generally show more sensitivity to and awareness of emotions than males, they may more easily offer self-reports about disturbing feelings, creating a misimpression that large sex differences exist in self-esteem, he suggests.

Although this potential "response bias" muddies the research waters, psychologist Daniel Offer of Northwestern University in Evanston, Ill., cites several possible explanations for the tendency among early-adolescent girls to report more self-dissatisfaction than boys.

One theory holds that since girls experience the biological changes of puberty up to 18 months before boys, they may suffer earlier and more pronounced self-esteem problems related to sexual maturity. Several studies have found that early-maturing girls report the most dissatisfaction with their physical appearance, a particularly sensitive indicator of self-esteem among females. Social pressures to begin dating and to disengage emotionally from parents may create additional problems for early-maturing girls, Offer says.

Other research suggests that, unlike their male counterparts, adolescent girls often maintain close emotional ties to their mothers that interfere with the development of a sense of independence and self-confidence, Offer says. In addition, parents may interrupt and ignore girls more than boys as puberty progresses, according to observational studies of families, directed by psychologist John P. Hill of Virginia Commonwealth University in Richmond.

Despite these findings, the director of the most ambitious longitudinal study of adolescent self-esteem to date says her findings provide little support for the substantial gender gap outlined in the AAUW survey, which took a single-point-in-time "snapshot" of self-esteem.

During the 1970s, sociologist Roberta G. Simmons of the University of Pittsburgh and her co-workers charted the trajectory of self-esteem from grades 6 through 10 among more than 1,000 youngsters attending public schools in Milwaukee and Baltimore. Simmons discusses the research in *Moving Into Adolescence* (1987, Aldine de Gruyter).

Overall, adolescents reported a gradual increase in self-esteem as they got older, she says, but many girls entering junior high and high school did experience drops in feelings of confidence and self-satisfaction.

Simmons agrees with Gilligan that adolescent girls increasingly strive for intimacy with others. Large, impersonal junior high schools throw up a barrier to intimacy that initially undermines girls' self-esteem, Simmons asserts. As girls find a circle of friends and a social niche, their self-esteem gradually rebounds, only to drop again when they enter the even larger world of high school.

"We don't know if that last self-esteem drop [in high school] was temporary or permanent," Simmons points out.

As in the AAUW survey, Simmons' team found that black girls, as well as black boys, consistently reported positive and confident self-images.

But given the increased acceptance of women in a wide variety of occupations since the 1970s, Simmons expresses surprise at how much the self-esteem of girls lagged behind that of boys in the AAUW survey.

A new study of 128 youngsters progressing through junior high, described in the February [1991] *Journal of Youth and Adolescence,* also contrasts with the AAUW findings. The two-year, longitudinal investigation reveals comparable levels of self-esteem among boys and girls, notes study director Barton J. Hirsch, a psychologist at Northwestern University. Hirsch and his colleagues used a global self-esteem measure much like the one in the AAUW survey.

The researchers gathered self-reports from boys and girls as the students neared the end of sixth grade, then repeated the process with the same youngsters at two points during the seventh grade and at the end of eighth grade. Students lived in a midwestern city and came from poor or middle-class families. Black children made up about one-quarter of the sample.

In both sexes, about one in three youngsters reported strong self-esteem throughout junior high school, the researchers report. These individuals also did well in school, maintained rewarding friendships and frequently participated in social activities.

Another third of the sample displayed small increases in self-esteem, but their overall psychological adjustment and academic performance were no better than those of the group with consistently high self-esteem.

Chronically low self-esteem and school achievement dogged 13 percent of the students, who probably suffered from a long history of these problems, Hirsch says.

But the most unsettling findings came from the remaining 21 percent of the youngsters. This group—composed of roughly equal numbers of boys and girls—started out with high self-esteem, good grades and numerous friends, but their scores on these measures plunged dramatically during junior high, eventually reaching the level of the students with chronically low self-esteem.

The data offer no easy explanations for the steep declines seen among one in five study participants, Hirsch says. An examination of family life might uncover traumatic events that influenced the youngsters' confidence and motivation, but this remains speculative, he says.

One of the most comprehensive longitudinal studies of the relation between child development and family life . . . suggests that particular parenting styles produce the most psychologically healthy teenagers. The findings indicate that parents who set clear standards for conduct and allow freedom within limits raise youngsters with the most academic, emotional and social competence.

Directed by psychologist Diana Baumrind of the University of California, Berkeley, the ongoing study has followed children from 124 families, most of them white and middle-class. At three points in the youngsters' lives—ages 3, 10 and 15—investigators assessed parental styles and the children's behavior at home and school.

Baumrind assumes that self-esteem emerges from competence in various social and academic tasks, not vice versa. For that reason, she and her colleagues track achievement scores and trained observers' ratings of social and emotional adjustment, not children's self-reports of how they feel about themselves.

In fact, Baumrind remains unconvinced that girls experience lower self-esteem than boys upon entering adolescence. Her study finds that girls in elementary grades show a more caring and communal attitude toward others, while boys more often strive for dominance and control in social encounters. But by early adolescence, she maintains, such differences largely disappear.

The gender-gap debate, however, shows no signs of disappearing. In a research field characterized by more questions than answers, most investigators agree on one point. "Most kids come through the years from 10 to 20 without major problems and with an increasing sense of self-esteem," Simmons observes.

Yet that trend, too, remains unexplained. "Perhaps the steady increase in self-esteem noted in late adolescence results more from progressive indoctrination into the values of society than from increasing self-acceptance," says Robson. "We simply do not have the empirical data necessary to resolve this question."   [1991]

Understanding the Reading

1. What does self-esteem mean?
2. What is the relationship between self-esteem and math and science?
3. How does race relate to self-esteem?
4. According to this article, how does Gilligan explain the educational gender gap?
5. What are the objections to her theory?
6. Why do girls and boys respond differently to scholastic difficulty?
7. What may explain girls' loss of self-esteem in adolescence?
8. What relationships are there between self-esteem and academic performance?
9. What did the Baumrind study show?

Suggestions for Responding

1. What factors do you think account for adolescent girls' loss of self-esteem?
2. How could schools be changed in order to provide an environment more responsive to girls' needs? ✦

18

I Want a Wife

JUDY SYFERS

I belong to that classification of people known as wives. I am A Wife. And, not altogether incidentally, I am a mother.

Not too long ago a male friend of mine appeared on the scene fresh from a recent divorce. He had one child, who is, of course, with his ex-wife. He is obviously looking for another wife. As I thought about him while I was ironing one evening, it suddenly occurred to me that I, too, would like to have a wife. Why do I want a wife?

I would like to go back to school so that I can become economically independent, support myself, and, if need be, support those dependent upon me. I want a wife who will work and send me to school. And while I am going to school I want a wife to take care of my children. I want a wife to keep track of the children's doctor and dentist appointments. And to keep track of mine, too. I want a wife to make sure my children eat properly and are kept clean. I want a wife who will wash the children's clothes and keep them mended. I want a wife who is a good nurturant attendant to my children, who arranges for their schooling, makes sure that they have an adequate social life with their peers, takes them to the park, the zoo, etc. I want a wife who takes care of the children when they are sick, a wife who arranges to be around when the children need special care, because, of course, I cannot miss classes at school. My wife must arrange to lose time at work and not lose the job. It may mean a small cut in my wife's income from time to time, but I guess I can tolerate that. Needless to say, my wife will arrange and pay for the care of the children while my wife is working.

I want a wife who will take care of *my* physical needs. I want a wife who will keep my house clean. A wife who will pick up after me. I want a wife who will keep my clothes clean, ironed, mended, replaced when need be, and who will see to it that my personal things are kept in their proper place so that I can find what I need the minute I need it. I want a wife who cooks the meals, a wife who is a *good* cook. I want a wife who will plan the menus, do the necessary grocery shopping, prepare the meals, serve them pleasantly, and then do the cleaning up while I do my studying. I want a wife who will care for me when I am sick and sympathize with my pain and loss of time from school. I want a wife to go along when our family takes a vacation so that someone can continue to care for me and my children when I need a rest and change of scene.

I want a wife who will not bother me with rambling complaints about a wife's duties. But I want a wife who will listen to me when I feel the need to explain a rather difficult point I have come across in my course of studies. And I want a wife who will type my papers for me when I have written them.

I want a wife who will take care of the details of my social life. When my wife and I are invited out by my friends, I want a wife who will take care of the babysitting arrangements. When I meet people at school that I like and want to entertain, I want a wife who will have the house clean, will prepare a special meal, serve it to me and my friends, and not interrupt when I talk about the things that interest me and my friends. I want a wife who will have arranged that the children are fed and ready for bed before my guests arrive so that the children do not bother us.

And I want a wife who knows that sometimes I need a night out by myself.

I want a wife who is sensitive to my sexual needs, a wife who makes love passionately and eagerly when I feel like it, a wife who makes sure that I am satisfied. And, of course, I want a wife who will not demand sexual attention when I am not in the mood for it. I want a wife who assumes the complete responsibility for birth control, because I do not want more children. I want a wife who will remain sexually faithful to me so that I do not have to clutter up my intellectual life with jealousies. And I want a wife who understands that *my* sexual needs may entail more than strict adherence to monogamy. I must, after all, be able to relate to people as fully as possible.

If, by chance, I find another person more suitable as a wife than the wife I already have, I want the liberty to replace my present wife with another one. Naturally, I will expect a fresh, new life; my wife will take the children and be solely responsible for them so that I am left free.

When I am through with school and have a job, I want my wife to quit working and remain at home so that my wife can more fully and completely take care of a wife's duties.

My God, who *wouldn't* want a wife?   [1972]

Understanding the Reading

1. According to Syfers, what are the seven main areas of wifely responsibility?
2. What objections "might" a wife have to each?

Suggestions for Responding

1. Since Syfers' analysis in the early 1970s, the traditional feminine role has undergone many changes. Analyze the role today. What re-

mains of Syfers' definition? What has been eliminated? What has been added? How do you judge the new role for women?

2. Try to write a piece like Syfers' entitled "Why I Want a Husband," presenting, from the male point of view, the demands and frustrations of either the traditional role or that of the "new man." ✦

19

Women and Names

CASEY MILLER AND KATE SWIFT

The photograph of the three bright, good-looking young people in the Army recruitment ad catches the eye. All three have a certain flair, and one knows just by looking at the picture that they are enjoying life and glad they joined up. They are typical Americans, symbols of the kind of people the modern Army is looking for. The one closest to the camera is a white male. His name, as can be seen from the neat identification tag pinned to the right pocket of his regulation blouse, is Spurgeon. Behind him and slightly to the left is a young black man. He is wearing a decoration of some kind, and his name is Sort—. Perhaps it is Sorter or Sortman—only the first four letters show. A young woman, who is also white, stands behind Spurgeon on the other side. She is smiling and her eyes shine; she looks capable. She is probably wearing a name tag too, but because Spurgeon is standing between her and the camera, her name is hidden. She is completely anonymous.

The picture is not a candid shot; it was carefully posed. The three models were chosen from thousands of possible recruits. They are the same height; they all have dark hair and are smiling into the camera. They look like students, and the copy says the Army will pay 75 per cent of their tuition if they work for a college degree. It is no accident that two are white, one black, or that two are male, one female. Nor is it an accident that Spurgeon stands in front of the others at the apex of a triangle, or that, since someone had to be anonymous, the woman was chosen.

In our society women's names are less impor-

tant than men's. The reasons why are not hard to identify, but the consequences for both men and women are more far-reaching than members of either sex, with a few notable exceptions, have been prepared to admit or even, until recently, to examine. Like other words, names are symbols; unlike other words, what they symbolize is unique. A thousand John Does and Jane Roes may live and die, but no bearer of those names has the same inheritance, the same history, or the same fears and expectations as any other. It therefore seems legitimate to ask what effect our naming customs have on girls and boys and on the women and men they grow into. Are the symbol-words that become our names more powerful than other words?

Few people can remember learning to talk. The mystery of language is rarely revealed in a single moment of electrifying insight like Helen Keller's, when suddenly, at the age of seven, the deaf and blind child realized for the first time the connection between the finger signals for w-a-t-e-r her teacher was tapping into her palm and "the wonderful cool something" that flowed from the pump spout onto her other hand.

From what scholars report about the way children normally acquire speech, it seems probable that "learning to talk" is actually the measured release, in conjuction with experience, of an innate capacity for language that is common to all human beings. We are no more likely to remember the process than we are to remember growing taller. What one may remember is a particular moment—seeing the yardstick exactly even with the latest pencil line marking one's height on the door jamb or learning a word for some particular something one had been aware of but could not name: tapioca, perhaps, or charisma, or a cotter pin. Anyone who has ever said, "so *that's* what those things are called," knows the experience.

When children are first learning to talk they go through a series of similar experiences. The very act of learning what a person or thing is called brings the object into the child's ken in a new way. It has been made specific. Later, the specific will also become general, as when the child calls any small, furry animal a "kitty." Words are symbols; their meanings can be extended.

Amanda, who is twenty months old, has spurts of learning names. "Mum," she says to her mother while pointing to the box. "Mum," she says again, pointing to the doorknob. "What is it?" she is asking without using words. "Tell me its name." When she calls her mother by a name, she knows her mother will respond to it. She knows that she, Amanda, has a name. It is important to her, for she has already become aware of herself as a thing different from everything else. As a psychologist might put it, her ego is emerging. Hearing her name, being called by it, is part of the process.

Amanda makes certain sounds, naming food or her bottle, that tell her parents she is hungry or thirsty. Before long she will speak of herself in the third person: "'Manda want apple." "'Manda come too." She may repeat her name over and over, perhaps mixing it with nonsense syllables. It is like a charm. It may be the first word she learns to spell. She will delight in seeing the letters of her name, this extension of herself, on her toothbrush or drinking mug. They belong to her, not to her brother or to her mother or father.

When children begin to play with other children and when they finally go to school, their names take on a public dimension. The child with a "funny" name is usually in for trouble, but most kids are proud of their names and want to write them on their books and pads and homework. There was a time when older children carved their names or initials on trees. Now that there are so many people and so few trees, the spray can has taken over from the jackknife, but the impulse to put one's identifying mark where all the world can see it is as strong as ever. The popularity of commercially produced name-on objects of every kind, from tee-shirts to miniature license plates, also attests to the importance youngsters (and a lot of grown-ups too) place on claiming and proclaiming their names.

Given names are much older than surnames, of course, probably as old as language itself. One can imagine that as soon as our ancient forbears started using sounds to represent actions or objects, they also began to distinguish each other in the same way. One might even speculate that the people who most often assigned sounds to others were those who produced and cared for the group's new members. Commenting on the assumption of philologists that the exchange of meaningful vocal sounds began among males as they worked and hunted together—hence the so-called "yo-heave-ho" and "bow-wow" theo-

ries of language origin—Ethel Strainchamps, a psycholinguist, notes that most philologists have in the past been men. Considering the importance to human survival of communication between mother and child when open fires, venomous reptiles, and other hazards were everywhere, "it might have occurred to a woman that a 'no-no' theory was more likely," Strainchamps says. Perhaps her suggestion should be taken a step further: who knows that it was not the creative effort of women, striving to communicate with each new baby, calling it by a separate and distinguishing sound, that freed the primordial human mind from the prison of animal grunts and led in time to the development of language?

Inevitably, some people dislike the names they have been given, and many children go through a phase of wanting to be called something else. For no apparent reason Anne announces that her name is really Koko and she will not answer to any other. For months nothing will change her resolve. She is Koko—and then one day she is Anne again. But if Cecil decides he wants to be called Jim, or Fanny elects to be known as Jill, the reasons may be less obscure: names do seem to give off vibrations of a sort, and other people's response to your name becomes a part of their response to you. Some psychologists think that given names are signals of parental expectations: children get the message and act on it either positively or negatively. One study claims to show, for example, that names can be "active" or "passive." If you call your son Mac or Bart he will become a more active person than if you call him Winthrop or Egbert. Your daughter is more likely to be outgoing and confident, according to this theory, if you call her Jody rather than Letitia. It follows, though, that if Jody prefers to be called Letitia, she is letting it be known that she sees herself in a more passive and dependent way than you anticipated.

Last names, too, can be positive or negative. Some carry a mystique of greatness or honor: Randolph, Diaz, Morgenthau, Saltonstall. Others are cumbersome, or they invite cruel or tasteless jokes. Many people decide, for one reason or another, to change their last names, but a great many more take pride today in being identified as a Klein or a Mackenzie, a Giordano or a Westervelt. The first-and-last-name mix which a person grows up with—that combination of particular and general, of personal and traditional—is not lightly exchanged for another.

Whether a name is self-chosen or bestowed at birth, making it one's own is an act of self-definition. When a former Cabinet member who had been involved in the Watergate scandal asked the Senate investigating committee to give back his good name, he was speaking metaphorically, for no one had taken his name away. What he had lost, justly or unjustly, was his public image as a person of integrity and a servant of the people. One's name also represents one's sense of power and self-direction. "I'm so tired I don't know my own name" is a statement of confusion and fatigue. *Your* name, the beginning of your answer to "Who am I?" is the outermost of the many layers or identity reaching inward to the real you. It is one of the significant differences between you and, let's say, a rose, which is named but does not know it. Yet it is one of the things a little girl grows up knowing she will be expected to lose if she marries.

The loss of women's last names may seem compensated for by a custom in first-naming that allows girls to be called by a version of their fathers' names, so that—after a fashion, at least—continuity is restored. In this post-Freudian age it would be bad form to give a boy a version of his mother's first name. Nevertheless, if a couple named Henrietta and Frank should decide to call their son Henry, chances are an earlier Henry, after whom Henrietta was named, provides the necessary male for him to identify with. In any case, the name has come back into its own: it stands foursquare and solid, which is seldom true of the derivative names given to girls. The strength of John is preserved in Joan and Jean, but these are exceptions. Names like Georgette and Georgina, Josephine, Paulette and Pauline, beautiful as they may sound, are diminutives. They are copies, not originals, and like so many other words applied to women, they can be diminishing.

A man in most Western societies can not only keep his name for his lifetime but he can pass it on intact to his son, who in turn can pass it on to *his* son. The use of a surname as a given name is also usually reserved for males, presumably on the grounds that such names do not have a sufficiently "feminine" sound for the "weaker sex." When tradition permits the giving of a family surname to daughters, as in the American South, a woman can at least retain her identification with that branch of her family. Once a surname has gained popularity as a girl's name, however, it is likely to face extinction as a boy's name. Shirley, for example, an old Yorkshire family name meaning "shire meadow," was once given as a first name only to boys. Not until Charlotte Brontë wrote *Shirley*—a novel published in 1849, whose central character, Shirley Keeldar, was modeled on Charlotte's sister Emily—was it used for a girl. Since then, Shirley has become popular as a girl's name but has dropped out of use as a boy's. Names like Leslie, Beverly, Evelyn, and Sidney may be traveling the same route. Once they have become popular as women's names, their histories as surnames are forgotten, and before long they may be given to girls exclusively.

In English, names like Charity, Constance, Patience, Faith, Hope, Prudence, and Honor no longer have popular equivalents for males, as they often do in other languages. The qualities described are not limited to females, of course, and yet to name a son Honor or Charity, even if doing so breaks no objective rule, would somehow run counter to social expectations. This may be true in part because such names are subjective, expressing more intimately than would seem appropriate for a boy the parents' expectations for their offspring. Or the principle that applied in the case of Shirley may apply here, for once a name or a word becomes associated with women, it is rarely again considered suitable for men.

One of the most useful functions of a given name is to serve as a quick identifier of sex. Nearly everyone, whether they admit it or not, is interested in knowing what sex an unknown person is. You get a postcard from a friend saying he will be stopping by to see you next week with someone named Lee, and chances are the first question that pops into your mind is not whether Lee is young or old, black or white, clever or dull, but whether Lee will turn out to be female or male. Still, natural curiosity does not entirely explain the annoyance or embarrassment some people seem to feel when women have names that are not specifically female by tradition or why names that become associated with women are thenceforth out of bounds for men.

If quick sex identification were the only consideration, the long male tradition of using initials in place of first names would not have come about. People with names like J. P. Morgan, P. T. Barnum, and L. L. Bean were always male—or were they? No one could stop women from sneaking under the flap of *that* tent, and in fact so many did that the practice had to be disallowed. In the early years of this century Columbia University, which in its academic bulletins identified male faculty members only by their surnames and initials, wrote out the names of women faculty members in full—lest anyone unintentionally enroll in a course taught by a woman.

Perhaps it is because of the transience of women's last names that their first names seem often to be considered the logical, appropriate, or even polite counterpart of men's surnames, and the news media frequently reflect this feeling. When Secretary of State Henry Kissinger and Nancy Maginnis were married, many news stories called them "Kissinger and Nancy" after the first paragraph. The usage is so accepted, and its belittling implications so subliminal, that it often persists in defiance of changes taking place all about it. In a magazine story on the atypical career choices of six graduate students, the subhead read "Stereotypes fade as men and women students . . . prepare to enter fields previously dominated almost exclusively by the opposite sex." Three women going into dentistry, business administration, and law were introduced by their full names, as were three men whose fields of study were nursing, library science, and primary education. The men were then referred to as Groves, White, and Fondow, while the women became Fran, Carol, and Pam.

Children, servants, and other presumed inferiors are apt to be first-named by adults and employers and by anyone else who is older, richer, or otherwise assumed to be superior. In turn, those in the first category are expected to address those in the second by their last names prefixed with an appropriate social or professional title. People on a fairly equal footing, however, either first-name each other or by mutual if unspoken agreement use a more formal mode of address.

As it happens, even though the average full-time working woman in the United States is slightly older than the average man who is employed full-time, she makes only slightly more than half the salary he makes. This may explain why a great many more women than men are called by their first names on the job and why, in offices where most of the senior and junior executives are men and most of the secretaries and clerks are women, the first-naming of all women—including executives, if any—easily becomes habitual. Or it could be that women are at least slightly less impressed by the thought of their own importance, slightly more inclined to meet their colleagues and employees on equal terms. When a reporter asked newly elected Governor Ella Grasso of Connecticut what she wanted to be called and she answered, "People usually call me Ella," a new benchmark for informality must have been set in the other forty-nine state capitals. Unless men respond in the same spirit, however, without taking advantage of what is essentially an act of generosity, women like Governor Grasso will have made a useless sacrifice, jeopardizing both their identity and their prestige.

In the whole name game, it is society's sanction of patronymy[1] that most diminishes the importance of women's names—and that sanction is social only, not legal. In the United States no state except Hawaii legally requires a woman to take her husband's name when she marries, although social pressures in the other states are almost as compelling. The very fact that until recently few women giving up their names realized they were not required to do so shows how universal the expectation is. Any married couple who agree that the wife will keep her own name are in for harassment, no matter how legal their stand: family, friends, the Internal Revenue Service, state and local agencies like motor vehicle departments and voter registrars, hotels, credit agencies, insurance companies are all apt to exert pressure on them to conform. One judge is quoted as saying to a married woman who wanted to revert to her birth name, "If you didn't want his name, why did you get married? Why didn't you live with him instead?" To thus equate marriage with the desire of some women to be called "Mrs." and the desire of some men to have "a Mrs." is insulting to both sexes; yet the equation is so widely accepted that few young people growing up in Western societies think in any different terms.

The judge just quoted was, in effect, defining what a family is in a patronymical society like ours where only males are assured permanent surnames they can pass on to their children. Women are said to "marry into" families, and families are said to "die out" if an all-female generation occurs. The word family, which comes from the Latin *famulus,* meaning a servant or slave, is itself a reminder that wives and children, along with servants, were historically part of man's property. When black Americans discard the names of the slaveholders who owned their forebears, they are consciously disassociating their sense of identity from the property status in which their ancestors were held. To adopt an African name is one way of identifying with freedom and eradicating a link to bondage. The lot of married women in Western society today can hardly be called bondage, but to the degree that people's names are a part of themselves, giving them up, no matter how willingly, is tantamount to giving up some part of personal, legal, and social autonomy.

Since a surname defines a family and identifies its members, a man who marries and has children extends his family, but a woman in marrying gives up her "own" family and joins in extending another's. She may be fully aware that she brings to her new family—to her children and grandchildren—the genetic and cultural heritage of her parents and grandparents, but the lineages she can trace are ultimately paternal. Anyone who decides to look up their ancestors through marriage and birth records in town halls and genealogical societies may find paternal lines going back ten or fifteen generations or more, whereas with few exceptions maternal ones end after two or three. The exceptions are interesting for they emphasize how important the lost information from maternal lines really is. Stephen Birmingham, writing about America's blue-blooded families, notes that "'Who is she?' as a question may mean, 'What was her maiden name?' It may also mean what was her mother's maiden name, and what was her grandmother's maiden name, and so on." Blue bloods, in other words, care a lot about "maiden names," and rightly so, considering that the inputs of maternal genes and culture have as great an effect on offspring as paternal inputs.

Obviously we all have as many female ancestors as male ancestors, but maternal lineages, marked with name changes in every generation, are far more difficult to trace. To most of us the identity of our mother's mother's mother's mother, and that of *her* mother, and on back, are lost forever. How is one affected by this fading out of female ancestors whose names have disappeared from memory and the genealogical records? Research on the subject is not readily available, if it exists at all, but it seems likely that daughters are affected somewhat differently from sons. If it is emotionally healthy, as psychologists believe, for a child to identify with the parent of the same sex, would it not also be healthy for a child to identify with ancestors of the same sex?

A boy, knowing he comes from a long line of males bearing the name Wheelwright, for example, can identify with his forefathers: Johnny Wheelwright in the 1970s, if he wants to, can imagine some medieval John in whose workshop the finest wheels in the land were fashioned, a John who had a son, who had a son, who had a son, until at last Johnny Wheelwright himself was born. No line of identifiable foremothers stretches back into the past to which his sister Mary can lay claim. Like Johnny, she is a Wheelwright, assigned by patronymy to descent from males. What neither boy nor girl will ever be able to trace is their equally direct descent from, let's say, a woman known as the Healer, a woman whose daughter's daughter's daughter, through the generations, passed on the skilled hands which both John and Mary may have inherited.

Imagine, in contrast to Johnny Wheelwright, a hypothetical woman of today whose name is Elizabeth Jones. If you were to ask, in the manner of a blue blood, "Who is she?" you might be told, "She was a Fliegendorf. Her people were Pennsylvania Dutch farmers who came over from Schleswig-Holstein in the seventeenth century." Actually, that tells a fraction of the story. This hypothetical Elizabeth Jones's mother—who met her father at an Army post during the Second World War—was a Woslewski whose father emigrated from Poland as a boy, lived in Chicago, and there married a Quinn whose mother came from Canada and was a Vallière. The mother of that Vallière was the great-great-granddaughter of a woman whose given name was the equivalent of "Deep Water" and who belonged to a group of native North Americans called the Têtes de Boule by French explorers.

Elizabeth Jones's father's mother, in Pennsylvania, had been a Bruhofer, whose mother had been a Gruber, whose mother, a Powell, was born in Georgia and was the great-great-granddaughter of a woman brought to this country from Africa in the hold of a slave ship.

Thus, although Elizabeth Jones is said to have been a Fliegendorf whose people came from Schleswig-Holstein in the sixteen hundreds, fewer than 5 per cent of her two thousand or so direct ancestors who were alive in that century had any connection with Schleswig-Holstein, and only one of those who made the passage to America was born with the name Fliegendorf. The same may be said, of course, of Elizabeth Jones's brother, Ed Fliegendorf's relationship to the Fliegendorf family or Johnny Wheelwright's relationship to the bearers of his name. Yet so strong is our identification with the name we inherit at birth that we tend to forget both the rich ethnic mix most of us carry in our genes and the arbitrary definition of "family" that ultimately links us only to the male line of descent.

This concept of family is one of the reasons why most societies through most of history have placed greater value on the birth of a male child than of a female child. Ours is no exception. A . . . survey reported in *Psychology Today* showed that a higher percentage of prospective parents in the United States would prefer to have a son than a daughter as a first or only child. The percentage who feel this way, however, has dropped from what it was [in 1956]. Responding to the report, a reader expressed his opinion that the change could be attributed to "a breakdown in the home-and-family ideal" among young parents today. "The son," he wrote in a letter to the editor, "and in particular the eldest son, is strongly tied to the archetypal family; first as its prime agent of continuation, and also as the future guardian and master of the home." Here, then, family and name are seen as synonymous, the male is the prime if not only progenitor, and even the order of birth among male children affects the model of an ideal family.

One could not ask for a better example of how patronymy reinforces the powerful myth that pervades the rest of our language—the myth that the human race is essentially male. The ob-

vious first reaction to such a statement may be to say, "But that's absurd. No one thinks of the race as essentially male." And yet we do. As the social critic Elizabeth Janeway has pointed out, a myth does not really describe a situation; rather, it tries to bring about what it declares to exist.

A childless couple adopted a baby girl. When asked why they chose a girl rather than a boy, they explained that if she did not live up to their expectations because of her genetic heritage, "at least she won't carry on the family." Journalist Mike McGrady states the myth of racial maleness even more tellingly in an article about sperm banking: "One customer . . . gave a reason for depositing sperm that may foreshadow the future: it was to carry on the family line should his male offspring prove sterile. What we are talking about here," McGrady said, "is not fertility insurance but immortality insurance." This customer, then, believes he cannot be linked to future generations through his female offspring, should they prove fertile. His immortality, one must conclude, is not in his sperm or his genes but in his name.

"One's name and strong devotion to it," wrote an Austrian philosopher, Otto Weininger, around the turn of the century, "are even more dependent on personality than is the sense of property. . . . Women are not bound to their names with any strong bond. When they marry they give up their own name and assume that of their husband without any sense of loss. . . . The fundamental namelessness of the woman is simply a sign of her undifferentiated personality." Weininger, whose book *Sex and Character* had a brief but powerful influence on popular psychology, is of historical interest because he articulated the myth of humanity's maleness at a time when the first wave of feminism was beginning to be taken seriously by governments, trade unions, and other institutions in England and the United States as well as in Europe. In describing the "fundamental namelessness" of woman as "a sign of her undifferentiated personality," Weininger was building support for his premise that "women have no existence and no essence . . . no share in ontological reality, no relation to the thing-in-itself, which, in the deepest interpretation, is the absolute, is God."

Otto Weininger was aware of the movement for women's rights and was deeply disturbed by it. He may well have heard of the noted American feminist Lucy Stone, whose decision to keep her birth name when she married Henry Blackwell in 1855 had created consternation on both sides of the Atlantic. An eloquent speaker with a free and fearless spirit, Stone was widely known as an antislavery crusader. After the Civil War her organizing efforts helped secure passage of the [Fifteenth] Amendment, which extended the vote to freed slaves who were men. She devoted the rest of her long, productive life to the cause of suffrage for women and founded and edited the *Woman's Journal,* for forty-seven years the major weekly newspaper of the women's movement.

It is especially relevant that among Lucy Stone's many important contributions to history she is best known today for her refusal to give up her name. Her explanation, "My name is the symbol of my identity and must not be lost," was a real shocker to anyone who had not considered the possibility that a married woman could have an individual identity—and in the nineteenth century that meant almost everyone. The law did not recognize such a possibility, as the famous English jurist William Blackstone made clear when he summarized the rule of "coverture," influencing both British and American law for well over a hundred years. "By marriage," he wrote, "the husband and wife are one person in the law—that is, the very being or legal existence of the woman is suspended during the marriage. . . ."

The suspended existence of the married woman came to be well symbolized in the total submersion of a wife's identity in her husband's name—preceded by "Mrs." The use of designations like "Mrs. John Jones" does not go back much before 1800. Martha Washington would have been mystified to receive a letter addressed to "Mrs. George Washington," for at that time the written abbreviation *Mrs.,* a social title applied to any adult woman, was used interchangeably with its spelled-out form *mistress* and was probably pronounced the same way. "Mistress George" would have made little sense.

Lucy Stone's example was followed in the late nineteenth and early twentieth centuries by small but increasing numbers of women, mostly professional writers, artists, and scientists. The Lucy Stone League, founded in New York in 1921, was the first organization to help women with the legal and bureaucratic difficulties involved in keeping their names after marriage. Its early leaders included Jane Grant, co-founder with her first husband, Harold Ross, of the *New Yorker* magazine, and journalist Ruth Hale who in 1926 asked rhetorically how men would respond to the suggestion that they give up *their* names. The suggestion does not often arise, but a psychologist recently described the reaction of one husband and father when someone in his family raised the possibility of changing the family name because they didn't like it:

"He suddenly realized that it was a traumatic thing for him to consider giving up his last name," according to Dr. Jack Sawyer of Northwestern University. "He said he'd never realized before that 'only men have real names in our society, women don't.' And it bothered him also that his name should be a matter of such consequence for him. He worried about his professional standing, colleagues trying to contact him—all kinds of things that women face as a matter of course when they get married. Men have accepted the permanency of their names as one of the rights of being male, and it was the first time he realized how much his name was part of his masculine self-image."

Lucy Stone, whose self-image was comfortably female but not feminine, agreed to be known as Mrs. Stone after her marriage. Through this compromise with custom she avoided the somewhat schizophrenic situation many well-known women face when they use their birth names professionally and their husband's names socially, thus becoming both Miss Somebody and Mrs. Somebody Else. The Pulitzer prize–winning novelist Jean Stafford wants to be "saluted as *Miss* Stafford if the subject at hand has to do with me and my business or as *Mrs.* Liebling if inquiries are being made about my late husband." Miss Stafford objects to being addressed as "Ms.," a title that Lucy Stone would probably have welcomed had it existed in her time.

During the nearly two centuries in which the use of the distinguishing marital labels Miss or Mrs. for women was rigidly enforced by custom, the labels tended to become parts of women's names, in effect replacing their given names. A boarding school founded by Sarah Porter in Farmington, Connecticut, soon became known as Miss Porter's School. After the actress Minnie Maddern married Harrison Grey Fiske, she became famous as Mrs. Fiske. In the following classroom dialogue, the columnist Ellen Cohn provides a classic example of how the custom works:

> *Question:* Who is credited with discovering radium?
> *Answer* (all together): Madam Curie.
> *Teacher:* Well, class, the woman (who was indeed married to a man named Pierre Curie) had a first name all her own. From now on let's call her Marie Curie.
> *Question:* Can Madam Curie ever be appropriately used?
> *Answer:* Of course. Whenever the inventor of the telephone is called Mr. Bell.

Through the transience and fragmentation that have traditionally characterized women's names, some part of the human female self-image has been sacrificed. It is hardly surprising, therefore, that the second wave of feminist consciousness brought a serious challenge to patronymy and to the assignment of distinguishing marital labels to women. To be named and defined by someone else is to accept an imposed identity—to agree that the way others see us is the way we really are. Naming conventions, like the rest of language, have been shaped to meet the interests of society, and in patriarchal societies the shapers have been men. What is happening now in language seems simply to reflect the fact that, in the words of Dr. Pauli Murray, "women are seeking their own image of themselves nurtured from within rather than imposed from without."   [1976]

Note

1. PATRONYMY: Receiving names from the male lineage.

Understanding the Reading

1. Explain the importance of one's name to one's identity.
2. What is the importance of the gendering of given names?
3. Why does it matter whether one is publicly called by one's first or last name?
4. How are surnames linked to our sense of family?

5. What examples do Miller and Swift give to illustrate the myth that the human race is essentially male?

Suggestions for Responding

1. Describe how society would be different if men rather than women gave up their names, or if both women and men retained their own names throughout their lives. What would be the benefits and disadvantages of such a new society?
2. Write an essay tracing your lineage back as far as you can through the various female lines.
3. Since this essay was written, some marrying couples have adopted alternative naming practices. Describe the ones you are familiar with, and explain why you support or object to this break with tradition. ♦

20

Static in Communication

AARON T. BECK, M.D.

Key conversational differences between men and women, which seem to be derived from the different subcultures of boys and girls, can be summarized as follows:

- Women seem to regard questions as a way to maintain a conversation, while men view them as requests for information.
- Women tend to connect "bridges" between what their conversational partner has just said and what it is that they have to say.
- Men do not generally follow this rule and often appear to ignore the preceding comment by their partner.
- Women seem to interpret aggressiveness by their partner as an attack that disrupts the relationship. Men seem to view aggressiveness simply as a form of conversation.
- Women are more likely to share feelings and secrets. Men like to discuss less intimate topics, such as sports and politics.
- Women tend to discuss problems with one

another, share their experiences, and offer reassurances. Men, on the other hand, tend to hear women (as well as other men) who discuss problems with them as making explicit requests for solutions, rather than as simply looking for a sympathetic ear.

These variations in the meaning of talk lead husbands and wives to have very different expectations. Women frequently want their partners to be a new, improved version of their best friend. They warm up when their husband tells them secrets, they enjoy being his confidante, and they are disturbed when their husband holds in his feelings.

Even though many husbands do not meet their wives' standards of intimacy, the fact remains that they are more likely to confide in their wives than in other people. When I have asked couples, "Whom do you most frequently confide in?" the husband generally responds, "My wife" and the wife says, "My best friend."

When it comes to talking out conflicts, again there is a sex difference. Many women, for example, take the attitude "The marriage is working as long as we can talk about it." Many husbands, on the other hand, have the view "The relationship is not working as long we keep talking about it."

Talking about problems makes some people (especially husbands) more and more upset; they would prefer to arrive at a quick, practical solution. But many people (especially wives) want to talk the problem out, because that is the way they get a sense of empathy, intimacy, and understanding.

Men and women tend to differ, too, in the way they respond to each other's problems. A wife, for example, may share a problem with her husband, hoping he will give her understanding and sympathy. Not infrequently, however, the husband fails to offer consolation. Instead, he is all business, trying to give his wife a practical solution; indicating areas in which she may be distorting or misinterpreting the situation; suggesting that she might be overreacting; and advising her how to avoid these problems in the future.

In these circumstances the wife may feel hurt or slighted. She is put out that her husband does not realize she knows perfectly well what to do about the situation, but merely wants his understanding—perhaps to tell her about similar experiences that he had. If the husband questions her interpretation of the problematic situation, she may read this reaction as criticism, indicating that there is something wrong with her. Instead, she wants him to convey to her in some way that she is not peculiar or wrong for reacting the way she does.

Husbands and wives frequently differ over what they consider important in what their mates tell them. For instance, a lawyer friend of mine, whose wife works in an art gallery, complains that she always wants to tell him "the trivial details about who said what to whom," while he would like to hear more about the kinds of paintings she is dealing with, her evaluation of them, and specific business details, such as purchasing strategies. He wants the facts and does not see the importance of his wife's conversations with her colleagues. To his wife, however, what happens between her and her associates at the gallery constitutes the fabric of her working life. Only a small proportion of her on-the-job attention is focused on details of the paintings themselves. Because she focuses on her interpersonal experiences—which strike him as trivial—the husband tends to cut her off. She is then hurt, because he seems to be telling her not only that what she says is unimportant and that her job is unimportant, but that *she* is unimportant.

The husband's chief satisfactions, on the other hand, come from talking about his law practice, politics, and sports. When he starts to discuss any of these areas, his wife thinks that he is lecturing her and is being condescending. Indeed, when I listen to his tone of voice, it is clear to me that there *is* a note of condescension, of which he is unaware. (Such sexist attitudes may be prominent among husbands and may become accentuated when their wives embark on their own careers.) In such a situation, the husband requires some consciousness raising in order to appreciate the importance his wife places on narrating her interpersonal work experiences. At the same time, he needs to modify his condescending way of instructing her, and to correct his estimation of her as intellectually inferior to him.   [1988]

Understanding the Reading

1. Explain what differences Beck sees in men's and women's conversational strategies.
2. Why does he think women and men conversationally handle conflicts and problems differently?
3. What kinds of topics do women and men consider conversationally important?
4. What do the different communication patterns show about female and male gender roles?

Suggestions for Responding

1. Do you think that Beck's analysis of gendered conversational styles is accurate? Why or why not?
2. How would the writers of two of the other readings in Part II account for Beck's five differences in the communication patterns of women and men? ◆

21

Dividing Lines

ANTHONY ASTRACHAN

CLASS

The class of gender crosses the boundaries of class defined by income, education, and power. Where the political and psychological dimensions intersect, men and women are indeed class enemies at many moments in their lives. (The oppressed class always sees the struggle more clearly than the dominant; so far, women have seen this more clearly than men.) But the human condition is that these enemies must love each other and often do.

The ways they love each other, the ways through this contradiction, this paradox, vary according to the familiar categories of class. Income and education do affect men's feelings about women's demands for independence and equality. So does power. Men treat women as equals more easily when they are sure of themselves and their money and power, or when questions of power are diffuse.

Blue-collar men feel the contradiction between their physical power and their place at the bottom of the male hierarchy, and they are more obvious than men in other classes about their need to treat women as underlings to compensate. They are more honest, or quicker to voice their anger and their fear, about changes in the balance of power and in sex roles, at work and at home. They find it harder than men with higher incomes and more education to overcome the traditions of their culture that prohibit treating women as equals, but some do so; at least one market researcher finds that blue-collar men express fewer traditional and macho values than stereotypes suggest, that some express higher expectations of intimacy and emotional support in relationships with women than middle-class men do. This sometimes translates from talk into action. Lower-income men in my small sample and in advertising surveys sometimes do more housework than middle-class men, I suspect for the simple reason that their wives work but they still can't afford maids.

Middle-class and upper-class men are more affected by the psychotherapy subculture and by commercial trends, both forces that make some try, and others pretend to try, to understand and accept what women are doing. A higher proportion of middle-class men than either blue-collar or upper-class men is genuinely supportive of women at work. A higher proportion is also more likely to take a real share in, or real responsibility for, child care and housework. In both cases it's still a small minority that reaches the stage of association. Many upper-class men talk about their devotion to equality, but few give it in business management and only slightly more in the professions. In both groups their economic, command, and prestige power is real and they don't want to lose it. They are probably sincere when they talk about equality in their personal lives, and the proportion who treat their wives as equals, while small, may be as great as in the middle-class. But with upper-class men, I can't escape the feeling that it's more a matter of principle than practice because they hire maids and nannies, almost always female.

Middle-class and upper-class men, I found in my interviews, are more likely than blue-collar men to sense that there is something wrong about our effort to monopolize power, to keep women powerless. (It's harder for blue-collar men because they are further from real power.) Part of it is cognitive dissonance[1] between our preaching democracy, human rights, and social mobility, and our practicing a kind of power politics that transforms gender and race into class. But I think our sense of wrong goes deeper than that. We know that mastery produces satisfaction, that competence means power and self-esteem. Conversely, we know that failure in mastery produces dissatisfaction, which turns into rage. We know that powerlessness, which we have made congruent with incompetence, is synonymous with low self-respect. We restrict women's mastery and deny them power even as they force us to recognize their competence.

RACE

The black experience of the gender revolution is different from white and Hispanic for several reasons. Black women have been working outside the home for so many generations that the idea of women in the workplace was not as revolutionary for them or their men as it was for other groups. Black women in general are still at the bottom of the economic ladder, but the proportion with better education, higher-status jobs, and higher salaries than men have is higher than it is among whites. This means the balance of economic and work power between men and women did not shift as dramatically for blacks as for others in recent years. Black women have been heading families in larger proportions for at least sixty years, so the balance of power at home did not shift so dramatically there either. In addition, the women's movement originated in and focused on the white middle class; it was the creation of white women whom many blacks see as a threat to black progress. So it did not touch black women as deeply as white, did not stimulate them to offer as many challenges as quickly to black men as white women did to white men.

Despite this, the balance at work and home for blacks *has* been affected by the changes of the past fifteen years. Many black men identify with women's demands as an outgrowth of the civil rights movement. The proportion who strongly resist women's demands is probably greater than the proportion of whites, however,

if only because they are more conscious of how little power they have and are therefore more sensitive to every erosion in it. Many middle-class black men think they see women with money and power all around them, and they are often more intensely hostile than their white counterparts. Many black women have come to recognize what they see as a double oppression, racial and sexual. So do many black men, like the Atlanta banking consultant who said, "Men have no control now, and they're looking for control. . . . You can't deal with your boss because he's white, and you can't control the home place because your wife is making as much as you do."

Among poorer blacks, many men simply do not "feel like a man" because of their inability to find a good job, earn good money, and do even half the providing for a family. They may feel impotent (and sometimes turn sexually impotent), or they may abandon the families they start and then feel even less like a man. They may displace their anger and resentment from the economy and the white world onto women—and all the more so when they see black women who earn decent money and provide single-handedly for families. The men's economic disability has many causes. Thomas Sowell, an economist, and William Wilson, a sociologist, are black conservatives who argue that the psychological legacy of the past is more important than anything in the society as a whole in blacks' failure to advance economically. Most blacks who have looked at the problem disagree, blaming continuing racial discrimination, real if not always intentional, visible in an array of facts: black men show greater increases in rates of chronic disease and mental illness than white men. Blacks are imprisoned at a rate four or five times higher than whites (and prison is not a place that trains men in sensitivity to women). The unemployment rate for black men officially is twice as high as the rate for white men and in fact may be much worse than that. (There is nearly a one-to-one correspondence in the increase in unemployment among black men and the increase in female-headed families over the years, according to Walter Allen, a sociologist at the University of Michigan.) Government welfare programs give no money to mothers and children if there is a man in the house. Yet many black men continue to maintain a connection with children even when they abandon the family in form or in reality—a sign that it may be possible to draw them into one of the main channels for men's participation in the gender revolution.

Hispanic attitudes resemble whites' more than blacks' because the place of *la mujer*[2] was so unquestionably in the home that the movement of women into the workplace was a dramatic change for Latins as it was for Anglos, indeed even more revolutionary in most Hispanic communities than in the majority society. The myth that women are not in the labor force persisted far longer for Chicanas[3] than for Anglos, though today the proportions for all women sixteen and over are similar. Hispanic men and women both insist that Latin machismo and the importance of the family are often misunderstood by Anglos, but their more accurate versions still emphasize the traditional importance of the father and the confinement of the mother to home, even if she demonstrates real strength there. A Hispanic woman who achieves an income or occupational level higher than her husband's arouses more agony in her spouse than occurs in any other ethnic group. Mexican-Americans often go on to say that the rebellion against the forces of machismo and family by Chicana women has created a change that may be greater in the long run than the changes among Anglos. But the forces of change are attenuated by the Hispanic birthrate, 75 percent higher than that of the rest of the population (25.5 births per thousand compared with 14.7 for non-Hispanics), with a higher percentage born to women under twenty, which keeps more women from finishing high school and from finding better jobs. The birthrate of course reflects Catholic doctrine, but it also reflects the belief of many, perhaps most Hispanic males that manhood is demonstrated by the number of children a man has. My impression is that while the dynamics of power change among Hispanics resemble the Anglos', the proportion and the intensity of male resistance approaches the blacks'.

AGE AND STAGES OF GROWTH

I did not find, as some of my friends expected, that older men uniformly tend to resist and younger men to support what women are doing, as though revolution depended primarily upon youth. It's true that men in their twenties today grew up with feminism in the air they breathed, and with an informality between the sexes that has many causes besides feminism. Many of them are freer of sex-role stereotypes than older men are. In surveys they profess more support for the equality of women than do older men or the male population as a whole, and a few studies say that (in much smaller proportions) they are more likely to live up to their professions. It's also true that men in their sixties are often more devoted to, or more the prisoner of, the habits that go with the old stereotypes. But in every season of a man's life from his twenties through his fifties, I found opponents, ambivalents, pragmatists, and supporters.

Looking at men under thirty, I found more who speak in terms of equality than those in any other age group, of equality within marriage and equality for women at work. But there are just as many in this group who assume power or privilege as there are true egalitarians. Many expect their wives to have careers, for instance, but also expect those careers to take second place to their own. Many become angry or fearful when they compete against women in the workplace. The under-thirties are traditional in tending to start relationships and initiate sex more often than the women they know, as the few women I interviewed confirm. They are often unsure how to treat single women and more cautious—from fear or anxiety—about marriage, so they postpone it. (The proportion of men between twenty-five and twenty-nine who are single grew from 23 to 38 percent between 1960 and 1984.) But young men are better able to say no to a woman's initiative than are their elders, and better able to maintain nonsexual friendships with women.

There are also some who reject tradition without moving toward equality—young men who seem ready to let women assume the kind of dominance that used to be male. I met two who talked about being househusbands; half-consciously they expect their wives to support them in a mirror image of the old wage-earner ethic, and they have no idea how much labor is involved in child raising. Three had little idea of how they wanted to earn a living, little concept of a career—like women before the recent changes. They are no doubt responding to the changes women are making, but hardly in an egalitarian fashion.

The most traditional of the under-thirties are blue-collar men for whom the factory is the place where they pass from the worlds of home and school, which they see as being run by women, to a world run by men. A woman personnel manager in [a] heavy equipment plant . . ., who dealt every day with the workers, saw this, and I heard her thought echoed in many men's conversations. She said:

> Women who come to work in the factory are violating not only the man's sense of family but his sense of order in the world. Look at the world the man-child grows up in: up to the eighth grade it's run almost entirely by women—his mother and his teachers. Even in high school, there are a lot of women teachers—and the girl students affect the boys, whether they behave themselves or go wild. Graduation from high school and coming to work in the plant is graduation from a woman's world and coming into a man's world. When they see a woman at work on the line, it looks like, "Oh, Lord, here comes Mother back again."

Many of these men, even though they grew up in a world much influenced by feminist ideas, still see women primarily as sex objects, not as fellow workers. Many are more self-centered and less helpful than their elders to any peer; they give less support to women on the job than some older men who are uncomfortable with the female presence but have been conditioned both to help their buddies and to help ladies. And, as the personnel manager saw, many younger men think of the shop as the first place they will be members of a male world. Not all blue-collar men under thirty are like this, but many are—enough to remind people not to jump to conclusions or ignore the intersection of age with class.

Many men in their thirties, men born between 1945 and 1955, were closer to what had been predicted: old enough to have acquired traditional attitudes but young enough to have felt the impact of feminist charges and changes. Some tried to respond positively. Others were too unsure of themselves to resolve questions in a way that satisfied them or the women in their lives. Women looking at young men and at the thirties

group often complain that they are getting neither what they asked nor the positive supports that accompanied the denial of equality in the old system.

Men in their late thirties and men in their forties were often in the position of marrying a homemaker and celebrating their tenth anniversary with a career woman. Some of these marriages ended in divorce, and the men in those that lasted probably struggled even harder to master the changing rules of the game. A *Ms.* magazine collective described both: "Some men who ran this gauntlet did not feel thanked enough. Some men who resisted change felt punished, angry, and occasionally guilty." That jibes completely with my interviews. *Ms.* added a point I didn't hear often, but which I find easy to believe: "Those feelings, once hidden, now surface as pained concern for the failures of feminism."

Men under forty provide the members of two groups who have achieved prominence in the media, yuppies and new men. Both occupy a bigger place in middle-class consciousness than they do in the population. Yuppies account for only 4 percent of the baby boom, the seventy-six million people between the ages of twenty-one and thirty-nine. This figure comes from an advertising agency measure of the consumer population; what could be more appropriate? J. Walter Thompson U.S.A. defines yuppies as people in this age group who combine higher education (five years, on the average) and high income (a median of $39,100). Despite the *u* for "urban" in yuppie, the agency finds that 56 percent of them live in the suburbs and only one in six is female. This figure may say more about their employers than about the yuppies themselves, but it provides an important reason for my observation that yuppies are unlikely to treat women as equals: they don't meet them as peers in large numbers.

Yuppies, by definition, are devoted to acquisitive and career pursuits, and appear (to me, at least) to be more selfish and narcissistic than the population as a whole. This may give them additional reason to postpone marriage and treasure the freedom of the single state. No doubt it also affects their behavior in marriage; I suspect that much of what I read about remodeling houses and finding new recipes for wholesome dishes reflects a yuppie attempt to substitute material ventures for some of the psychological effort needed to build intimacy and make a marriage last. I wonder if this makes for a more egalitarian marriage—it might, if the spouse were of the same kind—or a less. The first yuppies are now turning forty, and their behavior may change as they enter middle age and become more capable of thinking about others and integrating the masculine and feminine in themselves.

Thompson defines another 16 percent of the baby boom age group as would-bes, people with the same education as yuppies and presumably with yuppie values, but a median income of only $15,000—teachers, clergy, social workers, paramedics, college instructors. There's obviously considerable overlap between Thompson's would-bes and . . . service occupations, and a much higher proportion of would-bes than yuppies are women. Those two facts should make more of the male would-bes treat women as equals.

When I'm asked about yuppies, however, I think not only about that low 4 percent proportion of the baby boomers, but also of the downward mobility of the whole generation, including elite workers, workers, and housewives. Real after-tax income for families headed by a person aged twenty-five to thirty-four declined 2.3 percent between 1961 and 1982. The combined take-home pay of a two-earner couple in this age group is probably less than what each of their respective fathers earned on his own at the same age. Now, that's a good reason for having no, or fewer, children. But—thinking back to my expectations of a group with a high proportion of women and a lot of service jobs—a man may not treat his wife as an equal if he earns no more than she does; it may only fuel his anger and his anxiety.

The new man is someone whom feminists, social scientists, and advertisers all search for. Barbara Ehrenreich describes the prototype as twenty-five to forty years old, single, affluent, and living in a city, "for it is among such men that the most decisive break in the old masculine values is occurring." (I disagree on the single and I have doubts about the affluent.) He is usually able to

choose his clothes, decorate his apartment, and cook for himself—abilities that certainly distinguish him from traditional man, even if, as Ehrenreich says, he uses these skills to demonstrate his class status. They also enable him to stay independent of the women who used to take care of his domestic needs, and he does indeed tend to avoid commitment, in the current phrase. "Sensitivity" is a touchstone for the new man, who claims that he knows how to be "in touch with his feelings." Ehrenreich has her doubts. "Quite possibly," she says, "as sensitivity has spread, it has lost its moorings in the therapeutic experience and come to signify the heightened receptivity associated with consumerism: a vague appreciation that lends itself to aimless shopping."

That fits with marketing definitions of the new man. Playboy Marketing Services describes him as single, separated, divorced, widowed, living with someone who works or married with a working wife, and making purchasing decisions. It estimated in 1984 that 64.9 percent of all men meet this definition, rather different from my estimate of 5 to 10 percent who genuinely support women's demands for independence and equality. . . . Advertising agencies describe him similarly, in terms of his willingness to do household chores . . . and his propensity to make brand choices of products used in those chores, but they put him at 13 to 22 percent of all men.

All the surveys agree that men under thirty-five were more likely to show new-man characteristics than those over thirty-five. As I've said, I'm not so sure.

Hyatt & Esserman Research Associates did a poll for *Good Morning America* in 1980 that put the proportion of new men at 19 percent. They asked forty questions and defined the new man in terms of responses to the three that created the greatest division of opinion among the 752 men interviewed. The new man disagreed with the statement, "If women have children at home under six years of age, they should not work." He agreed that "when women marry, it's fine for them to keep their maiden names." And he agreed that "if both parents work, the wife and husband should take turns to stay home when the kids are sick."

But two thirds of *all* men in the Hyatt & Esserman survey disagreed with the statement, "A man should never cry in public," and six out of seven agreed that men can be just as good at changing diapers as women. Those figures show how men in general have been affected by change. They are evidence for my feeling that it will be hard to reverse the revolution. But neither they nor the 19 percent of Hyatt & Esserman's definition of new men are going to make the revolution succeed. That will take another kind of man, or this kind of new man after he has gone through or been put through profound struggle with himself and society.

Some new men are certainly over thirty-five, even over forty. Older men do seem to find it harder than younger men to accept women on the job, but there are so many exceptions to this that I mention it only with reluctance. I found several older men who were genuinely supportive of women's demands for equality and choice. It takes a man who is relatively sure of his own competence, his own achievement, and his own masculinity to feel and behave positively about the changes women are making. Not every successful man is positive about these changes; many hate them as denials of their own lives and values, their own manhood. But a large proportion of those men who do like what women are doing are successful in their own terms. That means many of them are middle-aged.

Older men who are egalitarian and younger men who aren't don't constitute a historical anomaly as much as they illustrate the process of adult development that Daniel Levinson outlined. A young man in his twenties, in early adulthood, is striving to take his place in the world as an adult male. He is apt to try to control or repress the feminine in himself. That often makes it harder for him to respond to women making changes, whom he sees as competing for places as adult "males." A man in his late thirties usually makes an intense effort to achieve a more senior, "manly" position in the world. That often makes him neglect or repress the feminine in himself

and also makes him more hostile to women engaged in the same effort. In the forties, the period of the mid-life transition and the famous mid-life crisis, a man becomes more able to integrate the masculine and feminine in himself—and, if he is not too much the victim of tradition, more able to accept and support women's efforts to achieve independence and choice.   [1986]

Notes

1. COGNITIVE DISSONANCE: Inconsistency or disparity in thinking; holding two contradictory ideas or beliefs.
2. *LA MUJER:* Spanish for woman.
3. CHICANAS: Mexican-American women.

Understanding the Reading

1. Describe the differences between blue-collar men, middle-class men, and upper-class men in their attitudes about women.
2. Why does Astrachan think men need to keep women powerless?
3. How does racial discrimination affect male-female relationships in the black community?
4. Characterize the relationship of Hispanic men and women.
5. Describe the ways that age and economic class affect men's attitudes about gender equality.
6. Who is "the new man"?

Suggestions for Responding

1. How has your economic class, race, or age influenced your attitudes about gender equality? Provide specific evidence to support your analysis, perhaps by contrasting yourself with someone in a different category (e.g., your parent, a co-worker, a neighbor, etc.).
2. Astrachan explores some of the ways in which gender roles are changing. Describe the roles he projects for the 1990s. ✦

SUGGESTIONS FOR RESPONDING TO PART II

1. The readings in this part have examined both traditional and changing gender roles in our society. As the introduction suggested, our socialization into gender-appropriate behavior is complex and is both subtle and overt. Consider how you learned to behave appropriately in terms of your gender. Think back to your earliest memories. When were you first aware of being male or female? How did your placement in your family (first-born, only child, etc.) affect your family's expectations about you as a girl or a boy? If you have siblings of the other sex, were they treated differently than you or held to different standards of behavior? At various points in your life you were probably quite self-consciously masculine or feminine. Can you explain those moments? Also, your attitudes toward your femininity or masculinity have probably undergone changes; record these changes and try to figure out what triggered them. After you have reflected on these matters, write an autobiography of your gender development.

2. The importance of gender in our society can scarcely be overstated. Whether we accept or reject all the social mandates of our assigned gender role, we cannot escape its influence. However, try to imagine that you were born the other sex. How would your life have been different, and what would you be like today? Think about specific moments in your life where the switch would have been especially important—from your earliest childhood through adolescence into adulthood. Consider how it would influence and alter your expectations for your own future. Write an autobiography of this imaginary you.

3. Many of the selections in Part II focused in one way or another on the difficulties of traditional femininity or masculinity, and yet most of us are quite content to be who we are. Write an essay about why you like being the sex you are. You probably want to look at both its advantages and rewards and the disadvantages and difficulties of the opposite sex.

III
Economics and the American Dream

THE AMERICAN DREAM! WE ALL KNOW WHAT THAT means—a good job with plenty of opportunity for advancement, a good family, a nice house with at least one car (probably two) in the driveway, plenty of good food and frequent dining out with enough money left over for the kids' education at good schools, a few luxuries, and an annual vacation. Each of us can add specific details—appliances, electronic games, and so on—but we would probably agree on the general features of the dream.

This dream arrived on our shores with the early Puritans, who held to the doctrine that God rewarded virtue with earthly wealth; to them economic success was a way to glorify God. Thus, the **Protestant work ethic** became a core principle of American culture. This ethic is the belief in the importance of hard work and productivity and the corresponding faith that this behavior will be rewarded appropriately. In the eighteenth century, national icon Benjamin Franklin and his "Poor Richard's" maxims advocating frugality, initiative, industry, diligence, honesty, and prudence secularized and popularized the doctrine. Franklin personified the ethic, both for his contemporaries and for succeeding generations, right up to today.

Franklin also represents another facet of the American dream: the ideal of the **self-made man** (who, of course, adheres to the Protestant work ethic). The self-made man has appeared throughout this country's history. In the nineteenth century, Horatio Alger made a fortune with his popular fictional heroes, who rose "from rags to riches" by "luck and pluck and hard work." One of the most admired American Presidents is the log-cabin-born, rail-splitting Abraham Lincoln, another self-made man. Recent Presidents also tend to flaunt their "humble origins": grocer's son Richard Nixon, peanut farmer Jimmy Carter, alcoholic's son Ronald Reagan; even George Bush prefers to be seen as an oil-field wildcatter rather than as a privileged Yale graduate. One might say that in America if you are self-made, you have "made it."

The myth of the American dream, based as it is on the assumption that opportunities are boundless and that success depends solely on one's character, has a flip side that makes the dream more like a nightmare for many Americans. If individuals are responsible for their own success, they must also be responsible for their own failure and therefore deserving of their fate. Even as the end of the twentieth century approaches, we still hold to these myths, which conceal the realities of class distinctions. We like to think of the United States as a **classless society;** we don't even like to talk about class, except to claim that we all belong to the middle class. This thinking makes it possible for us to ignore the problems created by inequitable economic distribution.

The disparity between the wealthiest and the poorest members of society is, in fact, extensive; Congressional figures indicate that the richest 5% of the American population own up to 83% of the wealth of the country. This disparity increases as the rich get richer and poor get poorer. Statistics released by the U.S. Congress show that from 1963 to 1983, the richest Americans saw their wealth increase 400 times faster than the rest of us did. The House Ways and Means Committee reports that from 1979 to 1987 the standard of living of the richest 20% of the population increased by 24%, while that of the poorest 20% fell by 12%. Yet there is resistance to changing the system because we have faith in **upward mobility,** the possibility that we will some day strike it rich ourselves—the good old American dream.

The first three selections in Part III speak to the issue of upward mobility. Gary Soto records his childhood awareness of the distance between his impoverished barrio life and the television portrayal of the upper-middle-class world to which he already aspires. Nonetheless, his faith in the American dream leads him to decide "to become wealthy, and right away!"

Norman Podhoretz recounts the efforts of a teacher who wants to polish him, a "filthy little slum child," so he can pursue a life of the mind at an Ivy League college; however, he also explains the cultural costs to him of such upward mobility and offers an interesting critique of the values of the middle class and those of his immigrant working-class family. Bebe Moore Campbell's story of Leanita McClain, a highly successful black woman reporter, reveals the dark side of upward mobility. Torn by the tension between the demands of the middle-class world in which she works and the impossibility of forgetting where she came from, she is propelled into ultimate despair and suicide.

The next five selections consider the lives of people who are not middle-class. Sallie Bingham explains the disadvantages of being a woman in a very wealthy family; she argues that such women are suppressed and controlled to serve the interests of the wealth to which they have only indirect access. In contrast, Lynda M. Glennon examines the experience of growing up as a member of the working class in a community dominated by an elite Ivy League university, of being virtually invisible to its privileged student population and excluded from most of its benefits and rewards.

Moving further down the economic scale, Ruth Sidel examines poverty in America in the early 1980s, focusing especially on its impact on women and children. Nicholosa Mohr puts a human face on Sidel's statistics. In her story, a Puerto Rican mother and child experience the humiliation of applying for welfare assistance; even a well-intentioned gesture by the social worker is degrading. At the very bottom of the economic heap is Gerald Winterlin; Peter Swet's interview with him helps us see that homeless people are hardworking Americans who just happen to fall between the cracks and want to pull themselves back up.

Finally, Robert Cherry examines how discrimination is **institutionalized;** that is, how the various parts of our social system work together to create, however unintentionally, a self-perpetuating cycle of discrimination and economic disadvantage. Lower educational levels limit access to good jobs with good pay, while affordable housing is available only in neighborhoods with poor schools, which means the next generation is doomed to lower education levels, perpetuating the cycle.

Although the myth of a classless, middle-class America is an appealing concept, the readings in Part III will reveal that it is a myth and not an accurate description of our nation. It masks many cruel realities that are embedded in our economic system. In addition, our faith in the American dream and its underlying principles of hard work and self-reliance allow us to ignore the problems of those who are ill-served by the system and even to *blame those victims* for their plight. On the other hand, upward mobility, while possible, exacts a considerable toll on those who are forced to choose between the behavior patterns, beliefs, values, and even family and friends of their original world in order to "move up," to enter a culture that is both alien and alienating. Thus, in many senses, class in our "classless" society is problematic.

22

Looking for Work

Gary Soto

One July, while killing ants on the kitchen sink with a rolled newspaper, I had a nine-year-old's vision of wealth that would save us from ourselves. For weeks I had drunk Kool-Aid and watched morning reruns of *Father Knows Best,* whose family was so uncomplicated in its routine that I very much wanted to imitate it. The first step was to get my brother and sister to wear shoes at dinner.

"Come on, Rick—come on, Deb," I whined. But Rick mimicked me and the same day that I asked him to wear shoes he came to the dinner table in only his swim trunks. My mother didn't notice, nor did my sister, as we sat to eat our beans and tortillas in the stifling heat of our kitchen. We all gleamed like cellophane, wiping the sweat from our brows with the backs of our hands as we talked about the day: Frankie our neighbor was beat up by Faustino; the swimming pool at the playground would be closed for a day because the pump was broken.

Such was our life. So that morning, while doing-in the train of ants which arrived each day, I decided to become wealthy, and right away! After downing a bowl of cereal, I took a rake from the garage and started up the block to look for work.

We lived on an ordinary block of mostly working class people: warehousemen, egg candlers,[1] welders, mechanics, and a union plumber. And there were many retired people who kept their lawns green and the gutters uncluttered of the chewing gum wrappers we dropped as we rode by on our bikes. They bent down to gather our litter, muttering at our evilness.

At the corner house I rapped the screen door and a very large woman in a muu-muu[2] answered. She sized me up and then asked what I could do.

"Rake leaves," I answered, smiling.

"It's summer, and there ain't no leaves," she countered. Her face was pinched with lines; fat jiggled under her chin. She pointed to the lawn, then the flower bed, and said: "You see any leaves there—or there?" I followed her pointing arm, stupidly. But she had a job for me and that was to get her a Coke at the liquor store. She gave me twenty cents, and after ditching my rake in a bush, off I ran. I returned with an unbagged Pepsi, for which she thanked me and gave me a nickel from her apron.

I skipped off her porch, fetched my rake, and crossed the street to the next block where Mrs. Moore, mother of Earl the retarded man, let me weed a flower bed. She handed me a trowel and for a good part of the morning my fingers dipped into the moist dirt, ripping up runners of Bermuda grass. Worms surfaced in my search for deep roots, and I cut them in halves, tossing them to Mrs. Moore's cat who pawed them playfully as they dried in the sun. I made out Earl whose face was pressed to the back window of the house, and although he was calling to me I couldn't understand what he was trying to say. Embarrassed, I worked without looking up, but I imagined his contorted mouth and the ring of keys attached to his belt—keys that jingled with each palsied step. He scared me and I worked quickly to finish the flower bed. When I did finish Mrs. Moore gave me a quarter and two peaches from her tree, which I washed there but ate in the alley behind my house.

I was sucking on the second one, a bit of juice staining the front of my T-shirt, when Little John, my best friend, came walking down the alley with a baseball bat over his shoulder, knocking over trash cans as he made his way toward me.

Little John and I went to St. John's Catholic School, where we sat among the "stupids." Miss Marino, our teacher, alternated the rows of good students with the bad, hoping that by sitting side-by-side with the bright students the stupids might become more intelligent, as though intelligence were contagious. But we didn't progress as she had hoped. She grew frustrated when one day, while dismissing class for recess, Little John couldn't get up because his arms were stuck in the slats of the chair's backrest. She scolded us with a shaking finger when we knocked over the globe, denting the already troubled Africa. She muttered curses when Leroy White, a real stupid but a great softball player with the gift to hit to all fields, openly chewed his host when he made his

First Communion; his hands swung at his sides as he returned to the pew looking around with a big smile.

Little John asked what I was doing, and I told him that I was taking a break from work, as I sat comfortably among high weeds. He wanted to join me, but I reminded him that the last time he'd gone door-to-door asking for work his mother had whipped him. I was with him when his mother, a New Jersey Italian who could rise up in anger one moment and love the next, told me in a polite but matter-of-fact voice that I had to leave because she was going to beat her son. She gave me a homemade popsicle, ushered me to the door, and said that I could see Little John the next day. But it was sooner than that. I went around to his bedroom window to suck my popsicle and watch Little John dodge his mother's blows, a few hitting their mark but many whirring air.

It was midday when Little John and I converged in the alley, the sun blazing in the high nineties, and he suggested that we go to Roosevelt High School to swim. He needed five cents to make fifteen, the cost of admission, and I lent him a nickel. We ran home for my bike and when my sister found out that we were going swimming, she started to cry because she didn't have the fifteen cents but only an empty Coke bottle. I waved for her to come and three of us mounted the bike—Debra on the cross bar, Little John on the handle bars and holding the Coke bottle which we would cash for a nickel and make up the difference that would allow all of us to get in, and me pumping up the crooked streets, dodging cars and pot holes. We spent the day swimming under the afternoon sun, so that when we got home our mom asked us what was darker, the floor or us? She feigned a stern posture, her hands on her hips and her mouth puckered. We played along. Looking down, Debbie and I said in unison, "Us."

That evening at dinner we all sat down in our bathing suits to eat our beans, laughing and chewing loudly. Our mom was in a good mood, so I took a risk and asked her if sometime we could have turtle soup. A few days before I had watched a television program in which a Polynesian tribe killed a large turtle, gutted it, and then stewed it over an open fire. The turtle,

basted in a sugary sauce, looked delicious as I ate an afternoon bowl of cereal, but my sister, who was watching the program with a glass of Kool-Aid between her knees, said, "Caca."

My mother looked at me in bewilderment. "Boy, are you a crazy Mexican. Where did you get the idea that people eat turtles?"

"On television," I said, explaining the program. Then I took it a step further. "Mom, do you think we could get dressed up for dinner one of these days? David King does."

"*Ay, Dios,*" my mother laughed. She started collecting the dinner plates, but my brother wouldn't let go of his. He was still drawing a picture in the bean sauce. Giggling, he said it was me, but I didn't want to listen because I wanted an answer from Mom. This was the summer when I spent the mornings in front of the television that showed the comfortable lives of white kids. There were no beatings, no rifts in the family. They wore bright clothes; toys tumbled from their closets. They hopped into bed with kisses and woke to glasses of fresh orange juice, and to a father sitting before his morning coffee while the mother buttered his toast. They hurried through the day making friends and gobs of money, returning home to a warmly lit living room, and then dinner. *Leave It To Beaver* was the program I replayed in my mind:

"May I have the mashed potatoes?" asks Beaver with a smile.

"Sure, Beav," replies Wally as he taps the corners of his mouth with a starched napkin.

The father looks on in his suit. The mother, decked out in earrings and a pearl necklace, cuts into her steak and blushes. Their conversation is politely clipped.

"Swell," says Beaver, his cheeks puffed with food.

Our own talk at dinner was loud with belly laughs and marked by our pointing forks at one another. The subjects were commonplace.

"Gary, let's go to the ditch tomorrow," my brother suggests. He explains that he has made a life preserver out of four empty detergent bottles strung together with twine and that he will make me one if I can find more bottles. "No way are we going to drown."

"Yeah, then we could have a dirt clod fight," I reply, so happy to be alive.

Whereas the Beaver's family enjoyed dessert in dishes at the table, our mom sent us outside, and more often than not I went into the alley to peek over the neighbor's fences and spy out fruit, apricots or peaches.

I had asked my mom and again she laughed that I was a crazy *chavalo*[3] as she stood in front of the sink, her arms rising and falling with suds, face glistening from the heat. She sent me outside where my brother and sister were sitting in the shade that the fence threw out like a blanket. They were talking about me when I plopped down next to them. They looked at one another and then Debbie, my eight-year-old sister, started in.

"What's this crap about getting dressed up?"

She had entered her profanity stage. A year later she would give up such words and slip into her Catholic uniform, and into squealing on my brother and me when we "cussed this" and "cussed that."

I tried to convince them that if we improved the way we looked we might get along better in life. White people would like us more. They might invite us to places, like their homes or front yards. They might not hate us so much.

My sister called me a "craphead," and got up to leave with a stalk of grass dangling from her mouth. "They'll never like us."

My brother's mood lightened as he talked about the ditch—the white water, the broken pieces of glass, and the rusted car fenders that awaited our knees. There would be toads, and rocks to smash them.

David King, the only person we knew who resembled the middle class, called from over the fence. David was Catholic, of Armenian and French descent, and his closet was filled with toys. A bear-shaped cookie jar, like the ones on television, sat on the kitchen counter. His mother was remarkably kind while she put up with the racket we made on the street. Evenings, she often watered the front yard and it must have upset her to see us—my brother and I and others—jump from trees laughing, the unkillable kids of the very poor, who got up unshaken, brushed off, and climbed into another one to try again.

David called again. Rick got up and slapped grass from his pants. When I asked if I could come along he said no. David said no. They were two years older so their affairs were different from mine. They greeted one another with foul names and took off down the alley to look for trouble.

I went inside the house, turned on the television, and was about to sit down with a glass of Kool-Aid when Mom shooed me outside.

"It's still light," she said. "Later you'll bug me to let you stay out longer. So go on."

I downed my Kool-Aid and went outside to the front yard. No one was around. The day had cooled and a breeze rushed the trees. Mr. Jackson, the plumber, was watering his lawn and when he saw me he turned away to wash off his front steps. There was more than an hour of light left, so I took advantage of it and decided to look for work. I felt suddenly alive as I skipped down the block in search of an overgrown flower bed and the dime that would end the day right.

[1985]

Notes

1. EGG CANDLERS: Workers who examine eggs for freshness in front of a light.
2. MUU-MUU: A long loose dress that hangs from the shoulders.
3. *CHAVALO*: Young man.

Understanding the Reading

1. List the details that illustrate the socioeconomic class of Soto's family.
2. In what ways does the boy illustrate the Protestant work ethic?
3. What is wrong with the school he attends?
4. What are the strengths of the Soto family's lifestyle?
5. Why did young Soto want to behave more like the families he saw on television?
6. Why are these children thought of as "unkillable kids"?

Suggestion for Responding

Compare the reality of your childhood with the portrayals of the families you saw on television as you were growing up. ✦

23

The Brutal Bargain

NORMAN PODHORETZ

One of the longest journeys in the world is the journey from Brooklyn to Manhattan—or at least from certain neighborhoods in Brooklyn to certain parts of Manhattan. I have made that journey, but it is not from the experience of having made it that I know how very great the distance is, for I started on the road many years before I realized what I was doing, and by the time I did realize it I was for all practical purposes already there. At so imperceptible a pace did I travel, and with so little awareness, that I never felt footsore or out of breath or weary at the thought of how far I still had to go. Yet whenever anyone who has remained back there where I started—remained not physically but socially and culturally, for the neighborhood is now a Negro ghetto and the Jews who have "remained" in it mostly reside in the less affluent areas of Long Island—whenever anyone like that happens into the world in which I now live with such perfect ease, I can see that in his eyes I have become a fully acculturated citizen of a country as foreign to him as China and infinitely more frightening.

That country is sometimes called the upper middle class; and indeed I am a member of that class, less by virtue of my income than by virtue of the way my speech is accented, the way I dress, the way I furnish my home, the way I entertain and am entertained, the way I educate my children—the way, quite simply, I look and I live. It appalls me to think what an immense transformation I had to work on myself in order to become what I have become: if I had known what I was doing I would surely not have been able to do it, I would surely not have wanted to. No wonder the choice had to be blind; there was a kind of treason in it: treason toward my family, treason toward my friends. In choosing the road I chose, I was pronouncing a judgment upon them, and the fact that they themselves concurred in the judgment makes the whole thing sadder but no less cruel.

When I say that the choice was blind, I mean that I was never aware—obviously not as a small child, certainly not as an adolescent, and not even as a young man already writing for publication and working on the staff of an important intellectual magazine in New York—how inextricably my "noblest" ambitions were tied to the vulgar desire to rise above the class into which I was born; nor did I understand to what an astonishing extent these ambitions were shaped and defined by the standards and values and tastes of the class into which I did not know I wanted to move. It is not that I was or am a social climber as that term is commonly used. High society interests me, if at all, only as a curiosity; I do not wish to be a member of it; and in any case, it is not, as I have learned from a small experience of contact with the very rich and fashionable, my "scene." Yet precisely because social climbing is not one of my vices (unless what might be called celebrity climbing, which very definitely *is* one of my vices, can be considered the contemporary variant of social climbing), I think there may be more than a merely personal significance in the fact that class has played so large a part both in my life and in my career.

But whether or not the significance is there, I feel certain that my long-time blindness to the part class was playing in my life was not altogether idiosyncratic. "Privilege," Robert L. Heilbroner has shrewdly observed in *The Limits of American Capitalism,* "is not an attribute we are accustomed to stress when we consider the construction of *our* social order." For a variety of reasons, says Heilbroner, "privilege under capitalism is much less 'visible,' especially to the favored groups, than privilege under other systems" like feudalism. This "invisibility" extends in America to class as well.

No one, of course, is so naïve as to believe that America is a classless society or that the force of egalitarianism, powerful as it has been in some respects, has ever been powerful enough to wipe out class distinctions altogether. There was a moment during the 1950's, to be sure, when social thought hovered on the brink of saying that the country had to all intents and purposes become a wholly middle-class society. But the emergence of the civil-rights movement in the 1960's and the concomitant discovery of the poor—to whom, in helping to discover them, Michael Harrington interestingly enough applied, in *The Other America,* the very word ("invisible") that Heilbroner later used with reference to the rich—has put at least a temporary end to that kind of talk. And yet if class had become visible again, it is only in its grossest outlines—mainly, that is, in terms of income levels—and to the degree that manners and style of life are perceived as relevant at all, it is generally in the crudest of terms. There is something in us, it would seem, which resists the idea of class. Even our novelists, working in a genre for which class has traditionally been a supreme reality, are largely indifferent to it—which is to say, blind to its importance as a factor in the life of the individual.

In my own case, the blindness to class always expressed itself in an outright and very often belligerent refusal to believe that it had anything to do with me at all. I no longer remember when or in what form I first discovered that there was such a thing as class, but whenever it was and whatever form the discovery took, it could only have coincided with the recognition that criteria existed by which I and everyone I knew were stamped as inferior: we were in the *lower* class. This was not a proposition I was willing to accept, and my way of not accepting it was to dismiss the whole idea of class as a prissy triviality.

Given the fact that I had literary ambitions even as a small boy, it was inevitable that the issue of class would sooner or later arise for me with a sharpness it would never acquire for most of my friends. But given the fact also that I was on the whole very happy to be growing up where I was, that I was fiercely patriotic about Brownsville (the spawning-ground of so many famous athletes and gangsters), and that I felt genuinely patronizing toward other neighborhoods, especially the "better" ones like Crown Heights and East Flatbush which seemed by comparison colorless and unexciting—given the fact, in other words, that I was not, for all that I wrote poetry and read books, an "alienated" boy dreaming of escape–my confrontation with the issue of class would probably have come later rather than sooner if not for an English teacher in high school who decided that I was a gem in the rough and who took it upon herself to polish me to as high a sheen as she could manage and I would permit.

I resisted—far less effectively, I can see now, than I then thought, though even then I knew that she was wearing me down far more than I would ever give her the satisfaction of admitting. Famous throughout the school for her altogether outspoken snobbery, which stopped short by only a hair, and sometimes did not stop short at all, of an old-fashioned kind of patrician anti-Semitism, Mrs. K. was also famous for being an extremely good teacher; indeed, I am sure that she saw no distinction between the hopeless task of teaching the proper use of English to the young Jewish barbarians whom fate had so unkindly deposited into her charge and the equally hopeless task of teaching them the proper "manners." (There were as many young Negro barbarians in her charge as Jewish ones, but I doubt that she could ever bring herself to pay very much attention to them. As she never hesitated to make clear, it was punishment enough for a woman of her background—her family was old-Brooklyn and, she would have us understand, extremely distinguished—to have fallen among the sons of East European immigrant Jews.)

For three years, from the age of thirteen to the age of sixteen, I was her special pet, though that word is scarcely adequate to suggest the intensity of the relationship which developed between us. It was a relationship right out of *The Corn Is Green,* which may, for all I know, have served as her model; at any rate, her objective was much the same as the Welsh teacher's in that play: she was determined that I should win a scholarship to Harvard. But whereas (an irony much to the point here) the problem the teacher had in *The Corn Is Green* with her coal-miner pupil in the traditional class society of Edwardian England was strictly academic, Mrs. K.'s problem with me in the putatively egalitarian society of New Deal[1] America was strictly social. My grades were very high and would obviously remain so, but what would they avail me if I continued to go about looking and sounding like a "filthy little slum child" (the epithet she would invariably hurl at me whenever we had an argument about "manners")?

Childless herself, she worked on me like a dementedly ambitious mother with a somewhat recalcitrant son; married to a solemn and elderly man (she was then in her early forties or thereabouts), she treated me like a callous, ungrateful adolescent lover on whom she had humiliatingly bestowed her favors. She flirted with me and flattered me, she scolded me and insulted me. Slum

child, filthy little slum child, so beautiful a mind
and so vulgar a personality, so exquisite in sensibility and so coarse in manner. What would she
do with me, what would become of me if I persisted out of stubbornness and perversity in the
disgusting ways they had taught me at home and
on the streets?

To her the most offensive of these ways was
the style in which I dressed: a tee shirt, tightly
pegged pants, and a red satin jacket with the legend "Cherokees, S.A.C." (social-athletic club)
stitched in large white letters across the back.
This was bad enough, but when on certain days
I would appear in school wearing, as a particular
ceremonial occasion required, a suit and tie, the
sight of those immense padded shoulders and
my white-on-white shirt would drive her to even
greater heights of contempt and even lower
depths of loving despair than usual. *Slum child,
filthy little slum child.* I was beyond saving; I deserved no better than to wind up with all the
other horrible little Jewboys in the gutter (by
which she meant Brooklyn College). If only I
would listen to her, the whole world could be
mine: I could win a scholarship to Harvard, I
could get to know the best people, I could grow
up into a life of elegance and refinement and
taste. Why was I so stupid as not to understand?

In those days it was very unusual, and possibly even against the rules, for teachers in public
high schools to associate with their students after
hours. Nevertheless, Mrs. K. sometimes invited
me to her home, a beautiful old brownstone located in what was perhaps the only section in the
whole of Brooklyn fashionable enough to be intimidating. I would read her my poems and she
would tell me about her family, about the schools
she had gone to, about Vassar, about writers she
had met, while her husband, of whom I was
frightened to death and who to my utter astonishment turned out to be Jewish (but not, as Mrs. K.
quite unnecessarily hastened to inform me, *my*
kind of Jewish), sat stiffly and silently in an arm-
chair across the room, squinting at his newspaper
through the first *pince-nez* I had ever seen outside the movies. He spoke to me but once, and
that was after I had read Mrs. K. my tearful editorial for the school newspaper on the death of
Roosevelt—an effusion which provoked him
into a full five-minute harangue whose blasphemous contents would certainly have shocked me

into insensibility if I had not been even more
shocked to discover that he actually had a voice.

But Mrs. K. not only had me to her house; she
also—what was even more unusual—took me
out a few times, to the Frick Gallery and the Metropolitan Museum, and once to the theater,
where we saw a dramatization of *The Late George
Apley,* a play I imagine she deliberately chose
with the not wholly mistaken idea that it would
impress upon me the glories of aristocratic
Boston.

One of our excursions into Manhattan I remember with particular vividness because she
used it to bring the struggle between us to rather
a dramatic head. The familiar argument began
this time on the subway. Why, knowing that we
would be spending the afternoon together "in
public," had I come to school that morning im-
properly dressed? (I was, as usual, wearing my
red satin club jacket over a white tee shirt.) She
realized, of course, that I owned only one suit
(this said not in compassion but in derision) and
that my poor parents had, God only knew where,
picked up the idea that it was too precious to be
worn except at one of those bar mitzvahs[2] I was
always going to. Though why, if my parents were
so worried about clothes, they had permitted me
to buy a suit which made me look like a young
hoodlum she found it very difficult to imagine.
Still, much as she would have been embarrassed
to be seen in public with a boy whose parents
allowed him to wear a zoot suit,[3] she would have
been somewhat less embarrassed than she was
now by the ridiculous costume I had on. Had I
no consideration for her? Had I no consideration
for myself? Did I want everyone who laid eyes on
me to think that I was nothing but an ill-bred little
slum child?

My standard ploy in these arguments was to
take the position that such things were of no concern to me: I was a poet and I had more important matters to think about than clothes. Besides,
I would feel silly coming to school on an ordinary
day dressed in a suit. Did Mrs. K. want me to look
like one of those "creeps" from Crown Heights
who were all going to become doctors? This
was usually an effective counter, since Mrs. K.
despised her middle-class Jewish students even
more than she did the "slum children," but probably because she was growing desperate at the
thought of how I would strike a Harvard inter-

viewer (it was my senior year), she did not respond according to form on that particular occasion. "At least," she snapped, "they reflect well on their parents."

I was accustomed to her bantering gibes at my parents, and sensing, probably, that they arose out of jealousy, I was rarely troubled by them. But this one bothered me; it went beyond banter and I did not know how to deal with it. I remember flushing, but I cannot remember what if anything I said in protest. It was the beginning of a very bad afternoon for both of us.

We had been heading for the Museum of Modern Art, but as we got off the subway, Mrs. K. announced that she had changed her mind about the museum. She was going to show me something else instead, just down the street on Fifth Avenue. This mysterious "something else" to which we proceeded in silence turned out to be the college department of an expensive clothing store, de Pinna. I do not exaggerate when I say that an actual physical dread seized me as I followed her into the store. I had never been inside such a store; it was not a store, it was enemy territory, every inch of it mined with humiliations. "I am," Mrs. K. declared in the coolest human voice I hope I shall ever hear, "going to buy you a suit that you will be able to wear at your Harvard interview." I had guessed, of course, that this was what she had in mind, and even at fifteen I understood what a fantastic act of aggression she was planning to commit against my parents and asking me to participate in. Oh no, I said in a panic (suddenly realizing that I *wanted* her to buy me that suit), I can't, my mother wouldn't like it. "You can tell her it's a birthday present. Or else I will tell her. If I tell her, I'm sure she won't object." The idea of Mrs. K. meeting my mother was more than I could bear: my mother, who spoke with a Yiddish accent and of whom, until that sickening moment, I had never known I was ashamed and so ready to betray.

To my immense relief and my equally immense disappointment, we left the store, finally, without buying a suit, but it was not to be the end of clothing or "manners" for me that day—not yet. There was still the ordeal of a restaurant to go through. Where I came from, people rarely ate in restaurants, not so much because most of them were too poor to afford such a luxury—although most of them certainly were—as because eating

in restaurants was not regarded as a luxury at all; it was, rather, a necessity to which bachelors were pitiably condemned. A home-cooked meal was assumed to be better than anything one could possibly get in a restaurant, and considering the class of restaurants in question (they were really diners or luncheonettes), the assumption was probably correct. In the case of my own family, myself included until my late teens, the business of going to restaurants was complicated by the fact that we observed the Jewish dietary laws, and except in certain neighborhoods, few places could be found which served kosher food; in midtown Manhattan in the 1940's, I believe there were only two and both were relatively expensive. All this is by way of explaining why I had had so little experience of restaurants up to the age of fifteen and why I grew apprehensive once more when Mrs. K. decided after we left de Pinna that we should have something to eat.

The restaurant she chose was not at all an elegant one—I have, like a criminal, revisited it since—but it seemed very elegant indeed to me: enemy territory again, and this time a mine exploded in my face the minute I set foot through the door. The hostess was very sorry, but she could not seat the young gentleman without a coat and tie. If the lady wished, however, something could be arranged. The lady (visibly pleased by this unexpected—or was it expected?—object lesson) did wish, and the so recently defiant but now utterly docile young gentleman was forthwith divested of his so recently beloved but by now thoroughly loathsome red satin jacket and provided with a much oversized white waiter's coat and a tie—which, there being no collar to a tee shirt, had to be worn around his bare neck. Thus attired, and with his face supplying the touch of red which had moments earlier been supplied by his jacket, he was led into the dining room, there to be taught the importance of proper table manners through the same pedagogic instrumentality that had worked so well in impressing him with the importance of proper dress.

Like any other pedagogic technique, however, humiliation has its limits, and Mrs. K. was to make no further progress with it that day. For I had had enough, and I was not about to risk stepping on another mine. Knowing she would subject me to still more ridicule if I made a point of my revulsion at the prospect of eating nonkosher food, I resolved to let her order for me and then to feign lack of appetite or possibly even illness when the meal was served. She did order—duck for both of us, undoubtedly because it would be a hard dish for me to manage without using my fingers.

The two portions came in deep oval-shaped dishes, swimming in a brown sauce and each with a sprig of parsley sitting on top. I had not the faintest idea of what to do—should the food be eaten directly from the oval dish or not?—nor which of the many implements on the table to do it with. But remembering that Mrs. K. herself had once advised me to watch my hostess in such a situation and then to do exactly as she did, I sat perfectly still and waited for her to make the first move. Unfortunately, Mrs. K. also remembered having taught me that trick, and determined as she was that I should be given a lesson that would force me to mend my ways, she waited too. And so we both waited, chatting amiably, pretending not to notice the food while it sat there getting colder and colder by the minute. Thanks partly to the fact that I would probably have gagged on the duck if I had tried to eat it— dietary taboos are very powerful if one has been conditioned to them—I was prepared to wait forever. And in fact it was Mrs. K. who broke first.

"Why aren't you eating?" she suddenly said after something like fifteen minutes had passed. "Aren't you hungry?" Not very, I answered. "Well," she said, "I think we'd better eat. The food is getting cold." Whereupon, as I watched with great fascination, she deftly captured the sprig of parsley between the prongs of her serving fork, set it aside, took up her serving spoon and delicately used those two esoteric implements to transfer a piece of duck from the oval dish to her plate. I imitated the whole operation as best I could, but not well enough to avoid splattering some partly congealed sauce onto my borrowed coat in the process. Still, things could have been worse, and having more or less successfully negotiated my way around that particular mine, I now had to cope with the problem of how to get out of eating the duck. But I need not have worried. Mrs. K. took one bite, pronounced it inedible (it must have been frozen by then), and called in quiet fury for the check.

Several months later, wearing an altered but respectably conservative suit which had been handed down to me in good condition by a bachelor uncle, I presented myself on two different occasions before interviewers from Harvard and from the Pulitzer Scholarship Committee. Some months after that, Mrs. K. had her triumph: I won the Harvard scholarship on which her heart had been so passionately set. It was not, however, large enough to cover all expenses, and since my parents could not afford to make up the difference, I was unable to accept it. My parents felt wretched but not, I think, quite as wretched as Mrs. K. For a while it looked as though I would wind up in the "gutter" of Brooklyn College after all, but then the news arrived that I had also won a Pulitzer Scholarship which paid full tuition if used at Columbia and a small stipend besides. Everyone was consoled, even Mrs. K.: Columbia was at least in the Ivy League.

The last time I saw her was shortly before my graduation from Columbia and just after a story had appeared in the *Times* announcing that I had been awarded a fellowship which was to send me to Cambridge University. Mrs. K. had passionately wanted to see me in Cambridge, Massachusetts, but Cambridge, England was even better. We met somewhere near Columbia for a drink, and her happiness over my fellowship, it seemed to me, was if anything exceeded by her delight at discovering that I now knew enough to know that the right thing to order in a cocktail lounge was a very dry martini with lemon peel, please.

Looking back now at the story of my relationship with Mrs. K. strictly in the context of the issue of class, what strikes me most sharply is the astonishing rudeness of this woman to whom "manners" were of such overriding concern. (This, as I have since had some occasion to notice, is a fairly common characteristic among members of the class to which she belonged.) Though she would not have admitted it, good manners to Mrs. K. meant only one thing: conformity to a highly stylized set of surface habits and fashions which she took, quite as a matter of course, to be superior to all other styles of social behavior. But in what did their superiority consist? Were her "good" manners derived from or conducive to a greater moral sensitivity than the "bad" manners I had learned at home and on the streets of Brownsville? I rather doubt it. The "crude" behavior of my own parents, for example, was then and is still marked by a tactfulness and a delicacy that Mrs. K. simply could not have approached. It is not that she was incapable of tact and delicacy; in certain moods she was; and manners apart, she was an extraordinarily loving and generous woman. But such qualities were neither built into nor expressed by the system of manners under which she lived. She was fond of quoting Cardinal Newman's[4] definition of a gentleman as a person who could be at ease in any company, yet if anything was clear about the manners she was trying to teach me, it was that they operated—not inadvertently but by deliberate design—to set one at ease *only* with others similarly trained and to cut one off altogether from those who were not.

While I would have been unable to formulate it in those terms at the time, I think I must have understood perfectly well what Mrs. K. was attempting to communicate with all her talk about manners; if I had not understood it so well, I would not have resisted so fiercely. She was saying that because I was a talented boy, a better class of people stood ready to admit me into their ranks. But only on one condition: I had to signify by my general deportment that I acknowledged them as *superior* to the class of people among whom I happened to have been born. That was the bargain—take it or leave it. In resisting Mrs. K. where "manners" were concerned, just as I was later to resist many others, I was expressing my refusal to have any part of so brutal a bargain. But the joke was on me, for what I did not understand, not in the least then and not for a long time afterward, was that in matters having to do with "art" and "culture" (the "life of the mind," as I learned to call it at Columbia), I was being offered the very same brutal bargain and accepting it with the wildest enthusiasm.

I have said that I did not, for all my bookishness, feel alienated as a boy, and this is certainly true. Far from dreaming of escape from Brownsville, I dreaded the thought of living anywhere else, and whenever my older sister, who hated the neighborhood, began begging my parents to move, it was invariably my howls of protest that kept them from giving in. For by the age of thirteen I had made it into the neighborhood big time, otherwise known as the Cherokees, S.A.C. It had by no means been easy for me, as a mediocre athlete and a notoriously good student, to win acceptance from a gang which prided itself mainly on its masculinity and its contempt for authority, but once this had been accomplished, down the drain went any reason I might earlier have had for thinking that life could be better in any other place. Not for nothing, then, did I wear that red satin jacket to school every day. It was my proudest possession, a badge of manly status, proving that I was not to be classified with the Crown Heights "creeps," even though my grades, like theirs, were high.

And yet, despite the Cherokees, it cannot be that I felt quite so securely at home in Brownsville as I remember thinking. The reason is that something extremely significant in this connection had happened to me by the time I first met Mrs. K.: without any conscious effort on my part, my speech had largely lost the characteristic neighborhood accent and was well on its way to becoming as neutrally American as I gather it now is.

Now whatever else may be involved in a nondeliberate change of accent, one thing is clear: it bespeaks a very high degree of detachment from the ethos of one's immediate surroundings. It is not a good ear alone, and perhaps not even a good ear at all, which enables a child to hear the difference between the way he and everyone else around him sound when they talk, and the way teachers and radio announcers—as it must have been in my case—sound. Most people, and especially most children, are entirely insensitive to such differences, which is why anyone who pays attention to these matters can, on the basis of a man's accent alone, often draw a reasonably accurate picture of his regional, social, and ethnic background. People who feel that they belong in their familiar surroundings—whether it be a place, a class, or a group—will invariably speak in the accent of those surroundings; in all likelihood, indeed, they will never have imagined any other possibility for themselves. Conversely, it is safe to assume that a person whose accent has undergone a radical change from childhood is a person who once had fantasies of escaping to some other world, whether or not they were ever realized.

But accent in America has more than a psychological or spiritual significance. "Her kerbstone English," said Henry Higgins of Eliza Doolittle, "will keep her in the gutter to the end of her days." Most Americans probably respond with a sense of amused democratic superiority to the idea of a society in which so trivial a thing as accent can keep a man down, and it is a good measure of our blindness to the pervasive operations of class that there has been so little consciousness of the fact that America itself is such a society.* While the broadly regional accents—New England, Midwestern, Southern—enjoy more or less equal status and will not affect the economic or social chances of those who speak in them, the opposite is still surely true of any accent identifiably influenced by Yiddish, Italian, Polish, Spanish—that is, the languages of the major post–Civil War immigrant groups, among which may be included American-Irish. A man with such an accent will no longer be confined, as once he would almost automatically have been, to the working class, but unless his life, both occupational and social, is lived strictly within the milieu in whose tone of voice he speaks, his accent will at the least operate as an obstacle to be overcome (if, for example, he is a schoolteacher aspiring to be a principal), and at the most as an effective barrier to advancement (if, say, he is an engineer), let alone to entry into the governing elite of the country. For better or worse, incidentally, these accents are not a temporary phenomenon destined to disappear with the passage of the generations, no more than

---

* On the other hand, the New York *Times* reported on May 8, 1966, that "A real-life Professor Higgins" had "descended upon Harlem in search of Eliza Doolittles." The *Times* went on: "Every Saturday afternoon the portly 45-year-old professor of comparative education at Teachers College of Columbia University, Dr. George Z. F. Bereday, directs 10 Negro girl seniors from Benjamin Franklin High School on the upper East Side in a series of classes in grooming, dress, make-up, speech, poise, rhythmics, and general deportment and culture." Explained Dr. Bereday: "The theory is that there are factors other than skin color in racial discrimination. These factors are class differences and they are more immediately manageable. They oil their hair and chew gum. Maybe a girl can get a good job as a secretary, but if her hair smells like coconut oil. . . ." (Dr. Bereday himself speaks with a thick Polish accent, which makes him acceptably foreign rather than unacceptably lower class.)

ethnic consciousness itself is. I have heard third-generation American Jews of East European immigrant stock speaking with thicker ethnic coloring even than their parents.

Clearly, then, while fancying myself altogether at home in the world into which I was born, I was not only more detached from it than I realized; I was also taking action, and of a very fundamental kind, which would eventually make it possible for me to move into some other world. Yet I still did not recognize what I was doing—not in any such terms. My ambition was to be a great and famous poet, not to live in a different community, a different class, a different "world." If I had a concrete image of what greatness would mean socially, it was probably based on the famous professional boxer from our block who had moved to a more prosperous neighborhood but still spent his leisure time hanging around the corner candy store and the local pool room with his old friends (among whom he could, of course, experience his fame far more sharply than he could have done among his newly acquired peers).

But to each career its own sociology. Boxers, unlike poets, do not undergo a cultural change in the process of becoming boxers, and if I was not brave enough or clever enough as a boy to see the distinction, others who knew me then were. "Ten years from now, you won't even want to talk to me, you won't even recognize me if you pass me on the street," was the kind of comment I frequently heard in my teens from women in the neighborhood, friends of my mother who were fond of me and nearly as proud as she was of the high grades I was getting in school and the prizes I was always winning. "That's crazy, you must be kidding," I would answer. They were not crazy and they were not kidding. They were simply better sociologists than I.

As, indeed, my mother herself was, for often in later years—after I had become a writer and an editor and was living only a subway ride away but in a style that was foreign to her and among people by whom she was intimidated—she would gaze wistfully at this strange creature, her son, and murmur, "I should have made him for a dentist," registering thereby her perception that whereas Jewish sons who grow up to be successes in certain occupations usually remain fixed in an accessible cultural ethos, sons who grow up into literary success are transformed almost beyond recognition and distanced almost beyond a mother's reach. My mother wanted nothing so much as for me to be a success, to be respected and admired. But she did not imagine, I think, that she would only purchase the realization of her ambition at the price of my progressive estrangement from her and her ways. Perhaps it was my guilt at the first glimmerings of this knowledge which accounted for my repression of it and for the obstinacy of the struggle I waged over "manners" with Mrs. K.

For what seemed most of all to puzzle Mrs. K., who saw no distinction between taste in poetry and taste in clothes, was that I could see no connection between the two. Mrs. K. knew that a boy from Brownsville with a taste for Keats was not long for Brownsville, and moreover would in all probability end up in the social class to which she herself belonged. How could I have explained to her that I would only be able to leave Brownsville if I could maintain the illusion that my destination was a place in some mystical country of the spirit and not a place in the upper reaches of the American class structure?

Saint Paul, who was a Jew, conceived of salvation as a world in which there would be neither Jew nor Greek, and though he may well have been the first, he was very far from the last Jew to dream such a dream of transcendence—transcendence of the actual alternative categories with which reality so stingily presents us. Not to be Jewish, but not to be Christian either; not to be a worker, but not to be a boss either; not—if I may be forgiven for injecting this banality out of my own soul into so formidable a series of fantasies—to be a slum child but not to be a snob either. How could I have explained to Mrs. K. that wearing a suit from de Pinna would for me have been something like the social equivalent of a conversion to Christianity? And how could she have explained to me that there was no socially neutral ground to be found in the United States of America, and that a distaste for the surroundings in which I was bred, and ultimately (God forgive me) even for many of the people I loved, and so a new taste for other kinds of people—how could she have explained that all this was inexorably entailed in the logic of a taste for the poetry of Keats and the painting of Cézanne and the music of Mozart?   [1967]

Notes

1. NEW DEAL: President Franklin Roosevelt's 1930s program for economic reform that included creation of the Social Security system.
2. BAR MITZVAH: The coming-of-age ceremony for 13-year-old Jewish males.
3. ZOOT SUIT: A suit with full-legged, tight-cuffed pants and a long coat with wide lapels and padded shoulders, popular in the 1940s.
4. CARDINAL NEWMAN: John Henry Newman, a nineteenth-century British theologian.

Understanding the Reading

1. What did Podhoretz like about his home neighborhood?
2. Why did his clothes so bother Mrs. K.?
3. What distinction did Mrs. K. make between her husband's Jewishness and that of Podhoretz?
4. What does eating in restaurants show about class values?
5. Why did Mrs. K. want to humiliate Podhoretz?
6. Why did he come to see Mrs. K. as rude, and why is this ironic?
7. Why are a person's speech and accent important features of identity?
8. Why could the famous boxer retain his ties to the old neighborhood when Podhoretz couldn't?
9. What does Podhoretz mean when he says that wearing the de Pinna suit would be like a religious conversion?
10. What does Podhoretz mean when, in the opening, he calls his upward mobility "treason"?

Suggestion for Responding

Everyone has lost or rejected some values and behaviors learned in childhood. Even though the shift may not be as dramatic as the one Podhoretz presents, describe such a change that you experienced; explain why you changed and how you feel about it now. ✦

24

To Be Black, Gifted, and Alone

BEBE MOORE CAMPBELL

By the time Leanita McClain was 32, the black journalist had won the Peter Lisagor Award from the Headline Club (the Chicago Chapter of Sigma Delta Chi, the national journalism honorary fraternity); the 1983 Kizzy Award for outstanding black women role models; and top honors from the Chicago Association of Black Journalists for commentary. She was also the first black to become a member of the *Chicago Tribune*'s editorial board in that newspaper's 137-year history: a prestigious position that carried with it a salary of approximately $50,000 and the opportunity to influence the attitudes of millions of people. In March 1984, McClain was selected by *Glamour* magazine as one of the ten most outstanding working women in America.

Two months later, on the evening of May 29, 1984—Memorial Day—McClain killed herself.

To many observers, McClain's accomplishments seemed even more astounding because she had grown up in a housing project in Chicago's predominantly black south side, an area known for gang warfare, poverty, and despair. Her success had netted her a posh address in the city's predominantly white, gentrified north side, but McClain wasn't entirely comfortable in her new setting. In October 1980, in *Newsweek*'s "My Turn" column, she wrote, "It is impossible for me to forget where I came from as long as I am prey to the jive hustler who does not hesitate to exploit my childhood friendship. I am reminded, too, when I go back to the old neighborhood in fear—and have my purse snatched—and when I sit down to a business lunch and have an old classmate wait on my table. I recall the girl I played dolls with who now rears five children on welfare, the boy from church who is in prison for murder, the pal found dead of a drug overdose in the alley where we once played tag. . . . Sometimes when I wait at the bus stop with my attaché case, I meet my aunt getting off the bus with other cleaning ladies on their way to do my neighbors' floors."

McClain realized that she couldn't go home again. Yet, despite her fair skin and sandy hair, despite her credentials and awards, she didn't have full access to her new world either. "I . . . have fulfilled the entry requirements of the American middle class, yet I am left, at times, feeling unwelcomed and stereotyped," she wrote.

She confided to a friend that she feared being a token on her job, and she worked at a frenzied pace to prove her competence.

Her dress-for-success uniform belied the fact that her emotional underpinnings had been created on the other side of town. "She got thrown into a white world and was expected to act the part," says a friend. "She was often fighting and grappling with her real self. She couldn't even write what she wanted. She had to bottle up her rage."

While McClain the journalist scaled corporate heights, her private life was conflicted, and her personal problems were exacerbated by her rapid professional rise. "She was sort of guilty about her success," says Monroe Anderson, a columnist and reporter for the *Chicago Tribune* and a close friend of McClain's. "Her parents still lived in the ghetto. Their problems were her problems."

But she had problems of her own as well. Her eight-year marriage to Clarence Page ended in 1982. Page, a journalist who has since been named to replace McClain on the *Tribune*'s editorial board, says the divorce was McClain's idea. "She began to express dissatisfaction with the marriage; she wanted love to come and hit her out of the blue. I told her, 'You're looking for something that's not there.'"

McClain found that her success could be intimidating. Her new-world expectations demanded that a mate match or better her salary and status. She dated a younger man, Keenan Michael Coleman, a computer salesman; their affair was stormy, yet McClain, desiring marriage, held on. She purchased an expensive house in Chicago's Hyde Park section, only to put it back on the market 24 hours later when her relationship dissolved.

As her personal desires eluded her and the values of her old and new worlds collided, close friends witnessed spells of hysterical crying, brooding silence, and mounting depression. She began stockpiling the potent antidepressant amitriptyline prescribed by her physician. For all of her accoutrements of professional success, McClain was as full of despair as any ghetto dweller.

On the night of what would have been her tenth wedding anniversary, McClain swallowed a huge overdose of amitriptyline and left both worlds behind.

It is rare for a black woman to ascend to the professional heights that McClain attained. Black women in corporate America are still scarce: According to the Bureau of Labor Statistic's report for 1984, among the classification "executive, administrative, managerial, and professional specialty," there were only 1,474,000 black women, 5.9% of the total, as opposed to 22,250,000 white women, 91% of the total number of working women in this category. Understandably, then, the loss of McClain's influence, power, and her ability to be a role model is perceived by some blacks as a group loss. "It hurt me to see a black woman who's achieved so much take it all away from us," says Paulette, a 38-year-old television producer in Los Angeles. Paulette is one of a small random sampling of black female executives—most working in upper middle management positions for large corporations and earning between $40,000 and $80,000 annually—who agreed to talk to SAVVY under a cloak of anonymity. These women admit that a black woman's climb to corporate power is at least as arduous as survival in the ghetto: They see a part of themselves in Leanita McClain's life, if not in her death.

Stress is the common experience these women all share. Not the Alka Seltzer stress of fighting deadlines and office politics while maintaining homes and families, this stress is from the oppressive combination of racism, sexism, and professional competition that separates black women not only from their white colleagues, but also insidiously pits them against their black male professional counterparts. The overload on black executive women often results in their pulling away from a cultural identity that includes family and old friends. Corporate racism, they expected. What was unexpected was the various degrees of culture shock, isolation, and alienation that black women experience as they attempt to acclimate professionally and to assimilate their culturally distinct selves into organizations that reward uniformity.

"I met Leanita a month or so before she died," says the director of a large, midwestern state agency. "We were both receiving the same award. When she sat down, I took one look at her and said to myself, 'The sister has problems.' I noticed it because I've been there before. . . . It was hard for me to believe that she committed suicide just because of job stress. When you're down there competing with white folks, you go through any number of changes. We've been brought up to expect that."

No one ever imagined the time when blacks would be insiders. Although Martin Luther King dreamed aloud of that day and Malcolm X railed against it, and thousands of blacks and whites marched, fought, and died to prevent or bring the moment closer, no one fully understood what overcoming the barriers of discrimination would mean for people who had been outsiders for centuries. Freedom, yes. But freedom to do what? To be whom?

When Leanita McClain began working for the *Chicago Tribune* in 1973, she was part of the first generation of corporate blacks that affirmative action[1] helped to create. Although it may have appeared that McClain easily glided from one world into another, her transition, like that of other black female executives, was far from smooth.

"I was very uneasy around whites when I first entered the corporation," says Yolanda, 35, a human resource manager for a large hair-care firm in New York City. "I come from a middle-class family. My father is a lawyer, and my mother is a teacher. My grandparents went to college. We were far from poor, yet I still grew up in a black world. My childhood was spent in a middle-class section of Los Angeles. I went to all-black schools from elementary school through college."

In 1970, Yolanda began her career as one of two blacks out of 40 people in a Sears management training program in Los Angeles. "Coming into big business, I had culture shock, but I didn't know it," Yolanda explains. "The sixties had just ended," she recalls, "and I was wearing my hair in a six-inch Afro. My consciousness was as high as my hair. One evening, my manager, a white man, took me aside and told me to wear jeans and a T-shirt to work the next day, because I'd be on the loading docks. Now I realize that working there was standard procedure, but I can remember wondering then if he was going to give me menial work to do because I'm black."

What some people would term Yolanda's "hypersensitivity" is a cultural orientation that most American blacks share and find difficult to shed: a tendency to be preoccupied with race and racism.

"Preoccupation with race can be very debilitating," says Ron Brown, Ph.D., a psychologist whose firm, Banks and Brown, counsels white and black managers from Fortune 500 companies on racial attitudes. "Back in the late sixties, it was obvious that black managers were having difficulty adjusting to the cues and norms of the corporate environment. Some of them were starting from ground zero. Blacks are trying to learn an ingrown system without coaching and mentoring. They can do it, but it takes longer. And some are paying a heavy price in stress."

Even after ten successful years in the corporate world, Yolanda still struggles with some degree of cultural unease "I'm still uncomfortable around whites in social situations," she says. "If I have to go to cocktail parties with whites, I don't feel completely at ease. We're all uncomfortable. When we're away from the job, the differences between us appear greater."

Many black executive women claim that in addition to the usual conformity that is required of all corporate professionals, if they want to succeed, they must make the whites around them feel comfortable, a difficult feat. Black women consciously choose their speech, their laughter, their walk, their mode of dress and car. They trim and straighten their hair, lest kinky curls or cornrows set them apart. At work, they try not to congregate in groups of more than two, so that white colleagues will not suspect a "plot."

McClain, fair and freckled as she was, couldn't blend in with her white co-workers even by changing her style. In *Newsweek* she declared, "I am painfully aware, that even with my off-white trappings, I am prejudged by my color. . . ." Although white women may chafe under corporate dress codes, behavioral constraints, and sexism, they don't have the additional burden of compromising their cultural selves. If black women, however, truly relinquish their cultural selves, they are unable to function

in the old world that still claims them. They learn to wear a mask.

"Each day, when I get into my car, I always begin the ride to work by turning on a black radio station so that it blares," says Karen, 35, a Harvard MBA who works for an Atlanta-based telecommunications corporation. "I boogey all the way down the highway. A few blocks from my job, I turn the music down and stop shaking my shoulders. When my building comes into view, I turn the music off, because I know the curtain is about to go up."

"I try hard not to be what they expect," says Estelle, 31, a fair-skinned black woman who is the vice president of the business division of a large bank in Los Angeles. "I don't misconjugate verbs. I don't wear a natural. . . . It probably helps that I'm not real dark-skinned. That's sad, but I know that kind of thing influences them."

Regardless of how black executive women may want to express themselves—and not all feel a conflict—they are pragmatic. Karen concludes, "The choice to enter the corporation is a choice to conform. Loudness, street talking, afros, flashy cars—that's not what white folks buy into. I've given up some self-expression. That trade-off for the salary is to play by the rules."

McClain knew the rules well. She came to work dressed for success and she wore her light brown hair in a straightened style. She lunched with white co-workers. She was articulate and pleasant. "Most whites thought Leanita was wonderful," says Monroe Anderson. "She was an actress around them."

As black executive women move up, they become isolated from those in their old world. McClain's parents and her two sisters were unaware of the pressures she was under. "Her sisters had no idea what bad shape she was in," one co-worker said. "She wasn't confiding in them." Many black executive women have few people to confide in. As they move up the corporate ladder they also become isolated from other blacks who work in lower positions in the same company.

"Not long ago, my division laid off several hundred people," says the 36-year-old director of career development for minorities at a New York television network. "Two of my closest friends were let go. There was nothing that I could have done to prevent it. I was hurting with them. Once they left, they told the other blacks in the company not to talk to me because I was management. I was very, very hurt. Blacks began to stay away from me. What could I do? I couldn't go to my boss about it. I felt as though I'd been ripped apart."

Some accept the isolation as par for the course. "The higher up you move, the more you'll be isolated," says the Los Angeles banker matter-of-factly. "I have less in common with those people who used to be my friends. I have more in common with those of the same class or income, be they black or white."

If some black women are pragmatic about assimilation, many are pained by the thought of "losing their blackness" and strive to maintain cultural ties. For Linda, a human resources manager for a fast-food chain headquartered outside of Chicago, the decision to remain in the black south side brings turmoil. "I firmly believe, although it's being chipped away, that if blacks don't live in the black community, there will be no role models for inner-city kids."

But Linda's voice is weary as she talks about the disadvantages. "I have a 35-mile one-way commute. Obviously, property values are much lower. And two company cars have been stolen from in front of my house. One was right in the driveway.

"I've been to the homes of whites I work with who live in the suburbs; I haven't invited them to mine."

Leanita McClain had felt guilty about moving away from her old friends; she felt awkward about fitting the militant blacks' stereotype of a "sell out." "I am not comfortably middle class," she wrote. "I am uncomfortably middle class."

Not assimilating into the corporate mold, which includes an acceptable lifestyle away from the job, isn't overlooked by companies. "Eventually, when upper management considers someone who maintains a visibly black lifestyle for increased responsibility, she might be ruled out as not being a 'good fit,'" says Ron Brown.

If being alienated from blacks brings stress, at the same time there are new pressures from those in the old world who view the executive woman as having made it. Black organizations demand time and money, as do friends and family. Some black executives find themselves alternately being used and abused as they are made to pay for their success. "I am a member of the black middle class who has had it with being patted on the head by white hands and slapped in the face by black hands," wrote McClain.

Isolated from blacks, black executive women often are alienated from the whites with whom they are supposed to assimilate. "When I was placed in a fast-track development program, I was really estranged from my white co-workers," says Cora, 33, who manages 105 people in a Chicago communications company. "I felt that they were all watching me. They had all worked their way up to management. I came in off the street into a management position. They knew I'd been tapped to move up. They were waiting for me to fall on my face. They resented me because I was black, female, young, and headed to be a company executive."

"I have to interpret what my white managers are saying two and a half times," says Yolanda, the hair-care manager." They filter out information because I'm a black woman."

McClain clearly questioned the ties that bound her to some of her white peers. She wrote, "Some of my 'liberal' white acquaintances hint that I am a freak, that my success is less a matter of talent than of luck and affirmative action. I may live among them, but it is difficult to live with them."

For some blacks, the mask they wear begins to crack under the pressure as their rage bubbles to the surface. When Chicago Mayor Harold Washington, a black man, was running for office, Chicago became a hate-filled city. In a series of columns, McClain vented her feelings of anger and disillusionment, but it was in *The Washington Post* that her article, "How Chicago Taught Me to Hate Whites," potently articulated the rage that she felt as the mayoral campaign progressed to what she called "a race war." Her anger was directed toward whites who spoke disparagingly of "the blacks." "'The blacks,'" McClain wrote. "It would make me feel like machine-gunning every white face on the bus."

McClain could powerfully externalize her fury, but most black women lack that access to public confrontation. They turn their rage inward. Nearly all of the women interviewed by SAVVY show a series of disturbing symptoms: hair loss, nervous exhaustion, chronic stomach pains, insomnia, and depression. "I thought I had high blood pressure," says the Los Angeles television producer. "My heart was beating fast and I had shortness of breath. I had migraines. The physician couldn't find anything wrong. Finally I went to a therapist and we discussed my negative feelings about my job and career. That gave me some relief."

"I see a high rate of alcoholism and cocaine and marijuana abuse. Lots of tranquilizers," says Audrey B. Chapman, a therapist and human relations trainer in Washington, D.C., who specializes in stress management seminars for female professionals. "The women exhibit a lot of psychosomatic pain in their backs and necks. They have severe menstrual cramps. The pain isn't so much physical as it is mental," says Chapman. "The stress leads to the real killers of black women—hypertension, diabetes, and strokes."

As prevalent as racism is, many black executive women declare that, at times, they are aware of discrimination because of gender even more than of race.

According to findings from Black Values in the American Workplace, a conference held in March 1984, funded by the Xerox Corporation and organized by John L. Jones, that company's director of affirmative action, sexism is a major problem for black executive women.

"I was in the hall talking with one of the big bosses, an older white guy," says the Los Angeles television producer. "As I turned to leave, he swatted me on my behind with a rolled-up newspaper. I was in a state of shock. If anybody ever does that to me again, I swear, I'll grab him by his collar and throw him up against a wall."

Although white males see them as fair game, black women complain that black males are most often the perpetrators of sexist behavior. "Most of my trouble came from black men," says the agency head from Illinois. "They had problems because I was a firm manager. I fired all of them eventually because they did a poor job. One of the men I let go came to me and said, 'Your problem is that you're just evil.' I told him, 'Evil is what your girlfriend or woman may be. I'm efficient.

And your ass is gone.' He couldn't believe that a woman would let him go."

If a black woman's managerial status is threatening to the black men with whom she works, so it is that her success may inhibit or spoil her personal relationships. No other group is as likely to be divorced: In 1983, according to the Census Bureau's report of marital status and living arrangements, 297 black women were divorced per 1,000 marriages—over twice the rate as for white women. The divorce rate for black women is 10% higher for those with college degrees, 15% higher with one year of graduate school, and 19% higher for those with two years of graduate school.

Among the never-married, the search for a "suitable" mate is frustrating. According to the 1980 Census figures, there are nearly 1.5 million more black females than males: the largest difference in male/female ratio of any racial group in the country. And, for many years, there have been more college-educated black females than males. According to Joyce Payne, director, Office for the Advancement of Public Black Colleges, between 1976 and 1981, the number of black women awarded professional degrees increased by 71%; there was a 12% decline for black males. The single women interviewed all told stories of failed relationships with professional black males. These women claim that the male/female ratio allows men to "romp"; they add that black professional men are intimidated by the success of the women.

"I've had long-term relationships that have ended, and the next thing I knew, my ex-boyfriend was dating a secretary," says the midwestern agency director. "I think that black professional women must be too honest. I was going with a man who headed a local agency and who was trying to go into business for himself. He had some good ideas, but he had some dumb ones, too. Maybe I should have just pretended that everything he said was wonderful. Also, he had this irritating habit. Whenever he'd come to my office, he'd close the door, sit in my chair, put his feet up on my desk, and say, 'Now, if I were the boss, this is how I'd run this agency.'"

"In the old days, black women who were professionals married pullman porters and postal workers, the only jobs most black men could get," says Chapman. "What today's women expect is less available." Still the hunt for the elusive black male professional continues.

Toward the end of her life, Leanita McClain's loneliness was perhaps a heavier burden than her professional struggles. The combination was, for her, unbearable.

"It wasn't a question of either her professional problems or her personal ones causing her the most difficulty," says Monroe Anderson, the *Tribune* reporter. "Her focus was on her personal life. What happened was that with her rapid success and her still not being happy, the personal came into focus. It's difficult for a black woman to make it without a personal relationship. Black women have to battle racism and sexism and then come home to loneliness, or again do battle. For the majority of professional black women, it's not good."

Yet, most black executive women admit that their brothers' quest for professional ascendancy is far more frustrating than their own. "Black men have a harder time," says one executive black woman, echoing most others, "because white males are intimidated by them."

The progress of black men is tied to the progress of black women. Black women cannot contribute the best of their talents to the corporation if they are placed in the position of being an affirmative action buffer zone, fulfilling federal government standards at the expense of professional opportunity for black men. Until black women develop strategies to overcome many of their own self-inflicted problems, they will be ensnared by their own success, forging ahead while straining under a staggering emotional load.

Leanita McClain finally laid her burden down and escaped the narrow alley located between pain and desire to another place. Her unanswered question continues to haunt her sisters.

"I have made it, but where?"   [1984]

Note

1. AFFIRMATIVE ACTION: A federal program requiring businesses to seek out qualified employees from traditionally excluded and underrepresented groups.

Understanding the Reading

1. What does Campbell mean when she says, "McClain realized that she couldn't go home again"?
2. What causes stress for McClain and other black women executives?
3. Why would differences between blacks and whites appear greater away from the job?
4. According to the article, what is the cultural self that black corporate women must relinquish? What does losing their blackness mean?
5. Why are relationships between successful black women and black men so problematic?

Suggestions for Responding

1. Describe how some facet of your heritage (in the broadest sense) put you into a double bind because of the expectations of two different groups. How did the tension make you feel, and how did you respond?
2. Why do you think Podhoretz was able to survive and thrive by his move into the middle class and McClain was destroyed by her move? ✦

25

The Truth About Growing Up Rich

SALLIE BINGHAM

Very few people think of rich women as being "highly vulnerable." We are usually portrayed as grasping and powerful, like Joan Collins's character in the television miniseries "Sins." Yet in reality, most rich women are invisible; we are the faces that appear behind well-known men, floating up to the surface infrequently, palely; the big contributors, often anonymous, to approved charities, or the organizers of fund-raising events. Rich women have been so well rewarded by an unjust system that we have lost our voices; we are captives, as poor women are captives, of a system that deprives us of our identities.

Growing up a daughter in a very rich family placed me in this special position. It was important to avoid all displays of pride; what made me unusual, after all, was not really my own. I hadn't earned it. It had been given to me, willy-nilly, along with a set of commandments, largely unspoken, that enforced my solitariness:

- Always set a good example.
- Do not condescend to those who have less.
- Never ask the price of anything.
- Avoid being conspicuous in any way.

These commandments were backed by fear. Rich women are always vulnerable to criticism; we do not share the justifications of the men who actually made the money. We neither toil, nor do we spin, yet we have access to a wide range of material comforts. But here there is a delicate line. The jewels must not be too big, nor the furs too obvious.

Often in a rich family the jewels are inherited, obscuring, with their flash and dazzle, the ambivalent feelings of the women who first wore them. In my family, attention was focused on a pair of engagement rings, one made of diamonds, the other of sapphires, which had belonged to our grandmothers. When the time came to divide the rings, my two older brothers, then adolescents, were allowed to choose. Knowing nothing about the value of jewels, but liking the color of the sapphires, the eldest chose it for his eventual bride; the younger brother took possession, by default, of the much more valuable diamonds.

Both those rings were conspicuous, which broke a cardinal tenet of my childhood. It was a rule I had broken before. All bright children are naturally conspicuous; they talk in loud voices and move about in unhampered ways. But when the whole world is watching for a mistake, this natural exuberance must be curbed. And when the child in question is a girl, the curbing is especially intense: as a sexual object, she represents the family's peculiar vulnerability to outsiders, predators—husbands. The little rich girl must learn to sit with her legs firmly crossed and her skirt prudently down at the same time she is learning to modulate both the tone of her voice and the color of her opinions. The result is paleness.

Her models are pale as well. The hard-driving ancestor who made the fortune is not a good choice for his retiring granddaughter. Yet her female relatives, because of their learned conformity, offer little color or originality to the small girl; their rebellions are invisible, their opinions matched to the opinions of their male counterparts. The most sympathetic woman may be a maid or nurse, but her educational and social limitations restrict her effectiveness as a model. This, in turn, can lead to a split between love and administration: the cozy, uneducated nurse is loved; the remote, perfect mother is admired. How can one satisfactory role be forged out of two contradictions?

The little rich girl realizes, with a chill, that she must treat the women around her differently. When I was a very small child, I kissed my nurse and the servants when I felt like it; as I grew older, I realized that such displays embarrassed them. As a very small child, I pitied my nurse because she had to work so hard, tending five children; a little later, I realized that such pity was inappropriate. The love doesn't change, but the little girl must look elsewhere for someone to imitate.

Obeying all the rules can never be enough, however. No amount of proper behavior can place a rich woman on comfortable terms with a world where there is so much poverty and suffering. She will always be suspect in a democracy, either as a decoration for a tyrant or a parasite with little feeling for women struggling to survive.

Another obligation is added to the role of the third- or fourth-generation heiress, whose male relatives have led lives nearly as protected as her own. From private boarding school and Ivy League college, these men return to the family fold and a lifetime career managing assets or running the family business. The harsh bustle and hard knocks of independent life have been avoided, at some cost. Yet since these sheltered individuals are men, they are expected to play roles of some importance in society, as executives or politicians, donors or secret political kingmakers. Unused to stress and criticism, they must be protected if they are to survive; here, the rich woman's role as peacemaker becomes crucial.

Most women are expected to balance demands for equity with a special sensitivity to human needs. We are asked to value compassion more than fairness, understanding more than critical judgment. Since family fortunes and family businesses usually descend to male heirs, this protective duty becomes essential to the maintenance of the whole structure. If the inheriting males are revealed as vulnerable and uncertain, the whole enterprise is likely to fall. And so the role of rich women becomes, essentially, that of buttressing rich men.

From this buttressing and sheltering springs an intolerance for conflict, for the harsh give-and-take that characterizes most families. A silken silence prevails, a nearly superhuman attempt to agree on every issue. This is the example provided for the children, who are at the same time secretly or openly competing for affection and favor. Emotional inhibition does not really quell raging emotional needs, which are seldom satisfied in families that value appearances highly. And since there can be no open conflict, no channels are carved out for carrying off animosity. Everything must go underground. This is a recipe for an explosion.

Explosions don't wreck most families. At worst, they cause hurt feelings and temporary alienation. But where there are no channels for the resolution of conflict, an explosion leaves nothing but desolation behind it. No one knows how to proceed.

In addition, explosions in rich families may cause a widespread tremor. Employees may be laid off, elaborate households may be dismembered because of a purely personal falling-out. The rich family supports a large number of dependents: domestics, poor relations, down-at-heel friends, the managers of charitable foundations and their grantees, enormous business ventures with their scaled layers of managers and employees, and a huge retinue of legal and financial advisers. All these people tremble when the family that supports them disagrees. This is a strong inducement to contrived peace.

But to preserve a contrived peace, some people will be permanently silenced. And since the point of view of women is generally less acceptable than the point of view of men, it will be women, in rich families, who are silenced for the sake of peace.

This leads to a good deal of distance between the women in such families. Young girls, like young boys, usually express some degree of rebellion. However, there is no way to express such a rebellion inside such a family without causing the tinkling of crystal chandeliers, which sounds too much like tears. And so the rebellious girl will never find an ally to moderate or encourage her in mother, sister, grandmother, or aunt. They have subscribed to a system that supports them in comfort, and so the system cannot be questioned. The rebel must learn silence or leave.

Rich families shed, in each generation, their most passionate and outspoken members. In the shedding, the family loses the possibility of renewal, of change. Safety is gained, but a safety that is rigid and judgmental. And the price, for the mothers, is terrible: to sacrifice their brightest, most articulate children to the dynasty.

So around the main fire of the wealthy family one usually sees the little winking campfires of the cast-out relatives. Lacking in skills, these relatives may spend their lives on the fringes of poverty, dependent on an occasional check from home. Often they retain emotional ties with the main fire, strengthened by unresolved conflicts; but they will never thrive either within its glow or in outer darkness. Some of these cast-out souls are women.

For no matter how well paid we are for our compliance, in the end, we do not inherit equally. Most rich families work on the English system and favor male heirs. There's an assumption that the women will marry well and be taken care of for life; there's an assumption that the men will do the work of the world, or of the family, and should be adequately compensated for it. When the will is read, the women inherit houses, furniture, and jewels; the men inherit cash, stocks, and securities. Yet the same commandments that rule out conspicuous behavior prevent rich women from fighting for their inheritance. Instead, we learn early to accept, to be grateful for what we are given. The slave mentality abounds in the palaces of the rich, even when the slave is decked in precious attire. We are dependent, after all, on the fickle goodwill of those who will never proclaim us their heirs.

What a fruitless arrangement this is for families, as well as for the society as a whole, may be seen in the absence of wealthy women from positions of power and influence. Without strong women models and allies, we sink into silence. Bribed by material comfort, stifled by guilt, we are not strong leaders, strong mothers, or strong friends. We are alone. And often, we are lost.

For what personal ethic can transcend, or transform, the ethic of the men in our lives? What sense of self-justification can grow out of a sheltered, private, silenced life?

A fine sense of decorum often prevents us from cherishing friendships with women, friendships that are often untidy, provocative, and intimate. The same sense of decorum makes us hesitate to join groups that may also contain unruly elements. Our good looks and fine clothes are separating devices as well; our smooth, sophisticated deportment doesn't encourage intimacies. And so the most envied women in this country today are probably the loneliest, the least effective, the most angry and forlorn. Yet we have everything. How do we dare to complain?

"Everything" is largely material. It's the charge cards, the jewelry, the clothes. We are not taught skills, self-discipline, or self-nurturing; we are left, by and large, to fend for ourselves inside prohibitions that discourage us from experimenting. And if we are unable to persuade or force our daughters to follow our example, we will lose them, in the end. And in the end, we may find ourselves totally dependent on our male relatives, for friendship, status, affection, a role in life—and financial support. Such total dependence breeds self-distrust, bitterness, and fear.

It doesn't have to be this way. But in order to change, the women in a rich family must realize that its covenants are simply self-perpetuating prejudices: a prejudging of events and individuals so that no untoward thought or action will upset the family's ethic, which is, first and foremost, to preserve the status quo.

Young girls growing up isolated by wealth must find their allies, whether inside or outside the family. They must get themselves educated and prepared for careers, not at the Eastern establishments that are geared to perpetuating male leadership, but at schools and colleges that are sympathetic to the special fears and vulnerabilities of women. And they must rid themselves of their guilt and their compulsion to smooth the way for the heirs.

This is a large bill. But the releasing of energy and hope, for this small group of wealthy women, would have results, in the country at large, far out of proportion to our numbers. What a difference it would make, for example, if rich women contributed their wealth to the causes that benefit poor women rather than to the sanitized, elitist cultural organizations favored by their fathers, brothers, and financial advisers.

What a difference it would make to women running for political office if they could draw on the massive resources of rich women, as men political candidates have drawn on the rich for generations.

What a difference it would make if wealthy women, who hire so many professionals, made sure those professionals were women lawyers, doctors, bankers, and advisers.

What a difference it would make to women as a whole if we, who are so misperceived, became visible, actively involved in working out our destiny.

Wealthy men have always influenced the course of this nation's history. Wealthy women have, at best, worked behind the scenes. We share our loneliness, our sense of helplessness, and our alienation from the male establishment with all our sisters. Out of our loneliness and alienation, we can learn to transform the world around us, with a passion for equality that we learned, at close hand, from observing the passionate inequalities practiced by wealthy families.   [1986]

Understanding the Reading

1. What does Bingham mean when she says rich women are captives?
2. What is the responsibility of a rich woman to her family, especially to its males?
3. Why is conflict especially difficult in rich families?
4. Why are rich women "silenced" and lonely?
5. What effects would changing the lives of rich women have on society?

Suggestions for Responding

1. Most of us dream that being rich would make us happy; however, as Bingham points out, wealth has disadvantages. What drawbacks, beyond those she describes, do you think you

might face if you were a female or a male member of a very wealthy family?

2. What are the advantages of the working-class lives Soto and Podhoretz describe over Bingham's upper-class life? ✦

26

Yale: Reflections on Class in New Haven

Lynda M. Glennon

For a long time I've avoided writing about my social-class experiences with Yale. What of my parents and friends back in New Haven? They will be scandalized by my unearthing this whole business of class conflict. But one of my personal and professional interests has become the study of social-class life styles, and, oh, how Yale plays a part in my personal struggles and in my very education!

YALE. Townspeople sound ambivalent when they say the word. "Yay'-illll," they intone, partly in resentment, partly in pride that the fancy university is in their home town. "Yay'-illll?" the stranger searches. "Oh yeah, that's that Ivy-League place, the one with the boola boola, bull-dog bow wow wow, Eli Yale and all that, from 'the tables down at Mory's to the place where Louie dwells.'" What these names meant few of us knew, even though they were familiar in our world of working-class New Haveners. As a child hearing "We are poor little lambs who have lost our way," I would think of Little Bo Peep, and of "Black sheep black sheep have you any wool, Yes sir (or mam), yes sir, three bags full." Whenever I would ask my mother, "Who's Louie, Ma?" or "Who's Mory?" she would say she didn't know. I didn't know until my college years that Mory's "restaurant" was an exclusive association located on York Street next to the Yorkside restaurant where we would go for coffee after the movies and football games and next to where the old Yale Co-op used to be. In those days the Co-op's clothing and sporting goods sections were located at the far end of the building on York Street.

I found magic in the window displays of blue-and-white striped scarves that Yale steadies wore and that for a time became the uniform of upper-middle-class females in New Haven, along with the required camel's hair polo coats. I could never afford to buy one, though I remember beginning to knit one and giving up after fifteen rows of the six feet required.

When I was a child I had only vague notions of what Yale was. I knew, of course, that it had a major presence in New Haven. "What's that building?" I'd ask my mother, spotting something that looked interesting. "Oh, that's part of Yale," she'd answer. "But what do they do in there?" I'd persist. "What's it for?" "I don't know; it's just part of Yale," she'd repeat. The tone of her voice would signal me to stop; I was treading on shaky grounds. I was not to ask her anything more about things she didn't know about and felt intimidated by. She did know Woolsey Hall, the Yale Bowl, and Peabody Museum. But these even I knew then. These were the buildings that entered into the daily lives of townspeople, even us working-class ones. Practically everybody knew Yale Bowl—the local radio station covered the games there, and besides we couldn't visit Aunt Josephine on those Saturdays when home football games were scheduled, the traffic was so bad. "Oh, it's Bowl traffic," was a common phrase. A lot of us knew that famous singers or musicians performed in Woolsey Hall from reading the placards in front of the building or their advertisements on the movie pages of *The New Haven Register*. And Peabody Museum was open to the public. We went there on Sunday afternoons once in a while, when my mother had exhausted the supply of stores that we could "window shop" in the downtown area of New Haven. Peabody Museum didn't have a "keep out" aura about it and we didn't feel unwelcome—there were too many other townspeople there for us to feel conspicuous, and lots of kids racing around hooting and hollering made the place very hang-loose. I never knew Yale had an art gallery until many years later when I was in college.

Somehow, even now, I can't imagine the presence of noisy, messy children at most of the rest of Yale. The images are just too contradictory. The only children I ever saw rode papoose style on their parents' backs even then, or they were the velvet-clad hothouse variety who looked like the twentieth-century version of Little Boy Blue.[1] These children were different from the children I grew up with, and, more than their clothing, their language style set them apart from the rest of us kids, a style that one now hears from articulate child actors on some television commercials. These children at Yale speak the Queen's English at ages five and six, by God: "Pardon me, Aunt Emily, but may I have another dollop of sour cream on my baked potato?" Most of the kids I grew up with could hardly manage to keep the food in their mouths at that age, and were constantly getting walloped verbally or manually and told to be quiet, sit still, mind your manners, and eat what's on your plate. The poor starving children in China (then) would suffer worse hunger pains if I didn't finish my yellow waxed beans and unseasoned potato. (So I tried to sit still, be quiet, and save the world with every mouthful.) This was not the scene at the Yale family table, though. That conversation was erudite, worldly wise, and had shape. Most working-class children learn to speak that way, if at all, as a second language.

Any unusual, old, or expensive-looking architecture in New Haven almost invariably turned out to be Yale-connected. My family, like most other working-class families in New Haven, came to know the Yale campus in fragmented but personally relevant ways. When I went to college I began to match such names as Vanderbilt and Wright with the freshman buildings in the quadrangle of the Old Campus. Until then I had thought that these somber structures, up by where we used to park the family car for movie matinees as young high school girls, were either classroom buildings where mysterious mathematical formulae covered the blackboards, or that these were the offices where all the administrators could be found. The Forestry School up on Prospect Street became real to me after I had gotten an after-school job of picking up and delivering dictaphone tapes to a woman in my neighborhood who transcribed them. I had half-expected to run into Paul Bunyan in the halls, and I was disappointed to find dull, ordinary-looking, bureaucratic types in there, although once I did catch a glimpse of a man in a red-and-black plaid flannel shirt and field boots that fed my fantasy for weeks about what went on in that

building. Ingalls Hockey Rink was built during my adolescence, and it was so unusual in shape that everybody in town commented on it. To some it was the whale, to some the turtle, to others Noah's Ark. "Ugh." my parents used to say, "that building is hideous, why would they ever build anything so crazy?" I thought it was kind of nice, partly in rebellion against my parents, partly because I was beginning to experience the social-class ambivalence that plagues working-class kids who find themselves in two social worlds.

My family came to know those Yale buildings in the passageways of our everyday life; buildings we passed on the way from our relatives' homes in one working-class district to our own in Fair Haven. Unlike the legally recognized East, West, and North Havens, Fair Haven was known only to old-time New Haveners, and sometimes only those who had some working-class ties, for it was the Irish-Italian enclave whose roots went back generations. It was thoroughly working-class in flavor; a few scattered lower-middle-class homes could be found there (lace-curtain Irish, especially), but the blood and guts were blue-collar. So when a Yale student asked me what part of New Haven I lived in, "Fair Haven" was never enough of a reply. At that time I thought merely that Yalies were out-of-towners and couldn't be expected to know the districts in a strange city. I realized much later that besides being out-of-towners they were also "out-of-classers." Certain knowing elites would reply, "Oh, how very interesting," with that tone all working-class people know, and then politely excuse themselves. I was the exception in their lives, just as they were in mine. But for them New Haven was synonymous with Yale, and the city's inhabitants were simply nuisances that got in their way from time to time. I was the one made to feel odd and out of place.

The Yalies were a lot of trouble to townspeople. They would practically take over at meal times the streets bounding their dining halls; at class-changing times the streets throughout the campus would be congested with moving bodies. Elm Street was always very bad, up by Liggetts at York and Elm down to College Street. The Yalies always seemed quietly ruthless and unselfconsciously confident in their khaki slacks, blue oxford-cloth shirts, sleeves rolled twice, ties flapping in the breeze, running off to classes or dinner, crossing Elm Street, not bothering about traffic, oblivious. The townspeople resented this terribly. My father called them "rich boys" or "smart alecks." My young working-class dates would get furious if a Yalie crossed in front of a car they were driving without seeming to notice. "Get a Yalie," they'd yell, revving up the engine, while I would cry, "Don't do that," or "Stop it," giving them the perfect excuse to spare the life of the enemy. It was a ritual we took for granted. As these working-class males grew older and calmer they stopped noticing the insult of going unnoticed, stopped hoping a Yalie would run in front of their cars. Then it would take a real affront for one of them to rile one of us; we learned to call them names rather than to wish their demise. So "wise guy" and "smart aleck" (and their obscene renditions) peppered the air down Elm Street every day at these regular intervals. It was especially marked at the dinner hour because then the working-class folks would be coming home from work—hard, uninspiring work in jobs that did not allow them to control the rhythm of work, the breaks, or the pacing. This is the most difficult thing to take, the thing that most social critics miss who have never themselves had to survive working-class jobs. It's seldom the repetitiveness or the monotony of the job that causes alienation and demoralization, that erodes one's sense of pride and independence. It's being told when to start work, when to have a cigarette break; it's having to make an issue out of going to the toilet, and having gongs, bells, or even music dictate what has to be done next. And then driving home in cars that are falling apart but not yet paid for, the last straw for these working-class people is for some smart-ass-rich-Yalie to cross in front of a car in defiance of traffic rules, courtesy, or decent responsibility. It is too much. These privileged creatures seemed to make the whole world stop for them, wait for them, fear them.

Yalies seemed to be oblivious of the feelings of the townspeople, particularly the working-class ones. They took it for granted that these were their streets, that cars were intruders that didn't belong there. Townspeople feel that Yalies are guests of the town, that they come and go, but the people stay on. Yalies seem to think that they are New Haven.

The "townie" syndrome is vicious, but it was a long time before I got the full impact of its class dynamics. Coming into puberty, I began to look at Yalies as something other than the "smart alecks" my father called them. I began to find them attractive. I first "discovered" Yale men one day in my first or second year of high school. Three of my girlfriends and I had gotten all the way to the College movie theatre ticket booth one Sunday afternoon when we discovered we were short of money. It was a freezing cold day in late September, and we began to look for shelter from the wind. We started to saunter into an entranceway, just past what I later came to identify as Bingham Hall on Chapel Street. We felt very brave, as ex-members of The Black Rebellion Girls' Club (after Brando's Black Rebellion Motorcycle club in *The Wild Ones*), and we were still wearing B.R.G.C. uniforms—skintight jeans, navy shirts over yellow turtlenecks, dungaree jackets, and brown Western-style ankle boots. We found ourselves surrounded by two- and three-story long buildings, old and ivy-covered. Like a spark hitting tinder the place was suddenly alive with hooting, hollering, catcalls, and whistling. Since this was the 'fifties, we were flattered. I thought, "Oh gee, I might get to meet a Yalie." They all seemed to be falling in love with us. "If you can't get a date get a Yalie"—a maxim that seemed to spring from a rage at being ignored—was forgotten in that instant. And I did not know then that while sex and love are polarities for many men, they are so especially for Yalies and townies.

We somehow sensed that parading through the campus getting whistled at was not a good idea, so we never repeated that first experience. We had a gut-level intuition that such conduct would get us into trouble, although no one of us ever articulated what was wrong. Other working-class girls may not have been so lucky as to have such a strong peer group. For example, around the time of my freshman year in college the story of a girl who regularly held "court" in Yale dormitories, and offered her services to a line of eager young Yalies, was published locally. Those men who were caught were dismissed from Yale. The girl was charged with "lascivious carriage," and because she was only fifteen or sixteen was remanded to juvenile authorities.

Just as in the Elizabeth Ray scandal,[2] one must understand that there is a strong pull by very virtue of class differences toward the men from the higher classes. It is not a matter of a woman's scanning several options and selecting the one that best advances self-interest. The life style of the working class does not include this middle-class emphasis on actively mastering one's environment, on rational calculation and primacy of self-interested action. In a society that makes those from the poorer classes feel shabby and as if they did not count for anything, it is easy for a girl to feel flattered by sexual attention from one of the privileged classes. Such attention can seem more desirable than being ignored, as though social class differences were temporarily equalized. The rude awakening comes much later when it becomes apparent that sex was mistaken for love. I struggled through these confusions along with my friends throughout adolescence. Any one of us might have come to the same fate had we not had the support of one another.

I used to find myself describing my home town to strangers as "New Haven—you know, the place where Yale is," with a sense of pride at having grown up next to so famous and fancy a place as Yale. I also used to say we had great cultural advantages—art, music, films, lectures, and theatre—"because of Yale." This went along with describing my alma mater, a small Catholic women's college (we called it "girls'" college in those days), Albertus Magnus, as intellectually superior because it had some Yale professors on the staff who were induced by economic pressure or by the personal pleading of the "good nuns" to teach a course or two there. I now wonder what those teachers thought of the Aggie Maggies, so polarized a bunch were we: the suave but not so bright upper-middle-class girls and the socially inept but bright working-class girls. The temper of the place has changed since my four years that bridged the 'fifties and 'sixties, but then the school was geared to the needs and interests of the upper middle class, socially at least, and we commuters were always made to feel as though we were the poor relatives. It was here that I learned that verbal proficiency could masquerade as intelligence. It took years for me to speak without self-consciousness, trying to make some sense of the confusion of speech between working class and upper middle class.

Most of the commuters were from working-class backgrounds. We had to be unusually bright in order for someone besides our parents,

already economically strapped and not enthusiastic about our spending four years in college, to notice us and spur us on to get a college education. I remember my mother's saying offhandedly that girls didn't really need to go to college; they could get good jobs without it. I just "happened" into college, having graduated second in my class in high school, and having taken to heart the assumption of everybody there that I should go to college. I was not a supermotivated achiever, although I liked theoretical discussions and social criticism, and had even then a satiric view of the world, having first been the leader of the B.R.G.C. and then in my senior year captain of cheerleaders.

By the time of my graduation from high school the teachers had convinced my parents that I needed a good academic college, and one that was Catholic, too. The nuns at high school and my parents communicated to me that if I went to a secular school I'd lose the faith (like a wallet or a pair of mittens, I thought). So I chose Albertus Magnus, where for the first time I was exposed to an upper-middle-class life style.

I was convinced during my first two years there that I was hopelessly stupid, that all the work I had done up until now had been completely misjudged, and that a terrible mistake had been made: that I was actually quite stupid, if not retarded. It wasn't until later in my junior year that I was discovered and defined as a nascent intellectual by three of my teachers, a philosopher, a sociologist, and an English professor. I had also by my junior year become the reigning bohemian at the college, the president of the debate club, and the distress of the administrators, who were constantly reminding me that I represented the college and that I would simply have to *do something* about my appearance and manner. That meant that I was to become more like the upper-middle-class students, the ones who talked "nice," dressed sedately, and who smiled when they got in sticky situations. The administration didn't know what to make of my black leotards and turtlenecks, waist-length hair, and direct, unsmiling eye contact. One of the deans, a lace-curtain-Irish nun, asked me in each of the many confrontations in her office, "What are you staring at?" Staring was an un-middle-class thing to do; it made her ill at ease. I had no idea why she was so upset. I have since come to understand better the profound differences between social classes on this whole matter of self-presentation.

The college threw me into direct contact with Yale, especially through the mixers it arranged or got us invited to in our freshman year. I remember one such mixer in particular, held at some official-looking hall at Yale during our freshman orientation week. It was just terrible. I was asked to dance by a guy who looked like Mack the Knife, very slick—very clean lines—but a bit leering and sinister. Those days the typical Yalie was light-haired and crew-cutted, wearing the basic Ivy League uniform: khaki slacks, muted blue oxford-cloth button-down shirt, dark or striped knit tie, brown loafers or maybe desert boots—decidedly low-key or what they now call "laid back." This guy I met at the mixer was another basic Yalie type: headed for a career in finance management or corporate law. I didn't like him at all. He was wearing a navy blue flannel blazer with a crest on the pocket, and a navy and maroon rep tie. He said he lived in New York. No, actually he said he lived in Manhattan. I remember thinking "How unusual, calling New York 'Manhattan'," and I picked up that habit myself right then and there, and kept it for years afterward. Being marginal, I was always alert to the nuances of language. At that time I was uncritical of the very idea of social hierarchy so I tried my best to erase any traces of my "lower station." And calling Manhattan "New York" seemed by his very tone to be a gaffe, a sign that one was not knowing, was not "shoe," or, in short, had no class. I, the working-class child, felt ill at ease.

The sensitivity to being "in," to not being gauche, is not restricted to, but is particularly acute for, the working-class youngster. As a matter of fact, some working-class kids have little or no contact with the world of the upper or middle class, except on television, and escape that conflict, because class oppression requires a person-to-person encounter to be experienced as personal pain. The marginal youngster is torn between the desire to be welcomed in the group judged superior, and the desire to repudiate the group completely for its strangeness and for its presumption in judging. So I began to call New York "Manhattan" because I was afraid I'd be found out as a clod. At the same time I was beginning to question the whole system of class differ-

ences that could do such injury to the spirits of those caught in the ambiguities of the hierarchy.

It took much more exposure to Yale to begin to detect the finer points of class membership, which were glaringly obvious to class insiders. But this working-class child, who was just beginning to recognize that the working-class was considered less good than people who lived in the fancy houses and bought their clothes from the little shops near the campus, was in very strange territory.

My dancing partner's preparatory school was Andover. I had a vague notion that finishing or preparatory schools were for those who were deficient scholastically, as summer school provided a second chance to pass courses flunked during the regular year. I also remembered that a boy I had gone to school with was admitted to Yale on a scholarship on condition that he spend a year in a preparatory school to make up subjects lacking in his background. He was bright enough, but I had prided myself on being brighter. I thought indeed that he was being penalized for not being bright enough; that he was being sent to some detention station for scholastic deficiency. So this was my image of preparatory schools. It took about two years in college, some further abrasive encounters with the elites, and a sociology course for me to begin to make sense out of this alien system.

So this guy that I met at the mixer had gone to Andover, and was smooth as oil. I was wearing a dress I had made from some paisley cotton fabric cut from a Vogue pattern. The picture on the package looked very elegant indeed, but the actual dress looked ordinary, if not downright dowdy. I was also wearing a pin made out of some brass-alloy type metal molded into a cuckoo clock, with pendulums hanging on little chains and a bird perched atop the roof, the whole thing one-and-a-half by two-and-a-half inches (four inches if you count the pendulums). The stiffly painful conversation between this guy and me went from bad to worse. He asked if my pin (he called it a "brooch") was an heirloom. Lord, I got it from a box of junk jewelry my Aunt gave us kids to play with years before. So I was wearing this piece of discarded jumk to hide the uneven stitching around the collar of my homemade dress and Mack the Elite asks me if it's an heirloom. I'll never forget how I felt. In my nervousness, I blurted out that it was my grandmother's. So then he talked about his grandmama and how she was very wealthy but in poor health, and that she was very slow to give out any of her precious jewelry for fear that the relatives would take advantage of her situation. Another blow. I tried to get the conversation back to my reality but to no avail. Saying that the pin was just "an old thing" didn't help much. Long silence. He then said he liked my dress. I said I had made it. Another long silence. He tried again with how nice it was to be able to sew; what a nice change it was from having to go and be fitted at tailor shops. Lord, I sewed because my parents couldn't afford any really decent dresses, what with taking out a loan for my tuition. I said his blazer was nice, but he just looked startled. I tried to change the conversation to sports. Did he play any, I asked. Oh yes, he leaped at this, he hoped to get on the lacrosse team. "What the hell is lacrosse?" I asked myself. And he was rather good at cricket, he added. I felt hopelessly unable to say I didn't have a clue as to what he was talking about. But it wasn't so much a lack of courage on my part; we just had no common ground whatsoever. Nowadays I have the presence of self to treat such differences as interesting, and the upper-class person as somewhat provincial and sheltered not to realize that such cultural oddities are just that to the majority of the population. But not then. I was thoroughly intimidated and all I wanted to do was to get out of there, to get to a place where I could feel comfortable and sure of my signals, where everything I said wouldn't be misread, where the assumptions about me and my background would be the correct ones. At some point in the encounter I noticed the slow turning of Mack the Elite. He began to look at me as though I was slightly untouchable. I began to feel vermin-ridden. It was not a good feeling.

Mack the Elite was one of the few genuine stereotypes I met at Yale. I did meet many Yalies during my college years, but out of that number only a few fit the pure type. The others were those on scholarship, or those who had become steadies of upper-middle-class students at Albertus Magnus, or those who had some tie with organizations I belonged to: political clubs and the debating team. The pure types—the upper-class WASP's who had impeccable credentials, prepped at the best schools, had had money in the family for generations, were listed in the Social Register, and had dinner rights to all the other families in the elite circle—these I would meet by some fluke. One such fluke might be that their hometown sweethearts were taken ill and couldn't visit that weekend, so the guy ended up at a fraternity party or room party, or occasionally at one of the two or three mixers the college sponsored for us our first few years there. (Dick Cavett[3] labeled Albertus Magnus, along with the Nursing School and Hillhouse High, as "frontiers of desperation" for dateless Yalies, in his memoirs, a piece of snobbery most take for granted at Yale.) I watched with dismay as several of my friends got their hearts broken as it finally dawned on them that their great loves at Yale only saw them during the week and that big weekends were reserved for their serious attachments back home. "We're a geographical convenience, that's all we are," one of my friends used to chant.

Two of my commuter friends and I were almost tossed out of school one time for sending personal invitations to a mixer in the old stable at the college. We decided that the general invitation to the Thomas More Club was just not good enough. We went through the Yale Directory of the Class of '62 and picked out the most attractive looking Yalies we found and sent out forty or so invitations. Our Dean of Students was appalled. One of us got the penalty of stuffing envelopes for fifteen hours in the Alumnae Office for this misdeed and we were spared suspension. Through this mixer, though, I met another one of the genuine articles. He even belonged to a secret society, housed in one of those coffins of a building, vaguely Egyptian, with no windows; it looked like a huge mausoleum, a tomb covered with ivy. One rumor among us kids as we were growing up was that the building was entirely filled with water—a cubic swimming pool, we imagined, that rose three stories. We half expected to see a Pharoah emerge dressed in Harris tweed with a pipe clenched in his teeth, wearing royal headdress, and leading a sphinx on a chain. When I was a child my fantasy hodge-podge had little relationship to reality once I moved outside my neighborhood. My comic-book diet ran to *Archie, Casper the Friendly Ghost, Little Lulu, Superman,* and *Wonder Woman,* with an occasional horror diversion or true romance saga. I did not grow up reading those educational books middle-class uncles and aunts give for birthday and Christmas presents, books about pyramids, butterflies, how airplanes work, and where Japan, Egypt, and the Persian Gulf are. Remember, also, that I didn't grow up with television. I was almost adolescent before my parents were convinced TV wasn't a crazy thing to buy, and had saved up enough for a down payment. Up until then I watched television only occasionally at a friend's whose father worked as a delivery man for an appliance store and got a discount on a set. On Sunday nights we would sometimes visit acquaintances of my parents who had a rumpus room (that is, a cellar with linoleum) and would tune into Ted Mack's Amateur Hour.

It was very difficult growing up in the shadow of Yale, attending a school that was on the receiving end of its class bias but yet was so totally uncritical of Yale and all it represented. Yale had, of course, professional giants, and perhaps even a few geniuses. No doubt many of its people were free from class bias, but the image it projected was one of cultural imperialism, impressing the young Yalies with its sophistication and erudition. They tried frantically to fit the style, but those I met came off like a bad imitation: silly, bitchy, or just plain unfunny.

A friend recently called my attention to an article in *The New York Times Magazine* (February 1, 1976) on Yale's elitism. In fact, the subject of the article was not Yale, but Brown. Such is my ambivalence still that I thought, first, "How could anyone confuse Yale with Brown! Yale stands alone," and then, as I skimmed the actual article and read about the fashionably initialed luggage, the mutual checking out of one another that takes place as students return to classes in September, I remembered the old feelings of being poor, of being judged unworthy of respect because I didn't have all those things the others had: the tailored tweeds, the little leather clutch bags, the Pendleton plaids, or any of those things that were advertised in *The New Yorker*. (Ah, *The New Yorker!* They put in all those cartoons to keep working-class people from getting completely depressed over the insurmountable gap between their life style and that represented by the commodities pictured in its ads.)

The Brown article triggered those old feelings of envy, inadequacy, and outrage I had growing up next to Yale. Yale's style was so alien to us

that it was almost like having another country in the middle of town. New Haven felt like an occupied zone. From this vantage point it is easy to understand the hatred colonized people have toward the colonizer. It is also easy to understand how colonized people have to struggle with the problem of identifying with the colonizers. I and most of my friends went through stages where we felt that the Yale way was superior; that that way of dressing, talking, holding conversations, being witty, entertaining, relaxing—the whole works—was better than ours. We all, at one time or another, felt that we were inferior, of no use at all; that their oak-paneled life was the best this world had to offer.

What nonsense all this has become. But as a child riding past its old, expansive, and mysterious-looking buildings I would almost feel the sacredness emanating. And the ivy-covered walls! God, those were really there, just as in all those old songs and stories. The buildings seemed too fine for me, and I would get the same feeling for the entire building that I would get if I dreamed of being in the wrong upper-middle-class home facing its little tea tables, the linen napkins, the crystal and silver nut dishes and porcelain ashtrays, the muted pastels, oriental rugs, bud vases, silk and velvet upholstery, and petits fours on silver dessert trays. An after-dinner-mint wonderland. I felt out of place, the bull in the china shop, the screaming red in a world of pastel gentility. Yale was much more solid oak, vibrant earth tones, marble and gold, parchment and antiquity. Nonetheless, I felt the same way in both social circles.

When I was a child these Yale buildings looked like magic castles, but after living with a sacred object so long, it becomes taken for granted. But some took longer to fade into acceptance than others. Woolsey Hall for a long time looked like a magnificent Byzantine mosque to me. It had huge pillars lining the entranceway, ten or fifteen of them, tile mosaic floors, and a massive dome all gold and gleaming. Once or twice our College Glee Club performed there, and I remember going to an Erich Fromm[4] lecture there once. The fortress-like entrances to the residential colleges had archways, each with a coat of arms emblazoned on the top, through which one peeped into another magic world of ivy and brick and neat rectangles of grass. Most entrances had formidable looking iron gates. I always had the feeling I would be arrested the minute I set foot past the gate, even those times that I was escorted by a Yalie date, by the gatekeepers who lived in little stone cubicles just past the iron gates.

The out-of-town women, or those who looked affluent and self-confident, like a rich Nancy Drew,[5] always seemed to float past such barriers. After the scandal of the young girl in the college, I and my working-class friends were questioned thoroughly if we went to meet our dates unescorted. Not Nancy Drew, though. She got a smile and was waved on. Her tweed skirt, Gucci shoes, camel's hair coat and Yale-striped scarf, like the one we used to ooh and aah over at the Yale Co-op, assured her immediate entry anywhere on campus. Her spring uniform in the early 'sixties consisted of the Cos Cob look, straight from the pages of *The New Yorker:* tiny rosebud prints in pastel on cream-colored duck fabric, pastel cashmere cardigans, A-lines and Peter Pan collars, accented with circle pins and matching barrettes. The style has changed now (working-class Mary Hartman[6] is dressed this way in the 'seventies, appropriately), but the manner is consistently self-confident and unself-conscious. These women looked Yale, we didn't, even though the guards had never been given instructions that Pendleton, Gucci, J. Press, Abercrombie and Fitch, and Cos Cob were to be given first-class treatment. They just knew, just as the rest of the society learns that there are different social classes and that people are to be treated as befits their station. Never in these words, though. The lesson is always couched in such terms as someone's belonging to a "better class of people," as someone else's being "rough-cut" or "unpolished," or as being "riff-raff." No matter. When these terms are correlated with specific status possessions and life styles it is social classes that are being referred to. All this in a country that declares that we have no social classes. This blindness to the realities of class is not an affliction of the average citizen alone. The head of all research activities at one of the major television networks recently told me that America had no social-class system at all. Having come from a European country where class distinctions are blatant he found America classless by contrast. But this is rather like declaring that

the Northern United States is free of racism because its manifestations are not so obvious as they are in the South. So too it is with social class, except that few are willing to define the problem as one of class. It seems to be a difficult step to take to substitute the terms lower, middle and upper classes for the folksy terms in use now. For if the objective conditions of class are understood as tied to social fate, we could stop assuming that ineptness, self-consciousness, and lack of polish are random, and that polish is a sign of moral superiority. The polish or lack of polish results simply from being born into a particular family at a particular time in history. Simply that.   [1978]

Notes

1. LITTLE BOY BLUE: A reference to *Blue Boy,* a famous eighteenth-century portrait by Thomas Gainsborough of a young man in a satin suit with knee britches and a large feathered hat.

2. ELIZABETH RAY SCANDAL: When it became public that Representative Wayne Hays of Ohio put his mistress, Ray, who had no secretarial skills, on his payroll, Hays accused her of harassment and extortion and of trying to destroy his image and his career; while he didn't seek reelection, the lawsuit against him was dismissed at the request of the Justice Department.

3. DICK CAVETT: A humorist and television talk show host.

4. ERICH FROMM: A German-born American psychoanalyst.

5. NANCY DREW: Upper-middle-class teenage heroine of a mystery-novel series.

6. MARY HARTMAN: The lead character in a satirical television series.

Understanding the Reading

1. Why didn't Glennon's mother know much about Yale?
2. In what ways did Yale students cause problems for the townspeople?
3. What makes working-class jobs difficult?
4. Explain the relationship between Yale men and local working-class girls.
5. What were Glennon's experiences as a student at Albertus Magnus College like?

6. In what ways is the class distance between Glennon and the Yalie she met at the mixer revealed?
7. What values are implicit in phrases like "colonized people," "better class of people," and "unpolished"?

Suggestions for Responding

1. Compare the upper class as Glennon sees it with the way Bingham does.
2. Describe class differences you experienced when you were growing up. ✦

27

Who Are the Poor?

RUTH SIDEL

Of poor people in the United States today, the vast majority are women and their children. According to the Census Bureau, in 1984, 14.4 percent of all Americans—33.7 million people—lived below the poverty line. From 1980 to 1984 the number of poor people increased by 4-1/2 million. For female-headed households in 1984, the poverty rate was 34.5 percent, a rate five times that for married-couple families. The poverty rate for white female-headed families was 27.1 percent, for black female-headed families, 51.7 percent, and for Hispanic families headed by women, 53.4 percent. The poverty rate for the elderly, most of whom are women, was 12.4 percent in 1984. Two out of every three poor adults are women, and the economic status of families headed by women is declining.

The impact of women's poverty on the economic status of children is even more shocking. The poverty rate for children under six was under 24 percent in 1984; in other words, nearly one out of every four preschool children lived in poverty. In the same year the poverty rate for children living in female-headed households was 53.9 percent. Among black children, the poverty rate was 46.3 percent; among black children living in female-headed families, 66.6 percent. Among Hispanic children, 39.0 percent were

poor; among Hispanic children living in female-headed families, the poverty rate was 70.5 percent.

What are the factors that are responsible for this "feminization" of poverty? In an era in which so many gains have been made by so many women, in a country as rich as the United States, why do millions of women and their children live without adequate resources for food, clothing, and shelter? Before discussing these issues, let us first examine how poverty and the number of people living in poverty are officially determined.

In 1795, according to the records of economist Bruno Stein, a group of English magistrates decided that "a minimum income should be the cost of a gallon loaf of bread, multiplied by three, plus an allowance for each dependent." The poverty level today is set in much the say way. In 1963 Mollie Orshansky and her colleagues at the Society Security Administration set the "official" poverty line by using, according to Michael Harrington, a "minimal diet—just sufficient to hold body and soul together—as the base." Since U.S. Department of Agriculture studies in 1955 indicated that the average American family spent approximately one-third of its net income on food, Orshansky took a low-cost food budget prepared by the USDA, multiplied it by three, and came up with a "poverty line" for a family of four. And thus, the first U.S. poverty line was established in 1964 at $3,000.

Between 1965 and 1974, the cost of the USDA Economy Food Plan was used in determining the poverty line; since 1974, a new Thrifty Food Plan has been the standard. It is important to note, as one observer has stated, "The USDA does not consider the Thrifty Food Plan to be nutritionally adequate for lone-term use, a fact that is simply ignored in setting the poverty line." Today, the U.S. government poverty line still equals the cost of a Thrifty Food Plan for a family of four, multiplied by three, with adjustments for family size and for changes in the consumer price index. In 1984 the poverty line for a family of four was set at $10,609.

There is considerable controversy over this line. Many analysts feel that the number of people in dire need is underestimated because the poverty line is set too low and that it is virtually impossible for an urban family of four to meet their basic needs of food, clothing, and shelter on less than $11,000 per year. Others, most notably officials in the Reagan administration, believe that the number of poor people is exaggerated because noncash income, such as the value of food stamps, public housing, Medicare, and Medicaid, is not included when calculating the number of Americans living in poverty.

If we look closely at what the poverty line means for a family of four, we see that families at this level are indeed barely surviving. If, as the basis for calculation of the poverty line assumes, a family of four spends one-third of its income on food, a family living at the 1984 poverty level of $10,609 would have $3,536 per year for food and $7,073 for everything else. This would mean that family members would have $68.00 a week, or $2.43 per person per day, to spend on food. The remainder, $589.40 a month, would have to cover rent, utilities, transportation costs—including automobile maintenance—clothing, medical and dental bills, educational expenses, entertainment, and taxes. As one analyst has stated, "In the real world, individuals who live at or below the poverty line live poorly, and they do so absolutely; they have considerable and persistent difficulty getting enough to eat, finding adequate shelter (with heat and light), securing appropriate clothing, and obtaining medical care." Moreover, most poor families live well below the threshold of poverty. If an employed adult is paid the minimum wage of $3.35 an hour, he or she will only earn $6,968 a year, far below this line as well. Aid to Families with Dependent Children (AFDC) recipients are maintained far below the poverty line. In fact, in 1982, of all families living below the poverty line, the average poor family had a cash income of $6,477.

But beyond the statistics, what is the meaning of poverty in an affluent society? What does it mean to be poor in a country as rich as the United States? When we think of poverty in poor countries, we think of emaciated or swollen-bellied children starving to death in Ethiopia, people dying by the side of the road in prerevolutionary China, large families huddling together in the squatters' settlements that exist in most Latin American cities, children begging outside opulent tourist hotels in countries as dissimilar as India and Haiti.

But what are the images of poverty in America? Being poor in the United States surely means standing in line for food in soup kitchens; it means living in welfare hotels; it means a homeless woman sleeping in a doorway, her possessions all around her; it means television programs about families in winter with no heat. These images are stark and real. This is absolute poverty.

But there are other forms of poverty in affluent countries. What does it mean, to others not quite so desperate, to be "poor" in a society as wealthy as this one? What constitutes poverty when every few minutes television advertisements drum out versions of the "good life"— middle-class families in comfortable homes keeping in touch by calling one another long distance; a young couple celebrating the building of their new home by drinking high-priced, high-status beer; sleek cars, invariably accompanied by the sleek women? What does it mean to be poor when magnificent photography, knowing voice-overs, and music that triggers just the right emotions have conditioned us to believe that it is our birthright to own that car; to experience the joy that is supposed to come with the good life and a good beer; to be able to buy this season's hottest, newest jeans—and, of course, have the body to go into them? For, while we have created a never-ending demand for goods, we have also created a group of outsiders who can only watch and long to be part of that golden world.

Singer Tina Turner articulates the anger felt by some of these outsiders:

> *A Night In Television Wonderland*
> *Another Fairytale About Some Rich Bitch*
> *Lying By The Swimming Pool*
> *It's the Golden School*
> *Living's Easy When You Make The Rules . . .*
>
> *Try To Get On Board, You Find The Lock*
>   *Is On The Door*
> *Well, I Say "No Way . . .*
> *Don't Try To Keep Me Out Or There'll*
>   *Be Hell To Pay . . .*

It may be clear what poverty means in Biafra, but what does it mean to a family in Youngstown, Ohio, whose primary breadwinner has been unemployed for eighteen months; or to a mother who is trying, on the salary of a chambermaid in a Boston hotel, to raise her children? What does it mean to a battered wife in Maine who is afraid to leave her husband because she knows she cannot possibly support their children herself; or to an elderly widow in Tucson who does not receive enough from Social Security to get through the month? And what does poverty mean for all those parents who are just getting by but know their children are not getting their share of the American dream—are not getting adequate medical and dental care, are attending inferior schools, have no money for the extras that mean so much to children? What does it mean to be poor in a rich society?

"Absolute poverty" and "relative poverty" must be distinguished. Absolute poverty means living below the official poverty line; absolute poverty is not having money for adequate food, clothing, and shelter. But relative poverty is much more difficult to define. Is not having a telephone in this society relative poverty? Is not having a car in rural Vermont relative poverty? Is relative poverty not having the money to buy the kind of sneakers, or running shoes, as they are now called, every other twelve-year-old boy in the community is wearing? Is relative poverty not having the money to buy your fourteen-year-old daughter designer jeans? And in a society in which what we consume defines who and what we are, what does living outside mainstream America do to people? . . .

To be poor in America is to let America down—to let that Pepsi image down; to let the American dream down; to not do your share, carry your weight, lift up your corner of the flag. The poor, simply by being, are besmirching that sunlight-on-a-tree-lined-street America, that wheat-blowing-in-the-breeze America, that we-can-do-it-no-matter-what America. And they know it.

According to the Canadian Council on Social Development, the concept of relative poverty

defines poverty, or deprivation, in terms of whether a household has considerably less income than others. This method views low income as entirely relative to other incomes in the community. If surrounding incomes are generally high, then the poverty level will also be high. To do otherwise, to maintain serious income distortions, is to make some households "stand out" by their more frugal lifestyles and deny their members roughly the same opportunities that average- and higher-income households have. The relative income approach springs more from the principle of equity than it does from a concern to provide simply for the basic necessities of life.

In the 1980s we don't hear much about equity in relation to the poor. The Bureau of Labor Statistics calculates the minimum income necessary for a family of four to participate in life in the United States at a "lower level," an "intermediate level," and a "higher level." In 1981, the last year that this figure was calculated, the "lower" income level for an urban family of four was $15,323. In the same year the poverty line was $8,450 for a nonfarm family. It is clear that the poverty line is the demarcation of absolute poverty in the United States—even though many economists, sociologists, and social welfare experts question whether that figure is indeed adequate—and the Bureau of Labor Statistics's "lower level" figure is the demarcation of relative poverty. The family trying to survive at this lower level is "poor relative to the rest of the population" but still "only one emergency or one accident away from truly dire straits."

If the United States were to estimate poverty in relative terms, we would clearly have a far higher percentage of our population officially designated as poor. In any case, counting only cash income, the number of Americans officially living in poverty rose from 26.1 million in 1979 to 33.7 million in 1984, an increase of nearly 30 percent. In 1979, 11.7 percent of the U.S. population was classified as poor; in 1984, 14.4 percent were classified this way.

The number of Americans living in poverty had increased to 35.5 million, 15.3 percent of the population, in 1983. This rise in 1983 to the highest level since the early 1960s was in large part caused by the 1982–1983 recession, which produced a sharp increase in the number of unemployed Americans. Between 1983 and 1984 the poverty rate decreased almost one percentage point. While the number of female-headed families living in poverty declined somewhat between 1983 and 1984, the drop in the poverty rate in 1984 was due largely to white male workers returning to the labor force. Nearly three-fourths of the families who escaped poverty were male-headed white families. The 1984 reduction in poverty is surely a positive and welcome development, but it is clear that all groups are not benefiting equally from the economic recovery. Female-headed families and children, particularly nonwhite children, remain especially vulnerable to poverty.

Except for 1982 and 1983, the 1984 poverty rate is the highest Americans have suffered since 1966. Moreover, the gap between rich and poor was wider in 1984 than at any time since the Census Bureau began collecting these statistics in 1947. According to the Center on Budget and Policy Priorities, a Washington-based research and advocacy group, the poorest 40 percent of U.S. families received just 15.7 percent of the national income in 1984, again the lowest percentage since 1947. In contrast, the top 40 percent received 67.3 percent of the national income, the highest percentage ever recorded. The median income for families in the poorest 40 percent of the population was $470 *lower* in 1984 than in 1980; the median income for families in the most affluent 40 percent was $1,800 *higher* in 1984 than in 1980. Furthermore, the number of families who might be described as the "poorest of the poor," those with incomes below $5,000 a year, has increased 43 percent since the late 1970s.

Who are the 33.7 million people who remain poor? Many Americans have a stereotype of a "typical" poor person. The poor are commonly thought of as black, urban females who have been dependent on welfare for many years and whose children will, in all likelihood, also be dependent on welfare. Many aspects of this stereotype are false. The poor, particularly the adult poor, are indeed typically female, and the majority are urban, because our society is overwhelmingly urban; but what is often not recognized [according to Greg Duncan] is that "persistent poverty falls disproportionately on . . . those living in rural areas and in the South." The other components, rooted in racism, in misinformation, and in an ideology that seeks to cast the poor in the least favorable light in order to justify our often heartless treatment of them, are far from the truth.

First, it must be stated that the poor are overwhelmingly white. Approximately four-fifths of all Americans are white; consequently, the ma-

jority of the poor, approximately two-thirds, are white. It is indeed true, however, that a far larger percentage of nonwhites are poor than are whites. For example, in 1984, 11.5 percent of whites were poor, while 28.4 percent of Hispanics and 33.8 percent of blacks were officially designated as poor.

Perhaps the most deeply rooted stereotype, however, is that the poor today are a different breed from the rest of us and from the poor of earlier generations. It is commonly thought that those who were poor when they first emigrated to this country eventually worked their way out of poverty into the working class or even beyond. Popular notions about the poor today are that they are a little-changing group caught in a never-ending cycle of poverty, early childbearing, inadequate job skills, and hopelessness. While this characterization is true for many poor people, it is not a valid description of the majority of poor Americans.

According to a recent study conducted by the Survey Research Center of the University of Michigan, "an astonishing amount of turnover takes place in the low income population." This study, conducted over a ten-year period, found that "only a little over one-half of the individuals living in poverty in one year are found to be poor in the next, and considerably less than one-half of those who experience poverty remain persistently poor over many years." The researchers found that only 2.6 percent of the population could be called "persistently poor" over the ten-year period from 1968 to 1978—*persistent poverty* was defined as being poor eight of the ten years. This means that among the poor who in 1978 made up approximately 12 percent of the population, only 2.6 percent had been poor during the previous decade.

Who are the "persistent poor"? One-third are elderly; approximately one-third are rural, and rural poverty seems to be "much more persistent than is urban poverty." And, overall, "The persistently poor are heavily concentrated into two overlapping groups: black households and female-headed households."

And who are the "temporarily poor"? This question becomes extremely important since the number of people who are only intermittently poor is substantial and the number who are persistently poor is considerably smaller. According to Greg Duncan, the author of the Michigan report, "*The temporarily poor do not appear to be very different from the population as a whole, appearing to differ from nonpoor families only in that they have one or two bad years.* [Italics mine.]" The study found that the demographic characteristics of the temporarily poor are much more similar to those of the population as a whole than to those of the persistently poor. . . .

While the Michigan report confirms that blacks, the elderly, women, and children are at greatest risk of poverty, it disputes the commonly held idea that if the poor had more positive attitudes, they would climb out of poverty much more rapidly. These findings are extremely important, not only for our understanding of the issue of poverty in America but also for the formulation of a social policy that will effectively meet the needs of the poor. But, first, why do women and children make up the overwhelming majority of poor people today?

The feminization of poverty, a phrase originally coined by sociologist Diana Pearce, has been caused over the past fifteen years by a convergence of several social and economic factors. These include the weakening of the traditional nuclear family; the rapid growth of female-headed families; the continuing existence of a dual-labor market that actively discriminates against female workers; a welfare system that seeks to maintain its recipients below the poverty line; the time-consuming yet unpaid domestic responsibilities of women, particularly child care; and an administration in power in Washington that is systematically dismantling or reducing funds for programs that serve those who are most in need. Broader social, political, and economic aspects of life in the United States in the waning days of the twentieth century, such as unemployment; continuing discrimination on the basis of race, class, and age; and the changing nature of the economy also contribute to the increasing impoverishment of women and children. One additional factor that must be mentioned, and will be discussed at a later point in some detail, is the continuing notion on the part of women that they will someday be taken care of by a man, that they do not really need to prepare themselves to be fully independent. This lingering remnant of another era is really an example of "culture lag," an idea, a set of beliefs that has lasted long

after the conditions that produced them have changed dramatically. This core of dependency is, of course, fostered by almost all the social institutions of our culture, so that breaking out of the traditional role becomes extremely difficult.

What is particularly disturbing about poverty in the United States over the past twenty years [1965–1985] is that there have been two simultaneous trends: The percentage of Americans who are poor has decreased, only to rise again during the Reagan administration, and the percentage of poor women and children has sharply increased. This means that as Americans as a whole were moving out of poverty, women and children were moving in.

Beginning in the 1960s the proportion of the population that was defined as poor decreased markedly. The poverty rate for male-headed families, however, declined much more sharply than for female-headed families. In addition, the number of female-headed families increased significantly. As a result, by 1981 the number of persons in poor families headed by women *increased* 54 percent, in contrast with the nearly 50 percent *decrease* in the number of persons in poor families headed by white men. Due to economic conditions, starting in the late 1970s the poverty rate among two-parent families began to climb rapidly once again, but female-headed families are still five times more likely to be poor than two-parent families.

In families headed by minority women, the statistics are even more disturbing. Data for Hispanics, available only since 1972, indicate that between 1972 and 1981 the number of poor Hispanics living in female-headed families doubled; between 1959 and 1981 the number of blacks living in poor, female-headed families more than doubled as well. As a recent report of the United States Commission on Civil Rights stated, "As a group, female-headed households are sheltering an increasing percentage of poor persons, and this trend shows no signs of abating."

One of the significant social phenomena of the 1970s and the early 1980s was the proliferation of female-headed families. Between 1970 and 1984 the number of families maintained by women mushroomed from 5.5 million in 1970 to 9.9 million in 1984, an increase of 80 percent. In 1984 single-parent families, 89 percent of which were headed by women, accounted for 26 percent of all families with children under 18. Women who headed families in 1970 were likely to be older women who had been widowed and had grown children who could provide some financial support; women heading families in the 1980s are far more likely to be several years younger, to have never married or to be divorced, and to have young children whom they need to support. Why did the number of female-headed families grow so dramatically during the 1970s?

According to the Michigan study, the "single most important factor accounting for changes in family well-being was a fundamental change in family structure: divorce, death, marriage, birth, or a child leaving home." The study indicates that women are far more affected by changes in family composition than men; it shows, furthermore, that women who remain married show improved economic status while women who divorce show a significant decline.

Over the past fifteen years, the divorce rate has soared. Nearly one out of every two marriages in the United States now ends in divorce, and the figures are even higher for teenage marriages. Between 1970 and 1981 the divorce rate more than doubled; the rate may be leveling off, however, for since 1981 it has declined for three consecutive years.

The impact of family disruption on the well-being of children is clear. Children who live in families that are disrupted by divorce or separation experience "severe drops in economic well-being. . . .":

> These children . . . carried a disproportionately large burden of economic misfortune, mirroring and magnifying the . . . devastating economic effects of divorce or separation on the mothers with whom they usually lived. The situations of these children are striking evidence of the far-reaching, unsolved economic problems posed by family disruption.

Furthermore, having and keeping a child outside of marriage has become far more acceptable during this period. During the 1970s families headed by never-married mothers climbed to 3.4 million, an increase of 356 percent. In 1983, almost 70 percent of families headed by never-married mothers were poor.   [1986]

Understanding the Reading

1. How are poverty and the number of people living in poverty determined?
2. What is "absolute poverty"?
3. Explain what Sidel means by "relative poverty."
4. What are the stereotypes of the poor, and how are they incorrect?
5. What does "persistent poverty" mean?
6. Why does someone become "temporarily poor"?
7. What are the causes of the "feminization of poverty"?

Suggestions for Responding

1. Sidel defines four kinds of poverty: absolute, relative, persistent, and temporary. Describe what life in one of these categories is like, and what can or should be done to help such people.
2. How does either Soto's or Glennon's essay illustrate Sidel's concept of "relative poverty"? ◆

28

Nilda at the Welfare Office

NICHOLASA MOHR

LATE NOVEMBER, 1941

Nilda looked at the big round clock on the wall facing the rows of benches in the large rectangular waiting room. They had left the apartment early that morning, taking the bus downtown to be at the Welfare Department by nine A.M., and it was now a quarter past eleven. The hands on the clock looked so still, as if they were never going to move on to the next number. She concentrated on the red second hand that jumped sporadically from black dot to black dot until it finally reached a number. Shutting her eyes, Nilda would open them quickly, hoping to catch the red second hand in action. At the beginning, she had lost almost every time, but after a while she was able to catch the second hand just as it landed on a dot. She began to figure out just how long it took the second hand to reach the next number, thereby causing the large black hand to move ever so slightly. The game was beginning to bore her and she lost interest. She leaned against her mother, who was shifting her weight from side to side, trying to find a more comfortable position on the hard bench.

"Mami," Nilda whispered, nudging her mother. "I'm tired. How much longer we gonna be?"

"Be still, Nilda," her mother answered quietly.

"I'm thirsty. Can I get another drink of water?"

"You been up to get water at least five times. Just be still; they'll call us soon. Everybody here is also waiting. You are not the only one that's tired, you know." Her voice was almost a whisper, but Nilda knew she was annoyed. Nilda hated to come to places like this where she felt she had to wait forever. It's always the same, she thought, wait, wait, wait! She remembered the long wait they'd had at the clinic last time. It was over five hours.

"Stop leaning on me, Nilda; you are not a baby. Ya basta! Sit up and be still!" This time her mother had turned to look at her and she knew she had better be still.

The only good thing is that I don't have to go to school, she thought. Her mother would give her an excuse note tomorrow, so she did not have to worry.

Nilda looked around the large room again; each long row of benches was filled with people sitting silently. There were no other children her age. Now and then someone new came in from the outside, walked up to the front desk and handed the clerk a card, then sat down on a bench, joining the silent group.

She looked at the grey-green walls: except for two posters, placed a few feet apart, and the big round clock, the walls were bare. She began to study the posters again; she knew them almost by heart. They were full of instructions. The one nearest Nilda had a lifelike drawing of a young, smiling white woman, showing how well she was dressed when she went to look for employment. The reader was carefully informed about proper clothing, using this figure as the perfect model. Her brown hat sat on her short brown hair. Her smiling face had been scrubbed clean, her white teeth brushed, and she wore very little makeup. Her brown suit was clean and her skirt was just about six inches below the knee. She

carried a brown handbag, wore clean gloves and nicely polished shoes as she strolled along a tree-lined street, confident about her interview. She sure looks happy, thought Nilda. She must be a teacher or something like that.

The second poster was a large faded color photograph of a proper breakfast. The photograph showed fresh oranges, cereal, milk, a bowl of sugar, a plate of bacon and eggs, toast with butter and jelly. The reader was warned that it was not good to leave the house without having had such a breakfast first. Looking at the food, Nilda began to remember that she was hungry. She had eaten her usual breakfast of coffee with boiled milk, sugar, and a roll. It seemed to her that she had eaten a long, long time ago, and her stomach annoyed her when she looked at the bacon and eggs. I hope they call us soon, she said to herself.

The lady clerk at the front desk looked up and read a name aloud from a card. "Mrs. Lydia Ramírez," she called out.

"Come on," her mother said as she stood up and walked past the benches full of waiting people. Nilda followed her up to the front.

The lady clerk pointed and said, "Into the next room. You will see Miss Heinz." She then handed her mother a card. Nilda walked with her mother into another large room lined with rows of desks. A woman, seated at a desk across the room, raised her arm and waved to them.

"Over here, please." They walked quickly up to the woman and waited. The social worker, without lifting her head, pointed to the empty chair at the side of her desk. Her mother sat down. The woman continued to write something on a form sheet. Nilda stood next to her mother and looked down at the social worker as she went on writing. Her head was bent over and Nilda could see that her hair was very white and fine, with tiny waves and ringlets neatly arranged under a thin grey hair net. The tiny grey hairpins, which were carefully placed to hold each little lump of ringlets together, were barely visible. Her pink scalp shone through the sparse hair. Nilda had never seen such a brilliant pink scalp before. I wonder what would happen if I touched her head, she thought; maybe it would burn my finger. Finally, after a while, the woman lifted her head, nodded, and, still holding the pencil she had been writing with, asked, "Mrs. Lydia Ramírez?" Before her mother could answer, the social worker turned to Nilda and said, "My name is Miss Heinz. Does your mother understand or speak English?" Nilda turned to her mother with a look of confusion.

"I speak English," her mother replied quickly. "Maybe not so good, but I manage to get by all right."

"Let me have your card, please," Miss Heinz said, holding out her hand. Nilda's mother bent forward and gave Miss Heinz the card she had been holding. "Well, that's a help. At least you can speak English. But then," pointing to Nilda she continued, "why is she here? Why isn't she in school? This is a school day, isn't it?"

Nilda could see her mother turning red. Her mother never liked to go to these places alone; she always brought Nilda with her. Ever since Nilda could remember, she had always tagged along with her mother.

"She wasn't feeling too well so I kept her with me. She goes to school of course," her mother said. Surprised, Nilda looked at her mother. She had not been sick at all.

"Well, she should be home in bed, not here! Or are you alone?"

"No, I am not alone," her mother bit her lips and went on, "but there was no one at home this morning." Nilda knew Aunt Delia was home with her stepfather, and so were Sophie and the baby. Pausing, her mother went on, "My husband is resting; he is sick. So, I just thought—"

"This is not going to do her any good," interrupted Miss Heinz. Looking at Nilda, she asked, "What's wrong with you?" Nilda looked at her mother wide-eyed.

"She had an upset stomach," her mother answered.

Miss Heinz, blinking her eyes, heaved a sigh and picked up a folder with the name *Ramírez, Lydia*. "Now let's get on with this. I'm way behind schedule as it is, you know. Plenty of other people to see. Mrs. Ramírez, you have one married son and four children in school, three boys and a daughter. Your husband suffered two heart attacks, his second leaving him incapacitated, and you want us to give you public assistance. Am I correct?"

"Yes," her mother said in a voice barely audible. "He can't work no more."

"Well, then, we'll have to ask you some questions. Now, are you legally married?"

"Yes."

"How long? I see that your boys have a different last name. They are named Ortega."

"I been married twelve years." Her mother wet her lips.

"Were you legally married the first time and, if so, are you a widow or a divorcée?"

"Divorce."

"In Puerto Rico or in this country?"

"I married in Puerto Rico, but I got divorced here."

"That was twelve years ago? Then is this your second husband's child?"

Her mother sat up straight and answered, "Yes." Nilda glanced at her mother. Surprised and confused, she knew that she had been almost three years old when her mother married her stepfather.

"Your oldest son, Victor, can he help out?"

"He goes to high school, but he gets something after, like a delivery boy sometimes, and he gives us what he can."

"You also have an aunt living with you. Does she help?"

"No, she's an older woman and she has a relief check, but it's very little, and she can only spare for food and medicine. You see, she's also hard of hearing and—"

"O.K.," she interrupted. "How is your health, Mrs. Ramírez?"

"I'm fine. O.K."

"Can't you find some employment?"

"I got a lot of people to care for and small children I cannot leave."

Nilda realized that she was tired of standing. Looking at the woman, Nilda saw her write something each time she asked another question. Her fine grey mesh hair net came down over her forehead and stopped abruptly at the spot where her eyebrows should be. Nilda carefully strained her eyes, focusing on that spot, looking for her eyebrows, but the woman didn't seem to have any. Her skin was very pink, with a variety of brownish freckles that traveled on her hands, arms, and neck, giving her skin the look of a discolored fabric. She wore a light beige dress with a starched white collar. On her right hand she wore a silver wristwatch and two silver rings. Nilda thought, She looks tightly sealed up. Like a package, only you can't see the wrapping because it's like see-through cellophane.

"How many rooms in your apartment?"

"We got six rooms." They went on talking

and Nilda felt her legs getting heavy under her and a sleepiness begin to overtake her.

"Let me see your hands! Wake up, young lady! Let me see your hands!" Startled, Nilda saw that Miss Heinz was speaking to her. Extending her arms and spreading out her fingers, she showed the woman her palms.

"Turn your hands over. Over, turn them over. Let me see your nails." Nilda slowly turned over her hands. "You have got filthy nails. Look at that, Mrs. Ramírez. She's how old? Ten years old? Filthy." Impulsively, Nilda quickly pushed her hands behind her back and looked down at the floor.

"Why don't you clean your nails, young lady?" Nilda kept silent. "How often do you bathe?" Still silent, Nilda looked at her mother. She wanted to tell her to make the woman stop, but she saw that her mother was not looking her way; instead she was staring straight ahead.

"Cat got your tongue?" Miss Heinz asked. "Why doesn't she answer me, Mrs. Ramírez?"

Without turning her head, her mother said, "Nilda, answer the lady."

"I take a bath when I need it! And I clean my nails whenever I feel like it!" Nilda exploded in a loud voice.

"No need to be impertinent and show your bad manners, young lady."

"Nilda!" Her mother turned around and looked at her. "Don't be fresh! Stop it!" Looking at Miss Heinz she said, "I'm sorry."

"That's quite all right, Mrs. Ramírez, I understand. Children today are not what they used to be. Young lady, you are no help to your mother. I hope you're proud of yourself."

Bending over, Miss Heinz moved her head, shaking the lumps of ringlets as she opened the center drawer of her desk. She searched around, moving paper clips, pencils, index cards wrapped in a rubber band, and finally pulled out a small shiny metal nail file. Holding it up in front of Nilda, she said, "Now Miss, this is for you. I want you to take this home with you so that you have no more excuse for dirty nails. This," and she shook the small shiny silver file, "is a nail file Have you ever seen one before?"

Still sulking, Nilda answered, "Yes, I know what it is."

"Good! Here, you may take it," she said, smiling as she handed the nail file to Nilda, who did not move.

"Take it!" her mother said. Nilda reached over and took the metal file. Miss Heinz looked at Nilda, who said nothing. "Nilda! What do you say?" her mother asked.

"Thank you," Nilda said in an irritated tone.

Miss Heinz turned away and, closing the folder, she said, "Before we can make any definite decision, we will have to have an investigator come out to your home for a visit. Since you have had public assistance before, you know the procedure I'm sure. It will take a little while, but we will let you know."

"Good-bye, Miss Heinz, and thank you very much."

"Not at all. Good-bye now," and she bent over her desk again. Nilda and her mother walked out of the room and out of the building.

Walking alongside her mother, Nilda could feel the cold sharp air of winter. She held the shiny cold metal nail file in her hand. That mean old witch, she thought. And Mama, she's mean too. Nilda felt her mother put her arm around her and she pulled away.

"What's the matter? You got a problem maybe, Nilda?"

"I don't have an upset stomach, Mama. Why did you let her talk like that to me? Why didn't you stop her?" Nilda felt the angry tears beginning to come down her face. "You should have done something. You don't care anything about me. You don't care."

"Nilda, stop it! I had to say what I did, that's all. I have to do what I do. How do you think we're gonna eat? We have no money, Nilda. If I make that woman angry, God knows what she'll put down on the application. We have to have that money in order to live."

"I don't care. I don't care at all!" Nilda screamed. Without warning, she felt a sharp pain going across the left side of her face, followed by a stinging feeling. Her mother was in front of her, looking at her furiously.

"I'll slap you again, only harder, if you don't shut up." Nilda began to cry quietly. They walked along silently to the bus stop.

Still holding the nail file, Nilda thought about Miss Heinz. Oh how I hate her. She's horrible, she said to herself. I would like to stick her with this stupid nail file, that's what. When no one was looking I would sneak up behind her and stick her with the nail file. Then she would begin to die. No blood would come out because she hasn't any. But just like that . . . poof! She would begin to empty out into a large mess of cellophane. Everybody in that big office would be looking for her. "Oh, where is Miss Heinz?" they would all say. They would be searching for her all over. Poor Miss Heinz. Oh, poor Miss Heinz. First her eyebrows disappeared. Did you know that? She had no eyebrows. And now she's all gone. Disappeared, just like that! Poor thing. My, what a pity.

The bus pulled up. As Nilda climbed inside she felt the nail file slipping between her fingers and heard a faint clink when it hit the pavement.
[1973]

Understanding the Reading

1. Why does Nilda's mother lie to the social worker?
2. Why is Nilda so interested in the social worker's appearance?
3. Why does the social worker give Nilda the nail file?
4. What underlying realities of the system does Nilda's revenge fantasy reveal?
5. What humiliations are built into the welfare system Mohr describes?
6. Why does Nilda throw away the nail file?

Suggestions for Responding

1. Which category of poverty that Sidel identifies best describes the Ramírez family? In what ways do they fit that description, and in what ways do they differ from it?
2. Describe a situation in your childhood when you felt betrayed by one of your parents, or when you felt publicly humiliated. ✦

29

"We're Not Bums"

PETER SWET

For more than three years, Gerald Winterlin, now in his 40s, was one of the estimated 3 million homeless Americans. Forced by joblessness to live in his car or abandoned buildings, he had to cope with a sense of hopelessness and despair that could, and occasionally did, destroy others like himself.

Now he lives in a warm, modest apartment near the University of Iowa, where he's a scholarship student working on his degree in accounting and maintaining a 3.9 average. I traveled to Iowa to speak with him, hoping to understand how this bright, well-spoken, typical-seeming American could ever have hit such a deep low in his life. Just as important, I wanted to know how he fought his way back.

On the first of two long nights we would spend talking together, the burly Winterlin sat at his kitchen table and recalled an incident that still haunts him.

"I was on the cashier's line at a supermarket," he began, "behind this young, healthy-looking black woman. When her groceries were rung up, she pulled out a bunch of food stamps. I said, 'Hey, get a job. I'm tired of having money taken from my paycheck for people like you!' I expected a sharp answer, but instead she looked embarrassed and said, 'There's nothing I'd like better than a job, but nobody will give me one.' 'Bull,' I shot back, then turned away. Twenty years later, I'd love to find that lady and tell her I'm sorry. Little did I realize that what happened to her could happen to anyone. It happened to me."

Winterlin was born in an area known as the Quad Cities, encompassing Davenport and Bettendorf on the Iowa side of the Mississippi River, with Rock Island and Moline on the Illinois side. One of four children of a tool-and-die man, he graduated from Bettendorf High and eventually began work at the International Harvester plant. "I worked there about eight years," he said, "till '82, after the farm recession hit. Quad Cities is a world center for manufacturing farm equipment, and over 18,000 people, including me, were laid off."

"At first we figured the government would help," he said, adjusting his large framed glasses. "Hell, they bailed out Chrysler, right? But, instead, weeks turned into months with no work. With only two or three weeks of unemployment left, my demands dropped real fast, from $15 an hour to begging to sweep floors—anything. One day I just picked up the phone book and started with the A's. I made a list of every company I applied to. The final number was 380, and I remember realizing that what few jobs there were went to younger people. Still, I'd go out all day looking."

Winterlin heaved a deep sigh and glanced out the window at the cold Iowa night. "I kept thinking there'd be a tomorrow. Late one night, I finally said, 'Well, Gerry, this is it. No tomorrow.' I packed what I hadn't already sold or pawned and walked out. I never planned on living in my car for long," he added, "but then, no one *plans* to be homeless."

What about his family—couldn't they help? "They'd have probably taken me in," he said, "but people who ask that don't understand how impossible it is to say, 'Hey, folks, here I am in my late 30s, such a pathetic loser I can't even take care of myself.' Besides, my old man had lost his own job after 25 years, just six months shy of a full pension."

I asked about welfare, and Winterlin laughed. "Don't get me started on that," he said. "Welfare is the fast route to nowhere. They give you everything except what you need—a job. Some people have no option, like women with kids, but guys like me who want just enough to get started again would rather freeze than fall into a system that gives you a roof but robs you of hope. You trade your individualism and spirit for survival, and for some of us that's not a fair trade. Homeless people are proud people too."

For months, Winterlin lived in his '60 Mercury with rags stuck in the rust holes. Finally, the car died, and he was forced to find shelter wherever he could. "Somehow I made it from day to day," he said. "I tried to look as good as I could, to keep clean. Sometimes I did odd jobs, but never enough to put a roof over my head. I kept trying, but before I knew it, three years of my life were gone."

"Unless you've been there, you can't understand the loneliness, the misery, the humiliation, the self-disgust at what you've been reduced to," Winterlin continued. "I knew guys who just couldn't take it anymore and did themselves in. We're talking big, proud men, not junkies or drunks. They killed themselves, but I say they died of broken hearts because they couldn't handle the way people look at you, the loss of self-respect."

We both fell silent for a moment, then I asked how he had managed to persevere. "When times got darkest," Winterlin answered, "when thoughts of death and feelings of hatred began to overwhelm me, I thought of the people in my life who have known how to give, not just take. One of them was Linda, the girl I should have married. I wish I could name all the others, but the good people know who they are. It's for them that I wanted to succeed."

"Anyway," he added, "I read about something called the Dislocated Workers Program, which was designed to help people from old, dying industries become trained in new technologies. They put me into Scott Community College in the Quad Cities. I got straight A's. Everything looked great, then the program was cut back after six months. I almost fell apart, but because my grades were so good a woman named Mary Teague took the time to care, to help me piece together enough funding to keep going."

I noted the framed scholarship certificates displayed proudly on the wall, and Winterlin smiled, putting a hand up to conceal the spaces where he'd once been forced to pull his own teeth. "No big secret to that," he laughed. "Just plain hard work." He studies 50 hours a week, besides attending classes and working 20 hours at a part-time job. He has no friends, he admitted, and spends weekends alone. "I know it wasn't my fault, but when you're homeless you lose so much self-respect, you stay away from people." I asked if he felt his fellow Americans understood the homeless problem.

"The thing most people *don't* understand," he replied, "is that most of the folks you see huddled in doorways in Eastern cities or living in parks in Santa Monica or begging for a roof right here in America's Heartland aren't there by *choice*. I didn't ask to lose my job. None of us did. We're not bums," he said pointedly, his voice rising. "We're good, hardworking Americans who happened to fall between the cracks."

How does he see his future? He hopes that, after receiving his degree, "at least one person out there will say, 'Hey, I hire a person by what he's got, not by his age or where he has been.'" He added, "I've got to prove I can be part of society again, that Gerald Winterlin and the millions of other homeless out there really do count. There are just five words I'm determined to leave behind me—words that no one can ever, ever take away from me. The words are 'Gerald Winterlin, summa cum laude.'" [1990]

Understanding the Reading

1. What beliefs underlie Winterlin's confrontation with the woman in the supermarket?
2. How did Winterlin initially respond to unemployment?
3. Why didn't he turn to his family for help or go on welfare?
4. Why do some homeless men commit suicide?
5. Why may Winterlin escape his homelessness permanently? What obstacles does he face?

Suggestions for Responding

1. Winterlin says that the welfare system "robs you of hope." In what ways does Mohr's story illustrate this point?
2. Imagine that you, like Winterlin, were suddenly made homeless due to unemployment. Describe the difficulties you would face, especially the obstacles to your pulling yourself out of it on your own. ✦

30

Institutionalized Discrimination

ROBERT CHERRY

Individuals and institutions may use decision-making procedures that inadvertently discriminate and reinforce inequalities. For example, income differentials can cause unequal access to education even though the school system does not intend to discriminate; locational decisions of firms may have the unintended impact of reducing access to jobs. Similarly, when housing is segregated by income (race), all individuals do not have equal access to job information, as higher-income (white) households will tend to have greater access to job information through personal contacts than lower-income (black) households. Thus, employers will have more higher-income white applicants than if housing was distributed without regard to race or income. Also, employers attempting to reduce their screening costs might rely on group stereotypes rather than more individualized information when deciding which applicants to interview.

In none of these instances is discrimination consciously undertaken, but disadvantaged groups, having unequal access to education, job information, and the interviewing process, are nonetheless harmed. Though unintentional, these problems reinforce the "vicious cycle" of poverty.

INCOME DIFFERENTIALS AND EDUCATIONAL ATTAINMENT

Income constraints place heavy burdens on the allocation decisions of low-income households. Often they must "choose" to do without many necessities, such as education. In addition, children from low-income households often have explicit household responsibilities that take time away from school activities. This may involve responsibility for household activities (baby-sitting, shopping, and so on) or earning income. In either case, economists would argue that on average low-income students have a greater opportunity cost[1] on their time than high-income students. Since their opportunity costs are greater, lower-income students rationally allocate less time to studying and school-related activities than equally motivated higher-income students.

At the college level, even the availability of low-cost public institutions does not necessarily equalize the economic cost of education to all students. Just as at the elementary and secondary school level, lower-income students have a greater opportunity cost on their time than comparable higher-income students. Even if family responsibilities are negligible, students still require income for their own support. This invariably requires lower-income students to work at least part-time while attending school and has often led to the sending of male but not female offspring to college.

The level of income required is influenced by whether the student can live at home while attending college. Historically, public colleges were located in rural areas. For example, none of the original campuses of the Big Ten or Big Eight colleges are located in the states' largest metropolitan areas. The original campus of the University of Illinois is not located in Chicago and the University of Missouri is not located in St. Louis or Kansas City. Thus, not only did lower-income students have to pay for room and board away from home, but it was usually difficult to find part-time employment in these rural communities. This implies that even the availability of low-cost public colleges did not necessarily place the lower-income student on an equal footing with more prosperous students.

Theoretically, low-income youths with appropriate abilities and motivation should be able to borrow money to finance their education. As long as the economic returns from schooling are greater than the interest rate, students will gain from borrowing rather than forgoing additional education. The equalizing of economic costs can occur only if all students of equal promise can borrow at the same rates. Financial institutions, however, cannot accept expectations or probabilities of future income as sufficient collateral for loans. They require bank accounts or other tradable assets, which are normally held by upper-income but not lower-income households. Thus, students from lower-income households cannot borrow readily for education without government intervention.

It also appears that schools in poorer neighborhoods tend to have larger classes and weaker teachers. John Owen found that within the same city, as the mean neighborhood income rose by 1 percent, class size decreased by 0.24 percent and the verbal ability of teachers rose by 0.11 percent. This inequality is even more glaring when comparisons are made between cities. Owen found that for each 1 percent increase in the mean income of a city, there was a rise of 0.73 percent in real expenditures per student and a 1.20 percent increase in the verbal ability of teachers. Thus, students living in poorer neighborhoods in poorer cities have a double disadvantage.

If higher opportunity costs and lower-quality education were not sufficient to discourage educational attainment, Bennett Harrison found that for black inner-city youths, incomes are hardly affected by increases in educational attainment. He notes, "[A]s their education increases, blacks move into new occupations, but their earnings are hardly affected at all by anything short of a college degree, and there is no effect whatever on their chances of finding themselves without a job over the course of the year." Thus, independent of conscious discrimination by the educational system, we should expect low-income minority youths to have lower educational attain-

ment than white youths, even when ability and motivation are held constant.

During the 1970s, a number of policies were implemented in an attempt to compensate for the influence of family income on educational attainment. First, legislatures began funding state universities in larger urban areas. Second, court rulings forced states to change funding formulas so that per capita funding from wealthy and poor communities within each state would become more equal. Third, guaranteed student loans reduced the disadvantage low-income students faced when attempting to finance their education.

DIFFERENTIAL IMPACT OF INCOMPLETE INFORMATION

In the most simplified labor models, it is assumed that workers and firms act with complete information: Workers know the jobs that are available, and firms know the productivity of job seekers. In this situation, competitive firms would hire the best applicants for the jobs available, and workers would gain the maximum wage obtainable.

Economists have recently developed models in which information has a price; it is only "purchased" up to the point at which its benefits are at least as great as its costs. Neither firms nor workers rationally attempt to gain complete information concerning the labor market opportunities available. Workers find that some additional job information is not worth its cost, while firms find that some information on the productivity of applicants is not worth the additional personnel expenses. Liberals have argued that when workers and firms rationally decide to act on the basis of optimal rather than complete information, biases are generated.

Let us begin by analyzing how firms decide the optimal productivity information they should obtain. A firm benefits from additional productivity information if it translates into hiring a more profitable work force. A firm must weigh this increased profitability against the cost involved in seeking the additional information. After some point, it is likely that the benefits from additional information are insufficient to outweigh its cost. Even though the firm realizes additional information would probably result in hiring a somewhat more productive worker than otherwise, it knows that the added screening expenses would be even greater.

When a strong profit motive and wide productivity differentials among applicants are present, extensive screening will occur. This is the case with professional sports teams, especially since television revenues have transformed ownership from a hobby to a profit-making activity. Liberals believe, however, that in the vast majority of situations, productivity differentials among applicants are quite small and benefits from extensive screening are minimal.

Liberals suggest that the initial screening of applicants is often done with very little individual productivity information available. For firms with a large number of relatively equally qualified applicants, there is no reason to spend much time determining which applicants should be interviewed. These firms simply take a few minutes (seconds) to look over applications and select a promising group to interview. The employer realizes that such a superficial procedure will undoubtedly eliminate some job applicants who are slightly more productive than those selected for interviews. Since productivity differentials are perceived to be minor, however, this loss is not sufficient to warrant a more extensive (expensive) screening procedure.

There would be no discrimination if the job applicants victimized were random, but let us see why the screening method might cause the consistent victimization of individuals from disadvantaged groups. Suppose a firm considering college graduates for trainee positions decides that it has many equally qualified candidates. Looking at résumés, the firm can quickly identify each applicant's race, sex, and college attended. If the firm has enough applicants from better colleges, it is likely to say, "All things being equal, students from these colleges are likely to be more qualified than applicants who attended weaker colleges." Thus, the firm dismisses applicants from the weaker colleges, even though it realizes that weaker schools produce some qualified applicants. The firm has nothing against qualified graduates of weaker colleges. It simply reasons that the extra effort required to identify them is not worth the expense.

However unintentional, highly qualified graduates from weaker schools are discriminated against. Discrimination occurs because this screening method determines the selection for interviews on the basis of group characteristics rather than individual information. More generally, highly qualified applicants from any group that is perceived to have below-average productivity would be discriminated against by this superficial screening method.

Suppose employers believe that black and female applicants are typically less productive than their white male counterparts. If the firm has sufficient white male applicants, it will not interview black or female applicants. The firm will decide that although there are some black and female applicants who are slightly more productive than some white male applicants, it is not worth the added expense to identify them. The process by which individuals are discriminated against when firms use group characteristics to screen individuals is usually called statistical discrimination.

Statistical discrimination can occur indirectly. A firm hiring workers for on-the-job training may be primarily interested in selecting applicants who will stay an extended period of time. The firm does not want to invest training in individuals who will leave the firm quickly. Presumably, if the firm had a sufficient number of applicants who worked more than four years with their previous employer, it would not choose to interview applicants with more unstable work experience. Again, the firm reasons that although there are likely to be some qualified applicants among those with an unstable work record, it is too costly to identify them. This method of screening is likely to discriminate because of the nature of seniority systems, which operate on a "last hired, first fired" basis. Many minorities and women have unstable work records because they are hired last and fired first. Thus, even when firms do not use racial or gender stereotypes, they discriminate, since women and minorities are more likely to come from weaker schools and have more unstable work records than equally qualified white male applicants.

FINANCIAL AND OCCUPATIONAL EFFECTS

Many economists believe the job market is divided between good (primary) and bad (secondary) jobs. Good jobs have characteristics such as on-the-job training and promotions through well-organized internal labor markets. Bad jobs have little on-the-job training and minimum chance for promotions; they are dead-end jobs. Since on-the-job training is a significant aspect of primary-sector jobs, employment stability and behavioral traits are often more important than formal education and general skills. Both conservative and liberal economists agree that workers who do not possess the proper behavioral traits, such as low absenteeism and punctuality, will not be employed in the primary sector. Most liberals believe that many women and minority workers who possess the proper behavioral traits also will not find jobs in the primary sector as a result of statistical discrimination.

Facing discrimination in the primary sector, many qualified female and minority workers shift to secondary labor markets. As a result, secondary employers have a greater supply of workers and can reduce wages and standards for working conditions. Primary employers and majority workers also benefit from statistical discrimination. Since majority workers face less competition, more of them will gain primary employment than they would in the absence of statistical discrimination.

Primary employers may have to pay somewhat higher wages and employ somewhat less productive workers as a result of statistical discrimination, but the reduced screening costs more than compensate for the higher wages and productivity losses. Moreover, many primary employers also hire secondary workers. For them, the higher cost of primary employees will be offset by the resulting reduction in wages paid to secondary workers and their somewhat higher productivity.

Since primary workers, primary employers, and secondary employers benefit from statistical discrimination, there are identifiable forces opposed to change. Thus, rather than the market disciplining decision makers, statistical discrimination creates groups having a financial stake in its perpetuation.

APPLICANTS AND THEIR SEARCH FOR JOB INFORMATION

For job seekers, the cheapest source of job information is personal contacts, including neighbors and relatives and their acquaintances. Additional information can be obtained from newspaper advertisements and government employment offices. The most costly information is obtained from private employment agencies. A significant difference in the cost of job information would occur if one individual had few personal contacts and was forced to use private employment services, while another individual had extensive personal contacts. All things being equal, the individual with the lower cost of obtaining information would be better informed and hence more likely to obtain higher earnings.

The job information minorities receive from their search effort is likely to be less valuable than the job information received by their white counterparts. The fact that an individual is recommended by a personal contact might be sufficient reason to grant the person an interview. Those who obtain information from newspaper ads or government employment services do not have this advantage. This distinction is summed up in the adage "It's not what you know but who you know that counts."

Low-income (minority) individuals tend to have fewer contacts than high-income (white) individuals of equal abilities and motivation. High-income (white) individuals tend to have many neighbors or relatives who have good jobs, own businesses, or are involved in their firm's hiring decisions. Low-income (minority) individuals, having few personal contacts, are forced to spend additional time and money to obtain job information. Even if the job information is as valuable as that obtained by their white counterparts, minorities might give up searching for employment sooner because it is more costly. They do not do so because they are less able or less motivated; they simply face greater expenses.

AFFIRMATIVE ACTION

Affirmative action legislation is the major government attempt at counteracting the discriminatory features of the hiring process. Affirmative action assumes that discrimination results from employment decisions based on incomplete information. The role of the government is simply to encourage firms to hire all qualified applicants by forcing them to gather individualized productivity information.

Guidelines stipulate that all government

agencies and private firms doing business with the government must publicly announce job openings at least forty-five days prior to the termination of acceptance of applications. This provision attempts to offset the information inequality disadvantaged workers face. More importantly, these employers must interview a minimum number of applicants from groups that tend to be victims of statistical discrimination.

It is important to remember the difference between affirmative action and quotas. Under affirmative action, there is no requirement to hire; employers are required only to interview female and minority applicants and make sure they have access to job information. Quotas are more drastic actions reserved for situations in which firms are not making good faith efforts to seek out and hire qualified female and minority applicants. For example, if a firm attempts to circumvent affirmative action guidelines by announcing job openings in papers that reached only the white community or, after interviewing applicants, uses discriminatory procedures to eliminate women from employment, the government can impose quotas. Thus, quotas are imposed only when it is demonstrated that the lack of female or minority employment reflects something more conscious than the unintentional effects of incomplete information.

Besides the government, some private groups have attempted to compensate for unequal access to information. Women's groups have attempted to set up networks to aid female job applicants for management positions. Female executives are encouraged to share as much information as possible with other women to offset the traditional networking done by men. In many areas, male networking is referred to as the old boy network, and entry into it has historically been critical to obtaining the most desirable jobs. Thus, the lack of personal contacts is at least partially offset by networks that direct job information to disadvantaged workers and provide low-cost productivity information to firms.

SKILL AND LOCATIONAL MISMATCHES

Many individuals reject the view that groups are held back due to external pressures by noting that "when we came to America, we faced discrimination but were able to overcome it." In particular, these individuals often believe that internal inadequacies are responsible for the seemingly permanent economic problems minorities face. One response is to argue that the discrimination minorities face is more severe and their economic resources fewer than those of European immigrants at the turn of the century. Another response dominated the U.S. Riot Commission's assessment of black poverty. This presidential commission, which was created to study the causes of the urban rebellions of the late 1960s, noted,

> When the European immigrants were arriving in large numbers, America was becoming an urban-industrial society. To build its major cities and industries, America needed great pools of unskilled labor. Since World War II . . . America's urban-industrial society has matured: unskilled labor is far less essential than before, and blue-collar jobs of all kinds are decreasing in numbers and importance as sources of new employment. . . . The Negro, unlike the immigrant, found little opportunity in the city; he had arrived too late, and the unskilled labor he had to offer was no longer needed.

This commission, commonly known as the Kerner commission, avoided blaming either the victims (culture of poverty) or society (discrimination) for black economic problems; they were simply the result of technological change. To compensate for the higher skill levels required for entry-level positions, the Kerner commission recommended extensive job-training programs. Supposedly, once these skills were obtained, blacks would enter the employment mainstream and racial income disparities would diminish.

Job-training programs became the centerpiece of the liberal War on Poverty initiated during the Johnson administration. To an extent, these job-training programs complemented compensatory educational programs. Whereas the compensatory programs attempted to develop general skills, job-training programs attempted to develop specific job-related skills. Whereas the compensatory programs were attempts to increase white-collar skills, job-training programs were attempts to increase blue-collar skills.

The government's involvement in job-training programs was pragmatic; it sought upward mobility in ways that would not conflict with the interests of other groups. Thus, it did not aggressively institute training programs that would conflict with the objectives of many craft unions. This meant that in many of the construction trades, which had historically restricted membership, the government accepted union prerogatives. Job-training success also was impeded by the seeming irrelevance of many of the skills taught, and there were complaints that training programs did not use the latest equipment and the newest methods.

Many liberals discounted these complaints. They agreed with conservatives that the problems disadvantaged groups faced stemmed from their internal inadequacies. These liberals thought the actual technical skills developed were irrelevant; what was critical was the development of the proper behavioral traits of punctuality and low absenteeism. These liberals also recommended more restrictive programs that would train only the least deficient of the disadvantaged group. In contrast, those liberals who believed that external pressures, particularly discrimination, were dominant proposed costly training programs and a more aggressive approach to craft unions.

Job-training success also was impeded by the shifting of blue-collar jobs out of Northeastern and Midwestern urban areas. After World War II, technological changes decreased the viability of central city locations. First, trucking replaced the railroads as the major transportation mode. When firms delivered their output (and received their input) on railcars, central city locations were ideal. When trucking became dominant, traffic tie-ups made those locations too costly. Indeed, recognizing these costs, the federal government built a new interstate highway system so that travelers could bypass congested central city areas.

Second, new technologies emphasized assembly-line techniques that required one-level production. No longer could manufacturing firms use factory buildings in which they operated on a number of floors. High land costs made it too expensive to build one-level plants in urban centers, so manufacturing firms began to locate in industrial parks near the new interstate highways on the outskirts of urban areas. This intensified minority employment problems, as most minorities continued to live in the inner city.

Minorities with the proper behavioral requirements, education, and skills have difficulty obtaining employment due to these locational mismatches. Inner-city residents are likely to lack the financial ability to commute to suburban jobs. They are unlikely to own a car or to earn a sufficient income to justify the extensive commuting required, even if public transportation is available. Minorities also are less likely to have access to these jobs because they have fewer personal contacts working in suburban locations.

Liberals have offered a number of recommendations to offset locational mismatches. Some economists have favored government subsidies to transportation networks that would bring inner-city workers to suburban employment locations. These subsidies would be cost-effective if the added employment generated greater income tax revenues and government spending reductions. Other economists have favored subsidizing firms to relocate in targeted inner-city zones. This approach was even endorsed by President Reagan under the catchy name "Free Enterprise Zones."   [1989]

Note

1. OPPORTUNITY COST: The relative proportion of time or resources that can be invested in a given activity.

Understanding the Reading

1. In what ways does having a lower income level limit one's educational attainment?
2. Explain what Cherry means by "purchasing information" and how it affects discriminatory employment practices or statistical discrimination.
3. What causes higher wages in the primary sector and lower wages in the secondary sector?
4. How are low-income people disadvantaged in their job searches?
5. Explain how affirmative action is supposed to work and how it differs from quotas.
6. What were the objectives and problems of job training as a solution to minority unemployment or underemployment?

Suggestion for Responding

Apply Cherry's analysis to the circumstances described in one of the other selections in Part III. ◆

SUGGESTIONS FOR RESPONDING TO PART III

1. At the opening of his essay, Norman Podhoretz says that class is about how one looks and lives. Most of the writers in Part III discuss in one way or another how family values and attitudes, language, leisure activities, manners, dress, possessions, and education influence and reflect socioeconomic class. Describe how your socioeconomic class was reflected in such features during your own childhood and youth. Since socioeconomic class is strongly influenced by race and ethnicity, some of your considerations may overlap with those you discussed in your ethnic heritage report for Part I. Careful thinking should help you sort out the economic factors and come to a fuller understanding of another of the complex factors that shape your identity.

2. If you no longer live in the socioeconomic class into which you were born, consider how and why the change took place. In what ways have you retained the influences of your earlier class experience? What characteristics, behaviors, and values of that class have you rejected, either consciously or unconsciously? Evaluate the strengths of both classes.

3. In recent years, homelessness has become a severe problem throughout the country. Research the manifestations of homelessness in your region. What are the estimated number and proportion of homeless people? What demographic categories—such as gender, age, racial and ethnic groupings, and so on—do they represent? To what causes can your local homelessness problem be attributed? What programs, both governmental and private-sector ones, exist to assist the homeless? What additional services are needed?

4. Your instructor may want you to make an oral presentation of your report. In preparation, review the suggestions about oral reports given at the end of Part I.

IV
Stereotypes and Prejudice

"I need a big, strong boy to help move these chairs."

"I'm switching to another calculus section. Too many Asians in here for me."

"Just like a Jewish mother!"

"A California blonde! Wow, sure I'll go!"

"You're an English teacher. I'd better watch the way I talk."

"A football player? No, I don't think so; I prefer someone I can talk to."

"Would you buy a used car from this man?"

"Take my mother-in-law, please!"

WE ALL HAVE HEARD OR EVEN MADE COMMENTS LIKE these. Each of these statements is based on a stereotype, on conjectures we make about a person when we know only one or two facts about them.

A **stereotype** is a set of assumptions and beliefs about the physical, behavioral, and psychological characteristics assigned to a particular group or class of people. If we know that someone belongs to a given group, we make other suppositions about that person by attributing to her or him those qualities and characteristics we associate with that group. Stereotypes exist for every class of people imaginable; they can be based on such identifiers as age, education, profession, regional origin, family role, interests, sexual orientation, disability, and so on. Stereo-

types assigned by gender and by race and ethnicity, however, are the ones most deeply embedded in our culture, and it is these that we examine in Part IV.

Even though we may not like to admit that we stereotype people, we all do it. Stereotyping makes it easier to function in a world filled with unknowns. We use the oversimplified and exaggerated generalizations of stereotypes to filter and interpret the complexities of reality. They provide us with an easy way both to respond to and interact with this often confusing world, and to structure our social relationships.

The trouble with stereotypes, however, is that the filter also blocks our perceptions. If we see people in terms of the standardized pictures we project onto a group to which they belong, we don't see or interact with them as individuals. Worse still, we usually block and deny any characteristics that don't fit our preconceived ideas. The word "stereotype" originally referred to the solid metal plate of type used in printing. This origin reveals the truth about stereotypes: Not only are they rigid and inflexible, they perpetuate unchanging images. As Robert L. Heilbroner puts it in the first selection in this part, we "typecast the world."

While some stereotypes may seem harmless enough, in general, stereotyping is hardly a benign process. This is made clear by the fact that none of us likes to be pigeonholed. We actively resist seeing ourselves and those with whom we are intimate in stereotypic ways; we insist on our individuality. We apply stereotypes only to others—to those who are unknown to us or who are different from us. And herein lies the rub.

Because difference often makes us uneasy and because we tend to fear the unknown, our collective characterizations of "others" incorporate many undesirable or less-valued traits or behaviors. This provides the basis for **prejudice** against members of those groups. Without knowledge of specific individuals or examination of how they present themselves, we make adverse judgments about them. We come to believe in their inferiority based solely on such traits as race, ethnicity, sex, class, age, disability, or sexual orientation.

Although stereotypes of any given group may change over time, individuals tend to have great difficulty transcending the prevailing cultural ideas about a group's identity. People tend to see us as they think we should be. They notice and remember what fits and supports their expectations and ignore or dismiss what doesn't fit. The irony is that even when we see people who contradict the stereotype, we either interpret their nonconformity in ways that adapt it to our expectations, or we dismiss them as "the exception that proves the rule."

The readings in Part IV explore some of our socially shared stereotypes, especially those of gender and racial and ethnic ones. They also look at the ways stereotypes are supported and sustained by various facets of our culture. Heilbroner's opening piece provides a general analysis of stereotyping, how it affects us, and what we can do to rid ourselves of this oversimplified thinking. The next two selections consider gender stereotypes. Doug Cooper Thompson describes the male stereotype and analyzes what men give up to conform to its expectations. Hilary M. Lips shows that the stereotypes of masculinity and femininity are actually based on white, middle-class norms. She describes how other characteristics—such as race, age, appearance, and disability—affect our gender assumptions.

Stereotypes are learned from and perpetuated by many socializing influences in our culture. The next two selections look at one force

that we take so for granted that we rarely think about it: language. Any of us may use language as an intentional weapon to attack other people; we can call them names or ascribe unpleasant characteristics to them. However, as Robert B. Moore shows, racial bias goes beyond deliberate slurs; it is built into the very way we speak. Although he draws on examples from the 1970s, his analysis shows how the connotations of the words we use and the way we state seemingly neutral ideas support and perpetuate racial stereotyping of African-Americans and Native Americans. Similarly, Alleen Pace Nilsen analyzes how English reinforces the gender stereotype that women are sex objects, weak and inferior to men, because the language itself characterizes women as passive and men active and teaches that masculine is positive and feminine negative.

Language isn't the only agent of socialization that teaches and supports stereotypes. We learn from virtually every aspect of social interaction, from our parents, peers, schools, religion, laws, and mass media. For example, the black "collectibles" that Kenneth W. Goings describes preserve and give physical reality to the evolving stereotypes of African-Americans. Carol Lee Sanchez shows how over the past 150 years, novels, movies, and even children's games have negated the humanity of American Indians. She also offers five actions non-Indians can take to counteract the stereotype—to everyone's benefit. Yin Ling Leung considers the negative impact of even seemingly positive stereotypes—in this case, the representation of Asian-Americans as the "model minority." She explains that this image not only misrepresents the experience of most members of this group, but it is creating backlash against which the group is mobilizing.

The last three selections portray in more personalized ways the problems caused by stereotyping and prejudice. Debra Swallow narrates her story of multigenerational experiences of prejudice against a Native American stereotype; like the organized Asian-Americans Leung describes, Swallow and her son fight back—both physically and psychologically. As the other two pieces illustrate, the other response to prejudice is to **internalize** it, to psychologically succumb to it. Cohen's anti-Semitic attack on Schwartz in Bernard Malamud's story is a satiric demonstration of self-hatred projected onto another member of one's own group. Brent Staples, on the other hand, responds to the prejudiced treatment he receives from being seen as a stereotypic threatening black male by empathizing with the prejudice and altering his behavior to project a more acceptable image.

Stereotypes provide an inaccurate picture of any group, and they tell us nothing about an individual member. Nonetheless, they survive, supported by language, media, jokes, and many of the artifacts with which we surround ourselves. Stereotypes provide rigid patterns of thinking that obscure the complexity of the world and keep us from appreciating the full potential of one another and ourselves. They inflict damage both on those who embrace and act on them and on the victims of the prejudice they bolster.

As pervasive as stereotypes are in our culture, they are neither inevitable nor unalterable. We all can act to reduce stereotyping and prejudice by identifying, exposing, and challenging them in our daily lives, by opening our eyes and others' to the richness of our shared humanity.

31

Don't Let Stereotypes Warp Your Judgments

Robert L. Heilbroner

Is a girl called Gloria apt to be better-looking than one called Bertha? Are criminals more likely to be dark than blond? Can you tell a good deal about someone's personality from hearing his voice briefly over the phone? Can a person's nationality be pretty accurately guessed from his photograph? Does the fact that someone wears glasses imply that he is intelligent?

The answer to all these questions is obviously, "No."

Yet, from all the evidence at hand, most of us believe these things. Ask any college boy if he'd rather take his chances with a Gloria or a Bertha, or ask a college girl if she'd rather blind-date a Richard or a Cuthbert. In fact, you don't have to ask: college students in questionnaires have revealed that names conjure up the same images in their minds as they do in yours—and for as little reason.

Look into the favorite suspects of persons who report "suspicious characters" and you will find a large percentage of them to be "swarthy" or "dark and foreign-looking"—despite the testimony of criminologists that criminals do *not* tend to be dark, foreign or "wild-eyed." Delve into the main asset of a telephone stock swindler and you will find it to be a marvelously confidence-inspiring telephone "personality." And whereas we all think we know what an Italian or a Swede looks like, it is the sad fact that when a group of Nebraska students sought to match faces and nationalities of 15 European countries, they were scored wrong in 93 percent of their identifications. Finally, for all the fact that horn-rimmed glasses have now become the standard television sign of an "intellectual," optometrists know that the main thing that distinguishes people with glasses is just bad eyes.

Stereotypes are a kind of gossip about the world, a gossip that makes us prejudge people before we ever lay eyes on them. Hence it is not surprising that stereotypes have something to do with the dark world of prejudice. Explore most prejudices (note that the word means prejudgment) and you will find a cruel stereotype at the core of each one.

For it is the extraordinary fact that once we have type-cast the world, we tend to see people in terms of our standardized pictures. In another demonstration of the power of stereotypes to affect our vision, a number of Columbia and Barnard students were shown 30 photographs of pretty but unidentified girls, and asked to rate each in terms of "general liking," "intelligence," "beauty" and so on. Two months later, the same group were shown the same photographs, this time with fictitious Irish, Italian, Jewish and "American" names attached to the pictures. Right away the ratings changed. Faces which were now seen as representing a national group went down in looks and still farther down in likability, while the "American" girls suddenly looked decidedly prettier and nicer.

Why is it that we stereotype the world in such irrational and harmful fashion? In part, we begin to type-cast people in our childhood years. Early in life, as every parent whose child has watched a TV Western knows, we learn to spot the Good Guys from the Bad Guys. Some years ago, a social psychologist showed very clearly how powerful these stereotypes of childhood vision are. He secretly asked the most popular youngsters in an elementary school to make errors in their morning gym exercises. Afterwards, he asked the class if anyone had noticed any mistakes during gym period. Oh, yes, said the children. But it was the *unpopular* members of the class—the "bad guys"—they remembered as being out of step.

We not only grow up with standardized pictures forming inside of us, but as grown-ups we are constantly having them thrust upon us. Some of them, like the half-joking, half-serious stereotypes of mothers-in-law, or country yokels, or psychiatrists, are dinned into us by the stock jokes we hear and repeat. In fact, without such stereotypes, there would be a lot fewer jokes. Still other stereotypes are perpetuated by the advertisements we read, the movies we see, the books we read.

And finally, we tend to stereotype because it helps us make sense out of a highly confusing world, a world which William James[1] once described as "one great, blooming, buzzing confusion." It is a curious fact that if we don't *know* what we're looking at, we are often quite literally unable to *see* what we're looking at. People who recover their sight after a lifetime of blindness actually cannot at first tell a triangle from a square. A visitor to a factory sees only noisy chaos where the superintendent sees a perfectly synchronized flow of work. As Walter Lippmann[2] has said, "For the most part we do not first see, and then define; we define first, and then we see."

Stereotypes are one way in which we "define" the world in order to see it. They classify the infinite variety of human beings into a convenient handful of "types" towards whom we learn to act in stereotyped fashion. Life would be a wearing process if we had to start from scratch with each and every human contact. Stereotypes economize on our mental effort by covering up the blooming, buzzing confusion with big recognizable cut-outs. They save us the "trouble" of finding out what the world is like—they give it its accustomed look.

Thus the trouble is that stereotypes make us mentally lazy. As S. I. Hayakawa, the authority on semantics, has written: "The danger of stereotypes lies not in their existence, but in the fact that they become for all people some of the time, and for some people all the time, *substitutes for observation*." Worse yet, stereotypes get in the way of our judgment, even when we do observe the world. Someone who has formed rigid preconceptions of all Latins as "excitable," or all teenagers as "wild," doesn't alter his point of view when he meets a calm and deliberate Genoese,[3] or a serious-minded high school student. He brushes them aside as "exceptions that prove the rule." And, of course, if he meets someone true to type, he stands triumphantly vindicated. "They're all like that," he proclaims, having encountered an excited Latin, an ill-behaved adolescent.

Hence, quite aside from the injustice which stereotypes do to others, they impoverish ourselves. A person who lumps the world into simple categories, who type-casts all labor leaders as "racketeers," all businessmen as "reactionaries," all Harvard men as "snobs," and all Frenchmen as "sexy," is in danger of becoming a stereotype himself. He loses his capacity to be himself—which is to say, to see the world in his own absolutely unique, inimitable and independent fashion.

Instead, he votes for the man who fits his standardized picture of what a candidate "should" look like or sound like, buys the goods that someone in his "situation" in life "should" own, lives the life that others define for him. The mark of the stereotype person is that he never surprises us, that we do indeed have him "typed." And no one fits this straitjacket so perfectly as someone whose opinions about *other people* are fixed and inflexible.

Impoverishing as they are, stereotypes are not easy to get rid of. The world we type-cast may be no better than a Grade B movie, but at least we know what to expect of our stock characters. When we let them act for themselves in the strangely unpredictable way that people do act, who knows but that many of our fondest convictions will be proved wrong?

Nor do we suddenly drop our standardized pictures for a blinding vision of the Truth. Sharp swings of ideas about people often just substitute one stereotype for another. The true process of change is a slow one that adds bits and pieces of reality to the pictures in our heads, until gradually they take on some of the blurriness of life itself. Little by little, we learn not that Jews and Negroes and Catholics and Puerto Ricans are "just like everybody else"—for that, too, is a stereotype—but that each and every one of them is unique, special, different and individual. Often we do not even know that we have let a stereotype lapse until we hear someone saying, "all so-and-so's are like such-and-such," and we hear ourselves saying, "Well—maybe."

Can we speed the process along? Of course we can.

First, we can become *aware* of the standardized pictures in our heads, in other peoples' heads, in the world around us.

Second, we can become suspicious of all judgments that we allow exceptions to "prove." There is no more chastening thought than that in the vast intellectual adventure of science, it takes but one tiny exception to topple a whole edifice of ideas.

Third, we can learn to be chary of generalizations about people. As F. Scott Fitzgerald once wrote: "Begin with an individual, and before you know it you have created a type; begin

with a type, and you find you have created—
nothing."

Most of the time, when we type-cast the
world, we are not in fact generalizing about
people at all. We are only revealing the embar-
rassing facts about the pictures that hang in the
gallery of stereotypes in our own heads.   [n.d.]

Notes

1. WILLIAM JAMES: An American philosopher
   and psychologist.
2. WALTER LIPPMANN: An American journalist
   and political analyst.
3. GENOESE: A native of Genoa, Italy.

Understanding the Reading

1. What is the relationship between stereotyping and prejudice?
2. Why do we stereotype the world?
3. What does "we define first, and then we see"
   mean?
4. Why don't our observations of people who
   don't fit our stereotyped assumptions cause
   us to alter our preconceptions?
5. How do our stereotyped assumptions affect
   us?
6. Why is the assumption that all categories of
   people are "just like everyone else" a stereotype itself?
7. How can we get beyond stereotyping?

Suggestion for Responding

Describe one facet of your identity (ethnicity,
gender, religion, age, economic status, job, etc.)
in terms of the stereotype others might apply to
you. Explain why the stereotype is fallacious. ♦

32

The Male Role Stereotype

DOUG COOPER THOMPSON

When you first consider that many men now feel
that they are victims of sex role stereotyping,

your natural response might be: "Are you kidding? Why should men feel discriminated
against? Men have the best jobs; they are the corporation presidents and the political leaders. Everyone says, 'It's a man's world.' What do men
have to be concerned about? What are their
problems?"

It is obvious that men hold most of the influential and important positions in society, and it
does seem that many men "have it made." The
problem is that men pay a high cost for the ways
they have been stereotyped and for the roles that
they play.

To understand why many men and women
are concerned, we need to take a look at the male
role stereotype. Here is what men who conform
to the stereotype must do.

CODE OF CONDUCT:
THE MALE ROLE STEREOTYPE

1. Act "Tough"
   Acting tough is a key element of the male role
   stereotype. Many boys and men feel that they
   have to show that they are strong and tough,
   that they can "take it" and "dish it out" as
   well. You've probably run into some boys
   and men who like to push people around,
   use their strength, and act tough. In a conflict,
   these males would never consider giving in,
   even when surrender or compromise would
   be the smartest or most compassionate
   course of action.
2. Hide Emotions
   This aspect of the male role stereotype
   teaches males to suppress their emotions and
   to hide feelings of fear or sorrow or tenderness. Even as small children, they are warned
   not to be "crybabies." As grown men they
   show that they have learned this lesson well,
   and they become very efficient at holding
   back tears and keeping a "stiff upper lip."
3. Earn "Big Bucks"
   Men are trained to be the primary source of
   income for the family. So men try to choose
   occupations that pay well, and then they stick
   with those jobs, even when they might prefer
   to try something else. Boys and men are

taught that earning a good living is important. In fact, men are often evaluated not on how kind or compassionate or thoughtful they are, but rather on how much money they make.

4. Get the "Right" Kind of Job

    If a boy decides to become a pilot, he will receive society's stamp of approval, for that is the right kind of a job for a man. But if a boy decides to become an airline steward, many people would think that quite strange. Boys can decide to be doctors, mechanics, or business executives, but if a boy wants to become a nurse, secretary, librarian, ballet dancer, or kindergarten teacher, he will have a tough time. His friends and relatives will probably try to talk him out of his decision, because it's just not part of the male role stereotype.

5. Compete—Intensely

    Another aspect of the male role stereotype is to be super-competitive. This competitive drive is seen not only on athletic fields, but in school and later at work. This commitment to competition leads to still another part of the male stereotype: getting ahead of other people to become a winner.

6. Win—At Almost Any Cost

    From the Little League baseball field to getting jobs that pay the most money, boys and men are taught to win at whatever they may try to do. They must work and strive and compete so that they can get ahead of other people, no matter how many personal, and even moral, sacrifices are made along the way to the winner's circle.

Those are some of the major features of the male stereotype. And certainly, some of them may not appear to be harmful. Yet when we look more closely, we find that many males who do "buy" the message of the male role stereotype end up paying a very high price for their conformity.

THE COST OF THE CODE: WHAT MEN GIVE UP

1. Men who become highly involved in competition and winning can lose their perspective and good judgment. Competition by itself is not necessarily bad, and we've all enjoyed some competitive activities. But when a man tries to fulfill the male stereotype, and compete and win at any cost, he runs into problems. You've probably seen sore losers (and even sore winners)—sure signs of overcommitment to competition. Real competitors have trouble making friends because they're always trying to go "one-up" on their friends. And when cooperation is needed, true-blue competitors have a difficult time cooperating.

    The next time you see hockey players hitting each other with their hockey sticks or politicians or businessmen willing to do almost anything for a Senate seat or a big deal, you know that you are seeing some of the problems of the male sex role stereotype: an overcommitment to competition and the need to win at any cost.

2. Hiding emotions can hurt. For one thing, hiding emotions confuses people as to what someone's real feelings are. Men who hide their emotions can be misunderstood by others who might see them as uncaring and insensitive. And men who are always suppressing their feelings may put themselves under heavy psychological stress. This pressure can be physically unhealthy as well.

3. The heavy emphasis that the male stereotype puts on earning big money also creates problems. Some men choose careers they really do not like, just because the job pays well. Others choose a job which at first they like, only later to find out that they would rather do something else. But they stay with their jobs anyway, because they can't afford to earn less money.

    In trying to earn as much as possible, many men work long hours and weekends. Some even take second jobs. When men do this, they begin to lead one-track lives—the track that leads to the office or business door. They drop outside interests and hobbies. They have less and less time to spend with their families. That's one reason why some fathers never really get to know their own children, even though they may love them very much.

4. Many men who are absorbed by competition, winning, and earning big bucks pay a terrible price in terms of their physical health. With

the continual pressure to compete, be tough, earn money, with little time left for recreation and other interests, men find themselves much more likely than women to fall victim to serious disease. In fact, on the average, men die 8 years sooner than women. Loss of life is a high cost to pay for following the code of the male role stereotype.

5. Those boys and men who do not follow the male code of conduct may also find their lives more difficult because of this stereotype. For example, some boys choose to become nurses rather than doctors, kindergarten teachers rather than lawyers, artists rather than electricians. Social pressure can make it terribly difficult for males who enter these nonstereotyped careers. Other boys and men feel very uncomfortable with the continual pressure to compete and win.

And some boys do not want to hide their feelings in order to project an image of being strong and tough. These males may be gentle, compassionate, sensitive human beings who are puzzled with and troubled by the male role stereotype. When society stereotypes any group—by race, religion, or sex—it becomes difficult for individuals to break out of the stereotype and be themselves.   [1985]

Understanding the Reading

1. How are the six characteristics of the male role stereotype connected?
2. What characteristics does Cooper Thompson omit, and how do they relate to his six?
3. Explain the costs to men of conforming to this stereotype.
4. What other costs might Cooper Thompson have included?

Suggestions for Responding

1. Have masculine and/or feminine stereotypes undergone changes in recent years? If you think so, describe those changes and explain what has caused them. If not, explain why you think they haven't.
2. Using Cooper Thompson's analysis as a model, analyze the "Code of Conduct" and the "Cost of the Code" of the female role stereotype. ◆

33

Gender and Other Stereotypes: Race, Age, Appearance, Disability

HILARY M. LIPS

When an individual completing a questionnaire to measure male–female stereotyping is asked about the "typical" woman or man, what kind of person comes to mind? An elderly black woman? A middle-aged Native American man confined to a wheelchair? A young woman who has trouble finding stylish clothing because she weighs 200 pounds? Most likely, the image is influenced by the person's tendency to define "typical" with reference to the self and the people most visible in the environment. Probably, as [H.] Landrine suggests, research participants cannot imagine a woman (or man) "without attributing a race, a social class, an age, and even a degree of physical attractiveness to the stimulus." The image, at least in North America, is likely to be of someone who is relatively young, white, able-bodied, neither too fat nor too thin, neither too short nor too tall, of average physical attractiveness. Thus, it is more than likely that our studies of the stereotypes that accompany gender are based on generalizations that systematically exclude middle-aged and old people, Asians, blacks, Chicanos, native peoples, disabled people, fat people, and people whose appearance diverges markedly from the norm. It is also likely that in holding to gender stereotypes based on the so-called typical man or woman, our society creates added difficulties for individuals already victimized by racism, ageism, an intolerance of disability, or society's obsession with attractiveness and thinness.

GENDER STEREOTYPES AND RACISM

It is only in recent years that researchers have tried to understand the workings of racism and sexism by comparing the experiences of different gender–race groups. It has been noted, for example, that the forms of racism directed at black women and black men may differ, and that sexism may be expressed toward and experienced by a woman differently as a function of her race.

According to the stereotypes held by the larger society, black women may be judged as less "feminine" than white women. Indeed, there appears to be a persistent stereotype of black women in the social science literature that encompasses strength, self-reliance, and a strong achievement orientation and [J.] Fleming has documented the existence of a "black matriarchy" theory among social scientists suggesting that black women are more dominant, assertive, and self-reliant than black males. While such a stereotype may appear positive at first glance, the narrow labeling of black women's strengths as "matriarchal" represents a refusal to conceptualize strong women in anything but a family context. Moreover, there has been a tendency to blame black women's strong, assertive behavior for some of the problems experienced by black men—a tendency that surely reflects stereotypic notions about what kinds of behavior are "proper" for women. Fleming's own investigations indicate that the black matriarchy theory is based largely on flawed or misleading evidence. She suggests that this particular stereotype may have arisen from the fact that "their long history of instrumentality in the service of family functioning may well have built in black women an air of self-reliance that arouses further stereotyping among those (largely white) social scientists more accustomed to white traditional norms for women."

Studies of gender stereotyping within racial groups other than whites are fairly rare. [V. E.] O'Leary and [A. O.] Harrison, comparing the gender stereotypes of black and white women and men, found that blacks endorsed fewer items that discriminated between the sexes than whites did, and that black respondents were less likely than whites to devalue females on stereotypic grounds. White subjects of both sexes rated the white woman more negatively than the black woman was rated by black subjects.

In an attempt to determine whether the often-reported stereotype of women is actually just a stereotype of middle-class white women, Landrine asked undergraduates to use a list of 23 adjectives to describe the stereotype of each of four groups of women: black and white middle-class women and black and white working-class women. She found that while the stereotypes differed significantly by both race and social class, with white women and middle-class women being described in ways most similar to traditional stereotypes of women, all four groups were rated in ways consistent with the feminine stereotype. White women were described as higher than black women on the most traditional of stereotypical terms: dependent, emotional, and passive. However, both groups were rated similar on many other adjectives: ambitious, competent, intelligent, self-confident, and hostile, for example. The findings suggest that race and social class are implicit in what have been described as gender stereotypes, but that to some extent, there is a set of expectations for women that transcends these variables.

GENDER STEREOTYPES AND AGE

The stereotypes of femininity and masculinity seem to apply most strongly to the young. As they age, both women and men describe themselves in less stereotypic terms, and older men rate older women as more active, involved, hardy, and stable than themselves.

Perhaps the reason why gender stereotypes become less pronounced for older people is that age stereotypes replace them. One of the widely accepted stereotypes about the elderly is that they are no longer interested in sexuality. But sexuality is one of the major underpinnings of social expectations about gender. One of the main reasons for a man to be masculine is to be sexually attractive to women, and vice versa. If sexuality becomes irrelevant, so, in a sense, do masculinity and femininity. While studies show that sexuality is *not,* in fact, irrelevant to older people, perhaps one accidentally beneficial consequence of this myth is that it is a partial release from the restrictions of gender stereotypes.

On the other hand, many writers have noted that there is a "double standard" of aging that places older women at a disadvantage with respect to older men. Since in contemporary North American society so much of a woman's worth tends to be defined in terms of her physical attractiveness to men, the aging woman may find that along with her "femininity" she is losing her value as a person. The changes in physical appearance that accompany aging, while often considered acceptable or even "distinguished" in men, move women farther and farther from current definitions of female beauty. For women, who often have few other sources of power and prestige than their attractiveness, these changes can signify a slide into decreasing social worth. Older men, who are less likely to have to rely on their appearance for power and prestige, may have wider access to sources of social worth through occupational achievement, money, and even relationships with younger women.

Research suggests that women who abandon the strict constraints of gender stereotypes to make nontraditional choices while they are young may find themselves better equipped than their more traditional counterparts to handle old age. Among 70-year-old women, work-centered mothers showed higher life satisfaction than women who were more exclusively family focused, and among women in their sixties, the most feminine women were the most critical of themselves.

APPEARANCE

Psychologists have become increasingly aware that physical appearance is a critical aspect of stereotyping. In terms of gender stereotypes, physical appearance may have strong implications for how masculine or feminine a person is thought to be. Many a tall, broad-shouldered woman has slouched and crouched through life in a vain effort to appear petite and thus "feminine," and many a short man has quietly cursed his diminutive stature because it seemed to detract from his ability to project a "masculine" image.

While physical appearance is important to both males and females, beauty is generally defined as a peculiarly feminine attribute, and preoccupation with one's appearance is seen as part of the feminine stereotype. In a recent exploration of the concept of femininity, Susan Brownmiller illustrates the powerful role played by physical appearance in cultural definitions of femininity. In various times and places, aspects of the female anatomy have become supposed signals of how feminine and how sexual a woman is. For example, she notes the way that others react to a young woman's breast development:

"Parents and relatives mark their appearance as a landmark event, schoolmates take notice, girlfriends compare, boys zero in; later a husband, a lover, a baby expect a proprietary share. No other part of the human anatomy has such semipublic, intensely private status. . . ." Why all the fuss? Brownmiller argues that breasts are used as a prime cue to a woman's sexuality. She notes the myth that a flat-chested woman is nonsexual and that a woman with large breasts is flaunting her sexuality and seeking attention. Small wonder that women sometimes become intensely self-conscious about this part of their anatomy!

Perhaps no aspect of appearance is the cause of more grief in our own society right now than weight. Dieting has become a North American obsession, with an estimated 52 million adults in the United States either dieting or contemplating a diet at any one time. Being fat is a subject of special concern to women. Thinness is a major aspect of the definition of attractiveness, and attractiveness increases perceived femininity. When female university students were asked what kinds of activities or situations would make them feel less feminine, by far the most frequently checked item was "being overweight," endorsed by more than 50% of the sample. So highly charged is the issue of weight for women that according to [E.] Hatfield and [S.] Sprecher women respondents in the early Kinsey surveys of sexual practices were more embarrassed when asked their weight than when asked "How often do you masturbate?" or "Have you ever had a homosexual affair?"

Research shows that physical attractiveness is a more central part of the self-concept for women than for men. Moreover, a test of a sample of college undergraduates indicated that weight and body shape, while important to men, were the *central* determinants of women's perception of their physical attractiveness. Women are less satisfied with their bodies than are men: College women report a greater discrepancy between their actual and ideal body image than men do. And women have good reason to be concerned about their weight and shape: Obesity seems to trigger more negative evaluations for women than for men. Researchers who showed silhouettes of fat and thin women and men to hundreds of passersby at a summer fair found that fat men were rated significantly less negatively than were fat women, while thin women were rated less negatively than their male counterparts.

There is some evidence that even among women who have rejected many of the traditional norms of femininity, the obsession with slenderness continues to exert a powerful force. Women who value nontraditional roles for women prefer a smaller, thinner female body shape and associate a larger, rounder form with the "wife and mother" stereotype.

GENDER AND DISABILITY

While the general stereotype of persons with disabilities involves helplessness, dependence, social isolation, and suffering, this stereotype seems to be moderated by the gender of the person with the disability. For women, who are already stereotyped as more passive and dependent than men, the disability stereotype can act to reinforce the image of dependence. Indeed, newly disabled women are far more likely than their male counterparts to be advised by their physicians to retire from paid employment. For men, on the other hand, the dependence on others that many disabilities enforce is perceived as a threat to their masculine image.

Physical attractiveness is another area in which gender and disability stereotypes interact. We have already noted that physical attractiveness is more central to femininity than to masculinity; it is also apparent that a woman who is visibly disabled, even if not disfigured in any way, falls short of the cultural ideal of beauty. Here, for example, is the reaction of a former executive of the Miss Universe contest to the notion of a paraplegic woman as a contestant: "Her participation in a beauty contest would be like having a blind man compete in a shooting match." However, 1987 saw the first entry of a wheelchair-bound woman, Maria Serrao, in a major American beauty contest.

Like the elderly, persons with disabilities are often stereotyped as asexual. However, even the slowly growing public awareness that disability does not imply a lack of sexual needs or interest has been channeled by gender stereotypes that say that sex is more important to men than to women. Much more has been studied and written on the subject of sexuality among disabled men than disabled women. However, statistics indicate that the popular presumption that disabled women are asexual does not protect them from sexual assault. In fact, disabled women may be more likely than other women to be sexually assaulted. Children of both sexes are at high risk for sexual abuse if they are disabled, because they are often less able to get away from an abuser and/or unable to communicate to others about what is happening. During both childhood and adulthood, females with disabilities are more likely than their nondisabled counterparts to experience sexual or physical abuse. In one small-scale study, 67% of disabled women, as compared to 34% of nondisabled women, reported that they had been physically abused or battered as children.

Gender stereotypes are pervasive, interacting with other stereotypes to shape social perceptions of persons of various races, ages, abilities, and appearances. Gender stereotyping both grows out of and reinforces the social relations between women and men, [and] the way it works is both complete and subtle.   [1988]

Understanding the Reading

1. How do we identify a "typical" man or woman?
2. What is problematic about the black matriarchy theory?
3. How does age affect gender stereotypes?
4. Explain how stereotypic assumptions about gender are influenced by appearance.
5. What is the paradox about gender stereotyping of people with disabilities, especially women?

Suggestions for Responding

1. What is your stereotype of an older man, an older woman, and of a man and a woman with disabilities? Analyze how you think you learned these stereotypes.
2. Describe your stereotype of black and white middle-class women and black and white working-class women, and analyze what this

reveals about your attitudes about race and social class as well as gender. ◆

34

Racism in the English Language

ROBERT B. MOORE

LANGUAGE AND CULTURE

An integral part of any culture is its language. Language not only develops in conjunction with a society's historical, economic and political evolution; it also reflects that society's attitudes and thinking. Language not only *expresses* ideas and concepts but actually *shapes* thought. If one accepts that our dominant white culture is racist, then one would expect our language—an indispensable transmitter of culture—to be racist as well. Whites, as the dominant group, are not subjected to the same abusive characterization by our language that people of color receive. Aspects of racism in the English language that will be discussed in this essay include terminology, symbolism, politics, ethnocentrism, and context.

Before beginning our analysis of racism in language we would like to quote part of a TV film review which shows the connection between language and culture.

> Depending on one's culture, one interacts with time in a very distinct fashion. One example which gives some cross-cultural insights into the concept of time is language. In Spanish, a watch is said to "walk." In English, the watch "runs." In German, the watch "functions." And in French, the watch "marches." In the Indian culture of the Southwest, people do not refer to time in this way. The value of the watch is displaced with the value of "what time it's getting to be." Viewing these five cultural perspectives of time, one can see some definite emphasis and values that each culture places on time. For example, a cultural perspective may provide a clue to why the negative stereotype of the slow and lazy Mexican who lives in the "Land of Mañana"[1] exists in the Anglo value sys-

tem, where time "flies," the watch "runs" and "time is money."

A SHORT PLAY ON "BLACK" AND "WHITE" WORDS

Some may blackly (angrily) accuse me of trying to blacken (defame) the English language, to give it a black eye (a mark of shame) by writing such black words (hostile). They may denigrate (to cast aspersions; to darken) me by accusing me of being blackhearted (malevolent), of having a black outlook (pessimistic, dismal) on life, of being a blackguard (scoundrel)—which would certainly be a black mark (detrimental fact) against me. Some may black-brow (scowl at) me and hope that a black cat crosses in front of me because of this black deed. I may become a black sheep (one who causes shame or embarrassment because of deviation from the accepted standards), who will be blackballed (ostracized) by being placed on a blacklist (list of undesirables) in an attempt to blackmail (to force or coerce into a particular action) me to retract my words. But attempts to blackjack (to compel by threat) me will have a Chinaman's chance of success, for I am not a yellow-bellied Indian-giver of words, who will whitewash (cover up or gloss over vices or crimes) a black lie (harmful, inexcusable). I challenge the purity and innocence (white) of the English language. I don't see things in black and white (entirely bad or entirely good) terms, for I am a white man (marked by upright firmness) if there ever was one. However, it would be a black day when I would not "call a spade a spade," even though some will suggest a white man calling the English language racist is like the pot calling the kettle black. While many may be niggardly (grudging, scanty) in their support, others will be honest and decent—and to them I say, that's very white of you (honest, decent).

The preceding is of course a white lie (not intended to cause harm), meant only to illustrate some examples of racist terminology in the English language.

OBVIOUS BIGOTRY

Perhaps the most obvious aspect of racism in language would be terms like "nigger," "spook," "chink," "spic," etc. While these may be facing increasing social disdain, they certainly are not dead. Large numbers of white Americans continue to utilize these terms. "Chink," "gook," and "slant-eyes" were in common usage among U.S. troops in Vietnam. An NBC nightly news broadcast, in February 1972, reported that the basketball team in Pekin, Illinois, was called the "Pekin Chinks" and noted that even though this had been protested by Chinese Americans, the term continued to be used because it was easy, and meant no harm. Spiro Agnew's widely reported "fat Jap" remark and the "little Jap" comment of lawyer John Wilson, during the Watergate hearings, are surface indicators of a deep-rooted Archie Bunkerism.[2]

Many white people continue to refer to Black people as "colored," as for instance in a July 30, 1975 *Boston Globe* article on a racist attack by whites on a group of Black people using a public beach in Boston. One white person was quoted as follows:

> We've always welcomed good colored people to South Boston but we will not tolerate radical blacks or Communists. . . . Good colored people are welcome in South Boston, black militants are not.

Many white people may still be unaware of the disdain many African Americans have for the term "colored," but it often appears that whether used intentionally or unintentionally, "colored" people are "good" and "know their place," while "Black" people are perceived as "uppity" and "threatening" to many whites. Similarly, the term "boy" to refer to African American men is now acknowledged to be a demeaning term, though still in common use. Other terms such as "the pot calling the kettle black" and "calling a spade a spade" have negative racial connotations but are still frequently used, as for example when President Ford was quoted in February 1976 saying that even though Daniel Moynihan had left the U.N., the U.S. would continue "calling a spade a spade."

COLOR SYMBOLISM

The symbolism of white as positive and black as negative is pervasive in our culture, with the black/white words used in the beginning of this essay only one of many aspects. "Good guys" wear white hats and ride white horses, "bad guys" wear black hats and ride black horses. Angels are white, and devils are black. The definition of *black* includes "without any moral light or goodness, evil, wicked, indicating disgrace, sinful," while that of *white* includes "morally pure, spotless, innocent, free from evil intent."

A children's TV cartoon program, *Captain Scarlet,* is about an organization called Spectrum, whose purpose is to save the world from an evil extra-terrestrial force called the Mysterons. Everyone in Spectrum has a color name—Captain Scarlet, Captain Blue, etc. The one Spectrum agent who has been mysteriously taken over by the Mysterons and works to advance their evil aims is Captain Black. The person who heads Spectrum, the good organization out to defend the world, is Colonel White.

Three of the dictionary definitions of white are "fairness of complexion, purity, innocence." These definitions affect the standards of beauty in our culture, in which whiteness represents the norm. "Blondes have more fun" and "Wouldn't you really rather be a blonde" are sexist in their attitudes toward women generally, but are racist white standards when applied to third world women. A 1971 *Mademoiselle* advertisement pictured a curly-headed, ivory-skinned woman over the caption, "When you go blonde go all the way," and asked: "Isn't this how, in the back of your mind, you always wanted to look? All wide-eyed and silky blonde down to there, and innocent?" Whatever the advertising people meant by this particular woman's innocence, one must remember that "innocent" is one of the definitions of the word white. This standard of beauty when preached to all women is racist. The statement "Isn't this how, in the back of your mind, you always wanted to look?" either ignores third world women or assumes they long to be white.

Time magazine in its coverage of the Wimbledon tennis competition between the black Australian Evonne Goolagong and the white American Chris Evert described Ms. Goolagong as "the dusky daughter of an Australian sheepshearer," while Ms. Evert was "a fair young girl from the middle-class groves of Florida." *Dusky* is a synonym of "black" and is defined as "having dark skin; of a dark color; gloomy; dark; swarthy." Its antonyms are "fair" and "blonde." *Fair* is defined in part as "free from blemish, imperfection, or anything that impairs the appearance, quality, or character; pleasing in appearance, attractive; clean; pretty; comely." By defining Evonne Goolagong as "dusky," *Time* technically defined her as the opposite of "pleasing in appearance; attractive; clean; pretty; comely."

The studies of Kenneth B. Clark, Mary Ellen Goodman, Judith Porter and others indicate that this pervasive "rightness of whiteness" in U.S. culture affects children before the age of four, providing white youngsters with a false sense of superiority and encouraging self-hatred among third world youngsters.

ETHNOCENTRISM OR FROM A WHITE PERSPECTIVE

Some words and phrases that are commonly used represent particular perspectives and frames of reference, and these often distort the understanding of the reader or listener. David R. Burgest has written about the effect of using the terms "slave" or "master." He argues that the psychological impact of the statement referring to "the master raped his slave" is different from the impact of the same statement substituting the words: "the white captor raped an African woman held in captivity."

> Implicit in the English usage of the "master-slave" concept is ownership of the "slave" by the "master," therefore, the "master" is merely abusing his property (slave). In reality, the captives (slave) were African individuals with human worth, right and dignity and the term "slave" denounces that human quality thereby making the mass rape of African women by white captors more acceptable in the minds of people and setting a mental frame of reference for legitimizing the atrocities perpetuated against African people.

The term slave connotes a less than human quality and turns the captive person into a thing. For example, two McGraw-Hill Far Eastern Publishers textbooks (1970) stated, "At first it was the slaves who worked the cane and they got only food for it. Now men work cane and get money." Next time you write about slavery or

read about it, try transposing all "slaves" into "African people held in captivity," "Black people forced to work for no pay" or "African people stolen from their families and societies." While it is more cumbersome, such phrasing conveys a different meaning.

PASSIVE [VOICE]

Another means by which language shapes our perspective has been noted by Thomas Greenfield, who writes that the achievements of Black people—and Black people themselves—have been hidden in

> the linguistic ghetto of the passive voice, the subordinate clause, and the 'understood' subject. The seemingly innocuous distinction (between active/ passive voice) holds enormous implications for writers and speakers. When it is effectively applied, the rhetorical impact of the passive voice— the art of making the creator or instigator of action totally disappear from a reader's perception—can be devastating.

For instance, some history texts will discuss how European immigrants came to the United States seeking a better life and expanded opportunities, but will note that "slaves *were brought* to America." Not only does this omit the destruction of African societies and families, but it ignores the role of northern merchants and southern slaveholders in the profitable trade in human beings. Other books will state that "the continental railroad *was built*," conveniently omitting information about the Chinese laborers who built much of it or the oppression they suffered.

Another example. While touring Monticello, Greenfield noted that the tour guide

> made all the black people at Monticello "disappear" through her use of the passive voice. While speaking of the architectural achievements of Jefferson in the active voice, she unfailingly shifted to passive when speaking of the work performed by Negro slaves and skilled servants.

Noting a type of door that after 166 years continued to operate without need for repair, Greenfield remarks that the design aspect of the door was much simpler than the actual skill and work involved in building and installing it. Yet his guide stated: "Mr. Jefferson designed these doors . . ." while "the doors *were installed* [italics mine] in 1809." The workers who installed those doors were African people whom Jefferson held in bondage. The guide's use of the passive [voice] enabled her to dismiss the reality of Jefferson's slaveholding. It also meant that she did not have to make any mention of the skills of those people held in bondage.

POLITICS AND TERMINOLOGY

"Culturally deprived," "economically disadvantaged" and "underdeveloped" are other terms which mislead and distort our awareness of reality. The application of the term "culturally deprived" to third world children in this society reflects a value judgment. It assumes that the dominant whites are cultured and all others without culture. In fact, third world children generally are bicultural, and many are bilingual, having grown up in their own culture as well as absorbing the dominant culture. In many ways, they are equipped with skills and experiences which white youth have been deprived of, since most white youth develop in a monocultural, monolingual environment. Burgest suggests that the term "culturally deprived" be replaced by "culturally dispossessed," and that the term "economically disadvantaged" be replaced by "economically exploited." Both these terms present a perspective and implication that provide an entirely different frame of reference as to the reality of the third world experience in U.S. society.

Similarly, many nations of the third world are described as "underdeveloped." These less wealthy nations are generally those that suffered under colonialism and neo-colonialism. The "developed" nations are those that exploited their resources and wealth. Therefore, rather than referring to these countries as "underdeveloped," a more appropriate and meaningful designation might be "over exploited." Again, transpose this term next time you read about "underdeveloped nations" and note the different meaning that results.

Terms such as "culturally deprived," "economically disadvantaged" and "underdeveloped" place the responsibility for their own conditions on those being so described. This is known as "Blaming the Victim." It places respon-sibility for poverty on the victims of poverty. It removes the blame from those in power who benefit from, and continue to permit, poverty.

Still another example involves the use of "non-white," "minority" or "third world." While people of color are a minority in the U.S., they are part of the vast majority of the world's population, in which white people are a distinct minority. Thus, by utilizing the term minority to describe people of color in the U.S., we can lose sight of the global majority/minority reality—a fact of some importance in the increasing and interconnected struggles of people of color inside and outside the U.S.

To describe people of color as "non-white" is to use whiteness as the standard and norm against which to measure all others. Use of the term "third world" to describe all people of color overcomes the inherent bias of "minority" and "non-white." Moreover, it connects the struggles of third world people in the U.S. with the freedom struggles around the globe.

The term third world gained increasing usage after the 1955 Bandung Conference of "non-aligned" nations, which represented a third force outside of the two world superpowers. The "first world" represents the United States, Western Europe and their sphere of influence. The "second world" represents the Soviet Union and its sphere. The "third world" represents, for the most part, nations that were, or are, controlled by the "first world" or West. For the most part, these are nations of Africa, Asia and Latin America.

"LOADED" WORDS AND NATIVE AMERICANS

Many words lead to a demeaning characterization of groups of people. For instance, Columbus, it is said, "discovered" America. The word *discover* is defined as "to gain sight or knowledge of something previously unseen or unknown; to discover may be to find some existent thing that was previously unknown." Thus, a continent inhabited by millions of human beings cannot be "discovered." For history books to continue this usage represents a Eurocentric (white European) perspective on world history and ignores the existence of, and the perspective of, Native Americans. "Discovery," as used in the Euro-American context, implies the right to take what one finds, ignoring the rights of those who already inhabit or own the "discovered" thing.

Eurocentrism is also apparent in the usage of "victory" and "massacre" to describe the battles between Native Americans and whites. *Victory* is defined in the dictionary as "a success or triumph over an enemy in battle or war; the decisive defeat of an opponent." *Conquest* denotes the "taking over of control by the victor, and the obedience of the conquered." *Massacre* is defined as "the unnecessary, indiscriminate killing of a number of human beings, as in barbarous warfare or persecution, or for revenge or plunder." *Defend* is described as "to ward off attack from; guard against assault or injury; to strive to keep safe by resisting attack."

Eurocentrism turns these definitions around to serve the purpose of distorting history and justifying Euro-American conquest of the Native American homelands. Euro-Americans are not described in history books as invading Native American lands, but rather as defending *their* homes against "Indian" attacks. Since European communities were constantly encroaching on land already occupied, then a more honest interpretation would state that it was the Native Americans who were "warding off," "guarding" and "defending" their homelands.

Native American victories are invariably defined as "massacres," while the indiscriminate killing, extermination and plunder of Native American nations by Euro-Americans is defined as "victory." Distortion of history by the choice of "loaded" words used to describe historical events is a common racist practice. Rather than portraying Native Americans as human beings in highly defined and complex societies, cultures and civilizations, history books use such adjectives as "savages," "beasts," "primitive," and "backward." Native people are referred to as "squaw," "brave," or "papoose" instead of "woman," "man," or "baby."

Another term that has questionable connotations is *tribe*. The Oxford English Dictionary defines this noun as "a race of people; now applied especially to a primary aggregate of people in a primitive or barbarous condition, under a headman or chief." Morton Fried, discussing "The Myth of Tribe," states that the word "did not become a general term of reference to American Indian society until the nineteenth century. Pre-

viously, the words commonly used for Indian populations were 'nation' and 'people.'" Since "tribe" has assumed a connotation of primitiveness or backwardness, it is suggested that the use of "nation" or "people" replace the term whenever possible in referring to Native American peoples.

The term tribe invokes even more negative implications when used in reference to African peoples. As Evelyn Jones Rich has noted, the term is "almost always used to refer to third world people and it implies a stage of development which is, in short, a put-down."

"LOADED" WORDS AND AFRICANS

Conflicts among diverse peoples within African nations are often referred to as "tribal warfare," while conflicts among the diverse peoples within European countries are never described in such terms. If the rivalries between the Ibo and the Hausa and Yoruba in Nigeria are described as "tribal," why not the rivalries between Serbs and Slavs in Yugoslavia, or Scots and English in Great Britain, Protestants and Catholics in Ireland, or the Basques and the Southern Spaniards in Spain? Conflicts among African peoples in a particular nation have religious, cultural, economic and/or political roots. If we can analyze the roots of conflicts among European peoples in terms other than "tribal warfare," certainly we can do the same with African peoples, including correct reference to the ethnic groups or nations involved. For example, the terms "Kaffirs," "Hottentot" or "Bushmen" are names imposed by white Europeans. The correct names are always those by which a people refer to themselves. (In these instances Xhosa, Khoi-Khoin and San are correct.)

The generalized application of "tribal" in reference to Africans—as well as the failure to acknowledge the religious, cultural and social diversity of African peoples—is a decidedly racist dynamic. It is part of the process whereby Euro-Americans justify, or avoid confronting, their oppression of third world peoples. Africa has been particularly insulted by this dynamic, as witness the pervasive "darkest Africa" image. This image, widespread in Western culture, evokes an Africa covered by jungles and inhabited by "uncivilized," "cannibalistic," "pagan," "savage" peoples. This "darkest Africa" image avoids the geographical reality. Less than 20 per cent of the African continent is wooded savanna, for example. The image also ignores the history of African cultures and civilizations. Ample evidence suggests this distortion of reality was developed as a convenient rationale for the European and American slave trade. The Western powers, rather than exploiting, were civilizing and christianizing "uncivilized" and "pagan savages" (so the rationalization went). This dynamic also served to justify Western colonialism. From Tarzan movies to racist children's books like *Doctor Dolittle* and *Charlie and the Chocolate Factory,* the image of "savage" Africa and the myth of "the white man's burden"[3] has been perpetuated in Western culture.

A 1972 *Times* magazine editorial lamenting the demise of *Life* magazine stated that the "lavishness" of *Life*'s enterprises included "organizing safaris into darkest Africa." The same year, the *New York Times'* C. L. Sulzberger wrote that Africa has "a history as dark as the skins of many of its people." Terms such as "darkest Africa," "primitive," "tribe" ("tribal") or "jungle," in reference to Africa, perpetuate myths and are especially inexcusable in such large circulation publications.

Ethnocentrism is similarly reflected in the term "pagan" to describe traditional religions. A February 1973 *Time* magazine article on Uganda stated, "Moslems account for only 500,000 of Uganda's 10 million people. Of the remainder, 5,000,000 are Christians and the rest pagan." *Pagan* is defined as "Heathen, a follower of a polytheistic religion; one that has little or no religion and that is marked by a frank delight in and uninhibited seeking after sensual pleasures and material goods." *Heathen* is defined as "Unenlightened; an unconverted member of a people or nation that does not acknowledge the God of the Bible. A person whose culture or enlightenment is of an inferior grade, especially an irreligious person." Now, the people of Uganda, like almost all Africans, have serious religious beliefs and practices. As used by Westerners, "pagan" connotes something wild, primitive and inferior—another term to watch out for.

The variety of traditional structures that African people live in are their "houses," not "huts." A *hut* is "an often small and temporary dwelling of simple construction." And to describe Africans as "natives" (noun) is derogatory terminology—as in, "the natives are restless." The dictionary definition of *native* includes: "one of a people inhabiting a territorial area at the time of its discovery or becoming familiar to a foreigner; one belonging to a people having a less complex civilization." Therefore, use of "native," like use of "pagan" often implies a value judgment of white superiority.

QUALIFYING ADJECTIVES

Words that would normally have positive connotations can have entirely different meanings when used in a racial context. For example, C. L. Sulzberger, the columnist of the *New York Times,* wrote, in January 1975, about conversations he had with two people in Namibia. One was the white South African administrator of the country and the other a member of SWAPO, the Namibian liberation movement. The first is described as "Dirk Mudge, who as senior elected member of the administration is a kind of acting Prime Minister. . . ." But the second person is introduced as "Daniel Tjongarero, an intelligent Herero tribesman who is a member of SWAPO. . . ." What need was there for Sulzberger to state that Daniel Tjongarero is "intelligent"? Why not also state that Dirk Mudge was "intelligent"—or do we assume he wasn't?

A similar example from a 1968 *New York Times* article reporting on an address by Lyndon Johnson stated, "The President spoke to the well-dressed Negro officials and their wives." In what similar circumstances can one imagine a reporter finding it necessary to note that an audience of white government officials was "well-dressed"?

Still another word often used in a racist context is "qualified." In the 1960's white Americans often questioned whether Black people were "qualified" to hold public office, a question that was never raised (until too late) about white officials like Wallace, Maddox, Nixon, Agnew, Mitchell, et al. The question of qualifications has been raised even more frequently in recent years as white people question whether Black people are "qualified" to be hired for positions in industry and educational institutions. "We're looking for a qualified Black" has been heard again and again as institutions are confronted with affirmative action goals. Why stipulate that Blacks must be "qualified," when for others it is taken for granted that applicants must be "qualified."

SPEAKING ENGLISH

Finally, the depiction in movies and children's books of third world people speaking English is often itself racist. Children's books about Puerto Ricans or Chicanos often connect poverty with a failure to speak English or to speak it well, thus blaming the victim and ignoring the racism which affects third world people regardless of their proficiency in English. Asian characters speak a stilted English ("Honorable so and so" or "Confucius say") or have a speech impediment ("rots or ruck," "velly solly," "flied lice"). Native American characters speak another variation of stilted English ("Boy not hide. Indian take boy."), repeat certain Hollywood-Indian phrases ("Heap big" and "Many moons") or simply grunt out "Ugh" or "How." The repeated use of these language characterizations functions to make third world people seem less intelligent and less capable than the English-speaking white characters.

WRAP-UP

A *Saturday Review* editorial on "The Environment of Language" stated that language

> . . . has as much to do with the philosophical and political conditioning of a society as geography or climate. . . . people in Western cultures do not realize the extent to which their racial attitudes have been conditioned since early childhood by the power of words to ennoble or condemn, augment or detract, glorify or demean. Negative language infects the subconscious of most Western people from the time they first learn to speak. Prejudice is not merely imparted or superimposed. It is metabolized in the bloodstream of society. What is needed is not so much a change in language as an awareness of the power of words to condition attitudes. If we can at least recognize the underpinnings of prejudice, we may be in a position to deal with the effects.

To recognize the racism in language is an important first step. Consciousness of the influence of language on our perceptions can help to negate much of that influence. But it is not enough to simply become aware of the affects of racism in conditioning attitudes. While we may not be able to change the language, we can definitely change our usage of the language. We can avoid using words that degrade people. We can make a conscious effort to use terminology that reflects a progressive perspective, as opposed to a distorting perspective. It is important for educators to provide students with opportunities to explore racism in language and to increase their awareness of it, as well as learning terminology that is positive and does not perpetuate negative human values.   [1976]

Notes

1. LAND OF MAÑANA: A stereotype of Mexico as a place where people "put things off until tomorrow."
2. ARCHIE BUNKERISM: A reference to "All in the Family," a 1970s television show that featured a blue-collar worker who held bigoted stereotypes about virtually every subgroup in America.
3. WHITE MAN'S BURDEN: A belief of Europeans and Euro-Americans that they had a responsibility to govern the nonwhite peoples of the world.

Understanding the Reading

1. What do their words relating to time reveal about different cultures?
2. Why doesn't the claim that no harm is meant by the use of ethnic slang terms excuse their use?
3. What is the significance of color symbolism?
4. How are the terms "slave" and "master" ethnocentric?
5. Explain the effects of using the passive voice in historical narrations.
6. What ethnocentric value judgments are revealed by political labels?
7. Explain how whites have used language to distort their relationship to Native Americans.
8. How has English been used to justify western exploitation of Africa?
9. What is wrong with qualifying adjectives?

Suggestions for Responding

1. Discuss why you think the English language is so prejudiced about color differences.
2. Find three examples of the kind of ethnocentric usages Moore describes—in children's books, current periodicals, old history texts, advertisements. Analyze their implications, and rewrite them to eliminate the biases.
3. Discuss whether or not you think language usage has changed since 1976, when Moore wrote this piece. Provide specific examples to support your position. ✦

35

Sexism in English: A 1990s Update

ALLEEN PACE NILSEN

Twenty years ago I embarked on a study of sexism inherent in American English. I had just returned to Ann Arbor, Michigan, after living for two years (1967–69) in Kabul, Afghanistan, where I had begun to look critically at the role society assigned to women. The Afghan version of the *chaderi*[1] prescribed for Moslem women was particularly confining. Afghan jokes and folklore were blatantly sexist, such as this proverb: "If you see an old man, sit down and take a lesson; if you see an old woman, throw a stone."

But it wasn't only the native culture that made me question women's roles, it was also the American community.

Most of the American women were like myself—wives and mothers whose husbands were either career diplomats, employees of USAID, or college professors who had been recruited to work on various contract teams. We were suddenly bereft of our traditional roles: some of us became alcoholics, others got very good at bridge, while still others searched desperately for ways to contribute either to our families or to the Afghans. The local economy provided few jobs for women and certainly none for foreigners; we were isolated from former friends and the social goals we had grown up with.

When I returned in the fall of 1969 to the University of Michigan in Ann Arbor, I was surprised to find that many older women were also questioning the expectations they had grown up with. In the spring of 1970, a women's conference was announced. I hired a babysitter and attended, but I returned home more troubled than ever. The militancy of these women frightened me. Since I wasn't ready for a revolution, I decided I would have my own feminist movement. I would study the English language and see what it could tell me about sexism. I started reading a desk dictionary and making notecards on every entry that seemed to tell something about male and female. I soon had a dog-eared dictionary, along with a collection of note cards filling two shoe boxes.

Ironically, I started reading the dictionary because I wanted to avoid getting involved in social issues, but what happened was that my notecards brought me right back to looking at society. Language and society are as intertwined as a chicken and an egg. The language a culture uses is telltale evidence of the values and beliefs of that culture. And because there is a lag in how fast a language changes—new words can easily be introduced, but it takes a long time for old words and usages to disappear—a careful look at English will reveal the attitudes that our ancestors held and that we as a culture are therefore predisposed to hold. My notecards revealed three main points. Friends have offered the opinion that I didn't need to read the dictionary to learn such obvious facts. Nevertheless, it was interesting to have linguistic evidence of sociological observations.

WOMEN ARE SEXY; MEN ARE SUCCESSFUL

First, in American culture a woman is valued for the attractiveness and sexiness of her body, while a man is valued for his physical strength and accomplishments. A woman is sexy. A man is successful.

A persuasive piece of evidence supporting the view are the eponyms—words that have come from someone's name—found in English. I had a two-and-a-half-inch stack of cards taken from men's names but less than a half-inch stack from women's names, and most of those came from Greek mythology. In the words that came into American English since we separated from Britain, there are many eponyms based on the names of famous American men: *Bartlett pear, boysenberry, diesel engine, Franklin stove, Ferris wheel, Gatling gun, mason jar, sideburns, sousaphone, Schick test,* and *Winchester rifle.* The only common eponyms taken from American women's names are *Alice blue* (after Alice Roosevelt Longworth), *bloomers* (after Amelia Jenks Bloomer), and *Mae West jacket* (after the buxom actress). Two out of the three feminine eponyms relate closely to a woman's physical anatomy, while the masculine eponyms (except for *sideburns* after General Burnsides) have nothing to do with the namesake's body but, instead, honor the man for an accomplishment of some kind.

Although in Greek mythology women played a bigger role than they did in the biblical stories of the Judeo-Christian cultures and so the names of goddesses are accepted parts of the language in such place names as Pomona from the goddess of fruit and Athens from Athena and in such common words as *cereal* from Ceres, *psychology* from Psyche, and *arachnoid* from Arachne, the same tendency to think of women in relation to sexuality is seen in the eponyms *aphrodisiac* from Aphrodite, the Greek name for the goddess of love and beauty, and *venereal disease* from Venus, the Roman name for Aphrodite.

Another interesting word from Greek mythology is *Amazon.* According to Greek folk etymology, the *a* means "without" as in *atypical* or *amoral,* while *mazon* comes from *mazos* meaning "breast" as still seen in *mastectomy.* In the Greek legend, Amazon women cut off their right breasts so that they could better shoot their bows. Apparently, the storytellers had a feeling that for women to play the active, "masculine" role the Amazons adopted for themselves, they had to trade in part of their femininity.

This preoccupation with women's breasts is not limited to ancient stories. As a volunteer for the University of Wisconsin's *Dictionary of American Regional English (DARE),* I read a western trapper's diary from the 1930s. I was to make notes of any unusual usages or language patterns. My most interesting finding was that the trapper referred to a range of mountains as *The Teats,* a metaphor based on the similarity between the shapes of the mountains and women's breasts. Because today we use the French word-

ing, *The Grand Tetons,* the metaphor isn't as obvious, but I wrote to mapmakers and found the following listings: *Nippletop* and *Little Nipple Top* near Mount Marcy in the Adirondacks; *Nipple Mountain* in Archuleta County, Colorado; *Nipple Peak* in Coke County, Texas; *Nipple Butte* in Pennington, South Dakota; *Squaw Peak* in Placer County, California (and many other locations); *Maiden's Peak* and *Squaw Tit* (they're the same mountain) in the Cascade Range in Oregon; *Mary's Nipple* near Salt Lake City, Utah; and *Jane Russell Peaks* near Stark, New Hampshire.

Except for the movie star Jane Russell, the women being referred to are anonymous—it's only a sexual part of their body that is mentioned. When topographical features are named after men, it's probably not going to be to draw attention to a sexual part of their bodies but instead to honor individuals for an accomplishment. For example, no one thinks of a part of the male body when hearing a reference to Pike's Peak, Colorado, or Jackson Hole, Wyoming.

Going back to what I learned from my dictionary cards, I was surprised to realize how many pairs of words we have in which the feminine word has acquired sexual connotations while the masculine word retains a serious businesslike aura. For example, a *callboy* is the person who calls actors when it is time for them to go on stage, but a *call girl* is a prostitute. Compare *sir* and *madam. Sir* is a term of respect, while *madam* has acquired the specialized meaning of a brothel manager. Something similar has happened to *master* and *mistress.* Would you rather have a painting by an *old master* or an *old mistress?*

It's because the word *woman* had sexual connotations, as in "She's his woman," that people began avoiding its use, hence such terminology as *ladies' room, lady of the house,* and *girls' school* or *school for young ladies.* Feminists, who ask that people use the term *woman* rather than *girl* or *lady,* are rejecting the idea that *woman* is primarily a sexual term. They have been at least partially successful in that today *woman* is commonly used to communicate gender without intending implications about sexuality.

I found two hundred pairs of words with masculine and feminine forms, e.g., *heir-heiress, hero-heroine, steward-stewardess, usher-usherette.* In nearly all such pairs, the masculine word is considered the base, with some kind of a feminine suffix being added. The masculine form is the one from which compounds are made, e.g., from *king-queen* comes *kingdom* but not *queendom,* from *sportsman-sportslady,* comes *sportsmanship* but not *sportsladyship.* There is one—and only one—semantic area in which the masculine word is not the base or more powerful word. This is in the area dealing with sex and marriage. When someone refers to a *virgin,* a listener will probably think of a female, unless the speaker specifies *male* or uses a masculine pronoun. The same is true for *prostitute.*

In relation to marriage, there is much linguistic evidence showing that weddings are more important to women than to men. A woman cherishes the wedding and is considered a bride for a whole year, but a man is referred to as a groom only on the day of the wedding. The word *bride* appears in *bridal attendant, bridal gown, bridesmaid, bridal shower,* and even *bridegroom. Groom* comes from the Middle English *grom,* meaning "man," and in the sense is seldom used outside of the wedding. With most pairs of male/female words, people habitually put the masculine word first, *Mr. and Mrs., his and hers, boys and girls, men and women, kings and queens, brothers and sisters, guys and dolls,* and *host and hostess,* but it is the *bride and groom* who are talked about, not the *groom and bride.*

The importance of marriage to a woman is also shown by the fact that when a marriage ends in death, the woman gets the title of *widow.* A man gets the derived title of *widower.* This term is not used in other phrases or contexts, but *widow* is seen in *widowhood, widow's peak,* and *widow's walk.* A *widow* in a card game is an extra hand of cards, while in typesetting it is an extra line of type.

How changing cultural ideas bring changes to language is clearly visible in this semantic area. The feminist movement has caused the differences between the sexes to be downplayed, and since I did my dictionary study two decades ago, the word *singles* has largely replaced such sex specific and value-laden terms as *bachelor, old maid, spinster, divorcée, widow,* and *widower.* And in 1970 I wrote that when a man is called *a professional* he is thought to be a doctor or a lawyer, but when people hear a woman referred to as *a professional* they are likely to think of a prostitute. That's not as true today because so many women have become doctors and lawyers that it's no longer incongruous to think of women in those professional roles.

Another change that has taken place is in wedding announcements. They used to be sent out from the bride's parents and did not even give the name of the groom's parents. Today, most couples choose to list either all or none of the parents' names. Also it is now much more likely that both the bride and groom's picture will be in the newspaper, while a decade ago only the bride's picture was published on the "Women's" or the "Society" page. Even the traditional wording of the wedding ceremony is being changed. Many officials now pronounce the couple "husband and wife" instead of the old "man and wife," and they ask the bride if she promises "to love, honor, and cherish," instead of "to love, honor, and obey."

WOMEN ARE PASSIVE; MEN ARE ACTIVE

The wording of the wedding ceremony also relates to the second point that my cards showed, which is that women are expected to play a passive or weak role while men play an active or strong role. In the traditional ceremony, the official asks. "Who gives the bride away?" and the father answers, "I do." Some fathers answer, "Her mother and I do," but that doesn't solve the problem inherent in the question. The idea that a bride is something to be handed over from one man to another bothers people because it goes back to the days when a man's servants, his children, and his wife were all considered to be his property. They were known by his name because they belonged to him, and he was responsible for their actions and their debts.

The grammar used in talking or writing about weddings as well as other sexual relationships shows the expectation of men playing the active role. Men *wed* women while women *become* brides of men. A man *possesses* a woman; he *deflowers* her; he *performs;* he *scores;* he *takes away* her virginity. Although a woman can *seduce* a man, she cannot offer him her virginity. When talking about virginity, the only way to make the woman the actor in the sentence is to say that "She lost her virginity," but people lose things by accident rather than by purposeful actions, and so she's only the grammatical, not the real-life, actor.

The reason that women tried to bring the term *Ms.* into the language to replace *Miss* and *Mrs.* relates to this point. Married women resent being identified only under their husband's names. For example, when Susan Glascoe did something newsworthy, she would be identified in the newspaper only as Mrs. John Glascoe. The dictionary cards showed what appeared to be an attitude on the part of the editors that it was almost indecent to let a respectable woman's name march unaccompanied across the pages of a dictionary. Women were listed with male names whether or not the male contributed to the woman's reason for being in the dictionary or in his own right was as famous as the woman. For example, Charlotte Brontë was identified as Mrs. Arthur B. Nicholls, Amelia Earhart as Mrs. George Palmer Putnam, Helen Hayes as Mrs. Charles MacArthur, Jenny Lind as Mme. Otto Goldschmit, Cornelia Otis Skinner as the daughter of Otis, Harriet Beecher Stowe as the sister of Henry Ward Beecher, and Edith Sitwell as the sister of Osbert and Sacheverell. A very small number of women got into the dictionary without the benefit of a masculine escort. They were rebels and crusaders: temperance leaders Frances Elizabeth Caroline Willard and Carry Nation, women's rights leaders Carrie Chapman Catt and Elizabeth Cady Stanton, birth control educator Margaret Sanger, religious leader Mary Baker Eddy, and slaves Harriet Tubman and Phillis Wheatley.

Etiquette books used to teach that if a woman had *Mrs.* in front of her name, then the husband's name should follow because *Mrs.* is an abbreviated form of *Mistress* and a woman couldn't be a mistress of herself. As with many arguments about "correct" language usage, this isn't very logical because *Miss* is also an abbreviation of *Mistress.* Feminists hoped to simplify matters by introducing *Ms.* as an alternative to both *Mrs.* and *Miss,* but what happened is that *Ms.* largely replaced *Miss,* to become a catch-all business title for women. Many married women still prefer the title *Mrs.,* and some resent being addressed with the term *Ms.* As one frustrated newspaper reported complained, "Before I can write about a woman, I have to know not only her marital status but also her political philosophy." The re-

sult of such complications may contribute to the demise of titles, which are already being ignored by many computer programmers who find it more efficient to simply use names, for example in a business letter: "Dear Joan Garcia," instead of "Dear Mrs. Joan Garcia," "Dear Ms. Garcia," or "Dear Mrs. Louis Garcia."

The titles given to royalty provide an example of how males can be disadvantaged by the assumption that they are always to play the more powerful role. In British royalty, when a male holds a title, his wife is automatically given the feminine equivalent. But the reverse is not true. For example, a *count* is a high political officer with a *countess* being is his wife. The same is true for a *duke* and a *duchess* and a *king* and a *queen.* But when a female holds the royal title, the man she marries does not automatically acquire the matching title. For example, Queen Elizabeth's husband has the title of *prince* rather than *king,* but if Prince Charles should become king while he is still married to Lady or Princess Diana, she will be known as the queen. The reasoning appears to be that since masculine words are stronger, they are reserved for true heirs and withheld from males coming into the royal family by marriage. If Prince Philip were called *King Philip,* it would be much easier for British subjects to forget where the true power lies.

The names that people give their children show the hopes and dreams they have for them, and when we look at the differences between male and female names in a culture, we can see the cumulative expectations of that culture. In our culture girls often have names taken from small, aesthetically pleasing items, e.g., *Ruby, Jewel,* and *Pearl. Esther* and *Stella* mean "star," *Ada* means "ornament," and *Vanessa* means "butterfly." Boys are more likely to be given names with meanings of power and strength, e.g., *Neil* means "champion," *Martin* is from Mars, the God of War, *Raymond* means "wise protection," *Harold* means "chief of the army," *Ira* means "vigilant," *Rex* means "king," and *Richard* means "strong king."

We see similar differences in food metaphors. Food is a passive substance just sitting there waiting to be eaten. Many people have recognized this and so no longer feel comfortable describing women as "delectable morsels." However, when I was a teenager, it was considered a compliment to refer to a girl (we didn't call anyone a *woman* until she was middle-aged) as a *cute tomato,* a *peach,* a *dish,* a *cookie, honey, sugar,* or *sweetie-pie.* When being affectionate, women will occasionally call a man *honey* or *sweetie,* but in general, food metaphors are used much less often with men than with women. If a man is called *a fruit,* his masculinity is being questioned. But it's perfectly acceptable to use a food metaphor if the food is heavier and more substantive than that used for women. For example, pin-up pictures of women have long been known as *cheesecake,* but when Burt Reynolds posed for a nude centerfold the picture was immediately dubbed *beefcake,* cf. *a hunk of meat.* That such sexual references to men have come into the language is another reflection of how society is beginning to lessen the differences between their attitudes toward men and women.

Something similar to the *fruit* metaphor happens with references to plants. We insult a man by calling him a *pansy,* but it wasn't considered particularly insulting to talk about a girl being a *wallflower,* a *clinging vine,* or a *shrinking violet,* or to give girls such names as *Ivy, Rose, Lily, Iris, Daisy, Camellia, Heather,* and *Flora.* A plant metaphor can be used with a man if the plant is big and strong, for example, Andrew Jackson's nickname of *Old Hickory.* Also, the phrases *blooming idiots* and *budding geniuses* can be used with either sex, but notice how they are based on the most active thing a plant can do which is to bloom or bud.

Animal metaphors also illustrate the different expectations for males and females. Men are referred to as *studs, bucks,* and *wolves* while women are referred to with such metaphors as *kitten, bunny, beaver, bird, chick,* and *lamb.* In the 1950s we said that boys went *tomcatting,* but today it's just *catting around* and both boys and girls do it. When the term *foxy,* meaning that someone was sexy, first became popular it was used only for girls, but now someone of either sex can be described as *a fox.* Some animal metaphors that are used predominantly with men have negative connotations based on the size and/or strength of the animals, e.g., *beast, bull-headed, jackass, rat, loanshark,* and *vulture.* Negative metaphors used with women are based on smaller animals, e.g., *social butterfly, mousey, catty,* and *vixen.* The feminine terms connote ac-

tion, but not the same kind of large scale action as with the masculine terms.

WOMEN ARE CONNECTED WITH NEGATIVE CONNOTATIONS; MEN WITH POSITIVE CONNOTATIONS

The final point that my notecards illustrated was how many positive connotations are associated with the concept of masculine, while there are either trivial or negative connotations connected with the corresponding feminine concept. An example from the animal metaphors makes a good illustration. The word *shrew* taken from the name of a small but especially vicious animal was defined in my dictionary as "an ill-tempered scolding woman," but the word *shrewd* taken from the same root was defined as "marked by clever, discerning awareness" and was illustrated with the phrase "a shrewd businessman."

Early in life, children are conditioned to the superiority of the masculine role. As child psychologists point out, little girls have much more freedom to experiment with sex roles than do little boys. If a little girl acts like a *tomboy,* most parents have mixed feelings, being at least partially proud. But if their little boy acts like a *sissy* (derived from *sister*), they call a psychologist. It's perfectly acceptable for a little girl to sleep in the crib that was purchased for her brother, to wear his hand-me-down jeans and shirts, and to ride the bicycle that he has outgrown. But few parents would put a boy baby in a white and gold crib decorated with frills and lace, and virtually no parents would have their little boys wear his sister's hand-me-down dresses, nor would they have their son ride a girl's pink bicycle with a flower-bedecked basket. The proper names given to girls and boys show this same attitude. Girls can have "boy" names— *Chris, Craig, Jo, Kelly, Shawn, Teri, Toni,* and *Sam*—but it doesn't work the other way around. A couple of generations ago, *Beverly, Francis, Hazel, Marion,* and *Shirley* were common boys' names. As parents gave these names to more and more girls, they fell into disuse for males, and some older men who have these names prefer to go by their initials or by such abbreviated forms as *Haze* or *Shirl.*

When a little girl is told to *be a lady,* she is

being told to sit with her knees together and to be quiet and dainty. But when a little boy is told to *be a man* he is being told to be noble, strong, and virtuous—to have all the qualities that the speaker looks on as desirable. The concept of manliness has such positive connotations that it used to be a compliment to call someone a *he-man,* to say that he was doubly a man. Today many people are more ambivalent about this term and respond to it much as they do to the word *macho.* But calling someone a *manly man* or a *virile man* is nearly always meant as a compliment. *Virile* comes from the Indo-European *vir* meaning "man," which is also the basis of *virtuous.* Contrast the positive connotations of both *virile* and *virtuous* with the negative connotations of *hysterical.* The Greeks took this latter word from their name for *uterus* (as still seen in *hysterectomy*). They thought that women were the only ones who experienced uncontrolled emotional outbursts, and so the condition must have something to do with a part of the body that only women have.

Differences in the connotations between positive male and negative female connotations can be seen in several pairs of words that differ denotatively only in the matter of sex. *Bachelor* as compared to *spinster* or *old maid* has such positive connotations that women try to adopt them by using the term *bachelor-girl* or *bachelorette.* *Old maid* is so negative that it's the basis for metaphors: pretentious and fussy old men are called *old maids,* as are the leftover kernels of unpopped popcorn, and the last card in a popular children's game.

Patron and *matron* (Middle English for *father* and *mother*) have such different levels of prestige that women try to borrow the more positive masculine connotations with the word *patroness,* literally "female father." Such a peculiar term came about because of the high prestige attached to *patron* in such phrases as *a patron of the arts* or *a patron saint.* *Matron* is more apt to be used in talking about a women in charge of a jail or a public restroom.

When men are doing jobs that women often do, we apparently try to pay the men extra by giving them fancy titles, for example, a male cook is more likely to be called a *chef* while a male seamstress will get the title of *tailor.* The armed forces have a special problem in that they recruit

under such slogans as "The Marine Corps builds men!" and "Join the Army! Become a Man." Once the recruits are enlisted, they find themselves doing much of the work that has been traditionally thought of as "women's work." The solution to getting the work done and not insulting anyone's masculinity was to change the titles as shown below:

waitress	orderly
nurse	medic or corpsman
secretary	clerk-typist
assistant	adjutant
dishwasher or kitchen helper	KP (kitchen police)

Compare *brave* and *squaw.* Early settlers in America truly admired Indian men and hence named them with a word that carried connotations of youth, vigor, courage. But they used the Algonquin's name for "woman" and over the years it developed almost opposite connotations to those of *brave.* *Wizard* and *witch* contrast almost as much. The masculine *wizard* implies skill and wisdom combined with magic, while the feminine *witch* implies evil intentions combined with magic. Part of the unattractiveness of both *witch* and *squaw* is that they have been used so often to refer to old women, something with which our culture is particularly uncomfortable, just as the Afghans were. Imagine my surprise when I ran across the phrases *grandfatherly advice* and *old wives' tales* and realized that the underlying implication is the same as the Afghan proverb about old men being worth listening to while old women talk only foolishness.

Other terms that show how negatively we view old women as compared to young women are *old nag* as compared to *filly,* *old crow* or *old bat* as compared to *bird,* and of being *catty* as compared to being *kittenish.* There is no matching set of metaphors for men. The chicken metaphor tells the whole story of a woman's life. In her youth she is a *chick.* Then she marries and begins *feathering her nest.* Soon she begins feeling *cooped up,* so she goes to *hen parties* where she *cackles* with her friends. Then she has her *brood,* begins to *henpeck* her husband, and finally turns into an *old biddy.*

I embarked on my study of the dictionary not with the intention of prescribing language change but simply to see what the language would tell me about sexism. Nevertheless I have been both surprised and pleased as I've watched the changes that have occurred over the past two decades. I'm one of those linguists who believes that new language customs will cause a new generation of speakers to grow up with different expectations. This is why I'm happy about people's efforts to use inclusive language, to say *he or she* or *they* when speaking about individuals whose names they do not know. I'm glad that leading publishers have developed guidelines to help writers use language that is fair to both sexes, and I'm glad that most newspapers and magazines list women by their own names instead of only by their husbands' names and that educated and thoughtful people no longer begin their business letters with "Dear Sir" or "Gentlemen," but instead use a memo form or begin with such salutations as "Dear Colleagues," "Dear Reader," or "Dear Committee Members." I'm also glad that such words as *poetess, authoress, conductress,* and *aviatrix* now sound quaint and old-fashioned and that *chairman* is giving way to *chair* or *head, mailman* to *mail carrier, clergyman* to *clergy,* and *stewardess* to *flight attendant.* I was also pleased when the National Oceanic and Atmospheric Administration bowed to feminist complaints and in the late 1970s began to alternate men's and women's names for hurricanes. However, I wasn't so pleased to discover that the change did not immediately erase sexist thoughts from everyone's mind, as shown by a headline about Hurricane David in a 1979 New York tabloid, "David Rapes Virgin Islands." More recently a similar metaphor appeared in a headline in the *Arizona Republic* about Hurricane Charlie, "Charlie Quits Carolinas, Flirts with Virginia."

What these incidents show is that sexism is not something existing independently in American English or in the particular dictionary that I happened to read. Rather, it exists in people's minds. Language is like an X ray in providing visible evidence of invisible thoughts. The best thing about people being interested in and discussing sexist language is that as they make conscious decisions about what pronouns they will use, what jokes they will tell or laugh at, how they will write their names, or how they will begin their letters, they are forced to think about the underlying issue of sexism. This is good because

as a problem that begins in people's assumptions and expectations, it's a problem that will be solved only when a great many people have given it a great deal of thought.　　[1991]

Note

1. *CHADERI:* The long black dresses and head veils worn in public by Moslem women.

Understanding the Reading

1. What is problematic about the metaphorical words that relate to female sexuality?
2. Why are changes in language usage since 1970 important?
3. Explain the implications of the various ways women have been and are named.
4. What do food, plant, and animal metaphors reveal about gender stereotypes?
5. What is the significance of the negative connotations of words associated with women and of positive ones with men?

Suggestions for Responding

1. Nilsen endorses recent changes in language and usage. If you agree with her, describe additional changes she omits or additional changes you would like to see; in either case, explain why such changes are important.
2. If you disagree with her, try to persuade her she is wrong; support your position with specific examples. ✦

36

Memorabilia That Have Perpetuated Stereotypes About African Americans

KENNETH W. GOINGS

In Ralph Ellison's great novel *Invisible Man,* the main character, a black person known as Invisible Man, comes across a piece of "early Americana," a "jolly nigger bank," and sees this gross caricature with its black skin, red lips, and white eyes staring up at him from the floor. Enraged at the object and at the insensitivity of his landlady for keeping such an image around, the Invisible Man inadvertently breaks the bank and tries to sneak the pieces into a neighbor's trash can, but the neighbor stops him. Then he casually tries to leave the bundled pieces along the street, but a good samaritan returns the package to him. Finally, he ends up carrying the pieces with him into his hiding place, underground.

The Invisible Man's attempt to dispose of the broken pieces of the bank is indicative of African America's attempt to throw off racial and gender stereotypes. Every time the stereotypes seem to disappear someone or something brings them back. The something in this case is black memorabilia—often known as black collectibles—which have reflected and perpetuated racial and gender stereotypes about African Americans for years. These objects, produced from the late 17th century to the present, have been almost universally derogatory, with exaggerated racial features that helped "prove" that African Americans were "different" and inferior.

They also have been commonplace, items one might find in any home or yard: housewares (such as Aunt Jemima and Uncle Mose salt and pepper shakers), postcards, advertising cards, toys, lawn ornaments, etc. The everyday nature of these items meant that they were heavily used (the wear and tear on the surviving collectibles attests to this) and that frequency of use reinforced the owners' conscious and unconscious acceptance of the stereotypes. These items of material culture gave a physical reality to ideas of racial inferiority. They were the props that helped reinforce the racist ideology that emerged after Reconstruction.[1]

While collectibles were produced from the late 17th century on, their real significance as icons of racial and gender stereotyping dates back only to the decades immediately after the Civil War, when slavery was no longer a status determiner for African Americans. This was the period from 1880 to 1930, arguably the worst time for black people and race relations in the United States, a time that encompassed the retreat from Reconstruction, the rise of the second Klan,[2] hundreds of lynchings, the Great Migration north, and the race riots during and after World War I. It is during this period that new structures and new routines had to be developed and practiced to create and sustain a "new" or different racial ideology based not on slavery, but on concepts of racial inferiority. Folk-art pieces, sheet music, tourist items, and some housewares dominated this period. Black people, male and female, were portrayed as very dark, generally bug-eyed, nappy headed, childlike, stupid, lazy, deferential but happy. Black women were portrayed in the Jemima/mammy motif: fat, silent, nurturing and taking care of the "masses."

From the 1930's to the early 1960's in the United States, racial attitudes began to relax, to soften. Americans, including African Americans, had fought Nazis and Fascists overseas. It became more difficult, consequently, for whites to hold to the hard racist views of the past. Black collectibles reflect this changed perspective. Items, particularly housewares, became more functional and decorative. The skin tones on the collectibles were brighter, and some of the images of black women were slimmed down. Still, African-American women were generally portrayed as mammies and domestic workers and, increasingly, as the harlot. African-American males were represented as harmless, sexless clowns, not as mature workers, except for the image of the old family retainer, Uncle Mose. Their images emerged on salt and pepper shakers, cookie jars, stringholders, utility brushes, games, toys, and cooking utensils.

The final period, from the 1960's to the present, is somewhat peripheral to the main body of collectibles, much like the late 17th century to the 1880's. The last three decades have seen the most radical changes in race relations and attitudes. African Americans began calling themselves "black." The activism of the civil-rights movement, the resistance to police brutality linked with the assertiveness of the Black Power movement made it almost impossible to portray African Americans as loyal, servile, but happy Aunt Jemimas and Uncle Moses. Americans had only to turn on their television sets: It was obvious that Aunt Jemima and Uncle Mose were out marching, battling police dogs, and burning down Watts.[3] The exaggerated characteristics of the collectibles began to disappear as it became clearly illiberal, if not downright racist, to possess these items. Collectibles became more political: buttons, posters, and bumper stickers abounded. Also, black artists began creating new, more realistic images to replace the distorted images of the past.

To some extent, however, new—albeit more positive—stereotypes simply replaced the old. The militant Angela Davis traded places with Aunt Jemima and Malcolm X attempted to put Uncle Mose to rest.

Black collectibles are a window into American history. As the nation and ideology changed, the image created of black people by white people changed. Black collectibles were props in the slave/racial ideology that has engulfed America from the 17th century to the present. They were the physical manifestation of a culture that continually negated and demeaned African Americans and their achievements. Manufacturers produced the props that gave physical reality to the racist ideology that had emerged, and they did so at a profit. Literally, images of black people were being bought, sold, and used much like the slaves of ante-bellum America.

Perhaps one day, unlike the Invisible Man, African Americans will be able to leave these images in a trash can for keeps.   [1990]

Notes

1. RECONSTRUCTION: The twelve-year period following the Civil War when the federal government controlled the South.
2. SECOND KLAN: The Ku Klux Klan had three periods of significant strength in American history: the latter part of the nineteenth century, the 1920s, and the 1950s and early 1960s.
3. BURNING DOWN WATTS: Violent race riots, accompanied by widespread arson, occurred in Watts, a predominantly black neighborhood of Los Angeles, in 1965.

Understanding the Reading

1. What is wrong with such objects as Aunt Jemima and Uncle Mose housewares?
2. What characterizes black stereotypes, and why are they objectionable?
3. What led to changes in racial attitudes from the 1930s to the 1960s?
4. How and why have the stereotypes changed since the 1960s?

Suggestions for Responding

1. Describe the current stereotype of African-Americans, and try to explain the historical and contemporary ideology on which it rests.
2. Discuss the relationship between the stereotyped memorabilia Goings describes and the linguistic stereotyping Moore analyzes. ✦

37

Sex, Class and Race Intersections: Visions of Women of Color

CAROL LEE SANCHEZ

> *"As I understand it," said the American Indian [to one of the Puritan Fathers], "you propose to civilize me."*
> *"Exactly."*
> *"You want to get me out of the habit of idleness and teach me to work."*
> *"That is the idea."*
> *"And then lead me to simplify my methods and invent things to make my work lighter."*
> *"Yes."*
> *"And after that I'll become ambitious to get rich so that I won't have to work at all."*
> *"Naturally."*
> *"Well what's the use of taking such a roundabout way of getting just where I started from? I don't have to work now."*
> —[American Jokelore]

To identify Indian is to identify with an invisible or vanished people; it is to identify with a set of basic assumptions and beliefs held by *all* who are not Indian about the indigenous peoples of the Americas. Even among the Spanish-speaking Mestizos or mezclados,[1] there is a strong preference to "disappear" their Indian blood, to disassociate from their Indian beginnings. To be Indian is to be considered "colorful," spiritual, connected to the earth, simplistic, and disappointing if not dressed in buckskin and feathers; shocking if a city-dweller and even more shocking if an educator or other type of professional. That's the positive side.

On the negative side, to be Indian is to be thought of as primitive, alcoholic, ignorant (as in "Dumb Indian"), better off dead (as in "the only good Indian is a dead Indian" or "I didn't know there was any of you folks still left"), unskilled, non-competitive, immoral, pagan or heathen, untrustworthy (as in "Indian-giver") and frightening. To be Indian is to be the primary model that is used to promote racism in this country.

How can that happen, you ask? Bad press. One hundred and fifty years of the most consistently vicious press imaginable. Newspapers, dime novels, textbooks and fifty years of visual media have portrayed and continue to portray Indians as savage, blood-thirsty, immoral, inhuman people. When there's a touch of social consciousness attached, you will find the once "blood-thirsty," "white-killer savage" portrayed as a pitiful drunk, a loser, an outcast or a mix-blood not welcomed by, or trusted by, either race. For fifty years, children in this country have been raised to kill Indians mentally, subconsciously through the visual media, until it is an automatic reflex. That shocks you? Then I have made my point.

Let me quote from Helen Hunt Jackson's book, *A Century of Dishonor* from the introduction written by Bishop H. B. Whipple of Minnesota, who charged that:

> the American people have accepted as truth the teachings that the Indians were a degraded, brutal race of savages, who it was the will of God should perish at the approach of civilization. If they do not say with our Puritan fathers that these are the Hittites[2] who are to be driven out before the saints of the Lord, they do accept the teaching that manifest destiny[3] will drive the Indians from the earth. The inexorable has no tears or pity at the cries of anguish of the doomed race.

This race still struggles to stay alive. Tribe by Tribe, pockets of Indian people here and there. One million two hundred thousand people who identify as Indians—raised and socialized as Indian—as of the 1980 census, yet Cowboys and Indians is still played every day by children all over America of every creed, color, and nationality. Well—it's harmless isn't it? Just kids playing kill Indians. It's all history. But it's still happening every day, and costumes are sold and the cheap western is still rolling out of Hollywood, the old shoot-'em-up westerns playing on afternoon kid shows, late night T.V. Would you allow your children to play Nazis and Jews? Blacks and KKKs? Complete with costume? Yes! It is a horrifying thought, but in thinking about it you can see how easy it is to dismiss an entire race of people as barbaric and savage, and how almost impossible it is, after this has been inculcated in you, to relate to an Indian or a group of Indians today. For example, how many famous Indians do you know offhand? Certainly the great warrior chiefs come to mind first, and of course the three most famous Indian "Princesses"—Pocahontas, Sacajawea and La Malinche. Did you get past ten? Can you name at least five Indian women you know personally or have heard about? That's just counting on one hand, folks.

As Indians, we have endured. We are still here. We have survived everything that European "civilization" has imposed on us. There are approximately 130 different Indian languages still spoken in North America of the some 300 spoken at contact; 180 different Tribes incorporated and recognized by the Federal Government of the approximately 280 that once existed, with an additional 15 to 25 unrecognized Tribes that are lumped together on a reservation with other Tribes. We still have Women's Societies and there are at least 30 active women-centered Mother-Rite Cultures[4] existing and practicing their everyday life in that manner, on this continent.

We have been displaced, relocated, removed, terminated, educated, acculturated and in our hearts and minds we will always "go back to the blanket"[5] as long as we are still connected to our families, our Tribes and our land.

The Indian Way is a different way. It is a respectful way. The basic teachings in every Tribe that exists today as a Tribe in the western hemisphere are based on respect for all the things our Mother gave us. If we neglect her or anger her, she will make our lives very difficult and we always know that we have a hardship on ourselves and on our children. We are raised to be cautious and concerned for the *future* of our people, and that is how we raise our children—because *they* are *our* future. Your "civilization" has made all of us very sick and has made our mother earth sick and out of balance. Your kind of thinking and education has brought the whole world to the brink of total disaster, whereas the thinking and education among my people forbids the practice of almost everything Euro-Americans, in particular, value.

Those of you who are socialists and marxists have an ideology, but where in this country do you live communally on a common land base from generation to generation? Indians, who have a way of life instead of an ideology, do live on communal lands and don't accumulate anything—for the sake of accumulation.

Radicals look at reservation Indians and get very upset about their poverty conditions. But poverty to us is not the same thing as poverty is to you. Our poverty is that we can't be who we are. We can't hunt or fish or grow our food because our basic resources and the right to use them in traditional ways are denied us. In order to live well, we must be able to provide for ourselves in such a way that we can continue living as we always have. We still don't believe in being slaves to the "domineering" culture systems. Consequently, we are accused of many things based on those standards and values that make no sense to us.

You want us to act like you, to be like you so that we will be more acceptable, more likeable. You should try to be more like us regarding communal co-existence; respect and care for all living things and for the earth, the waters, and the atmosphere; respect for human dignity and the right to be who they are.

During the 1930s, '40s and '50s, relocation programs caused many Indians to become lost in the big cities of the United States and there were many casualties from alcoholism, vagrancy and petty crime. Most Indians were/are jailed for assault and battery in barroom brawls because the spiritual and psychological violation of Indian people trying to live in the dominant (domineering) culture generally forces us to numb ourselves as frequently as possible. That is difficult, if not impossible, for you to understand. White science studies dead things and creates poisonous substances to kill and maim the creatures as well as the humans. You call that progress. Indians call it insanity. Our science studies living things; how they interact and how they maintain a balanced existence. Your science disregards—even denies—the spirit world: ours believes in it and remains connected to it. We fast, pray to our ancestors, call on them when we dance and it rains—at Laguna, at Acoma, at Hopi—still, today. We fight among ourselves, we have border disputes, we struggle to exist in a modern context with our lands full of timber, uranium, coal, oil,

gasoline, precious metals and semi-precious stones; full—because we are taught to take only what we need and not because we are too ignorant to know what to do with all those resources. We are caught in the bind between private corporations and the government—"our guardian"—because they/you want all those resources. "Indians certainly don't need them"—and your people will do *anything* to get their hands on our mineral-rich lands. They will legislate, stir up internal conflicts, cause inter-Tribal conflicts, dangle huge amounts of monies as compensation for perpetual contracts and promise lifetime economic security. If we object, or sue to protect our lands, these suits will be held in litigation for fifteen to twenty years with "white" interests benefiting in the interim. Some of us give up and sell out, but there are many of us learning to hold out and many many more of us going back to the old ways of thinking, because we see that our ancestors were right and that the old ways were better ways. So, more Indians are going "back to the blanket," back to "Indian time," with less stress, fewer dominant (domineering) culture activities and occupations. Modern Indians are recreating Indian ways once again. All this leads to my vision as an Indian woman. It is my hope:

1. that you—all you non-Indians—study and learn about our systems of thought and internal social and scientific practices, leaving your Patriarchal Anthropology and History textbooks, academic training and methodologies at home or in the closet on a dusty shelf.

2. that your faculties, conference organizers, community organizers stop giving lip service to including a "Native American" for this or that with the appended phrase: "if we only knew one!" Go find one. There are hundreds of resource lists or Indian-run agencies, hundreds of Indian women in organizations all over the country—active and available with valuable contributions to make.

3. that you will strongly discourage or STOP the publication of any and all articles *about* Indians *written by non-Indians,* and publish work written by Indians about ourselves—whether you agree with us, approve of us or not.

4. that you will *stop colonizing us* and reinterpreting *our* experience.

5. that you will *listen* to us and *learn* from us.

We carry ancient traditions that are thousands of years old. We are modern and wear clothes like yours and handle all the trappings of your "civilization" as well as ours; maintain your Christianity as well as our ancient religions, and we are still connected to our ancestors, and our land base. You are the foreigners as long as you continue to believe in the progress that destroys our Mother.

You are not taught to respect our perfected cultures or our scientific achievements which have just recently been re-evaluated by your social scientists and "deemed worthy" of respect. Again, let me re-state that 150 years of bad press will certainly make it extremely difficult for most white people to accept these "primitive" achievements without immediately attempting to connect them to aliens from outer space, Egyptians, Vikings, Asians and whatever sophisticated "others" you have been educated to acknowledge as those who showed the "New World" peoples "The Way." Interestingly, the only continents that were ever "discovered" (historically) where people already lived are North and South America. Who discovered Europe? Who discovered Africa? Who discovered Asia? Trade routes, yes—continents, no. Manifest Destiny will continue to reign as long as we teach our children that Columbus "discovered" America. Even this "fact" is untrue. He actually discovered an island in the Caribbean and *failed* to discover Cathay!

When we consistently make ourselves aware of these "historical facts" that are presented by the Conqueror—the White Man—only then can all of us benefit from cultural traditions that are ten to thirty thousand years old. It is time for us to *share* the best of all our traditions and cultures, all over the world; and it is our duty and responsibility as the women of the world to make this positive contribution in any and every way we can, or we will ultimately become losers, as the Native Race of this hemisphere lost some four hundred years ago.   [1988]

Notes

1. MESTIZOS OR MEZCLADOS: The Latin-American name for the offspring of a Native American and a Spaniard.
2. HITTITES: Ancient nonblack peoples of Asia Minor and Syria.

3. MANIFEST DESTINY: A nineteenth-century belief that white people had the duty and right to control and develop the entire North American continent.
4. MOTHER-RITE CULTURES: Societies in which motherhood is the central kinship bond and women are highly valued and have considerable influence.
5. "GO BACK TO THE BLANKET": A phrase used by missionaries and white educators referring to "educated" Indian children who rejected white "civilized" values and returned to their native culture.

Understanding the Reading

1. What are the positive and negative stereotypes of Indians?
2. What does Sanchez mean when she says "children of this country have been raised to kill Indians"?
3. How does Sanchez characterize the Indian way?
4. Why do you think Sanchez objects to "articles about Indians written by non-Indians"?
5. What point is Sanchez making by her list of hopes?

Suggestions for Responding

1. Name and identify all the Native Americans you can think of. What does your list show you?
2. Compare and contrast Sanchez's characterization of the Indian stereotypes and Moore's analysis of "'Loaded' Words and Native Americans." ♦

38

The Model Minority Myth: Asian Americans Confront Growing Backlash

YIN LING LEUNG

The once predominant media caricatures of Asians such as the effeminate Charlie Chan, the evil Fu Manchu, the exotic dragon-lady Suzy Wong or the docile, submissive Mrs. Livingston are giving way to a more subtle but equally damaging image. The emerging picture of Asians as hard-working, highly-educated, family-oriented, and financially successful—in short, a "model minority"—appears benign at first, even beneficial. However, Asians are experiencing a growing backlash against their "model minority" status. The pervasive perception that Asian Americans are "making it," even surpassing whites despite of their minority status, is resulting in discriminatory college admittance practices and a rise in anti-Asian sentiment.

What is now being coined the "model minority myth" began to take root in the late 1960s, after increasing numbers of Asian immigrants came to the U.S. under the Immigration Act of 1965. A 1966 *U.S. News and World Report* article, entitled "Success Story of One Minority Group in the U.S.," portrayed Asian Americans as hard-working and uncomplaining, and implied that discrimination is not an obstacle for Asian Americans. A rash of similar articles followed, each attempting to reveal the "formula" responsible for Asian American success and prosperity.

The increased numbers of Southeast Asian refugees (the Hmong, Vietnamese, Laotian, and Kampuchean/Cambodians) and the increased immigration from Taiwan, Korea and Hong Kong have made Asians the second-fastest-growing minority population in the U.S. With this increase in numbers, the media has increased its focus on the "success stories" of Asian Americans as a whole. Articles in popular magazines such as *Newsweek, U.S. News and World Report* and others, with titles like "Asian-Americans: A 'Model Minority,'" "The Drive to Excel," "A Formula for Success," "The Promise of America," and "The Triumph of Asian Americans," perpetuate a distorted image of universal Asian-American success. One article in *Fortune* magazine portrayed Asians as a super competitive force, or "super minority," outperforming even the majority white population.

MYTH VERSUS REALITY

A closer examination of the facts, however, reveals holes in both the "model minority" and "super minority" myths. For example, 1980 census figures place the mean family income for Asian

American families in the U.S. at $26,456—nearly $3,000 higher than white families. These figures dramatically change, however, if adjusted for the number of workers per family. Because Asians tend to have more workers per family, the total income of a family reflects less per individual. In addition, over 64 percent of Asian Americans live in urban areas of San Francisco, Los Angeles, New York and Honolulu, where the incomes and cost of living are correspondingly higher.

The model minority myth also masks the complexity of Asians in America and the different realities they face. In fact, Asian Americans come from sharply distinct backgrounds which determine their life in the U.S. Many of the "successful" Asian immigrants touted by the media as exemplifying the model minority phenomenon come from families that have been in the states for many generations or from aristocratic, elite, educated, economically-advantaged backgrounds in their home countries. For example, the early Vietnamese refugee boat people were from wealthier and more educated communities than the more recent refugees from Vietnam. In addition, immigrants from China, Japan, and Korea tend to come from relatively more privileged backgrounds.

The more recent immigrants from Southeast Asia, like the Hmong, Laotian, Kampuchean/ Cambodian, and the Vietnamese refugees arriving after 1976, do not mirror the image of instant success that the media perpetuates. These hundreds of thousands of Southeast Asian refugees suffer not only from language difficulties, but also from deep-seated emotional and psychological disorders, resulting from the trauma they experienced in the war-torn countries of Southeast Asia. Asian refugees also face limited work opportunities, substandard wages and lack of health benefits and unhealthy working conditions.

Another facet to [the] model minority myth is the belief that all Asians excel academically. There is no disputing that Asian Americans are "overrepresented" in the nation's colleges and universities. Asians make up approximately 3.7 million, or 1.6 percent of the total U.S. population, but comprise 8 to 18 percent of enrollment in the nation's top colleges and universities. At the University of California at Berkeley, Asian students make up a quarter of the student population.

The media links Asian "success" in education with their strong familial bonds. This is, to some extent, an accurate portrayal. Many Asian cultures believe that social mobility is directly tied to education and therefore spend a disproportionate amount of family income on education, as compared to white families. Because it is a considerable sacrifice for most immigrant families to send their children to college, Asian students are often urged by their parents to pursue "safer" professions, such as medicine, engineering and other fields where the economic payback is proportionate to the number of years (and dollars) invested in education.

Even in these "safe" professions, however, Asians are discovering that quiet achievement and good job performance may not amount to promotions. A *Newsweek* article recently pointed to a phenomenon of Asian middle-management professionals, especially in corporate business fields, who "top-out," reaching a plateau beyond which their employers will not promote them.

BACKLASH: ASIANS FACE DISCRIMINATION

Repercussions of the model minority myth on Asian Americans could be described as "the many being punished by the success of a few." Asians of all classes and generations are experiencing a rise in anti-Asian sentiment. This anti-Asian sentiment is expressed both through subtle, systematic discrimination, particularly in higher education, and through racially-motivated violence.

Because of the disproportionate numbers of Asian Americans in the nation's universities, some colleges are denying Asians affirmative action consideration. At Princeton University, for example, where Asians make up approximately 8.5 percent of the entering class, admissions officials no longer consider Asian Americans as a minority group, despite federal regulations which define them as a protected subgroup.

Other prestigious colleges and universities are systematically excluding qualified Asians through the application of heavily subjective criteria. At the University of California at Berkeley, for example, despite a 14 percent rise in applications between 1983 to 1985, the number of Asian Americans admitted to UCB dropped 20 percent in 1984.

The Asian American Task Force on UC Admissions, which conducted a seven-month study, found that the university had temporarily used a minimum SAT verbal score to disqualify applicants. While Asian Americans excel on the math sections of the SAT, their national average on the verbal portion of the test was under 400. The Task Force also found that UCB now relies more heavily on subjective criteria for freshmen admissions. For the fall of 1987, grades and test scores will determine only 40 percent of admittees, while 30 percent will be chosen by subjective factors which tend to operate against Asians.

According to Henry Der, executive director of Chinese for Affirmative Action: "Qualified Asian students are being excluded from the Berkeley campus in substantial numbers. It is apparent that UC policy changes are conscious attempts to limit the growth of Asian students, to the benefit of qualified white students."

Discriminatory practices at UC Berkeley point to a nationwide trend. At Harvard University, where Asians make up 10.9 percent of the first-year class, admitted Asian students had scores substantially higher than white students who were admitted. At Brown University, a study conducted by Asian-American students found that Asian-American admittance rates in the early 1980s had been consistently lower than the all-college admittance rate.

There is increasing evidence that these and other select schools are designing "hidden quotas" to exclude otherwise qualified Asian applicants. For example, a recent survey of Asian-American applicants at Stanford demonstrated that popular images of Asians as narrowly-focused math and science students influenced how admissions officers judged Asians for entrance to college campuses. Just as "regional diversity" was used as mechanism to keep Jews, who tended to be concentrated in metropolitan areas like New York and Los Angeles, out of elite institutions prior to World War II, "extra-curricular and leadership" criteria are functioning in similar manner for certain Asians. The Stanford study found that although Asian Americans participated in nearly the same proportion as whites in high school sports, in equal numbers in music and in greater numbers in social, ethnic and community organizations, "intentional or unintentional" biases have made many applicants the victims of racial stereotypes.

Black conservative Thomas Sowell and other neoconservatives applaud the divorce of Asians from their minority status. Sowell believes that this will cause schools to be just as rigorous in selecting Asian students as they are at selecting majority white students. In this way, he continues, students will not be mismatched with their schools, a problem he attributes to quota requirements.

ANTI-ASIAN SENTIMENT RISING

The model minority myth, coupled with the rising economic prowess of Pacific Rim Asian countries and the corresponding economic downturn in the U.S., has given rise to an increase in anti-Asian violence. In 1981, the Japanese American Citizens League recorded seven cases in which anti-Asian sentiment was expressed verbally, legislatively or physically; in 1982 they recorded four; in 1983, 20; in 1984, 30; in 1985, 48.

One explanation for this rise in anti-Asian violence is that Asians are being used as scapegoats for the nation's economic problems. Both business and labor have waged explicitly anti-Asian media campaigns portraying Japanese competition as an explanation for the ills of American industry.

The case of Vincent Chin dramatically demonstrates the potential impact of such campaigns. Chin, a 27-year-old Chinese-American resident of Detroit, was bludgeoned to death by two white unemployed auto workers. The two men, who were merely fined and put on probation, mistook him for Japanese. They saw Chin as a representative of the Japanese automobile imports business, which they blamed for the loss of their jobs. Violence against Asian refugees and immigrants who compete for scarce resources in low-income communities has also dramatically increased.

THE ASIAN COMMUNITY RESPONDS

Asian Americans are contradicting the very stereotype of the hard-working, uncomplaining minority by protesting the discriminatory practices in the nation's colleges and in the job market. For example, the Chinese American Legal Defense Fund, a Michigan-based organization, has filed suit against UC Berkeley and several other elite institutions, including Stanford, Princeton, Yale, and MIT. They charge that campuses have imposed "secret quotas" on Asians because of their growing enrollments. In another case, Yat-Pang Au, valedictorian of San Jose's Gunderson High School with "top test scores and an impressive array of extracurricular activities," is threatening a civil rights suit against UC Berkeley for denying his entrance to the competitive College of Engineering.

At least one school has responded to this pressure by re-examining its admittance policies. A recent study of Asian student admission at Stanford, Brown, Harvard, and Princeton by John H. Bunzel and Jeffrey K. D. Au, both from Stanford, found that Stanford was the only university to buck the trend of declining Asian admissions. The 1986 entering class of Asian Americans increased from 119 last year to 245 this year. Asians at Stanford make up 15.6 percent of the class, still lower than the UC Berkeley, where 26.5 percent of this year's entering class are Asian Americans.

Mobilizations against anti-Asian violence have also begun on the national and the community level. The Japanese American Citizens League, the Violence Against Asians Taskforce, Chinese for Affirmative Action, and other Asian groups have monitored incidents of anti-Asian violence and pressured the U.S. Commission on Civil Rights and other government bodies to confront and investigate the problem. Projects such as the Coalition to Break the Silence and the Community Violence Prevention Project, both in Oakland, CA, are fighting to raise community consciousness on the issue through community forums and legislative testimony. The Coalition to Break the Silence has also developed ties with other organizations doing similar work in Los Angeles, New York, and Boston.   [1987]

Understanding the Reading

1. Describe the stereotype of Asian-Americans as the model minority or the super minority.
2. How does the stereotype distort or misrepresent reality?
3. What negative consequences does the model minority stereotype lead to?
4. What are Asian-Americans doing to challenge the stereotype?

Suggestions for Responding

1. Investigate an earlier stereotype of Asian-Americans or the stereotype of Eastern European Jews in the early part of this century and compare it with the current model minority stereotype.
2. The model minority stereotype seems to penalize Asian-Americans for working hard to succeed within the American system. Describe a situation in which you found yourself in this kind of double bind, when you were unfairly deprived of the rewards for doing the right thing. ✦

39

A White Man's Word

DEBRA SWALLOW

The screen door slammed shut, and I just knew eighty flies came in. Then I heard wailing and gibberish and ran to see who it was. My nine-year-old son was running toward me with blood, tears and dirty sweat trickling off his chin, making my knees go weak.

"What happened? Who did this to you?" I asked, kneeling to wipe his round face with a cool, damp cloth.

"I got in a fight, Mom. Mom, what's a half-breed?"

I felt like my blood stopped running, and I closed my eyes to kill my tears, my mind opening up a day I'd almost forgotten.

I opened my eyes to see how under-water looked, and a sting like cactus tips closed them fast. Surfacing, I looked across the pool for my friend. The water shimmered turquoise blue, reflecting nothing but the painted concrete bottom and rectangles of green light from the roof. Forty or fifty pale faces and arms bobbed and floated above the water, but no sign of my friend's brown, familiar face.

"Maybe it's time to go," I thought and swam to the closest edge. Feeling the rough, slimy ce-

ment on the palms of my hands, I hauled myself out of the water. Unsure of my footing, I walked slowly toward the shower rooms.

Screams, giggles and little-girl conversation filled the room, along with spraying, splashing and draining water. Stooping to peek under the first shower stall, I saw two white feet and moved on to the second door. Also two white feet. Next door, four white feet. I could feel myself starting to shiver now and my breath felt trapped in my chest. "What if they left me? I don't know anybody here," I thought.

My friend and her mom took me with them to Rushville to swim. My first time alone away from my family, and here I was, scared among white people—the only Indian in sight.

I decided to just kind of stand around in the shower room. I knew she wasn't in the pool, so she had to come here, where our clothes were. Trying to be as unnoticeable as possible, I leaned against a cool, wet wall and watched the white girls in the room, curious because I'd never been around any before.

"My dad bought me a brand-new bike and it has a blue daisy basket on the handlebars," one girl whined to her friend. "Well, I already knew that, but did you know my dad bought me a new bed and it has a canopy on it!" she whined back in a sing-song voice. The two girls were probably eight years old like me, but both were chubby with blonde ringlets and painted toenails.

Spacing out their words, I was thinking about the bike Dad made my sister and me. He made it from all different parts he found at the trash pile, and it looked funny and rusty, but it worked real well. Daddy also made us a pair of stilts, a playhouse and a pogo stick, which all our friends wanted to play with. I knew my dad was better than theirs, he BUILT stuff for us.

I noticed the first girl was dressed now, and while waiting for her friend to finish, she pulled out a whole handful of red licorice and chewed on one while her friend jabbered, every once in a while glancing at me, not knowing my tongue ached to taste just one mouthful of her licorice. Every time she looked at me, I wanted to evaporate. I had on a borrowed swimsuit a size too big, dull and old-fashioned compared to the bright-colored flower or print-covered two-pieces all the other girls wore. My hair hung down my back, straight and thick and dark.

The first girl said, "Look, this Indian is staring

at us," and glared at me with icy blue eyes, her nose pointing to the ceiling. The second girl said, "Oh, she don't know what we're saying anyhow. Dirty Indians don't know anything." Her friend said, "I don't think she's really a real Indian. My dad says some of them are half-breeds. So she's not *all* dirty."

"Only half-dirty," her friend said, and they giggled together and laughed at me.

My face felt hot and my arms were heavy as I walked carefully across the wet, slippery floor towards them. I noticed from far away that the room's noises started to fade.

I grabbed one of them by her hair and threw her away, wrapped my arm around the other one's neck and wrestled her down, and sitting on her, I kept punching her till her friend grabbed me. I stood up, and jerking away, I tripped her, landing her by her friend. They were both still crying and screaming on the floor when I walked out, carrying my bundle of clothes under my arm.

Standing outside in the shade of the pool building, I was really scared. There was someone yelling, "Debi! Debi!" but I wouldn't look. Somehow I thought they found out my name and were going to do something to me. But it was my friend's mom; she and my friend went for popsicles and just got back. I ran to their car and told them what I did, so my friend's mom went in after the clothes my friend left in the shower room and we headed back for home.

Safe once again with my family, I told Mom and Dad I got in a fight.

"Daddy, what's a half-breed?" I asked him.

The house got quiet, the only sound was the wind. Daddy looked at me and his eyes were sad.

"My girl, you're an Indian. The way of living is Indian. Lakota."

I said, "Yes, but what is a half-breed?"

"A white man's word," is what he said. "It's just a white man's word."

Now, eighteen years later, I was wiping blood from my son's face, and his question made my body shake with anger, sadness, frustration and hatred. Opening my eyes, I answered, "You're Lakota, son. The way of living is Indian. You're Lakota." He looked at me with black eyes shining with tears he now refused to shed, and asked me again what a half-breed was.

"A white man's word," is what I said. "It's just a white man's word."   [1988]

Understanding the Reading

1. What does the term "half-breed" mean, and what connotations does it carry?
2. What characteristics do the white girls attribute to Indians?
3. What do her Daddy and she mean by the assertion that "half-breed" is "just a white man's word"?

Suggestions for Responding

1. There is a derogatory label for almost every group. At one time or another, we all have suffered from name-calling intended to reduce us to the confines of some stereotype. Describe such an incident you have experienced, how it made you feel, how you responded, and how you feel about it today.
2. How is the stereotype Swallow presents connected to Moore's analysis of "'Loaded' Words and Native Americans" and Sanchez's description of this stereotype? ✦

40

The Jewbird

BERNARD MALAMUD

The window was open so the skinny bird flew in. Flappity-flap with its frazzled black wings. That's how it goes. It's open, you're in. Closed, you're out and that's your fate. The bird wearily flapped through the open kitchen window of Harry Cohen's top-floor apartment on First Avenue near the lower East River. On a rod on the wall hung an escaped canary cage, its door wide open, but this black-type long-beaked bird—its ruffled head and small dull eyes, crossed a little, making it look like a dissipated crow—landed if not smack on Cohen's thick lamb chop, at least on the table, close by. The frozen foods salesman was sitting at supper with his wife and young son on a hot August evening a year ago. Cohen, a heavy man with hairy chest and beefy shorts; Edie, in skinny yellow shorts and red halter; and their ten-year-old Morris (after his father)—

Maurie, they called him, a nice kid though not overly bright—were all in the city after two weeks out, because Cohen's mother was dying. They had been enjoying Kingston, New York, but drove back when Mama got sick in her flat in the Bronx.

"Right on the table," said Cohen, putting down his beer glass and swatting at the bird. "Son of a bitch."

"Harry, take care with your language," Edie said, looking at Maurie, who watched every move.

The bird cawed hoarsely and with a flap of its bedraggled wings—feathers tufted this way and that—rose heavily to the top of the open kitchen door, where it perched staring down.

"Gevalt, a pogrom!"[1]

"It's a talking bird," said Edie in astonishment.

"In Jewish," said Maurie.

"Wise guy," muttered Cohen. He gnawed on his chop, then put down the bone. "So if you can talk, say what's your business. What do you want here?"

"If you can't spare a lamb chop," said the bird, "I'll settle for a piece of herring with a crust of bread. You can't live on your nerve forever."

"This ain't a restaurant," Cohen replied. "All I'm asking is what brings you to this address?"

"The window was open," the bird sighed; adding after a moment, "I'm running. I'm flying but I'm also running."

"From whom?" asked Edie with interest.

"Anti-Semeets."

"Anti-Semites?" they all said.

"That's from who."

"What kind of anti-Semites bother a bird?" Edie asked.

"Any kind," said the bird, "also including eagles, vultures, and hawks. And once in a while some crows will take your eyes out."

"But aren't you a crow?"

"Me? I'm a Jewbird."

Cohen laughed heartily. "What do you mean by that?"

The bird began dovening.[2] He prayed without Book or tallith,[3] but with passion. Edie bowed her head though not Cohen. And Maurie rocked back and forth with the prayer, looking up with one wide-open eye.

When the prayer was done Cohen remarked, "No hat, no phylacteries?"[4]

"I'm an old radical."

"You're sure you're not some kind of a ghost of dybbuk?"[5]

"Not a dybbuk," answered the bird, "though one of my relatives had such an experience once. It's all over now, thanks God. They freed her from a former lover, a crazy jealous man. She's now the mother of two wonderful children."

"Birds?" Cohen asked slyly.

"Why not?"

"What kind of birds?"

"Like me. Jewbirds."

Cohen tipped back in his chair and guffawed. "That's a big laugh. I've heard of a Jewfish but not a Jewbird."

"We're once removed." The bird rested on one skinny leg, then on the other. "Please, could you spare maybe a piece of herring with a small crust of bread?"

Edie got up from the table.

"What are you doing?" Cohen asked her.

"I'll clear the dishes."

Cohen turned to the bird. "So what's your name, if you don't mind saying?"

"Call me Schwartz."

"He might be an old Jew changed into a bird by somebody," said Edie, removing a plate.

"Are you?" asked Harry, lighting a cigar.

"Who knows?" answered Schwartz. "Does God tell us everything?"

Maurie got up on his chair. "What kind of herring?" he asked the bird in excitement.

"Get down, Maurie, or you'll fall," ordered Cohen.

"If you haven't got matjes, I'll take schmaltz,"[6] said Schwartz.

"All we have is marinated, with slices of onion—in a jar," said Edie.

If you'll open for me the jar I'll eat marinated. Do you have also, if you don't mind, a piece of rye bread—the spitz?"[7]

Edie thought she had.

"Feed him out on the balcony," Cohen said. He spoke to the bird. "After that take off."

Schwartz closed both bird eyes. "I'm tired and it's a long way."

"Which direction are you headed, north or south?"

Schwartz, barely lifting his wings, shrugged.

"You don't know where you're going?"

"Where there's charity I'll go."

"Let him stay, papa," said Maurie. "He's only a bird."

"So stay the night," Cohen said, "but no longer."

In the morning Cohen ordered the bird out of the house but Maurie cried, so Schwartz stayed for a while. Maurie was still on vacation from school and his friends were away. He was lonely and Edie enjoyed the fun he had, playing with the bird.

"He's no trouble at all," she told Cohen, "and besides his appetite is very small."

"What'll you do when he makes dirty?"

"He flies across the street in a tree when he makes dirty, and if nobody passes below, who notices?"

"So all right," said Cohen, "but I'm dead set against it. I warn you he ain't gonna stay here long."

"What have you got against the poor bird?"

"Poor bird, my ass. He's a foxy bastard. He thinks he's a Jew."

"What difference does it make what he thinks?"

"A Jewbird, what a chutzpah.[8] One false move and he's out on his drumsticks."

At Cohen's insistence Schwartz lived out on the balcony in a new wooden birdhouse Edie had bought him.

"With many thanks," said Schwartz, "though I would rather have a human roof over my head. You know how it is at my age. I like the warm, the windows, the smell of cooking. I would also be glad to see once in a while the *Jewish Morning Journal* and have now and then a schnapps[9] because it helps my breathing, thanks God. But whatever you give me, you won't hear complaints."

However, when Cohen brought home a bird feeder full of dried corn, Schwartz said, "Impossible."

Cohen was annoyed. "What's the matter, crosseyes, is your life getting too good for you? Are you forgetting what it means to be migratory? I'll bet a helluva lot of crows you happen to be acquainted with, Jews or otherwise, would give their eyeteeth to eat this corn."

Schwartz did not answer. What can you say to a grubber yung?[10]

"Not for my digestion," he later explained to Edie. "Cramps. Herring is better even if it makes you thirsty. At least rainwater don't cost anything." He laughed sadly in breathy caws.

And herring, thanks to Edie, who knew where to shop, was what Schwartz got, with an occasional piece of potato pancake, and even a bit of soupmeat when Cohen wasn't looking.

When school began in September, before Cohen would once again suggest giving the bird the boot, Edie prevailed on him to wait a little while until Maurie adjusted.

"To deprive him right now might hurt his school work, and you know what trouble we had last year."

"So okay, but sooner or later the bird goes. That I promise you."

Schwartz, though nobody had asked him, took on full responsibility for Maurie's performance in school. In return for favors granted, when he was let in for an hour or two at night, he spent most of his time overseeing the boy's lessons. He sat on top of the dresser near Maurie's desk as he laboriously wrote out his homework. Maurie was a restless type and Schwartz gently kept him to his studies. He also listened to him practice his screechy violin, taking a few minutes off now and then to rest his ears in the bathroom. And they afterwards played dominoes. The boy was an indifferent checker player and it was impossible to teach him chess. When he was sick, Schwartz read him comic books though he personally disliked them. But Maurie's work improved in school and even his violin teacher admitted his playing was better. Edie gave Schwartz credit for these improvements though the bird pooh-poohed them.

Yet he was proud there was nothing lower than C minuses on Maurie's report card, and on Edie's insistence celebrated with a little schnapps.

"If he keeps up like this," Cohen said, "I'll get him in an Ivy League college for sure."

"Oh I hope so," sighed Edie.

But Schwartz shook his head. "He's a good boy—you don't have to worry. He won't be a shicker[11] or a wifebeater, God forbid, but a scholar he'll never be, if you know what I mean, although maybe a good mechanic. It's no disgrace in these times."

"If I were you," Cohen said, angered, "I'd keep my big snoot out of other people's private business."

"Harry, please," said Edie.

"My goddamn patience is wearing out. That crosseyes butts into everything."

Though he wasn't exactly a welcome guest in the house, Schwartz gained a few ounces although he did not improve in appearance. He looked bedraggled as ever, his feathers unkempt, as though he had just flown out of a snowstorm. He spent, he admitted, little time taking care of himself. Too much to think about. "Also outside plumbing," he told Edie. Still there was more glow to his eyes so that though Cohen went on calling him crosseyes he said it less emphatically.

Liking his situation, Schwartz tried tactfully to stay out of Cohen's way, but one night when Edie was at the movies and Maurie was taking a hot shower, the frozen foods salesman began a quarrel with the bird.

"For Christ sake, why don't you wash yourself sometimes? Why must you always stink like a dead fish?"

"Mr. Cohen, if you'll pardon me, if somebody eats garlic he will smell from garlic. I eat herring three times a day. Feed me flowers and I will smell like flowers."

"Who's obligated to feed you anything at all? You're lucky to get herring."

"Excuse me, I'm not complaining," said the bird. "You're complaining."

"What's more," said Cohen, "even from out on the balcony I can hear you snoring away like a pig. It keeps me awake at night."

"Snoring," said Schwartz, "isn't a crime, thanks God."

"All in all you are a goddamn pest and free loader. Next thing you'll want to sleep in bed next to my wife."

"Mr. Cohen," said Schwartz, "on this rest assured. A bird is a bird."

"So you say, but how do I know you're a bird and not some kind of a goddamn devil?"

"If I was a devil you would know already. And I don't mean because your son's good marks."

"Shut up, you bastard bird," shouted Cohen.

"Grubber yung," cawed Schwartz, rising to the tips of his talons, his long wings outstretched.

Cohen was about to lunge for the bird's scrawny neck but Maurie came out of the bathroom, and for the rest of the evening until Schwartz's bedtime on the balcony, there was pretended peace.

But the quarrel had deeply disturbed Schwartz and he slept badly. His snoring woke him, and awake, he was fearful of what would become of him. Wanting to stay out of Cohen's way, he kept to the birdhouse as much as possible. Cramped by it, he paced back and forth on the balcony ledge, or sat on the birdhouse roof, staring into space. In evenings, while overseeing Maurie's lessons, he often fell asleep. Awakening, he nervously hopped around exploring the four corners of the room. He spent much time in Maurie's closet, and carefully examined his bureau drawers when they were left open. And once when he found a large paper bag on the floor, Schwartz poked his way into it to investigate what possibilities were. The boy was amused to see the bird in the paper bag.

"He wants to build a nest," he said to his mother.

Edie, sensing Schwartz's unhappiness, spoke to him quietly.

"Maybe if you did some of the things my husbands wants you, you would get along better with him."

"Give me a for instance," Schwartz said.

"Like take a bath, for instance."

"I'm too old for baths," said the bird, "My feathers fall out without baths."

"He says you have a bad smell."

"Everybody smells. Some people smell because of their thoughts or because who they are. My bad smell comes from the food I eat. What does his come from?"

"I better not ask him or it might make him mad," said Edie.

In late November Schwartz froze on the balcony in the fog and cold, and especially on rainy days he woke with stiff joints and could barely move his wings. Already he felt twinges of rheumatism. He would have liked to spend more time in the warm house, particularly when Maurie was in school and Cohen at work. But though Edie was good-hearted and might have sneaked him in in the morning, just to thaw out, he was afraid to ask her. In the meantime Cohen, who had been reading articles about the migration of birds, came out on the balcony one night after work when Edie was in the kitchen preparing pot roast, and peeking into the birdhouse, warned Schwartz to be on his way soon if he knew what was good for him. "Time to hit the flyways."

"Mr. Cohen, why do you hate me so much?" asked the bird. "What did I do to you?"

"Because you're an A-number-one trouble maker, that's why. What's more, whoever heard of a Jewbird! Now scat or it's open war."

But Schwartz stubbornly refused to depart so Cohen embarked on a campaign of harassing him, meanwhile hiding it from Edie and Maurie. Maurie hated violence and Cohen didn't want to leave a bad impression. He thought maybe if he played dirty tricks on the bird he would fly off without being physically kicked out. The vacation was over, let him make his easy living off the fat of somebody else's land. Cohen worried about the effect of the bird's departure on Maurie's schooling but decided to take the chance, first, because the boy now seemed to have the knack of studying—give the black bird-bastard credit—and second, because Schwartz was driving him bats by being there always, even in his dreams.

The frozen foods salesman began his campaign against the bird by mixing watery cat food with the herring slices in Schwartz's dish. He also blew up and popped numerous paper bags outside the birdhouse as the bird slept, and when he got Schwartz good and nervous, though not enough to leave, he brought a full-grown cat into the house, supposedly a gift for little Maurie, who had always wanted a pussy. The cat never stopped springing up at Schwartz whenever he saw him, one day managing to claw out several of his tailfeathers. And even at lesson time, when the cat was usually excluded from Maurie's room, though somehow or other he quickly found his way in at the end of the lesson, Schwartz was desperately fearful of his life and flew from pinnacle to pinnacle—light fixture to clothes-tree to door-top—in order to elude the beast's wet jaws. Once when the bird complained to Edie how hazardous his existence was, she said, "Be patient, Mr. Schwartz. When the cat gets to know you better he won't try to catch you any more."

"When he stops trying we will both be in Paradise," Schwartz answered. "Do me a favor and get rid of him. He makes my whole life worry. I'm losing feathers like a tree loses leaves."

"I'm awfully sorry but Maurie likes the pussy and sleeps with it."

What could Schwartz do? He worried but came to no decision, being afraid to leave. So he ate the herring garnished with cat food, tried hard not to hear the paper bags bursting like fire crackers outside the birdhouse at night, and lived terror-stricken closer to the ceiling than the floor, as the cat, his tail flicking, endlessly watched him.

Weeks went by. Then on the day after Cohen's mother had died in her flat in the Bronx, when Maurie came home with a zero on an arithmetic test, Cohen, enraged, waited until Edie had taken the boy to his violin lesson, then openly attacked the bird. He chased him with a broom on the balcony and Schwartz frantically flew back and forth, finally escaping into his birdhouse. Cohen triumphantly reached in, and grabbing both skinny legs, dragged the bird out, cawing loudly, his wings wildly beating. He whirled the bird around and around his head. But Schwartz, as he moved in circles, managed to swoop down and catch Cohen's nose in his beak, and hung on for dear life. Cohen cried out in great pain, punched the bird with his fist, and tugging at its legs with all his might, pulled his nose free. Again he swung the yawking Schwartz around until the bird grew dizzy, then with a furious heave, flung him into the night. Schwartz sank like stone into the street. Cohen then tossed the birdhouse and feeder after him, listening at the ledge until they crashed on the sidewalk below. For a full hour, broom in hand, his heart palpitating and nose throbbing with pain, Cohen waited for Schwartz to return but the broken-hearted bird didn't.

That's the end of that dirty bastard, the salesman thought and went in. Edie and Maurie had come home.

"Look," said Cohen, pointing to his bloody nose swollen three times its normal size, "what that sonofabitch bird did. It's a permanent scar."

"Where is he now?" Edie asked, frightened.

"I threw him out and he flew away. Good riddance."

Nobody said no, though Edie touched a handkerchief to her eyes and Maurie rapidly tried the nine times table and found he knew approximately half.

In the spring when the winter's snow had melted, the boy, moved by a memory, wandered in the neighborhood, looking for Schwartz. He found a dead black bird in a small lot near the river, his two wings broken, neck twisted, and both bird-eyes plucked clean.

"Who did it to you, Mr. Schwartz?" Maurie wept.

"Anti-Semeets," Edie said later.   [1963]

Notes

1. "GEVALT, A POGROM": "What do I do now! It's another officially sanctioned persecution and massacre of Jews."
2. DOVENING: The Orthodox Jewish prayer practice that involves rhythmic movement of the upper body.
3. TALLITH: A fringed prayer shawl used by Jewish men.
4. PHYLACTERIES: Small leather boxes containing scriptural quotations used in Jewish worship.
5. DYBBUK: A demon possessing a living person.
6. MATJES AND SCHMALTZ: Expensive and cheap herring, respectively.
7. SPITZ: The heel of a loaf of bread.
8. CHUTZPAH: Brazenness.
9. SCHNAPPS: Liquor.
10. GRUBBER YUNG: Crude joker.
11. SHICKER: Drinker.

Understanding the Reading

1. In what ways is Schwartz characterized as a stereotypic Jew?
2. In what ways does he challenge the stereotype?
3. Why does Cohen resent and dislike Schwartz?
4. Why is Cohen's campaign against Schwartz ironic?
5. In what ways is Edie correct in concluding that anti-Semitism was the cause of Schwartz's death?

Suggestions for Responding

Several readings in Part IV have raised the issue of how stereotypes can lead to self-hatred, the internalization of negative depictions of a group. Malamud satirically exaggerates Cohen's group hatred, but most people dissociate themselves from the negative stereotype attributed to a group with which they are associated—a woman who takes pride in being told she thinks like a man, African-Americans who prefer light skin or "good" (straighter) hair, gays who pass as heterosexuals, or German-Americans who changed their name during World War II.

1. Try to analyze why people act this way and what the personal and social costs of such behaviors are.
2. Describe a time or a situation when you wanted or tried to distance yourself from or deny stereotyped assumptions about a group with which you were associated. Were you successful or not? How did you feel then, and how do you feel about it now? ◆

41

Just Walk On By

BRENT STAPLES

My first victim was a woman—white, well dressed, probably in her early twenties. I came upon her late one evening on a deserted street in Hyde Park, a relatively affluent neighborhood in an otherwise mean, impoverished section of Chicago. As I swung onto the avenue behind her, there seemed to be a discreet, uninflammatory distance between us. Not so. She cast back a worried glance. To her, the youngish black man—a broad six feet two inches with a beard and billowing hair, both hands shoved into the pockets of a bulky military jacket—seemed menacingly close. After a few more quick glimpses, she picked up her pace and was soon running in earnest. Within seconds she disappeared into a cross street.

That was more than a decade ago. I was 22 years old, a graduate student newly arrived at the University of Chicago. It was in the echo of that terrified woman's footfalls that I first began to know the unwieldy inheritance I'd come into—the ability to alter public space in ugly ways. It was clear that she thought herself the quarry of a mugger, a rapist, or worse. Suffering a bout of insomnia, however, I was stalking sleep, not defenseless wayfarers. As a softy who is scarcely able to take a knife to a raw chicken—let alone hold it to a person's throat—I was surprised, embarrassed, and dismayed all at once. Her flight made me feel like an accomplice in tyranny. It also made it clear that I was indistinguishable from the muggers who occasionally seeped into the area from the surrounding ghetto. That first encounter, and those that followed, signified that a vast, unnerving gulf lay between nighttime pedestrians—particularly women—and me. And I soon gathered that being perceived as dangerous is a hazard in itself. I only needed to turn a corner into a dicey situation, or crowd some frightened, armed person in a foyer somewhere, or make an errant move after being pulled over by a policeman. Where fear and weapons meet—and they often do in urban America—there is always the possibility of death.

In that first year, my first away from my hometown, I was to become thoroughly familiar with the language of fear. At dark, shadowy intersections in Chicago, I could cross in front of a car stopped at a traffic light and elicit the *thunk, thunk, thunk, thunk* of the driver—black, white, male, or female—hammering down the door locks. On less traveled streets after dark, I grew accustomed to but never comfortable with people who crossed to the other side of the street rather than pass me. Then there were the standard unpleasantries with police, doormen, bouncers, cab drivers, and others whose business it is to screen out troublesome individuals *before* there is any nastiness.

I moved to New York nearly two years ago and I have remained an avid night walker. In central Manhattan, the near-constant crowd cover minimizes tense one-on-one street encounters. Elsewhere—visiting friends in SoHo, where sidewalks are narrow and tightly spaced buildings shut out the sky—things can get very taut indeed.

Black men have a firm place in New York mugging literature. Norman Podhoretz in his famed (or infamous) 1963 essay, "My Negro Problem—And Ours," recalls growing up in terror of black males; they "were tougher than we were, more ruthless," he writes—and as an adult on the Upper West Side of Manhattan, he continues, he cannot constrain his nervousness when he meets black men on certain streets. Similarly, a decade later, the essayist and novelist Edward Hoagland extols a New York where once "Negro bitterness bore down mainly on other Negroes." Where some see mere panhandlers, Hoagland

sees "a mugger who is clearly screwing up his nerve to do more than just *ask* for money." But Hoagland has "the New Yorker's quick-hunch posture for broken-field maneuvering," and the bad guy swerves away.

I often witness that "hunch posture," from women after dark on the warrenlike streets of Brooklyn where I live. They seem to set their faces on neutral and, with their purse straps strung across their chests bandolier style, they forge ahead as though bracing themselves against being tackled. I understand, of course, that the danger they perceive is not a hallucination. Women are particularly vulnerable to street violence, and young black males are drastically overrepresented among the perpetrators of that violence. Yet these truths are no solace against the kind of alienation that comes of being ever the suspect, against being set apart, a fearsome entity with whom pedestrians avoid making eye contact.

It is not altogether clear to me how I reached the ripe old age of 22 without being conscious of the lethality nighttime pedestrians attributed to me. Perhaps it was because in Chester, Pennsylvania, the small, angry industrial town where I came of age in the 1960s, I was scarcely noticeable against a backdrop of gang warfare, street knifings, and murders. I grew up one of the good boys, had perhaps a half-dozen fist fights. In retrospect, my shyness of combat has clear sources.

Many things go into the making of a young thug. One of those things is the consummation of the male romance with the power to intimidate. An infant discovers that random flailings send the baby bottle flying out of the crib and crashing to the floor. Delighted, the joyful babe repeats those motions again and again, seeking to duplicate the feat. Just so, I recall the points at which some of my boyhood friends were finally seduced by the perception of themselves as tough guys. When a mark cowered and surrendered his money without resistance, myth and reality merged—and paid off. It is, after all, only manly to embrace the power to frighten and intimidate. We, as men, are not supposed to give an inch of our lane on the highway; we are to seize the fighter's edge in work and in play and even in love; we are to be valiant in the face of hostile forces.

Unfortunately, poor and powerless young men seem to take all this nonsense literally. As a boy, I saw countless tough guys locked away; I have since buried several, too. They were babies, really—a teenage cousin, a brother of 22, a childhood friend in his mid-twenties—all gone down in episodes of bravado played out in the streets. I came to doubt the virtues of intimidation early on. I chose, perhaps even unconsciously, to remain a shadow—timid, but a survivor.

The fearsomeness mistakenly attributed to me in public places often has a perilous flavor. The most frightening of these confusions occurred in the late 1970s and early 1980s when I worked as a journalist in Chicago. One day, rushing into the office of a magazine I was writing for with a deadline story in hand, I was mistaken for a burglar. The office manager called security and, with an ad hoc posse, pursued me through the labyrinthine halls, nearly to my editor's door. I had no way of proving who I was. I could only move briskly toward the company of someone who knew me.

Another time I was on assignment for a local paper and killing time before an interview. I entered a jewelry store on the city's affluent Near North Side. The proprietor excused herself and returned with an enormous red Doberman pinscher straining at the end of a leash. She stood, the dog extended toward me, silent to my questions, her eyes bulging nearly out of her head. I took a cursory look around, nodded, and bade her good night. Relatively speaking, however, I never fared as badly as another black male journalist. He went to nearby Waukegan, Illinois, a couple of summers ago to work on a story about a murderer who was born there. Mistaking the reporter for the killer, police hauled him from his car at gunpoint and but for his press credentials would probably have tried to book him. Such episodes are not uncommon. Black men trade tales like this all the time.

In "My Negro Problem—And Ours," Podhoretz writes that the hatred he feels for blacks makes itself known to him through a variety of avenues—one being his discomfort with that "special brand of paranoid touchiness" to which he says blacks are prone. No doubt he is speaking here of black men. In time, I learned to smother the rage I felt at so often being taken for a criminal. Not to do so would surely have led to madness—via that special "paranoid touchiness"

that so annoyed Podhoretz at the time he wrote the essay.

I began to take precautions to make myself less threatening. I move about with care, particularly late in the evening. I give a wide berth to nervous people on subway platforms during the wee hours, particularly when I have exchanged business clothes for jeans. If I happen to be entering a building behind some people who appear skittish, I may walk by, letting them clear the lobby before I return, so as not to seem to be following them. I have been calm and extremely congenial on those rare occasions when I've been pulled over by the police.

And on late-evening constitutionals along streets less traveled by, I employ what has proved to be an excellent tension-reducing measure: I whistle melodies from Beethoven and Vivaldi and the more popular classical composers. Even steely New Yorkers hunching toward nighttime destinations seem to relax, and occasionally they even join in the tune. Virtually everybody seems to sense that a mugger wouldn't be warbling bright, sunny selections from Vivaldi's *Four Seasons*. It is my equivalent of the cowbell that hikers wear when they know they are in bear country.   [1986]

Understanding the Reading

1. What does Staples mean when he refers to himself as an "accomplice in tyranny"?
2. Why do people run from him, lock their car doors, or cross to the other side of the street?
3. What causes Staples' sense of alienation?
4. How does stereotyping contribute to his "power to frighten and intimidate"?
5. What causes black men's "special brand of paranoid touchiness"?
6. How do the expectations of others affect Staples' actual behavior?

Suggestions for Responding

1. Describe a time that you took evasive action like those Staples describes; rewrite the incident from the other person's point of view.
2. In what ways does Staples' essay support the theory of "self-presentation and self-fulfilling prophecy" that Lips describes?   ◆

SUGGESTIONS FOR RESPONDING TO PART IV

1. What stereotypes might others apply to you in terms of your racial, ethnic, gender, and economic class identities? How have you resisted conformity to these expectations, and how have you complied with them? What impact have they had on your sense of self, your identity?

2. Describe your versions of the female stereotype and the male stereotype. Then describe your ideal woman and your ideal man. Analyze the differences between the two pairs, and explain what this reveals about stereotypes and reality.

3. Collect a series of advertisements that feature men and women. Analyze the gender stereotypes they present. Then imagine that all the males are females and vice versa. Analyze what this reversal discloses about the realities of women and men in America today.

4. Research the evolution of the stereotype of one racial or ethnic group in America, for example, the image of Native Americans as noble savages evolving into the drunken Indian or the inscrutable Chinese into the model minority. Analyze how historical contexts influenced the various characterizations, and how each variation benefited the dominant culture.

5. For a week, monitor the front-page stories of your daily newspaper, or all articles in one issue of your favorite weekly newsmagazine, for stereotyping. Be particularly alert for the practices, identified by Moore and Nilsen, that treat females differently than males or people of color differently than white people. For instance, notice identifying labels, qualifying adjectives, references to stereotyped or "nontraditional" appearance or behavior, use of passive voice, loaded words, and so on. Analyze what your findings show about the absence or pervasiveness of stereotypic thinking.

6. Collect a dozen advertisements from popular magazines that represent men and women and/or people of color in nonstereotyped ways. Analyze them to show whether they are creating new stereotypes to replace the old, or whether they reveal more flexible thinking about roles. Evaluate the effectiveness of the ads, and try to explain the motivation of the advertisers for underwriting these changes.

SUGGESTIONS FOR RESPONDING TO IDENTITY

Apply the concepts you have explored in "Identity" to write an autobiographical report about how your present identity has been shaped by your race and ethnicity, your gender, your economic class, and stereotypes that others may apply to you. If you wrote in response to the first suggestion at the ends of Parts I–IV, this report will be a compilation of those four pieces. If you didn't, you may want to consult those instructions and suggestions to determine how to focus your report.

Power in its simplest sense means the ability to do, act, think, and behave as we like, to have control over our own lives. Because we are members of society as well as individuals, however, there are substantial restrictions on our actual ability to exercise this kind of personal power. Society influences who we are, what we can do, how we act, what we believe or think about, and, central to our purposes here, how we interact with others.

Power

Most interpersonal relationships reflect the relative power of the individuals involved, and the individual with the greater power can exercise greater control. We derive power from our capacity to distribute rewards or punishment, from being liked or admired, or from our position of authority or expertise. If, for example, John is more in love with Shelby than she with him, she can exercise power over him, like deciding where they go for dinner or how often they go out. She can reward him with her company or punish him by refusing to see him. Similarly, you may proofread a paper more carefully for a professor you like than for one whose lectures you find boring. Physicians and plumbers have power over their clients because they need their expert services. However, not all social power differentials are determined by or are under the control of the individual.

Our society is organized **hierarchically;** that is, it is structured according to rank and authority, and power is distributed unevenly within this hierarchy. Moreover, membership in a particular group, in and of itself, tends either to enhance or to reduce one's power, because some groups of people have more power and others have less. Access to power and our place in the social hierarchy both depend on a number of variable factors, including gender, race, sexual orientation, socio-economic class, age, and religion.

In our society, men generally have more power than women, white people more power than people of color, heterosexuals more than homosexuals, wealthy people more than workers, and so on. The intersection of these hierarchies confers the greatest social power on the group at the "top" of each scale: white heterosexual men *as a group*. Their power relative to other groups both rests on and reflects their greater wealth, more prestigious positions, and greater access to information and education. Thus, even though individual men may be relatively powerless (a gardener employed by a wealthy widow, for instance), *as a group* white, heterosexual men are better able to control their own lives, to influence and control others, and to act in their own interests.

People who have established power under any social system find it beneficial to retain that system and maintain the status quo. The interests and needs of members of less powerful social groups are not central to their purposes. In fact, within any social system, mechanisms operate to marginalize and subordinate its less powerful members.

In Part IV of "Identity," we saw how stereotypes can lead to prejudice, negative or hostile attitudes toward sexual, racial, ethnic, or economic outgroups. In "Power," we look at what happens when these prejudices are acted on. **Discrimination** is behavior that disadvantages one group in relation to another group and maintains and perpetuates conditions of inequality. In our culture it is practiced most often against women, minority men, and lesbians and gay men. Both individuals and organizations can discriminate, either consciously or unconsciously, and discrimination can be built into the system. Discrimination includes those policies, procedures, decisions, habits, and acts that overlook, ignore, or subjugate members of certain groups or that enable one group of people to maintain control over another group—lighter-skinned people over darker-skinned individuals or groups, men over women, heterosexuals over homosexuals. Such discrimination creates obstacles and barriers for its targets and provides unfair privileges for its beneficiaries.

In Part V, "Power and Racism," we examine the experience of racism, discrimination against and subordination of a person or group because of color. Part VI, "Power, Sexism, and Heterosexism," takes a comparable look at discrimination against and subjugation of women simply because of their sex, and the corollary mistreatment of lesbians and gays. Throughout our nation's history, racism and sexism have been embedded in our culture, and, as we see in Part VII, "Legal Discrimination," they have been sanctioned and enforced by the power of the law. Finally, Part VIII, "Violence," documents how brute force and physical intimidation are used to enforce racism and sexism.

We like to think of America as a place of liberty, equality, and justice for all, but, as the readings in "Power" document, this ideal has yet to be realized. Racism and sexism are not just problems for minorities and women; they are, as a bumper sticker declares, "a social disease." The more fully each of us understands the problems, the closer we will be to finding a cure.

V

Power and Racism

RACISM IS NOT SIMPLY A BLACK AND WHITE ISSUE; IT is the subordination of any person or group because of color. As we discussed in the introduction to Part I, racial identity is not as fixed and immutable as we think. It is a **social construct** that could be said to exist only in the eye of the beholder. At one point or another, many different peoples have been considered to be racial groups—Jews, Italians, Poles, Latinas/os, Native Americans, Asian-Americans, and African-Americans—and have been subjected to racist treatment.

With few exceptions, Americans agree that racism is a bad thing, but there is less consensus about precisely what racism is or how it actually operates. The U.S. Commission on Civil Rights identifies two levels of racism. The first, **overt racism,** is the use of color and other visible characteristics related to color as subordinating factors. The roots of overt racism lie in our national history: the institution of slavery, the belief in the "manifest destiny" of European-Americans to rule the entire North American continent, and the sense of America as a Christian nation, to name just three.

These beliefs provided the basis for and justification of racially discriminatory laws, social institutions, behavior patterns, language, cultural viewpoints, and thought patterns. Even after the Civil War and the abolition of slavery, new seg-

regationist laws and practices known as **Jim Crow** extended overt racism against African-Americans up to the middle of this century. Shifting federal policies—such as removals, the reservation system, Indian boarding schools—effectively destroyed much of the Native American culture and population. Exclusionary immigration laws and **restrictive covenants** (excluding members of certain groups from living in specified areas) limited the opportunities of Jews and Asian-Americans.

The civil rights movement of the 1950s and 1960s awakened most white Americans to the evils of overt racism. However, this change of attitude by itself has been inadequate to address the residual racial inequities that survive in the second level of racism, indirect institutional subordination. More subtle, often invisible, **institutionalized racism** does not explicitly use color as the subordinating mechanism. Instead, decisions are based on such other factors as skill level, residential location, income or education—factors that appear to be racially neutral and reasonably related to the activities and privileges concerned.

In reality, however, such practices continue to produce racist inequities because they fail to take into account the problems created by a 300-year history of overt racist practices. For example, having a parent with insufficient job training would likely mean that the child will grow up poor and attend poor schools, without access to sufficient job training, leading to another generation of deprivation and poverty. In this way, no matter how unintentionally, a wide variety of policies, procedures, decisions, habits, attitudes, actions, and institutional structures perpetuate racism, the subordination and subjugation of people of color.

Part IV showed how stereotypes provide the foundation for prejudices. Part V will examine the behavioral extension of racial prejudice: racial discrimination. One can be *prejudiced,* believing in the inferiority of certain kinds of individuals based on their membership in a certain group, but not *discriminate,* not act on those beliefs. As stated earlier, discrimination is individual, organizational, or structural behavior that disadvantages one group in relation to another group and that maintains and perpetuates conditions of inequality for members of the disadvantaged group.

Part V opens with selections that give a historical perspective on racism in America. Oscar Handlin provides a brief overview of late nineteenth- and early twentieth-century racism based on color, national origin, and religion. Robert Cherry reviews the various theories that historians have offered to explain one manifestation of religiously based racism: the widespread anti-Semitism of that same period. Racism permeates society in unexpected ways; not even such purportedly objective fields as science and statistics have escaped its influence. Stephen Jay Gould exposes the fallacies in Arthur Jensen's attempt to "prove" the intellectual inferiority of African-Americans by debunking his use of supposedly scientific evidence about IQ scores. Jewel Handy Gresham describes Secretary of State John Calhoun's use of faulty census figures in the 1840s to "prove" that slavery was a "natural" condition,

comparing it to the more recent reports on the decline of the African-American family by Daniel Patrick Moynihan and Bill Moyers.

The next two selections voice the pain and anger experienced by those who are personally subjected to racial prejudice and discrimination. As a Lakota Sioux, Barbara Cameron has encountered racist cruelty and rejection; despite that fact, she has come to understand that she herself is not free from racist feelings about other people of color. Gloria Yamato speaks about the various expressions of racism she has endured, but she provides some concrete suggestions for steps that individuals, both whites who want to be allies of people of color and people of color who are working through internalized racism, can take to combat racism.

The last two readings provide different insights into racism. Peggy McIntosh examines the invisible privileges that light-skinned people enjoy simply because of their skin color, and she recommends the extension of those positive advantages to all people. Finally, Jon A. Blubaugh and Dorthy L. Pennington analyze the power that minority group members have as a result of their "difference," their "potential," and even racial stereotypes.

Racism continues to exist in our society because the subordination of people of color benefits those who do the subordinating. These psychological, economic, and political benefits will be reduced if racism is eliminated. However, the social costs of excluding a substantial proportion of our population from full participation in society—contributing to as well as benefiting from its bounty—are immense. Hearing the voices of those subjected to racism gives us fuller and more sympathetic insight into the problem. Even those of us who personally reject overt racism need to work to loosen its less visible institutionalized tentacles.

42

Racism and Nationality

OSCAR HANDLIN

Discrimination was the permanent manifestation of the hostilities bred by racism. It had long since limited the rights of the Negro and, with the development of racist ideas and emotions, had, by 1918, come to apply with increasing frequency to other groups as well. In the decade after the end of the war it seriously abridged the privileges of men distinguishable by their color, like the Negroes and Japanese; by their religion, like the Jews and Catholics; and by their national origins, like the Italians and Poles. Discrimination then was supported by a well-developed code of practices, by the active agitation of political movements, and by an ideology that justified the separateness and the inferiority of the underprivileged. That complex survived until the middle of the 1930's; its collapse has created the situation in which the minorities now find themselves.

By 1918 a tightly meshed pattern of discriminatory practices put substantial portions of the American population at an enormous disadvantage in almost every aspect of life. The inferiority of which such people were often accused was well on the way to being forced upon them.

Of the groups marked off by color the Negroes were most important, by virtue of their numbers, of their long history in the country, and of the tragic injustices to which they had already been subject. Their progress since slavery had been painfully slow. Emancipation after the Civil War had stricken from them the shackles of legal bondage, but it had not succeeded in endowing them with rights equal to those of other citizens. Once the interlude of Reconstruction[1] had passed, the white South, redeemed, had developed a way of life that maintained and extended the actual inferiority of the blacks. In the last decade of the nineteenth century one device after another had deprived them of the ballot and of political power; their own lack of skill and of capital, as well as discrimination, had confined them to a submerged place in the economy; and

the rigid etiquette of segregation made their social inferiority ever clearer. In no aspect of his life could the Negro escape awareness that he was decisively below the white, hopelessly incapable of rising to the same opportunities as his former masters. If ever he lost sight of that fact central to his existence, the ever present threat of lynching and other forms of violence reminded him of it.

Progress in ameliorating their condition down to 1917 had been too slow to kindle the flame of hope among the Negroes, and the momentary flare of enthusiasm during the war quickly subsided. Thereafter there were few sober reasons for optimism. A slowly developing middle class offered the hope of personal improvement to a tiny handful. A gradual movement to the northern cities offered an escape from the South but not an escape from the problems of discrimination; poverty, violence, and disorder dogged their heels in Chicago and Harlem as they had in Alabama or Georgia. The limited degrees of improvement were minuscule in comparison with the way that still remained to go. And when the depression struck in the 1930's, the Negroes, who were first to suffer in both the North and the South, faced a future of desperate futility.

No other group suffered the total burden of discrimination the Negro bore. Yet the Japanese and the Indians, also set off by their color, had their share of grievances. For them also the postwar period brought no confidence that a remedy was within sight.

It was the same with some groups made distinctive by religious affiliation. Catholics were widely reproached for being un-American. The hostile sentiments stirred up by the American Protective Association (the APA) in the 1890's had never died down, and during the war there had been ugly rumors that the Pope was somehow favoring the Central Powers.[2] Was it possible that he intended ultimately to subvert American democracy? The suspicion ebbed and flowed, but never altogether receded; and stories remained current of arms stored in churches, of mysterious international emissaries, and of strange doings in convents and monasteries.

Catholicism was also a burden to its communicants. The presidential campaigns of 1924 and 1928, the savage hatreds that led numerous Democrats to desert their party, left many Catholics with the conviction that their faith was a distinct political liability. Nor were they likely to find reassurance in the efforts to outlaw parochial schools and otherwise to limit the rights of their co-religionists. In their day-to-day existence, too, boycotts of their businesses, discrimination in employment, and exclusion from important areas of social life embittered their relationships with other Americans.

The forces that generated the attacks against Catholics found another target in the Jews. From the 1800's onward a developing pattern of slights and formal barriers closed clubs and restaurants and hotels to these people and narrowed the range of their social contacts. Early in the twentieth century they began to feel the effects of discrimination in employment and of restriction in housing. After the end of the First World War they discovered also that their access to many educational institutions and to some of the professions, like medicine and engineering, was being limited.

By then, moreover, they were the victims of the full barrage of anti-Semitic accusations. The old stereotype of the Jew acquired a sinister connotation. He was the international banker, but also the inflamed radical responsible for Communist revolution in eastern Europe. Above all, he was the agent of a vast conspiracy designed to enslave America. Henry Ford's *International Jew* and the pages of his *Dearborn Independent*[3] exposed the plot of the elders of Zion[4] to conquer the whole world. Repercussions of the credulous acceptance of these charges poisoned the relationships of Jews with their neighbors throughout the decade.

The enemy now took the form of groups set off by their differences of national origin. In the twenty years before the First World War millions of newcomers had arrived in the United States from parts of Europe and Asia which had not theretofore produced a heavy volume of immigration. The host of aliens from Italy, from Poland, from Greece, and from Austria, disembarking in massive numbers within a very short period, evoked a reaction of shock and hostility from some Americans longer settled. All the findings of science cast doubt upon the capacity of these strange, outlandish people to adjust to the ways of American life. Totally unassimilable, they were bound to lower all national values. Beaten men from beaten stocks, they should not be en-

trusted with the equal rights they would, in any case, never be able to enjoy.

Possession of a Slavic or Italian name became a decisive liability. A widespread, if informal, network of discriminatory practices limited the opportunities of these people and gave subtle expression to a hostility that occasionally, as in West Frankfort, Illinois, in 1920, erupted in passionate violence.

The discriminatory practices against the minorities were supported and extended by organized movements of considerable strength aimed to make them more rigid and more consistent. The anti-Catholic APA had passed from the scene at the opening of the century. But its burden was taken up, in the South, by the followers of Tom Watson[5] and carried by a variety of smaller groups down to the outbreak of the war. There was an interval of relaxation during the war itself while all such energies and tensions were subsumed in the more general emotions of the struggle against Germany.   [1948]

Notes

1. RECONSTRUCTION: The twelve-year period following the Civil War when the federal government controlled the South.
2. CENTRAL POWERS: The World War I alliance of Germany, Austria-Hungary, Bulgaria, and Turkey.
3. *DEARBORN INDEPENDENT*: A very conservative, anti-Semitic magazine.
4. ELDERS OF ZION: An alleged international conspiracy of powerful Jews for world domination, purportedly "documented" in a propaganda tract known as *The Protocols*.
5. TOM WATSON: A southern leader of the Ku Klux Klan.

Understanding the Reading

1. What tactics did the white South use to enforce the inferiority of blacks?
2. What tactics did blacks use to resist?
3. Why and how were Catholics discriminated against?
4. How did discrimination affect Jews?
5. Why were turn-of-the-century immigrants discriminated against?

Suggestions for Responding

1. Write a paper speculating about how you would react if you were victimized by one or more of the discriminatory tactics that Handlin describes.
2. Research and report on one of the examples of discrimination Handlin mentions, such as the American Protective Association, Ford's *Dearborn Independent,* Tom Watson, or the West Frankfort, Illinois, incident. ✦

43

Anti-Semitism in the United States

ROBERT CHERRY

From most accounts, it appears that anti-Semitism was most intense during the period 1877 to 1927, from the time Joseph Seligman was refused admittance to the Grand Hotel in Saratoga, New York, until Henry Ford publicly apologized for anti-Semitic articles in his Dearborn Press.[1] Prior to this period, there were examples of anti-Semitism, beginning with the reluctance of Peter Stuyvesant to allow the first group of Jews to enter New York in 1654. Anti-Semitism also was part of the Know Nothing party's[2] anti-immigration campaign in the 1850s and General Grant's policies during the Civil War. However, anti-Semitism became widespread only during the latter part of the nineteenth century.

Oscar Handlin and Richard Hofstadter identify anti-Semitism with the short-lived agrarian Populist movement[3] of the 1890s. They contend that the Populists associated traditional Jewish stereotypes with the evils faced by the yeomanry. Increasingly forced into debt peonage, the yeomanry demanded elimination of the gold standard. However, President Cleveland pursued a scheme with the Rothschild banking empire[4] to protect the gold standard. This led many Populists to attack Jews for what they perceived as Jewish control of world finance. Also, the yeomanry often divided society into those who engaged in productive labor and those who did not.

Typically, Jews in rural areas were identified with nonproductive labor—that is, they were commercial and financial middlemen who gained income from the work of others.

Other historians claim that early twentieth century anti-Semitism was associated with xenophobic fears fueled by mass immigration. Later Jewish immigrants tended to be poorer, less skilled, and less urbanized than the Jews who had emigrated from Germany during the 1850s. They were considered a dangerous criminal element. In 1908 New York City's police commissioner Theodore Bingham suggested that half of all criminals were Jews. The 1910 report of the Dillingham commission claimed that large numbers of Jews scattered throughout the United States seduced and kept girls in prostitution and that many were petty thieves, pickpockets, and gamblers. The report stated, "Jews comprise the largest proportion of alien prisoners under sentence for offenses against chastity."

During this era, Jews were not pictured simply as petty criminals. The stereotypic Jewish businessman was one who manipulated laws and engaged in white-collar crimes, especially insurance fraud. [Michael N.] Dobkowski gives numerous examples of how these stereotypes became part of the popular culture. In describing a Jewish businessman, *Puck,* a popular New York City humor magazine, noted that "despite hard times, he has had two failures and three fires." It claimed, "There is only one thing [their] race hates more than pork—asbestos." So pervasive were these images that the Anti-Defamation League (ADL)[5] in 1913 noted, "Whenever a theatre producer wishes to depict a betrayer of the public trust, a white slaver or other criminal, the actor is directed to present himself as a Jew." Indeed, for more than fifty years, *Roget's Thesaurus* included the word *Jew* as a synonym for usurer, cheat, extortioner, and schemer.

Some historians, including John Higham, believe that anti-Semitism was more significant among the elite than among either the rural yeomanry or middle-class xenophobic nativists. Higham notes that the patrician class, typified by Henry and Brooks Adams, realized that the industrialization process was transforming the United States into a materialistic, pragmatic society that had less concern for tradition and culture than previously. This transformation, which meant the end of patrician hegemony over political and economic affairs, was thought to be the result of Jewish influence.

According to Higham, the patrician class believed that Jewish commercial values undermined basic American traditions. While most became defeatist, some, including Henry Cabot Lodge and John J. Chapman, attempted to reduce Jewish influence. In 1896 Lodge proposed legislation requiring immigrants to be literate in the language of their country of origin rather than in another language. Since most Polish and Russian Jews were literate in Yiddish but not in Polish or Russian, this would have made them ineligible for immigration. Lodge's legislative proposal was defeated, and Jewish immigration continued. Chapman was an active urban reformer who did not have anti-Semitic values until the time of World War I. Dobkowski contends that his inability to reform urban society led him to agree with Henry Adams that the reason for urban decay was growing Jewish influence.

Dobkowski documents how progressive muckrakers,[6] including George Kibbe Turner, Jacob Riis, and Emily Balch, echoed many of the charges against Jews made by the patrician class. Lamenting the decay of cities, Turner considered Jewish immigrants to be at the "core of this festering human cancer." Riis believed that the lack of social values among Jewish immigrants was overwhelming urban society. He thought that recent Jewish immigrants believed that "[M]oney is God. Life itself is of little value compared with even the leanest bank account." Even Balch, a leading defender of social welfare reforms, accepted negative Jewish stereotypes.

Liberal sociologist E. A. Ross believed that Jewish immigrants were cunning in their ability to use their wit to undermine business ethics and to commercialize professions and journalism. He claimed that attempts to exclude Jews from professional associations and social clubs had nothing to do with discrimination; instead they reflected a strong desire not to associate with individuals from an immoral culture. Tom Watson, a former Populist and later KKK leader, used Ross's writings to justify his organization's anti-Semitism.

These examples of anti-Semitic views sometimes provide the basis for contentions that Jews faced discrimination similar to that of other groups. Thomas Sowell implies this when he states, "Anti-Semitism in the United States assumed growing and unprecedented proportions in the last quarter of the nineteenth century with the mass arrival of eastern European Jews. . . . [H]elp wanted ads began to specify 'Christian,' as they had once specified 'Protestant' to exclude the Irish."

This is an incorrect assessment. During the last quarter of the nineteenth century, the United States adopted a reservation program for American Indians, an exclusionary policy for Orientals, Jim Crow laws for blacks, and an anti-immigration movement to harass Italian and Polish newcomers. In contrast, before World War I, Jewish immigrants faced few anti-Semitic barriers to their advancement. For example, in 1910 it was estimated that only 0.3 percent of employment advertisements specified Christians and no colleges had adopted restrictive entrance policies.

Only after World War I and the Bolshevik Revolution when xenophobic fears peaked did anti-Semitic restrictions become significant. Zosa Szakowski documents the vigorous attack on Jews during the anti-immigrant Palmer raids[7] in 1919. In 1920, 10 percent of employment ads specified Christians, rising to 13.3 percent by 1926. [Stephen] Steinberg summarizes the restrictive entrance policies many prestigious universities, including Columbia and Harvard, adopted at that time to reduce Jewish enrollment.

At about this time, Henry Ford began publishing anti-Semitic tracts in his Dearborn Press. Like Ross, Ford was a Progressive. He supported Wilson,[8] social legislation, antilynching laws, and urban reforms. Unlike Ross, Ford had nothing but praise for the ordinary Jewish businessman, and he could count Jews among his personal friends. However, Ford thought that industrialists were at the mercy of financial institutions controlled by international Jewry.

Adopting a similar perspective, Robert La Follette introduced a petition to Congress in 1923 assigning responsibility for World War I to Jewish international bankers. This petition also asserted that Wilson, Lloyd George, Clemenceau, and Orlando[9]—the officials in charge of negotiating the peace treaty at Versailles—were surrounded by Jewish advisors.

World's Work and other liberal publications

also complained that Jews were not 100 percent American. They not only identified Jews with draft dodgers and war profiteers, but also complained that Jews, though taking advantage of the opportunities given by democracy, had not taken "the one essential act of a democratic society. . . . They are not willing to lose their identity." By the end of the decade, however, after immigration restrictions laws had been passed and the anticommunist hysteria had subsided, anti-Semitism again subsided to a minimum level.

[1989]

Notes

1. DEARBORN PRESS: The publisher of the very conservative, anti-Semitic magazine, the *Dearborn Independent.*
2. KNOW NOTHING PARTY: A political movement in the mid-nineteenth century that was antagonistic to Catholics and immigrants.
3. POPULIST MOVEMENT: A political movement advocating the rights of the common people.
4. ROTHSCHILD BANKING EMPIRE: An international financial empire created by a Jewish banking dynasty during the first half of the nineteenth century.
5. ANTI-DEFAMATION LEAGUE (ADL): A Jewish civil rights organization.
6. MUCKRAKERS: Investigative reporters who focused on corruption.
7. PALMER RAIDS: Raids authorized by Attorney General A. Mitchell Palmer, who zealously enforced the Espionage Act of 1917 to suppress antiwar and socialist publications.
8. [WOODROW] WILSON: U.S. President, 1913–1921.
9. LLOYD GEORGE, CLEMENCEAU, AND ORLANDO: David Lloyd George, British Prime Minister, 1916–1922; Georges Clemenceau, French Premier, 1906–1909, 1917; Vittorio Emanuele Orlando, Italian Prime Minister, 1917–1919.

Understanding the Reading

1. Explain why the Populists attacked Jews.
2. What stereotypes were assigned to Jews in the early part of this century?
3. Why were the elites anti-Semitic?
4. What other justifications have been given to rationalize anti-Semitism?

Suggestions for Responding

1. Describe the Jewish stereotype that underlies the various beliefs Cherry discusses, and explain its inconsistencies.
2. Do you agree with the claim by *World's Work* that losing one's identity is "the one essential act of a democratic society"? Why or why not? ✦

44

Racist Arguments and IQ

STEPHEN JAY GOULD

Louis Agassiz, the greatest biologist of mid-nineteenth-century America, argued that God had created blacks and whites as separate species. The defenders of slavery took much comfort from this assertion, for biblical proscriptions of charity and equality did not have to extend across a species boundary. What could an abolitionist say? Science had shone its cold and dispassionate light upon the subject; Christian hope and sentimentality could not refute it.

Similar arguments, carrying the apparent sanction of science, have been continually invoked in attempts to equate egalitarianism with sentimental hope and emotional blindness. People who are unaware of this historical pattern tend to accept each recurrence at face value; that is, they assume that each statement arises from the "data" actually presented, rather than from the social conditions that truly inspire it.

The racist arguments of the nineteenth century were based primarily on craniometry, the measurement of human skulls. Today, these contentions stand totally discredited. What craniometry was to the nineteenth century, intelligence testing has been to the twentieth. The victory of the eugenics movement[1] in the Immigration Restriction Act of 1924 signaled its first unfortunate effect—for the severe restrictions upon non-Europeans and upon southern and eastern Europeans gained much support from results of the first extensive and uniform application of intelligence tests in America—the Army Mental Tests of World War I. These tests were engineered and administered by psychologist Robert M. Yerkes, who concluded that "education alone will not place the negro [*sic*] race on a par with its Caucasian competitors." It is now clear that Yerkes and his colleagues knew no way to separate genetic from environmental components in postulating causes for different performances on the tests.

The latest episode of this recurrent drama began in 1969, when Arthur Jensen published an article entitled, "How Much Can We Boost IQ and Scholastic Achievement?" in the *Harvard Educational Review*. Again, the claim went forward that new and uncomfortable information had come to light, and that science had to speak the "truth" even if it refuted some cherished notions of a liberal philosophy. But again, I shall argue, Jensen had no new data; and what he did present was flawed beyond repair by inconsistencies and illogical claims.

Jensen assumes that IQ tests adequately measure something we may call "intelligence." He then attempts to tease apart the genetic and environmental factors causing differences in performance. He does this primarily by relying upon the one natural experiment we possess: identical twins reared apart—for differences in IQ between genetically identical people can only be environmental. The average difference in IQ for identical twins is less than the difference for two unrelated individuals raised in similarly varied environments. From the data on twins, Jensen obtains an estimate of environmental influence. He concludes that IQ has a heritability of about 0.8 (or 80 percent) *within* the population of American and European whites. The average difference between American whites and blacks is 15 IQ points (one standard deviation). He asserts that this difference is too large to attribute to environment, given the high heritability of IQ. Lest anyone think that Jensen writes in the tradition of abstract scholarship, I merely quote the first line of his famous work: "Compensatory education has been tried, and it apparently has failed."

I believe that this argument can be refuted in a "hierarchical" fashion—that is, we can discredit it at one level and then show that it fails at a more inclusive level even if we allow Jensen's argument for the first two levels:

Level 1: The equation of IQ with intelligence. Who knows what IQ measures? It is a good predictor of "success" in school, but is such success a result of intelligence, apple polishing, or the assimilation of values that the leaders of society prefer? Some psychologists get around this argument by defining intelligence operationally as the scores attained on "intelligence" tests. A neat trick. But at this point, the technical definition of intelligence has strayed so far from the vernacular that we can no longer define the issue. But let me allow (although I don't believe it), for the sake of argument, that IQ measures some meaningful aspect of intelligence in its vernacular sense.

Level 2: The heritability of IQ. Here again, we encounter a confusion between vernacular and technical meanings of the same word. "Inherited," to a layman, means "fixed," "inexorable," or "unchangeable." To a geneticist, "Inherited" refers to an estimate of similarity between related individuals based on genes held in common. It carries no implications of inevitability or of immutable entities beyond the reach of environmental influence. Eyeglasses correct a variety of inherited problems in vision; insulin can check diabetes.

Jensen insists that IQ is 80 percent heritable. Princeton psychologist Leon J. Kamin has done the dog-work of meticulously checking through details of the twin studies that form the basis of this estimate. He has found an astonishing number of inconsistencies and downright inaccuracies. For example, the late Sir Cyril Burt, who generated the largest body of data on identical twins reared apart, pursued his studies of intelligence for more than forty years. Although he increased his sample sizes in a variety of "improved" versions, some of his correlation coefficients remain unchanged to the third decimal place—a statistically impossible situation.* IQ depends in part upon sex and age; and other studies did not standardize properly for them. An

---

*I wrote this essay in 1974. Since then, the case against Sir Cyril has progressed from an inference of carelessness to a spectacular (and well-founded) suspicion of fraud. Reporters for the *London Times* have discovered, for example, that Sir Cyril's coauthors (for the infamous twin studies) apparently did not exist outside his imagination. In the light of Kamin's discoveries, one must suspect that the data have an equal claim to reality.

improper correction may produce higher values between twins not because they hold genes for intelligence in common, but simply because they share the same sex and age. The data are so flawed that no valid estimate for the heritability of IQ can be drawn at all. But let me assume (although no data support it), for the sake of argument, that the heritability of IQ is as high as 0.8.

Level 3: The confusion of within- and between-group variation. Jensen draws a causal connection between his two major assertions—that the within-group heritability of IQ is 0.8 for American whites, and that the mean difference in IQ between American blacks and whites is 15 points. He assumes that the black "deficit" is largely genetic in origin because IQ is so highly heritable. This is a *non sequitur* of the worst possible kind—for there is no necessary relationship between heritability within a group and differences in mean values of two separate groups.

A simple example will suffice to illustrate this flaw in Jensen's argument. Height has a much higher heritability within groups than anyone has ever claimed for IQ. Suppose that height has a mean value of five feet two inches and a heritability of 0.9 (a realistic value) within a group of nutritionally deprived Indian farmers. High heritability simply means that short farmers will tend to have short offspring, and tall farmers tall offspring. It says nothing whatever against the possibility that proper nutrition could raise the mean height to six feet (taller than average white Americans). It only means that, in this improved status, farmers shorter than average (they may now be five feet ten inches) would still tend to have shorter than average children.

I do not claim that intelligence, however defined, has no genetic basis—I regard it as trivially true, uninteresting, and unimportant that it does. The expression of any trait represents a complex interaction of heredity and environment. Our job is simply to provide the best environmental situation for the realization of valued potential in all individuals. I merely point out that a specific claim purporting to demonstrate a mean genetic deficiency in the intelligence of American blacks rests upon no new facts whatever and can cite no valid data in its support. It is just as likely that blacks have a genetic advantage over whites. And, either way, it doesn't matter a damn. An individual can't be judged by his group mean.

If current biological determinism in the study of human intelligence rests upon no new facts (actually, no facts at all), then why has it become so popular of late? The answer must be social and political. The 1960s were good years for liberalism; a fair amount of money was spent on poverty programs and relatively little happened. Enter new leaders and new priorities. Why didn't the earlier programs work? Two possibilities are open: (1) we didn't spend enough money, we didn't make sufficiently creative efforts, or (and this makes any established leader jittery) we cannot solve these problems without a fundamental social and economic transformation of society; or (2) the programs failed because their recipients are inherently what they are—blaming the victims. Now, which alternative will be chosen by men in power in an age of retrenchment?

I have shown, I hope, that biological determinism is not simply an amusing matter for clever cocktail party comments about the human animal. It is a general notion with important philosophical implications and major political consequences. As John Stuart Mill wrote, in a statement that should be the motto of the opposition: "Of all the vulgar modes of escaping from the consideration of the effect of social and moral influences upon the human mind, the most vulgar is that of attributing the diversities of conduct and character to inherent natural differences."

[1977]

Note

1. EUGENICS MOVEMENT: A campaign at the beginning of this century to improve the human stock by genetic control.

Understanding the Reading

1. Explain how Jensen determined the genetic and environmental factors affecting IQ.
2. Why does Gould feel IQ can't be equated with intelligence?
3. Why does he think Jensen's claim that IQ is 80% heritable is wrong?
4. How does confusion of within-group and between-group variation flaw Jensen's argument?
5. Why does Gould object to the arguments of biological determinism?

Suggestions for Responding

1. Gould refers to the concept of "blaming the victim." Explain what that means, and describe at least one other example that illustrates the concept.
2. Research the eugenics movement and write a brief report on it. ✦

45

The Politics of Family in America

JEWELL HANDY GRESHAM

The past is not dead. It's not even past.
—William Faulkner

In April 1844, Secretary of State John Calhoun, the pre-eminent Southern philosopher of States' rights, directed a letter to the British ambassador in Washington attesting that where blacks and whites existed in the same society, slavery was the natural result. Wherever the states changed that providential relationship, the blacks invariably degenerated "into vice and pauperism accompanied by the bodily and mental afflictions incident thereto—deafness, blindness, insanity, and idiocy." In the slave states, in contrast, the blacks improved greatly "in number, comfort, intelligence, and morals."

To prove his point, Calhoun supplied statistics from the 1840 census. The data showed a shocking rate of black insanity in New England: one out of every fourteen in Maine, every twenty-eight in New Hampshire, every forty-three in Massachusetts, etc. The overall figure for the North was almost ten times the rate in the South, where only one "lunatic" for every 1,309 blacks was shown in Virginia, one in 2,447 in South Carolina, etc.

At the time Calhoun wrote that letter, one of the country's leading newspapers had just broken the scandal of the plot by President Tyler's Administration to annex Texas as slave territory—a potential constitutional crisis certain to inflame the bitter North-South conflict. In that context, Calhoun's statistics were intended less for the British than for Congress, to which he forwarded copies.

There was only one flaw in his argument: The figures were false. Dr. Edward Jarvis of Massachusetts General Hospital, a leading specialist in the incidence of insanity, immediately challenged them. Joined by the prestigious American Statistical Association, Jarvis conducted an exhaustive study of every town and county in the free states in which black insanity had been reported by the Census Bureau. In case after case, the number of "insane" blacks proved larger than the state's total black population!

The A.S.A.'s comprehensive study—forwarded to former President John Quincy Adams in the House of Representatives—concluded that "it would have been far better to have no census at all, than such a one as has been published" and urged Congress either to correct the data or "discard or disown" it "as the good of the country . . . and as justice and humanity shall demand." But when Adams, as recorded in his diary, confronted Calhoun at the State Department, the latter "answered like a true slavemonger. . . . He writhed like a trodden rattlesnake on the exposure of his false report to the House . . . and finally said that where there were so many errors they balanced one another, and led to the same conclusion as if they were all correct." The A.S.A. report—blocked by the Speaker and the proslavery majority in the House—never reached the floor.

While these developments unfolded, Southern slaves were of course in no position to challenge the claims [on] which their welfare was critical. Nor did the free blacks of New York City under the leadership of the distinguished black physician/abolitionist James McCune Smith stand a chance of having their memorial to Congress protesting the "calumnies against free people of color" recognized. For those who held political power, it was imperative that blacks simply not exist except as objects, and the truth or falsity of what was said was beside the point. What mattered, then as now, was not the *facts* but only that the semblance of "substance" be provided for a time sufficient to confuse the issue and carry the day.

"The Need to Segregate or Quarantine a Race"

After the Civil War, the Calhoun view of the inherent degeneracy of blacks, which held that they could not survive outside slavery, was tenaciously clung to by the outnumbered whites of Mississippi. In 1865 the *Meridian Clarion* asserted with unconcealed satisfaction that the black race was doomed: "A hundred years is a long time to one man; but to a nation or a race, it is but a limited period. Well, in that time the negro will be dead."

In due course, Mississipi produced figures to prove it: The 1866 state census showed a more than 12 percent decline in the black population. Unfortunately for the prophets, however, this data was as accurate as Calhoun's: The 1870 Federal census showed an *increase* of more than 7,000, which turned out to be an undercount of between 50,000 and 75,000, corrected in the 1880 Federal figures.

Nonetheless, in the 1880s, the Reverend C. K. Marshall, the most prominent preacher in the state, predicted that "by January, 1920 . . . except for a few old people [who] will linger as the Cherokees do on their reservation . . . the colored population of the south will scarcely be counted."

With the passage of more years without apparent visible diminution in black ranks, however, white theories of a built-in biological solution to the black "problem" obviously had to be augmented. In *The Plantation Negro as Freeman* (1889), the historian Philip A. Bruce used the black family as a device for attacking all blacks. Bruce, the scion of a former Virginia slaveowner, simply advanced Calhoun's thesis: With the end of slavery, the loss of white "supervision" led to a severe and menacing deterioration in blacks' social and moral condition. The black family as such did not exist, he announced; black children, accordingly, were born into a state of moral degeneracy.

Bruce viciously castigated black women. Alluding to the alleged propensity of black men to rape white women, he asserted that they found "something strangely alluring and seductive . . . in the appearance of a white woman" because of the "wantonness of the women of his own race." The "fact" that black women failed to complain of being raped by men of their race counted as "strong proof of the sexual laxness of plantation women as a class."

Herbert Gutman called Bruce's work perhaps the most important connecting link between the "popular" views of African-American degeneracy in the 1880s and the supportive pseudoscientific works of the ensuing decades before World War I. These latter writings rested heavily on the pseudoscientific data of Social Darwinism—the doctrine of survival of the fittest. The historian George Frederickson explains the relevance of such theories in his book *The Black Image in the White Mind:*

> If the blacks were a degenerating race with no future, the problem ceased to be one of how to prepare them for citizenship or even how to make them more productive and useful members of the community. The new prognosis pointed rather to the need to segregate or quarantine a race liable to be a source of contamination and social danger to the white community, as it sank ever deeper into the slough of disease, vice, and criminality.

The Device Updated

It was against these brutally repressive rationalizations still undergirding the Southern apartheid system after World War II that the civil rights revolution of the 1950s and 1960s erupted. And it was at the climactic stages of that struggle that Labor Department official Daniel Patrick Moynihan conceived, in December 1964, his supposedly secret "internal memorandum" on the black family.

Whether Moynihan knew his history or not, his report served the time-tested purpose: Whenever the system is in crisis (or shows signs of becoming transformed); whenever blacks get restless (or show strength); whenever whites in significant numbers show signs of coming together with blacks to confront their mutual problems (or enemies), the trick is to shift the focus from the real struggle for political and economic empowerment to black "crime," degeneracy, pathology and—in Moynihan's innovative twist—the "deterioration" of the black family (previously defined as nonexistent!).

Moynihan's report was subtitled "The Case for National Action." But just how much serious "action" it intended was made plain in the author's next "internal memo"—this time to Richard Nixon—counseling "benign neglect."

In the light of subsequent events it is interesting to discover in *Pat,* the Senator's biography, that it was presidential assistant Bill Moyers who, in May 1965, first brought the black family report, until then ignored, to Lyndon Johnson's attention and arranged for the President to deliver a major policy speech based on it.

Curiously, the Moyers-arranged speech bypassed all agencies of the government set up to aid the passage of the President's civil rights agenda. It was delivered at the graduation exercises of Howard University before an overwhelmingly black audience of thousands of students, parents, friends and dignitaries. Apparently few observers among the editors, journalists and scholars present found what Johnson did reprehensible. Howard was one of the colleges that had sent a sizable contingent of students into the revolutionary *nonviolent* Southern struggle which at that moment was galvanizing, inspiring and, in a thousand unforeseeable ways, transforming the nation. Before the young people whom he should have congratulated for the extraordinary example of sacrifice and heroism they were setting, the President emphasized the "historical" degenerate state of the families from which they came!

True, words of noble intent were there (as they were in Moynihan's original), and they heartened many. But so were the declarations of black degeneracy that reinforced the racism of many more and signaled the open-door policy for what was to come. Through the summer, however, the "secret" Moynihan report continued to be leaked to selected journalists. Then came the event that cemented its impact. Ten days after the August passage of the Voting Rights Act of 1965, Watts[1] exploded—and in a mad scramble for instant wisdom, journalists turned to the black family report and drew on its conclusions as explanations for the violent civil disorders.

What did it explain? What were the causes of Watts and the succeeding ghetto rebellions? Not, as the Kerner Commission[2] concluded in 1967, the division of America into two societies, separate and unequal. Not historical white racism, Depression-level unemployment and the intolerable conditions of the ghetto that cut short the dreams and lives of millions of black men, women and children. Not at all. "Ours is a society," offered Moynihan, "which presumes male leadership in private and public affairs. . . . A subculture such as that of the Negro American, in which this is not the pattern, is placed at a distinct disadvantage." To overcome that disadvantage, he said, the malaise of the black family, characterized by the unnatural dominance of a "black matriarchy," had to be cured.

In contrast, Moynihan wrote: "*The white family has achieved a high degree of stability and is maintaining that stability.*" (Emphasis added.) Against the backdrop of the next twenty-five years, this declaration would be hilarious were it not for the fact that, for untold millions of *white* working women—divorced, single and joint providers—the idealized patriarchal structure held up as an icon had always been a myth! Indeed, even as Moynihan wrote the words, the modern women's movement for equal rights and a sense of selfhood, submerged under the centuries-old domination of that very model, was being forged in the crucible of the civil rights struggle.

Those who found the Moynihan report useful were presumably unaware that the archetypal sexism on which it rests is inextricable from its racism. At any rate, the report signaled, at the very height of the civil rights movement, that Northern whites would pick up where the South was forced to leave off in blocking the long black struggle for parity with whites in American life.

LINE OF DESCENT

On January 25, 1986, Bill Moyers, Moynihan's original booster, invoked the full power of a prime-time, two-hour CBS Special Report to beam the old theme into millions of homes. The title: *The Vanishing Black Family—Crisis in Black America* (shades of the old Mississippi *Meridian Clarion!*). The East Texan, in sympathetic "liberal" guise, took cameras into a Newark, New Jersey, housing project for an "intimate" portrait of black teen-age welfare mothers, sexually irresponsible if not criminal youth, a smiling black male "superstud," and pervasive pathology all around. Moyers's report was directed not at the cause of the plight of the people whose confidences he elicited. Viewers were shown, rather, a pathology in black America so overwhelming and irredeemable as to leave the panel of blacks brought in at the end to "discuss" the subject helpless to dissipate the impact of the carefully selected imagery.

The result, whatever sympathy toward individual victims white viewers might have felt, and whatever responsibilities some might acknowledge that America has for its racist "past," could only be: First, to utterly terrify most as to the very nature of their fellow black citizens by reinforcing, with "liberal" authority, the most archetypal of racist myths, fears and stereotypes—a picture of "jungle" immorality and degeneracy, inarticulateness and sloth so rife that the onlookers could actually forget the terrible national corruption, wholesale public and private immorality, and other massive problems about them, in horrified fascination with the doings of these Others. And second, to make the situation seem so hopeless that "realistically" there is nothing to be done about it anyway. Racism is no longer the problem, self-destructiveness is. And if that is so, why continue to throw good taxpayer dollars after bad? In the words of the older black woman selected by Moyers to deliver the clincher at the end: "If Martin Luther King were alive, he would not be talking about the things I think he was talking about—labor and all that. He would be talking about the black family."

It is hard to believe that it was simply bad taste that led CBS to choose the very week of the first national celebration of King's birthday to televise his fellow Southerner's broadside. African-Americans had hardly had a moment to savor the honor to the martyred black minister before their psyches were so powerfully assaulted.

The extent of the commonplace manner in which deepseated black response is blocked out from the larger society may be seen in several postscripts to the broadcast beginning when the National Black Leadership Roundtable, comprising the chief executive officers of more than 300 national black organizations, directed a detailed letter to CBS to protest the "untimely and indeed . . . suspect" airing of an "unbalanced, unfair and frequently salacious" documentary.

The N.B.L.R. challenged the implication "that the *only* legitimate and sanctioned family form is nuclear and partriarchal," and observed:

One was left with the impression that black families generally do not have fathers in the home, but there was no serious examination of the reasons for the absence of the father within some black families. The unconscionable high levels of unemployment, underemployment, imprisonment, drug addiction and mortality among black men—effects of an economy which does not fully respond to the employment needs of all Americans—all play a role. . . . Single-parent families then, are not, as implied . . . the result of "immorality" or promiscuity, but rather are adaptive responses to economic and social forces.

Two months later CBS vice president of public affairs broadcasts Eric Ober, speaking for Moyers, replied. He refused to meet with Walter Fauntroy, N.B.L.R. president, or "any member of your group." And to the N.B.L.R. query as to what "experts" had been consulted within the black community, he replied that the "experts we consulted were primarily officials of *the Department of the Census*." (Emphasis added.) Little did he know the history.

The reinforcing white response was predictable. In early 1987, the Columbia University Graduate School of Journalism gave its highest award in broadcast journalism—the Alfred I. DuPont–Columbia University Gold Baton for the "program judged to have made the greatest contribution to the public's understanding of an important issue"—to CBS News for the Moyers Special Report on "the disintegration of black family life."

Moyers's contribution lies not only in his restoration to primacy of old images through the power of the television but in his encouragement of the willingness, indeed the eagerness, of large numbers of white Americans to have all that he portrayed be true at any cost so that the victims might deserve their fate. Such is the depth of the entrenched white desire to avoid facing the society's culpability for creating and maintaining the two ever more unequal "societies" the Kerner report asked us to face up to a generation before.

RESTRAINING THE "DARKER IMPULSES"

In such a climate, it is not surprising that politicians like "centrist" Democrat Charles Robb, L.B.J.'s[3] son-in-law and former Virginia Governor, now Senator, promptly picked up Moyer's cue. Once upon a time, black people were the victims of white racism, Robb conceded in his keynote speech to a conference on the Johnson presidency. But that time has passed. "It's time to shift the primary focus from racism, the traditional enemy from without, to self-defeating patterns of behavior, the new enemy within."

Approval by establishment opinion makers was swift to follow. A *New York Times* editorial endorsed Robb's brand of "hard truth," and journalists flung the name of the messenger into the public arena as a worthy candidate for President.

In such a climate, the level of public tolerance of the intolerable increased. Even years before, there had been little reaction when, at a speech in New Orleans to the International Association of Chiefs of Police, President Reagan had drawn "applause and some whoops of approval" for remarks that included the following:

> It has occurred to me that the root causes of our . . . growth of government and the decay of the economy . . . can be traced to many of the same sources of the crime problem. . . . Many of the social thinkers of the 1950s and '60s who discussed crime only in the context of disadvantaged childhoods and poverty-stricken neighborhoods were the same people who thought that massive government spending could wipe away our social ills. The underlying premise in both cases was a belief that there was nothing permanent or absolute about any man's nature—that he was a product of his material environment, and that by changing that environment . . . we could . . . usher in a great new era. The solution to the crime problem will not be found in the social worker's files, the psychiatrist's notes or the bureaucrat's budget. . . . Only our deep moral values and strong institutions can hold back that jungle and restrain the darker impulses of human nature.

Most black people knew immediately of which "jungle" and whose "darker impulses" Reagan was speaking, and that his words represented a not-so-subtle invitation to white-against-black terror.

Reagan's position was a *theological* one in the American Calvinist tradition, a division of the world into good and evil, with a scapegoat selected to serve as "sacrificial animal upon whose back the burden of unwanted evils is ritualisti-cally loaded," in Kenneth Burke's definition. Through such projections, the culture thus expiates its sins and receives absolution.

The Reagan rhetoric directed to the assembled police officers was a direct corollary of his theological labeling of the Soviet Union as an "evil empire" (a remark now implicitly withdrawn in the case of the Russians, but not that of African-Americans!). It indicates how high is the level of responsibility for nationwide police practices of treating black Americans as if they are foreign enemies and, with sickening regularity, eliminating many. And it also indicates the treatment of a variety of foreign "enemies"—now mostly desperately struggling Third World countries—on the basis of a "moral" stance rooted in the myths of a fatalistically corrupt domestic system.

It is on this level that the politics of family —which is to say the politics of power and domination—threatens not only domestic but world social, political and economic order.

It is likewise on this level that the political manipulation of the intermingled race/sex/religion syndrome of the society is irrevocably wedded to violence; in its ultimate form, militaristic. For the identities of those who create the monsters in the mind (Toni Morrison[4] calls the creations "grinning apes in the head") require ever vigilant attention to finding and confronting replicas in the external world.

It is this system of macho ethics that was successfully drawn upon in George Bush's march to the White House. True to tradition, the ultimate scapegoat tapped was a black male, the rapist Willie Horton (whether real or fancied does not traditionally matter), projected before millions via television and print.

Those who make use of such a repugnant and dangerous tactic—among them South Carolina's Lee Atwater, now chair of the Republican National Committee, and Texan James Baker 3d[5]—know these traditions well. And they know further that it is not possible for the image of a black man accused of rape to be flashed before black Americans by white men independent of the psychic association for blacks with lynchings. After the election, *The New York Times* not only contributed the verdict to history that the Bush campaign was "tough and effective," this preeminent sheet augmented that judgment with strident editorial criticism of black students at Howard for their successful protest action when Lee Atwater was suddenly named to the University's Board of Trustees.

While white perception of black criminality is readily evoked, white awareness of black anger or anguish has been not only historically avoided but, on the deepest psychic levels, guarded against. Existentially, the concept of black people as vulnerable human beings who sustain pain and love and hatreds and fears and joy and sorrows and degradations and triumphs is not yet permitted in the national consciousness. Hence the constant need of the dominant society, in age after age, to reinforce linguistic and ritualistic symbols that deny black humanity.

Historically, white terror is the sustaining principle of the system. Whether overtly applied or covertly threatened, not only has this basic device of subjugation never been nationally rejected, it has, on the contrary, always been sanctioned.

THE FAMILY AS UNIFYING PRINCIPLE

A few weeks after his election, George Bush addressed the Republican Governors Association in Alabama where, some months before, several black legislators had been arrested for trying to remove the Confederate Flag from above the State Capitol, presided over by Republican Governor Guy Hunt. The theme of the conference— "Century of the States"—resurrected overtones of Calhoun's old brand of States' rights. To this audience, a smiling Bush announced that building more prisons was a major domestic priority of his Administration (on education, he emphasized that the initiative would be left up to the states).

Only a few weeks later a smiling Bush assured a black gathering celebrating the birthday of Martin Luther King Jr. that he is committed to the fulfillment of King's dream of America, just as they are. That King's dream does not include the construction of prisons is immaterial. In the prevailing political realm, language does not matter: Symbols are all.

However, the renewed focus on the black family has introduced a sleeper. For the very technology of communication which carries the message of black pathology to white people conveys to blacks the unmistakable message that once again the dominant culture needs the assurance that black pathology prevails. Clearly, we must bestir ourselves to face the threat. Ironically, we have been handed a mighty weapon. To millions of ordinary human beings the family is not a symbol to be manipulated by opportunistic politicians but the essential nurturing unit from which they draw their being. For African-Americans (and for hundreds of millions of others), it is the institution around which our historical memories cling. Through the extended family of mothers, fathers, sisters and brothers, uncles and aunts, cousins and unsung numbers of others who simply "mothered" parentless children, black people "got over."

It is unbelievable that on the eve of the twenty-first century those who are still fashioning the political formula for WHO and WHAT make a family remain overwhelmingly male!

But it is women who give birth, and children who represent the one essential entity which must exist if the family does. It is simply inconceivable that women, that society, can any longer allow men to retain almost exclusive domain over the vital process of defining the human family.

The concept of "family" can and should be a unifying, rather than divisive, principle. Given the weight of U.S. history that we uniquely bear, black women should step forth collectively not only as blacks but as women, in the name of our lost children throughout history—including most urgently the present generation. One of the first steps is to confront, in all their ramifications, the racist/sexist myths historically concocted by opportunistic, ruthless or naïve white males in the interests of white-over-black and male-over-female dominance.

Never again should the future black children—or children anywhere in the world—be left in such hands!   [1989]

Notes

1. WATTS: A predominantly black community in Los Angeles.
2. KERNER COMMISSION: The Commission on Civil Disorders, appointed by President Lyndon Johnson, headed by Ohio Governor Otto Kerner, and charged with investigating racial outbreaks in the mid-1960s.

3. L.B.J.: President Lyndon B. Johnson.
4. TONI MORRISON: A black novelist.
5. LEE ATWATER AND JAMES BAKER 3D: Atwater was President Bush's campaign manager, Baker his Secretary of State.

Understanding the Reading

1. Why did whites want to believe that free blacks were prone to insanity, dramatic population declines, and degeneracy?
2. What does "benign neglect" mean?
3. Why does Gresham find President Johnson's speech at Howard University reprehensible?
4. What were the differences between the Kerner Commission Report and Moynihan's?
5. How is the Moynihan Report sexist?
6. Why does Gresham find Moyers' CBS Special Report reprehensible?
7. How did various groups and individuals respond to the Moyers report?
8. What does Gresham mean by calling Reagan's position theological?
9. What does she mean by saying that in the prevailing political realm, "Symbols are all"?

Suggestions for Responding

1. What is a family? Should there be a national or cultural definition of what makes a family? Why or why not?
2. Both Gould and Gresham describe incidents where false data were used to support policy decisions. Assuming that those involved are reasonable men, explain their motivations and how you think they could have justified their actions. ◆

46

"Gee, You Don't Seem Like an Indian from the Reservation"

BARBARA CAMERON

One of the very first words I learned in my Lakota language was *wasicu* which designates white people. At that early age, my comprehension of wasicu was gained from observing and listening to my family discussing the wasicu. My grandmother always referred to white people as the "wasicu sica" with emphasis on *sica,* our word for terrible or bad. By the age of five I had seen one Indian man gunned down in the back by the police and was a silent witness to a gang of white teenage boys beating up an elderly Indian man. I'd hear stories of Indian ranch hands being "accidentally" shot by white ranchers. I quickly began to understand the wasicu menace my family spoke of.

My hatred for the wasicu was solidly implanted by the time I entered first grade. Unfortunately in first grade I became teacher's pet so my teacher had a fondness for hugging me which always repulsed me. I couldn't stand the idea of a white person touching me. Eventually I realized that it wasn't the white skin that I hated, but it was their culture of deceit, greed, racism, and violence.

During my first memorable visit to a white town, I was appalled that they thought of themselves as superior to my people. Their manner of living appeared devoid of life and bordered on hostility even for one another. They were separated from each other by their perfectly, politely fenced square plots of green lawn. The only lawns on my reservation were the lawns of the BIA* officials or white christians. The white people always seemed so loud, obnoxious, and vulgar. And the white parents were either screaming at their kids, threatening them with some form of punishment or hitting them. After spending a day around white people, I was always happy to go back to the reservation where people followed a relaxed yet respectful code of relating with each other. The easy teasing and joking that were inherent with the Lakota were a welcome relief after a day with the plastic faces.

I vividly remember two occasions during my childhood in which I was cognizant of being an Indian. The first time was at about three years of age when my family took me to my first powwow. I kept asking my grandmother, "Where are the Indians? Where are the Indians? Are they going to have bows and arrows?" I was very curious and strangely excited about the prospect of seeing real live Indians even though I myself was one. It's a memory that has remained with me through all these years because it's so full of the

_____
* Bureau of Indian Affairs.

subtleties of my culture. There was a sweet wonderful aroma in the air from the dancers and from the traditional food booths. There were lots of grandmothers and grandfathers with young children running about. Pow-wows in the Plains usually last for three days, sometimes longer, with Indian people traveling from all parts of our country to dance, to share food and laughter, and to be with each other. I could sense the importance of our gathering times and it was the beginning of my awareness that my people are a great and different nation.

The second time in my childhood when I knew very clearly that I am Indian occurred when I was attending an all white (except for me) elementary school. During Halloween my friends and I went trick or treating. At one of the last stops, the mother knew all of the children except for me. She asked me to remove my mask so she could see who I was. After I removed my mask, she realized I was an Indian and quite cruelly told me so, refusing to give me the treats my friends had received. It was a stingingly painful experience.

I told my mother about it the next evening after I tried to understand it. My mother was outraged and explained the realities of being an Indian in South Dakota. My mother paid a visit to the woman which resulted in their expressing a barrage of equal hatred for one another. I remember sitting in our pick-up hearing the intensity of the anger and feeling very sad that my mother had to defend her child to someone who wasn't worthy of her presence.

I spent a part of my childhood feeling great sadness and helplessness about how it seemed that Indians were open game for the white people, to kill, maim, beat up, insult, rape, cheat, or whatever atrocity the white people wanted to play with. There was also a rage and frustration that has not died. When I look back on reservation life it seems that I spent a great deal of time attending the funerals of my relatives or friends of my family. During one year I went to funerals of four murder victims. Most of my non-Indian friends have not seen a dead body or have not been to a funeral. Death was so common on the reservation that I did not understand the implications of the high death rate until after I moved away and was surprised to learn that I've seen more dead bodies than my friends will probably ever see in their lifetime.

Because of experiencing racial violence, I sometimes panic when I'm the only non-white in a roomful of whites, even if they are my closest friends; I wonder if I'll leave the room alive. The seemingly copacetic gay world of San Francisco becomes a mere dream after the panic leaves. I think to myself that it's truly insane for me to feel the panic. I want to scream out my anger and disgust with myself for feeling distrustful of my white friends and I want to banish the society that has fostered those feelings of alienation. I wonder at the amount of assimilation which has affected me and how long my "Indianness" will allow me to remain in a city that is far removed from the lives of many Native Americans.

"Alienation," and "assimilation" are two common words used to describe contemporary Indian people. I've come to despise those two words because what leads to "alienation" and "assimilation" should not be so concisely defined. And I generally mistrust words that are used to define Native Americans and Brown People. I don't like being put under a magnifying glass and having cute liberal terms describe who I am. The "alienation" or "assimilation" that I manifest is often in how I speak. There isn't necessarily a third world language but there is an Indian way of talking that is an essential part of me. I like it, I love it, yet I deny it. I "save" it for when I'm around other Indians. It is a way of talking that involves "Indian humor" which I know for sure non-Indian people would not necessarily understand.

Articulate. Articulate. I've heard that word used many times to describe third world people. White people seem so surprised to find brown people who can speak fluent english and are even perhaps educated. We then become "articulate." I think I spend a lot of time being articulate with white people. Or as one person said to me a few years ago, "Gee, you don't seem like an Indian from the reservation."

I often read about the dilemmas of contemporary Indians caught between the white and Indian worlds. For most of us, it is an uneasy balance to maintain. Sometimes some of us are not so successful with it. Native Americans have a very high suicide rate.

When I was about 20, I dreamt of myself at the age of 25–26, standing at a place on my reservation,

*looking to the North, watching a glorious, many-
colored horse galloping toward me from the sky.
My eyes were riveted and attracted to the beauty
and overwhelming strength of the horse. The
horse's eyes were staring directly into mine, hyp-
notizing me and holding my attention. Slowly
from the East, an eagle was gliding toward the
horse. My attention began to be drawn toward the
calm of the eagle but I still didn't want to lose sight
of the horse. Finally the two met with the eagle sail-
ing into the horse causing it to disintegrate. The eagle flew gently on.*

I take this prophetic dream as an analogy of
my balance between the white (horse) and Indian (eagle) world. Now that I am 26, I find that
I've gone as far into my exploration of the white
world as I want. It doesn't mean that I'm going to
run off to live in a tipi. It simply means that I'm
not interested in pursuing a society that uses
analysis, research, and experimentation to con-
cretize their vision of cruel destinies for those
who are not bastards of the Pilgrims; a society
with arrogance rising, moon in oppression, and
sun in destruction.

Racism is not easy for me to write about because of my own racism toward other people of
color, and because of a complex set of "racisms"
within the Indian community. At times animosity exists between half-breed, full-blood, light-
skinned Indians, dark-skinned Indians, and non-
Indians who attempt to pass as Indians. The U.S.
government has practiced for many years its divisiveness in the Indian community by instilling
and perpetuating these Indian vs. Indian tactics.
Native Americans are the foremost group of
people who continuously fight against pre-
meditated cultural genocide.

I've grown up with misconceptions about
Blacks, Chicanos, and Asians. I'm still in the process of trying to eliminate my racist pictures of
other people of color. I know most of *my* images
of other races come from television, books, movies, newspapers, and magazines. Who can pinpoint exactly where racism comes from? There
are certain political dogmas that are excellent in
their "analysis" of racism and how it feeds the
capitalist system. To intellectually understand
that it is wrong or politically incorrect to be racist
leaves me cold. A lot of poor or working class
white and brown people are just as racist as the

"capitalist pig." We are *all* continually pumped
with gross and inaccurate images of everyone
else and we *all* pump it out. I don't think there
are easy answers or formulas. My personal attempts at eliminating my racism have to start at
the base level of those mind-sets that inhibit my
relationships with people.

Racism among third world people is an area
that needs to be discussed and dealt with honestly. We form alliances loosely based on the fact
that we have a common oppressor, yet we do not
have a commitment to talk about our own fears
and misconceptions about each other. I've noticed that liberal, consciousness-raised white
people tend to be incredibly polite to third world
people at parties or other social situations. It's almost as if they make a point to SHAKE YOUR
HAND or to introduce themselves and then
run down all the latest right-on third world or
Native American books they've just read. On
the other hand it's been my experience that if
there are several third world gay people at a
party, we make a point of avoiding each other,
and spend our time talking to the whites to show
how sophisticated and intelligent we are. I've always wanted to introduce myself to other third
world people but wondered how I would introduce myself or what would I say. There are so
many things I would want to say, except sometimes I don't want to remember I'm Third World
or Native American. I don't want to remember
sometimes because it means recognizing that
we're outlaws.

At the Third World Gay Conference in October 1979, the Asian and Native American people
in attendance felt the issues affecting us were not
adequately included in the workshops. Our representation and leadership had minimal input
which resulted in a skimpy educational process
about our struggles. The conference glaringly
pointed out to us the narrow definition held by
some people that third world means black
people only. It was a depressing experience to sit
in the lobby of Harambee House with other Native Americans and Asians, feeling removed from
other third world groups with whom there is supposed to be this automatic solidarity and empathy. The Indian group sat in my motel room
discussing and exchanging our experiences
within the third world context. We didn't spend
much time in workshops conducted by other

third world people because of feeling unwelcomed at the conference and demoralized by having an invisible presence. What's worse than being invisible among your own kind?

It is of particular importance to us as third world gay people to begin a serious interchange of sharing and educating ourselves about each other. We not only must struggle with the racism and homophobia of straight white america, but most often struggle with the homophobia that exists within our third world communities. Being third world doesn't always connote a political awareness or activism. I've met a number of third world and Native American lesbians who've said they're just into "being themselves," and that politics has no meaning in their lives. I agree that everyone is entitled to "be themselves" but in a society that denies respect and basic rights to people because of their ethnic background, I feel that individuals cannot idly sit by and allow themselves to be co-opted by the dominant society. I don't know what moves a person to be politically active or to attempt to raise the quality of life in our world. I only know what motivates my political responsibility . . . the death of Anna Mae Aquash—Native American freedom fighter—"mysteriously" murdered by a bullet in the head; Raymond Yellow Thunder—forced to dance naked in front of a white VFW club in Nebraska—murdered; Rita Silk-Nauni—imprisoned for life for defending her child; my dear friend Mani Lucas-Papago—shot in the back of the head outside of a gay bar in Phoenix. The list could go on and on. My Native American History, recent and past, moves me to continue as a political activist.

And in the white gay community there is rampant racism which is never adequately addressed or acknowledged. My friend Chrystos from the Menominee Nation gave a poetry reading in May 1980, at a Bay Area feminist bookstore. Her reading consisted of poems and journal entries in which she wrote honestly from her heart about the many "isms" and contradictions in most of our lives. Chrystos' bluntly revealing observations on her experiences with the white-lesbian-feminist-community are similar to mine and are probably echoed by other lesbians of color.

Her honesty was courageous and should be representative of the kind of forum our community needs to openly discuss mutual racism. A few days following Chrystos' reading, a friend who was in the same bookstore overheard a white lesbian denounce Chrystos' reading as anti-lesbian and racist.

A few years ago, a white lesbian telephoned me requesting an interview, explaining that she was taking Native American courses at a local university, and that she needed data for her paper on gay Native Americans. I agreed to the interview with the idea that I would be helping a "sister" and would also be able to educate her about Native American struggles. After we completed the interview, she began a diatribe on how sexist Native Americans are, followed by a questioning session in which I was to enlighten her mind about why Native Americans are so sexist. I attempted to rationally answer her inanely racist and insulting questions, although my inner response was to tell her to remove herself from my house. Later it became very clear how I had been manipulated as a sounding board for her ugly and distorted views about Native Americans. Her arrogance and disrespect were characteristic of the racist white people in South Dakota. If I tried to point it out, I'm sure she would have vehemently denied her racism.

During the Brigg's Initiative scare, I was invited to speak at a rally to represent Native American solidarity against the initiative. The person who spoke prior to me expressed a pro-Bakke sentiment[1] which the audience booed and hissed. His comments left the predominantly white audience angry and in disruption. A white lesbian stood up demanding that a third world person address the racist comments he had made. The MC, rather than taking responsibility for restoring order at the rally, realized that I was the next speaker and I was also T-H-I-R-D-W-O-R-L-D!! I refused to address the remarks of the previous speaker because of the attitudes of the MC and the white lesbian that only third world people are responsible for speaking out against racism. *It is inappropriate for progressive or liberal white people to expect warriors in brown armor to eradicate racism.* There must be co-responsibility from people of color and white people to equally work on this issue. It is not just MY responsibility to point out and educate about racist activities and beliefs.

Redman, redskin, savage, heathen, injun, american indian, first americans, indigenous peoples, natives, amerindian, native american, nigger, negro, black, wet back, greaser, mexican, spanish, latin, hispanic, chicano, chink, oriental, asian, disadvantaged, special interest group, minority, third world, fourth world, people of color, illegal aliens—oh yes about them, will the U.S. government recognize that the Founding Fathers (you know George Washington and all those guys) are this country's first illegal aliens?

We are named by others and we are named by ourselves.

Epilogue . . .

Following writing most of this, I went to visit my home in South Dakota. It was my first visit in eight years. I kept putting off my visit year after year because I could not tolerate the white people there and the ruralness and poverty of the reservation. And because in the eight years since I left home, I came out as a lesbian. My visit home was overwhelming. Floods and floods of locked memories broke. I rediscovered myself there in the hills, on the prairies, in the sky, on the road, in the quiet nights, among the stars, listening to the distant yelps of coyotes, walking on Lakota earth, seeing Bear Butte, looking at my grandparents' cragged faces, standing under wakiyan, smelling the Paha Sapa (Black Hills), and being with my precious circle of relatives.

My sense of time changed, my manner of speaking changed, and a certain freedom with myself returned.

I was sad to leave but recognized that a significant part of myself has never left and never will. And that part is what gives me strength—the strength of my people's enduring history and continuing belief in the sovereignty of our lives.

[1981]

Note

1. PRO-BAKKE SENTIMENT: Supportive of the Supreme Court ruling that universities cannot reserve slots for minority students only.

Understanding the Reading

1. How did white people seem to Cameron as a child?
2. Explain the two memories Cameron had of being aware of being an Indian.
3. How has racial violence affected her?
4. Why does she despise the words "alienation," "assimilation," and "articulate"?
5. What does Cameron say about her own racism and racism among third world people?
6. What special problems affect third-world gay people?
7. Why did she refuse to address the pro-Bakke remarks?

Suggestions for Responding

1. What words have been used by others to characterize, even in a positive way, a group to which you belong? Explain how you feel about each of them.
2. In American society it is almost impossible not to be affected in some way by racism. Write a critical analysis of some manifestation of your own racism. ◆

47

Something About the Subject Makes It Hard to Name

GLORIA YAMATO

Racism—simple enough in structure, yet difficult to eliminate. Racism—pervasive in the U.S. culture to the point that it deeply affects all the local town folk and spills over, negatively influencing the fortunes of folk around the world. Racism is pervasive to the point that we take many of its manifestations for granted, believing "that's life." Many believe that racism can be dealt with effectively in one hellifying workshop, or one hour-long heated discussion. Many actually believe this monster, racism, that has had at least a few hundred years to take root, grow, invade our space and develop subtle variations . . . this mind-funk that distorts thought and action, can be merely wished away. I've run into folks who really think that we can beat this devil, kick this habit, be healed of this disease in a snap. In a sincere blink of a well-intentioned eye, presto—poof—racism disappears. "I've dealt with my racism . . . (envision a laying on of hands) . . . Hallelujah! Now I can go to the beach." Well, fine. Go to the beach. In fact, why don't we all go to the beach and continue to work on the sucker over there? Cuz you can't even shave a little piece off this thing called racism in a day, or a weekend, or a workshop.

When I speak of *oppression,* I'm talking about the systematic, institutionalized mistreatment of one group of people by another for whatever reason. The oppressors are purported to have an innate ability to access economic resource, information, respect, etc., while the oppressed are believed to have a corresponding negative innate ability. The flip side of oppression is *internalized oppression.* Members of the target group are emotionally, physically, and spiritually battered to the point that they begin to actually believe that their oppression is deserved, is their lot in life, is natural and right, and that it doesn't even exist. The oppression begins to feel comfortable, familiar enough that when mean ol' Massa lay down de whip, we got's to pick up and whack ourselves and each other. Like a virus, it's hard to beat racism, because by the time you come up with a cure, it's mutated to a "new cure-resistant" form. One shot just won't get it. Racism must be attacked from many angles.

The forms of racism that I pick up on these days are (1) aware/blatant racism, (2) aware/covert racism, (3) unaware/unintentional racism, and (4) unaware/self-righteous racism. I can't say that I prefer any one form of racism over the others, because they all look like an itch needing a scratch. I've heard it said (and understandably so) that the aware/blatant form of racism is preferable if one must suffer it. Outright racists will, without apology or confusion, tell us that because of our color we don't appeal to them. If we so choose, we can attempt to get the hell out of their way before we get the sweat knocked out of us. Growing up, aware/covert racism is what I heard many of my elders bemoaning "up north," after having escaped the overt racism "down south." Apartments were suddenly no longer vacant or rents were outrageously high, when black, brown, red, or yellow persons went to inquire about them. Job vacancies were suddenly filled, or we were fired for very vague reasons. It still happens, though the perpetrators really take care to cover their tracks these days. They don't want to get gummed to death or slobbered on by the toothless laws that supposedly protect us from such inequities.

Unaware/unintentional racism drives usually tranquil white liberals wild when they get called on it, and confirms the suspicions of many people of color who feel that white folks are just plain crazy. It has led white people to believe that it's just fine to ask if they can touch my hair (while reaching). They then exclaim over how soft it is, how it does not scratch their hand. It has led whites to assume that bending over backwards and speaking to me in high-pitched (terrified), condescending tones would make up for all the racist wrongs that distort our lives. This type of racism had led whites right to my doorstep, talking 'bout, "We're sorry/we love you and want to make things right," which is fine, and further, "We're gonna give you the opportunity to fix it while we sleep. Just tell us what you need. 'Bye!!"—which *ain't* fine. With the best of intentions, the best of educations, and the greatest generosity of heart, whites, operating on the misinformation fed to them from day one, will behave in ways that are racist, will perpetuate racism by being "nice" the way we're taught to be nice. You can just "nice" somebody to death with naïveté and lack of awareness of privilege. Then there's guilt and the desire to end racism and how the two get all tangled up to the point that people, morbidly fascinated with their guilt, are immobilized. Rather than deal with ending racism, they sit and ponder their guilt and hope nobody notices how awful they are. Meanwhile, racism picks up momentum and keeps on keepin' on.

Now, the newest form of racism that I'm hip to is unaware/self-righteous racism. The "good wife" racist attempts to shame Blacks into being blacker, scorns Japanese-Americans who don't speak Japanese, and knows more about the Chicano/a community than the folks who make up the community. They assign themselves as the "good whites," as opposed to the "bad whites," and are often so busy telling people of color what the issues in the Black, Asian, Indian, Latino/a communities should be that they don't have time to deal with their errant sisters and brothers in the white community. Which means that people of color are still left to deal with what the "good whites" don't want to . . . racism.

Internalized racism is what really gets in my

way as a Black woman. It influences the way I see or don't see myself, limits what I expect of myself or others like me. It results in my acceptance of mistreatment, leads me to believe that being treated with less than absolute respect, at least this once, is to be expected because I am Black, because I am not white. Because I am (*you fill in the color*), you think, "Life is going to be hard." The fact is life may be hard, but the color of your skin is not the cause of the hardship. The color of your skin may be used as an excuse to mistreat you, but there is no reason or logic involved in the mistreatment. If it seems that your color is the reason; if it seems that your ethnic heritage is the cause of the woe, it's because you've been deliberately beaten down by agents of a greedy system until you swallowed the garbage. That is the internalization of racism.

Racism is the systematic, institutionalized mistreatment of one group of people by another based on racial heritage. Like every other oppression, racism can be internalized. People of color come to believe misinformation about their particular ethnic group and thus believe that their mistreatment is justified. With that basic vocabulary, let's take a look at how the whole thing works together. Meet "the Ism Family," racism, classism, ageism, adultism, elitism, sexism, heterosexism, physicalism, etc. All these ism's are systematic, that is, not only are these parasites feeding off our lives, they are also dependent on one another for foundation. Racism is supported and reinforced by classism, which is given a foothold and a boost by adultism, which also feeds sexism, which is validated by heterosexism, and so it goes on. You cannot have the "ism" functioning without first effectively installing its flipside, the internalized version of the ism. Like twins, as one particular form of the ism grows in potency, there is a corresponding increasing in its internalized form within the population. Before oppression becomes a specific ism like racism, usually all hell breaks loose. War. People fight attempts to enslave them, or to subvert their will, or to take what they consider theirs, whether that is territory or dignity. It's true that the various elements of racism, while repugnant, would not be able to do very much damage, but for one generally overlooked key piece: power/privilege.

While in one sense we all have power we have to look at the fact that, in our society, people are stratified into various classes and some of these classes have more privilege than others. The owning class has enough power and privilege to not have to give a good whinney what the rest of the folks have on their minds. The power and privilege of the owning class provides the ability to pay off enough of the working class and offer that paid-off group, the middle class, just enough privilege to make it agreeable to do various and sundry oppressive things to other working-class and outright disenfranchised folk, keeping the lid on explosive inequities, at least for a minute. If you're at the bottom of this heap, and you believe the line that says you're there because that's all you're worth, it is at least some small solace to believe that there are others more worthless than you, because of their gender, race, sexual preference . . . whatever. The specific form of power that runs the show here is the power to intimidate. The power to take away the most lives the quickest, and back it up with legal and "divine" sanction, is the very bottom line. It makes the difference between who's holding the racism end of the stick and who's getting beat with it (or beating others as vulnerable as they are) on the internalized racism end of the stick. What I am saying is, while people of color are welcome to tear up their own neighborhoods and each other, everybody knows that you cannot do that to white folks without hell to pay. People of color can be prejudiced against one another and whites, but do not have an ice-cube's chance in hell of passing laws that will get whites sent to relocation camps "for their own protection and the security of the nation." People who have not thought about or refuse to acknowledge this imbalance of power/privilege often want to talk about the racism of people of color. But then that is one of the ways racism is able to continue to function. You look for someone to blame and you blame the victim, who will nine times out of ten accept the blame out of habit.

So, what can we do? Acknowledge racism for a start, even though and especially when we've struggled to be kind and fair, or struggled to rise above it all. It is hard to acknowledge the fact that racism circumscribes and pervades our lives. Racism must be dealt with on two levels, personal and societal, emotional and institutional. It is possible—and most effective—to do both at the same time. We must reclaim whatever delight we have lost in our own ethnic heritage or heritages. This so-called melting pot has only succeeded in turning us into fast food-gobbling "generics" (as in generic "white folks" who were once Irish, Polish, Russian, English, etc. and "black folks," who were once Ashanti, Bambara, Baule, Yoruba, etc.). Find or create safe places to actually *feel* what we've been forced to repress each time we were a victim of, witness to or perpetrator of racism, so that we do not continue, like puppets, to act out the past in the present and future. Challenge oppression. Take a stand against it. When you are aware of something oppressive going down, stop the show. At least call it. We become so numbed to racism that we don't even think twice about it, unless it's immediately life-threatening.

Whites who want to be allies to people of color: You can educate yourselves via research and observation rather than rigidly, arrogantly relying solely on interrogating people of color. Do not expect that people of color should teach you how to behave non-oppressively. Do not give in to the pull to be lazy. Think, hard. Do not blame people of color for your frustration about racism, but do appreciate the fact that people of color will often help you get in touch with that frustration. Assume that your effort to be a good friend is appreciated, but don't expect or accept gratitude from people of color. Work on racism for your sake, not "their" sake. Assume that you are needed and capable of being a good ally. Know that you'll make mistakes and commit yourself to correcting them and continuing on as an ally, no matter what. Don't give up.

People of color, working through internalized racism: Remember always that you and others like you are completely worthy of respect, completely capable of achieving whatever you take a notion to do. Remember that the term "people of color" refers to a variety of ethnic and cultural backgrounds. These various groups have been oppressed in a variety of ways. Educate yourself about the ways different peoples have been oppressed and how they've resisted that oppression. Expect and insist that whites are capable of being good allies against racism. Don't give up. Resist the pull to give out the "people of color

seal of approval" to aspiring white allies. A moment of appreciation is fine, but more than that tends to be less than helpful. Celebrate yourself. Celebrate yourself. Celebrate the inevitable end of racism.   [1988]

Understanding the Reading

1. Explain oppression and internalized oppression.
2. Explain the four forms of racism Yamato describes.
3. How does internalized racism work?
4. How do power and privilege reinforce "the Ism Family"?
5. What steps does Yamato suggest need to be taken to combat racism?

Suggestions for Responding

1. Describe an incident when you were a victim of, witness to, or perpetrator of racism; then analyze what feelings you were forced to repress.
2. What power and privileges do you enjoy as a result of your race, class, age, gender, sexual orientation, and so forth? ✦

48

White Privilege: Unpacking the Invisible Knapsack

PEGGY MCINTOSH

Through work to bring materials from Women's Studies into the rest of the curriculum, I have often noticed men's unwillingness to grant that they are over-privileged, even though they may grant that women are disadvantaged. They may say they will work to improve women's status, in the society, the university, or the curriculum, but they can't or won't support the idea of lessening men's. Denials which amount to taboos surround the subject of advantages which men gain from women's disadvantages. These denials protect male privilege from being fully acknowledged, lessened or ended.

Thinking through unacknowledged male privilege as a phenomenon, I realized that since hierarchies in our society are interlocking, there was most likely a phenomenon of white privilege which was similarly denied and protected. As a white person, I realized I had been taught about racism as something which puts others at a disadvantage, but had been taught not to see one of its corollary aspects, white privilege, which puts me at an advantage.

I think whites are carefully taught not to recognize white privilege, as males are taught not to recognize male privilege. So I have begun in an untutored way to ask what it is like to have white privilege. I have come to see white privilege as an invisible package of unearned assets which I can count on cashing in each day, but about which I was 'meant' to remain oblivious. White privilege is like an invisible weightless knapsack of special provisions, maps, passports, codebooks, visas, clothes, tools and blank checks.

Describing white privilege makes one newly accountable. As we in Women's Studies work to reveal male privilege and ask men to give up some of their power, so one who writes about having white privilege must ask, "Having described it, what will I do to lessen or end it?"

After I realized the extent to which men work from a base of unacknowledged privilege, I understood that much of their oppressiveness was unconscious. Then I remembered the frequent charges from women of color that white women whom they encounter are oppressive. I began to understand why we are justly seen as oppressive, even when we don't see ourselves that way. I began to count the ways in which I enjoy unearned skin privilege and have been conditioned into oblivion about its existence.

My schooling gave me no training in seeing myself as an oppressor, as an unfairly advantaged person, or as a participant in a damaged culture. I was taught to see myself as an individual whose moral state depended on her individual moral will. My schooling followed the pattern my colleague Elizabeth Minnich has pointed out: whites are taught to think of their lives as morally neutral, normative, and average, and also ideal, so that when we work to benefit others, this is seen as work which will allow "them" to be more like "us."

I decided to try to work on myself at least by identifying some of the daily effects of white privilege in my life. I have chosen those conditions which I think in my case *attach somewhat more to skin-color privilege* than to class, religion, ethnic status, or geographical location, though of course all these other factors are intricately intertwined. As far as I can see, my African American co-workers, friends and acquaintances with whom I come into daily or frequent contact in this particular time, place, and line of work cannot count on most of these conditions.

1. I can if I wish arrange to be in the company of people of my race most of the time.
2. If I should need to move, I can be pretty sure of renting or purchasing housing in an area which I can afford and in which I would want to live.
3. I can be pretty sure that my neighbors in such a location will be neutral or pleasant to me.
4. I can go shopping alone most of the time, pretty well assured that I will not be followed or harassed.
5. I can turn on the television or open to the front page of the paper and see people of my race widely represented.
6. When I am told about our national heritage or about "civilization," I am shown that people of my color made it what it is.
7. I can be sure that my children will be given curricular materials that testify to the existence of their race.
8. If I want to, I can be pretty sure of finding a publisher for this piece on white privilege.
9. I can go into a music shop and count on finding the music of my race represented, into a supermarket and find the staple foods which fit with my cultural traditions, into a hairdresser's shop and find someone who can cut my hair.
10. Whether I use checks, credit cards, or cash, I can count on my skin color not to work

against the appearance of financial reliability.

11. I can arrange to protect my children most of the time from people who might not like them.

12. I can swear, or dress in second hand clothes, or not answer letters, without having people attribute these choices to the bad morals, the poverty, or the illiteracy of my race.

13. I can speak in public to a powerful male group without putting my race on trial.

14. I can do well in a challenging situation without being called a credit to my race.

15. I am never asked to speak for all the people of my racial group.

16. I can remain oblivious of the language and customs of persons of color who constitute the world's majority without feeling in my culture any penalty for such oblivion.

17. I can criticize our government and talk about how much I fear its policies and behavior without being seen as a cultural outsider.

18. I can be pretty sure that if I ask to talk to "the person in charge," I will be facing a person of my race.

19. If a traffic cop pulls me over or if the IRS audits my tax return, I can be sure I haven't been singled out because of my race.

20. I can easily buy posters, postcards, picture books, greeting cards, dolls, toys, and children's magazines featuring people of my race.

21. I can go home from most meetings of organizations I belong to feeling somewhat tied in, rather than isolated, out-of-place, outnumbered, unheard, held at a distance, or feared.

22. I can take a job with an affirmative action employer without having co-workers on the job suspect that I got it because of race.

23. I can choose public accommodation without fearing that people of my race cannot get in or will be mistreated in the places I have chosen.

24. I can be sure that if I need legal or medical help, my race will not work against me.

25. If my day, week, or year is going badly, I need not ask of each negative episode or situation whether it has racial overtones.

26. I can choose blemish cover or bandages in "flesh" color and have them more or less match my skin.

I repeatedly forgot each of the realizations on this list until I wrote it down. For me white privilege has turned out to be an elusive and fugitive subject. The pressure to avoid it is great, for in facing it I must give up the myth of meritocracy. If these things are true, this is not such a free country; one's life is not what one makes it; many doors open for certain people through no virtues of their own.

In unpacking this invisible knapsack of white privilege, I have listed conditions of daily experience which I once took for granted. Nor did I think of any of these perquisites as bad for the holder. I now think that we need a more finely differentiated taxonomy of privilege, for some of these varieties are only what one would want for everyone in a just society, and others give licence to be ignorant, oblivious, arrogant and destructive.

I see a pattern running through the matrix of white privilege, a pattern of assumptions which were passed on to me as a white person. There was one main piece of cultural turf; it was my own turf, and I was among those who could control the turf. *My skin color was an asset for any move I was educated to want to make.* I could think of myself as belonging in major ways, and of making social systems work for me. I could freely disparage, fear, neglect, or be oblivious to anything outside of the dominant cultural forms. Being of the main culture, I could also criticize it fairly freely.

In proportion as my racial group was being made confident, comfortable, and oblivious, other groups were likely being made inconfident, uncomfortable, and alienated. Whiteness protected me from many kinds of hostility, distress, and violence, which I was being subtly trained to visit in turn upon people of color.

For this reason, the word "privilege" now seems to me misleading. We usually think of privilege as being a favored state, whether earned or conferred by birth or luck. Yet some of the conditions I have described here work to systematically overempower certain groups. Such privilege simply *confers dominance* because of one's race or sex.

I want, then, to distinguish between earned strength and unearned power conferred systematically. Power from unearned privilege can look like strength when it is in fact permission to escape or to dominate. But not all of the privileges on my list are inevitably damaging. Some, like the expectation that neighbors will be decent to you, or that your race will not count against you in court, should be the norm in a just society. Others, like the privilege to ignore less powerful people, distort the humanity of the holders as well as the ignored groups.

We might at least start by distinguishing between positive advantages which we can work to spread, and negative types of advantages which unless rejected will always reinforce our present hierarchies. For example, the feeling that one belongs within the human circle, as Native Americans say, should not be seen as privilege for a few. Ideally it is an *unearned entitlement*. At present, since only a few have it, it is an *unearned advantage* for them. This paper results from a process of coming to see that some of the power which I originally saw as attendant on being a human being in the U.S. consisted [of] *unearned advantage* and *conferred dominance*.

I have met very few men who are truly distressed about systemic, unearned male advantage and conferred dominance. And so one question for me and others like me is whether we will be like them, or whether we will get truly distressed, even outraged, about unearned race advantage and conferred dominance and if so, what we will do to lessen them. In any case, we need to do more work in identifying how they actually affect our daily lives. Many, perhaps most, of our white students in the U.S. think that racism doesn't affect them because they are not people of color; they do not see "whiteness" as a racial identity. In addition, since race and sex are not the only advantaging systems at work, we need similarly to examine the daily experience of having age advantage, or ethnic advantage, or physical ability, or advantage related to nationality, religion, or sexual orientation.

Difficulties and dangers surrounding the task of finding parallels are many. Since racism, sexism, and heterosexism are not the same, the advantaging associated with them should not be seen as the same. In addition, it is hard to disentangle aspects of unearned advantage which rest more on social class, economic class, race, religion, sex and ethnic identity than on other factors. Still, all of the oppressions are interlocking, as the Combahee River Collective[1] Statement of 1977 continues to remind us eloquently.

One factor seems clear about all of the interlocking oppressions. They take both active forms which we can see and embedded forms which as a member of the dominant group one is taught not to see. In my class and place, I did not see myself as a racist because I was taught to recognize racism only in individual acts of meanness by members of my group, never in invisible systems conferring unsought racial dominance on my group from birth.

Disapproving of the systems won't be enough to change them. I was taught to think that racism could end if white individuals changed their attitudes. [But] a "white" skin in the United States opens many doors for whites whether or not we approve of the way dominance has been conferred on us. Individual acts can palliate, but cannot end, these problems.

To redesign social systems we need first to acknowledge their colossal unseen dimensions. The silences and denials surrounding privilege are the key political tool here. They keep the thinking about equality or equity incomplete, protecting unearned advantage and conferred dominance by making these taboo subjects. Most talk by whites about equal opportunity seems to me now to be about equal opportunity to try to get into a position of dominance while denying that *systems* of dominance exist.

It seems to me that obliviousness about white advantage, like obliviousness about male advantage, is kept strongly inculturated in the United States so as to maintain the myth of meritocracy, the myth that democratic choice is equally available to all. Keeping most people unaware that freedom of confident action is there for just a small number of people props up those in power, and serves to keep power in the hands of the same groups that have most of it already.

Though systemic change takes many decades, there are pressing questions for me and I imagine for some others like me if we raise our daily consciousness on the perquisites of being light-skinned. What will we do with such knowledge? As we know from watching men, it is an open question whether we will choose to use unearned advantage to weaken hidden systems of advantage, and whether we will use any of our arbitrarily-awarded power to try to reconstruct power systems on a broader base.   [1989]

Note

1. COMBAHEE RIVER COLLECTIVE: A group of black feminist women in Boston from 1974 to 1980.

Understanding the Reading

1. Why is it important to consider the concept of being overprivileged as well as the concept of being disadvantaged?
2. Explain what each of the conditions that arise from white privilege reveals about our cultural values.
3. Why are these privileges important?
4. What does McIntosh mean when she says she must give up the "myth of meritocracy"?
5. Which white privileges "give licence to be ignorant, oblivious, arrogant and destructive"?
6. What assumptions underlie white privilege?
7. What connections does McIntosh make between privilege, power, and dominance?
8. How is whiteness a racial identity?

Suggestion for Responding

What did you learn from McIntosh's analysis of racism and white privilege, and what did you begin to think about after reading it? What additional privileges can you add to McIntosh's list? What will you do with such knowledge? ✦

49

Power of Minorities

JON A. BLUBAUGH AND
DORTHY L. PENNINGTON

While [it may seem] . . . that the use of power in interracial communication has been one-sided, we can point out instances in which minorities exercise power over the majority. The power of minorities has been far from equal to that of whites in terms of interpersonal, institutional, or cultural influence.

DIFFERENCE AS POWER

We are most comfortable around those who are similar to us or around those who emulate our behavior. We, therefore, feel somewhat uncomfortable around those who are different. Their differences produce a threat, and an aura of mystery surrounds the "different" person until we find ways of reducing our uncertainty. In American society, minority group members are the "different" ones. Thus when a member of a minority group moves into a predominantly white neighborhood, the neighbors are unable to conceal their curiosity. They want to know who the newcomer is, where he works, what his background is, what kinds of activities he participates in, even more so than if he were of the same race. Minority group members have indicated to us how such curiosity surrounds their presence, especially since they do not feel equally as curious about their neighbors. A black friend tells of an incident in which his neighbors, apparently unsatisfied with the information they had obtained from him verbally, went on to do further research. To his surprise one day a neighbor, in passing, remarked, "We didn't know you taught Political Science in the university," and "You have your doctorate, too, don't you?" This neighbor's research had produced accurate findings.

What we are suggesting here is that minority group members seem to possess the power of differentia-as-threat. Because they look different and may be different in cultural orientation and values, they are perceived as threatening. In the context of power by the majority, when minorities do not emulate the behavior of the majority, the majority may feel disconcerted, especially if the majority believes they should have legitimate power over the minority. The difference of the minority may, therefore, cause discomfort. Or it may be ignored. The power of the minority may then be unconscious and have as its base the perception of the majority or other racial group.

On the other hand, minorities may use differentia-as-threat in strategic ways. They may wish to cause consternation or to make themselves be noticed. It is the use of difference as strategy, however, that is of questionable value for establishing authentic interracial communication. Differences that are genuine must be accepted and respected. An example of difference used as strategy may show a Mexican American person saying to a white, "I don't like you because you're white." In this instance, skin color, itself, becomes the basis for lack of interaction. The strategist is therefore capitalizing upon the difference in skin color and allowing the difference to serve as a barrier or as a screen through which all of his interaction will be filtered. Another way in which difference may serve as strategy may show a black person wearing his African garb to a white gathering primarily for the purpose of calling attention to himself. On the other hand, if he dons African garb as a cultural matter-of-fact, it should be less of an issue.

Thus the act may be the same, but the meaning it triggers may be different. When a communicative act with possible racial differences of interpretation (whether verbal or nonverbal) is used by either communicator to create power differences, then increased difficulty in interracial communication occurs. Such acts should be avoided by both communicators.

We have also observed that while being "different" has served as a basis of power for minorities, there are also racial differences in the perception of that "difference." Just as there are racial differences in the perception of the power possessed by whites, there seem to be racial differences in the perception of the power possessed by minorities. For example, a black male student felt that his being "different" from whites was a type of undefined power, but not a threat. One white female student remarked that she, in fact, perceived his difference as a threat, although (1) he did not intend to have his difference serve as a threat, and (2) had she not expressed her feelings, he would never have known that many of her reactions to him were based upon her perception of him as a threat.

We can note several problematic features about this communication situation relating to the need to constantly validate one's perceptions. First, the male did not intend to have his "difference" perceived as a threat. Second, had the female not expressed her feelings, the male would never have known that many of her reactions toward him were based upon her perceiving him as a threat. We can see how the problem could have snowballed had the female gone on to influence others with her impressions of him as a threat instead of arresting the problem by evaluating her perceptions of him. He, by the same token, could help to reduce the communication problem by checking the possible effects of his behaviors on others, especially those behaviors that can be interpreted differently by someone with a different frame of reference. Otherwise, when both operate on the basis of unverified assumptions as when receivers impute their own intent into the acts of senders, communication problems are likely to arise. In this case, the female was responding to an imaginary power which, for her, had become real. Because the feelings about power were brought into the open, the two communicators were able to recognize their different perceptions and communicate across them. The communication between them was less complicated since the power issue was lessened or resolved.

POTENTIAL AS POWER

Though minorities are believed to be less powerful than the majority, their potential for development and advancement is a source of power. Because the power of potential is somewhat undefined, it creates uncertainty, which is often threatening.

Thus the emphasis on equal employment in hiring has caused some whites to fear that minorities are going to replace them. The idea of quotas is often viewed negatively. Because of the power potential, a company's attempt to hire minorities is sometimes taken by majority employees as a threat to their jobs. Defensive behaviors result, and the climate for communication is closed. A white worker was once heard remarking of minority employees, "I don't mind having one or two around, but with larger numbers, we may find ourselves out of a job." "Yeah," agreed his listener, "they'll probably try to take over."

While there is power in potential, or put another way, the power of possibility, communication need not be hampered with a false alarm. Most minority members are not concerned with seizing the jobs of whites or with taking over the company. The concern seems to be more of having enough jobs created or with having an equal opportunity for securing them.

The power of potential has been common since the revolutionaries Denmark Vesey and Nat Turner[1] showed that passivity of the oppressed could not be taken for granted. The possibility always existed historically for an unannounced attack on the system. Such attacks seemed to be aimed, not at individuals, but at the system. They called attention to what was perceived as being wrong with the system. The power of potential as seen now is aimed at nothing more than the assurance that each person be allowed to reach his or her full potential, wherein race does not serve as a barrier to achieving that goal.

POWER BASED IN STEREOTYPES

We can note how stereotypes and projections have been allowed to create a mythical power of minorities, which, for some whites, has become real. Blacks, for example, have been thought to be athletically and physically superior to whites, and this myth has often led to superficial interracial sexual encounters. In other cases, this mythical power of blacks has caused avoidance behaviors on the part of whites. One white student indicated how he used to go to the other side of the street if several blacks were congregated near where he had to pass. Because blacks were perceived by him to be physically aggressive, his avoidance made attempts at communication difficult. Communication can only be achieved when we cease to allow the power of myths and stereotypes to determine our degree of interaction with members of another race.

The language and music of blacks have also exerted a type of power wherein vestiges of both have influenced the style of the majority. When whites use the words and phrases coined by blacks, we may refer to this as a type of referent power. The difference, however, comes in the degree of internalization and viable alternatives available. Because of the options open to them, whites do not have to internalize the style initiated by blacks. For example, whites can use the language of blacks when convenient and resort back to the mainstream of standard English

when desirable. We may note a similar kind of referent identification in whites who deliberately wear the "Afro" hair style. When worn by whites, the "Afro" is more or less a stylistic option rather than a way of life. The identification with blacks is less than reciprocal and of questionable value for purposes of establishing authentic communication. The suspicion surrounding such superficial means of identification often leads to perceived insincerity, a deterrent to real communication.

REACTIVE POWER OF MINORITIES

We have indicated how historically minorities were placed in the power role of reactionaries to the power wielders. Much of the power of minorities seems to be limited to a negative, reactionary posture as illustrated by the following case, which also shows how power can be communicated nonverbally:

> At a soft ice cream shop in a southern state a black male drove up in front and got out of his car to take his place in line behind the white woman and small white male who were already in line. When his turn came, the black male approached the window, only to have the white waitress slam it shut in front of him. She then motioned for him to come around to the back window, and, puzzled at what had just occurred, the male followed the nonverbal order of the waitress who snobbishly took his order, once he was at the back window. After not being able to elicit any verbal communication from the waitress concerning her action, the black male received his order of food, paid for it and left.

It may be helpful to know that this incident occurred after the passage of the public accommodations aspect of the Civil Rights Bill of [1964]. For those who may be unfamiliar with the southern code of ethics for interracial communication, the policy of front window for whites and back window for blacks was operating in this case. From the point of view of communication, several implicit assumptions are brought to focus here: (1) the male, not being from the area, assumed that, all things being equal, he could go in the same line as everyone else and be served; (2) the waitress assumed that this was an obvious attempt on the part of the male to defy the southern code of ethics and to step out of his role as the inferior on the power hierarchy; and (3) had the male been from the area, the passage of the Civil Rights Bill should theoretically have given him the privilege to be served at the front window. In reality, however, this was not so. The slamming of the window in the male's face was a way of nonverbally defining him as inferior and of reinforcing the existing power roles. The waitress further denied the complete humanity of the male by refusing to explain why she slammed the window shut. This was psychological as well as physical communication denial and represents a nonverbal way in which power is exercised over minority group members.

Now in terms of the power of the male, we may ask what were the channels of communication available to him. What were his alternatives? Was he virtually powerless?

Assuming that he was aware of what was being communicated by the waitress, he could have driven away after the closing of the window; he could have ordered the food at the back window and demanded that he receive it from the front window before paying for it (which hardly seems viable, since the waitress had already indicated by closing the window that she was indifferent to his patronage when it involved upsetting the existing power rules); he could have organized a boycott or demonstration of the business and others like it; he could have committed destruction to the property after hours; or he could have filed a discrimination suit.

While carrying out any of these options represents a potential power of the male, we can see that all of these choices represent a negative reactionary power. This seems to be one of the most significant types of power possessed by minorities—that of boycotting, protesting, demonstrating, walking out, or destroying. The alternative of filing a law suit provides no immediate power, for the time lapse required for litigation often promotes discouragement in advance. If we had reciprocal power in interracial communication, minorities would not be limited to a negative, reactionary type of power, but all groups would possess the possibility of a positive, proactive, or initiator power posture. We are suggesting a power interchangeability in which all groups could initiate positive influence and action and carry them out with equal influence and immediacy.   [1976]

Note

1. DENMARK VESEY AND NAT TURNER: Leaders of slave rebellions in South Carolina in 1822 and Virginia in 1831, respectively.

Understanding the Reading

1. How can difference confer power?
2. Why is potential a source of power?
3. How can stereotypes enhance individual power?
4. What does reactive power mean, and what are its disadvantages?

Suggestions for Responding

1. Describe an incident when you were either the wielder or the recipient of one kind of power Blubaugh and Pennington describe. Explain how it made you feel.
2. Compare and contrast Blubaugh and Pennington's analysis of minority power with McIntosh's analysis of white privilege. ◆

SUGGESTIONS FOR RESPONDING TO PART V

1. Research and report on a specific example of racism in American history, such as the Cherokee removal and the Trail of Tears, anti-Semitic quotas in admission to colleges like Harvard in the 1920s, restrictive covenants, or the "scientific" studies that "proved" racial inferiority on the basis of such characteristics as brain size or physique.

2. Investigate a minority "first" like baseball player Jackie Robinson; athlete James Thorpe; the "Moses" of the Underground Railroad, Harriet Tubman; Virginia Governor Eugene Wilder; Arctic explorer Matthew Henson; the woman whose action began the civil rights movement, Rosa Parks; Olympic athlete Jesse Owens; Olympic gold medalist Kristi Yamaguchi; Supreme Court Justice Thurgood Marshall; tennis champion Arthur Ashe; heavyweight boxing champion Joe Lewis; poet Phillis Wheatley; founder of Chicago, Jean Baptiste Point du Sable; Nobel Peace Prize winner Ralph Bunche; Congressional Representatives Hiram Fong and Daniel Inouye; Academy Award winner Sidney Poitier; Springfield, Ohio, Mayor Robert C. Henry; Senator Edward Brooke; physician who performed the first open-heart surgery, Dr. Daniel Hale Williams; or any of the many others. Report on their achievements, and focus on the racial barriers they faced and overcame.

3. Imagine you are a member of a different race, and write an autobiography in which you analyze the impact that your new race would have on your opportunities and accomplishments.

VI
Power, Sexism, and Heterosexism

SCARCELY MORE THAN A GENERATION AGO, TRADI-
tional gender roles were accepted as natural, normal, even inevitable. Men were to be strong,
unemotional, aggressive, competitive, and devoted to concerns of the outside world; women
were to be gentle, emotional, passive, nurturing,
and devoted to home and family. Those who violated these norms were labeled deviant. A man
whose eyes appeared to moisten in public was
immediately perceived as less than fully qualified
to be U.S. President. An ambitious middle-class
woman who wanted more than a domestic role
was declared by psychiatrists to be suffering from
a psychological personality disorder.

The word "sexism" didn't exist until 25 years
ago. In the early 1960s, everyone assumed that
women had the same rights and opportunities
that men had and that they were content with
their domestic role, caring for their homes and
families. Magazines, movies, television, school
textbooks, church leaders, politicians—everyone, everywhere, including most women—ex-
tolled the virtues of the traditional division of
labor: man the breadwinner and woman the
homemaker.

However, economic reality was already making this ideal more and more difficult for white
middle-class women to maintain. Increasingly,
they had to work outside the home, but working
women were also expected to continue to serve

as wife and mother. In the workplace, however,
they were restricted in the kinds of jobs they
could get. Newspapers printed ads under separate "Help Wanted—Male" and "Help Wanted—
Female" listings, shunting even women with
college degrees, for example, into secretarial
rather than professional positions. Paying less for
women's work was considered natural because
men were regarded as the family breadwinners.

In 1963, Betty Freiden published *The Feminine Mystique,* in which she investigated the
unhappiness and malaise that haunted the well-
educated suburban housewife. Suddenly, everybody began talking about the "woman problem." Women organized **consciousness-raising
groups,** where they shared their experiences as
women. Simple as this sounds, this sharing almost immediately altered the way people saw the
gendered social system. What had been considered personal problems were revealed to be actually part of a larger web of social limitations
that society imposed on women simply because
of their sex.

The value of women and a women-centered
perspective and the advocacy of social, political,
and economic equality for both women and men
became the widely accepted and widely debated
platform of modern **feminism.** Scrutinizing every facet of society through a feminist lens revealed that fundamental gender inequality was

(and still is) embedded in the entire social system. The system was exposed as **patriarchal,** meaning that it is hierarchical and that its structures of power, value, and culture are male-dominated. Every aspect of society—employment, education, religion, media, law, economic arrangements, and even the family—served to reinforce and maintain men's social superiority and women's social inferiority and subordination.

Once feminist analysis exposed the inherent inequities of this system, women organized to change it. Equating the position of all women with that of blacks, they coined the term *sexism* to emphasize the correspondence between racism and the discriminatory treatment to which women were subjected. **Sexism** is the subordination of an individual woman or group of women and the assumption of the superiority of an individual man or group of men, based solely on sex. Like racism, sexism is reflected in both individual and institutional acts, decisions, habits, procedures, and policies that neglect, overlook, exploit, subjugate, or maintain the subordination of an individual woman or all women.

Feminist activism throughout the past quarter of a century has changed society dramatically. Textbooks from basal readers to medical volumes are scrupulously edited to eliminate blatant sexism and gender stereotyping. Women today have access to higher education and professional training, and they are represented in nearly every occupation from carpentry and mining to the clergy and the securities market. Men are more likely to share housework and child-care responsibilities. Advertisements present women taking business trips (other than to the supermarket) and climbing telephone poles. However, as the readings in Part VI reveal, much sexism still remains.

Although men have become more aware of the disadvantages of the male gender role, that role continues to provide them with greater social power and prestige, and gender still disadvantages most women. Joseph H. Pleck analyzes this phenomenon in the first selection. According to Pleck, men have a psychological need for power over women because they benefit from women's emotional and male-validating powers; also, controlling women enhances their power over other men. He advocates a men's movement to complement the women's movement by help-

ing men cope more effectively with the changing world feminism is creating.

Men's power over women takes many forms. Historically, it was believed that good women remained in the home and women who ventured out into the world alone were of questionable moral character. This stereotype has survived even though massive numbers of women have entered the workforce. Men (who were already there) had difficulty seeing beyond the sexuality of their female co-workers. As a result, some men subject female co-workers over whom they exercise some power to sexual innuendo, touching, propositions, and other forms of **sexual harassment.** Women today may be more aware of sexual harassment and they may resist it more effectively than was the case in 1978 when Bernice Resnick Sandler wrote her piece; nonetheless, her definition of harassment is still accurate, and harassment continues to be a problem for many female workers and students.

Sexual harassment is just one example of ongoing sexism. According to Laurel Richardson, men still monopolize all aspects of political and economic power; they hold most positions of political and institutional power, control most of the nation's wealth, and command greater prestige. Janice Delaney, Mary Jane Lupton, and Emily Toth explain the historical oppression of women based on sexist assumptions made about one manifestation of their difference from men; the fact that women menstruate has been used to restrict their activities and opportunities.

Sexism is so innate in our culture that we all practice it despite our best intentions. Mary Beth Marklein describes how teachers unconsciously provide boys and girls with different educational experiences by holding them to different standards and responding to them differently according to their gender. This phenomenon doesn't occur only in the elementary grades; it affects higher education as well, and even controls what we know and how we think about the world. Sara Coulter, K. Edgington, and Elaine Hedges demonstrate how the models of thought we take for granted—the ideal of objectivity, dualism, our language, and our acceptance of norms based on male experience—distort what we assume to be reality and truth.

Both Margaret L. Andersen and Katrine Ames elaborate on this thesis. Andersen shows how men's domination of science has shaped the questions science asks and the ways in which answers are expressed. Ames describes how women's health issues have been ignored and how the claim that female hormones complicate research projects is used to justify this exclusion, a striking example of the principle of male-as-norm.

Sexism shapes public policy in other ways. Paula Giddings describes how Daniel Patrick Moynihan projected the white middle-class sexist gender stereotypes onto the black family and therefore identified the strength of women in the black family as the cause of racial unrest. From this analysis he went on to propose a sexist solution of empowering black men at the expense of black women.

The last two selections raise the issue of **sexual orientation,** an individual's physical and/or emotional attraction to members of the other sex (*heterosexuality*), the same sex (*homosexuality*), or both sexes (*bisexuality*). **Heterosexism** is the cultural assumption that heterosexuality is natural and the only proper sexual behavior. In our society, homosexuality and bisexuality present a challenge to gender identity, one's personal sense of maleness or femaleness. That identity rests on acceptance and internalization of appropriate and stereotypic gender behavior. Homosexuals are thought of as violating these stereotypes: The lesbian stereotype emphasizes her presumed mannishness, while the stereotype of the gay man claims that he is effeminate and womanish.

The hostility created by the perceived homosexual threat to the "normal," heterosexual order is generally referred to as **homophobia,** fear of being labeled homosexual and hatred of homo-sexuals. Homophobia is not always seen as a sexist issue. However, the well-documented fact that men tend to be more homophobic than women exposes its sexist underpinnings. Male homophobia seems to arise from men's fear of being assigned the inferior feminine identity, a clear expression of the sexist belief in male superiority and female subordination.

Warren J. Blumenfeld and Diane Raymond try to help us understand the position of gay men and lesbians in our society by comparing homosexuality to being left-handed in a world designed for the right-handed. They show that there is little agreement about why or how people become either left-handed or homosexual; nonetheless, historically members of both groups have been stereotyped, ostracized, and discriminated against. In the final selection, Audre Lorde asks how she can be expected to choose among the various facets of her identity; she feels equally oppressed by racism, sexism, and heterosexism, and she challenges all people to work to eliminate all forms of domination.

Today, it is not fashionable to express racist and, to a lesser extent, sexist attitudes. Although racism and sexism may have become less visible recently, both remain well entrenched in our culture and within ourselves. They continue to distort our perceptions of one another and to impair our interpersonal behavior. They constrict the educational, economic, social, and cultural opportunities of people of color, women, and gay men and lesbians. Bad as this situation is, worse is the use of laws and violence to oppress some groups and to serve the interests of others. Parts VII and VIII explore these more blatant manifestations of racism and sexism.

50

Men's Power With Women, Other Men, and Society

Joseph H. Pleck

MEN'S POWER OVER WOMEN, AND WOMEN'S POWER OVER MEN

It is becoming increasingly recognized that one of the most fundamental questions raised by the women's movement is not a question about women at all, but rather a question about men: Why do men oppress women? There are two general kinds of answers to this question. The first is that men want power over women because it is in their rational self-interest to do so, to have the concrete benefits and privileges that power over women provides them. Having power, it is rational to want to keep it. The second kind of answer is that men want to have power over women because of deep-lying psychological needs in male personality. These two views are not mutually exclusive, and there is certainly ample evidence for both. The final analysis of men's oppression of women will have to give attention equally to its rational and irrational sources.

I will concentrate my attention here on the psychological sources of men's needs for power over women. Let us consider first the most common and commonsense psychological analysis of men's need to dominate women, which takes as its starting point the male child's early experience with women. The male child, the argument goes, perceives his mother and his predominantly female elementary school teachers as dominating and controlling. These relationships *do* in reality contain elements of domination and control, probably exacerbated by the restriction of women's opportunities to exercise power in most other areas. As a result, men feel a lifelong psychological need to free themselves from or prevent their domination by women. The argument is, in effect, that men oppress women as adults because they experienced women as oppressing them as children.

According to this analysis, the process operates in a vicious circle. In each generation, adult men restrict women from having power in almost all domains of social life except child rearing. As a result, male children feel powerless and dominated, grow up needing to restrict women's power, and thus the cycle repeats itself. It follows from this analysis that the way to break the vicious circle is to make it possible for women to exercise power outside of parenting and parentlike roles and to get men to do their half share of parenting.

There may be a kernel of truth in this "mother domination" theory of sexism for some men, and the social changes in the organization of child care that this theory suggests are certainly desirable. As a general explanation of men's needs to dominate women, however, this theory has been quite overworked. This theory holds women themselves rather than men ultimately responsible for the oppression of women—in William Ryan's phrase, "blaming the victim" of oppression for her own oppression. The recent film *One Flew over the Cuckoo's Nest* presents an extreme example of how women's supposed domination of men is used to justify sexism. This film portrays the archetypal struggle between a female figure depicted as domineering and castrating and a rebellious male hero (played by Jack Nicholson) who refuses to be emasculated by her. This struggle escalates to a climactic scene in which Nicholson throws her on the floor and nearly strangles her to death—a scene that was accompanied by wild cheering from the audience when I saw the film. For this performance, Jack Nicholson won the Academy Award as the best actor of the year, an indication of how successful the film is in seducing its audience to accept this act of sexual violence as legitimate and even heroic. The hidden moral message of the film is that because women dominate men, the most extreme forms of sexual violence are not only permissible for men, but indeed are morally obligatory.

To account for men's needs for power over women, it is ultimately more useful to examine some other ways that men feel women have power over them than fear of maternal domination. There are two forms of power that men perceive women as holding over them which derive more directly from traditional definitions of adult male and female roles, and have implications which are far more compatible with a feminist perspective.

The first power that men perceive women having over them is *expressive power,* the power to express emotions. It is well known that in traditional male–female relationships, women are supposed to express their needs for achievement only vicariously through the achievements of men. It is not so widely recognized, however, that this dependency of women on men's achievement has a converse. In traditional male–female relationships, men experience their emotions vicariously through women. Many men have learned to depend on women to help them express their emotions, indeed, to express their emotions for them. At an ultimate level, many men are unable to feel emotionally alive except through relationships with women. A particularly dramatic example occurs in an earlier Jack Nicholson film, *Carnal Knowledge.* Art Garfunkel, at one point early in his romance with Candy Bergen, tells Nicholson that she makes him aware of thoughts he "never even knew he had." Although Nicholson is sleeping with Bergen and Garfunkel is not, Nicholson feels tremendously deprived in comparison when he hears this. In a dramatic scene, Nicholson then goes to her and angrily demands: "You tell him his thoughts, now you tell me *my* thoughts!" When women withhold and refuse to exercise this expressive power for men's benefit, many men, like Nicholson, feel abject and try all the harder to get women to play their traditional expressive role.

A second form of power that men attribute to women is *masculinity-validating power.* In traditional masculinity, to experience oneself as masculine requires that women play their prescribed role of doing the things that make men feel masculine. Another scene from *Carnal Knowledge* provides a pointed illustration. In the closing scene of the movie, Nicholson has hired a call girl whom he has rehearsed and coached in a script telling him how strong and manly he is, in order to get him sexually aroused. Nicholson seems to be in control, but when she makes a mistake in her role, his desperate reprimands show just how dependent he is on her playing out the masculinity-validating script he has created. It is clear that what he is looking for in this encounter is not so much sexual gratification as it is validation of himself as a man—which only women

can give him. As with women's expressive power, when women refuse to exercise their masculinity-validating power for men, many men feel lost and bereft and frantically attempt to force women back into their accustomed role.

As I suggested before, men's need for power over women derives both from men's pragmatic self-interest and from men's psychological needs. It would be a mistake to overemphasize men's psychological needs as the sources of their needs to control women, in comparison with simple rational self-interest. But if we are looking for the psychological sources of men's needs for power over women, their perception that women have expressive power and masculinity-validating power over them is critical to analyze. These are the two powers men perceive women as having, which they fear women will no longer exercise in their favor. These are the two resources women possess which men fear women will withhold, and whose threatened or actual loss leads men to such frantic attempts to reassert power over women.

Men's dependence on women's power to express men's emotions and to validate men's masculinity has placed heavy burdens on women. By and large, these are not powers over men that women have wanted to hold. These are powers that men have themselves handed over to women, by defining the male role as being emotionally cool and inexpressive, and as being ultimately validated by heterosexual success.

There is reason to think that over the course of recent history—as male–male friendship has declined, and as dating and marriage have occurred more universally and at younger ages—the demands on men to be emotionally inexpressive and to prove masculinity through relating to women have become stronger. As a result, men have given women increasingly more expressive power and more masculinity-validating power over them, and have become increasingly dependent on women for emotional and sex-role validation. In the context of this increased dependency on women's power, the emergence of the women's movement now, with women asserting their right not to play these roles for men, has hit men with a special force.

It is in this context that the men's movement and men's groups place so much emphasis on men learning to express and experience their emotions with each other, and learning how to validate themselves and each other as persons, instead of needing women to validate them emotionally and as men. When men realize that they can develop in themselves the power to experience themselves emotionally and to validate themselves as persons, they will not feel the dependency on women for these essential needs which has led in the past to so much male fear, resentment, and need to control women. Then men will be emotionally more free to negotiate the pragmatic realignment of power between the sexes that is underway in our society.

MEN'S POWER WITH OTHER MEN

After considering men's power over women in relation to the power men perceive women having over them, let us consider men's power over women in a second context: the context of men's power relationships with other men. In recent years, we have come to understand that relations between men and women are governed by sexual politics that exists outside individual men's and women's needs and choices. It has taken us much longer to recognize that there is a systematic sexual politics of male–male relationships as well. Under patriarchy, men's relationships with other men cannot help but be shaped and patterned by patriarchal norms, though they are less obvious than the norms governing male–female relationships. A society could not have the kinds of power dynamics that exist between women and men in our society without certain kinds of systematic power dynamics operating among men as well.

One dramatic example illustrating this connection occurs in Marge Piercy's recent novel *Small Changes*. In a flashback scene, a male character goes along with several friends to gang rape a woman. When his turn comes, he is impotent; whereupon the other men grab him, pulling his pants down to rape *him*. This scene powerfully conveys one form of the relationship between male–female and male–male sexual politics. The point is that men do not just happily bond together to oppress women. In addition to hierarchy over women, men create hierarchies and rankings among themselves according to criteria of "masculinity." Men at each rank of mascu-

linity compete with each other, with whatever resources they have, for the differential payoffs that patriarchy allows men.

Men in different societies choose different grounds on which to rank each other. Many societies use the simple facts of age and physical strength to stratify men. The most bizarre and extreme form of patriarchal stratification occurs in those societies which have literally created a class of eunuchs. Our society, reflecting its own particular preoccupations, stratifies men according to physical strength and athletic ability in the early years, but later in life focuses on success with women and ability to make money.

In our society, one of the most critical rankings among men deriving from patriarchal sexual politics is the division between gay and straight men. This division has powerful negative consequences for gay men and gives straight men privilege. But in addition, this division has a larger symbolic meaning. Our society uses the male heterosexual–homosexual dichotomy as a central symbol for *all* the rankings of masculinity, for the division on *any* grounds between males who are "real men" and have power and males who are not. Any kind of powerlessness or refusal to compete becomes imbued with the imagery of homosexuality. In the men's movement documentary film *Men's Lives,* a high school male who studies modern dance says that others often think he is gay because he is a dancer. When asked why, he gives three reasons: because dancers are "free and loose," because they are "not big like football players," and because "you're not trying to kill anybody." The patriarchal connection: if you are not trying to kill other men, you must be gay.

Another dramatic example of men's use of homosexual derogations as weapons in their power struggle with each other comes from a document which provides one of the richest case studies of the politics of male–male relationships to yet appear: Woodward and Bernstein's[1] *The Final Days.* Ehrlichman jokes that Kissinger is queer, Kissinger calls an unnamed colleague a psychopathic homosexual, and Haig jokes that Nixon and Rebozo are having a homosexual relationship. From the highest ranks of male power to the lowest, the gay–straight division is a central symbol of all the forms of ranking and power relationships which men put on each other.

The relationships between the patriarchal stratification and competition which men experience with each other and men's patriarchal domination of women are complex. Let us briefly consider several points of interconnection between them. First, women are used as *symbols of success* in men's competition with each other. It is sometimes thought that competition for women is the ultimate source of men's competition with each other. For example, in *Totem and Taboo* Freud presented a mythical reconstruction of the origin of society based on sons' sexual competition with the father, leading to their murdering the father. In this view, if women did not exist, men would not have anything to compete for with each other. There is considerable reason, however, to see women not as the ultimate source of male–male competition, but rather as only symbols in a male contest where real roots lie much deeper.

The recent film *Paper Chase* provides an interesting example. This film combines the story of a small group of male law students in their first year of law school with a heterosexual love story between one of the students (played by Timothy Bottoms) and the professor's daughter. As the film develops, it becomes clear that the real business is the struggle within the group of male law students for survival, success, and the professor's blessing—a patriarchal struggle in which several of the less successful are driven out of school and one even attempts suicide. When Timothy Bottoms gets the professor's daughter at the end, she is simply another one of the rewards he has won by doing better than the other males in her father's class. Indeed, she appears to be a direct part of the patriarchal blessing her father has bestowed on Bottoms.

Second, women often play a *mediating* role in the patriarchal struggle among men. Women get men together with each other and provide the social lubrication necessary to smooth over men's inability to relate to each other noncompetitively. This function has been expressed in many myths, for example, the folk tales included in the Grimms' collection about groups of brothers whose younger sister reunites and reconciles them with their kingfather, who had previously banished and tried to kill them. A more modern myth, James Dickey's *Deliverance,* portrays what happens when men's relationships with each other are not mediated by women. According to

Carolyn Heilbrun, the central message of *Deliverance* is that when men get beyond the bounds of civilization, which really means beyond the bounds of the civilizing effects of women, men rape and murder each other.

A third function women play in male–male sexual politics is that relationships with women provide men a *refuge* for the dangers and stresses of relating to other males. Traditional relationships with women have provided men a safe place in which they can recuperate from the stresses they have absorbed in their daily struggle with other men, and in which they can express their needs without fearing that these needs will be used against them. If women begin to compete with men and have power in their own right, men are threatened by the loss of this refuge.

Finally, a fourth function of women in males' patriarchal competition with each other is to reduce the stress of competition by serving as an *underclass.* As Elizabeth Janeway has written in *Between Myth and Morning,* under patriarchy women represent the lowest status, a status to which men can fall only under the most exceptional circumstances, if at all. Competition among men is serious, but its intensity is mitigated by the fact that there is a lowest possible level to which men cannot fall. One reason men fear women's liberation, writes Janeway, is that the liberation of women will take away this unique underclass status of women. Men will now risk falling lower than ever before, into a new underclass composed of the weak of both sexes. Thus, women's liberation means that the stakes of patriarchal failure for men are higher than they have been before, and that it is even more important for men not to lose.

Thus, men's patriarchal competition with each other makes use of women as symbols of success, as mediators, as refuges, and as an underclass. In each of these roles, women are dominated by men in ways that derive directly from men's struggle with each other. Men need to deal with the sexual politics of their relationships with each other if they are to deal fully with the sexual politics of their relationships with women.

Ultimately, we have to understand that patriarchy has two halves which are intimately related to each other. Patriarchy is a *dual* system, a system in which men oppress women, and in which men oppress themselves and each other. At one level, challenging one part of patriarchy inherently leads to challenging the other. This is one way to interpret why the idea of women's liberation so soon led to the idea of men's liberation, which in my view ultimately means freeing men from the patriarchal sexual dynamics they now experience with each other. But because the patriarchal sexual dynamics of male–male relationships are less obvious than those of male–female relationships, men face a real danger: while the patriarchal oppression of women may be lessened as a result of the women's movement, the patriarchal oppression of men may be untouched. The real danger for men posed by the attack that the women's movement is making on patriarchy is not that this attack will go too far, but that it will not go far enough. Ultimately, men cannot go any further in relating to women as equals than they have been able to go in relating to other men as equals—an equality which has been so deeply disturbing, which has generated so many psychological as well as literal casualties, and which has left so many unresolved issues of competition and frustrated love.   [1974]

Note

1. WOODWARD AND BERNSTEIN: Bob Woodward and Carl Bernstein, the *Washington Post* investigative reporters who first exposed the Watergate conspiracy. Other figures mentioned in the anecdote are (John) Ehrlichman, President Richard Nixon's Chief of Staff; (Henry) Kissinger, his Secretary of State and National Security Advisor; (Alexander) Haig, Chief of Staff following Ehrlichman; and (Bebe) Rebozo, a wealthy friend of President Nixon's.

Understanding the Reading

1. What effect does "maternal domination" have on men's relationships with women?
2. What is expressive power, and how does it affect male-female relationships?
3. What is masculinity-validating power?
4. What is the men's movement doing to respond to women's expressive power and masculinity-validating power?
5. What are the bases for the stratification of men?
6. How do women function in the male stratification system?

Suggestions for Responding

1. Pleck advocates men's learning to express and experience their emotions and to validate their own masculinity as a means of reducing the problem of sexism. Do you agree or disagree with him? Why or why not?
2. What does Pleck leave out of his analysis of men's relationships with each other? ✦

51

Sexual Harassment: A Hidden Issue

BERNICE RESNICK SANDLER

- A Yale undergraduate recently charged her political science professor with sexual harassment, alleging that he offered her an "A" in exchange for sexual favors. She refused, received a "C" in the course, and has since filed a lawsuit against the university.
- A senior communications major at a state university in California testified before the California State Legislature in 1973 that she knew of "at least 15 professors who offered students 'A's' for sex."
- A female cadet at West Point resigned from the military academy in 1977 after charging her male squad leader with improper sexual advances. The Academy dismissed her charges when the squad leader denied any wrongdoing.
- An administrative assistant at the Environmental Protection Agency (EPA) lost her job after refusing her boss' sexual advances. She sued, and the court ruled that sexual demands as a condition of employment are illegal. EPA settled out-of-court with a back pay award.
- A woman complained that her boss was continually embracing her shoulders and touching her arms and waist. When she protested, she was told that he was just being a "friendly fellow" and she, a poor sport.

Often women have been quiet about the problem of sexual harassment, assuming that nothing could be done. Many believe it is their own personal dilemma or "women's lot." Some believe that they somehow caused it to occur or that they should have been able to avoid it. In recent years, the issue has begun to be discussed more openly as women have evaluated their positions in the workforce and on the campus. What emerges is a growing awareness of the scope and complexity of the problem, as well as an increasing number of court cases brought by women. Yale University has the distinction of being the first institution to be sued for sexual harassment of students.

What Is "Sexual Harassment"?

This paper focuses on male harassment of female students and employees, for in most work and academic settings, the majority of supervisors or professors are men.

Sexual harassment is difficult to define. It may range from sexual innuendos made at inappropriate times, perhaps in the guise of humor, to coerced sexual relations. Although there may be instances of students who initiate or encourage sexual activities with male professors, harassment is distinct from "acceptable" flirting; however, on occasion this line may be difficult to draw. Harassment at its extreme occurs when a male in a position to control, influence, or affect a woman's job, career, or grades uses his authority and power to coerce the woman into sexual relations, or to punish her refusal. It may include:

- verbal harassment or abuse
- subtle pressure for sexual activity
- sexist remarks about a woman's clothing, body, or sexual activities
- unnecessary touching, patting, or pinching
- leering or ogling of a woman's body
- constant brushing against a woman's body
- demanding sexual favors accompanied by implied or overt threats concerning one's job, grades, letters of recommendation, etc.
- physical assault

Because the male is in a position of authority, as professor, mentor, or supervisor, a woman, therefore, may be at great risk if she objects to the behavior or resists the overtures. It is this context which underlies the gravity of the problem of sexual harassment.

Whereas in rape cases, the man overpowers a woman with a weapon or threat of loss of life, in sexual harassment he overtly or implicitly threatens her with loss of economic livelihood, or with academic failure and hence loss of future livelihood. A woman cannot freely choose to say yes or not to such sexual advances. The fear of reprisal looms formidably for many women when deciding how to react to sexual harassment. To refuse sexual demands may mean jeopardizing her future, her career, her grades. In the case of working women, the decision to simply quit a job is a luxury she may not be able to afford.

How Widespread Is Sexual Harassment?

SEXUAL HARASSMENT IN EMPLOYMENT

Prior to 1976, there were few reliable statistics on the incidence of sexual harassment. Most of the data collected since then has focused on women in the workplace. A *Redbook* magazine survey of 9,000 clerical and professional women provided the first national data: 92% of the respondents had experienced overt physical harassment, sexual remarks and leering, with the majority regarding this behavior as a serious problem at work; nearly 50% said that they or someone they knew had quit or been fired because of harassment; and 75% believed that if they complained to a supervisor, nothing would be done. In a study conducted in New York by the Working Women United Institute, 70% of those surveyed said they had been harassed. A U.S. Naval officer who distributed questionnaires to women at a Navy base and in the nearby town of Monterey, California, found that 81% of the women who participated in the survey had experienced some form of sexual harassment. Similarly, an Ad Hoc Group on Equal Rights for Women at the United Nations documented the problem of sexual harassment at the U.N. Numerous articles as well as court cases confirm that the problem of sexual harassment in the workplace may be far more extensive than previously realized.

SEXUAL HARASSMENT ON CAMPUS

The suit against Yale University for sexual harassment has raised the issue as to the extent of such problems on campus. If the examples cited at the beginning of this paper were merely exceptions to women's experiences as students, one might simply attribute these problems to an unfortunate situation in an otherwise fair and responsible work environment. But what if they are not exceptions? What if sexual harassment is a common occurrence?

- The Association for Women in Science, a national organization for women professionals and scientists, reported earlier this year that among those who attended its annual conference in Washington, DC—all recent Ph.D. recipients—a substantial number reported in their group sessions that as students and as professionals, they had experienced sexual harassment by men who were in a position to affect their careers. None had discussed the subject publicly before, and most had not realized how widespread the problem is.

- In 1977, Donna Benson, a social science major at the University of California at Berkeley, distributed a questionnaire to one-sixth of the female graduate student population. Of the over 50% who returned the questionnaire, 20% stated that they had received sexual attentions, either as sexual remarks, touching, or propositions, from their professors. Most responded that they were bewildered or confused about how to deal with the situation.

Although the data concerning the scope of the problem on campus is slim, it seems likely that the campus is not exempt from the hidden but serious problems of sexual harassment. Women as students, staff, and faculty are affected, but often are silent.

A college professor wields considerable influence over a student's academic success and future career. A teacher's assessment of a student may in a very real sense affect her "life's chances." Students depend upon their professors for grades, recommendations, job referrals, and research-related opportunities. Graduate students, in addition, rely on their professors for opportunities to attend special seminars and conferences and to co-author research papers, for introductions to colleagues in the field, for sponsorship in informal and formal academic societies and professional associations, and for recommendations for grants, fellowships, and faculty appointments. The female graduate student's working relationship with a faculty member is developed on a one-to-one basis within small seminars, research projects, independent study, and tutorials. The professor serves as an academic advisor, and is a key figure in her academic progress. As the job market tightens and competition for employment opportunities intensifies, faculty influence increases.

When harassment occurs, often the woman is unsure whether a real injustice has been committed, for the aggressor may make light of it, or pretend that she initiated the encounter. A graduate student complained to her college counselor as follows:

"What was it that I did that led him to believe I was interested in him in anything but a professional sense? I am quite outgoing and talkative; could that be interpreted wrongly? I realized how utterly vulnerable I was in a situation like this. He is an immensely powerful person with many contacts and if I insult him, he can harm me and my career in a hundred different ways. Everything that happened would be interpreted in his favor, if it ever came public. It would be said that I got my signals wrong, that he was just truly interested in helping me in my career. I realized that should he try to hurt my professional advancement as a result of this kind of situation, there would be no person or formal mechanism to carry my grievances, no person I could complain to that would have any real power to help me. I was left feeling frustrated and defenseless. . . ."

Lorna Sarrel, co-director of the Yale Human Sexuality Program, believes that some forms of sexual harassment in the classroom would be better described as "psychological coercion." With more women than ever aspiring to advanced degrees and specific career goals, grades become exceedingly important. Sarrel points out, however, that students tend to overestimate the authority and power of their professors. The professors in turn know this, and some may take unfair advantage of their position. The following example is typical: Bonnie, a senior at a small college was an "A" student who earned the praises of her teachers. One of her professors propositioned her, and she refused. "The next semester he lowered my grade," Bonnie complained, "although my test scores improved. Now I'm afraid he would write me a bad letter of recommendation unless I sleep with him."

Although a teacher is rarely explicit about retaliation of a student who turns down his sexual invitation, the student nevertheless fears academic reprisal.

One student admitted that she will simply find another professor to write her law school recommendation. "What good would my complaints do? Professor R. is famous, has tenure, adds to the reputation of his department. If he denies what I say, whom would they believe, him or me? I would endanger my own future by complaining." A graduate student who answered the Berkeley questionnaire stated that although the professor was her mentor, she had to "discontinue this important relationship."

As a result of not returning a professor's unwanted attentions, one student, also in the Berkeley survey, reported that she was "unable to get proper attention" to her requests, while another stated that her professor "became more critical" of her work.

Sexual harassment takes an emotional toll as well. A wide range of symptoms has been reported by victims of harassment: insomnia, headaches, neck and backaches, stomach ailments, decreased concentration, diminished ambition, listlessness, and depression. Sexual coercion makes the educational atmosphere intolerable, forcing the student, in many cases, to withdraw from a course of study or change her career plans. But the overwhelming feeling is that of helplessness—knowing that if one complains, nothing will likely be done or worse yet, she will be labeled a "troublemaker."

Why Are Women Reluctant to Talk About Sexual Harassment?

The answers are many. Like rape, sexual harassment has been a hidden problem, treated as a joke, or blamed on the victim herself. Because of a long history of silence on the subject, many women feel uncomfortable, embarrassed, or ashamed when they talk about personal incidents of harassment. They are afraid that it will reflect badly on their character, or that they will be seen as somehow inviting the propositions. "Because we have been wrongly taught to feel it is somehow our fault," says Susan Meyer and Karen Sauvigne, founders of the Working Women United Institute, "we rarely tell our friends, husbands, or family when it happens."

When women *do* speak out, they are often ignored, discredited, or accused of "misunderstanding" their superior's intentions. Many women attribute their silence to practical considerations. Only 18% of the women in the Working Women United Institute survey stated that they complained about the harassment. The most common reasons given for not reporting the incidents were that they believed nothing would be done (52%), that it would be treated lightly or ridiculed (43%), or that they would be blamed or suffer repercussions (30%).

Because most women fail to publicize their complaints, either formally or informally, university officials may believe that the absence of complaints indicates the absence of a problem. In an interview published in a student newspaper, a dean of students stated that no women students had ever complained to him about being propositioned by male professors. In the same article, the president of the university stated that "we have no evidence of anything like that going on." A faculty member at the same institution commented that "to be a teacher is to be a person with power. It is difficult to ignore the admiration many of your students feel about you, and I admit that I have used this power for selfish means."

Certainly not all women students experience harassment nor do most professors proposition their students. Some students and faculty do not regard sexual harassment as a problem. Others may not believe it exists. The question of teacher-student sex is a delicate issue. Some are quick to point to the apparently "seductive" behavior of some female students. Yet, a humanities professor summed up the problem this way: "Those of us who teach college deal with young people when they are most physically beautiful, most open to new thought and experience. All the while we get older. It's quite a lure."

Some college and university administrators feel that regardless of whether teacher-student sexual relations occur, it's nobody's business. Yet to the individual who feels coerced into such a relationship, the problem may be overwhelming, especially since few universities have a formal channel for her to complain. Given both the desire to do well in one's academic field and the seriousness of the charge of sexual harassment, most women find themselves in a rather untenable position.

Sexual harassment is not, of course, solely a women's issue. Both men and women—students and faculty—suffer under a system that fails to provide established remedies. An indirect result of sexual harassment on campus is that some male teachers may be so cautious or concerned about the possible implications of a friendship with their female students that the women are shut out from the friend/teacher relationships that provide an invaluable learning experience for male students. The result is that female students are afforded less academic opportunity than their male peers, and fewer opportunities to obtain good job recommendations. A law student who participated in the sexual harassment survey at the University of California at Berkeley wrote that "male law school teachers ignore female students. . . . This means that we are afforded less academic opportunities than male students. . . . The only teacher I know somewhat well is a woman. I think the only remedy for this is to hire more women law professors. . . ." It appears that whether they are confronted with sexual propositions or are left alone because of the potential for them, women are inhibited in their pursuit of educational and professional goals.   [1978]

Understanding the Reading

1. Define sexual harassment.
2. Why is sexual harassment a problem for women students?
3. Why has sexual harassment been a hidden problem?
4. Explain the quandary women students face because of the issue of sexual harassment.

Suggestions for Responding

1. Have you, or has someone you know, experienced or been witness to sexual harassment? Describe the incident, including the victim's response. Having read Sandler's analysis, what advice would you now give someone experiencing sexual harassment?
2. Investigate and report on the antiharassment policies and procedures on your campus. ✦

52
Inequalities of Power, Property, and Prestige

LAUREL RICHARDSON

Every society makes decisions about how it will reward its members; that is, every society is stratified. In addition, every society has the same set of rewards that it might proffer: These are power, property, and prestige. The greater one's access to and control over the distribution of goods outside the family, the greater are one's social rewards—the greater one's power, the more one's wealth, and the higher one's prestige.

Sociologists have been studying how one's gender affects one's receipt of valued social goods. They find that men and women end up with different amounts of power, property, and prestige. Let's look at how inequalities in power, property, and prestige in the contemporary United States [are] accomplished.

POWER

Power—the probability of having one's will done despite opposition—is a complex phenomenon. Some of the more visible means of power are economic power, political power, and even sheer physical power. A less visible but still critical basis for power may be interpersonal power. (The perceived importance of this type of power may be seen in the popularity of assertiveness-training courses and books for women.)

The result of a male monopoly over one or more of these power arenas depends in large part on the significance of that type of power for social subsistence. In contemporary industrialized societies, for example, the slight advantage held by males in physical size and strength has little bearing on actual social power, because society does not depend on these traits for daily survival. Rather, . . . power comes to those who control the distribution of goods outside the family. In the United States, this power rests in persons who hold key decision-making positions in corporations, labor, universities, foundations, the mass media, government, and political parties, and in those who control great wealth—or the *establishment*.

When the system by which values, goods, and services are distributed to members of the society remains unchallenged, the probability is high that the interests of the establishment are those that will be served. Only when *interest groups* become politically active in relationship to particular issues does the potential for impact on decision making on those issues shift away from the dominant group. This political activity may take the form of a social movement or of a coalition between diverse pressure groups. Without such political activity, however, the system will *de facto* profit those who are in positions to make decisions that are in their own interests.

In the United States the feminist movement has agitated for equal rights for women for nearly a century and a half. Some of the fruits of that labor include the extension of suffrage to women via the Nineteenth Amendment to the Constitution in 1920; passage of the Equal Pay Act in 1963; approval of Title VII of the Civil Rights Act of 1964, which prohibits sex discrimination in employment; and passage of Title IX of the Higher Education Act of 1972, which prohibits sex segregation in education. These along with other legislative reforms are evidence that women have joined together as an effective interest group with both political access to and influence over legislation. Women's rights organizations are recognized as representing legitimate interests, and they have won some major gains.

Despite such evidence of the gains that have been won by the movement, it has had its failures—most notably, the failure to ratify the Equal Rights Amendment. Even though Congress had overwhelmingly endorsed the amendment in 1972, and even though a majority of Americans favored its passage, when the deadline for ratification came in 1982, the pro-ERA forces were still three states short. The organization and funding of anti-ERA interest groups held sway, along with a conservative executive, legislative, and judicial stance.

But there is more to politics than trying to sway legislation. One can participate as a voter, or as an elected or appointed official. How do males and females compare in these arenas?

Government

An institution that obviously must be considered when discussing differential power in the representation of males and females is the government. Although it is simplistic to assume that a man will represent the interests of men and that a woman will represent the interests of women, it is a place to begin. As the black political force has recognized, there is greater likelihood of a black representing black interests than a white, and the likelihood of those interests being met increases with the number of black representatives. What, then, is the differential access to the legitimated power of the government office? We will first consider elected positions and then turn to the appointed ones.

No woman has ever held either of the top two executive positions—the presidency and vice-presidency—although Geraldine Ferraro, the 1984 Democratic vice-presidential candidate, made such an idea seem probable and not just some feminist dream. Both the U.S. Senate and the House of Representatives have historically been overwhelmingly male. In the One Hundredth Congress (1987–1988), women comprised four percent of the Senate seats (2 out of 100) and 5.3 percent of the House seats (23 out of 413). . . .

The representation is small; growth is slow; and the process of entry may be altering, particularly in the House. Before 1949, congresswomen entered via the right of widow's succession: "If power is thrust upon a woman by her husband's death, she may accept it without blame." Although female senators are still more likely to be appointed than elected to their first term, new women representatives are more likely to run on their own professional and political merit. However, simply being elected to halls of Congress does not insure the representative an active role in legislating. Influencing budgets, initiating legislation, taking part in investigative functions, and responding to the particular needs of one's constituency all depend upon one's seniority, committee assignments, and access to the informal communication network.

Longevity in office is one of the primary ways in which a representative moves along in the power hierarchy of the Congress. As one 67-year-old male freshman representative remarked upon his choosing not to run again for office, "Nobody listens to what you have to say until you have been there 10 or 12 years. . . . There are only about 40 out of the 435 members who call the shots. They're the committee chairmen and ranking members."

It is not until his or her fifth term in the House of Representatives, that a member of Congress might expect to have influence. From 1918 to 1973, only 17 women held their seats in the House for the minimum five terms. In the One Hundredth Congress, only six female representatives had retained their seats for five terms or more. The major exception in the Senate was Margaret Chase Smith, who served nearly a quarter of a century. (She entered politics by running for the House seat that her husband vacated due to serious illness.)

Committee assignments and leadership positions are further avenues to power within the Congress. No woman has held the important leadership positions, such as majority leader, Speaker of the House, or party whip. Further, not all committees have equal power and importance. Women are assigned to low-prestige and uninfluential committees, making their participation unequal to that of males.

The third path to successful influence in Congress is through the informal social network. As is true of most important policy making in business, much of the important work of government takes place on the golf course, the steam room table, and the men's clubs. These informal settings not only provide safe contexts for negotiating problems, they also provide environments in which personal allegiances and friendships can be built. The importance of these informal contexts in developing friendships has led at least one male administrative aid to contend, "No woman can quite make it. So much of the power is built [in the male-only preserves]. I doubt that the best or most able women can ever get to the inner circle, where there is complete acceptance."

Decision making in government goes on not only at the legislative and executive levels but also in a wide variety of bureaus, the functioning arms of the government. Emanating from these bureaus are policies, practices, and programs that encompass the entire dictionary of our social life, from atoms to zoos. Individuals in positions to make decisions at this level either have been appointed to or have worked their way up through civil service. The question is: Do males and females have differential access to these positions? Let us look at the highest level appointments.

The president's cabinet has access to the president and, presumably, the power to influence decisions at the executive level. Few women have ever held cabinet rank. Two cabinet level positions in the Reagan administration have been held by women—the positions of secretary of transportation and secretary of health and human services, although HHS Secretary, Margaret Heckler, was later pressured to resign. The appointment of Sandra Day O'Conner by President Reagan in 1981 placed the first woman justice on the Supreme Court in its history. Ambassadors and ministers to foreign states have been predominately male, as has been the hierarchy of civil employees who work for the federal government.

Voting Behavior

The lack of female representation in the government at all levels and in all branches is not the result of lack of female participation in politics at the level of voting. In fact, . . . the differential voting *turnout* of men and women is so slight as to bring forth a studied "ho hum" from political scientists; nor can it be explained by differential engagement at the campaign level. The women volunteers—in their canvassing, phoning, typing, and mailing—are the real armies of the night; they provide the free labor upon which campaigns depend.

Until quite recently, moreover, women and men voted the same way on candidates and issues. However, in the 1980 elections, the phenomenon that had been expected and feared by some with the granting of the vote to women in 1920 finally materialized. A *gender gap,* whereby voting behavior and positions on political issues is differentiated by sex, became apparent. In that presidential election 54 percent of the men voted for Reagan, while only 46 percent of the women did. This was the largest difference between the electoral choices of men and women since such statistics have been kept. Since that year, such statistics have become a standard component of political analyses in the United States, and evidence of such a gap persists.

In the 1982 elections, women voted the Democratic ticket in 33 of 44 of U.S. Senate and gubernatorial races, provided the winning margin in three of the gubernatorial races, and were responsible for some landslide victories among candidates regarded as pro women's rights. Public opinion polls demonstrate that the gender gap applies to issues, as well; for example, women have been more critical of the economic policies of President Reagan than have men, are more favorable toward peace initiatives and disapproving of the arms race, and are more favorable toward environmental protection initiatives.

Concern over the potential impact of the gender gap became so great among Republicans prior to the 1982 election (since the gender gap had thus far been more favorable toward Democratic candidates and party platforms) that one official, in responding to a question about how the election might be changed to benefit his party, proposed (jokingly, we assume) repeal of the Nineteenth Amendment.

The gender gap, although apparent in the 1984 presidential election, as well, was not great enough to result in the defeat of Ronald Reagan (males, 62 percent for Reagan; females, 54 percent). Thus, while there are indications that the political power of women is increasing slightly in the United States in the form of interest group voting, political participation, and representation, the impact of such changes has thus far been limited.

What about other forms of power, however, such as control over the valued good of property in the United States today? We turn, now, and examine economic indicators of equality.

PROPERTY

Property, or material or monetary compensation, is closely tied to political power in that politically powerful people tend to be wealthy and vice versa. In fact, economic power often translates into political power. In this section, we will look first at how wealth and political power are interconnected, and then at the distribution of wealth and earnings by sex in American society.

Wealth is a power resource if its owner controls its investment. Despite the common myth that women control the wealth, in fact, men earn, own, and control most of the wealth in this country. Fifty-eight percent of stock shares are owned by institutions whose boards of trustees and brokers are almost exclusively male. Individually, women own approximately 18 percent of privately held stock shares; men own approximately 24 percent. In terms of privately held real estate holdings, only 39 percent belong to women, despite the fact of female longevity. Approximately 60 percent of persons with financial assets over $60,000 are male.

These statistics are probably quite liberal estimates of the wealth of women, because it is common for men to place holdings in the names of their wives, daughters, or mothers for tax purposes. Women are neither wealthier than men, nor are they situated to use their wealth as a power resource.

Rather, it can be argued that the control of the wealth in this country rests in the hands of a very small elite—approximately one percent of the population that is composed of owners and managers of the megaconglomerates. Members of this elite own 25 to 30 percent of privately held wealth in America and 60 to 70 percent of all privately held corporate wealth. Further, the amount of wealth held by these people has been increasing and there is a remarkable continuity in the families that hold wealth.

Our nation's "upper crust" belongs to interlinking social, financial, and governmental networks. They attend the same prep schools and universities, revel at the same men's clubs and resort-retreats, and marry into each other's families; that is, not only do these persons share common financial interests, they are also socially and familially bound to one another.

The policy decisions of this elite are discussed informally in boardrooms and social clubs, and consensus is reached in their major policy-setting organizations, which themselves are "directed by the same men who manage major corporations and financed by corporation and foundation monies."

In turn, these decisions affect our government through a number of channels. First, many of the members of these corporate organizations serve in high-level government offices, commissions, and committees. Second, "hired experts intimately identified with these organizations serve as government advisors." Third, these organizations provide experts for testimony at congressional committees and for advising those committees. Fourth, many members of these corporate organizations are large contributors to campaigns and have, therefore, easy access to politicians.

The relationship of corporate executives and politicians is developed through informal modes of interaction, and these modes are exclusively male. One of the settings for the development of this social cohesion . . . are exclusive retreats—The Bohemian Grove, Rancheros Visitadores, Round Up—that "women are strictly forbidden to enter."

The weight of the evidence seems quite clear that the corporate economy is effectively controlled by a few megacompanies—banks, insurance corporations, and conglomerates.

Activities at these retreats, such as boozing, high jinks, calf roping, cross-country horseback caravans, stag movies, the Bulls' Balls Lunch (donated yearly by a cattle baron following the castration of his herd) liken the retreats to a transplanted "college fraternity system" or "an overgrown boyscout camp." But apart from the stereotypically masculine orientation of the fun and games, these retreats provide a context of intimacy wherein the corporate rich cement their social bonds with governmental officials, university chancellors, and presidents of television networks.

Within these encampments, policies are suggested, proposals are made, and appointments are discussed. Women are conspicuous in their absence. They are not presidents of financial institutions, members of boards of directors, high-placed corporate lawyers, nor are they in any other way situated to control the wealth of this country.

Without inherited wealth, the route to property—for men and women—is through participation in the labor force. People work for wages to acquire goods; money is the reward for one's toil. Presumably, the more valuable one's work, the more one will be rewarded—the greater will be one's salary. But to get the reward in the first place, you have to be in the labor market: You have to work outside the home for pay.

Since the turn of the century, women in American society have steadily increased their representation in the labor force. In 1900, 20 percent of all women were in the labor market, and they comprised 18 percent of all wage earners. By 1940, those numbers had grown to 28 percent and 25 percent, respectively. During the World War II years, female labor force participation grew faster than before, and in 1945 nearly 36 percent of all women were employed, and they comprised just over 29 percent of all workers. In the years following the war, this rate of participation dropped sharply as women were forced out of their wartime jobs; it was ten years before female representation in the labor market reached the 1945 levels.

The growth of female participation in the labor force has occurred primarily since 1940, with sequential waves of women from various backgrounds—immigrant, young black, older married, and, most recently, young married women, many with preschool children. The demographic characteristics of employed women have become increasingly similar to the characteristics of the entire population in terms of race, ethnicity, education, age, and marital and family status; that is, "it is becoming more difficult to consider working women as in some sense an unrepresentative or atypical group." It is not atypical for a woman to be employed outside the home, nor is the gainfully employed woman typically different in demographic characteristics than the full-time homemaker.

In the 1980s, the participation of women in the labor market has approached that of men. In 1984, 63 percent of women between the ages of 18 and 64 were employed and they constituted 43 percent of the total labor force. One might reasonably expect, with this evidence of increasing labor market activity on the part of women, that female wages as a consequence would expand relative to those of males, but this has not been the case. In fact, the median earnings of women have declined relative to those of men. In 1955, the median earnings for year-round, full-time female employees was 64 percent of those of males; in 1981, the percentage had fallen to 59 percent. As [Table 1] demonstrates, these wage discrepancies are not the result of differences in the educational attainment of women and men, as the wage inequities are consistent within each educational grouping by sex.

TABLE 1
MEDIAN INCOME BY YEARS OF EDUCATION AND GENDER FOR
YEAR-ROUND, FULL-TIME WORKERS OVER 25 YEARS OLD (1984)

Years of School	Median Income		Women's Earnings for Male Dollar
	Women	Men	
ELEMENTARY			
8 years	10,421	16,112	.64
HIGH SCHOOL			
1–3 years	12,134	20,067	.60
4 years	14,733	24,000	.61
COLLEGE			
1–3 years	17,114	26,302	.65
4+ years	22,089	28,089	.62

Source: Cynthia M. Tauber and Victor Valdisera. *Women in the American Economy.* Current Population Reports (1986) Special Series P-23, No. 146. U.S. Department of Commerce, Bureau of the Census.

The discrepancies are not the result of differences in general occupational category. In fact, education and job responsibility do not reduce the discrepancy between men's and women's incomes. Indeed, when education, occupation, years of experience, and other relevant variables are taken into account, men's salaries are still higher than women's.

There is also evidence that race stratification and sex stratification interact. While the income gap between white males and females has increased since 1955, the gap between black males and females has decreased. Although black women remain at the bottom of the hierarchy of income, recently, there has been an increasing convergence between the wages of black women and white women.

What then is the explanation for the extreme income discrepancies between women and men? Possibilities include direct wage discrimination, disruptions in female employment patterns, and occupational segregation by sex. Direct wage discrimination, where females are paid lower wages than men for the same work, can still be found and is evidenced by the number of suits that have been taken to court, some of which are still pending. Disruptions in female employment patterns as an explanation cannot be dismissed—either as women have a generally shorter tenure at their

jobs due to their late group entry into the labor market, or due to time out because of pregnancy, homemaking, and child-rearing responsibilities. These work disruptions, however, do not uniformly affect all women, and such disruptions are becoming less frequent due to lower fertility rates and increased use of child care services. We have seen, though, that the wage discrepancies between women and men are not abating as we would expect them to if women's erratic job histories were a primary causal factor of unequal pay. Rather, after controlling for many other factors, researchers find that the most powerful explanation is *occupational segregation* by sex. This factor affects the life chances of more women on a continuing basis than any other factor: Men and women have different occupations; the occupations that men have provide greater rewards than the occupations women have. Occupations are *sex typed*. Those that are sex typed female are devalued.

Males dominate in some categories, females in others. The categories that men dominate—such as dentists—are better paid than the categories that women dominate—such as nurses. Moreover, men are spread out among a greater number of occupations. Fully one-fourth of the employed women, though, are concentrated in only five occupations—secretary, bookkeeper, elementary-school teacher, waitress, and retail salesclerk. None of these occupations are noted for their financial remuneration.

The occupational placement of black females is especially skewed. Although 66 percent of white women are white-collar workers, only 52 percent of black women are so situated. While a high proportion of the white women are teachers, registered nurses, and secretaries, a high proportion of the black women are key punchers and file clerks—positions that are poorly paid. In addition, while approximately only 18 percent of white women are service workers, nearly 30 percent of black women are; over 5 percent of the employed black women work as domestics in private homes. Although this rate of employ as a domestic is high, it has been steadily declining, and black women are increasingly being employed in clerical positions. Yet, it is still true that "gender allocates black women to sex-typed occupations while their race separates them from white women within the female-intensive occupations." Overall, black women are relegated to the lowest-paid and lowest-status jobs.

Simply looking at the large occupation categories—such as *teacher* and *salesperson*—conceals more about sex segregation than it reveals. Within job classifications, there are male sex-typed and female sex-typed positions. Sales is a good example. Men are more likely to hold the higher-paying corporate and commission sales positions, while women are more likely to be retail salesclerks, often working for minimum wage. Even within retail sales, women will be selling clothing, notions, and linens, and will be working for an hourly wage, whereas men will be selling dishwashers, riding mowers, computers, and furniture, and will be working for a commission on high-ticket items. In many stores, shoes are commission items—and their departments are heavily male staffed. Perfumes and cosmetics are one of the few female-dominated sales areas that are sold on a commission basis, although the percentage is lower than for appliances or shoes, and, interestingly, more males are entering the sales fray.

In terms of earnings, then, women do not fare as well as men do. No matter how earnings differences are computed (or explained), the differences are not erased. Part-time women workers make about 47 percent of what part-time male workers make; and, a woman with a college degree can expect to make about the same income as a man who has dropped out of high school. What is the reason? She will work as a nurse or a teacher, and he as a union worker or a skilled craftsman.

There is another indicator, however, of where the economics of sex is clear—namely, poverty. The sex ratio differences of living in poverty are so great that a phrase has been coined to describe the situation: "the feminization of poverty."

Currently in the United States, two poor adults out of three are women. Among the aged population, two and a half times as many women live in poverty as men do. Fully one-half of all elderly black women are officially poor.

Hilda Scott defines the feminization of poverty as the complex of forces keeping women in an economically precarious situation. In her estimation, the forces that maintain this situation include the assignment of primary responsibility for child rearing to women and its effects following divorce, and the limits on women's income and economic mobility that result from occupational segregation, sex discrimination, and sexual harassment. A key feature of her analysis of women's poverty is the amount of unpaid work that is done by women. Such work—including child-rearing and homemaking responsibilities—lessens women's economic mobility in a variety of ways. For women who devote their full time to this type of work, it may increase their economic dependence on men and actually work to their disadvantage should they later decide to enter the labor market. For those women who perform these tasks while working outside the home for pay, the double duty of balancing both sets of responsibilities may impede advancement in the labor market or make it impossible to function effectively in both settings.

Finally, let us turn to sex inequities in the control over the valued good of prestige and its relationship to access to power and property.

PRESTIGE

Prestige is commonly used to denote the respect or esteem that is accorded an individual or a social category of persons. It is highly congruent with power and property in that individuals with a great deal of these valued attributes typically will carry a great deal of prestige, as well. Prestige is linked with social status in that a status, or a defined position in the social structure, is frequently thought of in terms of ranking from higher to lower. Statuses are of two types: An achieved status is one that is acquired through individual effort, while an ascribed status is one that is determined by birth, or that is automatically assigned on a systematic basis by others. While all women theoretically have the ability to influence, affect, or determine their achieved statuses, no one can control their sex assignment at birth. It is to the ascribed sex status of being a female in our society that we will now turn.

. . . The existence of sexist language, the extent of violence against women, and the nature of religious and clinical ideologies about women are all indicators of women's shared and devalued status as females. These indicators may be denied or ignored, but there is no getting around the fact that women are treated similarly as women. Edwin Shurr examines the consequences of such sex stereotyping in his book *Labeling Women Deviant*. He sees the status, female, as categorically constituting a master status, whereas the status, male, does not. A master status is one of such significance that it becomes the primary identity of the individual. All other statuses held by the individual are defined by the master status: "Individual women are perceived of and reacted to at least initially, and often primarily, in terms of their femaleness."

Schurr argues further that to be female in our society is by definition to be deviant and part of a devalued status group in four ways. First, due to their lower position in the stratification system, there is a tendency for women to be evaluated unfavorably as a group and for this placement to be explained as resulting from inherently female characteristics. Second is the widespread objectification of women as a group that occurs when women are treated as nonpersons or as interchangeable objects. Third is the extensive devaluation of women in cultural symbolism, such as in common language usage and the mass media. Finally, a further indication of the low value placed on femaleness is the special relationship women have with definitions of deviance—including the failure of society to condemn many male offenses against women and the double standard of deviance that is applied to males and females.

One indicator of the master status aspect of femaleness is what Shurr refers to as the "hyphenization phenomenon": the tendency of others to note instances when the achieved statuses of particular women are incongruent with the stereotypical features of the ascribed sex status, female. This phenomenon occurs every time a woman's sex is noted along with some other status as in "woman-doctor," "female-lawyer," "woman-athlete," or the typically disparaging label, "woman-driver." These remarks are also indications of status inconsistency; it would be unusual to hear labels such as "woman-nurse" or "female-secretary."

The low-prestige level of women can be seen clearly in the occupational sphere. Not only is there sex segregation in the labor market—but also in the job categories in which women predominate; they are among the lowest in occupational prestige. A further indication of the low-prestige level of women's work is that a great deal of the work that women do—primarily in the home—is unpaid labor. This work may be highly valued within a woman's family and by homemakers themselves, although it may actually count for nothing should such a woman later attempt to enter the labor market.   [1988]

Understanding the Reading

1. What is the establishment?
2. Why don't women have political power?
3. What is the gender gap?
4. Explain the connection between wealth and political power.
5. How does a small elite control the wealth in this country?
6. What are the causes of differentials between men's incomes and women's?
7. What is the "feminization of poverty"?
8. What is the difference between achieved status and ascribed status?
9. What indicates the low prestige of women?

Suggestions for Responding

1. Write an essay in which you consider how your gender has affected your personal access to power, wealth, and prestige.
2. Research one of the equal rights laws Richardson lists in her "Power" section. Write a brief report on how it was enacted and what its effects have been. ◆

53

Modern Menstrual Politics

Janice Delaney,
Mary Jane Lupton, and
Emily Toth

It was the last day of the long Senate debate over Joint Resolution 208, otherwise known as the Equal Rights Amendment. The leader of the opposition, the self-proclaimed protector of women from the implications of their equality, took the floor to offer still another set of amendments designed to weaken ERA. As was his custom, Senator Sam Ervin, later to be a hero of Watergate but now little more than an anachronism to the hundreds of women who lined the galleries, cited what he considered to be the ultimate authority for his argument:

> We find in Chapter 1, Verse 27 of the book of Genesis this statement which all of us know to be true: "God created man in his own image. In the image of God created He him. Male and female, created He them. . . ." When He created them, God made physiological and functional differences between men and women. These differences confer upon men a greater capacity to perform arduous and hazardous physical tasks.

Even on March 22, 1972, forty-nine years after the amendment had first been proposed to Congress, one of the most respected U.S. senators was linking the Bible with the old question of equal rights for women. The final vote that day, approving the resolution 84 to 8, reflected the legislators' ability to divorce religion from reality in matters of state. But Senator Ervin's use of the Bible (as well as a staggering number of articles in scholarly and legal journals) to prove women do not deserve to have equal protection and responsibilities under law is a perfect illustration of the power of one religious tradition to keep the "physiological and functional" differences between men and women in the forefront of all debate about women's intellectual and professional freedom.

Since the advent of modern science, the fears and prejudices surrounding menstruation have given way to an acceptance of it as a normal bodily process—at least in print. But the habits of centuries are not easily unlearned by men, who depend on woman's manifest physical differences to give a rationale for their belief in her emotional, economic, and social otherness. That is why the system we call *menstrual politics* has by no means disappeared with the twentieth century and the "emancipation" of women from their biologically determined roles.

For the sake of argument, in reviewing the last hundred years or so, we are going to leave in the background the multiple movements in U.S. history that produced the drive for full female equality and concentrate instead on the one constant fact about women: their menstruation. The resulting picture puts in sharp focus how far we've come—and how far we have yet to go.

Practitioners of menstrual politics have one basic tenet in common: They are convinced that women are naturally and irrevocably limited by the menstrual function. Since the early nineteenth century, menstrual politics has taken two positions with regard to menstruation and economic life: first, that *factories and businesses pose a fatal threat to women's reproductive life;* second, that *the menstrual cycle threatens the health of American capitalism.* The progression of ideas has been from the first to the second; as medicine began paying more attention to the facts of the menstrual cycle and medical excuses for the exclusion of women waned, the idea that menstruation was bad for business gained in popularity, and that is where we are now. In this second wave of the American woman's movement, at a moment in history when man has so mastered his universe that he is beginning to redefine even life and death, women are still hearing from people like Edgar Berman, a physician and Democratic party functionary, who announced in 1970 that he would not like to see a woman in charge of this country at a time of national crisis because her "raging hormonal imbalances" would threaten the life and safety of all.

But the first phase of American menstrual politics was no less insidious for all its creaky chivalry. On the one hand, it was instrumental in getting some legislative relief for the thousands of women employed in the sweatshops and "dark satanic mills" of the nineteenth century. On the other, the bodily weakness attributed to the menstrual function became a favored argument for restricting the participation of women in higher education and national affairs. A continuing monument to the politics of menstrual exclusion in this country is the body of "protective" legislation that restricts women's working hours, women's duties, and ultimately, women's pay and prestige.

Women had been working in the factories and mills since the industrial revolution. England and New England alike exploited young women and children, working them as much as sixteen hours a day for as little as a dollar a week. Only very gradually did women organize in the nineteenth and twentieth centuries to change these conditions. The fledgling labor movement, then as now, was more concerned with stabilizing conditions for men. Few women had power in the American Federation of Labor; perhaps their Victorian sense of obligation to their paternalistic employers prevented them from getting any real power on their own.

Meanwhile, some states, alarmed at the appalling working conditions endured by *both* sexes, had tried to legislate humane practices. One such law, a New York statute setting maximum hours of work for bakery employees, had been declared unconstitutional by the U.S. Supreme Court in 1905 (*Lochner v. New York* 198 U.S. 45). But in 1908, the Court sent down a decision whose implications would have a significant effect on the ratification of the ERA. It upheld the constitutionality of an Oregon law that restricted the employment of women in any mechanical establishment, or factory, or laundry to ten hours a day. What the Court believed set this law apart from the New York statute was the question of sex:

> That woman's physical structure and the performance of material functions place her at a disadvantage in the struggle for subsistence is obvious. This is especially true when the burdens of motherhood are upon her. *Even when they are not, by abundant testimony of the medical fraternity continuance for a long time on her feet at work, repeating this from day to day, tends to have injurious effects upon the body,* and as healthy mothers are essential to vigorous offspring, the physical well-being of women becomes an object of public interest and care in order to preserve the strength and vigor of the race. (*Muller v. Oregon* 202 U.S. 412 [1908], italics ours)

Regarded as a stunning victory for women in 1908, and progenitor of many state protective

laws, *Muller v. Oregon* was still being cited in the U.S. Senate in 1972 as an argument for the defeat of ERA. It made no distinction between pregnant and nonpregnant women and classified all women as mothers or potential mothers. The state's interest in the bodies of all women was established—for the good of the preservation of the race.

Labor-union women and others who fought for the protective laws were principally interested in gaining a minimum standard of working conditions. They believed that minimum standards for women would be merely a first step toward humane conditions for all. But because the Court made its decision on the basis of "woman's physical structure" and the "strength and vigor of the race," the laws that followed the 1908 decision tended to restrict women more than help them; whereas men's hours—and salaries—remained limitless. Laws after *Muller* restricted the number of pounds a woman might lift, the kind of place she might work in, the number of rest breaks she must take during the day.

The debate in the courts was accompanied by strident debate among doctors over the effects on menstruation of living an active life. One controversy threatened to undo the progress of higher education for women, which had also been gaining momentum early in the nineteenth century. In 1874, a small book by one Edward F. Clarke, M.D., proposed that educating women would mean the end of the human race. Titled *Sex in Education,* its thesis was that American girls were generally feebler than their European sisters because of the deplorable trend toward higher education for women. The college years, Clarke believed, followed too soon on the menarche, when the debilitating effects of the newly flowing menstrual blood made the body susceptible to disease and outside influence. Studying forced the brain to use up the blood and energy needed to get the menstrual process functioning efficiently. Allowing young women to continue their studies would thus result in the weakening of women and consequently the weakening of generations of Americans as yet unborn. For of course, woman, to Clarke, was defined by her uterus, as she was to the 1908 Supreme Court: "Let the fact be accepted that there is nothing to be ashamed of in a woman's organization, and let her whole education and life be guided by the divine requirements of her system."

The uproar caused by Clarke's book is a measure of the extent to which thinking people were in favor of the education of women and were willing to answer Clarke in his own language. Several rebuttals were published, among them *Sex and Education,* a collection of essays by distinguished educators and public figures, edited by Julia Ward Howe (author of "The Battle Hymn of the Republic"). Most significant in this volume was the testimony from colleges admitting women, Vassar, Antioch, Michigan, Oberlin among them. Alida C. Avery, Vassar's resident physician, assured Dr. Clarke that students were forbidden to attend gym classes during the first two days of their periods and were denied physical education if they suffered from dysmenorrhea (painful menstruation). But the reports from these institutions all supported the thesis that education and discipline and regular exercise improve menstrual health and general vigor, thus contributing to a healthier and more intelligent population of mothers.

While declaring the halls of ivy off limits to any female person, Clarke had not shown similar concern for the mills, factories, and sweatshops that were the college of thousands of unfortunate young women. Clarke had, in fact, declared that factory work was not so damaging to young girls as studying, for bodily strain did not tax the fragile new menstrual process the way mental exertion did. But in 1875, Dr. Azel Ames, in *Sex in Industry,* spoke of the evil results of "coordinated mental and physical activity on the menstrual function." He called for laws that would prevent the exploitation of cheap female labor. Nonetheless, the message of both men was the same: If you let women out of the home and into the man's world, their reproductive lives would be so damaged that the future of the human race would be irrevocably jeopardized.

And so the arguments went. The major theme seemed to be that emancipation of women would mean the destruction of their menstrual cycles and thus the end of the human race, for woman exists to bear children. Even the real need for labor reform could not mask the determination to keep woman "in her place" and to provide a physical basis for doing so, so that competence, skill, strength, or intelligence could have no bearing on her advancement.

The turning point seems to have come around the time women gained the vote; large percentages of the female population were gaining advanced degrees, entering the professions, and in general reaping the benefits of the "century of struggle" for legal and political equality. An enormously liberating factor in these advances was the mass marketing of disposable sanitary napkins after World War I. Before Kotex came on the market in 1921, women had been wearing garments similar to babies' diapers, which they washed and reused. Imagine the effect this cumbersome and unhygienic garment must have had on the average woman's workday outside the home, whether in a factory or in an office, and you have some idea of why women probably did not venture out of the house when they menstruated. Imagine, too, the real courage and determination of those who did enter the work force despite this handicap. Significantly, women nurses, not men, were the motivating force behind disposable sanitary protection.

Turn-of-the-century studies succeeded in convincing many women (and a few men) that their menstrual cycles need not be considered a disability. Clelia Duel Mosher's *Health and the Woman Movement* (1916) attempted to disprove the belief that increased activity would damage woman's health. Citing centuries of old wives' tales, she said:

> Certainly, there is no disputing the fact that the mind has a powerful, if unconscious, control of organic processes. Now for generations, if we have taught girls any thing at all in regard to menstruation, we have been instilling the idea that it is a periodic illness involving suffering and incapacity.

An especially convincing part of Mosher's thesis was her denunciation of women's clothing. Fashions, she found, were directly related to cramps. The heavy skirts and waist-pinching corsets of the nineteenth century would increase congestion and pain in the uterus, but "as the skirt grew shorter and narrower and the waist grew larger, the functional health of women improved." She also devised a set of exercises to accompany the flapper fashions and free girls and women from menstrual pain.

Twenty years earlier, Mary Putnam-Jacobi, M.D., had also spoken out against the listlessness and enforced rest for women during menstruation, claiming that nothing but custom and the wishes of men were at the root of it:

Thus one of the most essential apparent peculiarities of the menstrual process, its periodicity, that formerly was supposed to indicate the periodical increase in the vital forces of the female organism, has come to be considered as a mark of constantly recurring debility, decidedly as a fracture or paralysis.

In their work, both women were actually trying to persuade women that no one need suffer menstrual pain against her wishes. This must have been a revolutionary idea for women, who had been convinced that ill health at menstruation was "woman's lot." The fact that women themselves perpetuated this belief is related to the eternal question of menstrual isolation: Who makes and enforces the taboos: men or women? In the industrial nineteenth century, just as in some prehistoric villages, menstrual malingering may have been subtly encouraged by men to ensure their dominance in the social and economic hierarchy. Woman, caught in this vicious circle of cause and effect, accepts her lot and makes the most of the benefits men see fit to extend to her, such as the protective labor laws, even if their real effect is to protect society from the achievements of women who work.

By the twentieth century, society showed more concern for the dollars and work hours lost because of menstrual and premenstrual absences than for the health and vitality of unborn children and their mothers. The protective laws themselves were used as evidence that women were incapable of holding responsible positions, from factory forewoman to company president. Grace Naismith, in *Private and Personal* (1966), uses unsupported statistics to prove that billions of dollars are lost each year because of women staying home from work with dysmenorrhea. She says:

> Since one out of every three workers in American industry today is a woman—24.5 million in our labor force—menstrual problems assume major significance. Eight percent of absenteeism is due to dysmenorrhea. The economic loss is said to be equivalent to an entire year of work by 5800 women.

To combat such waste, she suggests expanded use of industrial programs in which female employees are sent routinely to gynecologists ("sometimes a woman") to answer questions about their periods. She claims that Paramount Studios and United Artists require a gynecological exam for each employee, as do many other enlightened companies. If a woman (always an employee, never the boss) is absent too much, her (male) boss has a right to ask if she is menstruating or is "really sick," for "it is in the business world that menstruation plays havoc with men and their money."

Naismith's book suggests that absenteeism caused by dysmenorrhea is all but out of control in twentieth-century America and that only the patient, kindly, fatherly bosses and gynecologists can save the economy from these bleeding subversives. Yet, every year, the U.S. Department of Labor statistics on absences from work prove this argument to be unfounded. In 1971, for example, men lost 5.1 days because of sickness or injury, and women lost 5.2. These figures remain about the same from year to year. That hardly heralds a massive breakdown of American industrial life, especially when coupled with the fact that women bear the responsibility for staying home with sick children—and husbands.

Another book with a similar argument is Katharina Dalton's *The Menstrual Cycle* (1969), which treats exhaustively the alleged effects on the economy of the emotional aspects of the premenstrual syndrome. Like Naismith, Dalton emphasizes an unproven correlation between menstruation and work loss but overlooks those studies and tests that tend to prove the opposite. Especially important are the myriad of tests conducted in the private sector and the public as early as the 1920s, all showing little or no difference in efficiency and absenteeism among women during fluctuations of the menstrual cycle.

This same approach prevails in women's athletics. Historically, the menstrual cycle has been the root of discrimination against women in sports, despite the fact that in the last three Olympics, says an article in the September 1974 *Ms.,* "women won gold medals and established new world records during all phases of the menstrual cycle." Although there is a dearth of research involving women's psychological endurance or performance in sports, those studies that do exist find that menstruation has little or no effect. A recent study by the American Medical Association of sixty-six Olympic sportswomen showed that 75 percent continued regular training during menstruation, and only 5 percent stopped entirely. Unless a woman's period is unusually painful, says the AMA, "there seems to be no medical reason not to train or compete during menstruation." Obviously, the menses did not interfere with the American Olympic swimmer who broke a world record and won three gold medals at the height of her period.

But, again, most of the popular reasons for discrimination are based on the *effect of the menstrual cycle on the sport*. For example, Dick Butera, owner of the Philadelphia franchise of the World Team Tennis League, was quoted in *Philadelphia* as saying that he plans to hire more women athletes than he needs at any one time: "What happens if Billie Jean wakes up the morning of a big match and she's got her period bad? What are you going to tell the fans?"

One thing that an athlete *can* do if she "gets her period bad" is take hormones to delay it until after an important contest. Birth control pills can be used for this purpose, or the male hormone testosterone can be administered. Both Dalton and Naismith refer to the latter practice, but Dalton points out that the effects of testosterone on a woman's bodily strength and endurance are so extensive that the injection is illegal in most athletic contests. At Olympic Games, hormone tests are required of all athletes to make sure men aren't competing in women's contests.

Most women who are nonprofessional athletes probably formed their attitudes toward menstruation and sports in their high school gym classes, where they shared the experience of a character in Alice Munro's *Lives of Girls and Women:* "We had hidden in the girls' toilet together when we had the curse at the same time and were afraid to do tumbling—one at a time, in front of the rest of the class—afraid of some slipping or bleeding, and too embarrassed to ask to be excused." Such fears have bothered young women for centuries and originate in the two principles of menstrual politics we have been discussing: Girls in any condition do not participate in strenuous exercise because it might harm their female organs, and women cannot compete successfully in sports because their menstrual blood might "stain" the playing fields.

It is impossible to escape the conclusion that menstrual politics has dominated social and economic relations between the sexes since the beginning of time. In all their struggles for equality—the suffrage movement, the labor movement, the struggle for ERA—women have been obliged to fight against an enemy who will not contend with them in the halls of Congress or the courts of law. The enemy is within every woman, but it is not her menstruation. Rather, it is the habit of mind regarding menstruation into which she has been led by centuries of male domination. She has been taught that menstruation is disabling, and so she has been disabled.

Even in terms of twentieth-century life, it is inaccurate to say that women "invented" menstrual politics. Neither in machine-age America nor in contemporary Stone Age societies have women had enough control over their own lives to manipulate and control the lives of the ruling men. As the servant learns to reinforce the prejudices of the master, so woman has learned well to echo the male menstrual prejudice born in fear of her mysterious functions.   [1988]

Understanding the Reading

1. Explain the significance of the Supreme Court's ruling in *Muller v. Oregon*.
2. How was menstruation used in the late nineteenth century to limit women's educational and employment opportunities?
3. Explain Naismith's argument about the economics of dysmenorrhea and what is wrong with it.
4. What is the relationship between menstruation and athletics?
5. Explain what the authors mean by menstrual politics and how it has hurt women.

Suggestions for Responding

1. Describe and analyze your beliefs about menstruation.
2. Other features that distinguish women from men have been used to disadvantage women. Investigate and report on one of these, such as the fact that only women get pregnant, only women can nurse babies, women's body shape differs from that of men, or any other one you are aware of. ✦

54

Learning to Give Girls Equal Classroom Attention

Mary Beth Marklein

They read from the same textbooks and sit in the same classrooms, yet girls are often shortchanged in education, studies show, because teachers pay more attention to boys.

Most educators don't do it on purpose; they're just unaware of it, say Myra and David Sadker, professors at American University in Washington, D.C., who conduct workshops on this subtle form of sexism around the country.

And what they show teachers is that educators, knowingly or not:

- Force boys to work out problems they don't understand, but tell girls what to do. "It reinforces the old stereotypes that girls must rely on others and boys must stand on their own," says Brenda Cloyd, who heads a gender equity program within the Department of Education in Virginia.
- Are easier on girls when dispensing discipline. "When they get into the business world, (boys) are more adept at receiving criticism," Cloyd says. "They learn to deal with failure, which we've all got to deal with."
- Reward girls for non-academic achievements, such as neat penmanship or getting along with others. "Grades are given sometimes for politeness, as kind of a compromise," Myra Sadker says. The result, she adds, "leads to a false sense of security," and may explain why girls consistently get better report cards but earn lower SAT scores than boys.

But the Sadkers also help teachers understand why this happens. Based on their own four-year study of sexism in classrooms from grade school through graduate school, the Sadkers found boys are:

- Eight times more likely to call out in class.
- Five times more likely to receive the most attention from teachers.

When teachers do call on girls, they give them considerably less feedback, positive or negative, the Sadkers say.

"In short, males are the more dominant figures in the classroom and they receive more of the valuable educational resources—the teacher's time and attention," David Sadker says.

For girls, the consequences go beyond academic achievement. By the time young women reach post-secondary levels, those who do speak up in class frequently couch their responses with self-effacing language.

"When you're actively involved, your achievement is likely to go up, and so is your self-esteem," Myra Sadker says. "Education is not a spectator sport."

Federal mandates have targeted most of the overt forms of sex discrimination, the researchers say.

Title IX, the landmark 1972 law that established a women's equity program within the Department of Education, has helped eliminate such problems as male-only athletics programs.

More recently, a 1984 law encourages women to pursue vocational education for jobs traditionally held by men, such as auto mechanics.

Still, the Sadkers contend that educators aren't angry enough about the problem.

In an article published last year in *Educational Leadership,* the Sadkers, with co-author Sharon Steindam, call such inequities "a national blind spot." Their analysis of 183 articles about education reform printed in professional journals from 1983 through 1986 found that only 1 percent of the content dealt with the problem of sex bias.

Education groups acknowledge the problem, but are working to correct it.

"We make sure our people have information on that." says Barbara Van Blake, director of human rights for the American Federation of Teachers.

Bernice Sandler, of the Association of American Colleges, says almost 25,000 requests have come in for a 1982 report on sex bias. Her group is now working on a guide to help colleges change professors' behavior.

In their workshops, the Sadkers found that teachers can significantly diminish the problem of favoring boys with conscious effort.

They encourage educators to videotape their classroom behavior and then analyze it objectively for biases. Most teachers, they add, are eager to change behavior—once they can see it.

John Phillips, a teacher at Thomas Jefferson

Intermediate School in Arlington, Va., recalls the day a colleague pointed out that all of the inspirational quotations he had tacked on the wall referred to he, him or his. Not one mentioned girls or women.

"I thought, 'Hmmm, let me think about that,'" recalls Phillips, who had chosen the sayings because they stressed self-esteem. He decided to add some female references.

"Over time, people are bombarded with messages that seem to be only referring to men," he reasoned. "What I'm trying to communicate by these messages would be somehow lessened if I didn't somehow recognize that."   [1990]

Understanding the Reading

1. How do teachers treat girls differently from boys, and how does this reflect intentional or unintentional sexism?
2. What can teachers do to reduce the problem?

Suggestions for Responding

1. Think about an instance when you were leader of a mixed-sex group, such as a class group project or being a counsellor at a summer day camp. Describe ways that you, like these teachers, may have responded differently to the males and females. What behaviors would you change now?
2. Monitor one of your present instructors to see if she or he treats women and men students differently. Write (but don't necessarily send) the instructor a letter reporting on your findings and suggesting alternative behaviors. ◆

55

Feminist Scholarship and the "Invisible Paradigms"

Sara Coulter,
K. Edgington, and
Elaine Hedges

[The] "invisible paradigms"[1] underlying the academic disciplines [are] those epistemological[2] and methodological assumptions that have led to the exclusion or devaluation of women's experience. The Conference speakers therefore presented a series of panel discussions in which they identified these invisible paradigms.

The Ideal of Objectivity

Underlying the disciplines is a belief that knowledge can be objectively arrived at, through procedures that are free of the gender, race, and class contexts inside of which we all live. Feminist scholarship, often described pejoratively as "subjective," questions this belief. Feminist scholars in science ask whether the choice of research topics, the nature of the experimental design, the interpretation of the data, and the choice of a theory may not be influenced by gender bias. Is gender bias evident, for example, in Francis Bacon's paradigm of a female earth dissected and mastered by a male investigator? Was Darwin's theory of sexual selection—which he described as a competition among powerful males for passive females—influenced by the codes and standards of his Victorian world? In the social sciences feminist scholars ask whether the model of the objective researcher, who is detached from the human subjects being studied, may not ignore the emotions as a part of social reality, and whether the attempt to achieve a "value free" social science by applying "objective" scientific method may not lead to a level of generalization and abstraction that in fact conceals gender bias. So too in the humanities, scholars question the assumption that esthetic standards are "universal," "transcendent," and objectively derived. Is esthetic value located in the text, or in the reader? Are our esthetic judgements influenced by our gender, race, and class, as well as by our historical circumstances? These are central questions being asked and explored.

Dualisms

Objectivity itself is one half of a dualism, and the new scholarship on women has been concerned with demonstrating not only the extent to which dualistic thinking pervades Western culture, but also the extent to which one term in each dualism, the term usually associated with women, is less valued, in effect creating a hierarchy. The separation of the observer from what is observed creates such a dualism, in science. In the social sciences basic theoretical constructs such as Gemeinschaft/Gesellschaft,[3] primary/secondary groups, public/private, and instrumental/expressive are examples of conceptual frameworks in which male forms of social relationships are seen as more advanced than those forms associated with females. Traditional theories in psychology are being examined for their polarization of key factors into dualistic opposites, including the key dualism, nature versus nurture. In the humanities, artists and works of art are categorized as "major" or "minor."

LANGUAGE

The new scholarship is also asking whether the languages of the disciplines themselves may not reflect gender ideology. Pronoun reference—the use of the generic "he" which implies a picture of the human race as essentially male and makes women invisible—is a problem in all of the disciplines, and one that points to pervasive bias in our language. Beyond this, scholars indicate other examples of gendered terminology. Biology describes an active sperm and passive ovum, or DNA as an active agent controlling a passive cytoplasm.[4] The official definition of "work" in the social sciences devalues women's unpaid work in the home by omitting it from the definition. Prefixes such as "non-white" and "non-western" make large population groups invisible. The language of literary criticism can make women marginal or invisible by the use of such terms and labels as "masterpiece," "masterwork," "seminal," "hero," and "feminine or weak rhyme." The question being asked is whether, if men have controlled the power of naming, women's experiences have been misnamed and are yet to be accurately named.

MALE AS NORM

The ideal of objectivity, dualistic thinking, and linguistic usage that privileges male activity and viewpoints [is], it is being suggested, [an] indication of a fundamental assumption underlying the disciplines that male experience and male behavior—and often more narrowly, white male experience and behavior—represent the norm in terms of which all human behavior and experience are to be judged. In psychology, where data has been collected primarily on males, theoretical models do not explain female behavior, which may as a result be termed "deviant." Biologist Ruth Bleier has suggested that a male perspective, with an emphasis on mastery and individualism, has influenced the formulation of scientific concepts, from models of primate behavior to theories of cellular development. In Health courses, major medical problems for women, such as endometriosis,[5] may go unmentioned if male biology and health are seen as the standard. The emphasis in history and political science on public events and public behavior, which are traditionally male areas of activity, defines women out of the subject matter. Power and authority, when seen as attributes more appropriate to males than females, create problems for women aspiring to be professional or business leaders.

These paradigms become visible in the process of analyzing why women have been omitted from the curriculum or relegated to special or minor categories when included. The need to reconceptualize the disciplines becomes increasingly apparent.   [1986]

Notes

1. PARADIGMS: Models.
2. EPISTEMOLOGICAL: Relating to the philosophy of the nature and origin of knowledge.
3. GEMEINSCHAFT/GESELLSCHAFT: Community/Society.
4. CYTOPLASM: The protoplasm outside a cell nucleus.
5. ENDOMETRIOSIS: The growth in other parts of the body of tissue that usually lines the uterus.

Understanding the Reading

1. Why do feminist scholars question the ideal of objectivity?
2. What does dualism mean, and what might be wrong with that kind of thinking?
3. Why does it matter that "men have controlled the power of naming"?
4. What is meant by "male as norm"?

Suggestions for Responding

1. Extend the analysis of one of the invisible paradigms the authors discuss to show how the assumptions underlying it affect your own thinking. For example, what other "norms" besides the male are accepted in our society, or what parts of life are devalued by the ideal of objectivity?

2. Explain how the two preceding readings by Marklein and by Delaney, Lupton, and Toth illustrate the paradigms described in this reading. ✦

56

Sexism, Science, and Society

MARGARET L. ANDERSEN

Scientific explanations are generally thought to be objective accounts that are uninfluenced by the values and interests of scientific thinkers. Thus, science has the image of being value-neutral and true to the facts. Objectivity in science is depicted as stemming from the calculated distance between the observer and the observed. In the scientific framework, personal characteristics of scientific observers are not expected to influence their results.

Yet, the world of science is overwhelmingly male—a fact that is well documented in studies revealing the small proportion of women in virtually every scientific field. It is therefore possible that science carries a distinctively masculine tone—one that values objective separation from the objects of research and, yet, is nonetheless gendered in the descriptions it offers and the explanations it creates.

In considering gender, we can find numerous examples showing that the ideals of scientific objectivity have, in fact, not been met in reaching specific research conclusions. Note, for example, the description of the experimental scientific method offered by Francis Bacon, one of the sixteenth-century founders of modern scientific thought:

For you have but to follow and as it were hound nature in her wanderings, and you will be able when you like to lead and drive her afterward to the same place again. . . . Neither ought a man to make scruple of entering and penetrating into those holes and corners, when the inquisition of truth is his whole object.

The emergence of modern science is founded upon an image of rational man as conquering the passions of nature, which is depicted as female. Consider Machiavelli's famed quotation regarding fortune:

Fortune is a woman and it is necessary if you wish to master her to conquer her by force; and it can be seen that she lets herself be overcome by the bold rather than by those who proceed coldly, and therefore like a woman, she is always a friend to the young because they are less cautious, fiercer, and master her with greater audacity.

Such depictions of science and nature might be dismissed as old-fashioned ramblings of patriarchal days gone by, except for the fact that gendered descriptions of biological phenomena continue to appear in scientific texts. One of the best examples comes from Alice Rossi's description of the way in which male fantasies of sexual power have been projected onto descriptions of biological reproduction. Rossi writes:

A good starting place to observe such fantasy is the initial coming together of sperm and ovum. Ever since Leeuwenhoek[1] first saw sperm under the microscope, great significance has been attached to the fact that sperm are equipped with motile flagella, and it was assumed that the locomotive ability of the sperm fully explained their journey from the vagina through the cervix and uterus to the oviduct for the encounter with the ovum. . . . [D. M.] Rorvik describes the seven-inch journey through the birth canal and womb to the waiting egg as equivalent to a 500-mile upstream swim for a salmon and comments with admiration that they often make the hazardous journey in under an hour, "more than earning their title as the most powerful and rapid living creatures on earth." The image is clear: powerful active sperm and a passive ovum awaiting its arrival and penetration, male sexual imagery structuring the very act of conception.

In fact, as Rossi points out, uterine contractions, stimulated by the release of the hormone oxytocin, propel the sperm through the female system so that "completely inert substances such as dead sperm and even particles of India ink reach the oviducts as rapidly as live sperm do."

Particularly when scientists are observing events that are connected to our social lives, it is easy for their descriptions to become contaminated by social assumptions about gender roles. This does not mean that these investigators are dishonest or engaged in conscious delusion, but only that our social values can easily be projected onto the observations, descriptions, and explanations that we make. If we are unconscious of those values, as has often been the case with gender bias, then we will have created descriptions of the world that merely reproduce what we take for granted. Thus, to produce truly objective knowledge of the social world requires knowing the social conditions in which science is produced and seeing how those conditions are reflected in scientific conclusions. In the case of scientific discussions of sex differences and sexuality, the problem has sometimes been a semantic one: The language in which ideas are communicated has been gender-biased. But in addition to eliminating sexist language, more substantive changes have been necessary, particularly when scientific thought has served ideological purposes that reflect its attempts to justify the status quo.

Sociologists use the concept of *ideology* to refer to systems of belief that distort reality so as to justify and maintain the status quo. Biological explanations of gender inequality are a case in point. It is interesting to note that biologically determinist[2] arguments tend to flourish in times of political conservatism, when powerful groups are working to maintain their own advantages. In such a setting, claims to scientific truth lend legitimacy and scientific authority to beliefs that otherwise would have a clear political bias.

In the history of social thought, Social Darwinism is a good example. Social Darwinism emerged at the turn of the twentieth century during a time of rapid expansion of capitalist wealth together with extensive exploitation of immigrant and racial minorities. Capitalists such as John D. Rockefeller were inspired by Social Darwinism—a doctrine that claimed that only the most fit would survive and rise to the top. Such a belief justified their own accumulation of wealth while fostering the racist belief that those who failed did so out of biological inferiority. Rockefeller declared in a Sunday school address:

> The growth of a large business is merely survival of the fittest. . . . The American Beauty rose can be produced in the splendor and fragrance which bring cheer to its beholder only by sacrificing the early [buds] which grew up around it. This is not an evil tendency in business. It is merely the working out of a law of nature and a law of God.

Social Darwinism justified the emergence of capitalism by claiming it to be the result of natural laws over which man has no control. Clearly, Rockefeller's arguments rested on both racist and class-bound claims. Similarly, analyses that explain gender inequality as naturally arising from differences between the sexes are an ideological defense of patriarchal privilege. They justify the rule of men over women while at the same time distorting women's actual experience, both in a biological and a social sense. When these distortions become part of the scientific record, then science clearly is serving an ideological purpose.

Freud's theory of the double orgasm is a case in point. Freud's argument, and one that was widely believed until very recently, was that women have two kinds of orgasm—clitoral and vaginal. Clitoral orgasm, in Freud's view, was less "mature." He maintained that adult women should transfer their center of orgasm to the vagina, where male penetration made their sexual response complete. Freud's theory of the double orgasm has no basis in fact. The center of female sexuality is the clitoris; female orgasm is achieved through stimulation of the clitoris, whether or not accompanied by vaginal penetration. But, for nearly a century, the myth of the double orgasm led women to believe that they were frigid—unable to produce a mature sexual response. During this period, psychiatrists (most of whom were male) reported frigidity as the single most common reason for women to seek clinical therapy. In fact, the emphasis on male penetration meant that most women were not sexually satisfied in heterosexual relations because sexual intercourse and the ideology that buttressed it served male interests. This fact, in turn, supported the attitude that women needed men for sexually mature relationships, even though, as recent research shows, women have higher rates of orgasm when they masturbate, have sex with another woman, or engage in cunnilingus. One study, in fact, reports higher rates of orgasm for female virgins (through mutual masturbation and cunnilingus) than for coitally experienced females.

The assumption that women need men to achieve a mature sexual response is related to the larger issue that women are dependent on men for their sexual, emotional, social, and economic well-being. This assumption not only legitimates "compulsory heterosexuality" as an institution but denigrates women's relationships with other women and subjects them to continued domination by men.

In sum, feminist research has unraveled the way that gender bias has infiltrated the scientific record. Feminist revisions have not only cast a new light on old assumptions about sex and biology but have shown how many of the "truths" alleged by scientific study merely reflect the interests of a male-dominated society. Feminist revisions in science aim for a more objective perspective by recognizing the interplay between scientific knowledge and the social systems in which it is produced: This perspective shows that culture influences the production of knowledge while at the same time . . . affecting actual biological processes.

The Interaction of Biology and Culture

It is easy to think of biological events as unaffected by the intervention of cultural systems. Yet, as scholars have discovered, the natural and social worlds often overlap. Events that we think of as physiological processes—such as aging, illness, and reproduction—are heavily influenced by the social-cultural systems in which they occur. This fact has particular significance for feminist studies because it demonstrates the inadequacies of explanations of sex differences that rest upon biological explanations alone.

Consider, for example, the biological process of aging—clearly one that is universal, inevitable, and based on human physiology. Research shows that how long one lives is strongly influenced by one's gender. Life expectancy is shorter

for men (71.1 years in 1980) than for women (76.3 years), and males have higher accidental death rates (in both childhood and adulthood) than do women. Men also have higher suicide and homicide rates than do women. Some research has shown that men with personalities marked by ambition, single-mindedness, and devotion to work are more prone to heart attacks than others. In fact, the risks associated with traditionally masculine roles are so great that one psychologist has called masculinity a "lethal role."

But even the physiological changes associated with aging are greatly affected by the social context in which aging occurs. Nutrition, for example, affects the biological health of aging persons, but social factors such as living alone or in an institution are known to affect dietary habits, as are factors such as income, cultural preferences for food, and exercise. Aging is also aggravated by stress—a condition generated by a variety of social and psychological difficulties.

For women, the aging process has its own strains. In a society in which women are valued for their youth and beauty, aging becomes a difficult social and psychological experience. Birthday cards that joke about women deteriorating after age twenty-nine and commercials for creams that "hide your aging spots" tell American women that they should be ashamed of growing old. It should be no surprise, then, that a biological process such as menopause becomes a difficult psychological experience. Research shows that menopause produces more anxiety and more depression in cultures that are less supportive of women as they age.

What we learn from looking at the interaction of biology and culture is that cultural beliefs about biological events imbue them with a significance greater than their physiological character. Menstruation, for example, is a universal phenomenon, yet one that in different cultures takes on very different meanings. In many cultures, menstruation is symbolic of the strength of women, and elaborate rituals and rites of passage symbolize that power. Yet, in other cultures, menstruation is seen as symbolic of defilement, and elaborate practices may be developed to isolate and restrict menstruating women. In the nineteenth century, for example, southeast Asian women could not be employed in the opium industry, for it was believed that, were a menstruating woman nearby, the opium would turn bitter. And, in contemporary American culture, menstruation is depicted as secretive and invisible, as best seen in the advertising industry, which advises menstruating women to keep their "secret" protected, yet to feel confident, secure, and free.

Work on menstrual moods shows, in another context, the interactive effect of culture and biological events. The Rossis' research studies college-aged men and women who were asked to rate their daily moods over a 40-day period. Women in the sample also noted their first day of menstruation as it occurred during the rating cycle. The Rossis then compared mood ratings as clocked by biological time (measured by phases in the menstrual cycle) and by calendar (or social) time. Surprisingly, the results show that men marked more days per month when they felt "achy," "crampy," and "sick" than did women. But, more to the point, the Rossis' results show that the most significant changes in moods occurred for women according to changes in the calendar week, not their menstrual cycles.

Women were more likely to feel "happy," "loving," and "healthy" on weekends and "depressed," "unhappy," and "sick" on "blue Wednesday." The research also finds no significant elevation of negative moods in the premenstrual phase for women; there was, however, an elevation of positive moods in the ovulatory phase of menstruation and an elevation of negative moods in the luteal phase (days 17–24 in a 28-day menstrual cycle). But, more important than the independent effects of biological and social time, this research finds that moods (especially positive moods) were most strongly affected when biological and social cycles were synchronized (e.g., when ovulation occurred on a weekend).

In another example of the interaction of biology and culture, something once dismissed as an old wives' tale now appears to have scientific validity. It appears that menstrual cycles become synchronized among women who live in close proximity to each other and as close friends. Although the explanation for this phenomenon is not yet clear, it is likely that *pheromones*—a generic term used to refer to communication by chemical signals—are responsible for synchronization of menstrual cycles. This phenomenon shows how cultural living arrangements can exert an influence on physiological processes such as menstruation.

Such conclusions demonstrate the simplicity of reductionist arguments that trace sex differences to biological causes alone. Research in biology and human evolution points to the extreme difficulty of separating biological from social causes. In an evolutionary sense, the biological basis for human life must be flexible enough to allow for environmental change and adaptation. Moreover, the opinion that sex differences are biologically caused seems to assume that environmental conditions are changeable, whereas biological conditions are not. Research that examines ways in which culture influences biological events shows that this is a false assumption.

The study of human culture shows that there is no fixed correspondence between innate human dispositions (if they exist) and human social forms. Whatever link exists between biology and social life is mediated by the influence of culture. Because culture is symbolic (its meaning is derived from social interaction), it cannot be found in the intrinsic properties of persons or objects. One of the unique characteristics of human societies is their freedom from natural relationships. For example, even though the act of human reproduction is a physical one, its significance lies as much, if not more, in its social meaning. Moreover, what we reproduce is not just a genetic object, but a human being whose life is part of a system of human groups.

This does not mean that the biological basis for human life is irrelevant or unimportant, but it stresses the mutual and interdependent influence of even biological events. With regard to sex differences, culture exerts a powerful influence on who we are and what we become.   [1983]

Notes

1. LEEUWENHOEK: Anton van Leeuwenhoek, a Dutch pioneering microscopist and biologist, 1632–1723.
2. BIOLOGICAL DETERMINISM: The theory that behavior is controlled by physical makeup.

Understanding the Reading

1. What is masculine or sexist in the historical quotations Andersen uses at the opening of her article?
2. Why does Andersen call Rockefeller's Social Darwinist arguments both racist and class-bound?
3. How does culture influence such biological processes as aging and menstruation?
4. How does culture affect biology?

Suggestions for Responding

1. Examine a textbook for a biology course or some other course and report on the examples of sexism in language, examples, research subjects, and so on that you can identify.
2. Compare Andersen's analysis of sexism in science with Gould's analysis of scientific racism in Part V. ✦

57

Our Bodies, Their Selves

KATRINE AMES

Heart disease kills women and men in almost equal numbers: it has no gender bias. Medical researchers have. In clinical trials for any number of health problems, including heart disease, they usually employ only male subjects—whether humans or rodents. In 1988, research on 22,071 male doctors revealed that aspirin reduces the risk of heart attacks. The benefit for women? Who knows? A study published this fall indicated that heavy coffee intake did not increase the incidence of heart attacks or strokes. The 45,589 subjects, aged 40 to 75, were men.

Such studies are firing up women's health activists and raising the profile of women's health issues. As women become more aware of inequities in medical research, they're mobilizing to put on the pressure. More women are entering the male-dominated research field, and publicly funded research is becoming more responsive to taxpayers' concerns. The sure way to build government support for women's health, says Rep. Patricia Schroeder, is to make it a political issue: "Women pay half the taxes. If they don't get a fair share of research, they ought to go after the guys who don't allow it to happen."

Congress, led by the Caucus for Women's Issues, is getting involved. Concerned that the National Institutes of Health had not monitored a 1986 policy that urged researchers to include women in their studies, the 150-member group—founded in 1977 and cochaired by Schroeder—requested that the General Accounting Office investigate. The result: a report on the NIH's insensitivity to women's concerns. Last September the NIH — which may soon have its first woman director, Dr. Bernadine Healy, former president of the American Heart Association —opened an office on women's health in Bethesda, Md.

Ignoring women's health issues, Schroeder says, is "a nonfeasance issue, not a malfeasance issue. In politics, folks fund what they fear, so almost anything dealing with women doesn't get funded." But politics—specifically, pressure from the right—may be what stymies some research. Government-funded fertility research is virtually nonexistent; there's no ob/gyn research program at NIH. Anti-choice activists helped derail fetal-tissue research in Parkinson's disease this year, after allegations that it would lead to abortions performed to obtain fetal tissue.

Many organizations and individuals are attempting to circumvent the politics. Last year Lilly Tartikoff, an adviser to Max Factor (a Revlon subsidiary) and the wife of NBC executive Brandon Tartikoff, secured a $2.4 million grant from Revlon to establish the Revlon/UCLA Women's Cancer Research Program. She told Revlon chairman Ronald O. Perelman, "We've been buying your products at the local drugstore since were 10 or 12, and I feel it's your responsibility to give back to the women who have been supporting your company."

"Blatant sexism": Researchers' justification for omitting women is that female hormonal changes "complicate" work and that there may be fetal risk if a participant is pregnant and doesn't know it. The explanation, which some women consider shaky at best, can be outright absurd—as when a major NIH study on aging initially excluded females, despite the fact that postmenopausal women vastly outnumber their male contemporaries. As Rep. Henry Waxman, chairman of a House subcommittee on health and the environment, says, "It's not discrimination by intent, but it certainly is by result."

Diane Curtis, a founding member of New York City-based Women's Health Action and Mobilization (WHAM), puts it more bluntly: "Saying that women's bodies are complicated is saying that there is a norm out there and that norm is the male body. It's such blatant sexism." The results of such sexism, accidental or not, can be devastating. Treatments developed to alleviate a host of problems are tested on men, but they're used by women. And in matters of health, what's good for the gander can be harmful, even fatal, for the goose.

Many women are focusing attention on breast cancer, but there are several other issues that could benefit from a shot of activism. Osteoporosis-related problems kill as many women every year as breast cancer does, yet the debilitating disease gets less than half the government funds allocated for breast cancer and scientists still know little about it. Menopause is a vast unstudied area. Chlamydia, a frequently asymptomatic sexually transmitted disease, leaves thousands of women sterile every year, yet remains a virtual unknown. AIDS is a growing concern for women. The World Health Organization predicts that within 10 years as much as 80 percent of all AIDS cases will be transmitted heterosexually—and a healthy woman who has sex with an infected man is 14 times more likely to contract the AIDS virus than a healthy man who sleeps with an infected woman. According to Dr. Patricia Kloser of University Hospital in Newark, N.J., laboratory studies of AZT, the only AIDS drug approved by the federal government, revealed a terrible side effect in female mice: vaginal cancer.

Scientists, women's groups and others are beginning to work together on agendas, but much remains to be done. Washington-based consultant Joanne Howes wants to bring drug companies and medical groups into the discussion. "The challenge is to continue to build knowledge and to identify the issues," she says. "Otherwise [all this activity] will just be a blip on the screen."

[1990]

Understanding the Reading

1. How do medical researchers show an insensitivity to women's health problems?
2. How are women responding to this sexist bias?
3. Why do researchers discriminate against women?

Suggestion for Responding

Research the incidence (the proportion of people with the disease) and mortality rates for women and for men of the diseases Ames mentions. Analyze what this comparison reveals. ◆

58

Strong Women and Strutting Men: The Moynihan Report

PAULA GIDDINGS

President Lyndon B. Johnson's "War on Poverty,"[1] the key to his Great Society program, was unprecedented in its conception. Not only did the federal government support the equality of Blacks as a right and in theory, but it acted to make equality a result and a fact. The War on Poverty was waged at a time when the percentage of Americans living in poverty had reached an all-time high (17.8 percent) and poor urban Blacks were setting cities on fire. It became clear that Black poverty had to be alleviated if legal rights were to mean anything. So an expert set about the study of how to make economic equality a fact.

The first step was to pinpoint the problem. And the conclusion, detailed in the subsequent Moynihan Report, was: "At the heart of the deterioration of the fabric of the Negro society is the deterioration of the Negro family. It is the fundamental cause of weakness in the Negro community. Unless the damage is repaired all the effort to end discrimination, poverty and injustice will come to little."

So the "case for national action" was no longer to concentrate on the external machinery of racism and discrimination, but on the internal problems of the Black family—as if the two were unrelated. Moynihan arrived at this conclusion through the slavery-specific thesis. The problems of the Black family began under slavery, he postulated, and were worsened by continued discrimination and the migration to cities. In the urban environment, Black men had experienced "disastrous" levels of unemployment since World War II. This fact, combined with the already slave-damaged family structure, resulted in abnormal prominence of women. "A fundamental fact of Negro American family life is the often reversed roles of husband and wife," Moynihan noted, citing studies showing that the wife was "dominant" in the majority of Black families while the reverse was true of Whites. This matriarchal pattern "reinforced" itself over the generations through the continued higher educational attainment of Black women and their greater representation in professional and semiprofessional jobs. All of this made Black men very dispirited, said the report. Consequently they were not good prospective marriage partners, and this translated into high rates of desertion, divorce, and female-headed families, then making up one fourth of the Black family population. This in turn added to the high rate of out-of-wedlock births (about a quarter of all Black urban births) which led to a "startling" increase in welfare dependency. Such circumstances, Moynihan observed, borrowing a phrase from Black sociologist Kenneth Clark, led to a "tangle of pathology," inextricably knotted by a matriarchal head of the household.

A question that might arise from these observations was why men, rather than women, seemed less able to fulfill family obligations under the pressure of racism and discrimination. The answer, Moynihan speculated, was that although all Blacks suffered, men suffered more: "It was the Negro male who was the most humiliated. . . . Segregation and the submissiveness it exacts, [are] surely more destructive to the male than the female personality." The reason for this evidently had to do with the inherent nature of the species: "The very essence of the male animal, from the bantam rooster to the four-star general, is to strut," was his scientific conclusion.

The report drew a storm of protest. Leaders such as George Wiley, founder of the National Welfare Rights Organization, criticized the emphasis on internal problems of the Black family at a time when racism was particularly virulent. William Ryan, a psychologist who offered one of the most detailed responses to the report, suggested that the race factor may have induced Moynihan to exaggerate the increase in female single-headed households (which was 5 percent from 1940 to 1960) and its causes. Furthermore, he challenged Moynihan's conclusion that Blacks were more entangled in pathology than Whites, especially as reflected in the number of out-of-wedlock births. Whites had a greater tendency to use birth control and to abort unwanted pregnancies, Ryan said. And, especially taking discrimination into account, Black families were not deteriorating at an any more alarming rate than White families were.

The most controversial aspect of the report concerned the Black matriarchy. In response, a number of Black sociologists, including Joyce Ladner and Andrew Billingsly, wrote books stressing the strengths of the nontraditional family. The idea had even greater currency at a time when the middle-class family was under general attack in the society. "One must question the validity of the white middle-class life-style from its very foundation because it has already proven itself to be decadent and unworthy of emulation," said Ladner. In any case, Blacks challenged the accuracy of the term *matriarchy,* which implied female dominance and male subordination within the family. What appeared as matriarchy, many argued, was in reality something else. Despite male economic instability, Ladner wrote, "It could indeed be argued that much of the 'strength' of the Black woman comes as a result of the sustained support she receives through her male partner." Even in slavery, Angela Davis asserted, the Black woman was "in no sense an authoritarian figure. . . . On the contrary, she herself had just been forced to leave behind the shadowy realm of female passivity in order to assume her rightful place beside the insurgent male."

Black sociologist Robert Staples called Black matriarchy a myth, suggesting that the Black woman actually had little power over the family or the society. She did make many decisions affecting the family, but that was because men often deferred to her greater knowledge about certain things, especially the bureaucratic structure with which many families had to deal. The tenacity of Black women was something to be proud of, Staples affirmed. "While White women have entered the history books for making flags and engaging in social work, black women have participated in the total black liberation struggle." Furthermore their assertiveness was part and parcel of a history that had deprived Black men of their ability to protect and provide for the family since slavery. But if that assertiveness had been translated into power and dominance, Staples asked, why did Black women earn an annual wage of $2,372 in 1960 compared to $3,410 for white women and $3,789 for Black men? Writer Albert Murray also criticized the report's thesis: "Moynihan's figures provide for more evidence of male exploitation of females, than of females hen-pecking males. . . . Negro family instability might more accurately be defined as a cycle of illegitimacy, matriarchy, and female victimization by gallivanting males who refuse to or cannot assume the conventional domestic responsibilities of husbands and fathers."

It is likely that no one was more shocked by the reaction to his report than Daniel Patrick Moynihan. He had taken pains to be racially sensitive. For example, he explicitly stated that the report concerned only a certain segment of the Black community and not the race as a whole. In fact, Moynihan cited evidence in the report that middle-class Black families put "a higher premium on family stability and the conserving of family resources than their White counterparts." Moynihan also praised the strength of Blacks as a race. Many other groups would not have survived the centuries-long ordeal they had undergone, he declared. As far as matriarchy was concerned, Moynihan's report stated that there was nothing inherently wrong or pathological about a woman-headed household, only that it was not the norm in the society and thus subject to disadvantage. No doubt Moynihan was put out by the knowledge that strategy for the War on Poverty in general, and aspects of his report in particular, had been "approved" by the civil rights establishment, including King [Martin Luther King, Jr.], Roy Wilkins,[2] and Whitney Young, head of the National Urban League. Moynihan had borrowed heavily from established Black sociologists. In fact, Moynihan was less harsh in his evaluation of the nontraditional family structure than E. Franklin Frazier had been in *The Negro Family in the United States.*

Like Frazier's, Moynihan's thesis suffered from myopia. Moynihan's was also particularly untimely, leaving Blacks with no option but to challenge it. Though many took issue with Moynihan's view of the problem, however, few criticized his suggestion for resolving it—which was even more malevolent. Moynihan concluded, as Frazier had done, that Black family stability could be achieved only if Black men could "strut," even, if need be, at the expense of women. This was epitomized in his program for eradicating Black poverty. He believed, as an analysis of the report points out, "that jobs had primacy and the government should not rest until every able-bodied Negro man was working *even if this meant that some women's jobs had to be redesigned to enable men to fulfill them.*" (Emphasis added.) Not *White men's* jobs, mind you— women's jobs. This, despite the growing number of female-headed families, the fact that the average two-income Black family still earned less than one-income White families, that college-educated Black males earned less than high-school–educated Whites, that Black women earned less than Black men, and that because of historical circumstances more urban Black women were prepared to fill positions in an era of increasing credentialism. The thinking seemed to be: Just make Black men the lords of their own castles and everything will be all right. To reach this utopia, of course, Black women would somehow have to slow down, become less achievement-oriented, give up much of their independence. By remaining assertive, they were ruining the family and so ruining the race.

It was a shortsighted thesis, but what could one expect in an era of male revolt, when Black and White men alike targeted the destructiveness of mothers and wives? The Moynihan Report was not so much racist as it was sexist. Although it can't be held responsible for the intense Black male chauvinism of the period, it certainly didn't discourage it, and the report helped shape Black attitudes. In its wake, an *Ebony* article unequivocally stated, "The immediate goal of Negro women today should be the establishment of a strong family unit in which the father is the dominant person." Dorothy Height, head of the NCNW,[3] said, "The major concern of the Negro woman is the status of the Negro man and his need for feeling himself an important person."

All well and good, but the question was: At what cost? At what point did making men feel good provide only diminishing returns?

Finding the answer required a change of focus, away from "why men leave home" and toward why Black women, who were fulfilling their responsibilities, were yet the most vulnerable and exploited group in the society. One should have asked why, despite their status, a larger percentage of Black women stayed in school longer, were disproportionately represented in the professions, and (if full-time workers) were experiencing the greatest percentage increase in median income of all race/sex groups. Finding the answers could have alleviated Black women's guilt and ambivalence.

The traditional value of education among Black women was one key to their success. That parents had historically encouraged their daughters to go to school was not just a racial phenomenon but a class one. In an economy where blue-collar men earned as much as or more than white-collar women, sons dropped out of school to support themselves and their families, while daughters *went* to school to do so. They went to school, in most instances, to prepare for traditionally female occupations. This was true among Blacks and Whites alike. The 1960 percentage of the Black female labor force in professional occupations was 7.2, as compared to 3.1 percent of Black men. However, as one analyst noted, if teaching, social work, and other typically feminine occupations were to be subtracted from the total of female professionals, the total number of Black professional men would "appear in a more favorable light." The same holds true for the White population. In the same year, 13.8 percent of White women were in the professions compared to 10.9 percent of men. But the latter figure was conveniently overlooked in the Moynihan Report. Perhaps because to include it would have begged the question of why the difference in professional representation had a greater effect on Black families?

The reason for the disparity was that Black men had been largely excluded from both the most desirable professional occupations and the lucrative blue-collar positions by big business and discriminatory labor unions. It has always been easier for Black women, often more educated and work-experienced than White women,

to enter the lower-paying women's professions than it was for Black men to enter the male professions. Historically, when Black women were allowed—or needed—in occupations like nursing, teaching, and government work they moved into them in disproportionate numbers. In 1965, for example, in the Department of Labor, 70 percent of Black employees, compared to 40 percent of Whites, were women. And in positions open to civil servants with modest credentials, Black women outnumbered men four to one.

In the sixties, as in the past, Black women were able to draw strength and advantage from a situation that oppressed them because of their race and their sex. Through collective effort, they struggled to make substantial gains—in a way Black men were unable to do—in those occupational areas relegated to them. An outstanding example of this was the organization of the National Union of Hospital and Health Care Employees in 1969.

The first focal point of the union effort was New York City's voluntary hospitals. Because voluntary hospitals are nonprofit institutions and thus exempt from minimum wage laws, their nonprofessional workers were woefully underpaid and exploited. They had no unemployment insurance or disability insurance. Consequently only the most marginal class of workers sought jobs in the voluntary hospitals: By the late fifties the overwhelming majority of them were Black and Hispanic women. The hospital and nursing home industry is the third largest employer in the country, and in no field are more Black women employed. Its 2.5 million workers, mostly Black women, constitute a group four times larger than the steelworkers.

In the fifties, the first foray came from New York City's Local 1199, which demanded better pay and working conditions, as well as recognition of the union as the workers' bargaining agent. For a decade the struggle continued. The obstinance of voluntary hospital administrators precipitated walkouts, and the increasingly bitter battle drew the attention of such civil rights leaders as Adam Clayton Powell, Jr., A. Philip Randolph, and Martin Luther King, Jr. The confluence of civil rights organizations, other unions, and the determination of the workers resulted in major concessions and pay raises for New York City voluntary hospital workers in 1968. But that was only the first chapter. Their success inspired the formation of a national organizing committee and other hospital workers throughout the country—most notably in Charleston, South Carolina.

When management discovered the women workers in Charleston were attempting to organize, the leaders of the group were immediately fired. The firings prompted a walkout of four hundred workers, leading to the most spectacular of the labor actions of the sixties. SCLC[4] and other civil rights organizations, along with labor unions and the Charleston Black community, were pitted against the southern establishment. The latter included all the anti-union effort that J. P. Stevens[5]—fearful of the implications of a successful strike—could muster. (His instincts were correct. Six years later a J. P. Stevens plant in Virginia voted to unionize, capping decades of struggle to do so. As with the hospital workers, increasing numbers of Blacks—and especially Black women—in the textile industry provided the crucial margin of victory for the pro-union vote.)

Resulting from the hospital workers' strike were massive rallies and massive arrests, the bringing in of the National Guard, "jail, no bail," and predictable violence. The leader of the Charleston workers was a twenty-seven-year-old Black woman named Mary Moultrie. And one of the most visible civil rights leaders participating was Coretta Scott King, who continued to be active on the workers' behalf even after the assassination of her husband. What had impressed her about the strike was not only the determination of the Black workers and the support of the Black community, but "the emergence of black women as a new breed of union leaders." Such women as Moultrie, Emma Hardin, and Rosetta Simmons were "following in the steps of Harriet Tubman, Sojourner Truth, Rosa Parks, Daisy Bates, and Fannie Lou Hamer,"[6] she noted.

A turbulent 113 days and 1,000 arrests later, the Charleston hospital strike was settled, with many gains to the workers. By 1969 the national union was established, and in subsequent years 2.5 million workers throughout the country were organized. As a result, Local 1199—now headed by Doris Turner—and the National Union of Hospital and Health Care Workers are counted among the most important unions for Black and Hispanic women in the country.

The relative success of Black women in the desirable "higher" professions, though more visible, was not as great. Although more Black women than Black men were listed under the general category of "professional" when Moynihan published his report, many more Black men than women were physicians, dentists, engineers, and so on. And that trend was continuing. In 1968, three years after the report was published, Black institutions conferred 91 percent of their professional doctoral degrees on men and only 9 percent on women. A 1969 Ford Foundation survey revealed that 94.5 percent of 1,096 Blacks who had attained doctorates (excluding medical degrees) were men and 5.5 percent were women. Furthermore, a good portion of the Black women who received doctorates got them in education (and their percentage was lower than the percentage of women in the total doctoral population). Nevertheless, the relative achievement of Black women seemed startling. The 1960 census showed, for example, that 7 percent of White physicians as opposed to 9.6 percent of Black physicians were women; 8 percent of Black lawyers, compared to 3 percent of White lawyers, were women. The same trend was apparent in a whole range of occupations. As extraordinary as these statistics were, one must keep in mind that they reflected not only the achievements of Black women but the *lack* of achievement of Black men and White women in these occupations.

Still, the disproportionate number of Black women in the professions deserves further study, for it has fueled the charges of Black women's advantage over Black men. In 1972 sociologist Cynthia Fuchs Epstein studied thirty-one Black women professionals, including lawyers, physicians, university professors, journalists, and public relations executives. What prompted her inquiry was the seeming inconsistency of Black women's success in a society that was both racist and sexist. Epstein discovered that achievement had little to do with advantage but a great deal to do with the attitudes of each woman's family, her sense of self-worth, the role of her mother, and her superiors' perception of her.

In virtually every instance, Black women professionals (unlike most of their White counterparts) grew up in homes where their mothers were doers. Of those interviewed, only four had mothers who had never worked (one of these mothers had thirteen children). Many of the women's mothers were in professional or semi-professional occupations themselves; they were teachers, professors, nurses, and one was a physician. Fewer (five out of the thirty) fathers of the women were professionals, and many others held stable jobs, such as postal employee or bricklayer. A description of the mother of one of the women was typical: "My mother was not the stronger of my parents but she was the most aggressive, always planning and suggesting ideas to improve the family's situation." The mother, a dressmaker, would often "slip out" and do domestic work if she had to make ends meet, without telling the father, a carpenter who was excluded from the union and laid off periodically.

Not surprisingly, Epstein found that the daughters of such Black women had a tremendous sense of confidence in themselves and their abilities. She cited a 1964 study of Black women college graduates which confirmed that Black women tended to be more confident of their own abilities than did their White peers. When asked if they had personalities suitable to careers as business executives, 74 percent of Black women thought that they did as compared to 49 percent of the Whites. Another study, conducted by the American Council of Education in 1971, noted that 62.1 percent of Black women college freshmen rated themselves "above average to achieve." This was higher than Black male freshmen (59.2 percent), White female freshmen (53.4 percent), *and* White male freshmen (50.6 percent). Mothers of the Black women in Epstein's study encouraged achievement almost without exception. One physician recalled that her goal was to be a nurse but her mother encouraged her to be a doctor. This was in contrast to White families, who had more ambivalence about their daughters' becoming overeducated and thus having difficulty finding husbands.

One can speculate that although some Black women shared these anxieties, their life expectations generally were different from those of most White women. Black women expected to have to work, whether they were married or not. They didn't often think of their careers as "supplemental" to those of their husbands.

Another interesting characteristic of Black women professionals, Epstein found, was that they seemed to have a higher regard for each other than White women professionals had for *their* peers. In a previous study she had found self-hatred among White women lawyers, including negative stereotypes about "aggressive, masculine" women, but Black women professionals had better attitudes toward each other. Whereas few White women favored other women professionals, Black women "never indicated doubts about the competence of other women, and some said that they favored women as colleagues because they were more reliable and more willing to work than the men they knew."

The attitudes of Black women professionals also affected how they were perceived by White male employers. Often they were regarded as more "serious" than White women, because of their strong career motivation. Black women were also less apt to become involved in the sexual politics of the office. Nevertheless it is often heard that Black women's success is due to the fact that they are perceived as less of a threat to White males. This is true, but that perception also has its disadvantages, for it indicates that whatever their abilities, Black women often progress so far and no farther. They are less apt than their male or White female peers to displace someone from the executive suite, because they are women and because they are Black. And the assumption that the most lucrative and favored positions will fall to men is borne out by statistics.

As we see, for Black women, double discrimination can cut two ways. On the one hand their status makes them the most apt to be unemployed and underemployed. As a result, Black women have had the lowest median income of all groups. On the other hand, the tremendous effort required to transcend the barriers of race and sex has catapulted full-time Black women workers into significant gains in the ever-widening women's sphere of economic activity. The rate of progress of this group has been startling to some, not because they threatened to overtake Black men but because of their proximity to them despite sex *and* race discrimination. Sociologists like Moynihan believed that the proximity made Black men too dispirited to be responsible heads of household.

His male-directed solution ignored the fact that Black women's income and occupational status compared more favorably to Black men because of the latter's inability to penetrate the more lucrative job market reserved for White men. The suggestion that Black *women* brake their progress, rather than eliminating the discrimination that kept Black men down, ignored the plight of disproportionate numbers of Black poor women, female heads of families, and the necessity for two decent incomes if Blacks were to have a quality of life comparable even to that of single-income White families.

By failing to isolate the true reasons for some Black women's relative success in the face of double discrimination, both the women's movement and the Black movement failed to benefit from the valuable lessons inherent in that achievement. Consequently, the failure effectively to challenge Moynihan's solution, with all its implications, retarded both movements.

[1984]

Notes

1. WAR ON POVERTY: A multifaceted federal program in the 1960s aimed at eliminating poverty in the United States; it included job training, Head Start, VISTA, and community action projects and was part of the Great Society, President Johnson's domestic policy, which included medical insurance for the elderly, urban housing, federal assistance for education, food stamps, and urban renewal.
2. ROY WILKINS: National Director of the National Association for the Advancement of Colored People (NAACP).
3. NCNW: National Council of Negro Women.
4. SCLC: Southern Christian Leadership Conference.
5. J. P. STEVENS: A textile manufacturer.
6. Harriet Tubman was a former slave who led more than 300 slaves north to freedom on the Underground Railroad. Sojourner Truth was a nineteenth-century abolitionist and advocate of women's rights. In 1955, Rosa Parks refused to surrender her bus seat to a white man, triggering the Montgomery, Alabama, bus boycott. Daisy Bates of the Arkansas NAACP led the fight to desegregate the state's public schools. Fannie Lou Hamer was a founder of the Mississippi Freedom party, which unsuccessfully challenged the seating

of an all-white Mississippi delegation to the 1964 Democratic National Convention.

Understanding the Reading

1. How did the Moynihan Report explain the problems of poor urban blacks?
2. What criticisms were made against Moynihan's analysis?
3. Why does Giddings find Moynihan's suggestion for solving the problem "even more malevolent" than his view of the problem?

Suggestions for Responding

1. Explain how sexism and racism influenced Moynihan's analysis.
2. How is Giddings' analysis of the Moynihan Report similar to and different from Gresham's analysis in Part V? ♦

59

A Discussion About Differences: The Left-Hand Analogy

WARREN J. BLUMENFELD AND
DIANE RAYMOND

What do left-handedness and homosexuality have in common? This [essay] explores some of the similarities which do in fact exist between the two. Though comparing handedness and sexual orientation might seem akin to comparing artichokes and jet planes, as we do so, many striking connections appear. Although this analogy in no way is meant to imply any sort of statistical correlation between left-handedness and homosexuality, it does aim to show how society transforms the meanings of what appear to be value-neutral personal characteristics into morally significant facts.

Every analogy attempts to make a point. Whether one does so successfully depends on how much the items being compared really resemble each other. This one suggests that there are crucial ways in which handedness and sexual orientation are similar. What follows here is a thumbnail sketch of some of those similarities. . . .

It is estimated that one out of every ten people is left-handed. In fact, this statistic probably holds true for all places and all times. That means there are approximately 25 million left-handed people in the United States alone; and, in a classroom of, say, thirty, at least three people are probably left-handed. Amazingly enough, the statistics are virtually the same for people who act on same-sex attractions.

Left-handed people have existed throughout the ages in all cultures, in all races, in all social classes, and in every country. Even the earliest cave drawings show left-handed figures. Similarly, same-sex acts have probably always existed. Even some of our most ancient literary fragments contain references to love between members of the same sex.

WHO IS LEFT-HANDED AND LESBIAN AND GAY?

Though it may seem obvious, it is not always easy to determine who is left-handed. Some people, for example, use different hands for different activities. Former President Gerald Ford uses his left hand to write while sitting and his right hand to write on blackboards while standing. Some people can successfully manage with either hand. In fact, it is probably true that most people aren't exclusively right-handed or left-handed. We usually, however, define our handedness in terms of whichever hand we use the most, especially in writing. Nevertheless, people in general exhibit a great variety of hand skills which covers a broad continuum between exclusive left-handedness and exclusive right-handedness.

The same difficulty exists when we try to apply labels referring to sexual orientation. Some people very early in their lives develop an awareness and acceptance of their attractions to members of their own sex. Others, though, may reach this stage later in life. Some people may be attracted to both sexes, defining themselves as "bisexual." In fact, it is probably true that most people aren't exclusively heterosexual or homosexual. Most of us, however, define our sexuality by the sex with which we feel the more comfort-

able and to which we experience the stronger attraction. Nevertheless, people's sexuality is fairly flexible, covering a broad continuum between exclusive homosexuality and exclusive heterosexuality.

So far, these facts might seem interesting, but not particularly noteworthy. But for those who are left-handed or gay or lesbian, it might be comforting to know that they are not alone. And for the majority, right-handed people and heterosexuals, it might be worth considering that not everyone is the same. What "righties" usually take for granted—cutting with scissors, working with most tools, even writing from left to right—often involves awkward adjustment for "lefties." Similarly, what "straights" usually take for granted—holding hands in public, going to school dances, introducing girlfriends or boyfriends to parents—also often involves awkward adjustments for lesbians and gays.

PREJUDICE AND DISCRIMINATION

Though *you* might not think your friend or mother or classmate is all that weird because she or he is left-handed, such tolerance has not always been the case. In fact, for centuries, left-handed people have been viewed with scorn and even, at times, with fear.

Such scorn was often justified with references to religious texts such as the Bible. Both the Old and New Testaments consider "the left" to be the domain of the Devil, whereas the "right" is the domain of God. For this reason, Jesus told his followers to "not let thy left hand know what they right hand doeth." (Matthew 6:3.) Jesus also describes God's process for separating good from evil in the Last Judgment: ". . . the King [shall] say unto them on His right hand, 'Come, ye blessed of my Father, inherit the Kingdom prepared for you from the foundation of the world. . . .' Then shall He say unto them on the left, 'Depart from me, ye cursed, into everlasting fire, prepared for the devil and his angels. . . .'" (Matthew 25: 32–41.)

Early Christians applied these categories so strictly that they even held that the saints, while still infants, were so holy that they would not suck from the left breasts of their mothers!

It is not only the Bible that condemns left-handedness. This was also the case in some ancient societies. The ancient Greeks and Romans shared this attitude. For example, the philosopher Pythagoras argued that left-handedness was synonymous with "dissolution" and evil, and Aristotle described good as "what is on the right, above, and in front, and bad what is on the left, below, and behind." The Romans further reinforced these beliefs by standardizing the right-handed handshake, and in Western countries alphabets favor right-handed people in being written from left to right.

Later, in the Middle Ages, left-handed people were sometimes accused of being witches or sorcerers. The present-day wedding custom of joining right hands and placing the gold ring on the third finger of the left hand began with the superstition that doing so would absorb the evil inherent in the left hand.

Though few people today condemn left-handedness, lesbians and gays continue to be feared and excluded. Such treatment is also often justified with references to religious texts such as the Bible. Though there is great disagreement over the interpretations of certain passages in the Bible, it is difficult to find anything positive in passages like the following: "If a man also lie with mankind, as he lieth with a woman, both of them have committed an abomination: they shall surely be put to death; their blood shall be upon them." (Leviticus 20:13.)

Early Christians expanded this to include women when St. Paul condemned women "who did change the natural use into that which is against nature." (Romans 1:26.)

Though homosexual relations were condoned for some males in Classical Greece, the Romans, beginning around the 4th century C.E. (Common Era), prescribed the death penalty for male homosexual behavior. Though sentences were rarely carried out, these laws were later used as the foundation for both Canon Law (the law of the Catholic Church) and many civil laws throughout Europe. During the High Middle Ages, beginning in the late 12th century, a number of governments punished people accused of same-sex eroticism with banishment, mutilation, and death by fire. People discovered engaging in same-sex acts were sometimes accused of being witches or sorcerers. In fact, the present-day term

"faggot" is said by many to come from the practice of capturing gay men and tying them together as if they were a bundle (or "faggot") of wood to ignite as kindling over which a woman suspected of being a "witch" would be burned at the stake. Homosexuality was a crime punishable by death in Colonial America, and in England until 1861. Following the American Revolution, Thomas Jefferson proposed that the penalty be reduced from death to castration. In the United States today, the Supreme Court has ruled that laws which prohibit private, consensual, adult sexual acts commonly associated with homosexuality are constitutional.

Even our terminology often reflects such biases. Words like *sinister* in Latin and *gauche* in French suggest a moral evil or physical awkwardness associated with left-handedness. (Note that their opposites, *dexter* in Latin and *droit* in French, mean "skillful," "artful," "clever," "correct," or "lawful.") In fact, the English word "left" comes from an old Dutch word (*lyft*) meaning "weak" or "broken," whereas "right" derives from an Anglo-Saxon word (*riht*) meaning "straight," "erect," or "just." The word "ambidextrous" literally means "being right-handed on both sides." Phrases like "left-handed compliment" are insults to left-handed people.

Correspondingly, there exists a heterosexual bias in the language we use. There are no common words like "husband" or "wife" that refer to same-sex partners. And words like "bachelor" and "spinster" often inaccurately label gay men and lesbians regardless of their relationship status. If a gay person is involved in a media story, newspapers or the evening news commonly use phrases like "avowed homosexual" or "homosexual affair"; in contrast, no equivalent terminology is used to identify the sexuality of a heterosexual person.

All right, you might respond, but what does this have to do with the treatment of left-handed people and lesbians and gays today? Regarding left-handers, most tools and utensils and most packaging of products are designed for the ease of right-handed people. These include phonograph arms, power saws, corkscrews, sewing machines, and even gum wrappers. Left-handed pilots are not allowed to sit on the right side of the cockpit to reach the controls in the center, even though to do so would make it easier for them.

In the case of lesbians and gays, most laws and ordinances are made to protect the rights of heterosexuals, and, in most states in the United States, these protections do not extend to gays and lesbians. Homosexual relationships do not have legal status. No state recognizes lesbian and gay marriages, people can be denied employment and housing in most areas simply because they happen to be lesbian or gay, and gays and lesbians are often prevented from serving as adoptive and foster parents.

No one really knows why a little more strength in one hand over the other or preference for one sex over the other has been the basis of wide-scale persecution of a minority group of human beings.

How did such social preferences arise? Some people argue that the preference for right-handedness began with the military. If all soldiers were right-handed, they would all pass to the right of their enemy, keeping the enemy on their left side, where they held their shields, and enabling them to maintain a uniform defensive posture. This practice then extended to rules of the road, except in countries such as England, where they drive on the left side of the road. But even there, the practice was established from a right-handed preference. Knights on horseback would keep their opponents to their right with their lances when jousting.

It is possible that the emphasis on heterosexuality began with the early Hebrews, who were under pressure from competing faiths and cultures. Male homosexuality was a religious practice of the holy men of the Canaanite cults[1] and it was an accepted activity in the early years of the Greek empire. In order to insure the survival of the Jewish faith, condemnations of many of the beliefs and practices of their neighbors, including that of homosexuality, were used to emphasize the differences between the Hebrews and their competition. Also, because their numbers were constantly depleted by drought, disease, and warfare with their neighbors, the early Hebrews placed restrictions on homosexual behavior to promote an increase in their birthrate.

Nowadays, we tend to think of these practices as "natural" and to overlook their origin in history and social necessity. Thus, what began as human diversity has been translated into moral pronouncements of all sorts.

CAUSES: BIOLOGY? ENVIRONMENT?

Any difference from the norm gets more attention from researchers. This is certainly the case with left-handedness and homosexuality. Few ask what causes right-handedness or hand orientation in general, or heterosexuality or sexual orientation in general.

Some theorists believe that the cause of left-handedness is biological, citing evidence that left-handed people are dominated by the right side (hemisphere) of the brain. Some researchers, though, dispute this view, arguing that the correlation does not hold true in many cases.

There is also evidence to suggest that left-handedness may be genetic—that it is inherited—since there is a higher statistical probability that two left-handed parents will have a left-handed child. Others maintain that left-handedness is a result of an imbalance in the mother's hormones while the fetus is developing *in utero*. Some theorists have suggested that a distinct preference for one side over the other is shown as early as the second day of life.

Some social scientists argue that left-handedness is environmentally determined and may be a form of mimicking or copying of the behavior of another left-handed family member by the developing child. And some people argue that left-handedness is a choice as opposed to being biologically determined, while others maintain that hand orientation is influenced both by heredity and environment, citing possible genetic factors that are then modified by cultural influences. Still others say that left-handedness is pathological, a result of trauma to the brain or stress to the mother during pregnancy.

Likewise, some believe that the cause of homosexuality is biological, that some people are born with this orientation. Some researchers suggest that homosexuality is genetic, that there is a gay or lesbian gene. Others maintain that homosexuality is the result of an hormonal imbalance in the fetus or the pregnant woman. Some theorists have suggested that sexual orientation toward one's own sex over the other sex is determined as early as the fourth or fifth year of life.

Some researchers posit that homosexuality is environmentally determined as a result of a certain family constellations. Some, though, argue that homosexuality is simply a choice a person makes, while others maintain that sexuality is influenced both by heredity and environment, citing possible genetic factors that are then modified by cultural influences. Still others say that homosexuality is a physical defect, perhaps a result of injury to the fetus or stress to the pregnant woman.

The fact remains that no one knows for sure the causal factors in the development of handedness or sexual orientation. The evidence that does exist tends to be inconsistent and often contradictory. It is therefore likely that there is no unitary explanation that applies in every instance.

Stereotypes abound in reference to both left-handed people and people with same-sex attractions. Left-handers are often labeled, for example, as willful and stubborn. Gays and lesbians are termed immature or sexually insatiable. Often, people have the notion that all left-handers are controlled by the right side of the brain, making them more visually oriented and artistic, while being less verbal and less inclined to grasp abstract concepts than right-handed people. In addition, some people even think that lefties are at greater risk of committing criminal offenses. Likewise, some people have the notion that all gay men are overly effeminate and prey on young children, and lesbians are man-haters who secretly want to be men.

IS IT NATURAL?

No one really knows why hand preference or sexual preference occurs. In nature, four-legged creatures do not seem to show a preference for a side. And more animals seem to have developed "bilaterally," meaning that they have matching equal pairs which may be used interchangeably. There seems to be no solid evidence to support the idea of an animal preference of either the right or the left side, except for a few species of animals and plants, and sometimes a few individuals of different species. The honeysuckle is one of the few plants that twines to the left. The morning glory twines to the right, and others twist either way depending on other variables. Gorillas seem to exhibit a slight left-handed bias. But why humans prefer one side over the other remains a mystery even today. And, in the universe overall, there seems to be no common law for inanimate objects in terms of motion and favoring sides.

With respect to sexuality, many varieties of insects and reptiles, almost every species of mammal, and many types of birds engage in some form of homosexual behavior both in the wild and in captivity. Also, in some cultures, homosexual activity not only exists but is often encouraged. For example, the Azande and Mossi people of the Sudan in Africa and various tribes in New Guinea consider same-sex relations to be the norm. Adult lesbian relationships are quite common among the Azande, the Nupe, the Haussa, and the Nyakyusa people of Africa, as are adolescent lesbian activities among the Dahomeyan, the !Kung, and Australian aborigines.

Overall, there seems to be no common law for the attraction of inanimate objects, though some people have postulated that only opposites attract. Though this may hold true for positive and negative electric charges, this theory is contradicted time and again. For example, in metallurgy, various metals which vary slightly chemically combine with little difficulty to form strong and stable unions. In addition, the concept of opposites is a subjective one, and males and females actually have quite a lot in common.

Why does all this matter anyway? Well, it matters to some who believe that certain kinds of differences are innately unnatural. This attitude has led many theorists to propose strategies for changing an exhibited hand or sexual preference. They have urged parents to encourage young children to emphasize their right hands, especially in writing. In some schools, teachers have even tied the youngsters' left hands behind their backs or made them sit on their left hands to promote use of the right hand. Even noted baby doctor Benjamin Spock once urged mothers to discourage the use of the left hand in their infants. This treatment often results in emotional outbursts, speech impairments such as stuttering, reading problems, and other learning disabilities. And some "lefties" have tried to conceal their orientation, to "pass" as right-handed in order to fit in with the dominant majority group.

Homosexuals have also been coerced into changing their sexuality. "Experts" have urged parents to encourage young children to manifest behaviors and to engage in activities which are considered to be "appropriate" to their sex. Schools have traditionally withheld teaching about the positive contributions made by lesbians and gays in all areas of society. Most sex education either omits any mention of alternatives to heterosexuality or presents homosexuality only as a form of deviance to be avoided. This often results, for those who are not heterosexual, in self-hatred and isolation. Like lefties, some gays and lesbians have tried to conceal their orientation, hoping to "pass" as heterosexual in order to be accepted by the majority.

These kinds of treatments have prompted some people to question the underlying assumptions of the superiority of the majority group. Some lefties have maintained that they are the same as righties and that there are as many different kinds of left-handed people as there are right. Similarly, some lesbians and gays have maintained that they too are the same as heterosexuals and that there are as many different kinds of homosexual people as there are heterosexuals—but that certain types tend to be more visible because they fit into our expectations.

Others, however, have maintained that "being different" endows its possessors with exceptional qualities such as intuitiveness, creativity, and the like. In actuality, there seem to be some areas in which left-handed people do have an advantage. Neurologists have shown that left-handed people adjust more readily to underwater vision, giving them an advantage in swimming. In the sports of baseball and tennis there is a significantly higher percentage of left-handed players. For instance, 40 percent of the top tennis professionals are left-handed, and 32 percent of all major-league batters, 30 percent of pitchers, and 48 percent of all those who play first base are left-handed. In fact, the term "southpaw" was coined to describe left-handed pitchers. In a typical major-league ballpark they pitch from east to west with their south, or left arm (home plate being located to the west to keep the sun out of the batter's eyes).

Gay and lesbian people also may have certain advantages. For example, they are generally less bound to gender-based role expectations within a relationship, they don't constantly have to worry about birth control, and by not being fully accepted within society, they may be more tolerant of difference and so can objectively critique their cultures.   [1988]

Note

1. CANAANITE CULTS: A Jewish sect of extremely zealous anti-Romans.

Understanding the Reading

1. How are left-handedness and homosexuality analogous?
2. What historical biases have discriminated against left-handed people?
3. What historical biases have discriminated against homosexuals?
4. How does our language reflect these two biases?
5. What theories have been suggested to explain left-handedness? To explain homosexuality?
6. What stereotypes are assigned to each group?
7. Why is the "naturalness" or "unnaturalness" of left-handedness and homosexuality an important issue?
8. What are the advantages of being left-handed and of being a gay man or lesbian?

Suggestions for Responding

1. Which theory or theories mentioned by Blumenfeld and Raymond do you think best account for one's handedness or sexual orientation? What evidence can you provide to support your position?
2. Many famous people have had same-sex relationships, including Socrates, Sappho, Plato, Julius Caesar, Leonardo da Vinci, Michelangelo, Hans Christian Anderson, Walt Whitman, Gertrude Stein, Radclyffe Hall, Rock Hudson, Kate Millett, and Barney Frank. Write a report on how their sexual orientation affected their lives and achievements. ✦

60

There Is No Hierarchy of Oppressions

AUDRE LORDE

I was born Black, and a woman. I am trying to become the strongest person I can become to live the life I have been given and to help effect change toward a liveable future for this earth and for my children. As a Black, lesbian, feminist, socialist, poet, mother of two including one boy and a member of an interracial couple, I usually find myself part of some group in which the majority defines me as deviant, difficult, inferior or just plain "wrong."

From my membership in all of these groups I have learned that oppression and the intolerance of difference come in all shapes and sizes and colors and sexualities; and that among those of us who share the goals of liberation and a workable future for our children, there can be no hierarchies of oppression. I have learned that sexism (a belief in the inherent superiority of one sex over all others and thereby its right to dominance) and heterosexism (a belief in the inherent superiority of one pattern of loving over all others and thereby its right to dominance) both arise from the same source as racism—a belief in the inherent superiority of one race over all others and thereby its right to dominance.

"Oh," says a voice from the Black community, "but being Black is NORMAL!" Well, I and many Black people of my age can remember grimly the days when it didn't used to be!

I simply do not believe that one aspect of myself can possibly profit from the oppression of any other part of my identity. I know that my people cannot possibly profit from the oppression of any other group which seeks the right to peaceful existence. Rather, we diminish ourselves by denying to others what we have shed blood to obtain for our children. And those children need to learn that they do not have to become like each other in order to work together for a future they will all share.

The increasing attacks upon lesbians and gay men are only an introduction to the increasing attacks upon all Black people, for wherever oppression manifests itself in this country, Black people are potential victims. And it is a standard of right-wing cynicism to encourage members of oppressed groups to act against each other, and so long as we are divided because of our particular identities we cannot join together in effective political action.

Within the lesbian community I am Black, and within the Black community I am a lesbian. Any attack against Black people is a lesbian and gay issue, because I and thousands of other Black women are part of the lesbian community. Any attack against lesbians and gays is a Black issue, because thousands of lesbians and gay men are Black. There is no hierarchy of oppression.

It is not accidental that the Family Protection Act,[1] which is virulently anti-woman and anti-Black, is also anti-gay. As a Black person, I know who my enemies are, and when the Ku Klux Klan goes to court in Detroit to try and force the Board of Education to remove books the Klan believes "hint at homosexuality," then I know I cannot afford the luxury of fighting one form of oppression only. I cannot afford to believe that freedom from intolerance is the right of only one particular group. And I cannot afford to choose between the fronts upon which I must battle these forces of discrimination, wherever they appear to destroy me. And when they appear to destroy me, it will not be long before they appear to destroy you.   [1983]

Note

1. FAMILY PROTECTION ACT: A 1981 congressional bill repealing federal laws that promote equal rights for women, including coeducational school-related activities and protection for battered wives, and providing tax incentives for married mothers to stay at home.

Understanding the Reading

1. What is the common source of sexism, heterosexism, and racism?
2. Why does Lorde feel it is important for all people to resist all forms of intolerance?

Suggestions for Responding

1. Do you think that in today's society there is or is not a hierarchy of oppression? In other words, do you think it is worse to suffer from discrimination based on one's race, one's sex, or one's sexual orientation? Why or why not?

2. In Part V, McIntosh listed the "privileges" attributed to her solely on the basis of her skin color. Do a parallel analysis of heterosexual privilege. ✦

SUGGESTIONS FOR RESPONDING TO PART VI

1. Write a research report on the male-female pay differentials in your career-choice field. If at all possible, try to control for differences in education and experience of the two groups. Compare your findings with the more general statistics Richardson presents.

2. Investigate the federal Women's Educational Equity Agency to find out what kinds of research they conduct and the kinds of services they provide to public schools. If there is a similar agency in your state or area school district, learn about its activities and services.

3. Arrange to visit a classroom in a local school to monitor a teachers' treatment of the boys and the girls. Take notes on what you observe, and write a report on your findings, comparing them with Marklein's report. (Such a project is often of great interest to the teacher involved, so be prepared to discuss your visit with her or him. Be tactful, but honest. Most teachers are in their line of work because they genuinely care about their students and they appreciate helpful feedback.)

4. Research the initial entry of women into higher education—in women's colleges such as Mount Holyoke in 1837 and Vassar in 1865 and at the coeducational Oberlin College in 1832. How did the educational and extracurricular experiences differ in the two kinds of institutions? How were women treated differently from men at Oberlin?

5. If you are heterosexual, attend a meeting of the gay and/or lesbian group or center on your campus. Find out what their priorities are, and explore ways that you could help reduce the prejudice and discrimination they face.

6. Title IX of the Education Amendments of 1972 prohibits sex discrimination in all federally funded educational programs. It has been particularly effective in encouraging equity in athletic programs, requiring colleges and universities to provide and equally support comparable sports offerings for women and men. See if your school is in compliance. How many sports are offered for women and for men? How many women and men participate? Are budgets for the two overall programs equitable? Are scheduling and access to facilities fair to both women and men? Do the number and rank of the coaches reflect appropriate gender balance?

VII

Legal Discrimination

"WE ARE A NATION GOVERNED BY LAW, NOT BY MEN," Americans proudly proclaim. Underlying this boast is the assumption that law is actually neutral and free of the prejudices that plague mere mortals. It ignores the reality that laws are made by men. With law, as with other assertions of power, the members of the dominant group are likely to use their power to confirm and maintain the legitimacy of their privilege. The Founding Fathers of the United States were no different. They saw themselves as just and able patriarchs who could look out for the interests of their subordinates and who, in fact, had the moral responsibility to do so.

Unfortunately, oppression is always more visible to those who are oppressed than it is to the oppressor. Thus, the exclusion of women, African-Americans, Native Americans, Asian-Americans, and other people of color from the political process has resulted in a system that treats members of those groups unfairly and unjustly. The readings in Part VII provide a brief glimpse of some of the most egregious forms of legal discrimination, some of which you may already be aware of and some that may never have occurred to you.

A good example of the recognition of the problems of subordination by the subordinate person is provided by Abigail Adams. In 1776, her husband, John, was in Philadelphia, partici-

pating in the preparation of the Declaration of Independence, which declared that "all Men are created equal." She wrote asking him to "remember the ladies" and not put "unlimited power into the hands of the husbands." She threatened that women were "determined to foment a rebellion" and would not "hold [them]selves bound by any laws in which [they] have no voice or representation." John laughed. After the war, the Founding Fathers created a Constitution with no provision for legal recognition of or representation for the female half of the population. In fact, women did not gain the right to vote until the passage of the Nineteenth Amendment in 1920, and even then it took a 75-year campaign to get it.

Women were legally oppressed in many other ways that touched their daily lives more personally than political disenfranchisement. Under the system of **common law,** as explained in 1769 by Englishman William Blackstone, in marriage "the husband and the wife are one person . . . and legal existence of the woman is suspended." In effect, this meant that a woman's husband owned all property she brought into the marriage and, if she were employed, her wages belonged to him, as did her children. In the first half of the nineteenth century, women waged numerous petition campaigns and state-by-state legislative battles before they secured, through the enactment of Married Women's Property Acts, the right to own what was theirs.

In 1848, a group of women called a meeting at Seneca Falls, New York, the first women's rights convention in the world, and passed a resolution called the **Declaration of Sentiments.** Modeled on the 1776 Declaration of Independence, it identified the "history of repeated injuries and usurpations on the part of man toward woman" and specified the rights women had been denied: voting, enjoying individual legal existence, owning property, getting child custody, entering the professions and other areas of employment, and having access to education. Fundamental as these rights seem to us today, women won each one only after a long and arduous series of struggles.

In fact, instead of working for women, laws, the Constitution, and Supreme Court rulings actually blocked their way at every step. In 1868, for example, Myra Colby Bradwell was prohibited from practicing law in Illinois despite the fact that she had passed the bar examination. She took her case to the Supreme Court, which declared that "the civil law, as well as nature herself, has always recognized a wide difference in the respective spheres and destinies of man and woman" and woman's "natural and proper timidity and delicacy" make her unfit "for many of the occupations of civil life." According to this ruling, women were not protected by the Fourteenth Amendment, which declares that "No State shall make or enforce any law which shall abridge the privileges or immunities of citizens of the United States."

America's "rule by law" oppressed people of color in a different manner. Starting with the infamous **three-fifths compromise,** the original Constitution gave official recognition to and endorsement of the institution of slavery and denial of the humanity of the enslaved people. Article I, Section 2 stipulated that representation and taxation were to be apportioned according to "the whole Number of free persons, including those bound to Service for a Term of Years, and excluding Indians not taxed, three fifths of all other Persons" (people in bondage). In the famous 1857 **Dred Scott decision,** the Supreme Court further asserted that the federal government was obliged to protect the ownership rights of slave holders even in "free" states, thus effectively legalizing

slavery throughout the country even though many states had banned it.

After the Civil War, the abolition of slavery, and the enfranchisement of African-American males, southern states enacted and enforced **Black Codes,** or **Jim Crow laws,** which maintained white supremacy by requiring segregation of the races in all aspects of life. Benjamin Quarles explains some implications of Jim Crow laws in his article and shows how the 1896 Supreme Court ruling in *Plessy v. Ferguson* gave Constitutional sanction to these laws. In its decision, the Court declared that **separate but equal** treatment was constitutional. Not until the 1954 case *Brown v. Board of Education of Topeka,* discussed in the reading from the Southern Poverty Law Center, did the Court reverse itself and rule that separate cannot be equal.

The Constitution provided little protection for other people of color as well. The European settlers displaced the indigenous native populations almost from the start. Laws and government policies kept shifting the relationship between whites and Native Americans, but generally they served white interests at the expense of Native American needs and values. Initially, policies were established by treaty with what were considered sovereign Indian Nations. However, as the white population increased and moved westward, the government dealt with what had come to be considered the "Indian problem" through federal legislation imposed on these people.

Established in 1836, the Indian Bureau of the U.S. Department of the Interior was supposed to set the federal policy. In reality, however, actual control of the Indians was given to the army. The Indian Removal Act of 1830, for instance, authorized President Andrew Jackson to designate areas west of the Mississippi to be occupied only by Indians for "permanent homelands" in exchange for Indian lands in the East. The Indians, notably the Seminole in Florida and the Cherokee in Georgia, resisted relocation; despite a Supreme Court decision that forceful removal was unconstitutional, President Jackson ordered the U.S. Army to enforce the policy, resulting in the death march known as the Trail of Tears.

In 1867, Congress established the reservation system, which forced the Indian nations to settle on designated tracts of land and to rely on government agents for provisions and on farming rather than hunting for sustenance. In 1887, Congress again changed Indian policy by passing the disastrous Dawes Act abolishing tribal organizations, allotting 160 acres of land to the head of each family, and opening all left-over reservation land to white purchasers. Only in 1924 did the federal government finally grant citizenship to the Indians and a decade later, the Indian Reorganization Act stopped the land allotments, restored surplus lands to the tribes, and granted Indians self-government. However, as Michael Dorris reports, the government has continued in this century to regulate and restrict Native Americans.

Even today, Native Americans face continued encroachment on their treaty rights. Most Americans are probably only vaguely aware that such rights exist; if we are aware, we are likely to assume incorrectly that, as Scott Kerr notes in his selection, these are rights granted by the U.S. government to the tribes, not rights retained by the Indians in exchange for their earlier territories, which is actually the case. Native Americans are not alone in their loss of land rights in violation of treaty protections. Armando Valdez explains how residents in what are now the southwestern states lost much of their land to European-Americans, through legal and illegal means, when Mexico ceded the territories in which they lived to the United States at the end of the Mexican War, in 1848.

Asian-Americans suffered a different kind of legal discrimination. As early as 1867, the federal courts declared Chinese ineligible for naturalization; later this restriction was extended to Japanese. As detailed in the U.S. Commission on Civil Rights report on immigration, the policy was codified in a series of *racial exclusion orders* beginning with the 1882 Chinese Exclusion Act, which was extended in 1924 to Japanese, Koreans, Burmese, Malayans, Polynesians, Tahitians, and New Zealanders. What the Civil Rights report doesn't include, however, is *anti-alien legislation*. These laws, enacted by ten western states in the second decade of this century, prohibited Asians from purchasing real estate. But the most chilling anti-Asian laws resulted in the evacuation of 40,000 Japanese aliens and 70,000 Japanese-American citizens from the entire West Coast to inland *relocation camps* during World War II. John Hersey describes in great detail the impact relocation had on Japanese-Americans and the process by which it was created.

The last four selections address issues that might not initially seem to reflect legal discrimination. Benjamin DeMott considers how tax laws and school systems are as discriminatory as affirmative action policies. The editors of *The New Republic* examine the issue of military exclusion of women from combat roles, which many people believe to be sound policy, not discrimination. Lindsy Van Gelder analyzes how prohibitions on same-sex marriage discriminate unfairly against gay men and lesbians. Finally, Beth Brant draws parallels between earlier policies that removed Indian children from their families to attend Indian boarding schools and the contemporary court bias against homosexuals as being unfit parents, resulting in the removal of their children.

The issues raised in Part VII are complex. Many of us tend to ignore legal issues, thinking of the law as too complex and arcane for our understanding. However, as the readings show, the law can have tremendous impact on our lives in many ways. Laws determine our enjoyment of even the most basic rights, such as owning property or the custody of our children. They ensure or deprive us of access to public services, education, and employment opportunities. They determine where, how, and with whom we may live. For these reasons, all of us have a vested interest in understanding the laws that govern our country. As the saying goes, "Ignorance of the law is no excuse."

61

"Jim Crow" Law

BENJAMIN QUARLES

If the Conservatives in the South were aided by the do-nothing policy of the Republican party, they were abetted in a more positive way by the Supreme Court. This high tribunal consistently interpreted the Fourteenth and Fifteenth Amendments in such a way as to weaken their protection of the Negro.

A variety of considerations moved the Court in its handling of the war amendments and the acts of Congress relating to the Negro. Rightly concerned with maintaining a proper balance between the power of the national government and those of the states, the Court tended to restrict federal powers which it felt were excessive. Moreover, the Courts of the nineteenth century did not regard the purely human factor as crucial as the assumed first principles of the law: the letter of the law took precedence over its spirit. And, finally, the men of the Supreme Court could not escape the influence of public opinion on matters of race and color; for all their apparent Olympian aloofness, the justices were subject to the all-pervasive temper of the times.

In a series of cases, the Court set up four basic principles that worked in the interests of the southern whites. To begin with, it decreed that the war amendments applied only to actions taken by states or their agents, and not to private parties. Hence if a private individual or group kept a Negro from voting, the latter had no recourse in the federal courts. Another principle related to the emphasis on appearance rather than reality: if a state law were not plainly discriminatory, the Court would not attempt to ascertain whether it was being applied alike to black and white. A third principle was that of holding the state's police power paramount and therefore more important that the rights given to the individual under the Fourteenth Amendment. The state's police power—its inherent right to protect the public health, safety, or morals—of necessity had to be broad. At any rate, the Court obligingly found that state "Jim Crow" laws were a valid exercise of this power. Finally, the Court favored

the white southerner in its ruling that there was a substantial difference between "race discrimination" and "race distinction," the latter not being contrary to the Constitution.

The two most publicized of the Court's decisions affecting Negroes were the Civil Rights Cases of 1883 and *Plessy v. Ferguson,* thirteen years later. The former related to the Civil Rights Act of 1875, a measure which sought to secure equal rights for all citizens at hotels, theaters, and other places of public amusement. It also stipulated that no person should be disqualified to sit on juries because of race. This bill had been strongly supported by Negroes, James T. Rapier of Alabama, in a speech in Congress, having called attention to the fact that there was "not an inn between Washington and Montgomery, a distance of more than a thousand miles, that will accommodate me to a bed or meal."

The Civil Rights Act remained on the books for only eight years before the Court struck it down. Negroes were up in arms, holding a series of indignation meetings, heaping ridicule and invective on the Court, and offering it lessons in constitutional law. Anxious to soften the blow to its colored population, many nonsouthern states, numbering eighteen by 1900, passed state civil rights bills. But the national legislature was not destined to pass another such measure until seventy-five years after the Court's adverse ruling in 1883.

After the Court's action in the Civil Rights Cases, no one should have been unprepared for the *Plessy* decision. The high-water mark of the constitutional sanction of state "Jim Crow" laws, this decision in 1896 upheld a Louisiana law calling for separate railroad accommodations for white and colored passengers. Revealing something of the popular belief in white superiority, the Court ruled that laws were "powerless to eradicate racial instincts or to abolish distinctions based upon physical differences." In his dissenting opinion, Justice John Marshall Harlan pointed out that the "Constitution is color-blind, and neither knows nor tolerates classes among citizens." He ventured the opinion that "the judgment this day rendered will, in time, prove to be quite as pernicious as the decision made by this tribunal in the *Dred Scott Case.*" Prophetic words, but in 1896, Justice Harlan's was a lone voice. "*Plessy* was bad law: it was not supported by precedent," writes Barton J. Bernstein. But it remained the law of the land for over half a century.

The Court's rulings encouraged the white South to launch a final bloodless offensive to relegate the Negro to his proper political and social sphere. Regarding voting, the white South felt that the time was ripe to exclude the Negro legally, that it could adopt better and more permanent techniques of disfranchisement than those of intimidation and violence.

Mississippi was the first state to employ the new devices. In 1890 her constitution established three conditions for voting: a residence requirement, the payment of a poll tax, and the ability to read or to interpret a section of the state constitution. Five years later South Carolina adopted these same requirements, adding to them a list of crimes—such as larceny, which had a high incidence among Negroes—which disfranchised the offender. Another requirement southern states found useful was the good-character test: an applicant seeking to become a voter had to produce a responsible witness to vouch for his worth and standing. In many states, tricky registration procedures were legalized, giving local registers broad powers to thwart the Negro applicant. "White primary" laws were passed, asserting that the Democratic party was a voluntary association of citizens and could therefore limit voting as it pleased in party elections.

So sweeping and effective were these measures to disfranchise the Negro that they caught in their dragnet a number of whites, particularly the poor and illiterate. Hence some southern states hastened to pass "grandfather clauses," bestowing the franchise upon those whose grandfathers had voted. This measure added to the total number of voters, but all the persons on whom it bestowed the vote were white, since no Negro's grandfather had voted or been eligible to vote. (Such measures were declared unconstitutional in 1915.)

The white South's grim determination to keep the Negro voteless was strengthened by a half-hearted, unsuccessful attempt by Congress in 1890 to pass a "Force Bill," which would enforce the section of the Fourteenth Amendment stipulating that if a state denied the suffrage to its adult population, its representation in the House would be proportionately reduced. The South was more angered than alarmed by the "Force Bill," but it aroused her spirit of defiance and thus fanned her zeal for Negro disfranchisement.

More than any other factor, the white South's determination to totally separate the Negro from the ballot stemmed from the Populist revolt. Populism was the outgrowth of an effort by the American farmer to improve his lot. Believing that both major political parties were the creatures of business interests in the North, the aroused farmers formed a People's Party.

In the South the leaders of the agrarian crusade—Tom Watson, for example—sought Negro support, holding that the poor white man and the poor colored man were in the same economic strait jacket. Seeking cooperation across the color line, many southern Populists appealed to the remaining Negroes who could vote and tried to obtain the vote for those Negroes from whom it had been wrested. Taking alarm, many of the businessmen and planters decided to fight fire with fire. They, too, sought the Negro vote, opening their pursestrings for barbecues and entertainment, and for the services of Negro spellbinders. Where Populism was successful at the polls, as in North Carolina, Negroes were placed in such offices as alderman, magistrate, deputy sheriff, and collector of the port. But this re-emergence of the Negro voter and officeholder as a power to be reckoned with during the mid-nineties was short-lived.

Reviving the cry of "Negro domination," defeated or ambitious politicians charged that the Populists were taking the South back to the days of the carpetbagger. The Populists were stigmatized as the lineal descendants of the Loyal Leaguers. Such charges spelled doom, for in the South no political accusation was more fatal than that of being the party of the Negro. Although the reform measures championed by the Populists were directly aimed to benefit the poor white farmer, he tended to forget everything else whenever someone shouted Negro, and the white South closed ranks, determined to eliminate the agrarians. Populism's failure in the South stemmed in large measure from its attempt to bridge the color line.

To Negroes the aftermath of the Populist revolt was particularly galling. Seeking a scapegoat, many of the party's former leaders turned on the Negro, blaming him for its downfall. Moreover, the growing political influence of the poor whites and their pronounced anti-Negro bias led to the widespread adoption of "Jim Crow" legislation. To bolster their own self-esteem, the lower-class whites insisted on their social superiority to the Negro, and even such titles as "Hon." or "Mr." for the exceptional Negro were abandoned. In most southern states this sentiment received more formal expression in the laws requiring that Negroes be segregated at inns, hotels, restaurants, theaters, and on public carriers. And, as was to be expected, those who advocated "Jim Crow" measures had no trouble in convincing themselves that segregation was in the Negro's own best interests—indeed, that it upheld a status that he himself wanted.   [1969]

Understanding the Reading

1. Why did the Supreme Court's decisions weaken the Fourteenth and Fifteenth Amendments' protection of Negroes?
2. Explain the four basic principles the Supreme Court established that favored the interests of southern whites.
3. What was the Civil Rights Act of 1875?
4. Explain the *Plessy v. Ferguson* decision.
5. How did southern states stop Negroes from voting?
6. Why did the Populists court the Negro vote, and why did they then turn against Negroes?

Suggestions for Responding

1. Why do you think the Supreme Court didn't protect the rights of African-Americans at the end of the nineteenth and beginning of the twentieth century?
2. Research the *Plessy v. Ferguson* decision and explain its impact on African-Americans for the subsequent 60 years. ◆

62

Free at Last

SOUTHERN POVERTY LAW CENTER

By 1910, blacks were caught in a degrading system of total segregation throughout the South. Through "Jim Crow" laws (named after a black minstrel in a popular song), blacks were ordered to use separate restrooms, water fountains, restaurants, waiting rooms, swimming pools, libraries, and bus seats.

The United States Supreme Court gave its approval to Jim Crow segregation in the 1896 case of *Plessy v. Ferguson*. The Court said separate facilities were legal as long as they were equal. In practice, Southern states never provided equal facilities to black people—only separate ones.

Frederick Douglass[1] tried to expose the inherent contradictions in the law of the land: "So far as the colored people of the country are concerned," he said, "the Constitution is but a stupendous sham . . . fair without and foul within, keeping the promise to the eye and breaking it to the heart."

Despite Douglass' eloquent arguments, it would be generations before the nation lived up to its promises.

FIGHTING JIM CROW

Just as slaves had revolted against being someone else's property, the newly freed blacks revolted peacefully against the forces of racism. Ida B. Wells began a crusade against lynching at age 19 that inspired a national gathering of black leaders in 1893 to call for an anti-lynch law.

George Henry White, the only black U.S. congressman at the turn of the century, was a bold spokesman for equal rights. The former slave from North Carolina sponsored the first anti-lynching bill and insisted that the federal government enforce the constitutional amendments. In a speech to his fellow congressmen, White asked, "How long will you sit in your seats and hear and see the principles that underlie the foundations of this government sapped away little by little?"

One of the strongest critiques of American racism was offered by W. E. B. DuBois, a Harvard-educated sociologist. In *The Souls of Black Folk,* DuBois said American society had to be transformed if blacks were to achieve full equality.

DuBois, along with other black and white leaders, established the National Association for the Advancement of Colored People in 1910. The NAACP launched a legal campaign against racial injustice, began documenting racist violence, and published a magazine called *Crisis*. By 1940, NAACP membership reached 50,000.

As blacks were organizing for reform, white supremacists were organizing to stop them. By the time the NAACP was 10 years old, two million whites belonged to the Ku Klux Klan.[2] During the 1920s, Klansmen held high positions in government throughout the country.

In the South, Klan violence surged. Blacks moved North in record numbers, hoping to escape racial terrorism and to find better jobs. Although they faced poverty, unequal education, and discrimination in the North as well, racial restrictions there were less harsh. Blacks could even vote in Northern states. Indeed, by 1944, the black vote was a significant factor in 16 states outside the South.

BRINGING DEMOCRACY HOME

With the election of President Franklin Delano Roosevelt, black Americans finally had an ally in the White House. Black leaders were included among the president's advisers. Roosevelt's New Deal made welfare and jobs available to blacks as well as whites. A more liberal Supreme Court issued rulings against bus segregation and all-white political primaries. Black labor leader A. Philip Randolph scored a major victory when he convinced President Roosevelt to issue an Executive Order banning racial discrimination in all defense industries.

The demand for equal rights surged after World War II, when black soldiers returned from battling the racist horrors of Nazi Germany only to find they remained victims of racism at home.

Determined to bring democracy to America, blacks sought new strategies. Seeing Mahatma Gandhi[3] lead the Indian masses in peaceful demonstrations for independence, the Congress of Racial Equality decided to put the philosophy of nonviolence to work in America.

After much training and discussion, black and white members of CORE entered segregated restaurants, quietly sat down, and refused to leave until they were served. They did not raise their voices in anger or strike back if attacked. In a few Northern cities, their persistent demonstrations succeeded in integrating some restaurants.

After the Supreme Court outlawed segregation on interstate buses in 1946, CORE members set out on a "Journey of Reconciliation" to test whether the laws were being obeyed. Blacks and whites rode together on buses through the South and endured harassment without retaliating.

While the sit-ins and freedom rides of the 1940s served as models for the next generation of civil rights activists, they did not capture the broad support that was necessary to overturn segregation. The CORE victories were quiet ones, representing the determination of relatively few people.

The major battles against segregation were being fought in courtrooms and legislatures. Growing pressure from black leaders after World War II forced President Harry Truman to integrate the armed forces and to establish a civil rights commission. In 1947, that commission issued a report called *To Secure These Rights* that exposed racial injustices and called for the elimination of segregation in America.

By that time, half a million blacks belonged to the NAACP. Lawsuits brought by the NAACP had forced many school districts to improve black schools. Then, in 1950, NAACP lawyers began building the case that would force the Supreme Court to outlaw segregated schools and mark the beginning of the modern civil rights movement.

A MOVEMENT OF THE PEOPLE

Linda Brown's parents could not understand why their 7-year-old daughter should have to ride long distances each day to a rundown black school when there was a much better white school in their own neighborhood of Topeka, Kansas. Harry Briggs of Clarendon, South Carolina, was outraged that his five children had to attend schools which operated on one-fourth the amount of money given to white schools. Ethel Belton took her complaints to the Delaware Board of Education when her children were forced to ride a bus for nearly two hours each day instead of walking to their neighborhood high school in Claymont. In Farmville, Virginia, 16-year-old Barbara Johns led her fellow high school students on a strike for a better school.

All over the country, black students and parents were angered over the conditions of their schools. NAACP lawyers studied their grievances and decided that it was not enough to keep fighting for equal facilities. They wanted all schools integrated.

A team of NAACP lawyers used the Topeka, Clarendon, Claymont and Farmville examples to argue that segregation itself was unconstitutional. They lost in the lower courts, but when they took their cause to the Supreme Court, the justices ruled they were right.

On May 17, 1954, the Supreme Court unanimously ruled that segregated schools "are inherently unequal." The Court explained that even if separate schools for blacks and whites had the same physical facilities, there could be no true equality as long as segregation itself existed. To separate black children "solely because of their race," the Court wrote, "generates a feeling of inferiority as to their status in the community that may affect their hearts and minds in a way very unlikely ever to be undone."

The *Brown v. Board of Education* ruling enraged many Southern whites who did not believe blacks deserved the same education as whites and didn't want their children attending schools with black children. Southern governors announced they would not abide by the Court's ruling, and White Citizens' Councils were organized to oppose school integration. Mississippi legislators passed a law abolishing compulsory school attendance. A declaration called the Southern Manifesto was issued by 96 Southern congressmen, demanding that the Court reverse the *Brown* decision.

Despite the opposition by many whites, the *Brown* decision gave great hope to blacks. Even when the Supreme Court refused to order immediate integration (calling instead for schools to act "with all deliberate speed"), black Americans knew that times were changing. And they were eager for expanded rights in other areas as well.

WALKING FOR JUSTICE

Four days after the Supreme Court handed down the *Brown* ruling, Jo Ann Robinson wrote a letter as president of the Women's Political Council to the mayor of Montgomery, Alabama. She represented a large group of black women, she said, and was asking for fair treatment on city buses.

Blacks, who made up 75 percent of Montgomery's bus riders, were forced to enter the buses in front, pay the driver, and re-enter the

bus from the rear, where they could only sit in designated "colored" seats. If all the "white" seats were full, blacks had to give up their seats.

Women and children had been arrested for refusing to give up their seats. Others who challenged the bus drivers were slapped or beaten. Hilliard Brooks, 22, was shot dead by police in 1952 after an argument with a bus driver.

Every day, black housekeepers rode all the way home after work, jammed together in the aisles, while 10 rows of "white" seats remained empty.

Blacks could shut down the city's bus system if they wanted to, Jo Ann Robinson told the mayor. "More and more of our people are already arranging with neighbors and friends to ride to keep from being insulted and humiliated by bus drivers."

The mayor said segregation was the law and he could not change it.

On December 1, 1955, Rosa Parks was riding home from her job as a department store seamstress. The bus was full when a white man boarded. The driver stopped the bus and ordered Mrs. Parks along with three other blacks to vacate a row so the white man could sit down. Three of the blacks stood up. Rosa Parks kept her seat and was arrested.

Jo Ann Robinson and the Women's Political Council immediately began to organize a bus boycott with the support of NAACP leader E. D. Nixon. Prominent blacks hurriedly formed the Montgomery Improvement Association and selected a newcomer in town, Dr. Martin Luther King Jr., to be their leader.

On the night of December 5, a crowd of 15,000 gathered at Holt Street Church to hear the young preacher speak. "There comes a time that people get tired," King told the crowd. "We are here this evening to say to those who have mistreated us so long that we are tired—tired of being segregated and humiliated; tired of being kicked about by the brutal feet of oppression. . . . We have no alternative but to protest.

"And we are not wrong in what we are doing," he said. "If we are wrong, the Supreme Court of this nation is wrong. If we are wrong, God Almighty is wrong!"

If the bus boycott was peaceful and guided by love, King said, justice would be won. Historians in future generations, King predicted, "Will have to pause and say, 'There lived a great people—a black people—who injected new meaning and dignity into the veins of civilization.'"

For 381 days, black people did not ride the buses in Montgomery. They organized car pools and walked long distances, remaining nonviolent even when harassed and beaten by angry whites. When Dr. King's home was bombed, they only became more determined. City officials tried to outlaw the boycott, but still the buses traveled empty.

On December 21, 1956, blacks returned to the buses in triumph. The U.S. Supreme Court had outlawed bus segregation in Montgomery in response to a lawsuit brought by the boycotters with the help of the NAACP. The boycotters' victory showed the entire white South that all blacks, not just civil rights leaders, were opposed to segregation. It demonstrated that poor and middle class blacks could unite to launch a successful protest movement, overcoming both official counterattacks and racist terror. And it showed the world that nonviolent resistance could work—even in Montgomery, the capital of the Confederate States during the Civil War.

King went on to establish an organization of black clergy, called the Southern Christian Leadership Conference, that raised funds for integration campaigns throughout the South. Black Southern ministers, following the example of King in Montgomery, became the spiritual force behind the nonviolent movement. Using the lessons of Montgomery, blacks challenged bus segregation in Tallahassee and Atlanta.

But when they tried to integrate schools and other public facilities, blacks discovered the lengths to which whites would go to preserve white supremacy. A black student admitted to the University of Alabama by federal court order was promptly expelled. The State of Virginia closed all public schools in Prince Edward County to avoid integration. Some communities filled in their public swimming pools and closed their tennis courts, and others removed library seats, rather than let blacks and whites share the facilities.

Blacks who challenged segregation received little help from the federal government. President Eisenhower had no enthusiasm for the *Brown* decision, and he desperately wanted to avoid segregation disputes.

Finally, in 1957, a crisis in Little Rock, Arkansas, forced Eisenhower to act.

NINE PIONEERS IN LITTLE ROCK

On September 4, 1957, Governor Orval Faubus ordered troops to surround Central High School in Little Rock, to keep nine black teenagers from entering. Despite the *Brown* ruling which said black students had a right to attend integrated schools, Governor Faubus was determined to keep the schools segregated.

That afternoon, a federal judge ordered Faubus to let the black students attend the white school. The next day, when 15-year-old Elizabeth Eckford set out for class, she was mobbed, spit upon and cursed by angry whites. When she finally made her way to the front steps of Central High, National Guard soldiers turned her away.

An outraged federal judge again ordered the governor to let the children go to school. Faubus removed the troops but gave the black children no protection. The nine black children made it to their first class, but had to be sent home when a violent white mob gathered outside the school. Faubus said the disturbance proved the school should not be integrated.

President Eisenhower had a choice: he could either send in federal troops to protect the children or allow a governor to defy the Constitution. Saying "our personal opinions have no bearing on the matter of enforcement," the president ordered in troops. For the rest of the school year, U.S. soldiers walked alongside the Little Rock nine as they went from class to class.

The next year, Governor Faubus shut down all the public schools rather than integrate them. A year later, the U.S. Supreme Court ruled that "evasive schemes" could not be used to avoid integration, and the Little Rock schools were finally opened to black and white students.

Although the Little Rock case did not end the long battle for school integration, it proved the federal government would not tolerate brazen defiance of federal law by state officials. It also served as an example for President John F. Kennedy who in 1962 ordered federal troops to protect James Meredith as he became the first black student to attend the University of Mississippi.

[1989]

Notes

1. FREDERICK DOUGLASS: An escaped slave who became a leading abolitionist.

2. KU KLUX KLAN: A terroristic white supremacist organization founded after the Civil War.
3. MAHATMA GANDHI: A Hindu nationalist and spiritual leader who led the "passive resistance" movement to get the British out of India.

Understanding the Reading

1. What were Jim Crow laws?
2. How did the newly freed blacks respond to them?
3. How did Franklin Roosevelt's presidency benefit black Americans?
4. What gains did CORE achieve?
5. Explain the Supreme Court ruling in *Brown v. Board of Education*.
6. What made the Montgomery bus boycott effective?
7. What tactics did whites employ to avoid school desegregation?

Suggestions for Responding

1. Imagine that you were an African-American in the south in the first half of this century. Choose one example of Jim Crow segregation (separate schools, restrooms, waiting rooms, drinking fountains; prohibitions on voting; having to ride in the back of the bus) and describe your experience. What would you realistically do in such circumstances?
2. Learn more details about one specific example of southern white resistance to school integration, and write a brief report on it. ✦

63

Native Americans v. the U.S. Government

MICHAEL DORRIS

The turn of the twentieth century was an unhappy time for the Native people of America. Their total population was at its lowest ebb, the vast majority of their land had been taken away, their religions were outlawed, their children removed from home and incarcerated in hostile institutions where it was deemed a crime to so much as speak in one's own language. In 1900 few Native Americans were citizens and as a group they constituted the poorest, unhealthiest, and least likely to survive—much less succeed — population in all of the United States. And yet they not only survived, but they survived as a culturally intact group of peoples; against all odds, tribes maintained their languages and wisdom, guarded their art and music and literature, and for the most part, chose to continue to be Indians rather than assimilate and disappear.

The United States government, however, continued to advocate a melting-pot policy, and in 1924 Congress passed the Curtis Act, which conferred American citizenship on all native-born Indians. In many areas, such a change in status did not mean automatic access to the ballot box, however, and Native "citizens" remained disenfranchised "persons under guardianship" in Arizona and New Mexico until 1948.

Nevertheless, citizenship did, in the minds of some congressmen and others, abrogate the rights to special status which were guaranteed through treaty. Questions like "How can we have treaties with our own citizens?" (with its correlative answer: "We can't, therefore throw out the treaties and open up the land!!") should have been asked and answered before any such act was passed. *If* it had been made clear that United States citizenship meant abandonment of Native American identity, and *if* the opinion of Native American people had been solicited, it is improbable that even a significant minority of Indian people would have opted for it in 1924.

In effect, the Curtis Act was tantamount to the American government deciding to celebrate the Bicentennial in 1976 by unilaterally declaring all inhabitants of the Western Hemisphere "American citizens" and then immediately forcing any (former) Brazilian, Canadian, or Venezuelan engaging in international trade to comply with United States tariff restrictions and oil prices. Such an expanded Monroe Doctrine precludes all argument. The American experiment with instant naturalization is not unique: The Portuguese tried it in Angola, the Belgians in Zaire, and the French in Algeria—but somehow most Africans apparently never *felt* like Europeans. Most Native Americans didn't either, but by the twentieth century they lacked the population or resources to successfully dispute the denial of their sovereignty.

Four years later, a blue-ribbon congressional committee chaired by Lewis Meriam issued a report on conditions in Indian country. Its aim was to assess the effects of the Dawes[1] and Curtis acts and to inform the government of the progress these pieces of legislation had made possible for Native American people. The situation on reservations in 1928, however, yielded little in the way of optimistic forecast. Since 1887 conditions had universally worsened: The educational level was in most cases lower, the poverty greater, the death rate higher (and for younger people) than at any time previous to the enactment of the "benevolent" policies. Federal enforcement of the misguided and totally unjust severalty laws[2] was, in effect, cultural genocide.

In 1934 President Roosevelt appointed the anthropologist John Collier as Commissioner of Indian Affairs. Unlike too many of his predecessors in office, Collier actually knew something of at least one Native society (Pueblo) and had long opposed the Allotment policy[3] both for its inhumanity and its naiveté. His major achievement was to assist in the development and passage of the Indian Reorganization Act (the Wheeler-Howard Act), a policy which sought to undo most of the provisions of the Dawes Act and begin to remedy the disasters recounted in the Meriam Report of 1928.

Almost half a century, however, was a long time, and it was beyond realistic possibility that either the land base or the cultural, educational, and economic health of Native American societies could be restored as they were in 1880.

The Wheeler-Howard Act aimed to revive the traditional "bilateral, contractual relationship between the government and the tribes." Commissioner Collier emphasized the Native American right to a kind of self-determination and banned any further allotment of tribal land. The Indian Reorganization Act further authorized severely limited appropriations to purchase new holdings and reclaim certain lost property; it also established a federal loan policy for Native groups and reaffirmed the concept of self-government on reservations.

Many tribes opposed this legislation, however, on the basis of the restrictions and regulations it placed on the participating tribes. The act,

for instance, prohibited any individual transfer of tribal land without governmental approval, and it required that all tribal governments conform to a single political system based on majority rule. No tribe was eligible for a single benefit of the act unless it agreed to it *in toto,* and therefore its acceptance necessarily became widespread.

The period following the Collier administration and extending into the early 1950's was one in which many Americans seemed to forget about Indians and assumed that *at last* "they" had finally vanished as predicted. The national interest was focused on World War II and the Korean War, and domestic treaties seemed a thing of the far-distant past.

After one of these "dormant cycles," the public and its government usually seem particularly piqued and frustrated to discover that Native Americans are still very much alive and intact. Once again in the 1950's, as in the 1880's, the presumptuous and thoroughly invalid assumption was made that if Indians had not chosen to disappear into the melting pot, something sinister was to blame. It seems never to have occurred to those in power that Crows or Yakimas, for instance, simply preferred being Crows or Yakimas!

As usual, the federal government, liberal "friends of the Indian," and rural land developers concluded that special status, and the reservation system in particular, were somehow retarding Native assimilation, and therefore it was decided, once again, to breach all legal precepts of international and United States law and unilaterally break treaty agreements. It was further concluded that if some Native Americans insisted that they didn't want to change their relationship with the government, they simply didn't know what was good for them. The rivers were still running, the grass was still growing, but the promises made by the American government and written to apply in perpetuity could not exist for even a century without twice being violated.

A committee was therefore appointed to divide, like Gaul,[4] all reservations into three parts: the "prosperous," the "marginal," and the "poor." Even with this license, only a handful of tribes could be found to fit, by any stretch of the imagination, into the first category, and these were marked for quick termination. The implications of this policy are clear: Apparently Congress regarded reservations as transitionary steps between "primitive" and "modern" society. As soon as a group achieved a margin of success (according to the ethnocentric standards of American culture), a reservation ceased to have a rationale for existence. This self-serving attitude totally ignores both the political circumstances which brought about the reservation system in the first place (e.g., aboriginal right of title), and the legal treaties and sanctions which supposedly protected it.

Two of the most economically self-sustaining tribes, the Klamath in Oregon and the Menominee in Wisconsin, were located in timberland areas and operated logging industries. The government exerted tremendous pressure, employing levers of doubtful legal and ethical practice, and the manipulation of misunderstanding, to force these tribes to submit to termination. Whether this consent was ever actually granted in either case is a debatable point, but it is clear that neither group, had it sufficiently understood the policy, would have agreed.

Termination meant the absolute cessation, in exchange for a monetary settlement, of any special treaty arrangements or status which existed between the tribe and its members and the United States government. Upon termination, the Menominees would be expected, in legal effect, to cease being Indians and to somehow turn themselves into Wisconsonians overnight. On a date set by the government, the dependent, sovereign Menominee Nation, hundreds of years old, would become simply another county within the state.

Historical retrospect clearly shows that in all cases the termination policy was even more ill-conceived and socially disruptive than the Allotment policy had been before it—and just as illegal. The net effects of termination were the loss of large amounts of valuable land by the tribes involved, plus an enormous psychological blow to thousands of Indian people. The fallacy of the policy was patently obvious so quickly that it was suspended shortly after implementation, sparing other tribes similar losses. To date, one of the victimized tribes, the Menominee, has, through persistent and valiant efforts of a group of its members, managed to be reestablished as a reservation in 1973. But as a direct result of termination, the new Menominee lands were much smaller and poorer than the reservation had been before 1953.

Subsequent government policies aimed at assimilating the Native American were more subtle. Among these were the urban relocation programs, often hastily conceived and poorly managed attempts to induce Native Americans to migrate to cities. A substantial percentage of the participants in these programs eventually returned, frustrated and cynical, to their reservations.   [1975]

Notes

1. DAWES ACT: A federal law that abolished tribal organizations and allotted 160 acres to the head of each family.
2. SEVERALTY LAWS: Laws mandating that land must be held by individuals rather than in common by the whole group.
3. ALLOTMENT POLICY: The distribution of reservation land under the Dawes Act and the opening of undistributed land to whites.
4. GAUL: An ancient name for what is now France and Belgium. Julius Caesar opened his history with the statement, "All Gaul is divided into three parts."

Understanding the Reading

1. What effect did the Curtis Act have on Native Americans?
2. What were conditions like on reservations in 1928?
3. What were the benefits and restrictions of the Indian Reorganization Act?
4. What was "termination," and what were its effects?

Suggestions for Responding

1. Dorris presents the analogy of the U.S. government unilaterally declaring all inhabitants of the Western Hemisphere to be American citizens. Suppose this actually happened, and write about how you would respond personally if you were a citizen of one of the annexed countries.
2. Research one of the governmental policies Dorris mentions, and explain what it was supposed to do and what it actually did. ◆

64

The New Indian Wars

Scott Kerr

In northern Wisconsin and a number of other areas around the country, confrontations—possibly violent confrontations—are expected to erupt once again this spring over the rights conferred on Native Americans by treaties negotiated long ago with the Government of the United States.

In constitutional terms, treaties are "the supreme law of the land." In practical terms, the 371 treaties entered into over the last couple of centuries with Indian nations are increasingly a matter of bitter contention between Native Americans and their neighbors, local and state authorities, and business interests eager to exploit the land on which Indians exercise their treaty rights.

For the tribes involved in these disputes, the treaty rights are all they have to show for the bargains they concluded with a Government that was able to back up its demands with overpowering military might. The Native Americans gave up their lands; now, they are pressed to yield their treaty rights as well.

The Lake Superior Chippewa, for example, ceded land under treaties of 1836, 1837, 1842, and 1854, but retained the right to harvest resources on that land. Indian rights to hunt, fish, and gather in the ceded territory were not "granted" by the U.S. Government; they were *retained* by the tribes. And the validity of those rights has recently been affirmed by Federal court decisions.

But when the Indians attempt this spring to exercise their rights by spearfishing on northern Wisconsin lakes, they are likely to be met—as they have been in recent years—by vocal and sometimes violent anti-treaty protesters. Save a Walleye. Spear a Pregnant Squaw was a common slogan in northern Wisconsin last spring. Anti-Indian protesters carried spears topped with fake Indian heads to illustrate their animosity.

Wisconsin's state government has responded to the conflict, which is widely perceived as a threat to the peace *and* to Wisconsin's tourist industry, by insisting that the solution lies in buying out or leasing the Indians' treaty rights in exchange for cash or government services. There are no other options, say Governor Tommy Thompson and Attorney General Don Hanaway.

"It is a logic which defies logic," says Walter Bresette, a Chippewa who has been outspoken in support of treaty rights. "Indians win rights, whites beat up Indians; therefore, the only solution is for the Indian to *sell* rights. What ever happened to the enforcement of laws?"

Last year, the state of Wisconsin offered an economic and developmental aid package worth more than $50 million to the northern tribes in exchange for suspension of their treaty rights. Some tribes rejected the offer, and others announced they had no intention of selling their rights at any price. Now the state government says it will make no more attempts at settlement. Instead, officials hope to persuade the Federal Government to "modernize" the treaties—presumably by act of Congress, though such revision would violate the constitutional status of the treaties.

"We need to forge a Federal policy that is comprehensive and brings the treaties and the way the Federal Government deals with the tribes into the Twentieth Century," says Mark Rogacki, executive director of the Wisconsin Counties Association, who recently attempted to organize a "national coalition of state associations for the purpose of modernizing Indian treaties."

To that end, county and state officials from thirteen states, constituted as a Conference on Federal Indian Policy, met last January in Salt Lake City. They brought along lists of "Indian problems" they wanted solved, including questions about jurisdiction and taxation as well as concerns over tribal rights to minerals, water, timber, game, and fish.

The officials met behind closed doors and under armed guard. Native Americans who attempted to attend were refused entry. One state delegation walked out, claiming to have been misinformed about the meeting's purposes. But the agenda was clearly anti-treaty. Said organizer Rogacki, "The exercise of [treaty] rights is not in tune with contemporary society."

"Whose contemporary society?" counters James Yellowbank of the Indian Treaty Rights

Committee in Chicago, who has combated anti-Indian rhetoric for the last twenty years. "Modernization," Yellowbank adds, "is just another word for abrogation" of the treaties.

Still, there is an impression among many whites that treaty rights are special privileges, and that claims of tribal sovereignty are inconsistent with constitutional concepts of due process and equal rights. Such thinking is assiduously cultivated by a growing anti-Indian network across the country, which organizes protests, disseminates misleading or patently false information, solicits contributions from a variety of sources, and lobbies as the voice of "grass-roots concerned citizens."

"The plain fact is they see elimination of the treaties as a way of solving problems that are largely economic, jurisdictional, and racial," says Rudy Ryser, chairman of the Center for World Indigenous Studies in Seattle. Ryser has studied the anti-Indian movement for fifteen years and has compiled some disconcerting evidence.

"It's apparent that the extreme right-wing organizational activities are beginning to merge with some of the anti-Indian group activities," Ryser says. "Extreme right-wingers, who might be identified with Christian Identity (white supremacist), Christian Patriots, the Populist Party, or the neo-Nazi stuff, are very interested in getting in with the people who are hurting—economically, socially, politically—and gaining access to recruits to their particular cause. They've begun to look to those who hurt on or near Indian reservations as potential allies to whom they can offer assistance.

"The Christian Patriot group sees itself as eventually finding a homeland for the white man. What better place to look for it than on Indian reservations where things are rather confused already." Ryser notes that far-right neo-Nazi groups have located near or on Indian reservations in Idaho, Washington, Michigan, Minnesota, Alaska, Wisconsin, Montana, and South Dakota. He predicts a continuing convergence of the Far Right and anti-Indian movements "in ways that might manifest themselves in violent activities."

In Wisconsin, while Indians spearfish, protesters hurl rocks and racial slurs. Two men were charged with criminal conspiracy to interfere with Chippewa civil rights by building and exploding a pipe bomb near spearfishers last spring. And the tension is mounting rather than subsiding. The bulletin board at a bowling alley in the northern Wisconsin town of Eagle River cautions against shooting Indians: "That will only get more sympathy for them, but if you put holes in their boats they can't spear and holes in their tires they can't get to the lakes. Stop being wimps. Yelling or simply watching will not intimidate anyone. . . . Force confrontation and overreactions, escalate. . . . Nothing will change until you escalate."

Though the Far Right is increasingly funding the anti-Indian network, Lew Gurwitz, a veteran Indian-rights attorney, asserts that the anti-treaty forces are but pawns in the larger game. "I think the ultimate manipulation is being done by the energy development companies," says Gurwitz. "They and their agents within the states are fanning the flames of racism to try to defeat the treaties."

The Citizens Equal Rights Alliance (CERA) is a national umbrella anti-Indian organization incorporating such groups as Washington state's and Wisconsin's Stop Treaty Abuse. Fred Hatch, a former Bureau of Indian Affairs lawyer who is now general counsel for Stop Treaty Abuse (STA) and its delegate to CERA, describes CERA as "a political lobby group of ranchers, doctors, lawyers, businessmen, and large corporations like Burlington Northern and Exxon, everybody's friend. . . . All of these companies are having problems with the Federal Indian policy."

James Klauser, a powerful former lobbyist whose clients included Exxon, Union Carbide, and FMC Corporation, has led state efforts to get tribes to trade treaty rights for cash and services. Now the right-hand man to Governor Thompson of Wisconsin, Klauser dismisses questions regarding his ongoing public and private meetings with anti-Indian groups.

Stop Treaty Abuse, which claims 3,000 members, has stated publicly that it intends "to pursue a course of disruption until the various forms of government protect our constitutional rights and state resources for the equal utilization of all citizens." The reference to resources is significant: Exxon holds mineral rights to $6 billion worth of zinc and copper lying on and adjacent to a Wisconsin Indian reservation, not far from STA's most heated anti-Indian demonstrations. Indian and environmental leaders point out that Exxon has put mining plans on hold mainly because of Indian opposition to likely environmental degradation.

"The only thing standing in the way of all-out, mindless corporate development in northern Wisconsin is the Indian treaties," says Lew Gurwitz.

Opposition to treaty rights has not been confined to fringe groups; Wisconsin law-enforcement officials have also taken a stand on the spearing issue. "We're not anti-Indian, we're anti-spearfishing," says Jim Williquette, sheriff of Vilas County. After the Lac du Flambeau band of the Chippewa nation voted down the state's spear-fishing rights buy-out, Williquette told a reporter, "Now we're facing an all-out war."

Governor Thompson and his top aides have repeatedly complained about the high costs of law enforcement to protect the civil liberties of the Chippewas and have cited the figures in support of their money-for-rights deals. At the same time, they have used the violence of anti-treaty activists as a bargaining point with the Indians. The road to peace, they have suggested, must be paved with the curtailed rights of the Chippewa.

"Indians are not talking about taking away anyone else's rights, they are seeking to exercise their own—unmolested," says activist Walter Bresette. "What is the practical difference whether someone is anti-treaty because he's a bigot, or because he wants to pollute the environment for profit, or because he wants to tinker with established Federal law just for fun? What is the difference to the Indian?"

An increasingly vocal and visionary movement has begun advocating co-management of the resources in question. Under co-management, tribal leaders and state government would have equal say on land-use and management decisions. Although co-management has worked in other states with treaty conflicts, Wisconsin Governor Thompson has ruled it out, insisting that "co-management is not even constitutionally possible."

"I have no idea what he's talking about—constitutionally," counters State Representative Frank Boyle. "Co-management is working other places; the model is set."

In the state of Washington, Boyle notes, "they fought in court for ten years, they beat each other up, they shot at each other, they hated each other. The entire Washington DNR [Department of Natural Resources] was tied up in court for ten years, during which the Indians never lost a case. And the resources were going to hell. There was no protection because they were all in court, fighting the Indians."

Since the state of Washington accepted co-management, however, $350 million in Federal grant money has been allocated to aid the fisheries, other resources, and co-management itself.

"Treaty rights are the greatest single protection for the environment in northern Wisconsin," says Rick Whaley of the Wisconsin Greens. Al Gedicks of the Wisconsin Resource Protection Society adds that "the defense of treaty rights and the defense of the environment have become inseparable."

Walt Bresette hopes the Chippewas' territory—roughly the northern third of Wisconsin—could be declared a "toxic-free zone" by the state and the tribes. Bresette envisions "a massive ten-year clean-up plan, with the goal of making the water, land, and air safe for humans, animals, and plants" and passing stringent laws preventing degradation below clean-up standards. If contamination continued, "the two jurisdictions would jointly file suit, using the power of the treaties as well as that of the state."

The ceded territory could evolve into a unique economic zone, based on cooperation between the tribes and the state, "for the development of a diversified and environmentally sound small-business economy," Bresette says.

James Yellowbank says that to many Indians, the fight to save the treaties is fundamentally a fight between the Great Spirit and what the Winnebago call the Imposter Spirit, which "takes without giving back."

"This is not some cute New Age notion," says Yellowbank. "It's been around as long as we have. Just how long can we take, take, take, without destroying ourselves, anyway?"   [1990]

Understanding the Reading

1. What is the legal status of Native American treaties?

2. What solution to the spearfishing controversy has the Wisconsin state government proposed?
3. What was the purpose of the Conference on Federal Indian Policy?
4. How do the anti-Indian protesters view Indian treaty rights?
5. What tactics do the Far Right groups advocate?
6. What is the purpose of the Citizens Equal Rights Alliance?
7. What is co-management?
8. How are treaty rights related to environmental concerns?

Suggestions for Responding

1. Decide which side of the treaty-rights controversy you would take if you were a Wisconsin resident. Write a letter to the editor to your local newspaper stating and justifying your position.
2. If you were a professional arbiter, how would you resolve the dispute between the Chippewa and the Wisconsin state government? Explain your reasoning. ✦

65

Brown Power

ARMANDO VALDEZ

Before considering the basis of the current conflict[1] in New Mexico, the ethnic designation for the Hispanic population of New Mexico must be clarified. Though the term "Spanish-American" is commonly used in New Mexico to denote persons of Hispanic heritage, the ethnic designation "Mexican-American" is more appropriate. It must be acknowledged that some residents of relatively isolated New Mexican villages are the direct descendants of Spanish colonists. However, to designate such persons as Spanish, either culturally or linguistically, is to negate the influences of Mexican and Indian elements which blended over the centuries with Spanish elements so that today a uniquely heterogeneous culture totally distinct from Spanish culture prevails in these regions. In essence, the adoption of the term, Spanish-American, gained prominence in New Mexico during the 1920's as a reaction to the great influx of Mexican immigrants into the United States during that decade. The "earlier" residents sought to dissociate themselves from the unskilled, uneducated "aliens." A similar identity transformation occurred in Texas during the same period and the term "Latin-American" made its debut. This phenomenon of self-reclassification is not without parallels in the history of European immigration to the United States, especially among the northern and western European immigrants of the late nineteenth century. An implicit factor in this phenomenon of self-reclassification is a dichotomy between the cultured (i.e. established, wealthy) and the non-cultured (i.e. foreign, poor). Therefore, to designate the Spanish-surname, Spanish-speaking population of New Mexico as "Spanish-American" is not only grossly contradictory to historical fact but is a vacuous ethnic taxonomy.

INSURRECTION

The question of an impending armed insurrection in New Mexico may best be examined by considering the current conflict in its historical context. Since insurrection is the product of a long period of ferment, [a] historical perspective is imperative if causation is to be established.

La Alianza's struggle stems from an effort to regain lands annexed to the United States by the Treaty of Guadalupe-Hidalgo[2] in 1848. This treaty guarantees the protection of the civil and property rights of the residents of the annexed territories. However, it is [a] historical fact that these rights—though guaranteed by treaty—were never meant to be taken seriously by the United States government. In fact, the Treaty of Guadalupe-Hidalgo was a treaty of conquest dictated by the United States upon a defeated Mexican government. The Mexican residents in annexed territories were accorded the treatment of a conquered people. Moreover, the annexed territories (greater in area than Germany and France combined, and representing about one-half of the territory then held by Mexico) were dealt with as spoils of war. These formerly Mexican, American citizens have been assigned the role of a subordinate citizen since their conquest.

The conduct of General Stephen W. Kearny, commander of the United States military expedition through New Mexico and eventually California, attests to the fact that the newly absorbed American citizens were considered and correspondingly treated as a conquered people. Kearny was the first United States official to declare to the people of New Mexico that their rights "of person and property" would be held inviolable. Simultaneously, Kearny was under orders to declare the residents of this territory citizens of the United States and to *demand their allegiance*. Kearny's sanguine chauvinism is forcefully conveyed by Phillip St. George Cooke in his narrative, *The Conquest of New Mexico and California,* in the following description of addresses by Kearny to the villagers of Tecolote and San Miguel, New Mexico, respectively:

. . . the general and suit[3] were conducted by the alcalde[4] to his house and there, through his interpreter, General Kearny, addressed him and the village notables, informing them of the annexation and its great advantages to them. *He required the alcalde to take the oath of allegiance.*

. . . the general and his staff, the alcalde and a priest, and a few others ascended a flat housetop overlooking the plaza; the general, through his interpreter, delivered his address with the advantage of its success at Tecolote, but whether the priest's influence, the crowd's, or his own peculiar firmness, the alcalde positively refused to take the oath. The general then enlarged upon the perfect freedom of religion under our government, mentioning that his chief of staff, then present, was a Roman Catholic. All persuasion failed, and at last *the old man was forced to go through the form and semblance of swearing allegiance.*

This attitude displayed by Kearny is merely an example of the subsequent attitudes and behavior of *gringos*[5] toward the incipient wards of the United States—Mexican-Americans. It established a precedence of Anglo domination, both political and cultural. This arrogance of the conquering nation has resulted in the loss to Mexican-Americans of over two million acres of

public land and seventeen hundred thousand acres of communal lands in New Mexico since 1854. Eighteen hundred thousand acres of these lands are now in the possession of the United States federal government. These and other equally significant land losses have occurred in violation of Articles VIII and IX of the Treaty of Guadalupe-Hidalgo which guarantees the security of "property of every kind to Mexicans in the acquired territory." Only six years after the Treaty of Guadalupe-Hidalgo, Congress enacted a law reserving congressional prerogative to pass upon private land claims in New Mexico by direct legislative enactment, an action diametrically opposed to the treaty. Provisions for adverse proceedings or for surveying the boundaries of tracts were completely excluded from this act. Since the [n]otion of Manifest Destiny characterized the United States during the mid-nineteenth century, it should come as no surprise that Congress enacted such a law. During this period Americans were convinced that they were the legitimate heirs of *all* North America and viewed their struggle with Mexico as a struggle for their heritage; their manifest destiny was to rule North America from Atlantic to Pacific. The armies of Fremont, Taylor, and Kearny realized this "American Dream."

ANGLO[6] LAW

A major factor in the transfer of land from Mexican to Anglo propriety was the change in legal jurisdiction. The manner in which the Anglo legal system was introduced into this territory and its impact on the indigenous population is historically paralleled only by the introduction of Christianity into this same region several centuries earlier. Both of these doctrines were equally unsolicited and equally forced upon their unsuspecting beneficiaries by equally fervent "missionaries" of a conquering political order. Both doctrines were employed as instruments for exploiting and dominating their conquered subjects.

Within the Mexican legal system, land ownership was based primarily upon traditional and recognized rights of occupancy. Grant lands were immune from taxation since the financial needs of the Mexican and, formerly, Spanish governments were met by taxes upon harvests and livestock increases. Accordingly, the concept of property taxation was totally remote and a system of land survey was unknown to the Mexican landowner. Land boundaries were vague and imprecise, and land titles were generally unregistered. Conversely, the Anglo concept of property taxation as the economic base of county government demanded an authoritative system of land survey and concomitant registration of land titles. Therefore, the mandatory transposition of largely antithetical legal systems experienced by the Mexican-American residents of the acquired territory placed their land ownership in a very precarious position. Under the jurisdiction of the Anglo legal system, property owned by Mexican-Americans became subject to property taxes, precise delineation of boundaries, and registration of land titles. Herein lies a major causal factor in the demise of Mexican-American land ownership.

Avaricious Anglos employed their legal system as an instrument of intimidation, fraud, and deceit. Obscure and unregistered land titles held by Mexican-Americans were challenged in Anglo courts by lawyers, surveyors, land recorders, as well as by no lesser personages than governors, state supreme court justices, state and national politicians. Anglo lawyers, particularly, saw the vulnerability of Mexican-American land ownership and proceeded with great enterprise (i.e. Yankee ingenuity) to defraud Mexican-Americans of their land. One very common practice, for example, involved legal partners jointly conspiring to obtain these lands. One legal partner would file suit against an unregistered parcel of land while his associate would offer his services for the defense of the land title, *agreeing to accept land as retribution for his services.* Regardless of the outcome of the case, both lawyers would win; the Mexican-American landowner would be the sole loser. Indicating the prevalence of this fraudulent practice is the fact that *one out of every ten* Anglos in New Mexico in the 1880's was a lawyer.

The policies of the federal government further contributed to the land losses of Mexican-Americans in New Mexico resulting from unregistered and obscure land titles. The Homestead Laws opened up *over one million acres* of these lands to Anglo settlers.

ANGLO TAXES

Prior to 1848, property taxes were totally absent from the socio-political system of the annexed territory. However, the advent of Anglo law was accompanied by the practice of land taxation. Accordingly, land taxation provided yet another source of facile land gain for Anglos. Tax-delinquent properties multiplied during the period immediately succeeding the Treaty of Guadalupe-Hidalgo. The extent of the property losses that ensued is exemplified by the subsequent demise of the Anton Chico grant near El Cerrito, New Mexico. By 1860, the property had become chronically tax delinquent and large parcels of the two hundred seventy thousand acres were sold to meet the taxes levied. In 1926, the New Mexico legislature passed a statute declaring that lands delinquent in taxes for three years would be sold for the cost of the delinquent taxes. A decade later, in 1939, only eighty-five thousand of the original two hundred seventy thousand acres remained under Mexican-American ownership. Moreover, twenty-two thousand acres of these remaining lands were under lease.

The most vicious form of deceit employed by Anglos was the practice of differential tax assessments. In an effort to dispossess Mexican-Americans of their property, tax assessments levied against them were greater than those levied against Anglos. Once the property was transferred to Anglo ownership, the tax assessment was reduced. In *North from Mexico,* Carey McWilliams cites incidences in which taxes of $1.50 per acre levied against grazing lands owned by Mexican-Americans were reduced to thirty and forty cents per acre when transferred to Anglo ownership.

Federal land reclamation projects, irrigation projects, and the establishment of forest reserves all directly contributed to the losses of vast expanses of Mexican-American properties. Though the landowners received retribution for their confiscated property, the severity of the losses assumed subtle forms. The enormous amount of land required for these projects greatly increased the competition for agri-land.[7] Powerful land corporations (generally Anglo-owned) seeking to expand their operations, incessantly strove to force out smaller landowners, frequently Mexican-Americans, by some strange coincidence.

Moreover, increased conservation and water-use costs heightened the pressures directed against these smaller landowners, who frequently were forced to sell at a great financial loss. Land losses due to these factors still occur today in the Albuquerque region and in the Mesilla Valley in the vicinity of Las Cruces, New Mexico.

The terms of the Treaty of Guadalupe-Hidalgo, ratified by Mexico and the United States on May 30, 1848, have been flagrantly violated by the United States. Anglo law served not to protect the rights of the Mexican-Americans but conversely served to intimidate and exploit them. The historical accounts of the duplicity and intimidation employed to defraud Mexican-Americans of their land endure as testimony of Anglo disregard for the property rights of the Mexicans residing within the territory annexed to the United States, particularly in New Mexico. Consequently, Mexican-Americans in New Mexico were from the onset disenfranchised of their rights and concomitant opportunities. Today the situation has not changed; Mexican-Americans largely occupy a subordinate position as citizens of New Mexico and are, in every sense of the word, a minority group.   [1967]

Notes

1. CURRENT CONFLICT: In the mid-1960s, New Mexico officials mobilized the National Guard in response to land protests by a group of Mexican-Americans, La Alianza Federal de Mercedes.
2. THE TREATY OF GUADALUPE-HIDALGO: The treaty ending the Mexican War, ceding what are now Texas, California, Nevada, and Utah, most of Arizona, New Mexico, and Colorado, and part of Wyoming to the United States.
3. SUIT: Entourage.
4. ALCALDE: Mayor or justice of the peace.
5. *GRINGOS:* A disparaging term used in Mexico and elsewhere in Latin America for North Americans.
6. ANGLO: British-American.
7. AGRI-LAND: Land that can be cultivated.

Understanding the Reading

1. Explain the distinctions Valdez makes between Spanish-American and Mexican-American.

2. How did the United States treat the newly acquired Mexican-American citizens?
3. Explain the differences between American and Mexican land ownership and how these differences were used to defraud the new Mexican-Americans out of their land.
4. How did land taxation serve to cheat Mexican-Americans?

Suggestions for Responding

1. What kind of protections should the U.S. government have provided the new citizens when it acquired the southwestern territory?
2. Compare the appropriation of the land of the Mexican-Americans with the contemporary treaty problems of the Wisconsin Chippewa. ◆

66

Historical Discrimination in the Immigration Laws

U.S. COMMISSION ON CIVIL RIGHTS

THE EARLY YEARS

During the formative years of this country's growth, immigration was encouraged with little restraint. Any restrictions on immigration in the 1700s were the result of selection standards established by each colonial settlement. The only Federal regulation of immigration in this period lasted only 2 years and came from the Alien Act of 1798, which gave the President the authority to expel aliens who posed a threat to national security.

Immigrants from northern and western Europe began to trickle into the country as a result of the faltering economic conditions within their own countries. In Germany, unfavorable economic prospects in industry and trade, combined with political unrest, drove many of its nationals to seek opportunities to ply their trades here. In Ireland, the problems of the economy, compounded by several successive potato crop failures in the 1840s, sent thousands of Irish to seaports where ships bound for the United States were docked. For other European nationals, the emigration from their native countries received impetus not only from adverse economic conditions at home but also from favorable stories of free land and good wages in America.

THE NATIVIST MOVEMENTS

As a result of the large numbers of Catholics who emigrated from Europe, a nativist movement began in the 1830s. It advocated immigration restriction to prevent further arrivals of Catholics into this country. Anti-Catholicism was a very popular theme, and many Catholics and Catholic institutions suffered violent attacks from nativist sympathizers. The movement, however, did not gain great political strength and its goal of curbing immigration did not materialize.

Immigrants in the mid-19th century did not come only from northern and western Europe. In China, political unrest and the decline in agricultural productivity spawned the immigration of Chinese to American shores. The numbers of Chinese immigrants steadily increased after the so-called Opium War, due not only to the Chinese economy, but also to the widespread stories of available employment, good wages, and the discovery of gold at Sutter's Mill,[1] which filtered in through arrivals from the Western nations.

The nativist movement of the 1830s resurfaced in the late 1840s and developed into a political party, the Know-Nothing Party. Its western adherents added an anti-Chinese theme to the eastern anti-Catholic sentiment. But once again, the nativist movement, while acquiring local political strength, failed in its attempts to enact legislation curbing immigration. On the local level, however, the cry of "America for Americans" often led to discriminatory State statues that penalized certain racially identifiable groups. As an example, California adopted licensing statues for foreign miners and fishermen, which were almost exclusively enforced against Chinese.

In the mid-1850s, the Know-Nothing Party lost steam as a result of a division over the question of slavery, the most important issue of that time. The nativist movement and antiforeign sentiment receded because of the slavery issue and the Civil War. It maintained this secondary role until the Panic of 1873 struck.

CHINESE EXCLUSION

The depression economy of the 1870s was blamed on aliens who were accused of driving wages to a substandard level as well as taking away jobs that "belonged" to white Americans. While the economic charges were not totally without basis, reality shows that most aliens did not compete with white labor for "desirable" white jobs. Instead, aliens usually were relegated to the most menial employment.

The primary target was the Chinese, whose high racial visibility, coupled with cultural dissimilarity and lack of political power, made them more than an adequate scapegoat for the economic problems of the 1870s. Newspapers adopted the exhortations of labor leaders, blaming the Chinese for the economic plight of the working class. Workers released their frustrations and anger on the Chinese, particularly in the West. Finally, politicians succumbed to the growing cry for exclusion of Chinese.

Congress responded by passing the Chinese Exclusion Act of 1882. That act suspended immigration of Chinese laborers for 10 years, except for those who were in the country on November 17, 1880. Those who were not lawfully entitled to reside in the United States were subject to deportation. Chinese immigrants were also prohibited from obtaining United States citizenship after the effective date of the act.

The 1882 act was amended in 1884 to cover all subjects of China and Chinese who resided in any other foreign country. Then in 1888, another act was enacted that extended the suspension of immigration for all Chinese except Chinese officials, merchants, students, teachers, and travelers for pleasure. Supplemental legislation to that act also prohibited Chinese laborers from reentering the country, as provided for in the 1882 act, unless they reentered prior to the effective date of the legislation.

Senator Matthew C. Butler of South Carolina summed up the congressional efforts to exclude Chinese by stating:

> [I]t seems to me that this whole Chinese business has been a matter of political advantage, and we

have not been governed by that deliberation which it would seem to me the gravity of the question requires. In other words, there is a very important Presidential election pending. One House of Congress passes an act driving these poor devils into the Pacific Ocean, and the other House comes up and says, "Yes, we will drive them further into the Pacific Ocean, notwithstanding the treaties between the two governments."

Nevertheless, the Chinese exclusion law was extended in 1892 and 1902, and in 1904 it was extended indefinitely.

Although challenged by American residents of Chinese ancestry, the provisions of these exclusion acts were usually upheld by judicial decisions. For example, the 1892 act mandated that Chinese laborers obtain certificates of residency within 1 year after the passage of the act or face deportation. In order to obtain the certificate the testimony of one credible white witness was required to establish that the Chinese laborer was an American resident prior to the passage of the act. That requirement was upheld by the United States Supreme Court in *Fong Yue Ting v. United States*.

LITERACY TESTS AND THE ASIATIC BARRED ZONE

The racial nature of immigration laws clearly manifested itself in further restrictions on prospective immigrants who were either from Asian countries or of Asian descent. In addition to extending the statutory life of the Chinese exclusion law, the 1902 act also applied that law to American territorial possessions, thereby prohibiting not only the immigration of noncitizen Chinese laborers from "such island territory to the mainland territory," but also "from one portion of the island territory of the United States to another portion of said island territory." Soon after, Japanese were restricted from free immigration to the United States by the "Gentleman's Agreement" negotiated between the respective governments in 1907. Additional evidence would be provided by the prohibition of immigration from countries in the Asia-Pacific Triangle as established by the Immigration Act of 1917.

During this period, congressional attempts were also made to prevent blacks from immigrating to this country. In 1915 an amendment to exclude "all members of the African or black race"

from admission to the United States was introduced in the Senate during its deliberations on a proposed immigration bill. The Senate approved the amendment on a 29 to 25 vote, but it was later defeated in the House by a 253 to 74 vote, after intensive lobbying by the NAACP.[2]

In 1917 Congress codified existing immigration laws in the Immigration Act of that year. That act retained all the prior grounds for inadmissibility and added illiterates to the list of those ineligible to immigrate, as a response to the influx of immigrants from southern and eastern Europe. Because of a fear that American standards would be lowered by these new immigrants who were believed to be racially "unassimilable" and illiterate, any alien who was over 16 and could not read was excluded. The other important feature of this statute was the creation of the Asia-Pacific Triangle, an Asiatic barred zone, designed to exclude Asians completely from immigration to the United States. The only exemptions from the zone were from an area that included Persia and parts of Afghanistan and Russia.

The 1917 immigration law reflected the movement of American immigration policy toward the curbing of free immigration. Free immigration, particularly from nations that were culturally dissimilar to the northern and western European background of most Americans, was popularly believed to be the root of both the economic problems and the social problems confronting this country.

THE NATIONAL ORIGINS QUOTA SYSTEM

Four years later, Congress created a temporary quota law that limited the number of aliens of any nationality who could immigrate to 3 percent of the United States residents of that nationality living in the country in 1910. The total annual immigration allowable in any one year was set at 350,000. Western Hemisphere aliens were exempt from the quota if their country of origin was an independent nation and the alien had resided there at least 1 year.

The clear intent of the 1921 quota law was to confine immigration as much as possible to western and northern European stock. As the minority report noted:

The obvious purpose of this discrimination is the adoption of an unfounded anthropological theory that the nations which are favored are the progeny of fictitious and hitherto unsuspected Nordic ancestors, while those discriminated against are not classified as belonging to that mythical ancestral stock. No scientific evidence worthy of consideration was introduced to substantiate this pseudo-scientific proposition. It is pure fiction and the creation of a journalistic imagination. . . .

The majority report insinuates that some of those who have come from foreign countries are non-assimilable or slow of assimilation. No facts are offered in support of such a statement. The preponderance of testimony adduced before the committee is to the contrary.

Notwithstanding these objections, Congress made the temporary quota a permanent one with the enactment of the 1924 National Origins Act. A ceiling of 150,000 immigrants per year was imposed. Quotas for each nationality group were 2 percent of the total members of that nationality residing in the United States according to the 1890 census. Again, Western Hemisphere aliens were exempt from the quotas (thus, classified as "nonquota' immigrants). Any prospective immigrant was required to obtain a sponsor in this country and to obtain a visa from an American consulate office abroad. Entering the country without a visa and in violation of the law subjected the entrant to deportation without regard to the time of entry (no statute of limitation). Another provision, prohibiting the immigration of aliens ineligible for citizenship, completely closed the door on Japanese immigration, since the Supreme Court had ruled that Japanese were ineligible to become naturalized citizens. Prior to the 1924 act, Japanese immigration had been subjected to "voluntary" restraint by the Gentleman's Agreement negotiated between the Japanese Government and President Theodore Roosevelt.

In addition to its expressed discriminatory provisions, the 1924 law was also criticized as discriminatory against blacks in general and against black West Indians in particular.

THE MEXICAN "REPATRIATION" CAMPAIGN

Although Mexican Americans have a long history of residence within present United States territory, Mexican immigration to this country is of relatively recent vintage. Mexican citizens began immigrating to this country in significant numbers after 1909 because of economic conditions as well as the violence and political upheaval of the Mexican Revolution. These refugees were welcomed by Americans, for they helped to alleviate the labor shortage caused by the First World War. The spirit of acceptance lasted only a short time, however.

Spurred by the economic distress of the Great Depression, Federal immigration officials expelled hundreds of thousands of persons of Mexican descent from this country through increased Border Patrol raids and other immigration law enforcement techniques. To mollify public objection to the mass expulsions, this program was called the "repatriation" campaign. Approximately 500,000 persons were "repatriated" to Mexico, with more than half of them being United States citizens.

EROSION OF CERTAIN DISCRIMINATORY BARRIERS

Prior to the next recodification of the immigration laws, there were several congressional enactments that cut away at the discriminatory barriers established by the national origins system. In 1943 the Chinese Exclusion Act was repealed, allowing a quota of 105 Chinese to immigrate annually to this country and declaring Chinese eligible for naturalization. The War Brides Act of 1945 permitted the immigration of 118,000 spouses and children of military servicemen. In 1946 Congress enacted legislation granting eligibility for naturalization to Filipinos and to races indigenous to India. A Presidential proclamation in that same year increased the Filipino quota from 50 to 100. In 1948 the Displaced Persons Act provided for the entry of approximately 400,000 refugees from Germany, Italy, and Austria (an additional 214,000 refugees were later admitted to the United States).

THE McCARRAN-WALTER ACT OF 1952

The McCarran-Walter Act of 1952, the basic law in effect today, codified the immigration laws under a single statute. It established three principles for immigration policy:

1. the reunification of families,

2. the protection of the domestic labor force, and

3. the immigration of persons with needed skills.

However, it retained the concept of the national origins system, as well as unrestricted immigration from the Western Hemisphere. An important provision of the statute removed the bar to immigration and citizenship for races that had been denied those privileges prior to that time. Asian countries, nevertheless, were still discriminated against, for prospective immigrants whose ancestry was one-half of any Far Eastern race were chargeable to minimal quotas for that nation, regardless of the birthplace of the immigrant.

"Operation Wetback"

Soon after the repatriation campaign of the 1930s, the United States entered the Second World War. Mobilization for the war effort produced a labor shortage that resulted in a shift in American attitudes toward immigration from Mexico. Once again Mexican nationals were welcomed with open arms. However, this "open arms" policy was just as short lived as before.

In the 1950s many Americans were alarmed by the number of immigrants from Mexico. As a result, then United States Attorney General Herbert Brownell, Jr., launched "Operation Wetback," to expel Mexicans from this country. Among those caught up in the expulsion campaign were American citizens of Mexican descent who were forced to leave the country of their birth. To ensure the effectiveness of the expulsion process, many of those apprehended were denied a hearing to assert their constitutional rights and to present evidence that would have prevented their deportation. More than 1 million persons of Mexican descent were expelled from this country in 1954 at the height of "Operation Wetback."

The 1965 Amendments

The national origins immigration quota system generated opposition from the time of its inception, condemned for its attempts to maintain the existing racial composition of the United States. Finally, in 1965, amendments to the McCarran-Walter Act abolished the national origins system as well as the Asiatic barred zone. Nevertheless, numerical restrictions were still imposed to limit annual immigration. The Eastern Hemisphere was subject to an overall limitation of 170,000 and a limit of 20,000 per country. Further, colonial territories were limited to 1 percent of the total available to the mother country (later raised to 3 percent or 600 immigrants in the 1976 amendments). The Western Hemisphere, for the first time, was subject to an overall limitation of 120,000 annually, although no individual per-country limits were imposed. In place of the national origins system, Congress created a seven category preference system giving immigration priority to relatives of United States residents and immigrants with needed talents or skills. The 20,000 limitation per country and the colonial limitations, as well as the preference for relatives of Americans preferred under the former selections process, have been referred to by critics as "the last vestiges of the national origins system" because they perpetuate the racial discrimination produced by the national origins system.

Restricting Mexican Immigration

After 1965 the economic conditions in the United States changed. With the economic crunch felt by many Americans, the cry for more restrictive immigration laws resurfaced. The difference from the 19th century situation is that the brunt of the attacks is now focused on Mexicans, not Chinese. High "guesstimates" of the number of undocumented Mexican aliens entering the United States, many of which originated from Immigration and Naturalization Service sources, have been the subject of press coverage.

As a partial response to the demand for "stemming the tide" of Mexican immigration, Congress amended the Immigration and Nationality Act in 1976, imposing the seven category preference system and the 20,000 numerical limitation per country on Western Hemisphere nations. Legal immigration from Mexico, which had been more than 40,000 people per year, with a waiting list 2 years long, was thus cut by over 50 percent.

RECENT REVISIONS OF THE
IMMIGRANT QUOTA SYSTEM

Although the annual per-country limitations have remained intact, Congress did amend the Immigration and Nationality Act in 1978 to eliminate the hemispheric quotas of 170,000 for Eastern Hemisphere countries and 120,000 for Western Hemisphere countries. Those hemispheric ceilings were replaced with an overall annual worldwide ceiling of 290,000.

In 1980 the immigrant quota system was further revised by the enactment of the Refugee Act. In addition to broadening the definition of refugee, that statute eliminated the seventh preference[3] visa category by establishing a separate worldwide ceiling for refugee admissions to this country. It also reduced the annual worldwide ceiling for the remaining six preference categories to 270,000 visas, and it increased the number of visas allocated to the second preference[4] to 26 percent.   [1980]

Notes

1. SUTTER'S MILL: The site where gold was discovered in 1848, precipitating the California gold rush.
2. NAACP: National Association for the Advancement of Colored People.
3. SEVENTH PREFERENCE: Refugee status.
4. SECOND PREFERENCE: Spouses and unmarried children of U.S. citizens.

Understanding the Reading

1. What were the nativist movement and the Know-Nothing Party?
2. Explain the Chinese Exclusion laws.
3. Explain the National Origins quota system.
4. What was Operation Wetback?
5. How do the 1965 amendments perpetuate racial discrimination?

Suggestions for Responding

1. Explain what current immigration policy is and why you think it is good and/or bad.
2. Research and report on one specific law or policy that was mentioned in the article. ✦

67

Behind Barbed Wire

JOHN HERSEY

On March 31, 1942, there appeared on notice boards in certain communities on the Western Seaboard of the United States a number of broadsides bearing the ominous title, "Civilian Exclusion Orders." These bulletins warned all residents of Japanese descent that they were going to have to move out of their homes. No mention was made of where they would have to go. One member of each family was directed to report for instructions at neighboring control stations.

The Japanese attack on Pearl Harbor had taken place a little less than four months earlier. These Exclusion Orders cast a wide net. There were about 125,000 persons of Japanese ancestry scattered along the coastal tier of states then, and 7 out of 10 of them, having been born there, were full-fledged citizens of the United States; yet no distinction between alien and native was made among those summoned to control stations. The United States had declared war on Germany and Italy, as well as Japan, but no German or Italian enemy aliens, to say nothing of German-Americans or Italian-Americans, were subjected to these blanket Exclusion Orders. Only "Japanese aliens and non-aliens," as the official euphemism put it.

Each person who responded to the summons had to register the names of all family members and was told to show up at a certain time and place, a few days later, with all of them, bringing along only such baggage as they could carry by hand—for a trip to a destination unknown. Names had become numbers.

"Henry went to the control station to register the family," wrote a Japanese-American woman years later. "He came home with 20 tags, all numbered 10710, tags to be attached to each piece of baggage, and one to hang from our coat lapels. From then on, we were known as Family No. 10710." "I lost my identity," another woman would assert, describing the replacement of her name by a number. "I lost my privacy and dignity."

There followed a period of devastating uncertainty and anxiety. "We were given eight days to liquidate our possessions," one of the evacuees testified at an investigation by the Department of Justice many years later. The time allowed varied from place to place. "We had about two weeks," another recalled, "to do something. Either lease the property or sell everything." Another: "While in Modesto, the final notice for evacuation came with a four-day notice." Under the circumstances, the evacuees had to dispose of their businesses, their homes and their personal possessions at panic prices to hostile buyers.

"It is difficult," one man would later testify, "to describe the feeling of despair and humiliation experienced by all of us as we watched the Caucasians coming to look over our possessions and offering such nominal amounts, knowing we had no recourse but to accept whatever they were offering because we did not know what the future held for us." One woman sold a 37-room hotel for $300. A man who owned a pickup truck, and had just bought a set of new tires and a new battery for $125, asked only that amount of a prospective buyer. "The man 'bought' our pickup for $25." One homeowner, in despair, wanted to burn his house down. "I went to the storage shed to get the gasoline tank and pour the gasoline on my house, but my wife . . . said don't do it, maybe somebody can use this house; we are civilized people, not savages."

By far the greatest number of Nisei—the term for first-generation Japanese-Americans that came to be used as the generic word for all ethnic Japanese living in America—were in agriculture, growing fruit, vegetables, nursery plants and specialty crops. They had worked wonders in the soil. They owned about one-fiftieth of the arable land in the three Pacific Coast states, and what they had made of their farms is suggested by the fact that the average value per acre of all farms in the three states in 1940 was roughly $38, while an acre on a Nisei farm was worth, on average, $280.

But now the farmers had to clear out in a matter of days. The Mother's Day crop of flowers, the richest harvest of the year, was about to be gathered; it had to be abandoned. An owner of one of the largest nurseries in southern California, unable to dispose of his stock, gave it all to the Veterans Hospital adjoining his land. A strawberry grower asked for a deferral of his evacuation summons for a few days, so he could harvest his crop. Denied the permission, he bitterly plowed the berries under. The next day, the Federal Bureau of Investigation charged him with an act of sabotage and put him in jail.

Assured by authorities that they could store property and reclaim it after the war, many put their chattels in impromptu warehouses—homes and garages and outbuildings—only to have the stored goods, before long, vandalized or stolen. Some leased their property but never received rents. Some were cheated by their tenants, who sold the property as if it were their own.

On the day of departure, evacuees found themselves herded into groups of about 500, mostly at railroad and bus stations. They wore their numbered tags and carried hand-baggage containing possessions that they had packed in fear and perplexity, not knowing where they were going. They embarked on buses and trains. Some trains had blacked-out windows. Uniformed guards carrying weapons patrolled the cars. "To this day," one woman recalled long afterward, "I can remember vividly the plight of the elderly, some on stretchers, orphans herded onto the train by caretakers, and especially a young couple with four preschool children.

"The mother had two frightened toddlers hanging on to her coat. In her arms, she carried two crying babies. The father had diapers and other baby paraphernalia strapped to his back. In his hands he struggled with duffel bag and suitcase."

Each group was unloaded, after its trip, at one of 16 assembly centers, most of which were located at fairgrounds and racetracks. There seeing barbed wire and searchlights, and under the guard of guns, these "aliens and non-aliens" were forced to realize that all among them— even those who had sons or brothers in the United States Army—were considered to be dangerous people. At the entrance to the Tanforan Assembly Center, one man later remembered, "stood two lines of troops with rifles and fixed bayonets pointed at the evacuees as they walked between the soldiers to the prison compound. Overwhelmed with bitterness and blind with rage, I screamed every obscenity I knew at the armed guards, daring them to shoot me." Most evacuees were silent, dazed. Many wept.

A typical assembly center was at the Santa Anita race track. Each family was allotted a space in the horse stalls of about 200 square feet, furnished with cots, blankets and pillows; the evacuees had to make their own pallets, filling mattress shells with straw. There were three large mess halls, in which 2,000 people at a time stood in line with tin plates and cups, to be served mass-cooked food that cost an average of 39 cents per person per day—rough fare, usually overcooked, such as brined liver, which, one testified, "would bounce if dropped."

"We lined up," another later wrote, "for mail, for checks, for meals, for showers, for washrooms, for laundry tubs, for toilets. . . ." Medical care, under jurisdiction of the Public Health Service, was provided by evacuee doctors and nurses who were recruited to serve their fellow inmates in an improvised clinic, supplied at first with nothing more than mineral oil, iodine, aspirin, sulfa ointment, Kaopectate and alcohol. Toilets were communal, without compartments. The evacuees bathed in what had been horse showers, with a partition between the men's and the women's section. When the women complained that men were climbing the partition and looking at them, a camp official responded, "Are you sure you women are not climbing the walls to look at the men?"

Toward the end of May 1942, evacuees began to be transferred from these temporary assembly centers to 13 permanent concentration camps—generally called by the more decorous name of "relocation centers"—where they would be held prisoner until several months before the end of the war. By Nov. 1, some 106,770 internees had been put behind barbed wire in six western states and Arkansas.

Thus began the bitterest national shame of the Second World War for the sweet land of liberty: the mass incarceration, on racial grounds alone, on false evidence of military necessity, and in contempt of their supposedly inalienable rights, of an entire class of American citizens—along with others who were not citizens in the country of their choice only because that country had long denied people of their race the right to naturalize. (A 1924 Federal law had cut off all Japanese immigration and naturalization; it was not rescinded until 1952.)

"My mother, two sisters, niece, nephew, and

I left" by train, one recalled in later years. "Father joined us later. Brother left earlier by bus. We took whatever we could carry. So much we left behind, but the most valuable thing I lost was my freedom."

The Manzanar camp was quickly built in the desert country of east-central California. Its second director, a humane and farsighted man named Ralph Merritt, realized that history ought to have some testimony of what its victims had managed to salvage from an unprecedented American social crime. He had seen the consummate artistry of photographs taken in nearby Yosemite National Park by a friend of his, Ansel Adams, and he invited the great photographer to come to the camp to capture its woes and its marvels on film.

"Moved," Adams would later write, "by the human story unfolding in the encirclement of desert and mountains, and by the wish to identify my photography . . . with the tragic momentum of the times, I came to Manzanar with my cameras in the fall of 1943."

Adam's photographs restore energy to the sorry record—and remind us that this very word "record" in its ancient origins meant "to bring back the heart."

But first it seems appropriate to re-engage the mind, for the stories of Manzanar and the other camps raise grave questions for the American polity: Could such a thing occur again? How did this slippage in the most precious traditions of a free country come about?

The Japanese attack on Pearl Harbor on Dec. 7, 1941, threw the American psyche into a state of shock. Despite four years' demonstration of the skill and dispatch—and cruelty—of the Japanese invasion of China, American military commanders in the Philippines and elsewhere had issued boastful statements, over and over again, about how quickly the "Japs," as they were scornfully called, would be wiped out if they dared attack American installations.

Then suddenly, within hours, the United States Pacific Fleet was crippled at anchor. Most of the United States air arm in the Philippines was wrecked on the ground. American pride dissolved overnight into American rage and hysteria—and nowhere so disastrously as on the country's Western shores.

President Franklin D. Roosevelt promptly

proclaimed, and Congress voted, a state of war against Japan, and within days the other Axis powers, Germany and Italy, also became belligerents. The President issued orders that classified nationals of those countries as enemy aliens. These orders gave responsibility for carrying out certain restrictions against enemy aliens of all three countries to Attorney General Francis Biddle and the Department of Justice. Biddle was given authority to establish prohibited zones, from which enemy aliens could be moved at will; to seize as contraband any weapons and other articles as required for national security; to freeze enemy aliens' funds, and to intern any of them who might be deemed dangerous. These were perfectly normal wartime precautions against enemy aliens only, for which there had been statutory precedent under President Woodrow Wilson in the First World War.

With great speed and efficiency, beginning on the very night of the attack, the Justice Department arrested certain marked enemy aliens of all three belligerent nations. Within three days, 857 Germans, 147 Italians and 1,291 Japanese (367 of them on the Hawaiian Islands, 924 on the continent) had been rounded up.

On the night of Dec. 8, when Pearl Harbor jitters were at their highest pitch, San Francisco suffered a false alarm of an air incursion. Military and/or naval radio trackers reported that enemy aircraft were soaring in over the Bay Area and later that they had turned back to sea without attacking. Planes of the Second Interceptor Command took off from Portland, Ore., and searched as far as 600 miles offshore for a nonexistent Japanese aircraft carrier, from which the enemy planes were assumed to have been launched. At the first alarm, sirens sounded a warning, and San Francisco was supposed to be blacked out at once. But skyscrapers blazed, neon lights winked at hundreds of night spots, and Alcatraz was like a heap of sparkling diamonds in the bay.

Enter, the next morning, to center stage, a military figure in a high state of excitation. As commanding officer of the Fourth Army and Western Defense Command, Lieut. Gen. John L. DeWitt was charged with making sure that there would be no Pearl Harbors on the West Coast. That morning, a meeting at City Hall was called with Mayor Angelo Rossi and 200 of the city's

civic leaders, and as *Life* magazine would put it, DeWitt "almost split with rage."

"You people," he said to them, "do not seem to realize we are at war. So get this: Last night there were planes over this community. They were enemy planes. I mean Japanese planes. And they were tracked out to sea. You think it was a hoax? It is damned nonsense for sensible people to think that the Army and Navy would practice such a hoax on San Francisco."

He shouted that it might have been "a good thing" if some bombs *had* been dropped. "It might have awakened some of the fools in this community who refuse to realize that this is a war."

On the night of this "air attack," one of DeWitt's subordinates, Maj. Gen. Joseph W. Stilwell, later to be the famous "Vinegar Joe" of the doomed campaigns in Burma and China, wrote in pencil in a dime-store notebook that he used as a diary, "Fourth Army"—obviously meaning its headquarters—"kind of jittery." Two nights later, DeWitt and his staff, hearing that there was to be an armed uprising of 20,000 Nisei[1] in the San Francisco area, whipped up a plan to put all of them in military custody. The plan fortunately was aborted by the local F.B.I.[2] chief of station, Nat Pieper, who told the Army that the "reliable source" for their news of the uprising was a flake whom Pieper had once employed and had had to dismiss because of his "wild imaginings."

Next, on Dec. 13, came "reliable information" that an enemy attack on Los Angeles was imminent, and DeWitt's staff drafted a general alarm that would have advised all civilians to leave the city. Fortunately, it was never broadcast. That night, General Stilwell wrote in his notebook that General DeWitt was a "jackass."

The first week of the war brought news of one setback after another. The Japanese struck at Midway, Wake, the Philippines, Hong Kong, the Malay Peninsula and Thailand. On Dec. 13, they captured Guam. The American dream of invulnerability had suddenly been replaced by a feeling that the Japanese could do just about anything they wanted to do—including landing at any point along DeWitt's vast coastal command.

Two days after Pearl Harbor, Navy Secretary Frank Knox went to Hawaii to try to find out what had gone wrong there. On Dec. 15, he returned to the mainland from his scouting trip and called a press conference at which he said, "I think the most effective fifth-column work[3] of the entire war was done in Hawaii, with the possible exception of Norway." He carried back to Washington this report of treachery by resident Japanese, "both from the shores and from the sampans," and his absurdly impracticable recommendation that all those with Japanese blood be evacuated from Oahu.

His charges were quickly denied, in confidential reports, by J. Edgar Hoover of the F.B.I.; by John Franklin Carter, a journalist whom Roosevelt had enlisted to give him intelligence reports; and, after a few days, by Lieut. Gen. Delos C. Emmons, the newly appointed commanding officer in the Hawaiian Islands. But Frank Knox's statement was never denied by the Government—which, from Pearl Harbor to V-J Day, would record not a single case of sabotage by a Japanese alien or a Japanese-American worse than the plowing under of strawberries.

In 1943, when General DeWitt would submit to the Secretary of War his "Final Report" on the removal of the Japanese from the West Coast, one of its first assertions would be: "The evacuation was impelled by military necessity." DeWitt wrote, "There were hundreds of reports nightly of signal lights visible from the coast, and of intercepts of unidentified radio transmissions."

Hoover scornfully ridiculed the "hysteria and lack of judgment" of DeWitt's Military Intelligence Division. An official of the Federal Communications Commission reported on the question of radio intercepts: "I have never seen an organization that was so hopeless to cope with radio intelligence requirements. . . . The personnel is unskilled and untrained. . . . As a matter of fact, the Army air stations have been reported by the Signal Corps station as Jap enemy stations."

DeWitt urged random spot raids on homes of ethnic Japanese to seize "subversive" weapons and cameras. Attorney General Biddle stipulated that raiders should follow the constitutional requirement of finding probable cause for arrest, but DeWitt argued that being of Japanese descent was in itself probable cause. He insisted on searches without warrants, even of the homes of

citizens. Yet the Justice Department concluded from F.B.I. reports: "We have not found a single machine gun, nor have we found any gun in any circumstances indicating that it was to be used in a manner helpful to our enemies. We have not found a camera which we have reason to believe was for use in espionage."

When it came right down to it, the mere fact of having Japanese blood and skin was, to DeWitt, enough basis for suspicion. When he wrote in his "Final Report" of the way the ethnic Japanese population was scattered through his Defense Command, he used the military term "deployed"—"in excess of 115,000 persons deployed along the Pacific Coast—as if these people, these farmers and merchants and house servants, had been posted by plan, poised for attack.

Testifying before a Congressional subcommittee, DeWitt would say, as if this alone proved the military necessity he was trying to assert, "A Jap is a Jap."

The news from the Pacific after the first shock of Pearl Harbor grew worse and worse, and nerves in the Presidio[4] tightened. On Dec. 24 and 25, 1941, the Japanese took Wake Island and Hong Kong. On Dec. 27, Manila fell, and United States forces retreated to the Bataan Peninsula.

On Dec. 19, DeWitt urged on the War Department "that action be initiated at the earliest practicable date to collect all alien subjects 14 years of age and over, of enemy nations and remove them" to inland places, where they should be kept "under restraint after removal." This recommendation covered only aliens—Germans and Italians as well as Japanese.

Toward the end of the month, according to Roger Daniels, who has written two authoritative books on the evacuation, DeWitt began talking by phone—outside the normal chain of command, without telling his superiors—with an officer he knew in Washington, Maj. Gen. Allen W. Gullion. Gullion was Provost Marshal General, the Army's top law enforcement officer. Since the fall of France in June 1940, he had been concerning himself with the question of how the military could acquire legal control over civilians in wartime—in case there should be a domestic fifth column—and DeWitt, evidently stung by the ridicule of his alarms by civilian agencies like the F.B.I. and the F.C.C.,[5] was much attracted by Gullion's views.

Gullion had the chief of his Aliens Division, Major Karl R. Bendetsen, draft a memorandum proposing that the President "place in the hands of the Secretary of War the right to take over aliens when he thought it was necessary."

In one of their turn-of-the-year conferences, Bendetsen outlined to DeWitt plans for surveillance and control of West Coast Nisei; if the Justice Department wouldn't do the job, Bendetsen told DeWitt, then it would be up to the Army—really, to the two of them—to do it. According to notes taken at the session, DeWitt went along with Bendetsen, saying that he had "little confidence that the enemy aliens are law-abiding or loyal in any sense of the word. Some of them, yes; many, no. Particularly the Japanese. I have no confidence in their loyalty whatsoever."

In organizations like the Native Sons of the Golden West and the American Legion, clamor for the incarceration of all Nisei was growing. Congressman Leland Ford of Los Angeles argued for their removal with a most peculiar logic. On Jan. 16, he wrote to Secretary of War Henry L. Stimson a formal recommendation "that all Japanese, whether citizens or not, be placed in inland concentration camps. As justification for this, I submit that if an American-born Japanese, who is a citizen, is really patriotic and wishes to make his contribution to the safety and welfare of this country, right here is his opportunity to do so.... Millions of other native-born citizens are willing to lay down their lives, which is a far greater sacrifice, of course, than being placed in a concentration camp."

There were, in fact, lots of patriotic Nisei. Many of them were fiercely and showily patriotic precisely because so many "real Americans" doubted their fidelity. Some had joined together in the Japanese-American Citizens League, which did all it could to flaunt its members' loyalty. Their idealistic creed, adopted before Pearl Harbor, said, "Although some individuals may discriminate against me, I shall never become bitter or lose faith, for I know that such persons are not representative of the majority of American people."

Nisei in many cities and towns helped with civil defense. Furthermore, many young Nisei volunteered for the Army. (In Italy and France, the Japanese-American 442d Combat Regimental Team would turn out to be one of the most decorated units in the entire United States Army—with seven Presidential Distinguished Unit Citations, one Congressional Medal of Honor, 47 Distinguished Service Crosses, 350 Silver Stars, 810 Bronze Stars and more than 3,600 Purple Hearts. President Truman, attaching a Presidential Distinguished Unit Citation to the regimental colors, would say, "You fought not only the enemy, but you fought prejudice. . . .")

DeWitt's anxieties, however, flowered more and more, and they soon bore fruit. On Jan. 21, 1942, he recommended to Secretary Stimson the establishment of 86 "prohibited zones" in California, from which all "enemy" aliens would be removed, as well as a handful of larger "restricted zones," where they would be kept under close surveillance.

On Jan. 25, persuaded by DeWitt's reports of danger, Stimson recommended to Biddle that these zones be established. Since this request touched only enemy aliens, and meant moving them in most cases for very short distances, Biddle acceded.

At the beginning of February, voices raised on the West Coast against Japanese-Americans became more and more shrill. The Los Angeles Times took up the cry that Japanese citizens were just as much enemies as Japanese aliens: "A viper is nonetheless a viper wherever the egg is hatched—so a Japanese-American, born of Japanese parents, grows up to be a Japanese, not an American." California's liberal Governor, Culbert L. Olson, who had earlier taken the position that Japanese-Americans should continue in wartime to enjoy their constitutional rights, reversed himself in a radio address. Evidently on information from DeWitt, he said: "It is known that there are Japanese residents of California who have sought to aid the Japanese enemy by way of communicating information, or have shown indications of preparation for fifth-column activities." He hinted that there might have to be large-scale removals.

Biddle wanted to issue a press release jointly with the Army, designed to calm public fears on the West Coast about sabotage and espionage, and on Feb. 4, he, Assistant Attorney General

James Rowe Jr., J. Edgar Hoover, Stimson, Mc-Cloy, Gullion and Bendetsen met to discuss it. Gullion later described this encounter:

"[The Justice officials] said there is too much hysteria about this thing; said these Western Congressmen are just nuts about it and the people getting hysterical and there is no evidence whatsoever of any reason for disturbing citizens, and the Department of Justice—Rowe started it and Biddle finished it—the Department of Justice will [have] nothing whatsoever to do with any interference with citizens, whether they are Japanese or not. They made me a little sore, and I said, well listen, Mr. Biddle, do you mean to tell me that if the Army, the men on the ground, determine it is a military necessity to move citizens, Jap citizens, that you won't help me? He didn't give a direct answer, he said the Department of Justice would be through if we interfered with citizens and writ of habeas corpus,[6] etc."

When DeWitt, on Feb. 9, asked for the establishment of much larger prohibited zones in Washington, Oregon and Arizona, Biddle refused to go along. "Your recommendation of prohibited areas . . . include the cities of Portland, Seattle, and Tacoma," he wrote, "and therefore contemplate a mass evacuation of many thousands. . . . No reasons were given for this mass evacuation. . . . The Department of Justice is not physically equipped to carry out any mass evacuation."

If there were to be any question of evacuating citizens, the Attorney General wanted no part of it—yet in washing his hands of this eventuality, he now conceded that the Army might justify doing this as a "military necessity. . . . Such action, therefore, should in my opinion, be taken by the War Department and not by the Department of Justice."

Two days later, Stimson went over Biddle's head to Roosevelt. Unable to fit an appointment into a busy day, the President talked with Stimson on the phone. The Secretary told Roosevelt that the Justice Department was dragging its feet and asked if he would authorize the Army to move American citizens of Japanese ancestry as well as aliens away from sensitive areas. Further, he asked whether the President would favor evacuating more than 100,000 from the entire West Coast; 70,000 living in major urban areas; or small numbers living around critical zones, such as air-craft factories, "even though that would be more complicated and tension-producing than total evacuation."

Right after Stimson hung up, Assistant Secretary John J. McCloy jubilantly called Bendetsen in San Francisco to say that the President had declined to make a specific decision about numbers himself but had decided to cut out the Justice Department and had given the Army "*carte blanche*[7] to do what we want to." Roosevelt's only urging was to "be reasonable as you can."

The very next day—so promptly as to suggest that there had been some orchestration—the most influential newspaper pundit in the country, Walter Lippmann, in a column entitled "The Fifth Column on the Coast," lay out the basis for advocating the removal of citizens as well as aliens. "The Pacific Coast," he wrote, "is in imminent danger of a combined attack from within and without. . . . It is a fact that the Japanese Navy has been reconnoitering the coast more or less continuously. . . . There is an assumption [in Washington] that a citizen may not be interfered with unless he has committed an overt act. . . . The Pacific Coast is officially a combat zone. Some part of it may at any moment be a battlefield. And nobody ought to be on a battlefield who has no good reason for being there. There is plenty of room elsewhere for him to exercise his rights."

The day after the Lippmann article, the entire Pacific Coast Congressional delegation signed and delivered to Roosevelt a resolution urging "the immediate evacuation of all persons of Japanese lineage and all others, aliens and citizens alike, whose presence shall be deemed dangerous or inimical to the defense of the United States from . . . the entire strategic areas of the states of California, Oregon, and Washington, and the Territory of Alaska."

On Feb. 14, freed by Roosevelt's green light to the Army, doubtless encouraged by Lippmann and by the vociferousness of the West Coast press and West Coast Congressmen, DeWitt finally submitted to Stimson his recommendation for "Evacuation of Japanese and Other Subversive Persons From the Pacific Coast," to be carried out by his command. In justifying the "military necessity" of such an action, DeWitt wrote that ". . . along the vital Pacific Coast over 112,000 potential enemies, of Japanese extraction, are at large today. There are indications that these are organized and ready for concerted action at a favorable opportunity. The very fact that no sabotage has taken place to date is a disturbing and confirming indication that such action will be taken."

Here was logic worthy of "Animal Farm":[8] Proof that all ethnic Japanese were "ready for concerted action" lay in their not having taken it yet.

On Feb. 17, Biddle, in a letter to the President, made a last-ditch protest. "My last advice from the War Department," he wrote, "is that there is no evidence of imminent attack and from the F.B.I. that there is no evidence of planned sabotage."

The protest came too late. By this time, the Attorney General—whose voice had been absolutely solo in reminding those in power of central values in the Bill of Rights—was not only ignored; he was brutally vilified. Congressman Leland Ford told later of a call to Biddle:

"I gave them 24 hours' notice that unless they would issue a mass evacuation notice I would drag the whole matter out on the floor of the House and of the Senate and give the bastards everything we could with both barrels. I told them they had given us the runaround long enough . . . and that if they would not take immediate action, we would clear the goddamned office out in one sweep. . . ."

On the day Biddle transmitted his final protest to Roosevelt, Stimson convened a meeting with War Department aides to plan a Presidential order enabling a mass evacuation under Army supervision. Gullion was sent off to draft it.

That evening, McCloy, Gullion and Bendetsen went to Biddle's house, and Gullion read his draft aloud to the Attorney General. The order was to be sweeping and open-ended. Basing the President's right as Commander in Chief to issue it on a war powers act that dated back to the First World War, it authorized "the Secretary of War, and the military commanders whom he may from time to time designate . . . to prescribe military areas . . . from which any or all persons may be excluded, and with respect to which, the right of any person to enter, remain in, or leave shall be subject to whatever restriction the Secretary of War or the appropriate military commander may impose in his discretion."

On Feb. 19, 1942, Roosevelt set his signature to Executive Order No. 9066, "Authorizing the Secretary of War to Prescribe Military Areas."

The next day, Secretary Stimson formally appointed DeWitt "the military commander to carry out the duties and responsibilities" under Executive Order 9066. He specified that DeWitt should not bother to remove persons of Italian descent. There was widespread affection for Italian-Americans. The Mayor of San Francisco was one, and the baseball stars Joe and Dom DiMaggio, whose parents were aliens, were among the most popular idols in the country. "I don't care so much about the Italians," Biddle later quoted Roosevelt as having said in his cavalier way. "They are a lot of opera singers. . . ."

Stimson took a slightly harder line on German aliens, though he never authorized evacuating German-Americans. Instructions to DeWitt were that German aliens who were "bona fide refugees" should be given "special consideration." In any case, the F.B.I. had long since taken into custody German aliens who had been marked as potentially subversive.

As to ethnic Japanese, the message was clear. Classes 1 and 2 of those who were to be moved out were "Japanese Aliens" and "American Citizens of Japanese Lineage." A sharp racist line had been drawn.

Congress had set up a Select Committee to investigate the need for what it euphemistically called "National Defense Migration." Testifying in San Francisco on Feb. 21, Earl Warren, then Attorney General of California, echoed DeWitt's amazing "proof" of trouble to come. "Unfortunately [many] are of the opinion that because we have had no sabotage and no fifth column activities in this State . . . that none have been planned for us," Warren said. "But I take the view that this is the most ominous sign in our whole situation. It convinces me more than perhaps any other factor that the sabotage we are to get, the fifth column activities we are to get, are timed just like Pearl Harbor was timed and just like the invasion of France, and of Denmark, and of Norway, and all of those other countries."

Two evenings later, almost as if designed to make irrational fears like these seem plausible, a Japanese submarine, the I-17, having recently returned to the coastal waters, fired about 25 five-and-a-half-inch shells at some oil storage tanks on an otherwise empty hillside west of Santa Barbara. There were no casualties. But was this a prelude to an invasion?

The next night, the Army detected nonexistent enemy airplanes over Los Angeles, and at 2:25 A.M., an antiaircraft battery opened fire. Other gun crews, hearing the explosions, began firing, and within a couple of hours, 1,430 three-inch shells had gone off above the city. Their fragments rained down, causing a fair amount of damage to automobiles. It took quite a while before this happening could be given the joking title it came finally to bear: "The Battle of Los Angeles." At the time, it reinforced the public's panic.

On Feb. 27, the Cabinet in Washington met to discuss how the evacuations should be carried out. Bendetsen had been arguing that the Army should not bear the burden of administering the removals because, as he said in a phone call to the State Department, the Army's job was "to kill Japanese, not to save Japanese." And indeed, the Cabinet did decide that day that the "resettlement" should be handled by a new civilian agency, which would eventually be called the War Relocation Authority. Milton S. Eisenhower, an official of the Department of Agriculture, brother of the popular general who would one day be elected President, was put in charge of it. The Army would round up the evacuees and move them to temporary collection centers, and then the civilian W.R.A. would settle and hold them for the duration of the war in permanent camps.

On March 2, DeWitt established as Military Area No. 1—the field of hottest imaginary danger—the entire western halves of Washington, Oregon and California, and the southern half of Arizona. Presumably somewhat cooler was Military Area No. 2, comprising the remainder of the four states.

DeWitt did not yet, however, issue any orders for actual removals, because in Washington, Gullion had realized that there was no law on the books that made a civilian's disobedience of a military command a crime, so there was no way for DeWitt to force anyone to move. Gullion's office therefore went to work drawing up a statute—something absolutely new in American legal history—that would invent such a crime. DeWitt urged that imprisonment be mandatory,

and that the crime be classified as a felony because, he argued, "you have a greater liberty to enforce a felony than you have to enforce a misdemeanor, *viz,* You can shoot a man to prevent the commission of a felony."

On March 9, Stimson submitted to Congress the proposed legislation, which would subject any civilian who flouted a military order in a military area to a year in jail and a fine of $5,000. Only one person in either House rose in debate to challenge the measure: the archconservative Senator Robert A. Taft of Ohio, who would be known in later years as "Mr. Republican." This bill, he said, was "the 'sloppiest' criminal law I have ever read or seen anywhere."

When it came to a vote, not a single member of either House voted against the bill, which was signed into law by Roosevelt on March 21. The way was cleared. On March 31, 1942, with the posting of Civilian Exclusion Orders, the cruel capture of the ethnic Japanese was set in motion.

By early 1943, McCloy and others in the War Department and Army had clearly seen that "military necessity" could no longer, by the wildest imagining, justify keeping loyal American citizens of Japanese ancestry—or loyal aliens—away from the West Coast in "pens." DeWitt was horrified, but the War Department had had enough of his obsessive fears and complaints. He was relieved of his Western Defense Command that fall.

In the spring of 1944, the War Department finally urged the President to dissolve the camps. Others, however, urged caution. "The question appears to be largely a political one," wrote Under Secretary of State Edward Stettinius Jr., in a memo to the President. Roosevelt would be running for a fourth term in November. The evacuees would have to wait.

At the first Cabinet meeting after Roosevelt's re-election, it was decided that all evacuees who passed loyalty reviews could, at last, go home.

They went home to a bitter freedom. It took more than a year to empty all the camps. Given train fare and $25, the evacuees returned to the coast, many to learn that their goods had been stolen or sold; their land had been seized for unpaid taxes; strangers had taken possession of their homes. Jobs were plentiful, but not for the returning detainees, who met with notices: "No

Japs Wanted." Housing was hard to find; whole families moved into single rooms.

One man, who had a brother still overseas with the 442d Regimental Combat Team, would testify that his mother "finally had enough money for a down payment on a house. We purchased the house in 1946 and tried to move in, only to find two Caucasian men sitting on the front steps with a court injunction prohibiting us from moving in because of a restrictive covenant.[9] If we moved in, we would be subject to a $1,000 fine and/or one year in the County Jail."

One ordeal had ended; another had begun.

[1988]

Notes

1. NISEI: Children born of Japanese immigrants.
2. F.B.I.: Federal Bureau of Investigation.
3. FIFTH-COLUMN WORK: Secret subversive activities aiding an invading enemy.
4. THE PRESIDIO: The U.S. Army base in San Francisco that served as DeWitt's headquarters.
5. F.C.C.: Federal Communication Commission.
6. WRIT OF HABEAS CORPUS: An order to release or bring a prisoner before a court.
7. CARTE BLANCHE: Unconditional authority.
8. "ANIMAL FARM": A satirical novel by George Orwell with the climactic slogan, "All animals are equal, but some animals are more equal than others."
9. RESTRICTIVE COVENANT: A law prohibiting certain ethnic groups from residing in a given area.

Understanding the Reading

1. What were the Civilian Exclusion Orders?
2. What was the economic impact of the orders?
3. How were the Japanese-Americans treated like criminals?
4. What were conditions like at the Assembly Centers?
5. What was Lieutenant General DeWitt's response to the supposed San Francisco flyover by Japanese planes?
6. What was the single case of sabotage by a Japanese-American?
7. What were some of the problems with the Military Intelligence Division?

8. What were some of the most bizarre justifications offered in support of the evacuation?
9. What was the 442d Combat Regimental Team, and what was its service record like?
10. What triggered the "Battle of Los Angeles"?
11. Why did evacuation have to wait for Congress to act?
12. What problems did Japanese-Americans face after they left the camps?

Suggestions for Responding

1. Hersey raises the question of whether such an incident as the relocation program could occur again. How would you answer him?
2. Imagine you were a Japanese-American attending a West Coast university at the time of the evacuation order. How would you react?
3. Explain DeWitt's role in the evacuation. ◆

68

Legally Sanctioned Special Advantages Are a Way of Life in the United States

BENJAMIN DEMOTT

During years of service on academic committees, I've read stacks of "autobiographical statements" composed by candidates for Rhodes scholarships and other prestigious fellowships. Almost by convention these achievers cite evidence attesting to their readiness to "try everything" in the way of learning—including private lessons in skills ranging from dressage, bassoon playing, and wilderness-survival techniques to ballet, ice dancing, tennis, chess, and Russian.

The point the achievers seem determined to get across is that they are venturesome. As one candidate put it in a homily that I have encountered in several versions: "There was only one rule in my family. You had to try everything. You had to give it a fair try and afterward, if you didn't like it, okay: Quit. But you had to *make the effort.*"

Such assertions convey an important self-concept—that of people independent, unafraid of embarrassment or failure, aware of the endless range of pleasures and satisfactions life offers to those eager to seize them, proud of the capacity for commitment. Usually students see that capacity—a shade self-deceivingly—as a purely personal trait; they habitually see expensive advantages and options as proof of individual merit.

This innocent self-deception comes to mind often as I follow the national debate on affirmative action. American rhetoric has long insisted that the rules for success are the same for everyone and that merit is the key to advancement. The rhetoric of merit figures prominently in the affirmative-action debate—*fairness, level playing field, preferential treatment, competition, fear of competition,* and so on. And one theme surfaces time and again, favored not only by representatives of the majority culture but also lately by some minority representatives, as well. The substance of the theme is that special advantages of any sort are alien to the American way.

In my view, this is a wrong-headed belief, disturbingly oblivious of the vast structure of legally sanctioned special advantages that undergirds many Americans' individual achievements and comforts. In numberless ways, public policy contravenes the rhetoric denigrating special advantages. The evidence is omnipresent. The weekly journal *Tax Notes* recently pointed out that the *non*-poor population of the United States will receive a government benefit worth $60-billion in 1991—a clear special advantage—thanks to the deductibility of mortgage interest and property taxes. As renters, most of the working poor are ineligible for this benefit.

Comparable provisions—special advantages for the non-poor partly paid for by the taxes of the working poor—abound throughout our tax code. In 1989, writing in the *Population Research and Policy Review,* sociologists Leonard Beeghley and Jeffrey Dwyer listed some 30 different forms of federal tax subsidies that are awarded to the non-poor; these subsidies are worth hundreds of billions of dollars each year. People whose annual income is under $75,000 are ineligible for many of these subsidies. Only about one black family in 25 has an income that large.

To those who qualify for them, American tax shelters appear benign, color-blind, "democratic." But along this democratic byway some people clearly are more equal than others. Because most whites earn more than blacks, tax shelters favor whites; in many instances the degree of favoritism is staggering. When the cash benefits of a government policy are 25 times more likely to go to white families than to black families, and when that pattern has been in place for decades with barely a whisper of public protest, it's preposterous to speak—as many do in arguments over affirmative action—as though the idea of special advantages were un-American.

No less preposterous is the notion that student superstardom in colleges and universities is a function solely of native brilliance and individual true grit. Once hailed as democracy's front line, this country's schools long ago ceased functioning as equalizers. During the last three to four decades, educational researchers and historians have labored to explain why this happened, measuring the distance between a meritocratic school system and the system as it now functions.

The pioneering contribution to this inquiry was *Elmtown's Youth,* August Hollingshead's 1949 study of how social and economic class affected the treatment of poor, middle-class, and upper-middle-class pupils by teachers and principals in one Midwestern high school. The most penetrating research was conducted for Congress by the Coleman Commission at the height of the civil-rights movement.

The Coleman Report, published in 1966, established that class influenced the achievement of students throughout their schooling because it shaped their attitudes toward teachers, their familiarity with the materials of learning, their study habits and the environment in which they studied, and their classroom participation. (In this context, it is clear that training in the skills and arts of commitment like that provided by private lessons, is an immense advantage to any student.) The most recent confirmation and updating of the Coleman Commission's report appeared in William Julius Wilson's 1987 book, *The Truly Disadvantaged: The Inner City, the Underclass & Public Policy.*

Other research has documented that well-off students with weak academic records are far more likely to attend college than hard-up students with strong records; that "multitrack" or "open transfer" school systems create permanent enclaves of students of the same social class instead of fostering mobility; and that state financing arrangements provide low subsidies for the least-advantaged students attending two-year colleges and high subsidies for the most-advantaged attending flagship universities. Still other studies have shown that scholarship funds, advertised as democratizing influences at private colleges and universities, often are awarded to students with extremely large family incomes.

A body of inquiry has established, furthermore, that teachers' conceptions of "ideal" pupils typically equate class-connected characteristics such as accent, appearance, manner, and deportment with "natural or inborn intelligence." Similar skewing has been noted in standards adopted by testing agencies. For example, the verbal behavior of middle- and upper-middle-class children identified as "intelligent" has become the yardstick for evaluating all students, with predictable consequences for speakers of "Black English."

The point of citing all this isn't to deny that pure merit sometimes receives a fair shake in elementary and secondary schools. Everyone who teaches knows of occasions when worth has risen despite obstacles; faith that a caring teacher can help in this process sustains thousands of academicians. But it's one thing to acknowledge the possibility that students can overcome the odds and quite another to condone the excessively moralized assumptions—the fantasies of unconditioned individual accomplishment ("I did it my way")—that turn up in student's life stories and in adults' critiques of affirmative action.

The affirmative-action cause has failings, of course. Manipulative politicos easily exploit them to drive a wedge between working-class whites and blacks. The country would be better off if its politics focused less on race and more on the ways in which bad schools, bad jobs, bad housing, and frightening crime rates wreck life for blacks *and* whites. And it certainly would be harder to denigrate affirmative-action programs if they helped the working poor of all races as much as they help middle-class members of minority groups.

But righting ancient wrongs is complex work, beset with anomaly; succeeding at it requires exceptionally high levels of self-awareness and social realism. That is why it makes sense to challenge people who think sweetheart deals, insider trading, and special advantages for particular groups are alien to the American way of life. Let's face up to the awkward truth: Special advantages are and have been for generations as American as blueberry pie.   [1991]

Understanding the Reading

1. Why does DeMott feel scholarship applicants are self-deceived when they claim credit for their personal achievements?
2. Why does he think that special advantages are not alien to the American way?
3. How and to whom do tax laws provide special advantages?
4. Why does schooling no longer serve as an equalizer?
5. Why does DeMott endorse affirmative action?

Suggestions for Responding

1. In what ways does DeMott's analysis clarify Podhoretz's story about Mrs. K. in Part III?
2. Have you or your family benefited from any special legal advantages, either those DeMott mentioned or others like educational loans or government services that aren't available to everyone? ◆

69

Soldier Boys, Soldier Girls

EDITORS OF *THE NEW REPUBLIC*

During the U.S. invasion of Panama, a female soldier who had been driving a truck for hours, ferrying troops into a combat zone amid sporadic enemy fire, was about to be pressed back into service when she started crying. Another woman, who had been performing the same job, approached her and, by some accounts, started crying too. Both were relieved of their duties—whether at their request or not remains unclear. After news of the incident reached the press, the Army took pains to convey that the women had not disobeyed orders or been derelict in their duty. On the contrary, according to an Army official quoted in the *Washington Post,* "They performed superbly."

There are a number of sympathetic and truthful things you can say about these two women. You can note that they exhibited an acute understanding of the dangers they faced, or that their behavior was no different from that of countless male soldiers who have been traumatized by war. But to call the overall performance of a soldier who breaks down and cries during combat "superb" is ludicrous, and patronizing.

This utterance embodies a particular form of disingenuousness that has clouded the debate over opening combat positions to women. Within the Pentagon there is deep opposition to the idea, but it almost never gets honestly expressed. High-ranking officers may, over a beer, list half a dozen things that scare them about a fully integrated military—one of which is that women might start crying during war. But when Pentagon officials are publicly asked about the issue, they generally shy away from honest doubts. And proponents of full integration seem no more eager for a thorough airing of possible pitfalls. Their working assumption is that the only real sources of opposition are sexism and the political cowardice of legislators who don't want to be seen as sending women to war.

The shallowness of the resulting debate is by itself a good argument for proceeding with Representative Pat Schroeder's plan to open some Army units in every type of combat specialty to women on a four-year test basis. Mere public discussion of the issue, it seems, is not going to get us very far.

To the extent that the exclusion of females from combat roles has a stated rationale, it is that women should not be put at risk of physical harm. Even a position classified as non-combat may, under current policy, be closed to women if, in the event of war, it would be dangerous. The logic here is puzzling. Does a woman's life have greater moral value than a man's? Does a wounded woman suffer more than a wounded man? Neither question has a valid ring to it, and both are best left for contemplation by those women who want to go to war.

To further confuse things, this warped rationale for combat exclusion is half ignored in practice. Women are not allowed to fly fighter planes, but they are free to fly AWAC radar planes—which

are so big, slow, and tactically important that they might as well have "Shoot me first" stenciled on their sides. Women can't fight in tanks, but they sit in communication trucks that may be in harm's way. They can't serve on destroyers, but they serve on supply ships that drop anchor alongside destroyers.

Individual paradoxes aside, the distinction between combat and non-combat jobs is, as Schroeder stresses, broadly eroding. In the era of cruise missiles and other "smart" weapons, front lines are not necessarily more vulnerable than rear supply lines. And in the Panama-style interventions that some see as the wave of the future, there is scarcely such a thing as a front line.

The only valid reason to keep women out of combat is if their presence is debilitating to what military types call the mission. This is a real possibility, but so far it hasn't been illuminated by much honest discussion. Opponents of the combat exclusion rule often act as if the only reasonable doubts about female soldiers have to do with physical strength and stamina. If so, of course, the solution is simple: women who pass all relevant physical tests can go to war. Thus a woman who can march, say, 30 miles with a 65-pound pack would be eligible for the infantry; a woman who can readily lift and load heavy artillery shells would be admitted to the field artillery. (Women are now permitted only in the longer-range "push-button" artillery, which fires, for example, Lance missiles.) The number of women passing relevant strength tests should grow over the years, as strength, in the increasingly technological military, declines in relevance.

But strength and stamina are not the only pertinent biological differences between men and women. Men are, statistically speaking, more aggressive than women, and at least some of this difference is inherent—due to the effect of the male hormone testosterone on the brain. It is less clear whether other observed differences—in the propensity to take physical risks, for example—are also genetically based. But the aggression gap alone means that even if the military were gender-blind and physical strength were irrelevant, full parity would be highly unlikely; barring genetic engineering, there will never be as many women who want to kill, and are good at it, as men.

As with physical strength, differences between the sexes in aggressiveness or bravery needn't stand in the way of individual women; insufficiently aggressive women (and for that matter insufficiently aggressive men) can, in principle, be weeded out. This may be tricky. You can't tell how mean someone is by counting push-ups. There is no systematic effort to gauge such psychological factors in basic training, but some such tests may be useful adjuncts to the Schroeder plan.

The ultimate test of such tests, though, can only come in combat. If women who reach certain combat positions have a markedly higher rate of failure under fire, then they will have to be barred from those jobs. This may be unfair, but try telling that to the soldiers whose lives hang in the balance.

The second big issue that cannot be definitively settled without bloodshed is the effect of women on previously all-male groups. The hypothesis, advanced by some anthropologists and evolutionary biologists, that men are genetically predisposed to fight in groups remains controversial. It is unclear whether the intense bonds formed during war, and all the valor and sacrifice they inspire, result from "male-bonding" or simply "person-under-fire bonding." Either way, there is no doubt that introducing a woman into a previously all-male platoon will change the group dynamics (just as there is no doubt that comparably diluting a previously all-female group will change things).

One source of change, of course, is romance, along with any attendant distractions, rivalries, and conflicts of interest. Another possible problem is the patronizing of women; there is anecdotal evidence from Israeli military history that men are inclined to linger over a wounded female comrade, to the detriment of the larger mission. The list of other possible changes is long, but the question, in the end, is simple: After all the adjustments have been made, and the group has found some new equilibrium, will the change have been for the better, the worse, or neither? Perhaps some insight into this question can be gained in peacetime—through, for instance, mock combat between all-male units and integrated units. But the only way to find out for sure is amid live ammunition: open some

Army combat units to women and wait for the next Panama.

The issue of women in combat may end up being much ado about very little. Surveys suggest that few of the 192,000 enlisted women in the military are yearning for combat duty. (The case is different for the 33,000 female officers, who know that their exclusion from combat commands hurts their careers.) In Canada, which recently opened all positions to women, the military initially spent $500,000 trying to recruit 249 women for field tests in combat posts, but only 26 signed up.

Among the reasons for holding a real-war test of full military integration is that, surprisingly, there is little germane evidence on the modern historical record. The role of women in Israel's War of Independence has been exaggerated; of 4,000 Israeli soldiers killed, only 114 were women. (Still, it may be noteworthy that the most commonly cited reasons for Israel's subsequent combat exclusion rule were not any deficiencies on the part of female soldiers, but the frequency with which they were raped when captured and the already mentioned tendency of male soldiers to worry excessively about wounded women.) During World War II Soviet women fought the Germans and seem to have acquitted themselves ably, but accounts are sketchy. Moreover, the women fought in segregated units. The few NATO armies that have opened all combat posts to women, such as Canada's and Denmark's, have managed to stay out of wars. (But the Canadian experience suggests that infantry is by far the hardest challenge for women; at last count, of 88 female infantry recruits, 78 had dropped out of basic training, and only one had graduated.)

The U.S. military has been fitfully heading toward full integration for nearly a century. The Army founded auxiliaries for nurses in 1901, and for decades thereafter kept women in what was deemed to be their place. They served in clerical posts during World War I; some were in the trenches as telephone operators, but not at the very front lines. In World War II the Army Air Corps used women as ferry pilots, flying radio operators, control tower specialists, and airplane mechanics, as well as stenographers and telephonists. Sixty-seven military nurses survived the horrors of Bataan and Corregidor and were held for three years in a Japanese prisoner-of-war camp. For the most part women were cordoned off in separate auxiliaries; their presence was thought temporary. WAVES, the acronym for the Navy's auxiliary, stood for "Women Accepted for Voluntary Emergency Service."

Postwar legislation sustained the women's auxiliaries, but it also put a ceiling on the number of female soldiers—only two percent of each service—and imposed the combat exclusion rule on the Navy and Air Force. (The Army's exclusion rule is Pentagon policy, modeled on the legislation.) The two percent ceiling was lifted in 1967, but only after Vietnam did the numbers rise to impressive levels—from under four percent in 1974 to more than eight percent by 1980.

It is probably not too much to say that women saved the post-Vietnam all-volunteer military, by making up for the critical shortage of "high quality" (i.e., competently educated) male enlistees during the 1970s. As the high unemployment rate of the early Reagan years enriched the pool of male recruits, efforts to recruit women slackened. But their numbers grew anyway, reaching nearly 11 percent in 1989, the highest of any NATO country.

West Point, like the other service academies, was integrated barely more than a decade ago. And this year the First Captain (the top-ranking cadet in the senior class) was a woman. Still, the zenith for women in the military, so far, was probably reached in Panama. The now-famous assault by Capt. Linda Bray's military police unit on the Panamanian guard-dog kennel was not, it turns out, quite as heroic or bloody as first advertised. But it appears to be the first time a woman has commanded a military unit in combat. And by all accounts she didn't bat an eyelash, much less shed a tear.   [1990]

Understanding the Reading

1. What is the difference between the private and public attitudes about women in combat held by military leaders?
2. What inconsistencies exist in the present exclusionary policy?
3. What is the "aggression gap"?
4. Why is the issue of male bonding relevant?

5. What can be learned from the use of women in combat by other countries?
6. What indicates that at least some women are interested in military service, including combat duty?

Suggestions for Responding

1. Do you believe women should qualify for combat positions? What support can you provide for your position?
2. Over history, the military has excluded or restricted participation of other groups, most notably African-Americans. Research and report on racial integration of the armed services.
3. Another military policy states that "homosexuality is incompatible with military service," so gays and lesbians are discharged even if they have commendable service records. Do you feel this policy should be changed? Why or why not? ✦

70

Marriage as a Restricted Club

LINDSY VAN GELDER

Several years ago, I stopped going to weddings. In fact, I no longer celebrate the wedding anniversaries or engagements of friends, relatives, or anyone else, although I might wish them lifelong joy in their relationships. My explanation is that the next wedding I attend will be my own—to the woman I've loved and lived with for nearly six years.

Although I've been legally married to a man myself (and come close to marrying two others), I've come, in these last six years with Pamela, to see heterosexual marriage as very much a restricted club. (Nor is this likely to change in the near future, if one can judge by the recent clobbering of what was actually a rather tame proposal to recognize "domestic partnerships" in San Francisco.[1]) Regardless of the *reason* people marry—whether to save on real estate taxes or qualify for married students' housing or simply to express love—lesbians and gay men can't obtain the same results should they desire to do so. It seems apparent to me that few friends of Pamela's and mine would even join a club that excluded blacks, Jews, or women, much less assume that they could expect their black, Jewish, or female friends to toast their new status with champagne. But probably no other stand of principle we've ever made in our lives has been so misunderstood, or caused so much bad feeling on both sides.

Several people have reacted with surprise to our views, it never having occurred to them that gay people *can't* legally marry. (Why on earth did they think that none of us had bothered?) The most common reaction, however, is acute embarrassment, followed by a denial of our main point—that the about-to-be-wed person is embarking on a privileged status. (One friend of Pamela's insisted that lesbians are "lucky" not to have to agonize over whether or not to get married.) So wrapped in gauze is the institution of marriage, so ingrained the expectation that brides and grooms can enjoy the world's delighted approval, that it's hard for me not to feel put on the defensive for being so mean-spirited, eccentric, and/or politically rigid as to boycott such a happy event.

Another question we've fielded more than once (usually from our most radical friends, both gay and straight) is why we'd want to get married in the first place. In fact, I have mixed feelings about registering my personal life with the state, but—and this seems to me to be the essence of radical politics—I'd prefer to be the one making the choice. And while feminists in recent years have rightly focused on puncturing the Schlaflyite[2] myth of the legally protected homemaker, it's also true that marriage does confer some very real dollars-and-cents benefits. One example of inequity is our inability to file joint tax returns, although many couples, both gay and straight, go through periods when one partner in the relationship is unemployed or makes considerably less money than the other. At one time in our relationship, Pamela—who is a musician—was between bands and earning next to nothing. I was making a little over $37,000 a year as a newspaper reporter, a salary that put me in the 42 percent tax bracket—about $300 a week taken out

of my paycheck. If we had been married, we could have filed a joint tax return and each paid taxes on half my salary, in the 25 or 30 percent bracket. The difference would have been nearly $100-a-week in our pockets.

Around the same time, Pamela suffered a month-long illness which would have been covered by my health insurance if she were my spouse. We were luckier than many; we could afford it. But on top of the worry and expense involved (and despite the fact that intellectually we believe in the ideal of free medical care for everyone), we found it almost impossible to avoid internalizing a sense of personal failure—the knowledge that *because of who we are, we can't take care of each other.* I've heard of other gay people whose lovers were deported because they couldn't marry them and enable them to become citizens; still others who were barred from intensive-care units where their lovers lay stricken because they weren't "immediate family."

I would never begrudge a straight friend who got married to save a lover from deportation or staggering medical bills, but the truth is that I no longer sympathize with most of the less tangible justifications. This includes the oft-heard "for the sake of the children" argument, since (like many gay people, especially women) I *have* children, and I resent the implication that some families are more "legitimate" than others. (It's important to safeguard one's children's rights to their father's property, but a legal contract will do the same thing as marriage.)

But the single most painful and infuriating rationale for marriage, as far as I'm concerned, is the one that goes: "We wanted to stand up and show the world that we've made a *genuine* commitment." When one is gay, such sentiments are labeled "flaunting." My lover and I almost never find ourselves in public settings outside the gay ghetto where we are (a) perceived to be a couple at all (people constantly ask us if we're sisters, although we look nothing like each other), and (b) valued as such. Usually we're forced to choose between being invisible and being despised. "Making a genuine commitment" in this milieu is like walking a highwire without a net—with most of the audience not even watching and a fair segment rooting for you to fall. A disproportionate number of gay couples do.

I think it's difficult for even my closest, most feminist straight women friends to empathize with the intensity of my desire to be recognized as Pamela's partner. (In fact, it may be harder for feminists to understand than for others; I know that when I was straight,—I often resented being viewed as one half of a couple. My struggle was for an independent identity, not the cojoined one I now crave.) But we are simply not considered *authentic,* and the reminders are constant. Recently at a party, a man I'd known for years spied me across the room and came over to me, arms outstretched, big happy-to-see-you grin on his face. Pamela had a gig that night and wasn't at the party; my friend's wife was there but in another room, and I hadn't seen her yet. "How's M——?" I asked the man. "Oh, she's fine," he replied, continuing to smile pleasantly. "Are you and Pam still together?"

Our sex life itself is against the law in many states, of course, and like all lesbians and gay men, we are without many other rights, both large and small. (In Virginia, for instance, it's technically against the law for us to buy liquor.) But as a gay couple, we are also most likely to be labeled and discriminated against in those very settings that, for most heterosexual Americans, constitute the most relaxed and personal parts of life. Virtually every tiny public act of togetherness—from holding hands on the street to renting a hotel room to dancing—requires us constantly to risk humiliation (I think, for example, of the two California women who were recently thrown out of a restaurant that had special romantic tables for couples), sexual harassment (it's astonishing how many men can't resist coming on to a lesbian couple), and even physical assault. A great deal of energy goes into just expecting possible trouble. It's a process which, after six years, has become second nature for me—but occasionally, when I'm in Provincetown or someplace else with a large lesbian population, I experience the *absence* of it as a feeling of virtual weightlessness.

What does all this have to do with my friends' weddings? Obviously, I can't expect my friends to live my life. But I do think that lines are being drawn in this "pro-family" Reagan era, and I have no choice about what side I'm placed on. My straight friends do, and at the very least, I expect them to acknowledge that. I certainly expect them to understand why I don't want to be among the rice-throwers and well-wishers at their weddings; beyond that, I would hope that they would commit themselves to fighting for my rights—preferably in personally visible ways, like marching in gay pride parades. But I also wish they wouldn't get married, period. And if that sounds hard-nosed, I hope I'm only proving my point—that not being able to marry isn't a minor issue.

Not that my life would likely be changed as the result of any individual straight person's symbolic refusal to marry. (Nor, for that matter, do all gay couples want to be wed.) But it's a political reality that heterosexual live-together couples are among our best tactical allies. The movement to repeal state sodomy laws has profited from the desire of straight people to keep the government out of *their* bedrooms. Similarly, it was a heterosexual New York woman who went to court several years ago to fight her landlord's demand that she either marry her live-in boyfriend or face eviction for violating a lease clause prohibiting "unrelated" tenants—and whose struggle led to the recent passage of a state rent law that had ramifications for thousands of gay couples, including Pamela and me.

The right wing has seized on "homosexual marriage" as its bottom-line scare phrase in much the same way that "Would you want your sister to marry one?" was brandished 25 years ago. *They* see marriage as their turf. And so when I see feminists crossing into that territory of respectability and "sinlessness," I feel my buffer zone slipping away. I feel as though my friends are taking off their armbands, leaving me exposed.   [1984]

Notes

1. As of 1990, San Francisco legally recognizes domestic partners.
2. SCHLAFLYITE: A reference to Phyllis Schlafly, who opposed the Equal Rights Amendment on the grounds that it would leave housewives with no legal protections.

Understanding the Reading

1. Why doesn't Van Gelder attend weddings and anniversary and engagement celebrations?

2. Why would gay men or lesbians want to marry?

3. What other legal and personal rights are denied to gay men and lesbians?

4. What strategies for improving the lives of homosexuals does Van Gelder offer?

Suggestions for Responding

1. Why do you think many men "come on" to a lesbian couple, or why do you think Van Gelder feels they do?

2. Do you think gay men and lesbians should be allowed to marry or at least declare a legally recognized domestic partnership? ◆

71

A Long Story

BETH BRANT

*Dedicated to my Great-Grandmothers
Eliza Powless and Catherine Brant*

About 40 Indian children took the train at this depot for the Philadelphia Indian School last Friday. They were accompanied by the government agent, and seemed a bright looking lot.
    —From THE NORTHERN OBSERVER
        Massena, N.Y. July 20, 1892

I am only beginning to understand what it means for a mother to lose a child.
    —Anna Demeter, LEGAL KIDNAPPING

1890. . . .

It has been two days since they came and took the children away. My body is greatly chilled. All our blankets have been used to bring me warmth. The women keep the fire blazing. The men sit. They talk among themselves. We are frightened by this sudden child-stealing. We signed papers, the agent said. This gave them rights to take our babies. It is good for them, the agent said. It will make them civilized, the agent said. I do not know civilized. I hold myself tight in fear of flying apart into the air. The others try to feed me. Can they feed a dead woman? I have

stopped talking. When my mouth opens, only air escapes. I have used up my sound screaming their names . . . She Sees Deer! Walking Fox! My eyes stare at the room, the walls of scrubbed wood, the floor of dirt. I know there are People here, but I cannot see them. I see a darkness, like the lake at New Moon, black, unmoving. In the center a picture of my son and daughter being lifted onto the train. My daughter wearing the dark blue, heavy dress. All of the girls dressed alike. Her hair covered by a strange basket tied under her chin. Never have I seen such eyes! They burn into my head even now. My son. His hair cut. Dressed as the white men, his arms and legs covered by cloth that made him sweat. His face, wet with tears. So many children crying, screaming. The sun on our bodies, our heads. The train screeching like a crow, sounding like laughter. Smoke and dirt pumping out of the insides of the train. So many People. So many children. The women, standing as if in prayer, our hands lifted, reaching. The dust sifting down on our palms. Our palms making motions at the sky. Our fingers closing like the claws of the bear. I see this now. The hair of my son is held in my hands. I rub the strands, the heavy braids coming alive as the fire flares and casts a bright light on the black hair. They slip from my fingers and lie coiled and tangled on the ground. I see this. My husband picks up the braids, wraps them in a cloth; takes the pieces of our son away. He walks outside, the eyes of the People on him. I see this. He will find a bottle and drink with the men. Some of the women will join them. They will end the night by singing or crying. It is all the same. I see this. No sounds of children playing games and laughing. Even the dogs have ceased their noises. They lay outside each doorway, waiting. I hear this. The voices of children. They cry. They pray. They call me. . . . Nisten ha. I hear this. Nisten ha.

1978. . . .

I am awakened by the dream. In the dream, my daughter is dead. Her father is returning her body to me in pieces. He keeps her heart. I thought I screamed . . . Patricia! I sit up in bed, swallowing air as if for nourishment. The dream remains in the air. I rise to go to her room. Ellen tries to lead me back to bed, but I have to see once again. I open her door . . . she is gone. The room empty, lonely. They said it was in her best interests. How can it be? She is only six, a baby who needs her mothers. She loves us. This is not happening. I will not believe this. Oh god, I think I have died. Night after night, Ellen holds me as I shake. Our sobs stifling the air in our room. We lie in our bed and try to give comfort. My mind can't think beyond last week when she left. I would have killed him if I'd had the chance. He took her hand and pulled her to the car. The look in his eyes of triumph. It was a contest to him. I know he will teach her to hate us. He will! I see her dear face. Her face looking out the back window of his car. Her mouth forming the word over and over . . . Mommy Mama. Her dark braids tied with red yarn. Her front teeth missing. Her overalls with the yellow flower on the pocket, embroidered by Ellen's hands. So lovingly she sewed the yellow wool. Patricia waiting quietly until she was finished. Ellen promising to teach her the designs . . . chain stitch, french knot, split stitch. How Patricia told everyone that Ellen made the flower just for her. So proud of her overalls. I open the closet door. Almost everything is gone. A few little things hang there limp, abandoned. I pull a blue dress from a hanger and take it back to my room. Ellen tries to take it away from me, but I hold on, the soft, blue cotton smelling like her. How is it possible to feel such pain and live? Ellen?! She croons my name . . . Mary . . . Mary . . . I love you. She sings me to sleep.

1890. . . .

The agent was here to deliver a letter. I screamed at him and sent curses his way. I threw dirt in his face as he mounted his horse. He thinks I'm a crazy woman and warns me . . . "you better settle down, Annie." What can they do to me? I am a crazy woman. This letter hurts my hand. It is written in their hateful language. It is evil, but there is a message for me. I start the walk up the road to my brother. He works for the whites and understands their meanings. I think about my brother as I pull my shawl closer to my body. It is cold now. Soon there will be snow. The corn has been dried and hangs from our cabin, waiting to be used. The corn never changes. My brother is changed. He says that *I* have changed and bring shame to our clan. He says I should accept the fate. But I do not believe in the fate of child-

stealing. There is evil here. There is much wrong in our village. He says I am a crazy woman because I howl at the sky every night. He is a fool! I am calling my children. He says the People are becoming afraid of me because I talk to the air, and laugh like the loon overhead. But I am talking to the children. They need to hear the sound of me. I laugh to cheer them. They cry for us. This paper in my hands has the stink of the agent. It burns my hands. I hurry to my brother. He has taken the sign of the wolf from over the doorway. He pretends to be like those who hate us. He gets more and more like the child-stealers. His eyes move away from mine. He takes the letter from me and begins the reading of it. I am confused. This letter is from two strangers with the names Martha and Daniel. They say they are learning civilized ways. Daniel works in the fields, growing food for the school. Martha cooks and is being taught to sew aprons. She will be going to live with the schoolmaster's wife. She will be a live-in girl. What is live-in girl? I shake my head. The words sound the same to me. I am afraid of Martha and Daniel. These strangers who know my name. My hands and arms are becoming numb. I tear the letters from my brother's fingers. He stares at me, his eyes traitors in his face. He calls after me . . . "Annie . . . Annie." That is not my name! I run back to the road. That is not my name! There is no Martha. There is no Daniel. This is witch work. The paper burns and burns. At my cabin, I quickly dig a hole in the field. The earth is hard and cold, but I dig with my nails. I dig, my hands feeling weaker. I tear the paper and bury the scraps. As the earth drifts and settles, the names Martha and Daniel are covered. I look to the sky and find nothing but endless blue. My eyes are blinded by the color. I begin the howling.

1978. . . .

When I get home from work, there is a letter from Patricia. I make coffee and wait for Ellen, pacing the rooms of our apartment. My back is sore from the line, bending over and down, screwing the handles on the doors of the flashy cars moving by at an incredible pace. My work protects me from questions. The guys making jokes at my expense. Some of them touching my shoulder lightly and briefly, as a sign of understanding. The few women, eyes averted or smiling at me in sympathy. No one talks. There is no time to talk. There is no room to talk, the noise taking up all space and breath. I carry the letter with me as I move from room to room. Finally I sit at the kitchen table, turning the paper around in my hands. Patricia's printing is large and uneven. The stamp has been glued on half-heartedly and is coming loose. Each time a letter arrives, I dread it, even as I long to hear from my child. I hear Ellen's key in the door. She walks into the kitchen, bringing the smell of the hospital with her. She comes toward me, her face set in new lines, her uniform crumpled and stained, her brown hair pulled back in an imitation of a french twist. She knows there is a letter. I kiss her and bring mugs of coffee to the table. We look into each others' eyes. She reaches for my hand, bringing it to her lips. Her hazel eyes are steady in her round face. I open the letter. Dear Mommy. I am fine. Daddy got me a new bike. My big teeth are coming in. We are going to see Grandma for my birthday. Daddy got me new shoes. She doesn't ask about Ellen. I imagine her father standing over her, watching the words painstakingly being printed. Coaxing her. Coaching her. The letter becomes ugly. I frantically tear it in bits and scatter them out the window. The wind scoops the pieces into a tight fist before strewing them in the street. A car drives over the paper, shredding it to mud and garbage. Ellen makes a garbled sound. "I'll leave. If it will make it better, I'll leave." I quickly hold her as the dusk swirls around the room and engulfs us. "Don't leave. Don't leave." I feel her sturdy back shiver against my hands. She begins to kiss my throat and her arms tighten as we move closer. "Ah Mary, I love you so much." As the tears threaten our eyes, the taste of salt is on our lips and tongues. We stare into ourselves, touching our place of pain; reaching past the fear, the guilt, the anger, the loneliness. We go to our room. It is beautiful again. I am seeing it as if with new eyes. The sun is barely there. The colors of cream, brown, green mixing with the wood floor. The rug with its design of wild birds. The black ash basket glowing on the dresser, holding a bouquet of dried flowers, bought at a vendor's stand. I remember the old woman, laughing and speaking rapidly in Polish as she wrapped the blossoms in newspaper. Making a present of her work. Ellen undresses me as I cry. My desire for her breaking through

the heartbreak we share. She pulls the covers back, smoothing the white sheets, her hands repeating the gestures done every day at work. She guides me onto the cool material. I watch her remove the uniform of work. An aide to nurses. A healer in spirit. She comes to me full in flesh. My hands are taken with the curves and soft roundness of her. She covers me with the beating of her heart. The rhythm steadies me. Heat is centering me. I am grounded by the peace between us. I smile at her face gleaming above me, round like a moon, her long hair loose and touching my breasts. I take her breast in my hand, bring it to my mouth; suck her as a woman, in desire . . . in faith. Our bodies join. Our hair braids together on the pillow. Brown, black, silver; catching the last face of the sun. We kiss, touch, move to our place of power. Her mouth, moving over my body, stopping at curves and swells of skin, kissing, removing pain. Closer, close, together, woven, my legs are heat, the center of my soul is speaking to her, I am sliding into her, her mouth is medicine, her heart is the earth, we are dancing with flying arms, I shout, I sing, I weep salty liquid, sweet and warm, it coats her throat, this is my life. I love you Ellen, I love you Mary, I love, we love.

1891. . . .

The moon is full. The air is cold. This cold strikes at my flesh as I remove my clothes and set them on fire in the withered corn field. I cut my hair, the knife sawing through the heavy mass. I bring the sharp blade to my arms, legs, and breasts. The blood trickles like small red rivers down my body. I feel nothing. I throw the tangled webs of my hair into the flames. The smell, like a burning animal, fills my nostrils. As the fire stretches to touch the stars, the People come out to watch me . . . the crazy woman. The ice in the air touches me. They caught me as I tried to board the train and search for my babies. The white men tell my husband to watch me. I am dangerous. I laugh and laugh. My husband is only good for tipping bottles and swallowing anger. He looks at me, opening his mouth, and making no sound. His eyes are dead. He wanders from the cabin and looks out at the corn. He whispers our names. He calls after the children. He is a dead man. But I am not! Where have they taken the children? I ask the question of each one who travels the road past our house. The women come and we talk. We ask and ask. They say there is nothing we can do. The white man is a ghost. He slips in and out where we cannot see. Even in our dreams he comes to take away our questions. He works magic that has resisted our medicine. This magic has made us weak. What is the secret about them? Why do they want our babies? They sent the Blackrobes many years ago to teach us new magic. It was evil! They lied and tricked us. They spoke of gods who would forgive us if we became like them. This god is ugly!! He killed our masks. He killed our men. He sends the women screaming at the moon in terror. They want our power. They take our children to remove the inside of them. Our power. It is what makes us Hau de no sau nee. They steal our food, our sacred rattle, the stories, our names. What is left? I am a crazy woman. I look in the fire that consumes my hair and I see their faces. My daughter. My son. They are still crying for me, though the sound grows fainter. The wind picks up their keening and brings it to me. The sound has bored into my brain. I begin howling. At night, I dare not sleep. I fear the dreams. It is too terrible, the things that happen there. In my dream there is wind and blood moving as a stream. Red, dark blood in my dreams. Rushing for our village, the blood moves faster and faster. There are screams of wounded People. Animals are dead, thrown in the blood stream. There is nothing left. Only the air, echoing nothing. Only the earth, soaking up blood, spreading it in the Four Directions, becoming a thing there is no name for. I stand in the field, watching the fire, the People watching me. We are waiting, but the answer is not clear yet. A crazy woman. That is what they call me.

1979. . . .

After taking a morning off work to see my lawyer, I come home, not caring if I call in. Not caring, for once, at the loss in pay. Not caring. My lawyer says there is nothing more we can do. I must wait. As if we have done anything else. He has custody and calls the shots. We must wait and see how long it takes for him to get tired of being mommy and daddy. So . . . I wait. I open the door to Patricia's room. Ellen keeps it dusted and cleaned, in case she will be allowed to visit us. The yellow and bright blue walls are a mockery. I walk to the windows, begin to systematically

tear down the curtains. I slowly start to rip the cloth apart. I enjoy hearing the sounds of destruction. Faster and faster, I tear the material into long strips. What won't come apart with my hands, I pull at with my teeth. Looking for more to destroy, I gather the sheets and bedspread in my arms and wildly shred them to pieces. Grunting and sweating, I am pushed by rage and the searing wound in my soul. Like a wolf, caught in a trap, gnawing at her own leg to set herself free, I begin to beat my breasts to deaden the pain inside. A noise gathers in my throat and finds the way out. I begin a scream that turns to howling, then turns to hoarse choking. I want to take my fists, my strong fists, my brown fists, and smash the world until it bleeds. Bleeds! And all the judges in their flapping robes, and the fathers who look for revenge, are ground, ground into dust and disappear with the wind. The word . . . lesbian. Lesbian. The word that makes them panic, makes them afraid, makes them destroy children. The word that dares them. Lesbian. *I am one.* Even for Patricia, even for her, I will not cease to be! As I kneel amidst the colorful scraps, Raggedy Anns smiling up at me, my chest gives a sigh. My heart slows to its normal speech. I feel the blood pumping outward to my veins, carrying nourishment and life. I strip the room naked. I close the door.   [1988]

Understanding the Reading

1. How did the government justify taking Indian children from their families in 1890?
2. Who took Mary's child, and why?
3. Why does "Annie" say that there is no Martha and no Daniel and that Annie is not her name?
4. Why do both mothers tear up the letters from their children?
5. Why does "Annie" cut her hair and skin and burn her clothes? Is she actually crazy?
6. Why does Mary destroy Patricia's room? Is she crazy?

Suggestions for Responding

1. Explain the similarities and differences between the experiences of these two women.
2. What role should the government play in the socialization and education of children, especially those from minority populations? ✦

SUGGESTIONS FOR RESPONDING TO PART VII

1. Research one of the major Supreme Court civil rights rulings, such as *People v. Hall* in 1854, *Dred Scott v. Sanford* in 1857, *Bradwell v. Illinois* in 1873, *United States of America v. Susan B. Anthony* in 1873, *Minor v. Happersett* in 1875, *Elk v. Wilkins* in 1884, *Plessy v. Ferguson* in 1896, *Muller v. Oregon* in 1908, *Korematsu v. United States* in 1944, *Brown v. Board of Education of Topeka* in 1954, *Griswold v. Connecticut* in 1965, *Phillips v. Martin Marietta in 1971, Reed v. Reed* in 1971, *Roe v. Wade* in 1973, *Griggs v. Duke Power Company* in 1976, *Nashville Gas Company v. Satty* in 1977, *Regents of the University of California v. Bakke* in 1978, *United States v. Weber* in 1979, *Bundy v. Jackson* in 1981, *Wards Cove Packing v. Antonio* in 1989, or *United Auto Workers v. Johnson Controls* in 1990. Write a report explaining the background of the dispute, how the Court ruled and on what grounds it based its decision, and the impact that the case had on the civil rights of the affected group.

2. Research one of the major civil rights laws, such as the nineteenth-century Married Women's Property Acts , the 1875 Civil Rights Act, the 1887 General Allotment Act (Dawes Act), the 1963 Equal Pay Act, the 1964 Civil Rights Act, Title IX of the Education Act of 1972, the 1974 National Fair Housing Act, the 1974 Women's Educational Equity Act, the 1974 Equal Credit Opportunity Act, the 1978 Pregnancy Discrimination Act, the 1983 Women's Economic Equity Act, the 1988–1991 Civil Rights Restoration Acts, or the various Voting Rights Acts of the past two decades. Explain the purpose of the law, its congressional history, its enforcement, and its impact on the affected group.

3. Research how affirmative action is defined in Executive Orders 11246 (1965), 11375 (1968), and 11478 (1971). Explain what affirmative action actually means. Discuss how it differs from what you thought it meant. Do you now support or oppose the concept? Why?

4. Trace the history of the Equal Rights [for Women] Amendment to the U.S. Constitution since 1920. Do you think it should have been ratified in the 1980s? Why or why not?

5. Write a biography on a leader in the Woman Suffrage movement (as it was called) such as Susan B. Anthony, Elizabeth Cady Stanton, Carrie Chapman Catt, Lucy Stone, or Alice Paul.

6. Find out what the Equal Employment Opportunity Commission (EEOC) is, how it operates, what its regulations cover (including the concept of Bona Fide Occupational Qualification, or BFOQ), and evaluate its effectiveness in protecting employment rights of minorities and women.

VIII
Violence

VIOLENCE, THE USE OF PHYSICAL FORCE TO CONTROL the behavior of another, is the most brutal assertion of power. The single purpose of a violent act is to exercise control and to compel another person to follow a certain course of action or enforced inaction. It is intended to coerce the victim into acting or thinking in whatever way the person with power dictates and to leave the victim with no alternative except compliance. Violence, the crudest power strategy, enforces the *dominance* of the perpetrator and the *subordination* of the victim.

Most of us think we abhor violence. When we hear about a particularly violent occurrence, we protest, "That's horrible! How could anyone do that?" But violence actually plays a central role in American culture. Many movies, for example, celebrate violence; we adore the shoot-out, thrill to the car chase, relish the hunt. However, we expect this fantasy violence to have a moral resolution; we want to know that the good guy is ultimately victorious and that in the end the bad guy will be punished (violently, of course).

In real life, however, violent behavior doesn't have such sanguine outcomes. Rather, violence and fear of the threat of violence are employed to serve the interests of the dominant group and to assert and maintain the existing status hierarchy. Because ours is a patriarchal society dominated by European-Americans, violence is practiced most frequently against women and people of color. This is not to deny that these groups never resort to violence themselves; such examples as minority youth gangs or abusive mothers spring to mind immediately. The point is that most white males generally don't have to restrict or alter their behavior to avoid violent encounters as women and people of color do.

Patriarchal ideology rests on the belief in male supremacy and the inferiority of females—on **sexism.** Within the patriarchal hierarchy, every man is expected to dominate the women with whom he is affiliated. Thus, patriarchal society sanctions and condones all kinds of behavior, including violence, that enforce male control. Remember that aggressiveness and control are central features of the traditional male gender role and passivity and weakness of the female role. This construct reinforces the potential for aggression against women in traditional male-female relationships. This is evident in the well-entrenched societal tolerance of male violence, blaming the victim: "What was she doing out so late by herself?" "Boys will be boys." "I wonder what she did to bring it onto herself." Not very long ago, men had legal authority to beat their wives; in fact, the expression "rule of thumb" refers to the nineteenth-century law that "protected" wives by limiting the thickness of the stick husbands could use.

Men use violence to exert and maintain their power over women; violence and fear of violence control every woman's behavior. The threat of **rape,** being forced to have sex without consent, keeps every woman from moving freely wherever she wants and from dressing however she likes. A woman learns to be cautious about every man she encounters, even if she already knows him. The threat is real. A woman is raped every six minutes, and one out of every three women will be raped in her lifetime. Studies of college-age men have revealed that up to half of them thought they might commit a rape if they could be sure of getting away with it. Notwithstanding the frequency with which this crime occurs, rape victims are still treated with skepticism, even by friends and family. If a rape survivor decides to press charges against her attacker and the case goes to trial, the defense may try to introduce her behavior into the proceedings and may well claim that she enticed her assailant or that she wanted or enjoyed it.

The first three selections in Part VIII address the issue of rape. One of the most important points James A. Doyle makes in the first reading is that rape is an act of dominance, not sex; he explains why, despite general recognition of this fact, society tends to **blame the victim,** accusing her of being somehow responsible for what was done to her. Doyle also examines how **pornography,** which links violence with female sexuality, contributes to the degradation of women. In the next reading, Kathleen Hirsh analyzes fraternity gang rape; she sees it as the effort of young men to establish their heterosexual identity and to create male bonds at the expense of women. She also contends that the tendency of universities to protect the perpetrators more than the victim silences women—the victim herself *and* all women on campus. Tipper Gore charges that the sexism and racism in rap music reinforce these prejudices, encouraging violence against women.

In addition to rape, women experience other kinds of violence, in particular **battery,** which is defined under law as beating another person. Commonly referred to as "domestic violence" but more accurately labeled as wife beating, this form of physical abuse is the most common and least reported crime in this country, afflicting women of all races and classes. According to FBI statistics, a woman is beaten by her husband or partner every 18 seconds. As the Center for Women Policy Studies reports, such battery isn't experienced only by married women. The CWPS report on premarital violence reveals a shocking reality of abuse—from shoving and slapping to closed-fist battery—among college-age couples; moreover, they found that at least one-quarter of these couples remain together despite the fact that abuse generally escalates over time.

Not just heterosexual women experience violence; both gay men and lesbians are being terrorized more and more by violent physical attacks, known as **gay bashing.** According to Victoria A. Brownworth, the number of such attacks made on lesbians is increasing at a more rapid rate than those against gay men. She analyzes why it is difficult to gather accurate statistics on lesbian hate crimes: Women are more reluctant than men to turn to male authorities for protection, and hatred of lesbians plays a role in attacks on heterosexual women as well.

Both **assault,** threatening to injure a person physically, and battery are illegal, but both are reality for people of color as well as for women and gay men. Violence has been used to dominate members of these groups to "keep them in their place" throughout the history of this country.

Not long after European-American colonialists began to arrive on the shores of the New World in substantial numbers, they began to dominate the native peoples. To accommodate their expanding population, whites required more and more space. When the indigenous people resisted encroachment onto their traditional homelands, land-hungry whites used both law and force, including military action, to remove them. Following the Civil War, the principal business of the U.S. Department of War became controlling the Native Americans. Since **war** is state-organized and state-authorized violence, it must always be seen as serving the interests of those who control the state. Therefore, the dominant white society considered the Indian Wars to be both necessary and honorable actions. However, as the article on the Wounded Knee bloodshed shows, Indians experienced these wars as genocidal violence.

African-Americans were also victims of state-authorized violence. Prior to the Civil War, it was completely legal for slaveholders to whip, maim, rape, or even kill the people they held in bondage. Even after the ratification of the Thirteenth Amendment, which made slavery illegal, whites not only enacted discriminatory laws to maintain their advantage, they also used illegal violence to intimidate African-Americans. This was the original aim of the white-supremacist Ku Klux Klan, which first formed in the South. As Stanley Coben explains, by the early part of this century the Klan had expanded its bigotry to include intolerance of Catholics, Jews, and practically everyone else who wasn't a white Anglo-Saxon Protestant (WASP); as a result, its constituency grew enormously in the northern states, where it was sometimes tolerated, sometimes not.

Racial violence isn't limited to the actions of such organized groups as the Klan. William Faulkner's dramatic story shows how mob hysteria can be whipped up by a single violent man who knows how to exploit the racism and sexism of his community. For nearly a century, such random acts of violence were practiced against African-Americans to intimidate them and to enforce their "Jim Crow" inferiority. Teenager Emmett Till was murdered and mutilated because he "thought he was as good as any white man," as the Southern Poverty Law Center reports; Till was only one of more than forty people murdered between 1955 and 1968 in Mississippi and Alabama by white terrorists who wanted to "set an example" to blacks and civil rights workers.

Even after the civil rights movement of the 1950s earned equal legal rights for all citizens, white racists continued to use violence to keep blacks from exercising those rights. Diane Oliver's story of the firebombing of one black family because of their decision to send their young son to an all-white school depicts the experiences of many blacks who took great personal risk to make racial integration a reality.

Racist violence continues today all over our country. Toni Cade Bambara's story reveals both the routine violence that envelops an entire urban slum community and the even more destructive force of racist police action. The Klanwatch Project reports on the extensiveness of white racist resistance to housing integration, and the Anti-Defamation League describes the activities of skinheads, dangerous racist terrorists who are recruiting schoolchildren and acquiring sophisticated weapons.

Sadly, whites are not the only group that commits racial violence. As new racial groups immigrate to the United States and try to establish new lives, they find themselves facing violent racial discrimination. Michael Laslett describes incidents of interracial violence experienced by recent Southeast-Asian refugees; he feels that ignorance about cultural differences, aggravated by the poverty of their own communities, leads to African-American and Latino resentment and violent actions against the new outsiders.

Because we have concentrated only on sexist and racist violence, we have not touched on the many other forms of violence that occur in our society. Cultural violence actually threatens all of us; anyone, regardless of race or gender, can be victimized by such violent crimes as incest, child abuse, elder abuse, robbery, mugging, and homicide. Violence threatens us on the streets, in our homes, at our places of work.

Violence is like a cancer on our society, and like cancer it is something we don't like to think about or talk about. But as with cancer, a cure is unlikely if we are not aware of the manifestations of the disease. The first step toward a cure of the disease of violence is learning about it and gaining insight into the suffering experienced by those many members of society who are forced to live daily with violence, leaving them feeling humiliated, vulnerable, and powerless. We cannot forget them because they are us.

72

Rape and Sexual Assault

JAMES A. DOYLE

Few words strike as much terror in a person's heart as rape. Few human acts are so fraught with misinformation and misconception as rape. Few other acts so degrade a human being as rape. And few other acts show the imbalance of power between men and women and men's quest for domination over women as rape does.

Rape is first and foremost an act of *violence,* an attempted or completed sexual assault instigated by one or more persons against another human being. The historical roots of rape run deep in the patriarchal tradition of male violence toward women. Rape, to be understood, must not be seen as simply a violent sexual act of a few lunatics or pathologically disordered persons, but rather a violent sexual act performed by many and reinforced by the dominant patriarchal values coming to the fore in their most twisted and disturbing forms in our culture. A few cultures may be less prone to violent sexual acts between males and females, but ours and most others are definitely "rape-prone" cultures. No discussion of power and its imbalance between women and men would be complete without a discussion of rape.

. . . We will first take up the issue of rape as an act of dominance (not sex) and of power (not pathology) that is ingrained in the very fiber of the male's gender role. Next we will attempt to put the statistics of rape in perspective by trying to give some scope to the enormity of the act of rape in the everyday lives of many women and some men. And then, we will note the rising concern and some of the actions taken among feminists and nonfeminists alike over the issue of rape as a social phenomenon of epidemic proportions and not merely an isolated criminal act affecting a few.

RAPE AND POWER

Throughout most of this century those who influenced what others thought about rape saw it as a "victim-precipitated phenomenon." Sigmund Freud, in his study of the female personality, theorized that the female was more "masochistic" than the male and that rape—either in fantasy or in fact—was the one sexual act wherein the female acted out her masochism to the utmost. However, such nonsense was soon dismissed by the psychiatric and psychological communities who began to speculate that rape was the result of a disordered or aberrant sexual impulse within a certain small group of men. Today, however, rape—whether the victim is female or male—is seen as an act of power or dominance of one person over another. Recently, some social scientists have noted that rape is one of the most terrifying means used by men to dominate other men inside and outside of prison. To focus on rape as a power or dominance act we need only analyze how rape is used in prison:

> Rape in prison is rarely a sexual act, but one of violence, politics and an acting out of power roles. "Most of your homosexual rapes [are] a macho thing," says Col. Walter Pence, the Chief of Security here at the Louisiana State Penitentiary at Angola. "It's basically one guy saying to another: 'I'm a better man than you and I'm gonna turn you out ["turn you out" is prison slang for rape] to prove it.' I've investigated about a hundred cases personally, and I've not seen one that's just an act of passion. It's definitely a macho/power thing among the inmates."

A prime ingredient in rape is the element of aggression that is so deeply embedded in the male's gender role. For many men, aggression is one of the major ways of proving their masculinity and manhood, especially among those men who feel some sense of powerlessness in their lives. The male-as-dominant or male-as-aggressor is a theme so central to many men's self-concept that it literally carries over into their sexual lives. Sex, in fact, may be the one area where the average man can still prove his masculinity when few other areas can be found for him to prove himself manly or in control, or the dominant one in a relationship. Diana Russell addresses this issue when she declares that rape is not the act of a disturbed male, but rather an act of an over-conforming male. She writes:

Rape is not so much a deviant act as an over-conforming act. Rape may be understood as an extreme acting-out of qualities that are regarded as super masculine in this and many other societies: aggression, force, power, strength, toughness, dominance, competitiveness. To win, to be superior, to be successful, to conquer—all demonstrate masculinity to those who subscribe to common cultural notions of masculinity, i.e., the *masculine mystique*. And it would be surprising if these notions of masculinity did not find expression in men's sexual behavior. Indeed, sex may be the arena where these notions of masculinity are most intensely played out, particularly by men who feel powerless in the rest of their lives, and hence, whose masculinity is threatened by this sense of powerlessness.

The fusion of aggression and sexuality for many men can be seen when we examine the area of sexual arousal as stimulated by graphic scenes of rape. Initially, researchers found that convicted rapists were more sexually aroused by depictions of violent sexuality than were men who had not raped. Thus it was thought that rapists must have a very low threshold for sexual arousal, and that the least little provocation would set off a male rapist (e.g., a woman who would assertively say "no" to sexual advances or even put up a fight was enough to trigger off a rapist, or so it was thought). In more recent studies, however, when men who had never raped were exposed to depictions of sexual assault, they reported a heightened sexual arousal from such scenes and an increase in their rape fantasies. Another disquieting note is that when nonrapist males were shown depictions of sexual assault, they reported the possibility that they would even consider using force themselves in their sexual relations. The research appears to suggest that most men (i.e., rapists and nonrapists) find violence a stimulant to heighten or arouse their sexual feelings. There is evidence that seems to indicate that males in general find sexuality related at some level to an expression of aggression, and in turn aggression heightens their sexual fantasies or actual sexual behaviors.

In summary, we can say that sexual assault or rape is first and foremost an act of sexual violence that to some degree draws upon the sexual fantasies of the rapist; it is linked to the rapist's need to show superiority and dominance over another.

THE PROBLEM OF NUMBERS

Rape is one of the most underreported of all serious crimes in the United States and in other countries as well. When we try to get a true picture of the enormity of its incidence, we find the issue complicated by the lack of reliable rape statistics. The crime of rape presents some uniquely confounding problems.

One problem we encounter is the simple fact that many, if not most, rape victims simply refuse to come forward and report to the authorities incidents of sexual violence. For many rape victims, a sense of shame or guilt or self-blame about their role in the rape assaults may be enough to prevent them from coming forward and pressing charges. Those who do press charges, however, are apt to meet with questions, accusations, and other degrading and humiliating experiences by the very authorities that are sworn to uphold the laws of society that make the rape of a person a serious felony.

Another problem is that when rape victims do press charges against their assailants, their life histories, especially sexual activities, are dragged before the public. In many instances, the public seems willing to blame the victim for the assault rather than the rapist. The reason for such an attribution of guilt to the victim rather than to the assailant seems to lie in the fact that many people have a tendency to blame others for their misfortunes, as if the world we live in was and is a "just world" where bad things happen only to those who somehow bring on or somehow deserve the consequences of their acts. Consequently, a likely result of such a "just world" orientation is that more often than not, the defenders of rapists will try to show that the rape victims acted in such a manner as to infer their complicity in the sexual assaults or that they "had it coming" because of their actions. We find such a courtroom tactic used by many defense attorneys, and it was one that apparently did not work in the much publicized 1984 New Bedford, Massachusetts, gang-rape case. There the rape-victim's motives for stopping at a bar were questioned and inferences were made impugning her behavior while in the bar. For example, during the trial, it was pointed out that the rape victim had talked with several of the accused rapists before the gang rape occurred. (If the mere act of talking is sufficient cause in some people's minds for a group of men to rape a woman, then we indeed have a twisted view of the causes of rape.) Thus, with all the barriers preventing the victims of sexual assault from coming forward, it is no wonder that rape continues to be one of the most underreported crimes. Even so, the Federal Bureau of Investigation reported that in the decade between 1967 and 1977 the number of reported rapes doubled in the United States. [I have] noted that:

> During 1977 alone, over 63,000 cases of rape were reported by the FBI. The most shocking feature of these statistics is that rape is considered by many experts in crime statistics to be one of the *least* reported violent crimes. The best available estimates suggest that for every one reported rape case there are anywhere from three to ten unreported cases. The conservative estimate of three means that over a quarter of a million women were forcibly raped in the United States in 1977!

While we have no absolute statistics for the total number of completed or attempted rapes committed annually in North America, we can estimate the probability of a woman being the victim of sexual assault during her lifetime. Allan Johnson estimated that "Nationally, a *conservative* estimate is that, under current conditions, 20–30 percent of girls now twelve years old will suffer a violent sexual attack during the remainder of their lives." Even with this estimate, however, we should keep in mind that this percentage excludes females under twelve, married women, and male rape victims. The enormity of the incidence of rape becomes even more staggering when we note that untold numbers of children under twelve are often the victims of sexual assault, as well as the many cases of male rape both inside and outside of prison.

RAPE AS A SOCIAL CONCERN

Due to the mounting concern over women's rights heralded by the reemergent women's movement, sexual assaults and their debilitating consequences for the victims have become one of the more pressing central issues of the 1970s

and 1980s. Consequently, many social scientists have turned their attention toward understanding the dynamics of rapists and their motives, the institutional and cultural factors promoting rape, and of course, the various factors affecting the assault on rape victims and their reactions.

To combat the growing number of rapes, more and more people are beginning to think in terms of prevention and not only of ways to deal with the debilitating aftermath of sexual assault. Many different ways have been suggested to stop the growing wave of sexual assaults in our society.

Two such preventive approaches commonly thought of are, first, a "restrictive approach" that focuses on women changing their life-styles (e.g., not going out alone or not talking to strangers), and second, an "assertive approach" that suggests that women learn martial arts in order to fight back if assaulted. Both of these approaches have, however, some drawbacks. The restrictive approach, asking women to change their pattern of living, is an affront to women. Do we ask merchants to stop keeping money in their cash registers to prevent robberies? Why then should women change, for example, their dress or their social habits? The assertive approach has one possible value: the demise of the myth of the "defenseless woman." However, one problem with this approach is that many times in order to coerce a victim a rapist uses a deadly weapon, which totally nullifies any preventive action or force a victim may take to ward off an assailant.

Along with teaching young children and women to skillfully defend themselves, it seems that a broader based attack against sexual assaults should be taken against the social and institutional factors that promote sexual violence in our society. Two additional areas should be addressed if we are to see a reduction and, hopefully, an elimination in sexual assaults in our society. First, we need to examine the male's gender role with its prescriptive aggressive element, especially aggression against women. Aggression and violence are still seen by many as an integral part of the male's gender role. One way to reduce sexual assault in our society would be to redefine the male gender role, incorporating nonaggressive or nonviolent elements rather than aggressiveness. Of course, many people would object to such a major change in the male role, fearing that our country would fall prey to its national enemies who may wish to attack a nation of non-aggressive men.

Another controversial change that would reduce the number of sexual assaults is an open attack on hard-core and violence-oriented pornography and the multi-million dollar business that supports it. First of all, we should dismiss the notion that only males find sexually explicit materials arousing. Research has found that men *as well as* women find various kinds of erotic material sexually stimulating. However, the pornography industry has mainly directed its sales to a male audience. Although some erotic material does not focus on violent sexual aggression, a large proportion of the male-oriented pornography that is sold in stores across our country portrays the female as the victim of physical and sexual assault.

Researchers Neil Malamuth and Edward Donnerstein have found that exposure to violent pornography generally increases sexual arousal as well as negative attitudes toward women and favorable attitudes toward sexual assault. Thus one possible way to reduce the sexual violence in our society against women would be to eliminate such material. However, those who oppose such a plan immediately bring up the issue of a person's First Amendment rights, which guarantee freedom of speech; such opposition, however, misinterprets the Constitution and its intent.

Would society be as accepting if various media presented graphic anti-Semitic portrayals of Jews being shoved into gas chambers or American Indians being shot for sport for their land? And yet many people support the multi-million dollar industry that shows women assaulted and maimed for the sake of sexual stimulation.

If our society is to rectify the age-old problem of unequal power between females and males, we need to challenge many of our behaviors, our attitudes, and our social institutions that continue to cast women in an inferior role. Until that day, the problem of inequality between the genders is everyone's concern.   [1985]

Understanding the Reading

1. How does rape reflect patriarchal values?
2. How have theories about rape changed during this century, and how is it viewed today?
3. How is rape an act of an overconforming male?
4. How are aggression and sexuality related for most men?
5. Why is it difficult to know accurately the incidence of rape?
6. Why do people tend to "blame the victim" of sexual assault?
7. Explain the difference between the "restrictive approach" and the "assertive approach" to rape prevention and what is wrong with each.
8. What social and institutional factors promote sexual violence?

Suggestions for Responding

1. Doyle proposes that the male role be changed to eliminate its emphasis on aggression. Do you think this is desirable or not? Why? How might we go about making such a change?
2. Doyle also proposes that eliminating violent pornography is one way to reduce violence against women, and he dismisses the claim that this would be an infringement of First Amendment rights. Do you agree or disagree with his position? Why? ✦

73

Fraternities of Fear

KATHLEEN HIRSCH

Some scenes from the ivory tower: Five lacrosse team buddies and another student at St. John's University in Queens, New York, allegedly invited friends in to watch, last March, while they brutally sodomized a female student. A full month went by before the police were notified by university officials, who claimed to be protecting the victim's privacy. Because of the charges, all six men were suspended for the duration of the academic year. The woman has withdrawn from school.

At Colgate University, in Hamilton, New York, two women reported that a student sexually harassed two women, then raped a third, during the course of one evening last February. A doctor presented physical evidence to the university's judicial board of the rape victim's condition, which was said to include severe bruising and a ripped vagina. The student was found "guilty." His punishment, suspension in abeyance, was changed following campus protest to suspension for two semesters. The public authorities were never contacted.

In 1987, two fraternity sophomores at the University of New Hampshire, in Durham, were accused of sexually assaulting a woman student in a dormitory. A university disciplinary board, comprised of students, faculty, and staff, found the men "not guilty" of sexual assault but suspended the men for a semester, because of disrespect to others. The lack of sterner sanctions led students to a sit-in protest at the dean of students' office; 11 activists were eventually arrested. In a criminal hearing, the accused men, pleading guilty to misdemeanor charges, were sentenced to what amounted to 90 days in jail. The woman withdrew from school; the men eventually graduated, their degrees safely in hand.

The bad news this fall is that college campuses are unsafe for women. This is not because violent crimes occur more frequently there than anywhere else—actually, in the case of sex crimes, the rate runs about the same as the general population. Rather, it is because colleges do almost nothing about their student aggressors. In case after case of campus rape, university officers rely on administrative judicial boards that mete out absurdly lenient punishments; they fail to file criminal complaints in an effort to ward off bad publicity; and they largely succeed in creating the impression that crimes against women are aberrations in otherwise civilized communities devoted to the refinement of the mind.

Here are the facts. One out of four women will be sexually assaulted on a college campus. At the very most, only one in ten of those will report it. Their attackers will be fellow students 80 percent of the time, and the most likely location of the attack will be a dormitory room or a fraternity house.

Fraternities in particular seem to be breeding grounds for campus sexual aggression, from jeering verbal abuse to acquaintance rape. A 1969 study by the dean's office at the University of Illinois at Urbana-Champaign found that frat men, a quarter of its male student population, perpetrated 63 percent of student sexual assault at the

institution. From such studies it is also becoming clear that fraternities promote the most heinous form of sexual assault, the gang rape. Unlike widely publicized gang rapes that conform to class and racial stereotypes, this crime, if committed behind a fraternity's doors, becomes a boy's prank—or even a sanctioned rite of passage into the grown-up world of male dominance, privilege, and power.

The fraternity gang rape almost always conforms to script. New, naive students, or women from a nearby college, are invited to their first frat party, usually early in the fall term (although gang rapes take place at *any* time of the year, with women of *any* age). Alcohol is plentiful. In some cases, drinking is a prerequisite to entering the actual party, either by consuming a few cocktails in an upstairs room or having successive ones in several rooms. The point is for women to become as inebriated as possible—without suspecting negative consequences.

The victim is selected, either before the party or soon after she arrives, by a frat brother, and is "worked over," in a perverse parody of seduction, relying on a variety of ruses from flattery to subtle threats. The woman may actually believe that the student is seriously interested in her, "unaware that the 'friendly' persuasion of the [brother] is actually a planned pursuit of easy prey," wrote Julie K. Ehrhart and Bernice R. Sandler, in the paper "Campus Gang Rape: Party Games?"

The woman is led to one of the frat rooms, under the impression that she'll be with one man, or left alone to "sleep off" the alcohol. She is assaulted as soon as she enters his room, where other brothers are waiting for her. Or, more frequently, she regains consciousness while she is being raped by several men.

It is not enough, sensitive observers say, to recognize the pattern of a gang rape in order to protect oneself or reduce its occurrence. Gang rape—like pornography—is pervasive, because it is a key feature of male bonding rituals within patriarchal societies.

Peggy Reeves Sanday, an anthropology professor at the University of Pennsylvania and the author of *Fraternity Gang Rape: Sex, Brotherhood, and Privilege on Campus* (New York University Press), found that fraternities attract a certain type of male, more insecure than average;

men whose psychological and social bonds to parents, especially their mothers, have not yet been broken.

The security delivered by the fraternity "alter ego" is a powerful allure for these young men. They voluntarily endure humiliating and often physically painful initiations designed to break family allegiances. Forcibly torn from one set of norms, they are inducted into new ones that promise self-assurance—provided that they comply with the brotherhood's tightly enforced conformity.

These new norms have been described as "highly masculinist" by two Florida State University sociologists, Patricia Yancey Martin and Robert A. Hummer, writing in *Gender and Society*. The world of fraternities is characterized chiefly by "concern with a narrow, stereotypical conception of masculinity and heterosexuality; a preoccupation with loyalty . . . and an obsession with competition, superiority, and dominance."

"Almost always, male bonding turns against women," Sanday said. "It's a matter of degree, not kind. The way in which men extract loyalty from one another almost always means that they elevate male bonding by making women the despised other, and the scapegoat."

During Sanday's interviews, men degraded the women they slept with, "using such terms as gash, horsebags, heifers, scum, scum bags, queen, swanks, scum buckets, scum doggies, wench, life-support systems, beasts, bitch, swatches, and cracks." Laura McLaughlin, a resident adviser at Colgate, says it isn't unusual for women visiting with friends to be greeted at a fraternity house with comments like "Who's the chick? Who'd you bring us?"

Degrading women unites men in a culture that requires them to compete intensely. But, more important, at an age when their sexual identity is still fluid and a source of profound anxiety, frat men alleviate any insecurities about homoerotic attachments—and satisfy them—by having sex in front of each other, by abusing and dehumanizing women. In short, through gang rape.

Incredible amounts of time and energy go into planning, executing, documenting (in frat logs), and recollecting these bonding rituals. An entire underground lexicon of these practices exists: "rude-hoggering" (bedding the "ugliest" woman at a party), "landsharking" (kneeling on the floor behind a woman and biting her buttocks), and "baggings" (a group of men cornering a woman, dropping their trousers, wriggling their penises, and offering to gang rape her).

"Men rape for other men," contends Claire Walsh, director of Sexual Assault Recovery Services at the University of Florida. "It's a way of maintaining the myth of macho masculinity; a way to confirm their feelings of sexual adequacy. If a man in the room didn't participate, his sexual capacity could be called into question."

Kristen Buxton's assault at Colgate University in 1987 was horribly typical. Although Buxton, entering her junior year, was no newcomer to the university's social scene, she accepted an invitation to Sigma Chi's end-of-summer party because she was at emotional loose ends: her grandmother had just died, and she just had ended a serious relationship that had enabled her to avoid the more raucous "singles" side of Colgate life.

As nightfall approached, the weather in Hamilton, New York, that Saturday in late August was "great," Kristen remembers. In the company of old friends, she was glad to be at the party.

Twelve hours later she sat in her mother's living room north of Boston, unable to speak.

"Her face was all swollen from crying," Marah Buxton says. "I assumed she was upset over my mother. She wasn't able to get any words out of her mouth. I looked at Andrew [the friend who'd driven her home], and I said, 'I'm frightened. Give me a clue.'"

He answered, "This is going to take a while."

According to Kristen, shortly before midnight she was shown to a second-floor bedroom of Sigma Chi where the party was taking place, and went to sleep. She was awakened when two freshman athlete recruits gang raped her. Her screams, loud enough to break through the party noise below, brought friends to her aid.

If Buxton's experience was typical, her response, however, was not. For one thing, she was clear about what happened and decided, from the beginning, to prosecute. In part because she had the good fortune to be taken to a hospital emergency room near her hometown, she was immediately put in touch with police officers who pursued the criminal case.

The vast majority of sexual assault survivors on campuses keep it to themselves—blaming themselves, either because they were drinking or because they were "stupid enough" to have been in the wrong place at the wrong time. Women also believe, erroneously, that because the man was a friend, it couldn't have been rape.

Survivors' silence plays directly into the self-protective impulses of university officials. The morning after her daughter's rape, Marah Buxton phoned the school to inform them of the crime. In the three traumatic years that have passed since then, she says, "only one dean called. They distanced themselves completely."

Traumatized and often physically injured victims who deal directly with college clinics and officials may discover impassive bureaucracies instead of supportive advocates. "It's a syndrome," says Jeffrey Newman, Kristen Buxton's attorney and an expert on campus sexual assault. "We hear this over and again. The clinic head usually sends them to the school administration. The administration usually meets with the parents, probably with the attorney from the school present, to explain the benefits of undergoing the judicial process within the school, as opposed to the outside."

"What they're trying to do," says Newman's associate, Rosanne Zuffante, "is intimidate the young woman into backing off. And they succeed most of the time."

University tactics can violate a woman's due process, says Howard Clery, of Security on Campus, Inc., who insists that "a university cannot adjudicate a felony." But, typically, colleges attempt to do just this. Once a victim is persuaded to keep her accusations within the university, a judicial board hears testimony from all involved. The boards, normally composed of several faculty members, were originally established to review plagiarism cases and honor code violations. Now they determine the "innocence" or "guilt" of accused rapists, and dole out any punishments they deem fit.

On many campuses, the penalty for rape is identical to, or less severe than, the sanctions for plagiarism—one year's suspension. Frequently, confessed rapists are not even removed from campus. They are placed on "probation." (In Buxton's case, the athletes accused of rape withdrew from Colgate.)

Brave women who, like Buxton, press charges with the local authorities face several hurdles. Advocates say that district attorneys are reluctant to handle campus rape cases, and it's not only because they are difficult to win.

"It's a political game," says Newman. "Usually there are strong connections between the D.A.'s office and the higher-ups in the university. Most of the time you find the D.A.'s drop the case or they never take it. They say, look, there's just not enough evidence."

Buxton says she came under severe pressure from her D.A. to agree to a plea bargain that resulted in misdemeanor convictions, probation punishments, and, worst of all, no trace of the crime on her assailants' records.

Even more pressure is applied by peers. Buxton sometimes thought she was in hell after she returned to campus that fall—reading news accounts of the incident, feeling as if everyone was looking at her differently—but never more so than when she was finally persuaded by friends to join them at a downtown Hamilton pub.

"A bunch of fraternity members surrounded my table and just kind of stood there," she recounts. "Another time, I was standing in the middle of the room and a couple of them came over and were joking: 'Oh, look who's out.' They tried to intimidate me a lot."

This isn't uncommon. "Most women feel that if they make a public statement they have to leave," admits Ann Lane, founder of Colgate's women's studies program. "They receive threats from frat brothers, obscene phone calls. One woman [at Colgate] got a rock thrown through her window."

It is the rare victim who is offered adequate counseling. At best, institutions run a support group moderated by a faculty adviser or a clinic staffer.

"There was never any support," Buxton says of her own case. "Just kind of a blank stare."

It is the female students who pay the price for institutional passivity. Victims drop out of the classes they share with their assailants. Their grades go down. They experience chronic depression and have trouble concentrating. Eventually, many women, like Buxton, leave school for a period of time, or drop out altogether.

The code of silence exerts a ripple effect, observers say, through the entire female student population. It diminishes everything from classroom assertiveness and performance to confidence levels. Overall, says Professor Sanday, it suppresses a woman's initiative.

"There's a lot of anxiety," says Colgate resident adviser McLaughlin. "Almost every woman you talk to has a story."

And, interviews reveal, many have stories about a botched university clinic "rape kit" (the semen, blood, and other physical evidence of the assault) or a member of the judicial board unversed in the legal definition of rape. The unofficial negligence of universities reveals itself on many, mutually reinforcing levels.

By ignoring rape victims and their needs, universities succeed in minimizing adverse press. Sex crimes, characterized as "isolated incidents," keep consumers (students and their parents) and donors (alumni) ignorant and happy. The boat doesn't get rocked, and another generation learns the dynamics of domestic violence.

According to Sanday, what's at stake is "Brotherhood. That's older males protecting younger males, protecting their lost youth, and protecting their actual fraternity brothers. Protecting the American dream. The dream in which the young man goes out with his buddies, works his way up, becomes head of everything, and makes a fortune. Along the way, if he has to rape a few people—competitors, women—that's sort of what we expect. The American dream is very misogynistic."

But victims, feminists, and advocates on campus are fighting back. Victims are suing universities in civil court—successfully claiming, in many cases, that the institution is liable for security breaches or rule infractions that contributed directly to the rape. Colgate is currently defending itself in a $10 million civil damage suit filed by Buxton, who charges that the school should have forbidden the Sigma Chi party, because the fraternity had already been sanctioned for serving alcohol to minors. (Despite several requests, university officials were unavailable for comment.)

After lawsuits, the most sweeping effort to make universities responsible for campus criminal activity has been legislative. In June, the House of Representatives passed the "Student Right To Know and Campus Security Act"—despite keen back-room opposition from organized education lobbyists. If it becomes law, the act will require all institutions receiving federal aid to release their yearly crime statistics. It will also allow

victims the right to know what happens to the perpetrators of crimes against them.

Howard and Connie Clery, whose own daughter was raped and murdered by a fellow student, urge any victim of campus rape to contact the police and the local district attorney's office. If possible, hire a lawyer. Security on Campus, their two-year-old organization in Gulph Mills, Pennsylvania, will provide the names of attorneys and other information needed to pursue a legal case.

Finally, protests, vigils, and marches by campus feminists have pushed administrators to take a more active stand against the abuse of women and overt institutional sexism. Thanks to them, and to a growing number of enlightened deans and college presidents, there is room for cautious optimism.

For example, at the University of Pennsylvania (the site of several highly publicized rapes) an ongoing rape education program, including films, regular discussions, and lectures, has increased the number of women reporting and asking for help.

After the 1987 protests at the University of New Hampshire, the institution developed the Sexual Harassment and Rape Prevention Program, geared toward averting sexual violence. The University of Illinois at Urbana-Champaign investigates every case of sexual assault and battery, whether the attack occurs on or off campus. The institution hired a victims' advocate, and requires all perpetrators found guilty of sexual assault to participate in counseling. It also is developing an educational program for men with a family history of domestic violence.

Inevitably, there is the question of the fraternities themselves. It would seem that women's obvious recourse is to avoid, even boycott, fraternity social events and seek entertainment elsewhere. But it isn't that simple. Most campuses with fraternities have virtually abdicated responsibility for social life to "the houses," which are among the few places where minors can find easy access to alcohol.

Instead of abolishing the system, some colleges have forced fraternities to grow up. At Bowdoin and Trinity colleges, coed frats have appeared. Colby College voted to abolish its eight fraternities and two sororities in 1984, and the University of Illinois has banned alcohol at after-hours frat parties, and a brother in most houses is trained to counsel and intervene when a potentially violent situation develops.

At Colgate, where fraternities have been an issue for the last ten years, more than 500 students and staff staged a protest last year against them; the faculty subsequently voted to abolish the system. "It's detrimental to humane learning in a very broad sense," says Colgate's Lane, who lobbied for change. "It's anti-intellectual in its core. Fraternities foster values that are in opposition to values we all uphold and respect."

In response, Colgate's board of trustees established a subcommittee to investigate the houses. Its report, with recommended solutions, should be delivered this fall.

One hopes that the board considers the many women who silently share Kristen Buxton's story. These are not alums who will remember their alma maters at giving time. Buxton graduated in May, a year behind the classmates with whom she entered. As she tries to assess her four years of college, she only begins to suggest the legacy of male aggression in America—even to society's most privileged and educated women:

"I'm a lot more hesitant about things, more cautious. I'm much more comfortable with things I'm used to. I think I'm probably more scared. Like, I'm much more comfortable just being home."   [1990]

Understanding the Reading

1. How do colleges and universities generally respond to rape and sexual assault? Why?
2. What is the "script" for a fraternity gang rape?
3. How are fraternity members characterized in this article?
4. How do they degrade women, and why?
5. Why are most campus rapes not prosecuted?
6. What effect does campus rape have on the victim and other women on campus?
7. Why don't universities play a more active role in fighting campus rape?
8. What steps have been taken to stop campus rape?

Suggestions for Responding

1. Why do colleges and universities treat rape differently than the law does? Should they?

2. Investigate and report on the procedures followed in sexual assault cases on your campus. ◆

74

Hate, Rape and Rap

TIPPER GORE

Words such as "bitch" and "nigger" are dangerous. Racial and sexual epithets, whether screamed across a street or camouflaged by the rhythms of a song, turn people into objects less than human—easier to degrade, easier to violate, easier to destroy. These words and epithets are becoming an accepted part of our lexicon. What's disturbing is that they are being endorsed by some of the very people they diminish, and our children are being sold a social dictionary that says racism, sexism and antisemitism are okay.

As someone who strongly supports the First Amendment, I respect the freedom of every individual to label another as likes. But speaking out against racism isn't endorsing censorship. No one should silently tolerate racism or sexism or antisemitism, or condone those who turn discrimination into a multimillion-dollar business justified because it's "real."

A few weeks ago, television viewers saw a confrontation of depressing proportions on the Oprah Winfrey show. It was one I witnessed firsthand; I was there in the middle of it. Viewers heard black American women say they didn't mind being called "bitches" and they weren't offended by the popular rap music artist Ice-T when he sang about "Evil E" who "f—ed the bitch with a flashlight/pulled it out, left the batteries in/so he could get a charge when he begins." There is more, and worse.

Ice-T, who was also on the show, said the song came from the heart and reflected his experiences. He said he doesn't mind other groups using the word "nigger" in their lyrics. That's how he described himself, he said. Some in the audience questioned why we couldn't see the humor in such a song.

Will our kids get the joke? Do we want them

describing themselves or each other as "niggers?" Do we want our daughters to think of themselves as "bitches" to be abused? Do we want our sons to measure success in gold guns hanging from thick neck chains? The women in the audience may understand the slang; Ice-T can try to justify it. But can our children?

One woman in the audience challenged Ice-T. She told him his song about the flashlight was about as funny as a song about lynching black men.

The difference is that sexism and violence against women are accepted as almost an institutionalized part of our entertainment. Racism is not—or at least, it hasn't been until recently. The fact is, neither racism, sexism nor antisemitism should be accepted.

Yet they are, and in some instances that acceptance has reached startling proportions. The racism expressed in the song "One in a Million" by Guns N' Roses sparked nationwide discussion and disgust. But an earlier album that featured a rape victim in the artwork and lyrics violently degrading to women created barely a whisper of protest. More than 9 million copies were sold, and it was played across the radio band. This is only one example where hundreds exist.

Rabbi Abraham Cooper of the Simon Wiesenthal Center, who also appeared on the Oprah Show, voiced his concerns about the antisemitic statements made by Professor Griff, a nonsinging member of the rap group Public Enemy; statements that gain added weight from the group's celebrity. "Jews are wicked," Professor Griff said in an interview with The Washington Times. ". . . [responsible for] a majority of wickedness that goes on across the globe."

The Simon Wiesenthal Center placed a full-page ad in Daily Variety calling for self-restraint from the music industry, a move that prompted hundreds of calls to the center. Yet Rabbi Cooper's concerns barely elicited a response from Oprah Winfrey's audience.

Alvin Poussaint, a black Harvard psychiatrist, believes that the acceptance of such degrading and denigrating images may reflect low self-esteem among black men in today's society. There are few positive black male role models for young children, and such messages from existing role models are damaging. Ice-T defends his reality: "I grew up in the streets—I'm no

Bryant Gumbel." He accuses his critics of fearing that reality, and says the fear comes from an ignorance of the triumph of the street ethic.

A valid point, perhaps. But it is not the messenger that is so frightening; it is the perpetuation—almost glorification—of the cruel and violent reality of his "streets."

A young black mother in the front row rose to defend Ice-T. Her son, she said, was an A student who listened to Ice-T. In her opinion, as long as Ice-T made a profit, it didn't matter what he sang. Cultural economics were a poor excuse for the South's continuation of slavery. Ice-T's financial success cannot excuse the vileness of his message.

In America, a woman is raped once every six minutes. A majority of children surveyed by a Rhode Island Rape Crisis Center thought rape was acceptable. In New York City, rape arrests of 13-year-old boys have increased 200 percent in the past two years. Children 18 and younger now are responsible for 70 percent of the hate crime committed in the United States. No one is saying this happens solely because of rap or rock music, but certainly kids are influenced by the glorification of violence.

Children must be taught to hate. They are not born with ideas of bigotry—they learn from what they see in the world around them. If their reality consists of a street ethic that promotes and glorifies violence against women or discrimination against minorities—not only in everyday life, but also in their entertainment—then ideas of bigotry and violence will flourish.

We must raise our voices in protest and put pressure on those who not only reflect this hatred but also package, polish, promote and market it. Let's send the message loud and clear through our homes, our streets and our schools, as well as our art and our culture.   [1990]

Understanding the Reading

1. Why are racial and sexual epithets objectionable?
2. What difference does Gore see between the use of sexist expressions and the use of racist ones in rap lyrics?
3. Why do so many blacks and women accept the denigrating and degrading images in rap lyrics?

Suggestion for Responding

Tipper Gore has been the driving force behind the movement to have warning labels on popular musical recordings. Do you think this is a good idea? Why or why not? ✦

75

Premarital Violence: Battering on College Campuses

CENTER FOR WOMEN POLICY STUDIES

Experts on family violence have called the marriage license a "hitting license," but according to three recent studies in Minnesota, Arizona, and Oregon, plenty of couples slap, kick, and punch each other without it. The studies, which queried students at three universities about violence in their dating relationships, found that physical abuse occurs in at least one out of every five collegiate relationships.

At St. John's University in Minnesota, James Makepeace, a professor of sociology, questioned 202 freshman and sophomore students in the spring of 1979 and found that 21.2 percent had been abused or had inflicted abuse in a premarital relationship at least once and that most victims of abuse were women. An additional 61.5 percent of the students had friends who were involved in violent relationships. Of the students who had been abused, 4 percent said they were assaulted with closed fists and 1 percent said they were strangled, choked, or had a weapon used against them. A total of 13 percent of the students said they had been pushed, while 12.9 percent said they were slapped, and 4 percent were punched.

"Although the percentages of the students who have experienced the more serious forms of violence may seem small, the students actually suggest a significant social problem," Makepeace states in his study. "If the 4 percent incidence of assault with closed fists is typical, then 800 students on a 20,000 student campus would have experienced this form of violence."

The violent incidents in the Minnesota study were most often sparked by sexual jealousy, disagreements over drinking, and anger over sexual denial. Makepeace speculates that much of the violence in premarital relationships derives from a lack of rules or limits in these relationships. "The adolescent world is gray—not black and white as it once was," Makepeace commented in an interview.

According to the study, which was published in the January 1981 issue of *Family Relations,* abused students rarely seek help. Only 5 percent of the battered students identified by the study called the police. "Violence among young unmarried couples may be even more underreported than spouse abuse," Makepeace stated, "because young people view their world as a closed system, apart from adults. Even if they are being abused, calling the police is ratting on a peer to an adult, and that is unacceptable."

At Oregon State University, almost a fourth of 355 students surveyed reported that they were involved in violent relationships with their boyfriends or girlfriends, according to Rodney M. Cate of the University's Family Life Department. Over half of those students revealed that they had remained in the violent relationship.

"We were surprised by the high incidence of abuse and also by the number of students who believed violence helps a relationship," Cate commented in an interview. Of the 53 percent who remained in abusive relationships, 37 percent said their relationships improved with abuse, 41 percent said the relationships did not change, and 22 percent believed that their relationships became worse after the first abusive incident.

"The idea 'he wouldn't hit me if he didn't love me' seems to be operating among abusive college couples," Cate suggested. "Of our respondents, 29 percent viewed abuse as signifying love while only 8 percent considered abuse as an expression of hate."

Rodney Cate and June Henton, authors of the study, are currently interviewing high school students to determine when violence in dating relationships begins.

In another study of premarital violence on college campuses, Mary Riege Laner, a sociologist at Arizona State University, found that over 60 percent of 371 students questioned in the fall of 1980 had been either a victim or perpetrator of abuse in a dating relationship. A total of 46 percent of the students who reported abuse said they were pushed or shoved, 19 percent were punched or kicked, and 21 percent were pushed to the floor. Students who were abused as children were more likely to report an abusive premarital relationship than students who did not have violent childhoods, according to the study.

The study concludes that physical abuse is more likely to occur in serious rather than casual dating relationships. Laner theorizes that violence occurs more often between serious courting couples because they, like married couples, have a greater presumed range of interests and activities, greater intensity of involvement, an implied right to influence one another, and an extensive knowledge of one another's social biographies which include vulnerabilities and fears that can be used for purposes of attack. While these characteristics by themselves do not lead to violence, when added to a tolerance of violent behavior fostered in childhood and sexism in the relationship, the situation is ripe for abuse, according to Laner.

"Our culture accepts violence in all its institutions—including marriage, courtship, and child-rearing," Laner commented. "We're taught to accept violence from those who say they love us—so violence comes to connote a depth of feeling. Until we can reduce our acceptance of violence as a means to an end, abuse in intimate relationships will continue to be a serious problem." [n.d.]

Understanding the Reading

1. How prevalent is physical abuse in couple relationships on campus?
2. What triggers such physical abuse?
3. Why do people stay in abusive relationships?
4. What factors foster violent relationships?

Suggestions for Responding

1. If someone you know has been or is in an abusive relationship, describe the kinds of behaviors involved and the reactions of the two partners.
2. If a close friend told you of being physically abused, how would you respond? ✦

76

Not Invisible to Attack

VICTORIA A. BROWNWORTH

When Sheila Jackson went running with her lover, Meredith Bishop, in the Brooklyn neighborhood they were visiting on an early spring night last month, she expected nothing but a strenuous five miles. But before the run was finished, both women had endured continuous verbal attacks by a group of young men, which culminated in violence. Jackson was beaten and Bishop sexually assaulted.

In June 1990, in Philadelphia, Bertha Oliver left her boyfriend of four years for another woman. She didn't know it would make her a statistic. Oliver's ex-boyfriend allegedly stabbed her and her teenage son to death, and critically wounded her teenage daughter, citing her lesbianism as the reason for his actions.

In May 1988, when Rebecca Wight and Claudia Brenner went hiking on the Appalachian Trail near Gettysburg, neither expected to become statistics. But before the trip ended, Wight was shot to death and Brenner critically wounded. The killer's defense was that the women "teased him" by making love together in the isolated woods where he lived.

These cases are examples of the rise in anti-lesbian violence. But, in addition to being examples of violent homophobia, they also explicate the larger issue of anti-lesbian violence—the impact of sexism on homophobia, making lesbians double targets of violence and threat. None of these cases was treated by legal authorities as an anti-lesbian attack, yet in each case the lesbianism of the women involved was defined by the perpetrators as the source of the assault. As "statistics," these women are categorized by the legal system as victims of violent crime, not victims of the growing category of anti-lesbian, anti-woman violence.

Violence against lesbians is at an all-time high, according to numerous new reports, including those released last month by the National Gay and Lesbian Task Force (NGLTF) and the San Francisco-based Community United Against Violence (CUAV). The CUAV report also shows an increase in anti-lesbian violence over violence against gay men—at a ratio of 63 percent to 125 percent from the previous year. In addition, certain types of violence perpetrated against both gay men and lesbians have been shown by some studies, such as that released by the Philadelphia Lesbian and Gay Task Force (PLGTF), to be more extreme when perpetrated against lesbians than against gay men. And some of the most extreme forms of violence, such as rape, are almost solely perpetrated against lesbians.

These reports raise a variety of questions about the nature of violence against lesbians, and beg the question regarding parallels between anti-gay and anti-woman violence. And the above cases illustrate how cases of extreme violence instigated because of a woman's lesbian identity are not reported as such.

The issue of the numbers of attacks and the numbers of actual reports has become an increasingly problematic one for those attempting to cope with the breadth of the violence. And with anti-woman violence at an all-time high nationally, an added complication is how to differentiate anti-lesbian violence from anti-woman violence, causing some experts to question whether such differentiation is even possible.

The U.S. Department of Justice, which will not begin keeping statistics on anti-gay/anti-lesbian violence until later this year, gives statistics on anti-woman violence that show women more likely to be victims of a violent crime, such as assault, rape and murder. Statistics presented before the Senate Hearings on Crimes Against Women in June 1990 showed an increase of 48 percent in violence against women under 25 while violence against men in the same age group decreased by 12 percent.

The connection between anti-woman and anti-lesbian violence is clear in some of the statistics released by the lesbian and gay organizations monitoring the problem. CUAV shows a 28 percent increase in violence against lesbians and gay men in the last year and a 55 percent increase in the last four years. San Francisco had the most reports of anti-gay/anti-lesbian violence of any city in the nation except New York with reports to CUAV totaling 425 for 1990. New York recorded 507. In the past three years, CUAV recorded an increase in anti-lesbian violence of 125 percent—compared to 63 percent for gay men.

But the overall rate of anti-gay/anti-lesbian violence in San Francisco is totally out of proportion to its standing as the 13th largest city in the U.S. with a population of 700,000. New York had fewer than 100 more reported cases, but its population is ten times that of San Francisco—8 million.

The proportional relationship of reported cases to population has more to do, some experts say, with knowledge of reporting techniques rather than with actual acts of violence. Philadelphia, with a population of over a million in the metropolitan area, has reported a significant increase in anti-gay/anti-lesbian violence over the past five years with over 200 reported cases per year. But in a survey conducted by PLGTF, many respondents indicated that they were unaware of either laws protecting lesbians and gays in the city, or that these acts of violence could be investigated as specific hate crimes.

The PLGTF statistics showed that the more extreme acts of violence were committed against lesbians, so that although only one in ten reports of violence perpetrated by police was from lesbians, 64 percent of the women reporting cited assaults by officers or intimidation with a weapon, compared with 38 percent of gay men. The study showed ten percent more lesbians experienced threats and verbal assaults as men and almost the same percentage of lesbians as gay men reported assaults with or without weapons.

But PLGTF Executive Director Rita Addessa notes that in all the surveys her organization has conducted, and in the agency's hotline coordination, lesbians are less likely, and show more reluctance, to report than do gay men. "And we *don't* get reports from heterosexual women of anti-lesbian language or other assaults, yet we know that those occur as well."

Such statistics are creating controversy among those who work in the field of anti-gay/anti-lesbian violence. Consideration of the link between homophobia and sexism as a basis for anti-gay/anti-lesbian violence has caused some rifts between groups usually in coalition over such issues.

One of those who sees a clear connection between sexism and homophobia is Kevin Berrill, director of the NGLTF Anti-Violence Project. Berrill, who has been working on the legal as well as the theoretical aspects of the increase in anti-lesbian violence, said not enough gay men make the connection. "Look at the words that are used against gay men in verbal assaults—they are all feminizing terms, like 'pussy'. The links are clearly there. And the fight against anti-gay violence has an obvious connection to anti-woman violence." As for how such issues are to be addressed, Berrill illuminated some of the problems. "There's a general understanding that the problems of anti-woman and anti-gay violence are linked. But when you begin to discuss gender-based crimes and hate-crimes, the criteria become problematic. The criteria used for hate crimes may be used to separate out certain gender-based crimes. For example, *every* rape is anti-woman. Do we say it is only a hate crime if it is perpetrated against a lesbian? So there are problems with applying the framework. It is equally difficult to determine whether people are simply reporting crimes more or they are actually happening more. According to our 1990 Violence Report released last month, people *are* reporting more, up 42 percent from 1989. But we tend to believe there are more crimes of violence happening against lesbians, simply because historically women have not reported crimes against themselves in the way men have. So we believe that the increase in reportage *is* equal to an increase in the actual crimes."

Chezia Carraway, coordinator of the New York City Task Force Against Sexual Assault, noted that few crimes of violence against women are reported, and violence against lesbians is even less frequently reported. Carraway said that "fewer than five percent of rapes get reported and fewer than ten percent of all crimes of battering." According to Carraway, lesbians are much more uncomfortable about reporting rapes and are "much less eager to deal with male authority types."

Roberta L. Hacker is executive director of Women in Transition (WIT), the nation's oldest resource organization for domestic violence, which also serves lesbians who are victims of battering. "It has taken far longer for lesbians to acknowledge battering in their relationships than it has taken heterosexual women, and there are still no laws even in process to address the lesbian battering issue. If it is harder for lesbians to acknowledge one type of assault against them, it would certainly follow that it would be difficult

for them to report other assaults against them. And let's face it, who are they going to be reporting to—male authority figures, primarily. Many lesbians may feel that this will add another aspect of assault to their trauma. That has certainly been the experience of women victims of rape, why wouldn't it also be true of lesbian victims of violence? We have to remember that in this society women are viewed as having brought crimes of violence on themselves—whether it's battering or rape or anti-lesbian violence. Women aren't perceived as innocents, they are perceived as being responsible in some way for the violence perpetrated against them."

Suzanne Pharr of the Arkansas Women's Project, who has worked on the issue of anti-lesbian violence with Berrill, spoke on the topic at Columbia University April 5. Pharr echoed Hacker's comments in her speech and enumerated some of the traditional reasons lesbians might not report such crimes. Citing the fact that women are raised to expect that they will be victims of violence, Pharr noted that they also don't expect the patriarchal system to respond to that violence. "The belief that violence is our due because of gender, combined with a history of women being blamed for the violence acted against us, leads many of us not to report the violence." Pharr cites statistics of low reporting of other anti-woman crimes with a fear of outing[1] themselves as yet another reason for low reportage from lesbians. She said that the fear of further invasions and reprisals may also contribute to reduced reportage.

Berrill said that lesbians have also been more invisible than gay men. "Increased visibility has meant increased violence. Lesbians are becoming more visible. There are also historically fewer lesbian-defined institutions for women to turn to. In our society and our own community gay means men and media images of gays are male. That's why more reports tend to come from men. Women are simply more reluctant to report. Ming Lu said to me that women tend to rely more on networking than on institutions. Gay men are still men—they are more used to dealing with authority and figures of authority, and they also tend not to have the kinds of personal supports that women have."

The numbers vary widely from city to city. In New York, the reports of anti-gay male violence are twice as frequent as reports of violence against lesbians, while in San Francisco, the exact opposite numbers are true. But most anti-violence task force groups agree that violence against lesbians is up, and that separating anti-lesbian and anti-woman violence is next to impossible.

"How we differentiate," said Rita Addessa, executive director of the Philadelphia Lesbian and Gay Task Force (PLGTF), "is by whether anti-lesbian or anti-gay language is used." But Addessa also agrees that anti-lesbian language is frequently used against heterosexual women in assaults as well, further strengthening the link Pharr, Berrill and others have delineated. Addessa also believes that the higher visibility of lesbians, as well as the increased number of lesbians in leadership positions, has led to a sort of violent backlash. "White men, no matter who they are, don't like to see women in power. Lesbians with power are doubly threatening because they don't 'need' men, they aren't reliant upon men. That threat often results in discrimination, why wouldn't it also result in violence?"

Said Pharr, "Violence against women issues directly from male power and control, they do it to keep a system of power in place. This system is white, male and heterosexual and all institutions are dominated and controlled by this group. Violence against gay men and lesbians is directly related to our connection to women."

Pharr cites violence as the primary means of subjugation of women and suggests that it is used similarly to subjugate gay men and lesbians. "Our gender alone brings extraordinary possibilities of violence into our lives, and when we experience it, we find it hard to sort out whether it comes because of our gender or our sexual identity."

Pharr is organizing a conference in October in New York to work with women on an inclusive agenda for anti-woman and anti-lesbian hate crimes. NGLTF will hold a conference in November in which a primary focus will be adding gender-based violence to the hate crime agenda.

One Philadelphia lesbian who was the victim of a sexual assault in February that included the use of anti-lesbian language summed up the problem. "As I was being raped I was called a dyke and a cunt. The rapist used those terms as if they were interchangeable. And as I talk to other women who have been raped—straight and gay—I hear similar stories. Was my attack anti-lesbian? Or was it anti-woman? I think the facts are simple. I was raped because as a woman I'm considered rapeable and as a lesbian I'm considered a threat. How can you separate those two things?"   [1991]

Note

1. OUTING: Having one's homosexuality publicly revealed against one's will.

Understanding the Reading

1. Why are lesbians double targets for violence?
2. Why is it difficult to establish clear figures on anti-lesbian violence?
3. Why would heterosexual women experience anti-lesbian assaults?
4. What is the connection between sexism and homophobia?
5. Why are lesbians less likely to report assaults than are heterosexual women and gay men?
6. Why do white men feel especially threatened by lesbians with power?

Suggestions for Responding

1. What differences are there between being anti-lesbian and being either anti-woman or anti-gay? How do you account for these differences?
2. Find a news article on anti-gay or anti-lesbian violence and one on a comparable incident involving racist or sexist bias. Compare the treatment of the two. ◆

77

Indians Mourn Wounded Knee Bloodshed

ASSOCIATED PRESS

WOUNDED KNEE, S.D. (AP)—Sam Eagle Staff still mourns the death of the several hundred Sioux who fell in a cold, grassy valley when U.S. cavalry troops opened fire on an Indian camp a century ago.

"We feel it was a murdering of our people without weapons," says Eagle Staff, whose uncle was one of the victims. "What happened there must have been a nightmare, something hard to live with if you were there."

The Dec. 29, 1890, bloodshed at Wounded Knee was the last major armed conflict between government troops and Indians. It also wiped out the Sioux's last dream of ridding their lands of white invaders.

The Army called it a battle.

The Sioux call it a massacre, a needless slaughter of mostly unarmed Indian men, women and children by cavalry troops seeking revenge for Lt. Col. George Custer's death at the Battle of the Little Big Horn in Montana more than a decade earlier.

Though they still feel hurt and sorrow, many Indians also see the 100th anniversary as a chance to mend the Sioux Nation's sacred hoop—the spiritual and cultural traditions.

Riders on horseback are retracing the trail Chief Big Foot took to Wounded Knee a century ago, and ceremonies will be held Saturday in memory of those slain at the southwestern South Dakota site.

The Lakota, which is what the Sioux call themselves, see new hope for better race relations since South Dakota Gov. George Mickelson proclaimed 1990 as the Year of Reconciliation between Indians and whites.

The anniversary offers the Sioux a chance to tell their side of the story and to continue their effort to recover land, particularly the nearby Black Hills, which they consider sacred.

"We want to send a note to everyone in the country and the world that this type of thing will never happen again to any Indians or any nationality," said Eagle Staff, a leader of a group of descendants of Wounded Knee victims.

The site lies in a valley flanked by pine-dotted ridges that provide the name for the Pine Ridge Indian Reservation, the home of the Oglala Sioux Tribe.

In a tiny cemetery atop a small knoll, a chain-link fence surrounds a mass grave where 146 Indians were buried in a long trench. A tattered white flag flies over the site, and pieces of cloth and bird feathers hang from the fence and flutter in the wind.

A stone monument for Big Foot and the people who died with him stands to the side of the burial trench. Part of the message carved in the stone says: "Many innocent women and children who knew no wrong died here."

What happened still is debated. Accounts from Indians and the cavalry differed greatly.

Government records show about 150 Indians were killed and 44 were wounded, while 30 or more soldiers died. The Sioux argue that at least 300 Indians and perhaps more than 400 were slain at Wounded Knee.

The Sioux had been the dominant tribe in the northern Plains for about a century after getting horses from other tribes and guns from French traders. The Sioux warrior society peaked in 1876, when they defeated Custer.

Their fortunes rapidly went downhill after that, however, when treaties stripped them of land and forced them onto reservations in South Dakota.

By 1890, the Ghost Dance religion had arisen with a promise that the land and the decimated buffalo herds would be restored to the Sioux and the white man would be swept away.

After Sioux leader Sitting Bull was killed, Miniconjou Chief Big Foot led a band of about 400 Sioux from central South Dakota to seek refuge at the Pine Ridge Indian Reservation in southwestern South Dakota.

Cavalry troops found Big Foot's band, and by Dec. 29, the rebuilt 7th Cavalry that Custer had commanded at the Little Big Horn joined the other soldiers. Big Foot's camp was flying a white flag.

Accounts differ as to who fired first, but the shooting began when the troops were collecting the Indians' guns. According to the most common story, two soldiers wrestled with an Indian holding a gun and the weapon fired.

Army officers said a warrior took a rifle hidden under a blanket and shot. When they heard that, the soldiers opened fire. The Ghost Dance shirts worn by some of the Indians did not protect them.

William Horn Cloud, 84, of Pine Ridge, heard the story of Wounded Knee from his father, who was 14 when he survived the fight. He and other descendants say soldiers drank heavily the night before and wanted to settle an old score.

"They wanted revenge for Custer," says Horn Cloud. "They were there for one reason, and I guess they had a barrel of whiskey with them."

Since they were in a circle, soldiers who died at Wounded Knee probably were killed by their own gunfire, Horn Cloud says—the same fusillade that cut down women and children as they tried to escape to a nearby ravine.

"Those soldiers were shooting those screaming kids down," he said.

Each December for the past four years, Alex White Plume and others have mounted horses and followed the trail that led Big Foot's band to their death. They rode, he said, because they wanted to change the future of the Sioux.

This year's trail ride is the last one.

White Plume, whose great-grandfather died at Wounded Knee, said Sioux holy man Black Elk described how the sacred hoop of the Sioux nation was shattered at Wounded Knee. Seven generations later, the Sioux must mend the sacred hoop and rebuild themselves, he said.

White Plume is not the only Sioux who is intent on looking forward.

"There is prejudice here in South Dakota. We hope to eliminate this some day," said Eagle Staff. "It can be done, but it's going to take a long, long time."   [1990]

Understanding the Reading

1. Why do the Army and the Sioux label the Wounded Knee attack differently?
2. How are the dead Sioux commemorated?
3. How does the Army account of what happened differ from the Sioux version?
4. What does "mending the sacred hoop" mean?

Suggestions for Responding

1. Do you think that the U.S. military still conducts racial wars comparable to the Battle of Wounded Knee? Why or why not?
2. While perhaps not as well known as Wounded Knee, a number of other battles between the U.S. Army and various native peoples are described quite differently by the two sides. Research and report on one of these. (Dee Brown describes a number of these battles in his book, *Bury My Heart at Wounded Knee: An Indian History of the American West.*) ◆

78

The Failure of the Melting Pot

STANLEY COBEN

Almost all the racial fears felt by white Americans after World War I were distilled and promulgated by one organization: the Ku Klux Klan. The Klan gave voice also to the traditional culture—such as the dangers carried by new ideas and moral standards. The KKK of that period was started by a small group in Atlanta during 1915. The time and place were chosen to coincide with excitement generated by the showing of the motion picture "The Birth of a Nation." In that tremendously popular epic, white-hooded Klansmen of the post–Civil War era were depicted redeeming the South and its most cherished values from the clutches of black Reconstruction.

Until the cultural crisis of 1919–1920, however, the twentieth-century Klan remained a small, southern organization. When it expanded, the professional publicists who managed the membership drive discovered that the largest potential source of Klan dues lay not in Georgia or South Carolina, nor even in Alabama and Mississippi, those traditional strongholds of vigilante justice for Negroes. The greatest response to the Klan's brand of racism appeared in growing cities of the Southwest and Midwest: Shreveport, Dallas, Youngstown, Indianapolis, Dayton, and Detroit; and in smaller cities like Joliet, Illinois; Hammond, Indiana; Oklahoma City; San Antonio; Babylon, New York; Camden, New Jersey; and Anaheim, California.

In areas where Klan organizers—or Kleagles, as the invisible empire called them—were most successful in recruiting, they entered towns instructed to discover the prejudices of prospective members, then to exploit these peoples' complaints. At first it was assumed that the Klan once again would be chiefly a device for keeping southern Negroes and their white friends in place. When he called together the first small group of Klansmen in 1915, William J. Simmons explained that Negroes were getting "uppity." Klan recruiting efforts played cleverly on the Reconstruction Klan's reputation for punishing ambitious Negroes and for protecting white women against threats to their purity. A Klan recruiting lecturer promised: "The Negro, in whose blood flows the mad desire for race amalgamation, is more dangerous than a maddened wild beast and he must and will be controlled."

However, when questions and applications from all over the country poured into Atlanta headquarters during 1920, Imperial Wizard Simmons readily conceded that Negroes were not the only enemies of 100 percent Americans. Furthermore, he announced: "Any real man, any native-born white American citizen who is not affiliated with any foreign institution (that is, not a Catholic) and who loves his country and his flag may become a member of the Ku Klux Klan, whether he lives north, south, east, or west." The only other requirement for membership was a man's willingness to part with a $10 initiation fee, of which $4 went to the Kleagle, $2 to Simmons, $2.50 to the publicists in Atlanta, and the rest to the local Grand Goblin. Further payments were extracted later for membership dues and for uniforms (sheets), which were supplied from Atlanta.

Throughout the nation, Kleagles discovered a fear of Catholics, Jews, and recent immigrants, as well as Negroes. They also found native Americans worried about the erosion of moral standards, and angry about widespread lawlessness. Frequently this laxity was associated with foreign or colored races. Violation of prohibition statutes especially was blamed on urban minorities. Established governmental institutions seemed incapable of handling these elements—incapable of protecting white, Anglo-Saxon Victorian civilization. So Kleagles received a warm welcome when they came to town and gave native Americans an opportunity to fight back. One of the most effective pieces of Klan recruiting literature read:

> Every criminal, every gambler, every thug, every libertine, every girl ruiner, every home wrecker, every wife beater, every dope peddler, every moonshiner, every crooked politician, every pagan Papist priest, every shyster lawyer, every K. of C.,[1] every white slaver, every Rome-controlled newspaper, every black spider—is fighting the Klan. Think it over, which side are you on?

Local chapters took action against what they considered indecent motion pictures and books.

They destroyed stills, and attacked prostitutes and gamblers. Groups of hooded men even invaded lovers' lanes and beat up the occupants of cars, in one case beating a young couple to death. This work was considered no less important than political efforts to destroy parochial schools, to enforce Bible reading in classrooms, and to defeat Catholic and Jewish candidates for public office.

Although membership figures remain largely shrouded in secrecy, available records indicate that the hooded empire probably enrolled over 5 million members during the 1920s, with a peak membership of about 2 million in 1924. Because members were concentrated so heavily in certain northern and western areas, the Klan won considerable political power in at least six states, and in large sections of about ten others.

In the great cities, however, and eventually in the country as a whole, the Klan discovered that the time had passed when an organization devoted to the supremacy of white Anglo-Saxon Protestants could operate both violently and safely. In some respects the whole movement for 100 percent Americanism was an anachronism in the post–World War I era: but the Klan especially depended upon a widespread delusion that this was still the world of Wade Hampton and the young Rudyard Kipling.[2]

The Klan's fate in New York City was pathetic—and illustrative. In the world's wealthiest city, the nation's largest by far, with a million native—born white Protestants among its inhabitants, the KKK was treated like a band of shabby criminals. The great majority of New York's population of 6 million were Catholics and Jews; and the Irish Catholics who dominated the city's politics and police force were especially offended when the Klan dared organize in New York. The city seethed with bigotry against Negroes, Catholics, and Jews, including considerable distaste within these groups directed at members of the others. But even among white Protestant New Yorkers eligible for Klan membership, few were so foolhardy during the 1920s as to identify themselves publicly with an organization so clearly marked for disaster. It was not an absence of racial prejudice that doomed the Klan in New York, but rather the fact that in most respects the city already was controlled by the "minority" groups which the Klan aimed to suppress.

A year after Kleagles entered the city, two grand juries commenced investigations of the secret order. Special legislation, directed at the KKK, forced all unincorporated associations to file annual membership lists. New York Mayor John F. Hylan denounced Klan members as "anarchists," and the city police force was ordered to "ferret out these despicable disloyal persons who are attempting to organize a society, the aims and purposes of which are of such a character that were they to prevail, the foundations of our country would be destroyed."

In most of New York City, the customary march of hooded Klansmen, carrying banners with messages that were so popular in Kokomo and Anaheim, would have been a feat of amazing courage. In certain sections—the lower east side and Harlem, for example—such a march would have been the most foolhardy event since General Custer's seventh cavalry left a day early for the Little Bighorn. New York's borough of Queens, however, remained predominantly suburban and Protestant in the 1920s. Although subject to hostile laws and unsympathetic policies there as in the rest of New York City, a Klan chapter continued to operate in Queens. In 1927, it received permission to take part in the Queens County Memorial Day Parade to the local Soldier's Monument.

Both the Boy Scouts and the Knights of Columbus withdrew from the patriotic celebration rather than march in the same line as the KKK. The New York police did their best to stop or divert the Klan members, but something less than their best to hold back angry crowds determined to halt the hooded patriots. After 1500 Klansmen and Klanswomen—included a 100-man paramilitary unit—broke through several police barricades, the police simply left the KKK to the parade audience. According to the *New York Times:* "Women fought women and spectators fought the policemen and the Klansmen, as their desire dictated. Combatants were knocked down. Klan banners were shredded. . . ." Five Klansmen were arrested during the melée. Finally the police ceased holding back traffic as the remnant of the Klan cavalcade passed, and motorists tried to run the white-robed marchers down. The Klan parade disintegrated, although three Klansmen in an automobile managed to reach the war memorial monument and placed a wreath with the KKK signature upon it. The wreath promptly was stolen.

Throughout the Northeast, the Klan found only mild support, and even that sometimes aroused the kind of mob violence for which the Klan itself was so well known in the South. In Boston, Mayor James Michael Curley incited crowds by speaking before flaming crosses—the Klan's favorite symbol—and pointing to the cross while he shouted to his predominantly Irish Catholic audiences: "There it burns, the cross of hatred upon which Our Lord, Jesus Christ, was crucified—the cross of human avarice, and not the cross of love and charity. . . ." Curley declared Klan meetings illegal even in private homes, and in Boston he obtained support in his crusade not only from the City Council, but also from city's Catholic and Jewish leaders. It was just as well for the Klan that they did not meet in Boston; houses of people only suspected of being Klan members were attacked with bricks and stones.

In Pittsburgh, another center of Catholic population, Kleagles enjoyed great success in recruiting members. Ten thousand Klansmen from the area, led by the national Imperial Wizard, Hiram Wesley Evans, gathered outside the nearby town of Carnegie for an initiation rally in August 1923. When they marched into town, however, they were met not with cheers, but with angry shouts and a hail of rocks and bottles. The Klansmen continued until a citizen started shooting and a Klan member fell dead. There were no further Klan parades in the Pittsburgh area. The Klan chapter in Perth Amboy, New Jersey, obtained substantial police protection for its meetings; but guards availed little in that heavily Catholic and Jewish industrial and resort area. The entire city police and fire department, protecting a meeting of 500 Knights of the Secret Order, were overwhelmed by a mob of 6000 on the evening of August 30, 1923, and Ku Kluxers were beaten, kicked, and stoned as they fled.

When the Klan reached its peak strength in 1924, less than 4 percent of its members lived in the Northeast—the entire area from Portland, Maine, through Baltimore, Maryland—despite strenuous organizational efforts. The Klan itself claimed that over 40 percent of its membership lived in the three midwestern states of Indiana,

Illinois, and Ohio. Even in that hospitable area, however, the Klan's brand of racism was not welcome everywhere.

For a while it appeared that white Protestants in Chicago, disturbed by a rapid influx of Negroes and immigrants, and by the city's infamous lawlessness during the 1920s, might make it the hub of the Klan empire. By 1922, Chicago had more Klan members than any other city, and initiation fees continued to flow from the midwestern metropolis into Atlanta. When Imperial Kleagle Edward Young Clarke visited the city in June 1922, he announced that 30,000 Chicagoans already belonged to the Klan, and implied that the branch soon would be large enough to help enforce the law in Chicago, thus reducing the city's alarming crime rate. In smaller communities, where violators of Klan mores were easier to intimidate, bootleggers were forced to obey Prohibition laws, and gamblers and other sinners were punished by the secret order. When a major civic association started investigating crime in Chicago, however, the group's leader—a prominent clergyman—was found shot to death in Cicero, Illinois, then the center of Al Capone's operations. After Clarke returned to Atlanta, the Chicago Klan wisely continued to leave the war against crime to the police, the FBI, and the Treasury Department, even though these organizations were overwhelmed by the task.

As soon as the Klan's strength in Chicago became known, powerful enemies sprang up to protect the threatened minority groups. Mayor "Big Bill" Thompson, elected with crucial aid from Negro votes, denounced the Klan. The City Council opened an investigation of the society, and made its findings available to other state and local political bodies. One consequence was a bill prohibiting the wearing of masks in public, that passed the Illinois House of Representatives by a vote of 100 to 2, and the State Senate by 26 to 1. The City Council itself resolved by a vote of 56 to 2 to rid the city's payroll of Kluxers. Within a week, two firemen were suspended and the Klan's attorney had to be rushed from Atlanta to take legal steps halting the purge. Meanwhile the American Unity League, dominated by Catholics, started publishing the names of Klan members, concentrating on those in business and the professions. Salesmen, milkmen, and even a bank

president were forced out of their jobs when their customers refused to deal with Klan members. The disheartened bank president, complying with his board of directors' request that he resign, explained, "I signed a petition for membership in the Klan several months ago, but did not know it was anything else than an ordinary fraternal order." He may not have realized either how many Jewish, Irish, and Negro depositors had placed their money in his bank.

A counterattack was also launched in the press. In a front-page editorial headlined "To Hell with the Ku Klux Klan!" the Chicago *Defender,* the nation's leading Negro newspaper, advised readers to get ready to fight "against those who now try to win by signs and robes what their fathers lost by fire and sword." A prominent rabbi warned that "Protestantism is on trial. Protestantism must destroy Ku Kluxism or Ku Kluxism will destroy Protestantism."

Political candidates backed publicly by the Klan fared badly in Chicago. Enough excitement was generated during the city election of 1924 to bring forth a series of threatening letters from the Klan. Some of these went to Chicago's largest Negro church, which was completely destroyed one night by fire. On the other hand, bombs demolished a shop just vacated by the Klan journal, *Dawn,* and other bombs were exploded against offices of Klan members and of advertisers in Klan periodicals.

The accumulation of outside pressures on the Klan in Chicago—political, economic, and physical—served to increase internal dissension in the order. Although the Klan enrolled well over 50,000 members in Chicago by 1924, at the end of that year the organization was practically dormant in the city. For similar reasons it already was on the way to destruction as a major political and social force throughout the United States. The failure of the KKK, after temporary success in the immediate postwar years, should not be interpreted as a sign that racism was waning. The Klan simply had tried to take on too many enemies. The "minorities" which the Klan was organized to suppress possessed far more members, votes, wealth, and almost every other kind of power than the Klan itself. The order's fate should have served as a warning to the American people of the changes taking place in a world in which white Protestants were far outnumbered; but it did not.   [1970]

Notes

1. K. OF C.: Knights of Columbus, a Catholic benevolent society.
2. WADE HAMPTON AND RUDYARD KIPLING: A Confederate war hero who restored Southern white rule to South Carolina and a British writer who romanticized colonial India, respectively.

Understanding the Reading

1. How did the Klan recruit new members in the 1920s, and where was it most successful? Why?
2. Why did the Klan have trouble organizing in New York City and other large cities in the Northeast?
3. How was the Klan defeated in Chicago?

Suggestions for Responding

1. Explain why the Ku Klux Klan appealed to more than five million Americans in the 1920s.
2. The Klan still exists today in some areas of the country. Find out if there is a Klan group near you, and report on them and their activities. ◆

79

Dry September

WILLIAM FAULKNER

Through the bloody September twilight, aftermath of sixty-two rainless days, it had gone like a fire in dry grass—the rumor, the story, whatever it was. Something about Miss Minnie Cooper and a Negro. Attacked, insulted, frightened: none of them, gathered in the barber shop on that Saturday evening where the ceiling fan stirred, with-

out freshening it, the vitiated air, sending back upon them, in recurrent surges of stale pomade and lotion, their own stale breath and odors, knew exactly what had happened.

"Except it wasn't Will Mayes," a barber said. He was a man of middle age; a thin, sand-colored man with a mild face, who was shaving a client. "I know Will Mayes. He's a good nigger. And I know Miss Minnie Cooper, too."

"What do you know about her?" a second barber said.

"Who is she?" the client said. "A young girl?"

"No," the barber said. "She's about forty, I reckon. She aint married. That's why I don't believe—"

"Believe, hell!" a hulking youth in a sweat-stained silk shirt said. "Wont you take a white woman's word before a nigger's?"

"I dont believe Will Mayes did it," the barber said. "I know Will Mayes."

"Maybe you know who did it, then. Maybe you already got him out of town, you damn niggerlover."

"I dont believe anybody did anything. I dont believe anything happened. I leave it to you fellows if them ladies that get old without getting married dont have notions that a man cant—"

"Then you are a hell of a white man," the client said. He moved under the cloth. The youth had sprung to his feet.

"You dont?" he said. "Do you accuse a white woman of lying?"

The barber held the razor poised above the half-risen client. He did not look around.

"It's this durn weather," another said. "It's enough to make a man do anything. Even to her."

Nobody laughed. The barber said in his mild, stubborn tone: "I aint accusing nobody of nothing. I just know and you fellows know how a woman that never—"

"You damn niggerlover!" the youth said.

"Shut up, Butch," another said. "We'll get the facts in plenty of time to act."

"Who is? Who's getting them?" the youth said. "Facts, hell! I—"

"You're a fine white man," the client said. "Aint you?" In his frothy beard he looked like a desert rat in the moving pictures. "You tell them, Jack," he said to the youth. "If there aint any white men in this town, you can count on me, even if I aint only a drummer[1] and a stranger."

"That's right, boys," the barber said. "Find out the truth first. I know Will Mayes."

"Well, by God!" the youth shouted. "To think that a white man in this town—"

"Shut up, Butch," the second speaker said. "We got plenty of time."

The client sat up. He looked at the speaker. "Do you claim that anything excuses a nigger attacking a white woman? Do you mean to tell me you are a white man and you'll stand for it? You better go back North where you came from. The South dont want your kind here."

"North what?" the second said. "I was born and raised in this town."

"Well, by God!" the youth said. He looked about with a strained, baffled gaze, as if he was trying to remember what it was he wanted to say or to do. He drew his sleeve across his sweating face. "Damn if I'm going to let a white woman—"

"You tell them, Jack," the drummer said. "By God, if they—"

The screen door crashed open. A man stood in the floor, his feet apart and his heavy-set body poised easily. His white shirt was open at the throat; he wore a felt hat. His hot, bold glance swept the group. His name was McLendon. He had commanded troops at the front in France and had been decorated for valor.

"Well," he said, "are you going to sit there and let a black son rape a white woman on the streets of Jefferson?"

Butch sprang up again. The silk of his shirt clung flat to his heavy shoulders. At each armpit was a dark halfmoon. "That's what I been telling them! That's what I—"

"Did it really happen?" a third said. "This aint the first man scare she ever had, like Hawkshaw says. Wasn't there something about a man on the kitchen roof, watching her undress, about a year ago?"

"What?" the client said. "What's that?" The barber had been slowly forcing him back into the chair; he arrested himself reclining, his head lifted, the barber still pressing him down.

McLendon whirled on the third speaker. "Happen? What the hell difference does it make? Are you going to let the black sons get away with it until one really does it?"

"That's what I'm telling them!" Butch shouted. He cursed, long and steady, pointless.

"Here, here," a fourth said. "Not so loud. Dont talk so loud."

"Sure," McLendon said; "no talking necessary at all. I've done my talking. Who's with me?" He poised on the balls of his feet, roving his gaze.

The barber held the drummer's face down, the razor poised. "Find out the facts first, boys. I know Willy Mayes. It wasn't him. Let's get the sheriff and do this thing right."

McLendon whirled upon him his furious, rigid face. The barber did not look away. They looked like men of different races. The other barbers had ceased also above their prone clients. "You mean to tell me," McLendon said, "that you'd take a nigger's word before a white woman's? Why, you damn niggerloving—"

The third speaker rose and grasped McLendon's arm; he too had been a soldier. "Now, now. Let's figure this thing out. Who knows anything about what really happened?"

"Figure out hell!" McLendon jerked his arm free. "All that're with me get up from there. The ones that aint—" He roved his gaze, dragging his sleeve across his face.

Three men rose. The drummer in the chair sat up. "Here," he said, jerking at the cloth about his neck; "get this rag off me. I'm with him. I dont live here, but by God, if our mothers and wives and sisters—" He smeared the cloth over his face and flung it to the floor. McLendon stood in the floor and cursed the others. Another rose and moved toward him. The remainder sat uncomfortable, not looking at one another, then one by one they rose and joined him.

The barber picked the cloth from the floor. He began to fold it neatly. "Boys, dont do that. Will Mayes never done it. I know."

"Come on," McLendon said. He whirled. From his hip pocket protruded the butt of a heavy automatic pistol. They went out. The screen door crashed behind them reverberant in the dead air.

The barber wiped the razor carefully and swiftly, and put it away, and ran to the rear, and took his hat from the wall. "I'll be back as soon as I can," he said to the other barbers. "I cant let—" He went out, running. The two other barbers followed him to the door and caught it on the rebound, leaning out and looking up the street after him. The air was flat and dead. It had a metallic taste at the base of the tongue.

"What can he do?" the first said. The second one was saying "Jees Christ, Jees Christ" under his breath. "I'd just as lief be Will Mayes as Hawk, if he gets McLendon riled."

"Jees Christ, Jees Christ," the second whispered.

"You reckon he really done it to her?" the first said.

II

She was thirty-eight or thirty-nine. She lived in a small frame house with her invalid mother and a thin, sallow, unflagging aunt, where each morning between ten and eleven she would appear on the porch in a lace-trimmed boudoir cap, to sit swinging in the porch swing until noon. After dinner she lay down for a while, until the afternoon began to cool. Then, in one of the three or four new voile dresses which she had each summer, she would go downtown to spend the afternoon in the stores with the other ladies, where they would handle the goods and haggle over the prices in cold, immediate voices, without an intention of buying.

She was of comfortable people—not the best in Jefferson, but good people enough—and she was still on the slender side of ordinary looking, with a bright, faintly haggard manner and dress. When she was young she had had a slender, nervous body and a sort of hard vivacity which had enabled her for a time to ride upon the crest of the town's social life as exemplified by the high school party and church social period of her contemporaries while still children enough to be unclassconscious.

She was the last to realize that she was losing ground; that those among whom she had been a little brighter and louder flame than any other were beginning to learn the pleasure of snobbery—male—and retaliation—female. That was when her face began to wear that bright, haggard look. She still carried it to parties on shadowy porticoes and summer lawns, like a mask or a flag, with that bafflement of furious repudiation of truth in her eyes. One evening at a party she heard a boy and two girls, all schoolmates, talking. She never accepted another invitation.

She watched the girls with whom she had grown up as they married and got homes and children, but no man ever called on her steadily until the children of the other girls had been calling her "aunty" for several years, the while their mothers told them in bright voices about how popular Aunt Minnie had been as a girl. Then the town began to see her driving on Sunday afternoons with the cashier in the bank. He was a widower of about forty—a high-colored man, smelling always faintly of the barber shop or of whisky. He owned the first automobile in town, a red runabout; Minnie had the first motoring bonnet and veil the town ever saw. Then the town began to say: "Poor Minnie." "But she is old enough to take care of herself," others said. That was when she began to ask her old schoolmates that their children call her "cousin" instead of "aunty."

It was twelve years now since she had been relegated into adultery by public opinion, and eight years since the cashier had gone to a Memphis bank, returning for one day each Christmas, which he spent at an annual bachelors' party at a hunting club on the river. From behind their curtains the neighbors would see the party pass, and during the over-the-way Christmas day visiting they would tell her about him, about how well he looked, and how they heard that he was prospering in the city, watching with bright, secret eyes her haggard, bright face. Usually by that hour there would be the scent of whisky on her breath. It was supplied her by a youth, a clerk at the soda fountain: "Sure; I buy it for the old gal. I reckon she's entitled to a little fun."

Her mother kept to her room altogether now; the gaunt aunt ran the house. Against that background Minnie's bright dresses, her idle and empty days, had a quality of furious unreality. She went out in the evenings only with women now, neighbors, to the moving pictures. Each afternoon she dressed in one of the new dresses and went downtown alone, where her young "cousins" were already strolling in the late afternoons with their delicate, silken heads and thin, awkward arms and conscious hips, clinging to one another or shrieking and giggling with paired boys in the soda fountain when she passed and went on along the serried store fronts, in the doors of which the sitting and lounging men did not even follow her with their eyes any more.

III

The barber went swiftly up the street where the sparse lights, insect-swirled, glared in rigid and violent suspension in the lifeless air. The day had died in a pall of dust; above the darkened square, shrouded by the spent dust, the sky was as clear as the inside of a brass bell. Below the east was a rumor of the twice-waxed moon.

When he overtook them McLendon and three others were getting into a car parked in an alley. McLendon stooped his thick head, peering out beneath the top. "Changed your mind, did you?" he said. "Damn good thing; by God, tomorrow when this town hears about how you talked tonight—"

"Now, now," the other ex-soldier said. "Hawkshaw's all right. Come on, Hawk; jump in."

"Will Mayes never done it, boys," the barber said. "If anybody done it. Why, you all know well as I do there aint any town where they got better niggers than us. And you know how a lady will kind of think things about men when there aint reason to, and Miss Minnie anyway—"

"Sure, sure," the soldier said. "We're just going to talk to him a little; that's all."

"Talk hell!" Butch said. "When we're through with the—"

"Shut up, for God's sake!" the soldier said. "Do you want everybody in town—"

"Tell them, by God!" McLendon said. "Tell every one of the sons that'll let a white woman—"

"Let's go; let's go: here's the other car." The second car slid squealing out of a cloud of dust at the alley mouth. McLendon started his car and took the lead. Dust lay like fog in the street. The street lights hung nimbused as in water. They drove on out of town.

A rutted lane turned at right angles. Dust hung above it too, and above all the land. The dark bulk of the ice plant, where the Negro Mayes was night watchman, rose against the sky. "Better stop here, hadn't we?" the soldier said. McLendon did not reply. He hurled the car up

and slammed to a stop, the headlights glaring on the blank wall.

"Listen here, boys," the barber said; "if he's here, dont that prove he never done it? Dont it? If it was him, he would run. Dont you see he would?" The second car came up and stopped. McLendon got down; Butch sprang down beside him. "Listen, boys," the barber said.

"Cut the lights off!" McLendon said. The breathless dark rushed down. There was no sound in it save their lungs as they sought air in the parched dust in which for two months they had lived; then the diminishing crunch of McLendon's and Butch's feet, and a moment later McLendon's voice:

"Will! . . . Will!"

Below the east the wan hemorrhage of the moon increased. It heaved above the ridge, silvering the air, the dust, so that they seemed to breathe, live, in a bowl of molten lead. There was no sound of nightbird nor insect, no sound save their breathing and a faint ticking of contracting metal about the cars. Where their bodies touched one another they seemed to sweat dryly, for no more moisture came. "Christ!" a voice said; "let's get out of here."

But they didn't move until vague noises began to grow out of the darkness ahead; then they got out and waited tensely in the breathless dark. There was another sound: a blow, a hissing expulsion of breath and McLendon cursing in undertone. They stood a moment longer, then they ran forward. They ran in a stumbling clump, as though they were fleeing something. "Kill him, kill the son," a voice whispered. McLendon flung them back.

"Not here," he said. "Get him into the car." "Kill him, kill the black son!" the voice murmured. They dragged the Negro to the car. The barber had waited beside the car. He could feel himself sweating and he knew he was going to be sick at the stomach.

"What is it, captains?" the Negro said. "I aint done nothing. 'Fore God, Mr. John." Someone produced handcuffs. They worked busily about the Negro as though he were a post, quiet, intent, getting in one another's way. He submitted to the handcuffs, looking swiftly and constantly from dim face to dim face. "Who's here, captains?" he said, leaning to peer into the faces until they could feel his breath and smell his sweaty reek. He spoke a name or two. "What you all say I done, Mr. John?"

McLendon jerked the car door open. "Get in!" he said.

The Negro did not move. "What you all going to do with me, Mr. John? I aint done nothing. White folks, captains, I aint done nothing: I swear 'fore God." He called another name.

"Get in!" McLendon said. He struck the Negro. The others expelled their breath in a dry hissing and struck him with random blows and he whirled and cursed them, and swept his manacled hands across their faces and slashed the barber upon the mouth, and the barber struck him also. "Get him in there," McLendon said. They pushed at him. He ceased struggling and got in and sat quietly as the others took their places. He sat between the barber and the soldier, drawing his limbs in so as not to touch them, his eyes going swiftly and constantly from face to face. Butch clung to the running board. The car moved on. The barber nursed his mouth with his handkerchief.

"What's the matter, Hawk?" the soldier said.

"Nothing," the barber said. They regained the highroad and turned away from town. The second car dropped back out of the dust. They went on, gaining speed; the final fringe of houses dropped behind.

"Goddamn, he stinks!" the soldier said.

"We'll fix that," the drummer in front beside McLendon said. On the running board Butch cursed into the hot rush of air. The barber leaned suddenly forward and touched McLendon's arm.

"Let me out, John," he said.

"Jump out, niggerlover," McLendon said without turning his head. He drove swiftly. Behind them the sourceless lights of the second car glared in the dust. Presently McLendon turned into a narrow road. It was rutted with disuse. It led back to an abandoned brick kiln—a series of reddish mounds and weed- and vine-choked vats without bottom. It had been used for pasture once, until one day the owner missed one of his mules. Although he prodded carefully in the vats with a long pole, he could not even find the bottom of them.

"John," the barber said.

"Jump out, then," McLendon said, hurling the

car along the ruts. Beside the barber the Negro spoke.

"Mr. Henry."

The barber sat forward. The narrow tunnel of the road rushed up and past. Their motion was like an extinct furnace blast: cooler, but utterly dead. The car bounded from rut to rut.

"Mr. Henry," the Negro said.

The barber began to tug furiously at the door. "Look out, there!" the soldier said, but the barber had already kicked the door open and swung onto the running board. The soldier leaned across the Negro and grasped at him, but he had already jumped. The car went on without checking speed.

The impetus hurled him crashing through dust-sheathed weeds, into the ditch. Dust puffed about him, and in a thin, vicious crackling of sapless stems he lay choking and retching until the second car passed and died away. Then he rose and limped on until he reached the highroad and turned toward town, brushing at his clothes with his hands. The moon was higher, riding high and clear of the dust at last, and after a while the town began to glare beneath the dust. He went on, limping. Presently he heard cars and the glow of them grew in the dust behind him and he left the road and crouched again in the weeds until they passed. McLendon's car came last now. There were four people in it and Butch was not on the running board.

They went on; the dust swallowed them; the glare and the sound died away. The dust of them hung for a while, but soon the eternal dust absorbed it again. The barber climbed back onto the road and limped on toward town.

IV

As she dressed for supper on that Saturday evening, her own flesh felt like fever. Her hands trembled among the hooks and eyes, and her eyes had a feverish look, and her hair swirled crisp and crackling under the comb. While she was still dressing the friends called for her and sat while she donned her sheerest underthings and stockings and a new voile dress. "Do you feel strong enough to go out?" they said, their eyes bright too, with a dark glitter. "When you have had time to get over the shock, you must tell us what happened. What he said and did; everything."

In the leafed darkness, as they walked toward the square, she began to breathe deeply, something like a swimmer preparing to dive, until she ceased trembling, the four of them walking slowly because of the terrible heat and out of solicitude for her. But as they neared the square she began to tremble again, walking with her head up, her hands clenched at her sides, their voices about her murmurous, also with that feverish, glittering quality of their eyes.

They entered the square, she in the center of the group, fragile in her fresh dress. She was trembling worse. She walked slower and slower, as children eat ice cream, her head up and her eyes bright in the haggard banner of her face, passing the hotel and the coatless drummers in chairs along the curb looking around at her: "That's the one: see? The one in pink in the middle." "Is that her? What did they do with the nigger? Did they—?" "Sure. He's all right." "All right, is he?" "Sure. He went on a little trip." Then the drug store, where even the young men lounging in the doorway tipped their hats and followed with their eyes the motion of her hips and legs when she passed.

They went on, passing the lifted hats of the gentlemen, the suddenly ceased voices, deferent, protective. "Do you see?" the friends said. Their voices sounded like long, hovering sighs of hissing exultation. "There's not a Negro on the square. Not one."

They reached the picture show. It was like a miniature fairyland with its lighted lobby and colored lithographs of life caught in its terrible and beautiful mutations. Her lips began to tingle. In the dark, when the picture began, it would be all right; she could hold back the laughing so it would not waste away so fast and so soon. So she hurried on before the turning faces, the undertones of low astonishment, and they took their accustomed places where she could see the aisle against the silver glare and the young men and girls coming in two and two against it.

The lights flicked away; the screen glowed silver, and soon life began to unfold, beautiful and passionate and sad, while still the young men and girls entered, scented and sibilant in the half dark, their paired backs in silhouette delicate and sleek, their slim, quick bodies awkward, divinely young, while beyond them the silver dream accumulated, inevitably on and on. She began to laugh. In trying to suppress it, it made more noise than ever; heads began to turn. Still laughing, her friends raised her and led her out, and she stood at the curb, laughing on a high, sustained note, until the taxi came up and they helped her in.

They removed the pink voile and the sheer underthings and the stockings, and put her to bed, and cracked ice for her temples, and sent for the doctor. He was hard to locate, so they ministered to her with hushed ejaculations, renewing the ice and fanning her. While the ice was fresh and cold she stopped laughing and lay still for a time, moaning only a little. But soon the laughing welled again and her voice rose screaming.

"Shhhhhhhhhhhh! Shhhhhhhhhhhhhhhh!" they said, freshening the icepack, smoothing her hair, examining it for gray: "poor girl!" Then to one another: "Do you suppose anything really happened?" their eyes darkly aglitter, secret and passionate. "Shhhhhhhhhh! Poor girl! Poor Minnie!"

V

It was midnight when McLendon drove up to his neat new house. It was trim and fresh as a birdcake and almost as small, with its clean, green-and-white paint. He locked the car and mounted the porch and entered. His wife rose from a chair beside the reading lamp. McLendon stopped in the floor and stared at her until she looked down.

"Look at that clock," he said, lifting his arm, pointing. She stood before him, her face lowered, a magazine in her hands. Her face was pale, strained, and weary-looking. "Haven't I told you about sitting up like this, waiting to see when I come in?"

"John," she said. She laid the magazine down. Poised on the balls of his feet, he glared at her with his hot eyes, his sweating face.

"Didn't I tell you?" He went toward her. She looked up then. He caught her shoulder. She stood passive, looking at him.

"Don't, John. I couldn't sleep . . . The heat; something. Please, John. You're hurting me."

"Didn't I tell you?" He released her and half struck, half flung her across the chair, and she lay there and watched him quietly as he left the room.

He went on through the house, ripping off his shirt, and on the dark, screened porch at the rear he stood and mopped his head and shoulders with the shirt and flung it away. He took the pistol from his hip and laid it on the table beside the bed, and sat on the bed and removed his shoes, and rose and slipped his trousers off. He was sweating again already, and he stooped and hunted furiously for the shirt. At last he found it and wiped his body again, and, with his body pressed against the dusty screen, he stood panting. There was no movement, no sound, not even an insect. The dark world seemed to lie stricken beneath the cold moon and the lidless stars.   [1950]

Note

1. DRUMMER: A traveling salesman.

Understanding the Reading

1. Explain how the men in the barber shop came to accuse Will Mayes.
2. Why did most of the men join McLendon?
3. What was Minnie like, and how had she changed since she was a young woman?
4. Why didn't the men listen to Hawk?
5. Why did Hawk hit Will?
6. Why did Hawk get into the car with Mayes? Why did he jump out?
7. Why did Minnie go to the picture show?
8. What made her laugh hysterically?
9. What does McLendon's treatment of his wife show about the use of violence?

Suggestions for Responding

1. Using examples from this story, explain how mob psychology works.
2. Speculate on what the townspeople will have to say in the morning about the principal characters: McLendon, his wife, Hawk, Will Mayes, and Minnie. ◆

80

Emmett Louis Till, 1941–1955

SOUTHERN POVERTY LAW CENTER

Mamie Till was a devoted, well-educated mother who taught her son that a person's worth did not depend on the color of his or her skin. Nevertheless, when she put 14-year-old Emmett on a train bound for Mississippi in the summer of 1955, she warned him: "If you have to get down on your knees and bow when a white person goes past, do it willingly."

It was not in Emmett Till to bow down. Raised in a working-class section of Chicago, he was bold and self-assured. He didn't understand the timid attitude of his Southern cousins toward whites. He even tried to impress them by showing them a photo of some white Chicago youths, claiming the girl in the picture was his girlfriend.

One day he took the photo out of his wallet and showed it to a group of boys standing outside a country store in Money, Mississippi. The boys dared him to speak to a white woman in the store. Emmett walked in confidently, bought some candy from Carolyn Bryant, the wife of the store owner, and said "Bye baby" on his way out.

Within hours, nearly everyone in town had heard at least one version of the incident. Some said Emmett had asked Mrs. Bryant for a date; others said he whistled at her. Whatever the details were, Roy Bryant was outraged that a black youth had been disrespectful to his wife. That weekend, Bryant and his half-brother J. W. Milam went looking for Till. They came to the cotton field shack that belonged to Mose Wright, a 64-year-old farmer and grandfather of Emmett Till's cousin. Bryant demanded to see "the boy that did the talking." Wright reluctantly got Till out of bed. As the white men took Emmett Till away, they told Wright not to cause any trouble or he'd "never live to be 65."

A magazine writer later paid Milam to describe what happened that night. Milam said he and Bryant beat Emmett Till, shot him in the head, wired a 75-pound cotton gin fan to his neck and dumped his body in the Tallahatchie River.

When asked why he did it, Milam responded:

"Well, what else could I do? He thought he was as good as any white man."

SO THE WORLD COULD SEE

Till's body was found three days later—a bullet in the skull, one eye gouged out and the head crushed in on one side. The face was unrecognizable. Mose Wright knew it was Till only because of a signet ring that remained on one finger. The ring had belonged to Emmett's father Louis, who had died ten years earlier, and bore his initials L.T.

Mamie Till demanded the body of her son be sent back to Chicago. Then she ordered an open-casket funeral so the world could see what had been done to Emmett. *Jet* magazine published a picture of the horribly disfigured corpse. Thousands viewed the body and attended the funeral.

All over the country, blacks and sympathetic whites were horrified by the killing. Thousands of people sent money to the NAACP[1] to support its legal efforts on behalf of black victims.

In the meantime, J. W. Milam and Roy Bryant faced murder charges. They admitted they kidnapped and beat Emmett Till, but claimed they left him alive. Ignoring nationwide criticism, white Mississippians raised $10,000 to pay the legal expenses for Milam and Bryant. Five white local lawyers volunteered to represent them at the murder trial.

Mose Wright risked his life to testify against the men. In a courtroom filled with reporters and white spectators, the frail black farmer stood and identified Bryant and Milam as the men who took Emmett away.

Wright's act of courage didn't convince the all-white jury. After deliberating just over an hour, the jury returned a verdict of not guilty.

The murder of Emmett Till was the spark that set the civil rights movement on fire. For those who would become leaders of that movement, the martyred 14-year-old was a symbol of the struggle for equality.

"The Emmett Till case shook the foundations of Mississippi," said Myrlie Evers, widow of civil rights leader Medgar Evers, ". . . because it said even a child was not safe from racism and bigotry and death."

NAACP Executive Director Roy Wilkins said white Mississippians "had to prove they were superior . . . by taking away a 14-year-old boy."

Fred Shuttlesworth, who eight years later would lead the fight for integration in Birmingham, said, "The fact that Emmett Till, a young black man, could be found floating down the river in Mississippi just set in concrete the determination of the people to move forward . . . only God can know how many Negroes have come up missing, dead and killed under this system with which we live."   [1989]

Note

1. NAACP: National Association for the Advancement of Colored People.

Understanding the Reading

1. What did Emmett Till do to provoke the white Southerners?
2. What did Bryant and Milam do to Till?
3. What were the charges and the verdict against Bryant and Milam?
4. Nationally, what effect did Till's death produce, and why?

Suggestion for Responding

Compare the motives of Bryant, Milam, and other white Mississippians in the Till case with those of McLendon and the townspeople in Faulkner's story. ✦

81

Neighbors

DIANE OLIVER

The bus turning the corner of Patterson and Talford Avenue was dull this time of evening. Of the four passengers standing in the rear, she did not recognize any of her friends. Most of the people tucked neatly in the double seats were women, maids and cooks on their way from work or secretaries who had worked late and were riding from the office building at the mill. The cotton mill was out from town, near the house where she worked. She noticed that a few men were riding too. They were obviously just working men, except for one gentleman dressed very neatly in a dark grey suit and carrying what she imagined was a push-button umbrella.

He looked to her as though he usually drove a car to work. She immediately decided that the car probably wouldn't start this morning so he had to catch the bus to and from work. She was standing in the rear of the bus, peering at the passengers, her arms barely reaching the over-head railing, trying not to wobble with every lurch. But every corner the bus turned pushed her head toward a window. And her hair was coming down too, wisps of black curls swung between her eyes. She looked at the people around her. Some of them were white, but most of them were her color. Looking at the passengers at least kept her from thinking of tomorrow. But really she would be glad when it came, then everything would be over.

She took a firmer grip on the green leather seat and wished she had on her glasses. The man with the umbrella was two people ahead of her on the other side of the bus, so she could see him between other people very clearly. She watched as he unfolded the evening newspaper, craning her neck to see what was on the front page. She stood, impatiently trying to read the headlines, when she realized he was staring up at her rather curiously. Biting her lips she turned her head and stared out of the window until the downtown section was in sight.

She would have to wait until she was home to see if they were in the newspaper again. Sometimes she felt that if another person snapped a picture of them she would burst out screaming. Last Monday reporters were already inside the pre-school clinic when she took Tommy for his last polio shot. She didn't understand how anyone could be so heartless to a child. The flashbulb went off right when the needle went in and all the picture showed was Tommy's open mouth.

The bus pulling up to the curb jerked to a stop, startling her and confusing her thoughts. Clutching in her hand the paper bag that contained her uniform, she pushed her way toward the door. By standing in the back of the bus, she was one of the first people to step to the ground.

Outside the bus, the evening air felt humid and uncomfortable and her dress kept sticking to her. She looked up and remembered that the weatherman had forecast rain. Just their luck— why, she wondered, would it have to rain on top of everything else?

As she walked along, the main street seemed unnaturally quiet but she decided her imagination was merely playing tricks. Besides, most of the stores had been closed since five o'clock.

She stopped to look at a reversible raincoat in Ivey's window, but although she had a full time job now, she couldn't keep her mind on clothes. She was about to continue walking when she heard a horn blowing. Looking around, half-scared but also curious, she saw a man beckoning to her in a grey car. He was nobody she knew but since a nicely dressed woman was with him in the front seat, she walked to the car.

"You're Jim Mitchell's girl, aren't you?" he questioned. "You Ellie or the other one?"

She nodded yes, wondering who he was and how much he had been drinking.

"Now honey," he said leaning over the woman, "you don't know me but your father does and you tell him that if anything happens to that boy of his tomorrow we're ready to set things straight." He looked her straight in the eye and she promised to take home the message.

Just as the man was about to step on the gas, the woman reached out and touched her arm. "You hurry up home, honey, it's about dark out here."

Before she could find out their names, the Chevrolet had disappeared around a corner. Ellie wished someone would magically appear and tell her everything that had happened since August. Then maybe she could figure out what was real and what she had been imagining for the past couple of days.

She walked past the main shopping district up to Tanner's where Saraline was standing in the window peeling oranges. Everything in the shop was painted orange and green and Ellie couldn't help thinking that poor Saraline looked out of place. She stopped to wave to her friend who pointed the knife to her watch and then to her boyfriend standing in the rear of the shop. Ellie nodded that she understood. She knew Sara wanted her to tell her grandfather that she had to work late again. Neither one of them could figure out why he didn't like Charlie. Saraline had finished high school three years ahead of her and it was time for her to be getting married. Ellie watched as her friend stopped peeling the orange long enough to cross her fingers. She nodded again but she was afraid all the crossed fingers in the world wouldn't stop the trouble tomorrow.

She stopped at the traffic light and spoke to a shrivelled woman hunched against the side of a building. Scuffing the bottom of her sneakers on the curb she waited for the woman to open her mouth and grin as she usually did. The kids used to bait her to talk, and since she didn't have but one tooth in her whole head they called her Doughnut Puncher. But the woman was still, the way everything else had been all week.

From where Ellie stood, across the street from the Sears and Roebuck parking lot, she could see their house, all of the houses on the single street white people called Welfare Row. Those newspaper men always made her angry. All of their articles showed how rough the people were on their street. And the reporters never said her family wasn't on welfare, the papers always said the family lived on that street. She paused to look across the street at a group of kids pouncing on one rubber ball. There were always white kids around their neighborhood mixed up in the games, but playing with them was almost an unwritten rule. When everybody started going to school nobody played together any more.

She crossed at the corner ignoring the cars at the stop light and the closer she got to her street the more she realized that the newspaper was right. The houses were ugly, there were not even any trees, just patches of scraggly bushes and grasses. As she cut across the sticky asphalt pavement covered with cars she was conscious of the parking lot floodlights casting a strange glow on her street. She stared from habit at the house on the end of the block and except for the way the paint was peeling they all looked alike to her. Now at twilight the flaking grey paint had a luminous glow and as she walked down the dirt sidewalk she noticed Mr. Paul's pipe smoke added to the hazy atmosphere. Mr. Paul would be sitting in that same spot waiting until Saraline came home. Ellie slowed her pace to speak to the elderly man sitting on the porch.

"Evening, Mr. Paul," she said. Her voice sounded clear and out of place on the vacant street.

"Eh, who's that?" Mr. Paul leaned over the rail. "What you say, girl?"

"How are you?" she hollered louder. "Sara said she'd be late tonight, she has to work." She waited for the words to sink in.

His head had dropped and his eyes were facing his lap. She could see that he was disappointed. "Couldn't help it," he said finally. "Reckon they needed her again." Then as if he suddenly remembered he turned toward her.

"You people be ready down there? Still gonna let him go tomorrow?"

She looked at Mr. Paul between the missing rails on his porch, seeing how his rolled up trousers seemed to fit exactly in the vacant banister space.

"Last I heard this morning we're still letting him go," she said.

Mr. Paul had shifted his weight back to the chair. "Don't reckon they'll hurt him," he mumbled, scratching the side of his face. "Hope he don't mind being spit on though. Spitting ain't like cutting. They can spit on him and nobody'll ever know who did it," he said, ending his words with a quiet chuckle.

Ellie stood on the sidewalk grinding her heel in the dirt waiting for the old man to finish talking. She was glad somebody found something funny to laugh at. Finally he shut up.

"Goodbye, Mr. Paul," she waved. Her voice sounded loud to her own ears. But she knew the way her head ached intensified noises. She walked home faster, hoping they had some aspirin in the house and that those men would leave earlier tonight.

From the front of her house she could tell that the men were still there. The living room light shone behind the yellow shades, coming through brighter in the patched places. She thought about moving the geranium pot from the porch to catch the rain but changed her mind. She kicked a beer can under a car parked in the street and stopped to look at her reflection on the car door. The tiny flowers of her printed dress made her look as if she had a strange tropical disease. She spotted another can and kicked it out of the way of the car, thinking that one of these days some kid was going to fall and hurt himself. What she wanted to do she knew was kick the car out of the way.

Both the station wagon and the Ford had been parked in front of her house all week, waiting. Everybody was just sitting around waiting.

Suddenly she laughed aloud. Reverend Davis' car was big and black and shiny just like, but no, the smile disappeared from her face, her mother didn't like for them to say things about other people's color. She looked around to see who else came, and saw Mr. Moore's old beat up blue car. Somebody had torn away half of his NAACP[1] sign. Sometimes she really felt sorry for the man. No matter how hard he glued on his stickers somebody always yanked them off again.

Ellie didn't recognize the third car but it had an Alabama license plate. She turned around and looked up and down the street, hating to go inside. There were no lights on their street, but in the distance she could see the bright lights of the parking lot. Slowly she did an about face and climbed the steps.

She wondered when her Mama was going to remember to get a yellow bulb for the porch. Although the lights hadn't been turned on, usually June bugs and mosquitoes swarmed all around the porch. By the time she was inside the house she always felt like they were crawling in her hair. She pulled on the screen and saw that Mama finally had made Hezekiah patch up the holes. The globs of white adhesive tape scattered over the screen door looked just like misshapen butterflies.

She listened to her father's voice and could tell by the tone that the men were discussing something important again. She rattled the door once more but nobody came.

"Will somebody please let me in?" Her voice carried through the screen to the knot of men sitting in the corner.

"The door's open," her father yelled. "Come on in."

"The door is not open," she said evenly. "You know we stopped leaving it open." She was feeling tired again and her voice had fallen an octave lower.

"Yeah, I forgot, I forgot," he mumbled walking to the door.

She watched her father almost stumble across a chair to let her in. He was shorter than the light bulb and the light seemed to beam down on him, emphasizing the wrinkles around his eyes. She could tell from the way he pushed open the

screen that he hadn't had much sleep either. She'd overhead him telling Mama that the people down at the shop seemed to be piling on the work harder just because of this thing. And he couldn't do anything or say anything to his boss because they probably wanted to fire him.

"Where's Mama?" she whispered. He nodded toward the back.

"Good evening, everybody," she said looking at the three men who had not looked up since she entered the room. One of the men half stood, but his attention was geared back to something another man was saying. They were sitting on the sofa in their shirt sleeves and there was a pitcher of ice water on the window sill.

"Your mother probably needs some help," her father said. She looked past him trying to figure out who the white man was sitting on the end. His face looked familiar and she tried to remember where she had seen him before. The men were paying no attention to her. She bent to see what they were studying and saw a large sheet of white drawing paper. She could see blocks and lines and the man sitting in the middle was marking a trail with the eraser edge of the pencil.

The quiet stillness of the room was making her head ache more. She pushed her way through the red embroidered curtains that led to the kitchen.

"I'm home, Mama," she said, standing in front of the back door facing the big yellow sun Hezekiah and Tommy had painted on the wall above the iron stove. Immediately she felt a warmth permeating her skin. "Where is everybody?" she asked, sitting at the table where her mother was peeling potatoes.

"Mrs. McAllister is keeping Helen and Teenie," her mother said. "Your brother is staying over with Harry tonight." With each name she uttered, a slice of potato peeling tumbled to the newspaper on the table. "Tommy's in the bedroom reading that Uncle Wiggily book."

Ellie looked up at her mother but her eyes were straight ahead. She knew that Tommy only read the Uncle Wiggily book by himself when he was unhappy. She got up and walked to the kitchen cabinet.

"The other knives dirty?" she asked.

"No," her mother said, "look in the next drawer."

Ellie pulled open the drawer, flicking scraps of white paint with her fingernail. She reached for the knife and at the same time a pile of envelopes caught her eye.

"Any more come today?" she asked, pulling out the knife and slipping the envelopes under the dish towels.

"Yes, seven more came today," her mother accentuated each word carefully. "Your father has them with him in the other room."

"Same thing?" she asked picking up a potato and wishing she could think of some way to change the subject.

The white people had been threatening them for the past three weeks. Some of the letters were aimed at the family, but most of them were directed to Tommy himself. About once a week in the same handwriting somebody wrote that he'd better not eat lunch at school because they were going to poison him.

They had been getting those letters ever since the school board made Tommy's name public. She sliced the potato and dropped the pieces in the pan of cold water. Out of all those people he had been the only one the board had accepted for transfer to the elementary school. The other children, the members said, didn't live in the district. As she cut the eyes out of another potato she thought about the first letter they had received and how her father just set fire to it in the ashtray. But then Mr. Belk said they'd better save the rest, in case anything happened, they might need the evidence for court.

She peeped up again at her mother, "Who's that white man in there with Daddy?"

"One of Lawyer Belk's friends," she answered. "He's pastor of the church that's always on television Sunday morning. Mr. Belk seems to think that having him around will do some good." Ellie saw that her voice was shaking just like her hand as she reached for the last potato. Both of them could hear Tommy in the next room mumbling to himself. She was afraid to look at her mother.

Suddenly Ellie was aware that her mother's hands were trembling violently. "He's so little," she whispered and suddenly the knife slipped out of her hands and she was crying and breathing at the same time.

Ellie didn't know what to do but after a few seconds she cleared away the peelings and put the knives in the sink. "Why don't you lie down?" she suggested. "I'll clean up and get Tommy in bed." Without saying anything her mother rose and walked to her bedroom.

Ellie wiped off the table and draped the dishcloth over the sink. She stood back and looked at the rusting pipes powdered with a whitish film. One of these days they would have to paint the place. She tiptoed past her mother who looked as if she had fallen asleep from exhaustion.

"Tommy," she called softly, "come in and get ready for bed."

Tommy sitting in the middle of the floor did not answer. He was sitting the way she imagined he would be, crosslegged, pulling his ear lobe as he turned the ragged pages of *Uncle Wiggily at the Zoo.*

"What you doing, Tommy?" she said squatting on the floor beside him,. He smiled and pointed at the picture of the ducks.

"School starts tomorrow," she said, turning a page with him. Don't you think it's time to go to bed?"

"Oh Ellie, do I have to go now?" She looked down at the serious brown eyes and the closely cropped hair. For a minute she wondered if he questioned having to go to bed now or to school tomorrow.

"Well," she said, "aren't you about through with the book?" He shook his head. "Come on," she pulled him up, "you're a sleepy head." Still he shook his head.

"When Helen and Teenie coming home?"

"Tomorrow after you come home from school they'll be here."

She lifted him from the floor thinking how small he looked to be facing all those people tomorrow.

"Look," he said breaking away from her hand and pointing to a blue shirt and pair of cotton twill pants, "Mama got them for me to wear tomorrow."

While she ran water in the tub, she heard him crawl on top of the bed. He was quiet and she knew he was untying his sneakers.

"Put your shoes out," she called through the door, "and maybe Daddy will polish them."

"Is Daddy still in there with those men? Mama made me be quiet so I wouldn't bother them."

He padded into the bathroom with bare feet and crawled into the water. As she scrubbed him they played Ask Me A Question, their own version of Twenty Questions. She had just dried him and was about to have him step into his pajamas when he asked: "Are they gonna get me tomorrow?"

"Who's going to get you?" She looked into his eyes and began rubbing him furiously with the towel.

"I don't know," he answered. "Somebody I guess."

"Nobody's going to get you," she said, "who wants a little boy who gets bubblegum in his hair anyway—but us?" He grinned but as she hugged him she thought how much he looked like his father. They walked to the bed to say his prayers and while they were kneeling she heard the first drops of rain. By the time she covered him up and tucked the spread off the floor the rain had changed to a steady downpour.

When Tommy had gone to bed her mother got up again and began ironing clothes in the kitchen. Something, she said, to keep her thoughts busy. While her mother folded and sorted the clothes Ellie drew up a chair from the kitchen table. They sat in the kitchen for a while listening to the voices of the men in the next room. Her mother's quiet speech broke the stillness in the room.

"I'd rather," she said making sweeping motions with the iron, "that you stayed home from work tomorrow and went with your father to take Tommy. I don't think I'll be up to those people."

Ellie nodded. "I don't mind," she said, tracing circles on the oil cloth covered table.

"Your father's going," her mother continued. "Belk and Reverend Davis are too. I think that white man in there will probably go."

"They may not need me," Ellie answered.

"Tommy will," her mother said, folding the last dish towel and storing it in the cabinet.

"Mama, I think he's scared," the girl turned toward the woman. "He was so quiet while I was washing him."

"I know," she answered sitting down heavily. "He's been that way all day." Her brown wavy hair glowed in the dim lighting of the kitchen. "I told him he wasn't going to school with Jakie and Bob any more but I said he was going to meet some other children just as nice."

Ellie saw that her mother was twisting her wedding band around and around on her finger.

"I've already told Mrs. Ingraham that I wouldn't be able to come out tomorrow." Ellie paused, "She didn't say very much. She didn't even say anything about his pictures in the newspaper. Mr. Ingraham said we were getting right crazy but even he didn't say anything else."

She stopped to look at the clock sitting near the sink. "It's almost time for the cruise cars to begin," she said. Her mother followed Ellie's eyes to the sink. The policemen circling their block every twenty minutes was supposed to make them feel safe, but hearing the cars come so regularly and that light flashing through the shade above her bed only made her nervous.

She stopped talking to push a wrinkle out of the shiny red cloth, dragging her finger along the table edges. "How long before those men going to leave?" she asked her mother. Just as she spoke she heard one of the men say something about getting some sleep. "I didn't mean to run them away," she said smiling. Her mother half-smiled too. They listened for the sound of motors and tires and waited for her father to shut the front door.

In a few seconds her father's head pushed through the curtain. "Want me to turn down your bed now, Ellie?" She felt uncomfortable staring up at him, the whole family looked drained of all energy.

"That's all right," she answered. "I'll sleep in Helen and Teenie's bed tonight."

"How's Tommy?" he asked looking toward the bedroom. He came in and sat down at the table with them.

They were silent before he spoke. "I keep wondering if we should send him." He lit a match and watched the flame disappear into the ashtray, then he looked into his wife's eyes. "There's no telling what these fool white folks will do."

Her mother reached over and patted his hand. "We're doing what we have to do, I guess," she said. "Sometimes though I wish the others weren't so much older than him."

"But it seems so unfair," Ellie broke in, "sending him there all by himself like that. Everybody keeps asking me why the MacAdams didn't apply for their children."

"Eloise." Her father's voice sounded curt. "We aren't answering for the MacAdams, we're trying to do what's right for your brother. He's not old enough to have his own say so. You and the others could decide for yourselves, but we're the ones that have to do for him."

She didn't say anything but watched him pull a handful of envelopes out of his pocket and tuck them in the cabinet drawer. She knew that if anyone had told him in August that Tommy would be the only one going to Jefferson Davis they would not have let him go.

"Those the new ones?" she asked. "What they say?"

"Let's not talk about the letters," her father said, "Let's go to bed."

Outside they heard the rain become heavier. Since early evening she had become accustomed to the sound. Now it blended in with the rest of the noises that had accumulated in the back of her mind since the whole thing began.

As her mother folded the ironing board they heard the quiet wheels of the police car. Ellie noticed that the clock said twelve-ten and she wondered why they were early. Her mother pulled the iron cord from the switch and they stood silently waiting for the police car to turn around and pass the house again, as if the car's passing were a final blessing for the night.

Suddenly she was aware of a noise that sounded as if everything had broken loose in her head at once, a loudness that almost shook the foundation of the house. At the same time the lights went out and instinctively her father knocked them to the floor. They could hear the tinkling of glass near the front of the house and Tommy began screaming.

"Tommy, get down," her father yelled.

She hoped he would remember to roll under the bed the way they had practiced. She was aware of objects falling and breaking as she lay perfectly still. Her breath was coming in jerks and then there was a second noise, a smaller explosion but still drowning out Tommy's cries.

"Stay still," her father commanded. "I'm going to check on Tommy. They may throw another one."

She watched him crawl across the floor, pushing a broken flower vase and an iron skillet out of his way. All of the sounds, Tommy's crying, the breaking glass, everything was echoing in her ears. She felt as if they had been crouching on the floor for hours but when she heard the police car door slam, the luminous hands of the clock said only twelve-fifteen.

She heard other cars drive up and pairs of heavy feet trample on the porch. "You folks all right in there?"

She could visualize the hands pulling open the door, because she knew the voice. Sergeant Kearns had been responsible for patrolling the house during the past three weeks. She heard him click the light switch in the living room but the darkness remained intense.

Her father deposited Tommy in his wife's lap and went to what was left of the door. In the next fifteen minutes policemen were everywhere. While she rummaged around underneath the cabinet for a candle, her mother tried to hush up Tommy. His cheek was cut where he had scratched himself on the springs of the bed. Her mother motioned for her to dampen a cloth and put some petroleum jelly on it to keep him quiet. She tried to put him to bed again but he would not go, even when she promised to stay with him for the rest of the night. And so she sat in the kitchen rocking the little boy back and forth on her lap.

Ellie wandered around the kitchen but the light from the single candle put an eerie glow on the walls making her nervous. She began picking up pans, stepping over pieces of broken crockery and glassware. She did not want to go into the living room yet, but if she listened closely, snatches of the policemen's conversation came through the curtain.

She heard one man say that the bomb landed near the edge of the yard, that was why it had only gotten the front porch. She knew from their talk that the living room window was shattered completely. Suddenly Ellie sat down. The picture of the living room window kept flashing in her mind and a wave of feeling invaded her body making her shake as if she had lost all muscular control. She slept on the couch, right under that window.

She looked at her mother to see if she too had realized, but her mother was looking down at Tommy and trying to get him to close his eyes. Ellie stood up and crept toward the living room trying to prepare herself for what she would see. Even that minute of determination could not make her control the horror that she felt. There were jagged holes all along the front of the house and the sofa was covered with glass and paint. She started to pick up the picture that had toppled from the book shelf, then she just stepped over the broken frame.

Outside her father was talking and, curious to see who else was with him, she walked across the splinters to the yard. She could see pieces of the geranium pot and the red blossoms turned face down. There were no lights in the other houses on the street. Across from their house she could see forms standing in the door and shadows being pushed back and forth. "I guess the MacAdams are glad they just didn't get involved." No one heard her speak, and no one came over to see if they could help; she knew why and did not really blame them. They were afraid their house could be next.

Most of the policemen had gone now and only one car was left to flash the revolving red light in the rain. She heard the tall skinny man tell her father they would be parked outside for the rest of the night. As she watched the reflection of the police cars returning to the station, feeling sick on her stomach, she wondered now why they bothered.

Ellie went back inside the house and closed the curtain behind her. There was nothing anyone could do now, not even to the house. Everything was scattered all over the floor and poor Tommy still would not go to sleep. She wondered what would happen when the news spread through their section of town, and at once remembered the man in the grey Chevrolet. It would serve them right if her father's friends got one of them.

Ellie pulled up an overturned chair and sat down across from her mother who was crooning to Tommy. What Mr. Paul said was right, white people just couldn't be trusted. Her family had expected anything but even though they had practiced ducking, they didn't really expect anybody to try tearing down the house. But the funny thing was the house belonged to one of them. Maybe it was a good thing her family were just renters.

Exhausted, Ellie put her head down on the table. She didn't know what they were going to do about tomorrow, in the day time they didn't need electricity. She was too tired to think any more about Tommy, yet she could not go to sleep. So, she sat at the table trying to sit still, but every few minutes she would involuntarily twitch. She tried to steady her hands, all the time listening to her mother's sing-songy voice and waiting for her father to come back inside the house.

She didn't know how long she lay hunched against the kitchen table, but when she looked up, her wrists bore the imprints of her hair. She unfolded her arms gingerly, feeling the blood rush to her fingertips. Her father sat in the chair opposite her, staring at the vacant space between them. She heard her mother creep away from the table, taking Tommy to his room.

Ellie looked out the window. The darkness was turning to grey and the hurt feeling was disappearing. As she sat there she could begin to look at the kitchen matter-of-factly. Although the hands of the clock were just a little past five-thirty, she knew somebody was going to have to start clearing up and cook breakfast.

She stood and [tiptoed] across the kitchen to her parents' bedroom. "Mama," she whispered, standing near the door of Tommy's room. At the sound of her voice, Tommy made a funny throaty noise in his sleep. Her mother motioned for her to go out and be quiet. Ellie knew then that Tommy had just fallen asleep. She crept back to the kitchen and began picking up the dishes that could be salvaged, being careful not to go into the living room.

She walked around her father, leaving the broken glass underneath the kitchen table. "You want some coffee?" she asked.

He nodded silently, in strange contrast she thought to the water faucet that turned with a loud gurgling noise. While she let the water run to get hot she measured out the instant coffee in one of the plastic cups. Next door she could hear people moving around in the Williams' kitchen, but they too seemed much quieter than usual.

"You reckon everybody knows by now?" she asked, stirring the coffee and putting the saucer in front of him.

"Everybody will know by the time the city paper comes out," he said. "Somebody was here last night from the *Observer*. Guess it'll make front page."

She leaned against the cabinet for support watching him trace endless circles in the brown liquid with the spoon. "Sergeant Kearns says they'll have almost the whole force out there tomorrow," he said.

"Today," she whispered.

Her father looked at the clock and then turned his head.

"When's your mother coming back in here?"

he asked, finally picking up the cup and drinking the coffee.

"Tommy's just off to sleep," she answered. "I guess she'll be in here when he's asleep for good."

She looked out the window of the back door at the row of tall hedges that had separated their neighborhood from the white people for as long as she remembered. While she stood there she heard her mother walk into the room. To her ears the steps seemed much slower than usual. She heard her mother stop in front of her father's chair.

"Jim," she said, sounding very timid, "what we going to do?" Yet as Ellie turned toward her she noticed her mother's face was strangely calm as she looked down on her husband.

Ellie continued standing by the door listening to them talk. Nobody asked the question to which they all wanted an answer.

"I keep thinking," her father said finally, "that the policemen will be with him all day. They couldn't hurt him inside the school building without getting some of their own kind."

"But he'll be in there all by himself," her mother said softly. "A hundred policemen can't be a little boy's only friends."

She watched her father wrap his calloused hands, still splotched with machine oil, around the salt shaker on the table.

"I keep trying," he said to her, "to tell myself that somebody's got to be the first one and then I just think how quiet he's been all week."

Ellie listened to the quiet voices that seemed to be a room apart from her. In the back of her mind she could hear phrases of a hymn her grandmother used to sing, something about trouble, her being born for trouble.

"Jim, I cannot let my baby go." Her mother's words, although quiet, were carefully pronounced.

"Maybe," her father answered, "it's not in our hands. Reverend Davis and I were talking day before yesterday how God tested the Israelites, maybe he's just trying us."

"God expects you to take care of your own," his wife interrupted. Ellie sensed a trace of bitterness in her mother's voice.

"Tommy's not going to understand why he can't go to school," her father replied. "He's going to wonder why, and how are we going to tell him

we're afraid of them?" Her father's hand clutched the coffee cup. "He's going to be fighting them the rest of his life. He's got to start sometime."

"But he's not on their level. Tommy's too little to go around hating people. One of the others, they're bigger, they understand about things."

Ellie still leaning against the door saw that the sun covered part of the sky behind the hedges and the light slipping through the kitchen window seemed to reflect the shiny red of the table cloth.

"He's our child," she heard her mother say. "Whatever we do, we're going to be the cause." Her father had pushed the cup away from him and sat with his hands covering part of his face. Outside Ellie could hear a horn blowing.

"God knows we tried but I guess there's just no use." Her father's voice forced her attention back to the two people sitting in front of her. "Maybe when things come back to normal, we'll try again."

He covered his wife's chunky fingers with the palm of his hand and her mother seemed to be enveloped in silence. The three of them remained quiet, each involved in his own thoughts, but related, Ellie knew, to the same thing. She was the first to break the silence.

"Mama," she called after a long pause, "do you want me to start setting the table for breakfast?"

Her mother nodded.

Ellie turned the clock so she could see it from the sink while she washed the dishes that had been scattered over the floor.

"You going to wake up Tommy or you want me to?"

"No," her mother said, still holding her father's hand, "let him sleep. When you wash your face, you go up the street and call Hezekiah. Tell him to keep up with the children after school, I want to do something to this house before they come home."

She stopped talking and looked around the kitchen, finally turning to her husband. "He's probably kicked the spread off by now," she said. Ellie watched her father, who without saying anything walked toward the bedroom.

She watched her mother lift herself from the chair and automatically push in the stuffing underneath the cracked plastic cover. Her face looked set, as it always did when she was trying hard to keep her composure.

"He'll need something hot when he wakes up. Hand me the oatmeal," she commanded, reaching on top of the icebox for matches to light the kitchen stove.   [1966]

Note

1. NAACP: National Association for the Advancement of Colored People.

Understanding the Reading

1. What is Ellie's neighborhood like?
2. What were the men in the living room discussing?
3. Why were people sending letters to Tommy's family?
4. Why was Ellie reluctant to go into the living room after the bombing?
5. As the family sits in the kitchen in the morning, what is the unasked question on all their minds?
6. Why do they decide to send Tommy to school in spite of their reservations?

Suggestions for Responding

1. If you had been Tommy's parents, would you have sent him to school? Why or why not?
2. Compare the use of violence in the Faulkner story with that in Oliver's. Consider the motives of the perpetrators and the responses of both the victims and the community. ◆

82

The Hammer Man

TONI CADE BAMBARA

I was glad to hear that Manny had fallen off the roof. I had put out the tale that I was down with yellow fever, but nobody paid me no mind, least of all Dirty Red who stomped right in to announce that Manny had fallen off the roof and that I could come out of hiding now. My mother dropped what she was doing, which was the laundry, and got the whole story out of Red. "Bad enough you gots to hang around with boys," she said. "But fight with them too. And you would pick the craziest one at that."

Manny was supposed to be crazy. That was his story. To say you were bad put some people off. But to say you were crazy, well, you were officially not to be messed with. So that was his story. On the other hand, after I called him what I called him and said a few choice things about his mother, his face did go through some piercing changes. And I did kind of wonder if maybe he sure was nuts. I didn't wait to find out. I got in the wind. And then he waited for me on my stoop all day and all night, not hardly speaking to the people going in and out. And he was there all day Saturday, with his sister bringing him peanut-butter sandwiches and cream sodas. He must've gone to the bathroom right there cause every time I looked out the kitchen window, there he was. And Sunday, too. I got to thinking the boy was mad.

"You got no sense of humor, that's your trouble," I told him. He looked up, but he didn't say nothing. All at once I was real sorry about the whole thing. I should've settled for hitting off the little girls in the school yard, or waiting for Frankie to come in so we could raise some kind of hell. This way I had to play sick when my mother was around cause my father had already taken away my BB gun and hid it.

I don't know how they got Manny on the roof finally. Maybe the Wakefield kids, the ones who keep the pigeons, called him up. Manny was a sucker for sick animals and things like that. Or maybe Frankie got some nasty girls to go up on the roof with him and got Manny to join him. I don't know. Anyway, the catwalk had lost all its cement and the roof always did kind of slant downward. So Manny fell off the roof. I got over my yellow fever right quick, needless to say, and ventured outside. But by this time I had already told Miss Rose that Crazy Manny was after me. And Miss Rose, being who she was, quite naturally went over to Manny's house and said a few harsh words to his mother, who, being who she was, chased Miss Rose out into the street and they commenced to get with it, snatching bottles out of the garbage cans and breaking them on the johnny pumps and stuff like that.

Dirty Red didn't have to tell us this. Everybody could see and hear all. I never figured the garbage cans for an arsenal, but Miss Rose came up with sticks and table legs and things, and Manny's mother had her share of scissor blades and bicycle chains. They got to rolling in the streets and all you could see was pink drawers and fat legs. It was something else. Miss Rose is nutty but Manny's mother's crazier than Manny. They were at it a couple of times during my sick spell. Everyone would congregate on the window sills or the fire escape, commenting that it was still much too cold for this kind of nonsense. But they watched anyway. And then Manny fell off the roof. And that was that. Miss Rose went back to her dream books and Manny's mother went back to her tumbled-down kitchen of dirty clothes and bundles and bundles of rags and children.

My father got in on it too, cause he happened to ask Manny one night why he was sitting on the stoop like that every night. Manny told him right off that he was going to kill me first chance he got. Quite naturally this made my father a little warm, me being his only daughter and planning to become a doctor and take care of him in his old age. So he had a few words with Manny first, and then he got hold of the older brother, Bernard, who was more his size. Bernard didn't see how any of it was his business or my father's business, so my father got mad and jammed Bernard's head into the mailbox. Then my father started getting messages from Bernard's uncle about where to meet him for a showdown and all. My father didn't say a word to my mother all this time; just sat around mumbling and picking up the phone and putting it down, or grabbing my stickball bat and putting it back. He carried on like this for days till I thought I would scream if the yellow fever didn't have me so weak. And then Manny fell off the roof, and my father went back to his beer-drinking buddies.

I was in the school yard, pitching pennies with the little boys from the elementary school, when my friend Violet hits my brand-new Spaudeen over the wall. She came running back to tell me that Manny was coming down the block. I peeked beyond the fence and there he was all right. He had his head all wound up like a mummy and his arm in a sling and his legs in a cast. It looked phony to me, especially that walking cane. I figured Dirty Red had told me a tale just to get me out there so Manny could stomp me, and Manny was playing it up with costume and all till he could get me.

"What happened to him?" Violet's sisters whispered. But I was too busy trying to figure out how this act was supposed to work. Then

Manny passed real close the fence and gave me a look.

"You had enough, Hammer Head," I yelled. "Just bring your crummy self in this yard and I'll pick up where I left off." Violet was knocked out and the other kids went into a huddle. I didn't have to say anything else. And when they all pressed me later, I just said, "You know that hammer he always carries in his fatigues?" And they'd all nod waiting for the rest of a long story. "Well, I took it away from him." And I walked off nonchalantly.

Manny stayed indoors for a long time. I almost forgot about him. New kids moved into the block and I got all caught up with that. And then Miss Rose finally hit the numbers and started ordering a whole lot of stuff through the mail and we would sit on the curb and watch these weird-looking packages being carried in, trying to figure out what simpleminded thing she had thrown her money away on when she might just as well wait for the warm weather and throw a block party for all her godchildren.

After a while a center opened up and my mother said she'd increase my allowance if I went and joined because I'd have to get out of my pants and stay in skirts, on account of that's the way things were at the center. So I joined and got to thinking about everything else but old Hammer Head. It was a rough place to get along in, the center, but my mother said that I needed to be be'd with and she needed to not be with me, so I went. And that time I sneaked into the office, that's when I really got turned on. I looked into one of those not-quite-white folders and saw that I was from a deviant family in a deviant neighborhood. I showed my mother the word in the dictionary, but she didn't pay me no mind. It was my favorite word after that. I ran it in the ground till one day my father got the strap just to show how deviant he could get. So I gave up trying to improve my vocabulary. And I almost gave up my dungarees.

Then one night I'm walking past the Douglas Street park cause I got thrown out of the center for playing pool when I should've been sewing, even though I had already decided that this was going to be my last fling with boy things, and starting tomorrow I was going to fix my hair right and wear skirts all the time just so my mother would stop talking about her gray hairs, and Miss Rose would stop calling me by my brother's name by mistake. So I'm walking past the park and there's ole Manny on the basketball court, perfecting his lay-ups and talking with himself. Being me, I quite naturally walk right up and ask what the hell he's doing playing in the dark, and he looks up and all around like the dark had crept up on him when he wasn't looking. So I knew right away that he'd been out there for a long time with his eyes just going along with the program.

"There was two seconds to go and we were one point behind," he said, shaking his head and staring at his sneakers like they was somebody. "And I was in the clear. I'd left the man in the backcourt and there I was, smiling, you dig, cause it was in the bag. They passed the ball and I slid the ball up nice and easy cause there was nothing to worry about. And. . . ." He shook his head. "I muffed the goddamn shot. Ball bounced off the rim. . . ." He stared at his hands. "The game of the season. Last game." And then he ignored me altogether, though he wasn't talking to me in the first place. He went back to the lay-ups, always from the same spot with his arms crooked in the same way, over and over. I must've gotten hypnotized cause I probably stood there for at least an hour watching like a fool till I couldn't even see the damn ball, much less the basket. But I stood there anyway for no reason I know of. He never missed. But he cursed himself away. It was torture. And then a squad car pulled up and a short cop with hair like one of the Marx Brothers came out hitching up his pants. He looked real hard at me and then at Manny.

"What are you two doing?"

"He's doing a lay-up. I'm watching." I said with my smart self.

Then the cop just stood there and finally turned to the other one who was just getting out of the car.

"Who unlocked the gate?" the big one said.

"It's always unlocked," I said. Then we three just stood there like a bunch of penguins watching Manny go at it.

"This on the level?" the big guy asked, tilting his hat back with the thumb the way big guys do in hot weather. "Hey you," he said, walking over to Manny. "I'm talking to you." He finally grabbed the ball to get Manny's attention. But that didn't work. Manny just stood there with his arms out waiting for the pass so he could save the

game. He wasn't paying no mind to the cop. So, quite naturally, when the cop slapped him upside his head it was a surprise. And when the cop started counting three to go, Manny had already recovered from the slap and was just ticking off the seconds before the buzzer sounded and all was lost.

"Gimme the ball, man." Manny's face was all tightened up and ready to pop.

"Did you hear what I said, black boy?"

Now, when somebody says that word like that, I gets warm. And crazy or no crazy, Manny was my brother at that moment and the cop was the enemy.

"You better give him back his ball," I said. "Manny don't take no mess from no cops. He ain't bothering nobody. He's gonna be Mister Basketball when he grows up. Just trying to get a little practice in before the softball season starts."

"Look here, sister, we'll run you in too," Harpo said.

"I damn sure can't be your sister seeing how I'm a black girl. Boy, I sure will be glad when you run me in so I can tell everybody about that. You must think you're in the South, mister."

The big guy screwed his mouth up and let one of them hard-day sighs. "The park's closed, little girl, so why don't you and your boyfriend go on home."

That really got me. The "little girl" was bad enough but that "boyfriend" was too much. But I kept cool, mostly because Manny looked so pitiful waiting there with his hands in a time-out and there being no one to stop the clock. But I kept my cool mostly cause of that hammer in Manny's pocket and no telling how frantic things can get what with a big-mouth like me, a couple of wise cops, and a crazy boy too.

"The gates are open," I said real quiet-like, "and this here's a free country. So why don't you give him back his ball?"

The big cop did another one of those sighs, his specialty I guess, and then he bounced the ball to Manny who went right into his gliding thing clear up to the backboard, damn near like he was some kind of very beautiful bird. And then he swooshed that ball in, even if there was no net, and you couldn't really hear the swoosh. Something happened to the bones in my chest. It was something.

"Crazy kids anyhow," the one with the wig

said and turned to go. But the big guy watched Manny for a while and I guess something must've snapped in his head, cause all of a sudden he was hot for taking Manny to jail or court or somewhere and started yelling at him and everything, which is a bad thing to do to Manny, I can tell you. And I'm standing there thinking that none of my teachers, from kindergarten right on up, none of them knew what they were talking about. I'll be damned if I ever knew one of them rosy-cheeked cops that smiled and helped you get to school without neither you or your little raggedy dog getting hit by a truck that had a smile on its face, too. Not that I ever believed it. I knew Dick and Jane was full of crap from the get-go, especially them cops. Like this dude, for example, pulling on Manny's clothes like that when obviously he had just done about the most beautiful thing a man can do and not be a fag. No cop could swoosh without a net.

"Look out, man," was all Manny said, but it was the way he pushed the cop that started the real yelling and threats. And I thought to myself, Oh God here I am trying to change my ways, and not talk back in school, and do like my mother wants, but just have this last fling, and now this—getting shot in the stomach and bleeding to death in Douglas Street park and poor Manny getting pistol-whipped by those bastards and whatnot. I could see it all, practically crying too. And it just wasn't no kind of thing to happen to a small child like me with my confirmation picture in the paper next to my weeping parents and schoolmates. I could feel the blood sticking to my shirt and my eyeballs slipping away, and then that confirmation picture again; and my mother and her gray hair; and Miss Rose heading for the precinct with a shotgun; and my father getting old and feeble with no one to doctor him up and all.

And I wished Manny had fallen off the damn roof and died right then and there and saved me all this aggravation of being killed with him by these cops who surely didn't come out of no fifth-grade reader. But it didn't happen. They just took the ball and Manny followed them real quiet-like right out of the park into the dark, then into the squad car with his head drooping and his arms in a crook. And I went on home cause what the hell am I going to do on a basketball court, and it getting to be nearly midnight?

I didn't see Manny no more after he got into that squad car. But they didn't kill him after all cause Miss Rose heard he was in some kind of big house for people who lose their marbles. And then it was spring finally, and me and Violet was in this very boss fashion show at the center. And Miss Rose bought me my first corsage—yellow roses to match my shoes.   [1972]

Understanding the Reading

1. What details reflect the violence inherent in this neighborhood?
2. Why do other family members get involved in the dispute between the narrator and Manny?
3. What does the center mean by labeling her family and her neighborhood "deviant"?
4. Why did the narrator stay to watch Manny practice lay-ups?
5. What makes the narrator "warm," and why does she say Manny was her brother at that moment?
6. Why did the police arrest Manny?

Suggestions for Responding

1. The narrator says that she plans to be a doctor. Do you think this is a realistic goal? What factors work against her? What might make it possible?
2. Compare the behavior of these policemen with the police in Oliver's story. How do you account for the differences in their treatment of African-Americans? ✦

83

Terror in Our Neighborhoods

THE KLANWATCH PROJECT OF THE SOUTHERN POVERTY LAW CENTER

Imagine. It's your first night in your new home, on a quiet street where no one knows your name. Every sound seems strange; everything looks and feels different. You think about the children as you try to sleep. Will they like their new school? Will they find new friends?

And then it happens. The sound of a gasoline explosion, the blinding light of flames. You look outside your window and see a cross on fire.

Shock turns to fear, and finally, when the flames have died, to overwhelming sadness. How will you explain this to the children?

You can't believe it still happens.

But it does. It happened to a Chinese-American family in California last year, and a Jewish family in Connecticut. It happened to a 67-year-old black woman in Virginia who lived alone, and to a white woman in New Jersey whose children happen to have a black friend. And it happens to black families and interracial families all over the country.

Not only cross burnings, but vandalism, arsons, threats, and assaults greet minorities who choose to live in mostly white neighborhoods.

"Of all the incidents of hate violence which occur in this country, the terrorism of minorities in white neighborhoods is probably the most common, and the most devastating," said Pat Clark, Director of the Klanwatch Project of the Southern Poverty Law Center. "It destroys the security of families and breeds an environment of mistrust and resentment where there should be community."

Last year, Klanwatch documented a significant increase in the incidence of housing violence—attacks by neighbors upon neighbors because of race, color, religion, or ethnic background. Most of these attacks were directed at minorities who had recently moved into predominantly white neighborhoods. Others were aimed at people who had been living quietly in the neighborhood for years. And a significant number were only the latest in a long series of harassment against the same victims.

"Throughout the 1980s, about a third of the racial violence incidents we tracked were housing-related," said Clark. "Then in 1989, we saw a tremendous increase in neighborhood attacks. By the end of the year, incidents of housing violence accounted for roughly half of all the racial violence incidents we reported. This was particularly alarming because 1989 was also the year we saw a surge in hate violence of all types."

Of 289 hate crimes documented by Klanwatch, 130 were housing-related. "What we have to remember, though," said Clark, "is that the reports we receive are only a sampling of the overall problem. Since there is no national data collection on hate crime, our figures are necessarily incomplete, so we are probably looking at only a fraction of the violence that actually occurred."

The lack of reliable data on hate crimes has always hampered efforts to understand and address the problem of housing violence, but a new law will soon require police agencies to keep track of all bias-motivated crimes. Once the new monitoring procedures are in place, experts believe, the number of documented hate crimes will skyrocket.

The U.S. Department of Justice, the agency charged with implementing the Hate Crimes Statistics Act, has already witnessed a dramatic rise in hate crime cases in its jurisdiction. While all racial violence cases prosecuted by the Justice Department have gone up in recent years, cases involving housing violence have increased at a much higher rate. Statistics for combined fiscal years 1988 and 1989 show that housing violence cases comprised 75 percent of all federally-prosecuted racial violence cases.

HOUSING DISCRIMINATION PERSISTS

The rise in housing violence is clearly related to a hard-core resistance to integrated neighborhoods that has persisted in this country despite decades of racial progress in other areas.

While they may sit beside blacks at work, in schools and in restaurants, many whites still believe they have a right to keep their own neighborhoods segregated. And anyone who attempts to change that pattern of segregation is taking a risk.

The evidence of residential segregation has been substantiated across the country:

- A nationwide Washington Post survey conducted in 1989 showed that a third of white respondents believed they should have the right to refuse to sell their homes to blacks, despite federal housing laws that prohibit housing discrimination.

- A 1984 study by the U.S. Department of Housing and Urban Development, based on national and regional audits conducted in 1979, showed that blacks had a 27 percent chance of encountering discrimination in rental housing, and a 15 percent overall chance of discrimination in real estate sales. (The 15 percent figure does not include instances of "steering," the illegal practice of leading minority buyers or renters away from property in white neighborhoods.) A report scheduled for release by HUD this fall will update the 1979 data.

- A statistical analysis of metropolitan housing patterns conducted by University of Pennsylvania researchers in 1987 showed that between 1970 and 1980, blacks and whites made almost no progress toward integrated living. "Blacks may have won political freedom, and may have made substantial progress in attaining their economic goals, but they have not yet achieved the freedom to live wherever they want."

TERROR AT HOME

The greatest obstacle to that freedom is fear—the terror that comes from being victimized, often many times over, by your own neighbors.

That terror comes in many forms—"KKK" scrawled on the sidewalk, garbage thrown in the front yard, shouts from passing cars, anonymous harassing phone calls, doors painted with swastikas, windows broken.

Sometimes the incidents seem "minor" to an outsider, said Sgt. Bill Johnston, head of the Boston Police Department Bias Investigation Unit. "The mistake I first made, and a lot of people make, is you look at the crime, and you say 'it's only a broken window.'

"But I remember talking to one father of a family that had numerous broken windows. He had bought a house that was going to be his dream house, and during the course of the years it turned into a nightmare. Vandals were trying to force him out. He had already had more than a dozen incidents there, and then one night in February, it happened again. He had one child in the bathroom calling for him, another watching TV, and his wife was in the kitchen preparing dinner. And 18 windows in his house go out at once. His children and his wife started screaming for him, and he didn't know who to run to first. He was just paralyzed."

When Johnston arrived on the scene, he said,

the man had tears in his eyes. He asked Johnston to talk to his wife, because his wife was frantically asking him to do something. "Will you explain to her," the man asked Johnston, "that if I go outside that door, I am going to kill somebody or somebody is going to kill me?"

"Until we put our heads inside the broken windows we have no idea how traumatic these incidents are," said Johnston.

SHOCK IS THE FIRST RESPONSE

The first time a family is victimized, their reaction is "almost always extreme surprise," said Patrick Kelly of the Neighbors Network, a volunteer organization that works with housing violence victims in Georgia. "For the most part, victims are hardworking people that think because they are hardworking people that no one would mind where they lived. Often they say, 'we didn't even look to see if all our neighbors were white.'"

Richard Nichols and his wife lived in their Olathe, Mo., home for two years without any trouble. Then someone painted "KKK" on their garage door last Halloween. "It's kind of shocking," said Nichols. "It's something we've seen happen to other people and heard about, but when it happens to you, you feel violated and hurt. It makes you wonder who's out to get you."

A white woman who shared a house with a black coworker in Jacksonville, Fla., said, after a series of vandalisms and a cross-burning, "It's like being raped. I feel just as black as she does."

After her car was doused with paint thinner in a Los Angeles suburb, a black mother of three said, "It makes you paranoid. If I see someone on the street, I don't know if I want to talk to them. It makes me less open."

In families with small children, one of the first concerns of victims is to help their children understand what happened to them and why. Sometimes they understand it all too well. It means they are not wanted.

When racial slurs and threats were painted on the door of Mr. and Mrs. William Cromer's new home on Staten Island, Mrs. Cromer said "It didn't really get to me but it got to my daughter. Now she is scared to go outside; she said 'you see, there's nobody else here like us.'"

About two-thirds of families who are victimized move, said Kelly. They see initial acts of harassment as warnings of trouble to come, and they are not willing to risk their family's safety.

Former U.S. Marine George Lewis wanted to move his family back to his home of Jackson, Miss., from Florida. He got a job in Jackson and found a brick house big enough for his wife and three children. Then one day, before the family had moved in, Lewis went to check on the house. "When I went to the back, I saw some writing on the outside in some kind of black ink. 'Nigger Go Home.' I couldn't believe it." Lewis quit his job and returned to Florida.

A 32-year-old Portsmouth, Va., man who found his car covered with racial slurs decided to move out of the mostly white neighborhood he was living in. "If somebody is bold enough to come up into my front yard and destroy my car, then the next move is to burglarize my house," said E. Brian Ashton.

Others "feel they have to stay," said Kelly, often as a way of showing their children how to stand up for their rights despite the risks involved.

"It's not something you'd expect in a million years," said another black woman who had a cross burned on her lawn in Modesto, Calif. "I thought Modesto was quiet. But they can come back—we're not leaving." When her home was burned down by arsonists, Audrey Goodwin of Rantoul, Ill., said, "I'm not gonna budge from this spot," and made plans to rebuild the house that she had lived in for 11 years.

ENFORCING THE LAW

Most acts of neighborhood terrorism are covered by a variety of state and federal laws. In addition to the standard criminal charges available for assault, arson, threats and vandalism, the federal Fair Housing Act gives broad protection to minorities who are victims of neighborhood attacks.

The Fair Housing Act, amended last year, outlaws any act designed to intimidate or frighten someone away from a neighborhood because of their race, color, religion, sex, handicap, familial status, or national origin. Violators can be fined up to $1,000 or sentenced to a year in prison, or both; and if bodily injury results the maximum fine increases to $10,000 and the maximum

prison term to ten years. In addition, individual victims may bring civil action under the provision of the federal law.

Despite the laws, many acts of neighborhood terrorism go unprosecuted. Victims often do not report initial incidents, and sometimes simply move away rather than take their battle to court. Others in the neighborhood may be reluctant to provide information on the perpetrators for fear of being the next victim. Police in some areas do not pursue neighborhood terrorism as aggressively as other crimes.

One repeated victim of housing violence in Temperance, Mich., had little help from his local police. Charles Wilder not only had a cross burned at his house last March, but he was also allegedly beaten by police officers. His problems finally got the attention of U.S. Rep. John Conyers, who called for a federal investigation into the case.

Sometimes, the victims themselves are not aware of their housing rights.

"For many recent arrivals to this country," said Boston Police Sgt. Bill Johnston, "civil rights laws aren't even in their vocabulary, and the police don't even find out about the problem until after the second, third or fourth incidents."

MAKING A DIFFERENCE

Better law enforcement, Johnston and others believe, begins with education—not only for communities, but for police as well. A program begun this year by the Boston Police Department sends officers into schools to show videotapes of actual bias crimes and teach children about civil rights laws. So far, 2,000 students in kindergarten through high school have heard the message that bias crimes in Boston will be punished.

In addition, Johnston and Northeastern University sociologist Jack McDevitt conduct training for police around the country in bias crime investigation, and will be advising the U.S. Justice Department in its efforts to establish a national monitoring system.

"No amount of education will stop people from committing hate crimes, as long as there are people who believe the rights they have should not be available to others," said Klanwatch Director Pat Clark. "But better data on the problem, heightened law enforcement attention to housing violations, and community support networks can make big difference in terms of opening up our neighborhoods to people of all colors, religions and nationalities."

"There's two places you should be able to shut the door and feel secure," said Johnston. "One is your place of worship and the other is your home. No matter how bad the world is out there, you should be able to close your door and say I'm home."   [n.d.]

Understanding the Reading

1. What is the cause of rising housing violence?
2. Why has there been little progress in integrating housing?
3. Why is "minor" damage actually very serious?
4. How do blacks respond to this harassment?
5. Explain the federal Fair Housing Act.
6. Why is its protection ineffective?
7. What can be done to stop neighborhood harassment and violence?

Suggestions for Responding

1. If there were a hate crime committed against a neighbor, how would you respond? If you knew the perpetrator was "an all-right guy" except when he's had a "little too much to drink," what would you do?
2. Compare the kind of incidents discussed here with the experience of the black family in the Oliver story. ✦

84

Skinheads Target the Schools

ANTI-DEFAMATION LEAGUE OF B'NAI B'RITH

For the past two years the Anti-Defamation League has closely monitored the rise in the United States of neo-Nazi Skinheads. An import from Great Britain, the Skinhead movement first attracted our attention when a shaven-headed gang from Chicago calling itself "Romantic Violence" took part in a 1985 national conference of white supremacists in Michigan. Promoting a hoped-for American tour of a British white-power band (which never materialized), members of this group displayed all the by-now familiar characteristics: shaven heads, neo-Nazi tattoos, Doc Marten work boots[1] and an outspokenly vulgar advocacy of racism and violence.

Although non-racist Skinheads (often called "baldies" or "two-tones") considerably outnumber racist ones in most areas of the country, a fact we have noted in all our earlier reports, a new nationwide ADL survey shows racist Skinheads active today in thirty-one states—compared with twenty-one last fall—numbering a total of about 3,000 members. The southeastern states have experienced the greatest amount of membership growth since the last ADL survey. The national figure of 3,000, as compared with 2,000 eight months ago, represents a 50% increase, and a still disturbingly high rate of growth. Even more troubling was the fact that the overall high level of violence continued apace. Since the time of our last report in October, 1988 there have been three additional murders attributed to Skinheads, two of them racially motivated. Assaults on members of minority groups as well as heavy vandalism of religious institutions (particularly synagogues) have continued.

Our recently-completed survey also indicates that two new trends are adding to the dangers posed by racist Skinheads: a growing pattern of recruitment and activity in high schools and the acquisition of deadlier weaponry.

SCHOOLS

Skinheads have been responsible for a variety of racially-motivated incidents in schools, often creating an atmosphere of tension and fear among students. Such was the case at Groves High School in Birmingham, a suburb of Detroit, which was the site of a racial brawl in late November, 1988. It began when three non-student Skinheads walked into the school and, joining with three students, roamed the halls, eventually confronting two other students, one black and the other white. A brawl broke out—finally brought to a halt by school coaches—and Groves remained tense for several days afterward with rumors of revenge. Police ringed the school during this period. Skinhead students were ex-pelled and transferred to Seaholm High School, where officials were concerned because of the presence there of another small Skinhead group.

But the problems at Groves were far from over. In mid-April, racist flyers were found taped to a tree, fence, telephone pole and to doors outside the school. Two weeks later, several black students found the word "Nigger" scrawled across their lockers. Other lockers were defaced with swastikas. On May 14, the outside of the high school was spray-painted with swastikas and [the] words "White Power" and "Skins." Police believe Skinheads to be responsible for these acts.

In Camarillo, located in Ventura County, California, Skinhead flyers have been found in schools where Skinheads have clashed with a non-Skinhead group called the "Suicidals." Ventura County Skinheads have tried to recruit elementary school students, reportedly beating those whom they had befriended but who refused to partake in their activities.

Douglas County High School in Castle Rock, Colorado, has a group of approximately a dozen racist Skinheads who were responsible for a number of racial incidents during the past school year. In February, 1989, a black student was harassed by Skinheads shouting racial epithets at her. They followed her to a nearby store where they pushed and threatened her. In early May, the same student was harassed in the hall by the leader of the gang. Two weeks later, the Skinheads harassed the artist of an anti-racist poster with threats such as "any day now, any time now, we're going to get you." These Skinheads, reportedly heavy drug users, are considered a powerful presence on campus. An incident during homecoming weekend last fall in which a noose was hung on a black student's locker along with a sign "Wanted: Three Blacks, Reward," could not be pinned on members of the group, but it is believed that they were the perpetrators.

At Sprayberry High School, located in Cobb County, Georgia (suburban Atlanta), a larger group of over two dozen Skinheads have reportedly hurled "Heil Hitler!" salutes during recitation of the Pledge of Allegiance. The group's members have Nazi insignias scrawled on their lockers and books, as well as their jackets. Members of a Harrisburg, Pennsylvania, Skinhead group called "Blitzkrieg" are reportedly active in the Central Dauphin School District. Parents of both white and black children are said to be afraid to send their children to school.

RECRUITMENT

Skinheads have tried, with varying levels of success, to recruit students directly on school campuses. They have distributed literature and even, in one case, sent a mass mailing to parents. This occurred in Waco, Texas, where parents of students at Waco High School received a letter from the Dallas-based Confederate Hammer Skins last fall. Addressed to "proud parents," the message warned of "the dangers posed by minority gangs and drug pushers," adding that "it is time that the common White Americans stand up and demand that their children attend schools not polluted with drugs, gangs, and anti-Christian immorality." The letter closed by offering those who write to the group additional information about the organization "and what we are doing to help the White schoolchildren of America."

Students in at least eight eastern Oregon school districts as well as youngsters in four communities in the western part of the state were selected to receive a special "Skinhead movement" newsletter by long-time neo-Nazi activist Ricky Cooper. Cooper also sent the publication, a special edition of his "NSV Report" (named after his group, the National Socialist Vanguard), to youngsters in two Idaho communities, Bonner's Ferry and Weiser. Cooper obtained the names from local newspapers by clipping honor roll lists and articles about student leaders and sports participants. He has indicated that the mailings will continue until "the climate is ripe" for young people to rally around the hate movement.

On June 2, 1989, students, teachers, and administrators arrived at Oak Ridge High School in Orlando, Florida, to find two flags had been raised above the school, one proclaiming "White Power," the other bearing the insignia of the American Front, a San Francisco-based Skinhead group. Portable classrooms located on the school's premises were spraypainted with swastikas. The east coast organizer of the group, David Lynch, has been an active Skinhead recruiter in various parts of Florida, and has attempted, with limited success, to make inroads in Orlando area high schools.

Lynch also attempted to recruit last year at two high schools located in Orange County, New York, where his mother once lived. According to authorities, he had little success there, despite his claims that he recruited 20 students for an Orange County chapter of the American Front. (Lynch, 18, was arrested in Edgewater, Florida, in early May along with two other Skinheads for carrying concealed weapons, possession of drug paraphernalia, and other offenses.)

Recruitment efforts in high schools have also been made in the following communities: Phoenix, Arizona; Austin and Houston, Texas; and McKeesport, Pennsylvania. Scattered attempts at recruitment on college campuses have met with little success. Much of this effort has taken place at three universities in Ohio: Ohio State, the University of Ohio, and the University of Cincinnati, which are located in communities where Skinhead activity has stepped up in recent months.

WEAPONRY

The favored weapons of Skinheads continue to be simple and crude: knives, bats, chains and steel-toed Doc Marten boots. Nonetheless, possession of handguns, shotguns and semi-automatic weaponry is becoming more common among Skinheads, and there are disturbing signs that their weaponry is becoming increasingly deadly:

- In May, four Skinheads were stopped [in] Taveras, Florida, after two had pulled guns on an elderly couple. Police uncovered two AR-15's, two 9mm handguns, two shotguns, and live ammunition.
- When law enforcement authorities searched the home of a member of the Arizona White Battalion, a Skinhead group based in Phoenix, they found gunpowder, pipes and detonators.
- At an event for Skinheads in Napa County, California, in March, participants came equipped with semi-automatic weapons, including [an] AR-15, an AK-47, automatic pistols, and shotguns.

When three Portland Skinheads confronted Mulugeta Seraw, an Ethiopian immigrant in front of his apartment last November and clubbed him to death, their weapon was a simple baseball bat.

One month later, when three Skinheads drove through a neighborhood in the Northeast section of Reno, Nevada, looking for a black person to kill, one displayed a small round of ammunition and reportedly said, "This is a dead black man." He placed these bullets in a gun, and one of them hit a young black man named Tony Montgomery and killed him. Six other bullets riddled two nearby homes, missing a child by five feet.

The most recent murder attributed by authorities to Skinheads took place in Denver on March 18, when 33-year-old David Timoner was shot to death with a 9mm weapon and his car set afire. During a police chase the following day, one of the two Skinheads involved took a hostage and held him while brandishing a .22 caliber handgun, telling a police negotiator that he wanted "to go out in a blaze of glory."

WEAPONS TRAINING

The acquisition of sophisticated weaponry by Skinheads is to some degree the result of the influence which organized hate groups continue to exercise. For example, Tom Metzger of the White Aryan Resistance (WAR) and his son, John, traveled to Phoenix in January to lead Skinheads in a march to commemorate the birthday of Robert Matthews, founder of The Order. Later, they accompanied members of the Arizona White Battalion into the nearby desert where they engaged in weapons training with semi-automatic weapons. Notices for the Metzger-sponsored "Aryan Woodstock" announced that there would be a "Grand Prize drawing of a fine new firearm." (The drawing never actually took place.)

In April, following Richard Butler's Skinhead fest held at the Aryan Nation's compound in Idaho, authorities found a .30 caliber carbine rifle and a 12-gauge shotgun in the trunk of a car driven by two Skinheads who spun their car out of the compound and swerved into a ditch. One, Wyatt J. Brooks, 19, was charged with driving with a suspended license. (Brooks, a private first class, is a member of the 44th Inner Defense Artillery Station in Fort Lewis, Washington. Army authorities are said to be weighing whether his participation at the conference violated military regulations.)

In Casper, Wyoming, 18-year old Skinhead David Spethman was indicted in April by a federal grand jury for illegal possession of a sawed-off shotgun. Spethman served as campaign treasurer for the congressional candidacy of Daniel Johnson, author of the PACE Amendment, a blueprint for purging the U.S. of its minority population. At the time of Spethman's indictment, he was being held for another charge (unspecified because of his juvenile status in Wyoming). Because Spethman turned 18 this year he will be charged as an adult under federal law. According to U.S. Attorney Richard Stacey, the barrel and stock of the gun were cut off after it was purchased. He described the weapon as "a very short sawed-off shotgun" and added that it is "nothing more, nothing less than an anti-personnel weapon."

Long Island, New York, organizer Kenneth Hill was arrested in late May for illegal weapons possession. He was carrying a 9mm handgun and an AR-15 assault weapon in the commercial van he was driving. On April 1 of this year [1990], the leader of the Indianapolis National White Resistance, Matthew Myer, was arrested and charged with recklessness with a dangerous weapon (an AK-47 assault rifle).

The Confederate Hammer Skins of Dallas have stockpiled approximately a dozen shotguns and handguns. "Anthony," a leader of the CHS-affiliated Memphis area Skinheads, boasts ownership of a Mossberg 12-gauge pump-action shotgun, which he says he carries in his car along with a combat knife. According to Anthony, his group does not seek out confrontation, "but we are prepared."

LINKS AMONG SKINHEADS

Both the Chattanooga group, which calls itself the Chattanooga Area Confederate Hammer Skinheads and the Memphis group, MASH, are closely aligned with the Dallas-based Confederate Hammer Skins. That group has been at the core of Skinhead recruiting efforts in other states, including Arizona, Oklahoma, and Wisconsin, and maintains close ties to Tom and John Metzger. (During his trial on charges of attacking and vandalizing a Dallas synagogue and Jewish Community Center, CHS member Daniel Alvis Wood testified that he had discussed his problems with Tom Metzger on several occasions.)

One of the more active Skinhead groups of late has been the Old Glory Skins, based in Atlanta. One of its leaders, Terence Georges, has traveled to Orlando, Florida, to set up a branch of his organization. Another member, Robert von Sura, has traveled to Birmingham to forge a link with the Birmingham Area Skinhead (BASH). Members of BASH were present at both the Democratic National Convention in Atlanta last July and at the annual Klan gathering at Stone Mountain on Labor Day Weekend, where they were joined by members of the Atlanta Skinhead group. Two Skinheads from the Fort Lauderdale area and another from Daytona Beach have also linked up with the Old Glory group, and a chapter was established this spring in Charlotte. The leaders of Old Glory have also developed a friendly relationship with the Metzgers.

Although the Confederate Hammer Skins and Old Glory Skins have succeeded in establishing a level of organization more sophisticated than most Skinhead groups, it is not uncommon for Skinheads to establish ties to others in different parts of the country. This usually takes the form of correspondence about points of common interest (particularly White Power music) and about movement activities. Skinheads also seek out their counterparts when they travel to other cities, often staying at communal residences.

WAR YOUTH

Much of the Skinhead organizing has centered around a number of charismatic figures (most in their twenties and therefore somewhat older than the rank and file) who have brought together Skinheads in different cities under a single umbrella. The most successful of these has been John Metzger (himself not a Skinhead), whose WAR Youth works in tandem with John's father Tom of the White Aryan Resistance to organize Skinheads throughout the country. But there are others, most notably Robert Heick, leader of the San Francisco-based American Front, and the aforementioned Michael Palasch. Heick has organized in Southern California, Florida and Maryland. Palasch, who heads the National White Resistance of Metairie, Louisiana, has formed chapters in Indianapolis, Cincinnati, Columbus and on New York's Long Island. NWR literature printed in Metairie has been distributed by Palasch's local affiliates with local addresses to contact for further information.

Metzger, Heick and Palasch have gained something of "celebrity" status through their numerous appearances on television talk shows, most notoriously on the installment of Geraldo Rivera's program where a brawl broke out, resulting in injury to the show's host. These programs have apparently been judged by their producers to be successful vis-à-vis audience ratings, because many have continued to invite Skinhead leaders to appear on them, resulting in a boon for Skinhead recruitment. John Metzger has claimed that he received about a thousand letters after appearing as a guest on both "Donahue" and "Oprah," some of his fans sending as much as a $500 contribution. He also says that thanks to national exposure, he possesses a list of "a thousand different people that would drop ten, twenty bucks if I told them to." (Both claims are probably exaggerated.)

Given their lack of discipline and anti-organizational impulses, it is unlikely that the Skinheads will unite as a single national entity. Nevertheless, the growth in the number of Skinhead networks reflects the movement's increasing ability to organize, a factor which should contribute to its long-term survival.

NON-RACIST SKINHEADS

As indicated earlier in this report, non-racist Skinheads considerably outnumber the racist ones in most areas of the country. Careful observation of the Skinhead scene over the past several years, however, leads to the conclusion that the distinction between the racist and non-racist variety is often blurred. Some "baldies," for example, openly express hostility toward homosexuals and have been arrested for violently assaulting gays ("fag-bashing"). Furthermore, it is not unusual for Skinheads who claim they are not racists to avow a belief in "white pride," a notion which is intrinsically racist. It is not surprising therefore that a good many Skinheads started out as "baldies," but eventually joined a neo-Nazi gang.

At the same time, there is no doubt that many non-racist Skins do proudly and genuinely eschew bigotry. Indeed, it is not unusual for blacks and Hispanics to be members of non-racist groups. But this does not signify that the groups are non-violent. On the contrary, they often boast about how tough they are and how many scraps they've been involved in with neo-Nazi Skins. In fact, the entire Skinhead scene is a violent one. Eric Andrew Anderson, whose masters thesis at Washington State University focused on the Skinheads in Great Britain and San Francisco, has pointed out that violence and machismo are central ingredients of the Skinhead culture. The record of Skinhead activity throughout the country confirms the correctness of his view. Skinheads have beaten, stomped and stabbed other Skinheads, punk rockers, long-haired hippies, gays and, in the case of the racist Skins, members of racial and religious minorities. Often these battles have taken place in clubs, leading the owners to bar the Skinheads or the authorities to close down the clubs altogether.

CONCLUSIONS AND COUNTERACTIVE MEASURES

The movement of Skinheads from the streets into the schools coming as it does at a time when the nation's schools are already wrestling with a host of difficulties, is a serious development. The evidence shows its impact not only on the students directly involved—the Skinheads and those closest to them—but on the entire school community. Events such as assaults on minority students; the appearance of racist graffiti on lockers, walls and doors; the shouting of racial epithets and the distribution of racist flyers have the effect of poisoning the entire atmosphere in a school and making orderly study exceedingly difficult. Beyond that, the Skinheads' recruiting efforts have involved exploiting racial tensions which they themselves have helped to create, triggering a self-generating destructive cycle.

When such problems have arisen, school administrators have coped with them as best they could, using whatever techniques they have judged appropriate, with varying results. The one approach, however, that has proven singularly ineffectual has been the "head-in-the-sand" policy. Principals who have tended to ignore the problem, out of concern, perhaps, for their school's reputation, have found that rather than going away, the problem has festered. The wiser course is a candid recognition that the problem exists and a sober consideration of possible remedies.

The second trend disclosed by the new ADL survey is the acquisition by racist Skinheads of increasingly dangerous weapons. A growing number of neo-Nazi Skinheads are adding firearms, some of them semi-automatic, to their stockpile of weapons. Heretofore the typical Skinhead instrument of assault has been a baseball bat, a knife or a steel-toed Doc Marten boot. Even these primitive weapons in the hands of Skinheads have been shown to be capable of murdering innocent victims. With the acquisition of such weapons as AR-15's and sawed-off shotguns, plainly the danger grows.

Any firearms in the hands of political extremists need to be taken seriously. The history of the past several decades shows that revolutionaries of the far right and the far left have been responsible for numerous fatal shootings and bombings. But there is something especially troubling about the possession of weapons of death by volatile youngsters filled with racial and religious hatred. All the more reason why the dangers posed by neo-Nazi Skinheads warrants the urgent attention of parents, educators, community leaders and law enforcement officials.

The Anti-Defamation League has taken a number of steps to inform communities about the nature of the Skinhead threat. Our reports are widely distributed to law enforcement officials, educators, and the press. We continue to regard the growth of the Skinhead movement as both a national and local problem requiring an effective response at both levels.

In January a high-level ADL delegation met with U.S. Attorney General Dick Thornburgh and received assurances that the Department of Justice regards with concern the racially and religiously motivated violence committed by Skinheads against individuals and institutions. Last month, a federal grand jury was convened in Dallas, signalling a U.S. Justice Department investigation of Skinhead crime described by spokeswoman Deborah Wade as "a showcase effort." The grand jury inquiry and a related state-federal investigation of Skinhead crime are being conducted jointly by the F.B.I., the Dallas Police Department, the Civil Rights Division of the Justice Department and the Dallas County District Attorney's Office. ADL has provided information to investigators.

In addition to supplying information on an ongoing basis to law enforcement agencies investigating criminal acts committed by Skinheads, ADL officials have briefed police personnel at conferences in Arizona, California, Georgia, Ohio, and New Mexico as well as states' attorneys in Illinois and the Prosecuting Attorneys Research Council, a group of district attorneys from around the country. We continue to promote the adoption and use by prosecutors of ADL's Model Hate Crime Statute, a form of which is now in effect in some 20 states. These statutes increase penalties for bias-related crimes. They have begun to be used in a number of jurisdictions to prosecute Skinheads. Finally, we have established reward funds for information leading to the arrest and conviction of Skinheads responsible for criminal activity, a tactic which has proven successful in a number of cases.

A measure that would help considerably in reducing the potential danger of Skinhead violence would be the adoption of legislation outlawing the sale of semi-automatic assault weapons. As this report has documented, these weapons are increasingly falling into the hands of racist Skinheads, a trend which could climax in tragedy.   [n.d.]

Note

1. DOC MARTEN WORK BOOTS: Heavy, steel-tipped leather boots.

Understanding the Reading

1. What kind of acts do Skinheads perform in schools?
2. What recruitment tactics do they employ?
3. What kind of weapons do they use?
4. How are they organizing nationally, and why is this important?
5. Why are nonracist Skinheads also problematic?
6. What can and should be done in response to the growing numbers of Skinheads?

Suggestions for Responding

1. Do you think we should be alarmed by the growth of the Skinhead movement? Why or why not?

2. Compare the kind of racial hatred and acts of violence attributed to the Skinheads with the kind of racial harassment and violence described in one of the previous selections in Part VIII. ✦

85

Inter-Racial Violence: Conflicts of Class and Culture

MICHAEL LASLETT

On March 14, 1987, a Black assailant shot and killed Mo Yi, a Korean merchant who owned a corner store in Anacostia, Maryland, a predominantly Black suburb of Washington, DC. The attacker also shot Yi's wife in the arm, shattering her elbow, and shot Yi's 20-year-old daughter in the shoulder. The gunman and his accomplice returned later that evening and emptied the cash register and took food and cigarettes. Yi was one of three Korean merchants killed in Washington since October, 1986. In 1986, at least 11 Korean-owned businesses were firebombed in Anacostia.

Over the past two years in Tacoma, Washington, Black youth have beaten several Southeast Asian students and an elderly Cambodian man, and the tires of Southeast Asian-owned cars are slashed on a regular basis. Tom Dixon, president of the Tacoma Urban League, says that this type of conflict is common among poor people. Referring to the growing poverty in the United States and the slashing of social services by the Reagan administration, Dixon remarks: "When poor people have less they strike out at each other. It's happening all over the city, all over America. The priorities of the country are upside down, and things are going to get worse before they get better."

These outbreaks of violence are not isolated incidents. The past five years have seen a sharp rise in the number of conflicts between recent Asian immigrants and refugees and the Black, Latino and other poor communities they move into. For example:

- On November 4, 1986, 30 to 40 Black youth assaulted seven Cambodian high school students as they walked home from school through Olney, a predominantly Black neighborhood in Philadelphia.
- In the fall of 1986, two incidents of inter-racial violence occurred in East Dallas, Texas: in the first, three Latino men dragged a Cambodian man from his car, beat him and took his money; in the second, a group of Latinos fired, unprovoked, into a crowd of Cambodians standing on the street.
- In the western section of Oakland, California, conflict between the Black and Southeast Asian Refugee populations has led to the deaths of two Blacks and one Southeast Asian.

In spite of the growing pattern of Black and Latino violence against Asians, many minority community leaders and activists insist that the problem not be viewed simply as one of racial antagonism. Black and Latino aggression against newly-arrived Asians is far more complex: it is the consequence of differences in economic class, of language barriers and cultural misunderstandings, and of the government's inadequate preparation of low-income residents for the sudden influx of Asian immigrant and refugees into their communities.

IMMIGRANTS AND REFUGEES: TWO DISTINCT GROUPS

The complexity of this issue deepens when one takes into account the diversity of the Asian population and their relationships to other racial groups in the U.S. Contrary to popular belief, the Asian community is neither homogeneous nor monolithic. Some Asians enter the United States as immigrants with education, financial resources and skills. The majority, however, are impoverished refugees fleeing war and repression. When these diverse populations arrive, they occupy different positions in the communities they live in and enter into different economic and social relationships with the long-term residents they encounter. Given this diversity, it follows that the motivations behind an attack on Korean or Chinese merchants in the Black community are not identical with those behind a physical assault on Southeast Asian refugees in the schools or on the streets.

One factor which differentiates segments of the Asian population in the U.S. is when they arrived. The Asian population in the United States more than doubled between 1970 and 1980. In 1970 nearly 90 percent of Asian Americans were of Japanese, Chinese, or Filipino descent. By 1980, census reports listed 19 distinct Asian and Pacific Island populations, with the three largest groups comprising only 62 percent of the total.

The first wave of Southeast Asians arrived in the U.S. in 1975 following the U.S. defeat in Vietnam. In that year 133,633 Indochinese were admitted into the U.S. Between 1976 and 1978 the numbers dropped considerably, followed by an increase to 80,700 in 1979, to 166,700 in 1980 and to more than 200,000 between 1981 and 1982. Although the majority of Southeast Asians are from Vietnam, the proportion of Cambodians and Laotians has increased in recent years, particularly since 1980.

In contrast to the Indochinese refugees, Asian immigrants such as the ethnic Chinese from Vietnam, China, Hong Kong and Singapore, as well as many recently-arrived Koreans, come from relatively privileged backgrounds in their own countries. It is largely by virtue of this fact that they are able to afford the cost and negotiate the paperwork necessary to come to the U.S. in the first place. The Chinese and Koreans also have pre-existing communities and support systems in the United States. Many do not have to be able to speak English to get a job because they can work within the Korean or Chinese communities.

Since many of these immigrants were merchants and shopowners in their home countries, this background, coupled with fear of discrimination in the American job market, makes it logical for them to work as small entrepreneurs. By pooling their financial resources extended family networks are able to gather the initial start-up capital needed to open a business.

Communal traditions help these families to reduce costs. Asian immigrants will often reduce living expenses by eating inexpensively and by crowding several families into one house or apartment. Likewise, Asian merchants often reduce labor costs by employing family members. The free labor supplied by their large families also allows Asian immigrants to maintain very long hours. These factors are crucial to their businesses' viability. The low rents and abandoned storefronts available in poor minority communities make these areas a logical choice for Asian merchants to locate their businesses.

Southeast Asian refugees follow a very different path into minority communities. Most of them spend years in refugee camps in Southeast Asia waiting for their turn to move to the United States. When they arrive they are distributed around the country by the federal government. The only assistance they receive is provided by the Refugee Act of 1978. Under the Act, the State Department allocates $565 per refugee, distributed through local agencies. Local agencies are then obligated to help the refugees obtain food, housing, transportation and other living expenses for their [first] 30 days in the U.S. After that period, if they have not found work, the refugees are placed in the general category of welfare recipients with no special assistance or privileges.

Most Southeast Asian refugees, unlike the Asian immigrants, are not urban people. They are peasants with no formal education and little previous contact with western culture and customs. Unlike the Chinese and Koreans, Southeast Asian refugees have no pre-established communities to join. They enter the U.S. on the lowest rung of American society and move into poor and minority neighborhoods and housing projects.

POVERTY + SUSPICION = TENSION

When refugees arrive they often enter a minority community which has been homogeneous for many years. The residents, who are generally given no warning or preparation for the influx of a population so completely different from any group they have known, view the newcomers with suspicion.

Wayne Luk of the Southeast Asian Refugee Center in San Francisco tells of a typical scenario of escalating Black-Asian tension in a poor Black community. In 1981 several Southeast Asian families were moved into a housing project in Hunter's Point, a predominantly Black area of San Francisco. Part of the housing project had been closed for renovations and several Black families were forced to move out. When it re-opened and Southeast Asians moved in, it appeared to the Blacks that the Asians had received preferential treatment. What they did not know was that the refugees had waited three years, just like everyone else, to get into the project. The lack of preparation necessary to adjust both the Asian and the Black communities to living with each other, coupled with the resentment Blacks felt toward the perceived preferential treatment of the Asians, led to several incidents of Black-on-Asian violence at Hunter's Point.

Many poor minority communities view the Asian refugees as competitors for already scarce resources. "They're taking over," says one Black man in Tacoma, Washington. "They're getting our housing, they're taking our jobs." While any addition to a poor community stretches resources a little thinner, there is debate over whether the refugees take jobs that would otherwise go to long-time community residents. As Booker Neal, a member of the Eastbay Violence Against Asians Taskforce and a community conciliation worker with the Justice Department, points out, many refugees will accept wages, hours and working conditions that a Black community member would refuse: "A job here at $3.50 an hour is a step up the ladder from a war-torn country and refugee camps. But to a black in that neighborhood that job is the same old poverty—probably the last step on the ladder."

Sam Cacas, a Filipino community activist in Oakland, California, and former director of the Community Violence Prevention Project, claims that most American citizens feel that they have the first right to jobs and services over immigrants, and that Asians are seen as foreigners no matter how long they have lived in the U.S. Recent immigrants have always been pitted against other low-income groups by having to compete with each other at the bottom of American society, Cacas argues. In the case of Asians, the friction is made worse by a long tradition of anti-Asian racism, a tradition in which Blacks, as well as whites, participate.

Although there are isolated incidents of refugees getting help from their sponsors, most receive little additional assistance after their first month in the U.S. However, these isolated incidents fuel the perception among poor minorities that refugees get preferential treatment and generate resentment in poor neighborhoods. For example, when an arson fire destroyed the home of four Cambodian families and one Black family in Tacoma, Washington, the Asians found tempo-

rary shelter with their sponsors, who also helped them find new housing. The Black family had to rely on the Red Cross, which provided a motel room for months while the family looked for a permanent place to live.

In East Dallas, Blacks and Latinos have witnessed a predominantly Anglo church, which sponsors Southeast Asian refugees, bring the refugees food and clothing, take them to the clinic and help them find jobs.

Long-time residents are also angered by the perception that Asian newcomers succeed soon after they arrive in a community, while Blacks continue to struggle. As Booker Neal explains, the community watches as the Asians move in and within a year have a job and after two years have a new car. What the community does not see, however, is that often ten families contribute to buy the car. The new car masks the daily sacrifices made to buy it: the long working hours, the mostly-rice diet and the cramped living quarters.

The hope and enthusiasm of upward mobility in the 'land of opportunity' motivates newly-arrived refugees to strive in neighborhoods where, according to Booker Neal, Blacks experience only frustration. This frustration is most acute among teenagers, who suffer the highest levels of unemployment—nearly 40 percent. It is not surprising, says Neal, that the majority of attacks on Asian refugees within the Black community are committed by teenagers. "In an area of unemployment, drugs, crime, and poverty, you're not going to have some sixteen-year-old trying to learn about the culture, problems, and history of Laotian immigrants," Neal points out.

Many Southeast Asian refugees become victims because they are seen as passive and unwilling to fight back, behavior which is in part integral to their cultures, and in part a survival skill learned while living under repressive regimes in Southeast Asia. Many are unwilling to call the police because of the violent nature of police in their home countries.

Mary Cousar, a Black woman who is chairperson of the Logan Multi-Cultural Task Force in Philadelphia, also points out that the Southeast Asians are targets because they have darker skin than the Chinese and Koreans. "I've heard little black children refer to Cambodians as 'nigger Chinese,'" she says.

General disorientation in a new culture also makes the refugees targets for harassment. Yang Sam, the executive director of the Philadelphia Southeast Asian Mutual Aid Assistance Association Coalition, argues that "the way [Asian refugees] walk in the street" reflects their "insecurity and makes them easy targets of crime. [They] are not really comfortable, not confident yet in themselves" in the United States.

Sam Cacas argues that the current resurgence of anti-Asian sentiment is also reinforced by general ignorance, among all sectors of the American population, of the history of Asians in the United States. Most people are unaware of anti-Asian laws such as the Chinese Exclusion Act[1] or the internment of Japanese-Americans during World War II, and that most people think of racism as purely a Black/white problem, Cacas argues. He compares the unequal media coverage of the Howard Beach attack[2] and the killing of Vincent Chin[3] as evidence of this perception.

Cacas also points out that both the Black and Asian communities absorb the racist beliefs prevalent in society at large. While Blacks accept the model minority myth,[4] many Asians generalize from their experience in Black neighborhoods, as well as from images of Blacks in the media that all Blacks are prone to crime and violence. Many Asians are also unaware of the history of oppression that Blacks have suffered in the United States. Wayne Luk points out that before coming to the U.S., many Asian refugees and immigrants were unaware of the racial diversity in the United States, and have a distrust of Blacks.

ASIAN MERCHANTS: A CONFLICT OF CLASS

The tension between low-income minorities and the Chinese and Korean merchants who operate small businesses in their communities is in some respects similar to the conflicts between Blacks and Southeast Asian refugees. There are the same misunderstandings, cultural ignorance on both sides, and the vulnerability of the Asian shopowners as newcomers. But there are also significant differences.

According to Professor Edna Bonacich, a sociologist at the University of California at Riverside who has studied the growing phenomenon of Asian merchants, the Asian shopowners have entered into a fundamentally antagonistic economic relationship with the community. That antagonism, she says, is due primarily to class, not race or culture.

By definition, argues Bonacich, merchants of any race make their living by making a profit from their customers, in this case poor minorities. Since the merchants do not live in the community, no portion of their profits is reinvested into the community. Because the stores are family-run operations, they also provide no employment to the community. In addition, Asian merchants often operate businesses which are antithetical to the community's general welfare. Bonacich cites the example of Korean merchants opening numerous liquor stores in Watts, Los Angeles, despite the complaints of community leaders. "The Korean storeowners don't have to live with the increased amount of alcohol circulating in the community" says Bonacich. "They are willing to open any store that makes money."

Asian merchants, however, play a role that Bonacich describes as "middleman minority." These merchants are 'middlemen,' Bonacich argues, because while they are exploiting the community, they are also being exploited by the large, corporate manufacturers. Since large department stores and supermarket chains have evacuated poor and minority areas for more profitable, less turbulent neighborhoods, small minority-owned businesses have become the sole outlets for the products of manufacturing corporations in minority communities, which represent an important consumer market. The corporations also benefit from the free labor provided by Asian extended families, which allows the stores to stay open longer, Bonacich points out. In a paper on immigrant entrepreneurship Bonacich writes: "Their long hours mean that even the dribble-in trade will be picked up. . . . More of the producers' goods are sold, and thus more profits are made from the immigrants' activities."

As middlemen, it is the Asian merchants, not the corporate manufacturers, who must endure personal attacks and absorb the costs of operating a business in a crime-filled area. Small business also lends itself to self-exploitation, says Bonacich. Families have to devote their entire lives to keeping the business afloat. Often the entire first generation of an Asian immigrant family is sacrificed to allow the children to go to college and move up the economic ladder.

Although they make a profit from the community, most Asian merchants are far from rich. Some of their profit is taken by corporate manufacturers, as Bonacich points out. Michael Perez of the Minority Business Development Agency, an arm of the U.S. Commerce Department, explains that close to 35 percent of Asian-owned businesses earn less than $5,000 a year.

However, Asian merchants are the 'frontline' representatives of large corporate business in minority communities and therefore face the anger of a poor population. When minority communities respond, it is sometimes with political organizing. For example, the Black community in Harlem called a boycott of Asian stores in part because Black community members accused the merchants of taking dollars out of their community. However, the firebombings and beatings of Asian merchants in Philadelphia and Washington, DC, are examples of another, more common expression of anger and frustration.

Is Reconciliation Possible?

Sam Cacas has worked closely with several efforts to address the problems of Black/Asian tension. As director of the Community Violence Prevention Project, Cacas participated in a successful campaign to make emergency assistance more accessible to recent immigrants and refugees. In response to this community pressure the Alameda County Board of Supervisors approved a translation service for the 911 emergency assistance number in late 1986. The service includes more than 80 languages, which Cacas hopes will particularly help recently-arrived Asians who are the victims of intimidation or attack.

To resolve conflicts between the Asian and Black communities, Cacas advocates legislation requiring the police to keep statistics on racially-motivated crimes so that evidence of such attacks is easier to accumulate. He also argues for effective human relations commissions to mediate community conflicts and for increasing 'sensitivity training' for service providers who handle racial conflict.

Educational projects in schools stressing ethnic studies and interracial relationships are also necessary, says Cacas. Often aggressors are ignorant about who their victims are, what their problems are, and how they share common interests.

Asian merchants and Blacks are peacefully coexisting in one Black neighborhood in Philadelphia. There, Korean business-owners are participating in efforts to improve the community. Says Jewel Williams, president of the Susquehanna Neighborhood Advisory Council: "Ever since 1980, we have been trying to assist people who are needy, and the Koreans have been helping. Susquehanna Avenue has been a blighted area since the 1960's, since the riots in 1964. We've asked business people to come in here and make Susquehanna live again. The Koreans are the only ones who came. They've come in and done a good job. If they weren't here, it would be blighted again."

An innovative program at Fremont High School in East Oakland, California, has successfully begun to address the specific problem of tension between Blacks and Southeast Asian refugees. The project, jointly conceived by Asian Community Mental Health Service (ACMHS) and Conciliation Forums of Oakland (CFO), trains students to mediate the conflicts of other students. The mediators, who take a 26-hour preparation course, learn what CFO project coordinator Millie Cleveland calls "active listening." They validate and empathize with both sides of the conflict and they summarize what was said back to the hostile parties.

For every complaint or report of a conflict, a panel of trained student mediators is established. Each panel is chosen to insure that both people in conflict feel confident that their point of view will be fairly heard. For many students, says Cleveland, this is the first time they have been able to tell their side to a sympathetic ear. They express anger and other feelings about the conflict, and in the course of talking the disputants begin to communicate with each other.

According to Cleveland, this process enables both sides to see each other as individuals, to see the other person's point of view, and to psychologically prepare themselves for compromise. Cleveland explains how the hostile parties began to express regret for the conflict and talk about "how they would act next time" in a similar situation. The parties then sign a contract, drawn from the comments of the disputants, which formalizes their agreement to use communication and compromise to resolve conflicts. Often, says Cleveland, it becomes clear that the conflict is between two individuals rather than between representatives of different ethnicities or nationalities.

Since the implementation of the Fremont High project, there have been no reoccurances of conflict between students who took their problem to a panel, says Cleveland. "All the disputants agreed that it was worth coming, and that in absence of the panel something worse would have happened," she says.   [1987]

Notes

1. CHINESE EXCLUSION ACT: A law that prohibited Chinese from immigrating to the United States.
2. HOWARD BEACH ATTACK: Three young African-Americans were attacked and beaten at a pizza parlor in the white community of Howard Beach, New York; one was killed by a car when he ran onto a highway to escape.
3. VINCENT CHIN: A Chinese-American mistaken for a Japanese, who was clubbed to death by white autoworkers in Detroit.
4. MODEL MINORITY MYTH: The stereotype that all Asian-Americans are both academically and financially successful.

Understanding the Reading

1. What relationship does Tom Dixon see between poverty and racial conflict?
2. What are the differences between Asian immigrants and Asian refugees?
3. How do existing minority communities respond to newcomers from Southeast Asia?
4. Do Asian refugees take jobs away from other minority people?
5. Why are Asian newcomers likely to seem prosperous to blacks and Latinos?
6. Why are Asian refugees easy targets of violence and harassment?
7. Why are Asian shopkeepers especially resented by the minority community?
8. What can be done to reduce interracial violence?

Suggestions for Responding

1. Explain the complex web of causes of bias against Asians and Asian-Americans within the minority communities.
2. How is anti-Asian violence similar to and different from white violence against African-Americans? ◆

SUGGESTIONS FOR RESPONDING TO PART VIII

1. Research a specific civil rights campaign, such as the Birmingham bus boycott, integration of a school district in a southern city, integration of a southern university, the Freedom Rides, Freedom Summer, or voter registration in Mississippi, and report on the kinds of violence to which the civil rights workers were subjected.
2. In addition to nationally recognized Martin Luther King, Jr., more than forty people were murdered between 1955 and 1968 by white terrorists who opposed the civil rights movement. Write a biography of one of these martyrs, such as Lamar Smith, James Chaney, Andrew Goodman, Michael Schwerner, Rev. James Reeb, Viola Gregg Liuzzo, or Willie Brewster.
3. Investigate and report on a governmental or volunteer organization formed to protect rape victims or victims of domestic violence to learn what support is available to women in your area.
4. The Ku Klux Klan is not the only white-supremacist group active today; others include Identity, Liberty Lobby (Populist Party), the National Association for the Advancement of White People, and the Nationalist Movement, as well as such neo-Nazi groups as the American Nazi Party, Aryan Nation, Aryan Youth Movement, National Alliance, National

Socialist Vanguard, New Order, SS-Action Group, and White Aryan Resistance. Research and report on the beliefs and activities of one or more of these groups.

5. Among civil rights groups in active opposition to race hatred and interracial violence are the Southern Poverty Law Center, its Klanwatch Project, the Anti-Defamation League of B'nai B'rith, the Center for Third World Organizing, the National Association for the Advancement of Colored People, and the American Civil Liberties Union. Research one of these organizations, and report on its structure and principles and some of its recent activities.

6. In the 1890s, Ida Wells Barnett exposed and fought the racist use of lynching to control Negro males, especially those who were perceived as economic threats to local whites. Report on her work, including statistics on the incidence of lynching when she initiated her campaign and after it was underway.

7. Beulah Mae Donald is known as the "woman who beat the Klan." On March 21, 1981, her son Michael was beaten, had his throat cut, and was finally hanged by Klan members in Alabama. Research this case and report on the circumstances of Michael's murder, the investigation, the trial, and the final court verdict.

SUGGESTION FOR RESPONDING TO POWER

Research one manifestation of racism, sexism, classism, or homophobia that you read about in this book. As an individual you will want to focus on what may seem to be a very small part of the problem, but a group could investigate a broader problem, breaking it into its component parts, with each group member assuming responsibility for one aspect.

As a group you could investigate sexual harassment; as an individual, you might focus on something like sexual harassment on your campus. A group could look at housing segregation; individually you could consider red-lining (refusing credit to residents and businesses in certain locations) in your community. A group could research the issue of domestic battery, but individually you would research the cycle of violence. Or a group could examine current incidents of racial or homophobic harassment, but one person would concentrate on his or her campus or community.

Other broad areas for research include government policies affecting Native Americans; "scientific proof" of the inferiority of a racial, religious, or gender group; racist, sexist, or homophobic social policies; the race and/or gender wage gap; some facet of the history of racism or sexism in American law; organized racism, historically or at present; a manifestation of discrimination in education or employment.

Report on both the causes and the effects of the problem. Also include information about efforts that have already been made to alleviate or at least ameliorate the problem, and discuss how effective or unsuccessful they have been and why.

If your instructor plans to have you develop a "plan for action" in response to "Change," you probably want to select a topic for this assignment about which you are particularly concerned and which you would like to see changed.

As with earlier assignments, your instructor may ask you or your group to present your findings orally to your classmates. If this makes you uncomfortable, review the suggestions at the end of Part I on how to prepare for such a presentation.

Change is not only possible; it is an inevitable part of life. Seasons pass. We grow older. This kind of natural change is beyond our control. We adjust to many changes without taking much notice. On the other hand, much change is **social change,** caused and controlled by people acting individually and collectively.

Most of us think of social change as resulting from mass **social movements,** coalitions of groups and individuals seeking to revise social policies and transform social institutions. We recognize the strategies and achievements of the major American social movements that have affected the groups we have been reading about: abolition and civil rights, labor unions and consumer rights, woman suffrage and women's liberation, and gay and lesbian rights. This kind of direct collective action is probably the most effective way to promote social change, but it requires the strong commitment of many people who agree and will act on common objectives. However, social change doesn't necessarily depend on large-scale political activism. In fact, each of us in our daily life participates in the processes of social change.

Change

You may think this doesn't really apply to you. For example, you may never have been interested in social issues, much less consider yourself a social activist; but this doesn't mean you have no impact on the shape of society. You may not consider yourself prejudiced, but when a friend tells you a racial joke, you might laugh so you won't offend her. Your laughter, however, indicates your approval of the joke's racist assumptions and without your being aware of it, you have added one more stitch to the racist fabric of our society. In contrast, had you made a quiet comment that you don't care for that kind of joke, you could have begun to unravel at least one little thread. Both what you do and what you *don't* do influence social values.

Many of the issues raised in the first two divisions of this book are very disturbing. Because stereotypes are arbitrary oversimplifications, they blind us to the individuality of members of stereotyped groups and the rich potentiality of our diverse society. Prejudice, in turn, rests on such stereotyped thinking and encourages discrimination, sexism, racism, heterosexism, and classism. These "isms" support the beliefs and behaviors that lead to the pervasive neglect, exploitation, subordination, and oppression of women, minorities, lesbians, gay men, and the poor. This is a problem not just for members of these groups but for all Americans, because systemic exclusion of so many people from full participation diminishes society by depriving us of their full skills, talents, wisdom, and creativity. Moreover, prejudiced convictions, and the behaviors that grow out of them, violate the most basic tenets of American society, the principles of freedom, equality, and justice.

As troubling and discouraging as an awareness of these social problems may be, we don't need to accept them as inevitable or unalterable. They can be changed, and we can be instrumental in the process of effecting such change. We have already begun that process by learning about the issues, for we cannot begin to address a problem until we see and understand it. But such knowledge is only the first step.

This division, "Change," is intended to show how to make the changes we want. Part IX, "Taking Action," gives us an understanding of the nature and dynamics of social change. By learning the step-by-step process of creating social change, we can see how to be more effective contributors to society. Part X, "Change Makers," explores how people have worked to change their own lives and the world around them. Together these readings will increase our sense of our ability to control our own lives and to influence the society in which we live.

IX
Taking Action

AT ONE TIME OR ANOTHER, WE ALL WANT TO CHANGE something—our looks, our behavior, what happens to us or to others. This is one reason why you are in school: You want your life to be different than it otherwise would be. Part IX provides information about how to make change—how to think about problems, how to plan what we want to do, and how to do it. When we understand the way to approach change logically, we are better able to initiate and effect change ourselves.

In the first reading, Larry Letich presents the six main steps anyone should take to make any orderly change, whether it be in one's personal life or in society at large. Letich applies these steps to the problem of men's traditional lack of personal male friends, but they are equally applicable to making any desired change. The rest of the readings illustrate and elaborate on these six steps. By the end of Part IX, you will understand both how social change is created and how to make a change yourself.

The first basic step in the process is **identifying the problem.** We tend initially to see a problem in its broadest form, like the general issue of homelessness, for example. But that problem is so extensive that it feels overwhelming, so we are likely just to shrug our shoulders and dismiss it. After all, "What can one person do?" We *can* do something though. First, we must learn as much as we can about the specific issues that underlie the larger problem. This information will help us identify and define a specific, concrete issue to work on. Homelessness, for example, has numerous causes to consider: an apartment fire, or high rents and low incomes in the community; or, on a personal level, job loss or family breakup. Another way of thinking about this issue is to think about its consequences, such as lack of economic resources, sanitary facilities, or safety.

The next three selections focus on this step, each identifying a problem thoughtfully and precisely. Barbara Lawrence examines the sexist foundations of obscene language; William Snider explains why we need to be concerned about Latino undereducation; and the National PTA and the Council on Interracial Books for Children focus on why the problem of homophobia must be addressed in the classroom.

The second step in the change process is **identifying the desired outcome**—that is, defining what specific change we would like to see. Arturo Madrid considers his personal experiences of being seen as the "other" and concludes that America and Americans must come to terms with the diversity of our society, his desired outcome. Eloise Salholz, on the other hand, reports on the need for political awareness and activism in the Hispanic community. Considering the example of homelessness discussed above, one potential outcome might be finding a way to help the unemployed homeless find work. This would be the goal, the desired outcome.

The third step is **developing strategies** for realizing the goal. The first thing we think of is probably not the best idea we can come up with. We're better off considering many alternatives. *Brainstorming*—letting our minds wander freely — is a good approach. Take plenty of time, alone or with a group, to generate as many different ideas as possible. At this stage, don't censor yourself in any way; in fact, try to be as imaginative and creative as possible, because what might at first seem an unrealistic strategy can sometimes trigger an original, workable solution. This is what Charlotte Bunch is doing as she explores ways of bringing her feminist vision to bear on the public arena. Her "anything is possible" approach results in her suggesting many inventive tactics that most of us never would have dreamed of. Similarly, Andrew Kimbrell explores ways that men can work for change in their relationships with their families, with the environment, and in the community. Try brainstorming ways that could be used to help the homeless get jobs; see how many you can list. You might realize, for instance, that without a home, even qualified people have nowhere to receive responses to job applications. You could help solve this problem by figuring out a way to provide them with a mailing address.

Step four is **developing a plan for action.** Select the most appropriate strategies from your brainstorming and figure how to implement them. Be realistic. Consider what resources you have access to: time, energy, people, money, materials, and so on. Think about how you can augment them. After brainstorming about everything that needs to be done, develop a *timeline*—a schedule of what needs to be done and in what order. In his article, John D'Emilio presents a plan of action, including policies and other considerations, for colleges and universities that want to assure fair and equal treatment for gay men and lesbians on their campuses.

What could you do to help the homeless receive mail service? Probably very little by yourself, but if you interested others in working with you, you might create an effective solution. For example, you could solicit funds to pay rent on a post office box and distribute its contents at a prearranged location once a day. You could approach a church that already has a soup kitchen to feed the homeless and offer to help them establish a mail service for homeless job seekers at their address. There are many other ways to tackle this problem. Once you settle on your approach, develop your plan: the resources you need, your time frame, the people you need to work with you, and so on.

Once you have carefully mapped out your action project, your next step, the fifth, is **implementing the plan.** One major difficulty you will face at this stage is motivating people, getting them to act, to agree with you or your analysis of the problem, to support or perhaps even just to accept the desirability of the change you wish to implement. This is often the most crucial part of effecting social change. People resist change because we all tend to be more comfortable with the familiar, even when we realize that it isn't perfect; we all value the security of living with what we already know.

As you read Kathleen Ryan's analysis of the reasons for and signs of *resistance,* think about your own responses to the readings in this book and consider how you felt resistance to some of them—to the value system on which they are based, to the strategies they advocate, and so on. This will give you some insight into how some people may respond to (and resist) your own plan of action. If you can accurately anticipate the kinds of resistance you are likely to encounter, you can devise ways to respond to or counteract that resistance (and probably incorporate some of them into your plan for action).

The next two readings describe different approaches to creating social change. It is easiest, of course, if you have the power and authority to require people to change their attitude and behavior. Daniel Goleman, for example, explains how educators, without making their purpose explicit, can help students overcome racism by having them work in racially and ethnically mixed teams. This is the "top-down" model of making change. However, seemingly powerless people can also create tremendous changes by organizing and working together. For example, Cynthia Diehm and Margo Ross describe how people have identified the problem of domestic violence and taken steps to alleviate it through grass-roots activism. Throughout the country, small groups of people have worked together to set up shelters and to change laws and even the criminal justice system.

The final step in any good plan for social change is **evaluating your actions:** assessing the effectiveness of your endeavor and identifying the reasons for its successes and its disappointments. This is a very important step. Appraising the degree of your achievement can enhance your sense of a job well done, contributing to the satisfaction of everyone working with you. Identifying weaknesses in your project can help you plan better strategies to use in future actions. Evaluation isn't simply a matter of determining whether or not the plan worked; it is much more a function of one's beliefs and expectations. People determine the relative success of a project based on a wide variety of standards, values, attitudes, and expectations. What one person may consider a success another may perceive to be a failure.

Evaluative judgments differ when they rest on different priorities or value systems. In the last two readings, two law professors evaluate college and university policies that prohibit racist, sexist, and other types of harassing language or acts on their campuses. Gerald Gunther opposes them because he believes they violate our Constitutional freedom of speech. Charles R. Lawrence III supports them on the grounds that such offensive speech deprives its targets of Constitutionally protected equal educational opportunities. Each presents a persuasive case for his point of view and is clearly convinced that his policy is best, based on his values.

An awareness of the six steps makes it easier for us to work for social changes that we desire. However, change is never easy. Each of the steps requires a substantial investment of time and thought, and the more basic or extensive the desired change is, the more difficult it will be to achieve. Successful action demands thorough research, careful thought, strong motivation, extensive planning, and lots of time. If you commit yourself, however, you can do more than you probably think you can.

86

Do You Know Who Your Friends Are?

LARRY LETICH

"You gotta have friends," sang Bette Midler. But most men past the age of 30 don't have friends —not really. They have colleagues and work buddies, golf partners and maybe a "couple" friend or two, where the bond is really between the wives. If they say they *do* have a best friend, often it turns out to be an old friend whom they see or speak to once every few years.

Sadly, for most men in our culture, male friendship is a part of their distant past. One man spoke for many at a recent men's conference in Montclair, N.J., when he lamented, "I haven't made a new friend in 25 years."

Why is this so? All sorts of theories are thrown around, from "homophobia" to the absurd idea that men are biologically geared to competitiveness, which precludes friendship. But the major reason for the shortage of true friendship among men in America is that our culture discourages it.

Male friendship is idealized in the abstract (think of *Butch Cassidy and the Sundance Kid* and numerous other "buddy movies"), but if a man manages to have any true emotional attachment to another man, a lot of subtle pressures are placed on him to eliminate it. The most obvious time this happens is when a man gets married (especially if he's still in his 20s). Think of the impression that comes to mind from a thousand movies and TV shows about the guy who "leaves his wife" for the evening to "go out with the guys." Invariably, the other guys are shown as both immature *and* lower-class, losers who'll never amount to anything in life. The message is clear—no self-respecting middle-class man hangs out regularly with his friends.

In fact, friendship between men is rarely spoken of at all. Instead, we hear about something called male bonding, as if all possible non-sexual connection between men is rooted in some crude, instinctual impulse. More often than not, male friendship, reduced to male bonding, is sniggered at as something terribly juvenile and possibly dangerous.

This denigration of male friendship fits well into Reagan- and Thatcher-style capitalism. The decline in blue-collar jobs and the great white-collar work speed-up of the 1980s made no man's job safe. And money—not the richness of a man's relationship with family, friends, and community—became even more so the universally accepted value of a man's worth.

In this system, men (at least those men without golden parachutes[1]) are put in the position of constantly, and often ruthlessly, competing with all other men for the limited number of positions higher up the ladder—or even to hold onto their jobs at all. Men are encouraged not to trust one another, and are frankly told never to band together. (For example, in most places it is a serious faux pas, and often a dismissable offense, simply to tell a fellow worker what you make for a living; supposedly it is "bad for morale.") Naturally, this keeps men—and women, too—constantly knocking themselves out for the next promotion rather than demanding real changes, like cutting the CEO's[2] million-dollar salary down to size.

Given the kind of sterile, high-pressure work environments men are expected to devote themselves to, it's not surprising that the ideal American man is supposed to feel little or no passion about anything. As Robert Bly[3] has pointed out, the most damaged part of the psyche in modern man is the "lover," meaning not just the ability to make love, but the ability to love life, to feel, to be either tender or passionate. But passion—and with it the capacity for intimacy—is absolutely essential for friendship.

It's also not surprising that our society's ideal man is not supposed to have any emotional needs. Since few men can actually live up to that ideal, it's considered acceptable, even laudable, for him to channel all his emotional needs in one direction—his wife and children. A man who has any other important emotional bonds (that are not based on duty, such as an ailing parent) is in danger of being called neglectful, or irresponsible, or weak, because forging emotional bonds with others takes time—time that is supposed to be spent "getting ahead."

Small wonder that the only friendships allowed are those that serve a "business" purpose or those than can be fit effortlessly into one's leisure time. Maintaining one's lawn is more important than maintaining one's friendships. In keeping with this, there are no rituals and no respect given a man's friendships. When was the last time you heard a grown man talk proudly about his best friend?

Despite all these obstacles, it *is* possible to develop a real male friendship—the kind men remember from their childhood, high school, college, or military days—after the age of 30. My best friend today, with whom I share a deep and abiding bond, is a man I met five years ago when I was 30. But to forge real male friendships requires a willingness to *recognize* that you're going against the grain, and the *courage* to do so. And it requires the sort of conscious, deliberate campaign worthy of a guerrilla leader. Here are step-by-step guerrilla tactics to forge, maintain, and deepen male friendships in a hostile environment:

1. **First, you have to want it** [desired outcome]. Sounds simple and obvious, but isn't. You have to want it badly enough to work at getting it, just as you would a job or a sexual relationship. Right away, this causes anxiety, because it goes against the male self-sufficiency myth. You have to remind yourself *often* that there's nothing weird or effeminate about wanting a friend. Let your wife and children know about your quest. It's good for your sons, especially, to know what you're trying to do. They might even have some good suggestions!

2. **Identify a possible friend** [develop strategies]. Men in men's groups and others who seem in some way to be questioning society's view of masculinity and success are possible candidates. Don't look for men so upstanding and "responsible" they never have a second to themselves. Stuart Miller, author of the book *Men & Friendship,* suggested in a recent interview reconnecting with your old friends from childhood or adolescence.

3. **Be sneaky** [plan for action]. Once you've identified the guy you want to make your friend, do you say, "Hey , I want to be your friend, let's do lunch?" No. One of you will probably soon get threatened and pull away. Instead, get involved in a project with him, preferably non-work-related. For my best friend Mike and me, it was a newsletter we were working on. You need structured time just to be together, feel each other out, and get used to each other without the pressure of being "friends."

4. **Invite him to stop for a beer or a cup of coffee** [implementation]. Ask personal questions. Find out about his wife, his children, his girlfriend, his job. Find out what's really bugging him in his life. Look for common likes and dislikes. And risk being personal about yourself as well. Do this several times, each time risking a little more honesty.

5. **Call just to get together** [implementation] after a few months of this. Arrange to get together at least once a month, even if only for a few hours. Expect to always be the caller and arranger, especially in the beginning.

6. **Sit down and talk about your friendship** [evaluation]. It may take some time to reach this point. But while it's typical for men to leave things unsaid, this step is crucial. In a society that treats friendships as replaceable, you have to go against the tide by declaring the value of this special friendship between you. Only then will it survive life's stresses, such as a serious disagreement or one of you moving away. [1991]

Notes

1. GOLDEN PARACHUTE: A generous benefit package offered to high-level business executives to encourage them to retire.
2. CEO: Chief Executive Officer.
3. ROBERT BLY: Author of *Iron John* and advocate of the men's movement, which emphasizes men's exploring their inner maleness and bonding with other men.

Understanding the Reading

1. How does our culture discourage male friendship?
2. Explain the six steps required to forge and maintain male friendship.

Suggestion for Responding

Apply Letich's six steps to a personal problem you are experiencing. ◆

87

Four-Letter Words Can Hurt You

BARBARA LAWRENCE

Why should any words be called obscene? Don't they all describe natural human functions? Am I trying to tell them, my students demand, that the "strong, earthy, gut-honest"—or, if they are fans of Norman Mailer,[1] the "rich, liberating, existential"—language they use to describe sexual activity isn't preferable to "phony-sounding, middle-class words like 'intercourse' and 'copulate'?" "Copy You Late!" they say with fancy inflections and gagging grimaces. "Now, what is *that* supposed to mean?"

Well, what is it supposed to mean? And why indeed should one group of words describing human functions and human organs be acceptable in ordinary conversation and another, describing presumably the same organs and functions, be tabooed—so much so, in fact, that some of these words still cannot appear in print in many parts of the English-speaking world?

The argument that these taboos exist only because of "sexual hangups" (middle-class, middle-age, feminist), or even that they are a result of class oppression (the contempt of the Norman conquerors for the language of their Anglo-Saxon serfs), ignores a much more likely explanation, it seems to me, and that is the sources and functions of the words themselves.

The best known of the tabooed sexual verbs, for example, comes from the German *ficken,* meaning "to strike"; combined, according to Partridge's etymological dictionary *Origins,* with the Latin sexual verb *futuere;* associated in turn with the Latin *fustis,* "a staff or cudgel"; the Celtic *buc,* "a point, hence to pierce"; the Irish *bot,* "the male member"; the Latin *battuere,* "to beat"; the Gaelic *batair,* "a cudgeller"; the Early Irish *bualaim,* "I strike"; and so forth. It is one of what etymologists sometimes call "the sadistic group of words for the man's part in copulation."

The brutality of this word, then, and its equivalents ("screw," "bang," etc.), is not an illusion of the middle class or a crotchet of Women's Liberation. In their origins and imagery these words carry undeniably painful, if not sadistic, implications, the object of which is almost always female. Consider, for example, what a "screw" actually does to the wood it penetrates; what a painful, even mutilating, activity this kind of analogy suggests. "Screw" is particularly interesting in this context, since the noun, according to Partridge, comes from words meaning "groove," "nut," "ditch," "breeding sow," "scrofula" and "swelling," while the verb, besides its explicit imagery, has antecedent associations to "write on," "scratch," "scarify," and so forth—a revealing fusion of a mechanical or painful action with an obviously denigrated object.

Not all obscene words, of course, are as implicitly sadistic or denigrating to women as these, but all that I know seem to serve a similar purpose: to reduce the human organism (especially the female organism) and human functions (especially sexual and procreative) to their least organic, most mechanical dimension; to substitute a trivializing or deforming resemblance for the complex human reality of what is being described.

Tabooed male descriptives, when they are not openly denigrating to women, often serve to divorce a male organ or function from any significant interaction with the female. Take the word "testes," for example, suggesting "witnesses" (from the Latin *testis*) to the sexual and procreative strengths of the male organ; and the obscene counterpart of this word, which suggests little more than a mechanical shape. Or compare almost any of the "rich," "liberating" sexual verbs, so fashionable today among male writers, with that much-derided Latin word "copulate" ("to bind or join together") or even that Anglo-Saxon phrase (which seems to have had no trouble surviving the Norman Conquest) "make love."

How arrogantly self-involved the tabooed words seem in comparison to either of the other terms, and how contemptuous of the female partner. Understandably so, of course, if she is only a "skirt," a "broad," a "chick," a "pussycat" or a "piece." If she is, in other words, no more than her skirt, or what her skirt conceals; no more than a breeder, or the broadest part of her; no more than a piece of a human being or a "piece of tail."

The most severely tabooed of all the female descriptives, incidentally, are those like a "piece of tail," which suggest (either explicitly or through antecedents) that there is no significant difference between the female channel through which we are all conceived and born and the anal outlet common to both sexes—a distinction that pornographers have always enjoyed obscuring.

This effort to deny women their biological identity, their individuality, their humanness, is such an important aspect of obscene language that one can only marvel at how seldom, in an era preoccupied with definitions of obscenity, this fact is brought to our attention. One problem, of course, is that many of the people in the best position to do this (critics, teachers, writers) are so reluctant today to admit that they are angered or shocked by obscenity. Bored, maybe, unimpressed, aesthetically displeased, but—no matter how brutal or denigrating the material—never angered, never shocked.

And yet how eloquently angered, how piously shocked many of these same people become if denigrating language is used about any minority group other than women; if the obscenities are racial or ethnic, that is, rather than sexual. Words like "coon," "kike," "spic," "wop," after all, deform identity, deny individuality and humanness in almost exactly the same way that sexual vulgarisms and obscenities do.

No one that I know, least of all my students, would fail to question the values of a society whose literature and entertainment rested heavily on racial or ethnic pejoratives. Are the values of a society whose literature and entertainment rest as heavily as ours on sexual pejoratives any less questionable?   [1973]

Note

1. NORMAN MAILER: An American writer.

Understanding the Reading

1. What arguments are made in support of tabooed obscene words?
2. Why is the etymology of tabooed sexual verbs important?
3. Why does Lawrence advocate the sexual terms derived from Latin?
4. How does sexual slang dehumanize women?
5. Why is obscene language an important social problem?

Suggestion for Responding

Conduct an etymological investigation of the derivation of three of your favorite obscene words, and analyze the implications of your findings. ◆

88

The Need to Improve Hispanic Education

WILLIAM SNIDER

WASHINGTON—The Children's Defense Fund has joined in the call for "an all-out effort" to improve educational services for Hispanic youths, in a new report documenting the plight of the nation's fastest growing but most undereducated ethnic group.

"Until recently," the report released here last week notes, "both their small numbers and America's melting-pot perspective kept the story of Latino youths contained within the broader discussion of the plight and the progress of American minorities."

Citing demographers' projections that the number of Hispanic youths—and potential entrants into the labor force—will surpass that of blacks early in the next century, the report argues that "this general perspective can no longer be justified."

Hispanic advocacy groups, led by the National Council of La Raza, used this argument in persuading President Bush last December to form a high-level task force to focus on Hispanic education issues.

The new report, "Latino Youths at a Crossroads," assembles in one place a broad array of demographic, economic, and educational data that portray the extent of the challenges facing this ethnic group. It includes recommendations for action to address those issues.

Its publication, C.D.F. officials said, marks the return of education issues to the forefront of the Defense Fund's agenda after almost a decade in which it concentrated on children's health and welfare issues.

"We won our early battles over improving access to education services for poor and minority children, but access isn't enough if the quality isn't there," said Kati Haycock, the group's executive vice president. "We're getting out of preventing damage, and turning to promoting achievement."

HUGE ATTAINMENT GAPS

In comparing the current educational attainment of young Latinos and those of other ethnic groups and whites, the report notes that Latinos lag significantly on three indicators:

- The percentage of Hispanics who fail to receive a high-school diploma is almost three times the rate found among whites, and almost twice that of blacks. They also tend to drop out much earlier. In 1988, more than half of Hispanic dropouts between the ages of 16 and 24 had not even completed the 9th grade, and 31 percent had not completed the 7th grade.
- Hispanics are more likely than blacks and far more likely than whites to be two or more grades behind in school; the percentage who were that far behind increased by several points between 1981 and 1986. By age 17, one in six Hispanic students is at least two years behind expected grade level, and two in five are one year behind.
- Only 7 percent of Hispanics who graduated from high school in 1980 had completed a four-year college degree by 1986, compared with 18 percent of black and 21 percent of white graduates.

Other statistics, however, including improvements in Hispanic test scores, give reason for optimism, according to the report's authors, Karen Pittman and Luis Duany. Ms. Pittman is director of educational improvement and adolescent-pregnancy prevention for the C.D.F.

HISPANIC CHARACTERISTICS

Although Hispanics share several common characteristics, the report says, there are significant differences in both the problems and progress of the major Hispanic subgroups: Mexican-Americans, Cuban-Americans, Puerto Ricans, Central and South Americans, and others.

Within each of these groups, it says, are major differences in characteristics such as place of birth, length of U.S. residence, English-language proficiency, and socioeconomic status.

"Popular theories [used to explain Hispanic underachievement]—including recent immigration and language barriers—may have far less impact than factors such as family poverty, low educational attainment of parents, or segregation in low-quality schools," it suggests.

Hispanic families are less likely than black families to exhibit characteristics linked with lower educational attainment, including living in poverty or having heads of households who are single or unemployed.

But Hispanic students are far more likely than whites or blacks to have undereducated parents, which is also considered a major factor influencing a child's educational progress. Forty percent of Hispanic household heads have less than nine years of schooling, compared with only about 10 percent among white and black families.

Another factor explaining Hispanic underachievement, according to the report, is the fact that Latinos are now more likely than black students to be attending predominantly minority schools. Such schools, it notes, tend to have less-experienced teachers and "watered down" curricula.

Cultural factors less easy to quantify may also play a role, it says.

"Some argue that the differences result from Latino adherence to cultural values that place women in the home, not in the college classroom or the workplace, and encourage young men to enter the work force as soon as possible," the authors write.   [1990]

Understanding the Reading

1. Why is the undereducation of Hispanic youth an important national issue?
2. What are the three indicators that reveal a Latino educational lag?
3. What characteristics are popularly used to account for Hispanic underachievement?
4. What factors are more likely to lead to Latino underachievement?

Suggestion for Responding

The Children's Defense Fund believes that the undereducation of Latino children is a critical issue. Explain their position and argue for or against it. ✦

89

Why CIBC Is Dealing With Homophobia

NATIONAL PTA AND THE COUNCIL ON INTERRACIAL BOOKS FOR CHILDREN

Phobia is defined in Webster's dictionary as "an exaggerated and often disabling fear." "Homophobia" [may] not yet [be] found in [all] dictionaries, but its meaning is clear—a fear and hatred of homosexuals. CIBC has prepared this special *Bulletin* on homophobia and education for three reasons: First, homophobia oppresses at least one-tenth of our population, and we feel that education should be a vehicle for counteracting *all* forms of oppression. Second, homophobia is the ultimate weapon in reinforcing rigid sex-role conformity, and we believe that sex-role conformity oppresses all females and limits male options as well. Third, young people are generally appallingly misinformed about homosexuality, whereas education should provide accurate information about realities in this world.

1. **Homophobia and oppression:** Gay men and lesbians—approximately one out of every ten people, according to current research—face discrimination, particularly in jobs and housing. They also face name-calling, taunting, hatred and violence. Much of the violence is carried out by groups of fourteen- to nineteen-year-olds, and such violence is escalating sharply. Attacks by young people represent a clear failure of our schools and other social institutions to educate against violence and against homophobia.

Educators committed to "justice for all" and human rights need to examine their own responsibilities in this situation. There are children in almost every classroom who are gay or lesbian. Many children have gay or lesbian parents. These children need support and protection. Other targets of societal oppression, such as children of color or children with disabilities, can count on support from their family and community. Few gay children have any support or guidance. While gay teachers could offer guidance and serve as reassuring role models for these youngsters, most gay teachers cannot risk "coming out"[1] for fear of losing their jobs. It is the responsibility of non-gay teachers to help gay students —and to help their gay colleagues—by working to counteract heterosexism in their school. . . . [H]eterosexism is a belief in the inherent superiority of one pattern of loving over all others and thereby its right to dominance.

2. **Homophobia and sex-role conformity:** The second reason for educators to deal with this topic is that homophobia serves to reinforce rigid sex-role behaviors. Boys who fail to display prescribed "masculine" traits are called "sissy"—even before kindergarten, and any child will define a sissy as someone who is fearful, a crybaby or who "acts like a girl." Later they're called "fag." The fear of such name-calling makes boys toe the gender line and refrain from any display of caring and nurturing emotions. That fear also encourages them to develop aggressive, domineering behaviors.

Similarly, name-calling—from "tomboy" to "lezzie"—inhibits girls from developing their strengths or acting as equals to boys. Homophobia thus prevents the broadening of sex-role options. In fact, the women's movement is frequently attacked as "just a bunch of lesbians." This attack is calculated to make women toe the gender line. Until such time as non-gay people defend the rights and humanity of gay people and learn to shrug off homophobic labels, such name-calling will continue to oppress and inhibit everyone.

3. **Homophobia and misinformation:** CIBC's third reason for wanting to counteract homophobia in the classroom is that we believe all children—gay and non-gay—are entitled to honest information about sexuality or any other topic of relevance to their lives.

Educators can provide factual information to help counter the misinformation that promotes homophobia and to assist *all* children who are in the process of coming to terms with their sexuality.

It is important to note that those most actively involved in trying to prevent objective discussions of homosexuality are the same white right-wing fundamentalists who seek to prevent students from learning about racism, sexism, poverty and movements for social change. Norma Gabler, a leader of the white fundamentalist right's attack on textbooks, criticized a textbook discussion of homosexuality as being in "direct contradiction to the fact that God has identified this act as wrong regardless of the beliefs or actions of society about this abnormal relationship."

We must be wary of those who use religion to justify oppression. Similar arguments have been used to legitimize slavery, racial segregation, anti-Semitism and the domination of women by men. (It is also important to note that many religious groups advocate the civil rights of lesbians and gay men, and organized caucuses of different faiths are working towards increased rights for, and acceptance of, gays and lesbians within religious communities.)

To even raise the subject of homophobia in these pages, never mind in the classroom, is certain to elicit some outrage. Any consideration of homosexuality or heterosexism can often evoke profound fears and an insistence that homosexuality be rejected as "unnatural."

Our perception of what is "natural" is all too often a product of socialization. What has long been proscribed, legislated and condemned can come to be seen as "unnatural." It is instructive to note, for example, that homosexuality was considered "natural" in most European societies until the 13th century, when church and state began a concerted effort to declare it unnatural.

Before concluding, it is necessary to deal with the question of "proselytizing," since this concern is frequently raised when efforts are made to discuss homosexuality. Many educators (and this of course includes parents) fear that such discussions will somehow "lure" youngsters from heterosexuality. Many believe that being gay or lesbian is a matter of free choice—not of pre-determination. They imagine that they have the power to guide children to make the "proper"—that is, heterosexual—choice, and they do not want to be accused of influencing young people to become gay.

Though the direction of one's sexual activity *is* a matter of choice for a small percentage of adults, the majority of lesbians and gay men become aware that they are somehow "different" from the heterosexual "norm" when they are quite young. This awareness generally occurs in profoundly anti-gay social settings and in spite of a heterosexist society that "proselytizes" the superiority of heterosexuality and the inferiority of homosexuality. Given the pervasiveness of heterosexual influences (the media, the educational system, countless role models, etc.), the fact that lesbians and gay men succeed in discovering their identities at all provides a strong argument that sexual orientation is not influenced by "proselytizing."

To date, science has not determined how sexual orientation develops. We know only that homosexuality, like heterosexuality, has existed in all types of families, in all societies and cultures throughout history. (Asking why homosexuality develops is based on the heterosexist assumption that homosexuality is an "abnormality" with a specific cause or causes.) The evidence indicates that it is a difference—like left-handedness —and that it represents part of the range of human sexual affectional expression. For young people who are gay or lesbian, it is as much a "condition of their being" as the color of their skin, their gender or their age. CIBC believes that no one should be oppressed for their "condition of being."

If we truly intend to eliminate oppression and achieve human liberation, heterosexism and homophobia must be addressed. As in the struggle against racism and sexism, courage, commitment and integrity are required.   [1983]

Note

1. "COMING OUT": Making one's homosexuality known publicly.

Understanding the Reading

1. How does homophobia oppress gay men and lesbians?
2. How is it used to enforce gender-role conformity?
3. How do the National PTA and the CIBC editors answer those who object to discussing sexuality and homosexuality in the classroom?

4. What steps have they undertaken to effect change, and what ones have they not yet taken to achieve their goals?

Suggestions for Responding

1. Do you think homosexuality should be discussed in school? Why or why not?
2. Identify and analyze a social problem that you feel requires action. ✦

90

Diversity and Its Discontents

ARTURO MADRID

My name is Arturo Madrid. I am a citizen of the United States, as are my parents and as were my grandparents and my great-grandparents. My ancestors' presence in what is now the United States antedates Plymouth Rock, even without taking into account any American Indian heritage I might have.

I do not, however, fit those mental sets that define America and Americans. My physical appearance, my speech patterns, my name, my profession (a professor of Spanish) create a text that confuses the reader. My normal experience is to be asked, "And where are *you* from?" My response depends on my mood. Passive-aggressive, I answer, "From here." Aggressive-passive, I ask, "Do you mean where I am originally from?" But ultimately my answer to those follow-up questions that will ask about origins will be that we have always been from here.

Overcoming my resentment I try to educate, knowing that nine times out of ten my words fall on inattentive ears. I have spent most of my adult life explaining who I am not. I am exotic, but—as Richard Rodriguez of *Hunger of Memory* fame so painfully found out—not exotic enough . . . not Peruvian, or Pakistani, or whatever. I am, however, very clearly the *other*, if only your everyday, garden-variety, domestic *other*. I will share with you another phenomenon that I have been a part of, that of being a missing person, and how I

came late to that awareness. But I've always known that I was the *other*, even before I knew the vocabulary or understood the significance of otherness.

I grew up in an isolated and historically marginal part of the United States, a small mountain village in the state of New Mexico, the eldest child of parents native to that region, whose ancestors had always lived there. In those vast and empty spaces people who look like me, speak as I do, and have names like mine predominate. But the *americanos* lived among us: the descendants of those nineteenth-century immigrants who dispossessed us of our lands; missionaries who came to convert us and stayed to live among us; artists who became enchanted with our land and humanscape and went native; refugees from unhealthy climes, crowded spaces, unpleasant circumstances; and, of course, the inhabitants of Los Alamos,[1] whose sociocultural distance from us was accentuated by the fact that they occupied a space removed from and proscribed to us. More importantly, however, they—*los americanos*—were omnipresent (and almost exclusively so) in newspapers, newsmagazines, books, on radio, in movies, and, ultimately, on television.

Despite the operating myth of the day, school did not erase my otherness. It did try to deny it, and in doing so only accentuated it. To this day what takes place in schools is more socialization than education, but when I was in elementary school—and given where I was—socialization was everything. School was where one became an American, because there was a pervasive and systematic denial by the society that surrounded us that we were Americans. That denial was both explicit and implicit.

Quite beyond saluting the flag and pledging allegiance to it (a very intense and meaningful action, given that the United States was involved in a war and our brothers, cousins, uncles, and fathers were on the frontlines), becoming American was learning English, and its corollary: not speaking Spanish. Until very recently ours was a proscribed language, either *de jure*—by rule, by policy, by law—or *de facto*—by practice, implicitly if not explicitly, through social and political and economic pressure. I do not argue that learning English was not appropriate. On the contrary. Like it or not, and we had no basis to make any judgments on that matter, we were Americans by virtue of having been born Americans and English was the common language of Americans. And there was a myth, a pervasive myth, to the effect that if only we learned to speak English well—and particularly without an accent—we would be welcomed into the American fellowship.

Sam Hayakawa[2] and the official English movement folks notwithstanding, the true text was not our speech, but rather our names and our appearance, for we would always have an accent, however perfect our pronunciation, however excellent our enunciation, however divine our diction. That accent would be heard in our pigmentation, our physiognomy, our names. We were, in short, the *other*.

Being the *other* involves contradictory phenomena. On the one hand being the *other* frequently means being invisible. Ralph Ellison wrote eloquently about that experience in his magisterial novel, *Invisible Man*. On the other hand, being the *other* sometimes involves sticking out like a sore thumb. What is she/he doing here?

For some of us being the *other* is only annoying; for others it is debilitating; for still others it is damning. Many try to flee otherness by taking on protective colorations that provide invisibility, whether of dress or speech or manner or name. Only a fortunate few succeed. For the majority of us otherness is permanently sealed by physical appearance. For the rest, otherness is betrayed by ways of being, speaking, or doing.

The first half of my life I spent downplaying the significance and consequences of otherness. The second half has seen me wrestling to understand its complex and deeply ingrained realities; striving to fathom why otherness denies us a voice or visibility or validity in American society and its institutions; struggling to make otherness familiar, reasonable, even normal to my fellow Americans.

I spoke earlier of another phenomenon that I am a part of: that of being a missing person. Growing up in northern New Mexico I had only a slight sense of us being missing persons. *Hispanos,* as we called (and call) ourselves in New Mexico, were very much a part of the fabric of the society, and there were *hispano* professionals everywhere about me: doctors, lawyers, schoolteachers, and administrators. My people owned

businesses, ran organizations, and were both appointed and elected public officials.

My awareness of our absence from the larger institutional life of the society became sharper when I went off to college, but even then it was attenuated by the circumstances of history and geography. The demography of Albuquerque still strongly reflected its historical and cultural origins, despite the influx of Midwesterners and Easterners. Moreover, many of my classmates at the University of New Mexico were *hispanos,* and even some of my professors. I thought that would obtain at UCLA, where I began graduate studies in 1960. Los Angeles had a very large Mexican population and that population was visible even in and around Westwood and on the campus. Many of the groundskeepers and food-service personnel at UCLA were Mexican. But Mexican-American students were few and mostly invisible, and I do not recall seeing or knowing a single Mexican-American (or, for that matter, African-American, Asian, or American Indian) professional on the staff or faculty of that institution during the five years I was there. Needless to say, people like me were not present in any capacity at Dartmouth College, the site of my first teaching appointment, and of course were not even part of the institutional or individual mind-set. I knew then that we—a we that had come to encompass American Indians, Asian-Americans, African-Americans, Puerto Ricans, and women—were truly missing persons in American institutional life.

Over the past three decades the *de jure* and *de facto* types of segregation that have historically characterized American institutions have been under assault. As a consequence, minorities and women have become part of American institutional life. Although there are still many areas where we are not to be found, the missing persons phenomenon is not as pervasive as it once was. However, the presence of the *other,* particularly minorities, in institutions and in institutional life resembles what we call in Spanish a *flor de tierra* (a surface phenomenon): we are spare plants whose roots do not go deep, vulnerable to inclemencies of an economic, or political, or social nature.

Our entrance into and our status in institutional life are not unlike a scenario set forth by my grandmother's pastor when she informed him that she and her family were leaving their mountain village to relocate to the Rio Grande Valley. When he asked her to promise that she would remain true to the faith and continue to involve herself in it, she asked why he thought she would do otherwise. "Doña Trinidad," he told her, "in the Valley there is no Spanish church. There is only an American church." "But," she protested, "I read and speak English and would be able to worship there." The pastor responded, "It is possible that they will not admit you, and even if they do, they might not accept you. And that is why I want you to promise me that you are going to go to church. Because if they don't let you in through the front door, I want you to go in through the back door. And if you can't get in through the back door, go in the side door. And if you are unable to enter through the side door I want you to go in through the window. What is important is that you enter and stay."

Some of us entered institutional life through the front door; others through the back door; and still others through side doors. Many, if not most of us, came in through windows, and continue to come in through windows. Of those who entered through the front door, some never made it past the lobby; others were ushered into corners and niches. Those who entered through back and side doors inevitably have remained in back and side rooms. And those who entered through windows found enclosures built around them. For, despite the lip service given to the goal of the integration of minorities into institutional life, what has frequently occurred instead is ghettoization, marginalization, isolation.

Not only have the entry points been limited, but in addition the dynamics have been singularly conflictive. Gaining entry and its corollary, gaining space, have frequently come as a consequence of demands made on institutions and institutional officers. Rather than entering institutions more or less passively, minorities have of necessity entered them actively, even aggressively. Rather than waiting to receive, they have demanded. Institutional relations have thus been adversarial, infused with specific and generalized tensions.

The nature of the entrance and the nature of the space occupied have greatly influenced the view and attitude of the majority population within those institutions. All of us are put into the same box; that is, no matter what the individual reality, the assessment of the individual is inevitably conditioned by a perception that is held of the class. Whatever our history, whatever our record, whatever our validations, whatever our accomplishments, by and large we are perceived unidimensionally and dealt with accordingly. I remember an experience I had in this regard, atypical only in its explicitness. A few years ago I allowed myself to be persuaded to seek the presidency of a well-known state university. I was invited for an interview and presented myself before the selection committee, which included members of the board of trustees. The opening question of that brief but memorable interview was directed at me by a member of that august body. "Dr. Madrid," he asked, "why does a one-dimensional person like you think he can be the president of a multidimensional institution like ours?"

Over the past four decades America's demography has undergone significant changes. Since 1965 the principal demographic growth we have experienced in the United States has been of peoples whose national origins are non-European. This population growth has occurred both through birth and through immigration. A few years ago discussion of the national birthrate had a scare dimension: the high—"inordinately high"—birthrate of the Hispanic population. The popular discourse was informed by words such as "breeding." Several years later, as a consequence of careful tracking by government agencies, we now know that what has happened is that the birthrate of the majority population has decreased. When viewed historically and comparatively, the minority populations (for the most part) have also had a decline in birthrate, but not one as great as that of the majority.

There are additional demographic changes that should give us something to think about. African-Americans are now to be found in significant numbers in every major urban center in the nation. Hispanic-Americans now number over 15 million people, and although they are a regionally concentrated (and highly urbanized) population, there is a Hispanic community in almost every major urban center of the United States. American Indians, heretofore a small and rural population, are increasingly more numerous and urban. The Asian-American population, which has historically consisted of small and concentrated communities of Chinese-, Filipino-, and

Japanese-Americans, has doubled over the past decade, its complexion changed by the addition of Cambodians, Koreans, Hmongs, Vietnamese, et al.

Prior to the Immigration Act of 1965,[3] 69 percent of immigration was from Europe. By far the largest number of immigrants to the United States since 1965 have been from the Americas and from Asia: 34 percent are from Asia; another 34 percent are from Central and South America; 16 percent are from Europe; 10 percent are from the Caribbean; the remaining 6 percent are from other continents and Canada. As was the case with previous immigration waves, the current one consists principally of young people: 60 percent are between the ages of 16 and 44. Thus, for the next few decades, we will continue to see a growth in the percentage of non-European-origin Americans as compared to European-Americans.

To sum up, we now live in one of the most demographically diverse nations in the world, and one that is increasingly more so.

During the same period social and economic change seems to have accelerated. Who would have imagined at mid-century that the prototypical middle-class family (working husband, wife as homemaker, two children) would for all intents and purposes disappear? Who could have anticipated the rise in teenage pregnancies, children in poverty, drug use? Who among us understood the implications of an aging population?

We live in an age of continuous and intense change, a world in which what held true yesterday does not today, and certainly will not tomorrow. What change does, moreover, is bring about even more change. The only constant we have at this point in our national development is change. And change is threatening. The older we get the more likely we are to be anxious about change, and the greater our desire to maintain the status quo.

Evident in our public life is a fear of change, whether economic or moral. Some who fear change are responsive to the call of economic protectionism, others to the message of moral protectionism. Parenthetically, I have referred to the movement to require more of students without in turn giving them more as academic protectionism. And the pronouncements of E. D. Hirsch and Allan Bloom[4] are, I believe, informed by intellectual protectionism. Much more serious,

however, is the dark side of the populism[5] which underlies this evergoing protectionism—the resentment of the *other*. An excellent and fascinating example of that aspect of populism is the cry for linguistic protectionism—for making English the official language of the United States. And who among us is unaware of the tensions that underlie immigration reform, of the underside of demographic protectionism?

A matter of increasing concern is whether this new protectionism, and the mistrust of the *other* which accompanies it, is not making more significant inroads than we have supposed in higher education. Specifically, I wish to discuss the question of whether a goal (quality) and a reality (demographic diversity) have been erroneously placed in conflict, and, if so, what problems this perception of conflict might present.

As part of my scholarship I turn to dictionaries for both origins and meanings of words. Quality, according to the *Oxford English Dictionary,* has multiple meanings. One set defines quality as being an essential character, a distinctive and inherent feature. A second describes it as a degree of excellence, of conformity to standards, as superiority in kind. A third makes reference to social status, particularly to persons of high social status. A fourth talks about quality as being a special or distinguishing attribute, as being a desirable trait. Quality is highly desirable in both principle and practice. We all aspire to it in our own person, in our experiences, in our acquisitions and products, and of course we all want to be associated with people and operations of quality.

But let us move away from the various dictionary meanings of the word and to our own sense of what it represents and of how we feel about it. First of all we consider quality to be finite; that is, it is limited with respect to quantity; it has very few manifestations; it is not widely distributed. I have it and you have it, but they don't. We associate quality with homogeneity, with uniformity, with standardization, with order, regularity, neatness. All too often we equate it with smoothness, glibness, slickness, elegance. Certainly it is always expensive. We tend to identify it with those who lead, with the rich and famous. And, when you come right down to it, it's inherent. Either you've got or you ain't.

Diversity, from the Latin *divertere,* meaning to

turn aside, to go different ways, to differ, is the condition of being different or having differences, is an instance of being different. Its companion word, diverse, means differing, unlike, distinct; having or capable of having various forms; composed of unlike or distinct elements. Diversity is lack of standardization, of regularity, of orderliness, homogeneity, conformity, uniformity. Diversity introduces complications, is difficult to organize, is troublesome to manage, is problematical. Diversity is irregular, disorderly, uneven, rough. The way we use the word diversity gives us away. Something is too diverse, is extremely diverse. We want a little diversity.

When we talk about diversity, we are talking about the *other,* whatever that other might be: someone of different gender, race, class, national origin; somebody at a greater or lesser distance from the norm; someone outside the set; someone who possesses a different set of characteristics, features, or attributes; someone who does not fall within the taxonomies we use daily and with which we are comfortable; someone who does not fit into the mental configurations that give our lives order and meaning.

In short, diversity is desirable only in principle, not in practice. Long live diversity . . . as long as it conforms to my standards, my mind set, my view of life, my sense of order. We desire, we like, we admire diversity, not unlike the way the French (and others) appreciate women; that is, *Vive la différence!*—as long as it stays in its place.

What I find paradoxical about and lacking in this debate is that diversity is the natural order of things. Evolution produces diversity. Margaret Visser, writing about food in her latest book, *Much Depends on Dinner,* makes an eloquent statement in this regard:

> Machines like, demand, and produce uniformity. But nature loathes it: her strength lies in multiplicity and in differences. Sameness in biology means fewer possibilities and therefore weakness.

The United States, by its very nature, by its very development, is the essence of diversity. It is diverse in its geography, population, institutions, technology; its social, cultural, and intellectual modes. It is a society that at its best does not consider quality to be monolithic in form or finite in quantity, or to be inherent in class. Quality in our society proceeds in large measure out of the stimulus of diverse modes of thinking and act-ing; out of the creativity made possible by the different ways in which we approach things; out of diversion from paths or modes hallowed by tradition.

One of the principal strengths of our society is its ability to address, on a continuing and substantive basis, the real economic, political, and social problems that have faced and continue to face us. What makes the United States so attractive to immigrants is the protections and opportunities it offers; what keeps our society together is tolerance for cultural, religious, social, political, and even linguistic difference; what makes us a unique, dynamic, and extraordinary nation is the power and creativity of our diversity.

The true history of the United States is one of struggle against intolerance, against oppression, against xenophobia, against those forces that have prohibited persons from participating in the larger life of the society on the basis of their race, their gender, their religion, their national origin, their linguistic and cultural background. These phenomena are not consigned to the past. They remain with us and frequently take on virulent dimensions.

If you believe, as I do, that the well-being of a society is directly related to the degree and extent to which all of its citizens participate in its institutions, then you will have to agree that we have a challenge before us. In view of the extraordinary changes that are taking place in our society we need to take up the struggle again, irritating, grating, troublesome, unfashionable, unpleasant as it is. As educated and educator members of this society we have a special responsibility for ensuring that all American institutions, not just our elementary and secondary schools, our juvenile halls, or our jails, reflect the diversity of our society. Not to do so is to risk greater alienation on the part of a growing segment of our society; is to risk increased social tension in an already conflictive world; and, ultimately, is to risk the survival of a range of institutions that, for all their defects and deficiencies, provide us the opportunity and the freedom to improve our individual and collective lot.

Let me urge you to reflect on these two words—quality and diversity—and on the mental sets and behaviors that flow out of them. And let me urge you further to struggle against the notion that quality is finite in quantity, limited in its manifestations, or is restricted by considerations of class, gender, race, or national origin; or that quality manifests itself only in leaders and not in followers, in managers and not in workers, in breeders and not in drones; or that it has to be associated with verbal agility or elegance of personal style; or that it cannot be seeded, nurtured, or developed.

Because diversity—the *other*—is among us, will define and determine our lives in ways that we still do not fully appreciate, whether that other is women (no longer bound by tradition, house, and family); or Asians, African-Americans, Indians, and Hispanics (no longer invisible, regional, or marginal); or our newest immigrants (no longer distant, exotic, alien). Given the changing profile of America, will we come to terms with diversity in our personal and professional lives? Will we begin to recognize the diverse forms that quality can take? If so, we will thus initiate the process of making quality limitless in its manifestations, infinite in quantity, unrestricted with respect to its origins, and more importantly, virulently contagious.

I hope we will. And that we will further join together to expand—not to close—the circle.

[1990]

Notes

1. LOS ALAMOS: The military installation where scientists developed the atomic bomb.
2. SAM HAYAKAWA: The former chancellor of the University of California at Berkeley and an outspoken opponent of bilingual education.
3. IMMIGRATION ACT OF 1965: A federal law that abolished the national-origins quota system of immigration.
4. E. D. HIRSCH AND ALLAN BLOOM: Authors, respectively, of *Cultural Illiteracy* and *The Closing of the American Mind,* both of which advocate a traditional curriculum.
5. POPULISM: A political philosophy that gives primacy to the needs of common people.

Understanding the Reading

1. Why does Madrid resent being asked where he is from?
2. What does he mean by being "other"?
3. What does he mean by referring to himself as "invisible" or a "missing person"?

4. What is the distinction between a school's erasing otherness and denying it?
5. Why did his grandmother's pastor feel that it was important for her to enter the church and stay?
6. What does Madrid mean by saying he is perceived unidimensionally?
7. Why does he find "breeding" an offensive term?
8. What point is Madrid making by giving the various dictionary meanings of "quality" and "diversity"?

Suggestion for Responding

Do you agree or disagree with Madrid that diversity is the basis for the "quality" of the United States? Why? •

91

The Push for Power

ELOISE SALHOLZ

It will be months before demographers at the Census Bureau produce their portrait of who we are in the waning years of the American Century. But when the results from the 1990 count are finally in, one statistic should come as no surprise: the number of Hispanics—the nation's fastest-growing group—could be approaching 25 million, or 10 percent of the total U.S. population. Latino leaders say the census will be their community's ticket to fuller participation in American life than ever before. It seems all the more ironic, then, that the forms arriving in mailboxes across the country recently were printed only in English—another reminder that, despite their vast legions, Hispanics remain an invisible minority.

Latinos were poised to make their mark once before. "The 1980s will be the decade of the Hispanics," declared Raúl Yzaguirre, president of the National Council of La Raza, in 1978. Pollsters predicted that Hispanics would soon become a "voting time bomb." But a dozen years later, Latinos have proved largely incapable of translating their numeric strength into political and economic clout. Today Yzaguirre says, "If anything, we retrogressed in the '80s." Reagan-era cutbacks and recession pushed many Hispanics deep into poverty, while the conservative social climate permitted passage of "English Only" laws aimed at Spanish speakers. Last week, a report from Congress's General Accounting Office confirmed what Hispanics have been saying for years: the landmark 1986 immigration law,[1] which penalized employers of illegal aliens, has produced a widespread "pattern of discrimination" against job applicants with a "foreign appearance or accent"—even citizens and green-card[2] holders.

Disappointed by their lack of progress in the last decade, Hispanics are now determined to salvage the 1990s. Activists have adopted a grassroots strategy that has already led to successes in school reform and political redistricting. The Latino leadership is looking ahead to 1992, the 500th anniversary of Columbus's discovery of the Americas. The date holds great emotional significance for Spanish-speaking Americans, and activists hope it will lure diverse Hispanics—from cosmopolitan Miami and inner-city barrios to the planting fields of California—under a single political and cultural umbrella.

But the forces that made the "decade of the Hispanics" a nonevent continue to vex the Latino community. The first problem is one of definition. The term Hispanic is an imposed label, and remains more convenient than precise: it includes Mexicans, Cubans, Puerto Ricans and others who, apart from speaking Spanish, often have little in common. And the black-white dichotomy that characterizes American thinking on minorities leaves little room for Latino concerns.

Though Latinos have had a continuous presence in this country for centuries, they have been slow to gain recognition. "Hispanic" appeared as a census term only in 1980. Relative to their numbers, they remain seriously underrepresented—there are no Hispanic senators and only 10 congressmen. A 1989 study by the Southwest Voter Registration Education Project found that Latinos vote less, attend fewer political rallies and make fewer campaign contributions than other Americans. One reason is the extreme youth of the population. Young people generally are relatively uninvolved politically; with a median age of 25, many Hispanics are also simply too young to vote. And unlike blacks, whose churches and organizations provided an institutional base

for the fight against segregation, Hispanics have lacked a political superstructure and a common enemy.

The few attempts at putting together a national platform have proved ineffective. In 1987, political and corporate leaders headed by Henry Cisneros, then the mayor of San Antonio, Texas, presented the presidential candidates with a National Hispanic Agenda. Although the document drew attention to concerns about employment, education and housing, the group proved somewhat ineffectual on account of bickering between Mexican-Americans and Puerto Ricans. Because Mexicans represent more than 60 percent of the Hispanic population, committee members felt they should have greater control over the document. In general, the nation's various Hispanic groups have complained about having to compete for attention and scarce government and philanthropic funds.

To be sure, Latinos have made some impressive strides on the local level: they have won elections in many predominantly Spanish-speaking areas and were crucial to the victory of Harold Washington in Chicago and, more recently, David Dinkins in New York. But there hasn't yet been a break-through, national leader. Latino political aspirations suffered a serious setback in the fall of 1988, when Cisneros announced he wouldn't seek re-election, then confessed to an extramarital affair with a political fund raiser (he is still married and living with his wife). Cisneros, 42, once touted as a Democratic vice presidential candidate in 1984, had been the ethnic group's great hope. As it happened, polls a month after the scandal showed only a slight drop in his popularity and he remains, says Hispanic Rep. Bill Richardson, "our most logical leader." But his temporary fall from grace was unsettling. "There is no savior that will lead the Latino community to some political, economic and social promised land," says Segundo Mercado-Llorens, a labor official in Washington. "It depends upon a community of leaders who work together."

Latino talent: From New York to California, a new generation of Latino talent has emerged. Meanwhile, local leaders have set their sights close to home. "Hispanics are going to galvanize around a set of issues more than race," says Daniel Solis, head of Chicago's United Neighborhood Organization (UNO). "And because we're made up of different nationalities and different opinions, we're being forced to do it the hard way—at the grass-roots level, with local institutions." Hispanics are being elected in growing numbers to city councils and school boards—or, as one activist put it, the "front line of democracy."

Last year's school fight in Chicago, which is more than 20 percent Hispanic, illustrates the new grass-roots strategy. Angry over the city's appalling public education, busloads of Hispanics descended on the state capitol with a reform plan centered on greater parental control. They proceeded to win nearly 25 percent of the seats on newly created parent councils. Partly as a result of their efforts, some 50 principals lost their jobs. In a key legal victory, the Texas Supreme Court last year ordered a more equitable distribution of school funding—a decision that will be an automatic boost to Hispanics.

Latino leaders are now vesting their hopes for the future in the 1990 census. A vast increase in the population should bring Hispanics new funds and additional political representation. Because the 1980 census resulted in a large undercount of Hispanics—perhaps 10 percent—a number of activists have formed a program called Hágase Contar (Make Yourself Count) to ensure a more accurate picture. They have their work cut out for them. Spanish speakers have to call to request a form in their native tongue. That alone could discourage Hispanics from participating in the count.

Up for grabs: Time and numbers may be on the side of Latinos as they sail toward the 1992 anniversary. Voter registration climbed 21 percent from 1984 to 1988. At the same time, voter turnout has dropped slightly. Hispanic organizers attribute the decline to the difficulty of keeping up with a 25 percent increase in the voting-age population, though political consultants wonder whether they simply can't get out the vote. In the coming decade, some 5 million Hispanics will become eligible for citizenship, thanks in part to the amnesty program that granted legal residency to undocumented immigrants who had lived in the United States for five years. Both the Democrats and the GOP have strengthened their outreach programs to win Hispanic votes, which are viewed as being up for grabs.

But Hispanic leaders have failed to galvanize their armies before. The '90s will be a make-or-break test of their political maturity. "We either get this nation's attention," says Elaine Coronado, Quincentennial Commission director, "or we continue being perceived as a second-rate minority group." Says Cisneros: "We don't want to ever look at a decade again and say, 'Where did it go?'"   [1990]

Notes

1. 1986 IMMIGRATION LAW: A federal law providing residency to illegal aliens who could prove they had resided in the United States for at least five years; it also made it illegal for employers to employ undocumented workers.
2. GREEN CARD: A government permit allowing an alien to be employed.

Understanding the Reading

1. In what ways have Hispanics "retrogressed in the '80s"?
2. Why has it been difficult for Latinos to organize themselves politically?
3. What actions are they taking to increase their political clout?

Suggestions for Responding

1. What can Latinos do to make themselves more central to the American political system?
2. Describe what you feel would be a desirable outcome for the social problem you analyzed in response to the CIBC reading. ◆

92

Going Public With Our Vision

CHARLOTTE BUNCH

TRANSFORMATIONAL
POLITICS AND PRACTICAL VISIONS

To bring the feminist vision to bear on all issues and to counter the right-wing agenda for the future, require that we engage in multiple strategies for action. We must work on many fronts at once. If a movement becomes a single issue or single strategy, it runs the danger of losing its overall vision and diminishing its support, since different classes of people feel most intensely the pressure of different issues. So while we may say at any given moment that one issue is particularly crucial, it is important that work be done on other aspects of the changes we need at the same time. The task is not finding "the right issue," but bringing clear political analysis to each issue showing how it connects to other problems and to a broad-based feminist view of change in society.

Feminist concerns are not isolated, and oppression does not happen one-by-one-by-one in separate categories. I don't experience homophobia as a separate and distinct category from economic discrimination as a woman. I don't view racism as unconnected to militarism and patriarchal domination of the world.

In order to discuss the specific strategies necessary to get through this transition and bring feminism into the public arena more forcefully, we must first be clear that feminism is a transformational politics. As such, feminism brings a perspective to *any* issue and cannot and must not be limited to a separate ghetto called "women's issues." When dealing with any issue, whether it is budgets or biogenetics or wife battering, feminism as a political perspective is about change in structures—about ending domination and resisting oppression. Feminism is not just incorporating women into existing institutions.

As a politics of transformation, feminism is also relevant to more than a constituency of women. Feminism is a vision born of women that we must offer to and demand of men. I'm tired of letting men off the hook by saying that we don't know whether they can be feminists. Of course they can struggle to be feminists, just as I can and must struggle to be antiracist. If feminism is to be a transforming perspective in the world, then men must also be challenged by it.

This does not mean that we do not also need spaces and organizations for women only. Women need and want and have the right to places where we gather strength and celebrate our culture and make plans only with women. But as a political vision, feminism addresses the future for men as well as for women, for boys as well as for girls, and we must be clear that it is a

politics for the future of the world, not just for an isolated handful of the converted.

If we are clear about feminism as a transformational politics, we can develop viable public alternatives to Reaganism and all patriarchal policies. These would be policy statements of how we think the world could be organized in various areas if a feminist approach is taken.

We need feminist budgets for every town, state, and nation. For example, you could take the state budget in Montana, whatever it is, take the same amount of money and prepare a budget of how you would reorganize the use of that money if feminists had control of the state government. When you finish that one, you can do a federal budget. And when you finish that, take on the UN budget! Budgets are good indicators of priorities. If we publicized our approaches, people could see that there are alternatives, that we are talking about something different, and they would get a clearer idea of what a feminist perspective means in practical terms.

I would also like to see feminist plans for housing, transportation, criminal justice, child care, education, agriculture, and so on. We need serious discussion as feminists about how we deal with the issues of defense, not only by doing critiques of militarism, but also by deciding how to cope with the competing powers and threats in this world, as they exist right now. We're not going to solve many of the problems immediately, but we have to put forward other policies and practices, so people can see the difference. If we start with how things are now, then we can talk about how to move, step-by-step, toward policies that are based on very different assumptions and values.

To use such feminist policy statements, when we engage in electoral politics for example, would give people a clear and public statement of what it means to elect a feminist. We would also have something concrete to hold a candidate accountable to after election. To work to elect feminists with clear policy content makes a campaign focus on feminism as a transforming politics rather than just on personality or on adding women without clear political statements of what they represent. It can make electoral politics part of a strategy for change rather than isolated from the movement or a substitute for other action.

Developing such policies is particularly

important now because the Reagan crowd is also about a "revolution" in social policies. We could call it reactionary, but if revolution means massive change in government policies, that is what Reagan is pulling off right now. We need a creative counter to these policy changes that is not just a return to where we were in the past. We have to put forward approaches that both deal with the problems that we had before Reagan, and reveal the antiwoman, patriarchal, racist, and sexist assumptions of the right wing.

ORGANIZING FOR ACTION

Perhaps the most important thing that we need to do which underlies everything I've said, is organize. Organize. Organize. Organize. All the great ideas in the world, even feminist budgets, will mean little if we don't also organize people to act on them. We have to organize in a variety of ways.

We need to take what has been the decentralized strength of the women's movement—a multitude of separate women's projects and individuals whose lives have been radically affected by feminism—and find lasting forms for bringing that to more political power. The feminist movement has a wonderful array of creative small groups and projects. Nevertheless, when these don't have any voice in something larger, a lot of their potential power is lost simply because what is learned and done is limited to a small circle and has no larger outlet to affect the public. I don't want to abandon the small-group approach to working, but those groups need to band together into larger units that can have a political impact beyond their numbers. This can take the form of citywide or issue-based alliances, which still preserve each group's autonomy. Such feminist alliances then become the basis for coalitions—as a feminist force—with other progressive groups. If we organize ourselves to join coalitions as a community, rather than having women going into other groups one by one, we have a better chance of keeping our feminist values and perspectives in the forefront of that coalition work.

We can utilize the grass-roots decentralized nature of feminism well in organizing around policy changes today, because it is at the state and local level where most of the battles with the right wing are presently focused. But to do that effectively we have to learn how to get our supporters out—to be visible about their politics. If we are trying to influence policy, the policymakers must know that our people are reliable; if we say that a hundred thousand women will be in Washington, D.C., or a thousand in Billings, Montana, they have to know that they will be there.

The agenda for change is often set by the kind of organizing that goes on around specific issues—particularly ones that are very visible and of considerable interest to people, such as reproductive rights or the Family Protection Act.[1] Whatever the issue, as long as it is one that affects people's lives, the task of the organizer is to show how it connects to other issues of oppression, such as racism, and also to illustrate what that issue means in terms of a vision for the future. The Family Protection Act has demonstrated well these connections as its supporters have sought to bring back the patriarchal order through policies against gays, against assistance to battered women and children, against freedom in the schools, and against the organizing of workers into unions, and so on. It provides a clear case for discussing feminist versus antifeminist perspectives on life.

Another task of organizers is to devise strategies to activate people who care, but who aren't politically active. I saw a chain letter circulating among women artists, which instead of having people send a dollar, said: "Write a letter to Senator So and So (participating in the hearings on abortion), and then send this letter to eight of your friends who want reproductive rights but who aren't doing anything about it."

One mistake we often make is to act as if there is nothing that supporters can do politically if they can't be activists twenty-four hours a day, seven days a week. We must provide channels of action for people who have ten minutes a day or an hour a week, because that very action ties them closer to caring and being willing to risk or move toward a feminist vision. We must mobilize the constituency we have of concerned individuals, recognizing that many of them are very busy just trying to survive and care for their children or parents.

One of Jerry Falwell's[2] organizations sends a little cardboard church to its local supporters, who deposit a quarter a day, and at the end of the week, they dump the money out and send it to Falwell. We can learn something from this approach, which provides a daily connection to one's supporters. When I see community resources—health clinics, women's centers, whatever—closing because they're no longer getting outside support, I worry about our connections to our supporters. This movement did not start with government money. This movement started in the streets and it started with the support of women, and it can only survive if it is supported by us.

I have no objections to feminists getting government money or applying for grants as long as we remember that when they don't give us the money, we have to figure out other ways to do what has to be done by ourselves. We have to go back to our own resources if we believe in what we're doing. If the peasants of Latin America have supported the Catholic Church over the centuries, I don't see any reason why the feminists and gay men and lesbians of North America cannot support our movements.

COALITIONS: THE BOTTOM LINE

Coalitions with other progressive groups are important, but we must be clear about what makes them viable. The basis of coalitions is integrity and respect for what each group describes as its bottom line. Now that's not always easy. But with honest struggle over what each group feels is its necessary, critical minimum demand, coalitions can work. If we are to make compromises on where we put our time and energy, it has to be within that framework. Coalitions don't succeed simply for ideological or charitable reasons. They succeed out of a sense that we need each other, and that none of our constituencies can be mobilized effectively if we abandon their bottom-line concerns. Therefore, we have to know where the critical points are for each group in a coalition.

This is a difficult process, but I saw it work in Houston at the National Women's Conference[3] in 1977. As one of the people organizing the lesbian caucus, I can tell you there were moments in that process when I was ready to scream over the homophobia we encountered. But we knew our bottom line and were clear about what compromises we could and could not accept. If it had

been an event comprised only of feminists, we would have said more about lesbianism. But as a large, diverse conference, we saw our task as coalescing a critical mass recognition and support of the issue of sexual preference through working as part of the broad-based feminist coalition there.

In order to get this recognition, we had to organize our constituency so that other groups would want our support. We were clear that we would not support a compromise that left us out—that we had to have that mutual respect to make the coalition work. But the success of lesbians was based on the fact that we had organized at the state and local level as well as nationally. Our people were there and others knew we had the numbers. Many women realized that they had a lot more to gain by mobilizing our support for the overall plan by including us, than by alienating us, and creating a very public nuisance. Coalitions are possible, but they are only effective when you have mutual respect; when you have a clearly articulated bottom line; and when you have your own group mobilized for action. If you haven't got your own group organized, your own power base, when the crunch comes, no matter how politically correct or charitable people feel, they are going to align with the groups they feel will make them stronger.

We need more feminist alliances or coalitions that do not coalesce around only one event, but that establish themselves over time as representing a variety of groups and types of action, from electoral and media work to demonstrations or public education. Such ongoing political action groups are usually multi-issue and their strength lies in bringing groups together for concerted action on a city- or statewide basis. These groups then become a reliable basis for coalitions with other progressive organizations.

GOING PUBLIC

I think that it is crucial for the feminist movement to become more public. By going public, I mean we need to move beyond the boundaries of our subculture. This does not mean giving up the women's community, which remains our strength, our base, the roots of our analysis and of our sustenance. But to go more public in actions that are visible beyond our circles, demonstrating to the world that feminists have not rolled over and played dead as the media sometimes implies.

Going public involves statements about our visions for change. This can be through vehicles such as feminist policy statements on housing or the budget, as well as by demonstrating the passion of our visions with militancy, such as the civil disobedience and fasting women did in the struggle for ratification of the ERA.[4] Such actions make our issues dramatically visible, seen as matters of life and death. These also capture the public imagination and re-create some of that spirit of discovery that accompanied the early years of women's liberation. We need more creative community or media-oriented events that bring that instant recognition of what is at stake and inspire people to talk about those issues.

One of the important things that I remember about the early days of the women's movement is that we talked about feminism—incessantly. We talked in the laundromat, we talked on our jobs, we talked to everybody because we were so excited about what we were discovering. And that talk spread—it excited other women, whether they agreed with us or not. The primary method by which women have become feminists is through talk, through consciousness-raising, and through talk with other feminists. It was not through the government or even the media, but through ourselves. And they cannot take that away. They can deny us money, but they cannot take away ourselves, and the way that this movement has grown is through our "beings"—through being active in the world and being visible.

We have to go public by moving out of what may be comfortable places and engage with women who don't necessarily call themselves feminists. You can go public a hundred different ways—whether that is through media-oriented action or by talking to women on the job or at established women's places. In going public, we risk the vulnerability that goes with such interaction, but the rewards are worth it. The challenge to our ideas that comes with it enables us and our ideas to expand and be more inclusive and more powerful. The interaction that comes with seeing feminism in relation to situations that are not familiar to us, or seeing women of different class or race or geographic backgrounds taking feminism

in new directions, is a very good tonic for "tired feminists."

The growth of feminism depends precisely on this interaction—of different generations of feminists and of challenges that make our ideas change and go farther than when they started. If we believe that our visions are visions for the world and not just for a cult, then we have to risk them. For if our ideas cannot survive the test of being engaged in the world more broadly, more publicly, then feminism isn't developed enough yet, and that engagement will help us to know how to remold feminism and make it more viable. For if feminism is to be a force for change in the world, it too must grow and change; if we hoard it or try to hang onto it, we will only take it to the grave with us.

Going public with our visions is ultimately the only way that feminism can become a powerful force for change. There is no way that we can get more people wanting to be feminists and supporting and expanding our visions, if they can't even see them, if they never even hear about feminism from feminists rather than the media, and if they don't sense what we care about and believe in. To be seen as an alternative vision for the world, we first have to be seen. It's that simple and it's that important.

Another part of going public is coming out as feminists—in places where we might feel more comfortable not using the word or even discussing the ideas. An academic study has shown what movement activists have said for years—that the most effective counter to homophobia is "knowing one"—that is, people's antigay ideas change most when they realize that they know and care about someone who is gay. But this change would never occur if no one came out, and therefore most people could go on not realizing that they know one of "us" and accepting society's homophobia unchallenged.

"Coming out" as feminists has a similar power. It forces people to get beyond their media stereotypes and deal concretely with a feminist person and with ideas and visions as embodied by that person. Just as coming out for lesbians and gay men has to be decided on a personal basis, so too does coming out as a feminist. Still, it is important to recognize the political power of the personal action and to see that it is useful in advancing feminism and combating the power of the right wing, which includes the effort to intimidate us into going back into closets of fear and adopting apolitical life-styles.

Coming out and going public make it possible for us to communicate our feminist visions to people—the majority of whom I believe would welcome alternatives to the state of the world and have not necessarily accepted the right-wing's visions. They want alternatives to living behind closed doors in fear of violence on the streets and contamination in the air; they want decent work that does not destroy or demean them; they want to be able to affirm freedom and justice, but they may not believe that it is possible. We have to show them that we care about those same things and that our movement is about feminist struggles to create visions of new possibilities in the world, beginning with the struggle for possibilities for women and moving outward from there.

We need to invite people to join us in this struggle, approaching them with something to offer, rather than rejecting them as if they were enemies, or ignoring them as if they were not what we think they should be. If we invite them to join us in trying to become and create something different, we engage in politics as a process of seduction as well as of confrontation. Feminism must be a process of seeing and invoking the best in people as well as in confronting the worst. In this we may discover new ways of moving politically that will enable feminist visions to emerge and to provide the leadership so desperately needed to prevent the patriarchal militaristic destruction of the planet.

This is our challenge in the '80s. It is the particular moment that we have been given in human evolution and in the struggle between the forces of justice and domination. We are the inheritors of a proud and living tradition of creators, dreamers, resisters, and organizers who have engaged in the struggle before us, and we shall pass it on to the next generation. However long each of us lives, that's how much time we have, for this is a lifetime process and a lifetime commitment.   [1987]

Notes

1. FAMILY PROTECTION ACT: A 1981 Congressional bill to repeal federal laws that promote equal rights for women, including coeducational school-related activities and protection for battered wives, and providing tax incentives for married mothers to stay at home.
2. JERRY FALWELL: Founder of the Moral Majority, a conservative political organization.
3. NATIONAL WOMEN'S CONFERENCE: As part of the United Nations Decade for Women, each member country held a meeting to establish its national priorities for improving the status of women.
4. ERA: Equal Rights Amendment.

Understanding the Reading

1. Why does Bunch believe that feminism should not be limited to women's issues?
2. What does "transformational politics" mean?
3. List Bunch's strategies for achieving a feminist transformation.
4. What actions does she suggest?
5. What advantages does she see in "going public"?

Suggestion for Responding

Choose one strategy Bunch suggests, such as a feminist budget or coalition formation, and explore the social effects it could have. ✦

93

A Manifesto for Men

ANDREW KIMBRELL

As many of us come to mourn the lost fathers and sons of the last decades and seek to re-establish our ties to each other and to the earth, we need to find ways to change the political, social, and economic structures that have created this crisis. A "wild man" weekend in the woods, or intense man-to-man discussions, can be key experiences in self-discovery and personal empowerment. But these personal experiences are not enough to reverse the victimization of men. As the men's movement gathers strength, it is critical that this increasing sense of personal liberation be channeled into political action. Without significant changes in our society there will only be continued hopelessness and frustration for men. Moreover, a coordinated movement pressing for the liberation of men could be a key factor in ensuring that the struggle for a sustainable future for humanity and the earth succeeds.

What follows is a brief political platform for men, a short manifesto with which we can begin the process of organizing men as a positive political force working for a better future. This is the next step for the men's movement.

FATHERS AND CHILDREN

Political efforts focusing on the family must reassert men's bonds with the family and reverse the "lost father" syndrome. While any long-term plan for men's liberation requires significant changes in the very structure of our work and economic institutions, a number of intermediate steps are possible: We need to take a leadership role in supporting parental leave legislation, which gives working parents the right to take time from work to care for children or other family members. And we need to target the Bush administration for vetoing this vital legislation. Also needed is pro-child tax relief such as greatly expanding the young child tax credit, which would provide income relief and tax breaks to families at a point when children need the most parental care and when income may be the lowest.

We should also be in the forefront of the movement pushing for changes in the workplace including more flexible hours, part-time work, job sharing, and home-based employment. As economic analyst William R. Mattox Jr. notes, a simple step toward making home-based employment more viable would be to loosen restrictions on claiming home office expenses as a tax deduction for parents. Men must also work strenuously in the legal arena to promote more liberal visitation rights for non-custodial parents and to assert appropriateness of the father as a custodial parent. Non-traditional family structures should also be given more recognition in our society, with acknowledgment of men's important roles as stepfathers, foster fathers, uncles, brothers, and mentors. We must seek legislative ways to recognize many men's commitments that do not fit traditional definitions of family.

ECOLOGY AS MALE POLITICS

A sustainable environment is not merely one issue among others. It is the crux of all issues in our age, including men's politics. The ecological struggles of our time offer a unique forum in which men can express their renewed sense of the wild and their traditional roles as creators, defenders of the family, and careful stewards of the earth.

The alienation of men from their rootedness to the land has deprived us all of what John Muir[1] called the "heart of wilderness." As part of our efforts to re-experience the wild in ourselves, we should actively become involved in experiencing the wilderness first hand and organize support for the protection of nature and endangered species. Men should also become what Robert Bly[2] has called "inner warriors" for the earth, involving themselves in non-violent civil disobedience to protect wilderness areas from further destruction.

An important aspect of the masculine ethic is defense of family. Pesticides and other toxic pollutants that poison our food, homes, water, and air represent a real danger, especially to children. Men need to be adamant in their call for limitations on the use of chemicals.

Wendell Berry[3] has pointed out that the ecological crisis is also a crisis of agriculture. If men are to recapture a true sense of stewardship and husbandry and affirm the "seedbearing," creative capacity of the male, they must, to the extent possible, become involved in sustainable agriculture and organic farming and gardening. We should also initiate and support legislation that sustains our farming communities.

MEN IN THE CLASSROOMS AND COMMUNITY

In many communities, especially inner cities, men are absent not only from homes but also from the schools. Men must support the current efforts by black men's groups around the country to implement male-only early-grade classes taught by men. These programs provide role models and a surrogate paternal presence for young black males. We should also commit ourselves to having a far greater male presence in all elementary school education. Recent studies have shown that male grade school students have a higher level of achievement when they are taught by male teachers. Part-time or full-time home schooling options can also be helpful in providing men a great opportunity to be teachers—not just temperaments—to their children.

We need to revive our concern for community. Community-based boys' clubs, scout troops, sports leagues, and big brother programs have achieved significant success in helping fatherless male children find self-esteem. Men's groups must work to strengthen these organizations.

MEN'S MINDS, MEN'S BODIES, AND WORK

Men need to join together to fight threats to male health including suicide, drug and alcohol abuse, AIDS, and stress diseases. We should support active prevention and education efforts aimed at these deadly threats. Most importantly, men need to be leaders in initiating and supporting holistic and psychotherapeutic approaches that directly link many of these health threats to the coercive nature of the male mystique and the current economic system. Changes in diet, reduction of drug and alcohol use, less stressful work environments, greater nurturing of and caring for men by other men, and fighting racism, hopelessness, and homelessness are all important, interconnected aspects of any male health initiative.

MEN WITHOUT HOPE OR HOMES

Men need to support measures that promote small business and entrepreneurship, which will allow more people to engage in crafts and human-scale, community-oriented enterprises. Also important is a commitment to appropriate, human-scale technologies such as renewable energy sources. Industrial and other inappropriate technologies have led to men's dispossession, degradation—and increasingly to unemployment.

A related struggle is eliminating racism. No group of men is more dispossessed than minority men. White men should support and network with African-American and other minority men's groups. Violence and discrimination against men because of their sexual preference should also be challenged.

Men, who represent more than four-fifths of the homeless, can no longer ignore this increasing social tragedy. Men's councils should develop support groups for the homeless in their communities.

THE HOLOCAUST OF MEN

As the primary victims of mechanized war, men must oppose this continued slaughter. Men need to realize that the traditional male concepts of the noble warrior are undermined and caricatured in the technological nightmare of modern warfare. Men must together become prime movers in dismantling the military-industrial establishment and redistributing defense spending toward a sustainable environment and protection of family, school, and community.

MEN'S ACTION NETWORK

No area of the men's political agenda will be realized until men can establish a network of activists to create collective action. A first step might be to create a high-profile national coalition of the men's councils that are growing around the country. This coalition, which could be called the Men's Action Network (MAN), could call for a national conference to define a comprehensive platform of men's concerns and to provide the political muscle to implement those ideas.

A MAN COULD STAND UP

The current generation of men face a unique moment in history. Though often still trapped by economic coercion and psychological co-option, we are beginning to see that there is a profound choice ahead. Will we choose to remain subservient tools of social and environmental destruction or to fight for rediscovery of the male as a full partner and participant in family, community, and the earth? Will we remain mesmerized by the male mystique, or will we reclaim the true meaning of our masculinity?

There is a world to gain. The male mystique, in which many of today's men—especially the most politically powerful—are trapped, is threatening the family and the planet with irreversible destruction. A men's movement based on the recovery of masculinity could renew much of the world we have lost. By changing types of work and work hours, we could break our subordination to corporate managers and return much of our work and lives to the household. We could once again be teaching, nurturing presences to our children. By devoting ourselves to meaningful work with appropriate technology, we could recover independence in our work and our spirit. By caring for each other, we could recover the dignity of our gender and heal the wounds of addiction and self-destruction. By becoming husbands to the earth, we could protect the wild and recover our creative connections with the forces and rhythms of nature.

Ultimately we must help fashion a world without the daily frustration and sorrow of having to view each other as a collection of competitors instead of a community of friends. We must celebrate the essence and rituals of our masculinity. We can no longer passively submit to the destruction of the household, the demise of self-employment, the disintegration of family and community, and the desecration of our earth.

Shortly after the First World War, Ford Madox Ford, one of this century's greatest writers, depicted 20th century men as continually pinned down in their trenches, unable to stand up for fear of annihilation. As the century closes, men remain pinned down by an economic and political system that daily forces millions of us into meaningless work, powerless lives, and self-destruction. The time has come for men to stand up.   [1991]

Notes

1. JOHN MUIR: An American naturalist and conservationist.
2. ROBERT BLY: Author of *Iron John* and advocate of the men's movement, which emphasizes men's exploring their inner maleness and bonding with other men.
3. WENDELL BERRY: A contemporary American writer and university professor who has a special interest in the environment.

Understanding the Reading

1. Why does Kimbrell think men need to focus on family?

2. Why would environmental activism be especially beneficial to men?
3. What can men do to improve their communities?
4. How can men improve their health?
5. Why should men be concerned about war?
6. What does Kimbrell see as the benefits men would gain by implementing his program?

Suggestions for Responding

1. Do you agree or disagree with Kimbrell that men have been victimized by society? Why or why not?
2. Brainstorm strategies you could use to realize the outcome you identified in response to the Salholz selection. ◆

94

The Campus Environment for Gay and Lesbian Life

JOHN D'EMILIO

Just over twenty years ago, a new generation of feminists coined the phrase "the personal is political." Although the slogan has carried different meanings for those who use it, one implication has been to challenge our notions of private and public. Feminists have argued, and rightly so, that defining women's sphere and women's concerns as "private" has effectively excluded women from full and equal participation in the "public realm." As more and more women in the 1970s and 1980s fought for entry into academic life, higher education institutions increasingly have had to deal with a host of issues that were once safely tucked away in the private domain.

Colleges and universities in the pre-feminist era addressed privacy only in the breach, particularly with respect to matters of sexual identity. Consider the following examples:

• In 1959, at a small midwestern college, a student told her faculty adviser that one of her friends was a homosexual. The adviser informed a dean, who called in the student in question and pressured him into naming others. Within twenty-four hours, three students had been expelled; a week later, one of them hung himself.

- About the same time, a faculty member at a Big Ten[1] school was arrested in mid-semester on a morals charge (at that time, *all* homosexual expression was subject to criminal penalties). The police alerted the administration, and the professor was summarily told to leave the campus. He never appeared before his classes again.
- At an elite college in the Northeast, male students in the 1960s were in the habit of training a telescope on the windows of the women's dormitories. In one instance, they spied two female students erotically engaged. The women—not the men—were disciplined.
- At a women's college in New England, where accusations of lesbianism were periodically leveled against roommates in the 1960s, the standard solution was to separate the accused by housing them in different dorms.

I could list many more such examples. They came to me not through research but through the gay and lesbian academic grapevine. Stories like these are the substance of an oral tradition by which gay academics who came of age before the 1970s warned one another of the dangers they faced and socialized their younger peers into necessary habits of caution and discretion.

The point, I trust, is clear. For gay men and lesbians, the past is a history of privacy invaded, of an academy that enforced, maintained, and reproduced a particular moral order—a moral order aggressively antagonistic toward homosexual expression.

Since 1969, when the Stonewall Riots[2] in New York City ushered in the gay liberation movement, activists across the country have challenged that order. We have formed organizations by the thousands, lobbied legislatures, initiated public education campaigns, engaged in civil disobedience, and promoted self-help efforts. We have attempted to emancipate gays and lesbians from the laws, policies, scientific theories, and cultural attitudes that have consigned us to an inferior position in society.

When one considers that the political climate for most of the last twenty years has been conservative, and that this new conservatism has taken shape largely through an appeal to "traditional" notions of family, sexuality, and gender roles, the successes of the gay movement appear rather impressive. Half the states have repealed their sodomy laws.[3] Many of the nation's largest cities have enacted some form of gay civil rights ordinance, and a number of states are seriously debating the issue. The American Psychiatric Association has removed homosexuality from its list of mental disorders. Several religious denominations are revising their positions on the morality of homosexual relationships. And lesbian and gay organizations around the country are better financed and more stable now than at any point in their past.

Those of us associated with institutions of higher education have contributed to this movement and have benefited from it as well. Because the birth of gay liberation was so closely tied to the social movements of the 1960s, student groups have been part of the gay political and social landscape from the beginning. Currently, more than four hundred of these groups exist, in community colleges and research universities, in public institutions and private ones. Braving the ostracism and harassment that visibility sometimes brings, these young women and men have often had to battle for recognition and funding. In the process, their struggles have created a substantial body of judicial opinion that protects gay student groups as an expression of First Amendment rights of speech and assembly.

Faculty members, too, have organized. Initially forming separate organizations, such as the Gay Academic Union, they have increasingly turned to their professional associations as venues for action. Most social science and humanities disciplines now have lesbian and gay caucuses that publish newsletters, review current literature, and sponsor well-attended sessions at annual meetings. A vibrant new scholarship has emerged in the last decade that is substantial enough to spark a movement for gay studies programs in institutions as diverse as San Francisco City College, Yale University, and the City University of New York.

If one's reference point is university life a generation ago, one can say that things *are* getting better for gay faculty, students, administrators, and staff. Grit, courage, and determination have opened up some space in which it is possible to live, breathe, and work openly. Our situation no longer appears uniformly grim.

Nevertheless, being openly gay on campus still goes against the grain. Despite the changes in American society in the last two decades, gay people are still swimming in a largely oppressive sea. Most campuses do not have gay student groups. Most gay faculty members and administrators have not come out. Even on campuses that have proven responsive to gay and lesbian concerns, progress has often come through the work of a mere handful of individuals who have chosen to be visible. And, although I do not have statistics to measure this precisely, I know that there are still many, many campuses in the United States where no lesbian or gay man feels safe enough to come out. From a gay vantage point, something is still wrong in the academy.

Oppression in its many forms is still alive, and the university is not immune to it. Indeed, as the gay population has become a better organized and stronger force in the 1980s, we have also become easier to target. In recent years, harassment, violence, and other hate-motivated acts against lesbians and gay men have surfaced with alarming frequency on campuses across the country. Institutions such as the University of Kansas and the University of Chicago, to name just two, have witnessed campaigns of terror against their gay members. At Pennsylvania State University, a report on tolerance found that bias-motivated incidents most frequently targeted gay people.

Unlike many other groups—women and African Americans, for instance—in which one's identity is clear for the world to see, most gay men and lesbians have the option to remain invisible. I cannot fault individuals who choose that path: the costs of visibility often can be high. Yet the fear that compels most gay people to remain hidden exacts a price of its own. It leads us to doubt our own self-worth and dignity. It encourages us to remain isolated and detached from our colleagues and peers, as too much familiarity can lead to exposure. And it often results in habitual patterns of mistrust and defensiveness because anyone, potentially, may cause our downfall. Hence, speaking about gay oppression involves not only addressing injustice in the abstract but also acknowledging the emotional toll it levies

on particular individuals and the institutions of which they are a part.

For reasons that I cannot quite fathom, I still expect the academy to embrace higher standards of civility, decency, and justice than the society around it. Having been granted the extraordinary privilege of thinking critically as a way of life, we should be astute enough to recognize when a group of people is being systematically mistreated. We have the intelligence to devise solutions to problems that appear in our community. I expect us also to have the courage to lead rather than follow.

Although gay oppression has deep roots in American society, the actions that would combat it effectively on campuses are not especially difficult to devise and formulate. What sort of policies would make a difference? What would a gay-positive institution look like?

One set of policies would place institutions of higher education firmly on the side of equal treatment. Gay faculty, administrators, staff, and students need to know that their school is committed to fairness, to treating us on the basis of our abilities. At a minimum that would mean:

A nondiscrimination policy, formally enacted, openly announced, and in print wherever the institution proclaims its policy with regard to race, gender, and religion. Such a policy would apply to hiring, promotion, tenure, admissions, and financial aid. Because of the history of discrimination in this country, it is not enough for an administration to claim that it subscribes to the principle of fairness for everyone. Sexual orientation, sexual preference, sexual identity, or whatever term one chooses to adopt, needs to be explicitly acknowledged.

Spousal benefits for the partners of gay men and lesbians, at every level of institutional life and for every service that is normally provided to husbands and wives. These benefits include health insurance, library privileges, access to the gym and other recreational facilities, listings in school directories if spouses are customarily listed, and access to married students' housing for gay and lesbian couples.

An approach to gay student groups that is identical to that for all other groups with regard to recognition procedures, funding, and access to facilities. Administrators who place obstructions in the way of these groups are doing a costly disservice to their institutions since courts have uniformly sustained the rights of gay students to organize.

Subscribing to the above policies would simply place lesbians and gays in a *de jure*[4] position of parity. Implementing these measures would go a long way toward alleviating the fears that we live with, integrating us fully into the life of the campus, and letting us know that we are valued and "welcomed."

The university's responsibility towards its gay members goes well beyond these elementary procedures of fairness, however. Administrators will need to take an activist stance to counteract the misinformation about gays and lesbians that many members of the university community have, the cultural prejudices that are still endemic in the United States, and the growing problem of hate-motivated incidents. The following areas need attention:

1. One of the prime locations where harassment occurs is in residence halls. Dormitory directors and their assistants need to be sensitized about gay issues and trained in how to respond quickly and firmly to instances of oppressive behavior and harassment. In an age when heterosexual undergraduates routinely hold hands, walk arm-in-arm, and engage in other simple displays of affection, lesbian and gay students need to know that they will not have their rooms ransacked, or their physical safety endangered, for doing the same. They also need reassurance that campus activism on gay issues will not come back to haunt them when they return to their dorms each night.

2. Student affairs programming is an important tool in fostering toleration, understanding, and enthusiasm for differences in culture and identity. Resources should be made available to sponsor special gay awareness week events, as well as to integrate gay films, public lectures, and other events and activities into the regular programming.

3. Late adolescence is an especially stressful time for gay men and lesbians. These may be the years when they become sexually active, form their first relationships, and grapple with issues of identity. School counseling services need personnel who are sensitive to these issues and who can foster self-acceptance and self-esteem rather than reinforce self-hatred.

4. Because the issues and situations affecting lesbians and gay men range widely across the structure of large and medium-size campuses, hiring an "ombudsperson" for gay and lesbian concerns makes good institutional sense. Someone who can think expansively about these issues, provide a resource where needed, and intervene decisively in emergencies can move a whole campus forward.

5. When hate-motivated incidents occur—and the evidence of the last few years suggests that they happen with greater frequency than we care to admit—the *highest* officers of the university need to exercise their *full* authority in condemning the attacks and correcting the underlying problems which encourage such incidents. Bias-motivated incidents are awful, but they also offer a unique opportunity for raising consciousness and for shifting the climate of opinion on a campus.

6. An institution that prohibits discrimination against gays ought not to countenance the presence on campus of institutions and organizations that engage in such discrimination. The government intelligence agencies and the military are the most egregious perpetrators of anti-gay bias. Recent actions by the military against its gay and lesbian personnel amount to a form of terrorism. Military recruiters and ROTC programs ought to be banned from American campuses until the armed forces change their policies.

7. Last, but not least, is the issue of research. The 1980s have witnessed an efflorescence of scholarship on gay and lesbian issues in several disciplines. Yet many topics go begging for researchers because faculty members know that prejudiced department heads and tenure committees will label such work trivial and insignificant. Gay scholarship, opening as it does a new window on human experience, must be encouraged.

On sunny mornings, I am optimistic that the 1990s will see a dramatic improvement in the quality of life for gay men and lesbians in higher education: the body of scholarship is growing and pressure for gay studies programs will mount; academics in many disciplines have created stable and permanent caucuses which will strengthen our networks; regional associations of gay student groups are forming to reinforce those groups already established on individual campuses. In addition, the National Gay and Lesbian Task Force in Washington, D.C., recently initiated a campus-organizing project so that gay men and lesbians on each campus no longer have to reinvent the wheel.

Of equal importance, perhaps, some administrators are moving beyond the most elementary issues of visibility and recognition. They are addressing the key areas of equal treatment and deep-rooted prejudice. Such a stance—on every campus—is long overdue.   [1990]

Notes

1. BIG TEN: The major midwestern universities.
2. STONEWALL RIOTS: After a raid on a gay bar in New York City called the Stonewall, gays rioted in protest against police brutality.
3. SODOMY LAWS: Laws criminalizing anal intercourse.
4. *DE JURE:* According to law.

Understanding the Reading

1. Explain the distinctions between private and public.
2. What strategies has the gay liberation movement employed?
3. What effects has gay liberation had on academic institutions?
4. What problems do gay men and lesbians face on college campuses?
5. Explain D'Emilio's plan for combatting gay and lesbian oppression on college campuses.

Suggestions for Responding

1. Argue for or against one of the policies or practices D'Emilio recommends.
2. Develop a plan for action to implement one strategy or a group of strategies you identified in response to the Kimbrell reading. ◆

95

Resistance to Change

KATHLEEN RYAN

Resisting change is a very natural behavior; it is neither "good" nor "bad." Everyone does it from time to time. In many ways, resisting change is like driving in fog. When drivers enter a patch of

fog, they should slow down, get a feel for the conditions, and then proceed at an appropriate pace. People making their way through the ambiguity and disorder of change have similar reactions. Their attitude is affected by their past experiences, their confidence in their skills, and by whether they interpreted the situation as an adventure or a problem. Their pace is influenced by how much they can learn about the change, their freedom to make decisions, and their ability to take action. In an ideal situation, past and present circumstances combine to give individuals the necessary confidence, freedom, and skills to move successfully and comfortably through a time of change. Unfortunately, few of us operate within ideal situations; we are often slowed down and encumbered by a variety of unanswered questions and unsettled concerns.

Handling resistance effectively is the unspoken challenge faced by anyone who wants to do things differently. Never knowing when it might actually surface, the change agent nevertheless needs to be ready for resistance. He or she needs to be able to:

1. Recognize resistance when it occurs;
2. Respond to the resistant person(s) in ways that identify the reasons behind the resistance;
3. Work, to whatever degree possible, with the resistant person(s) to answer the questions and ease the concerns which form the source of the resistance.

RECOGNIZING RESISTANCE

To recognize resistance when it occurs, one needs to have a sense of how resistance looks, feels, and sounds. Language and behavior are two of the primary means for identifying the source of resistance. At times the clues they give are very visible, allowing the underlying issue to be recognized easily. At other times, the source of the resistance is essentially hidden, hard to identify or connect to an event or situation.

To better understand *visible resistance,* imagine a discussion of the way the advertising media influence current images of men and women. As the conversation becomes increasingly animated, one person becomes quite hostile in [her] comments. Finally, in a burst of frustration, she suddenly stands and shouts, "This is the most ridiculous discussion I've ever been in!'' She leaves the room and slams the door on her way out. The exclamation of frustration, the departure, and the slamming of the door are all rather dramatic signs of resistance to a particular point or issue being discussed: They are *visible* signs of resistance.

The less obvious, *hidden resistance* is of course more difficult to identify. Consider the hypothetical case of a supervisor and a male employee. Because of a recent decision to rotate jobs temporarily, the male employee will be assigned to an all-female work crew for three months. After announcing the decision, the supervisor notices that the employee's participation in staff meetings is less enthusiastic. Even though the employee has sometimes spoken positively about the change, his general attitude on the job is less pleasant, he is less patient, and he does not seem to produce the usual amount or quality of work. In this case, the employee's small changes in attitude and behavior—extended over a period of time—can be interpreted as signs of resistance to the new job assignment. Until the supervisor confronts the employee, however, he or she has no way of knowing whether the resistance actually exists, and if so, what its cause might be.

The more skilled you become at listening and watching for signs of resistance to change, the better you will be at managing change. Simply put, if you are unable to recognize resistance when it occurs, it will be very difficult for you to take action to overcome it.

REASONS AND CLUES

People resist change for a variety of reasons. The first clues about resistance are usually found in the words people speak and in their behavior. While behavioral signs of resistance are more general, language often gives very direct clues to the reasons for resistance. The material presented in this section is designed to expand your awareness of how people's language and behavior can be tied to very specific reasons for resisting change. As you read through the following lists, think of those with whom you live and work. Think of yourself as well. Note any familiar linguistic or behavioral clues to resistance to change.

REASONS FOR RESISTANCE	WORDS OF RESISTANCE
1. Information. People don't have enough or accurate information about the change.	"I've never heard of a man who's been very successful in that kind of role." "Well, I'm sorry, but I won't go along with this until somebody can show me an example of where she's been successful with this idea before."
2. Influence. People have a strong desire to influence what happens to them in their work and their environment. If they cannot influence these decisions, they may resist because they feel left out.	"Nobody consulted me before bringing these women down here in the shop." "I'll never understand why they don't talk to the people who are really doing the work before they make their decisions."
3. Feelings. People have emotional reactions to change. For example, they may become angry, frustrated, or scared by something new. These feelings often remain unspoken and trigger resistance.	"I'm worried about how those guys are going to react to me. I frankly don't know if it's worth the effort or not." "My child is not going through any program like that. I'll take him out of school before I let them teach him about *those* kinds of things."
4. Control. People have a need to control information, decisions, or other people. If they cannot do so, they may resist.	"How do you expect me to do my part when I don't have access to the information I need?" "I haven't had enough time to coach her on the budgeting issues. I don't think she's ready for the promotion just yet."
5. Benefits. People don't see any advantage to changing.	"I wish someone would tell me what they think is so great about this new plan." "Why in the world do you want to go back to school? You're already overqualified for half the jobs you apply for!"

REASONS FOR RESISTANCE	WORDS OF RESISTANCE
6. Stress. People feel over-loaded; they don't want the added stress of an-other change.	"If you tell the line manag-ers that they've got to be responsible for this EEO[1] training, you'll have a revolt on your hands. They've al-ready got too much to handle." "You want me to be the first woman to go out on the line? Forget it. I don't need that kind of hassle."
7. Desire to be right. People think that if they change, all their previ-ous effort will be "wrong." They have a strong desire to be "right" in their thinking and behavior.	"I told you all along, women don't want this 'sen-sitive male' stuff. They want a man who can tell them what to do." "I don't know exactly what to do. I'd hate to take a po-sition that really upsets the way things are done around here."
8. Ability. People are not confident about their ability to handle new responsibilities or per-form new tasks re-quired by a change.	"Oh, I could never do that!" "Nobody told me that when I volunteered for this posi-tion I'd have to play nurse-maid to a bunch of prima donnas. I just want to get the job done. They keep slowing things down with all their new ideas. I don't know how to handle them."
9. Routine. People don't want to alter their living or working conditions or routine.	"You mean to tell me we may have to talk different around here?" "There's something you need to know if you're go-ing to fit in here. There are certain things that have al-ways been done certain ways."
10. Status. People don't want to lose their status, authority, or power.	"What do you mean they want a female engineer out there in the field? Don't you know what they will do to morale?"

REASONS FOR RESISTANCE	WORDS OF RESISTANCE
	"Why do we need all these experts to tell us what to do? We're doing just fine."
11. Structure. People have a need for structure. Change can create con-fusion about roles, re-sponsibilities, and procedures.	"The new policy is clear on this issue. You can't expect me to ignore it." "Was this your father's idea?"
12. Values. People disagree with the basic values or concepts behind the change. They may think that the change violates a basic belief about people or work, or that the change will have an undesirable effect.	"But what about the person who'll use this law to dam-age someone's career? If we tell our employees about this, all we're going to be doing is investigating complaints." "Schools should not have anything to do with teach-ing children about sexuality and family decision-making. That's the parents' job."

While words are an important part of any-one's communication, they are not the only way we communicate. Behavior—nonverbal com-munication—can be just as important as words in identifying the source of resistance to change. Behavioral signs of resistance, especially when unaccompanied by words, are often very difficult to tie to resistance. Because of this, it is wise to become familiar with some of the behavioral clues to visible and hidden resistance. Some of those clues are listed here:

Behavioral Clues to Resistance to Change

VISIBLE RESISTANCE	HIDDEN RESISTANCE
• name-calling	• increased illnesses
• loud sighing	• acting "dumb"
• unusual non-participation	• blasé, disinterested attitude
• unexpected cool, aloof manner	• delaying tactics
• argumentative behavior	• losing things
• obvious avoidance	• pretending to lack information
• walking away	• not passing along information
• walking out	• work slow-down
• deliberately changing the subject	

VISIBLE RESISTANCE	HIDDEN RESISTANCE
• missing appointments	• indirect communication (innuendo)
• no follow-through on specific commitments	• not returning phone calls
• sullen posture	• being placed last on a busy agenda
• critical jokes	• unnecessarily referring a question to someone else
• quitting	• consistent day-dreaming
• angry outbursts	• lack of thorough preparation
• telling others it won't work	• tardiness
• poor attendance	• forgetting
• constant excuses for poor performance	• procrastination
• deliberately distorting information	• appearing agreeable, but taking no action
• cynical expression and tone	• signs of depression or sadness
• complaining to others	• unusual swearing
	• negative facial expressions
	• spreading gossip

If we were physicians, we would look for the symptoms of a disease or illness. We would observe those symptoms carefully and use them as a basis for our diagnosis. We would not treat the disease without first considering its underlying cause. The words and behaviors listed above should be regarded in the same manner—as symptoms of resistance and clues to its cause, clues that must be considered in context of the situation in which they appear.

The most direct way to understand why a person is resisting a change is to ask the person. For example:

> You are a mid-level manager working in a large organization which has become increasingly public about its commitment to equal opportunity for women and minorities. You have been asked to join a task force which will investigate possible pay discrepancies between job classifications—including those which have been traditionally held by female employees. You become aware that your task force meetings seem to get bogged down with reports and discussions of procedures, rather than with defining critical problems and addressing questions that need attention. The task force chairperson is a colleague of yours and is known for her skillful facilitation of meetings, and it is more and more difficult to find a time when everyone can meet. You decide, because of her behavior, that the task force chairperson is somehow resisting the potential changes involved in this work. You decide to investigate further, to see if you are right.

In such a case, you might say:

> "Jane, I get the feeling you're not very comfortable with your role on this task force. You don't seem to be approaching the facilitation with your usual flair."

Or:

> "Tell me what you think about where all this work will lead."

Or:

> "I'll bet you're feeling some extra pressure because of chairing this task force, Jane. Do you have the kind of clerical support to be able to handle this and your regular work too?"

In cases such as these, you want to create an opportunity for the person who you think is resisting to talk. If this person trusts and respects you, you have a relatively good chance to discover whether your suspicions about the resistance are correct or not. Once you confirm that resistance exists, you should identify the reason for it. This information is critical for any action you subsequently take to overcome the resistance. In this case, Jane may be resisting because of:

> *Values.* She believes the organization could work on other issues which would better, and more immediately, promote equal opportunity.
>
> *Benefits.* Because of previous experiences with other task forces, Jane believes that in the end, no one will benefit from all this work, and no substantial changes will really take place.
>
> *Stress.* She has too many other responsibilities to give this project the attention it needs.

Because you are not Jane's superior, your role in helping her to overcome her resistance is somewhat limited. There are some very positive things you could do, however:

> *Values.* If you believe the work of this task force *is* critical for developing equal opportunity, say so. Present your reasons. along with information about studies in other organizations which have increased wage equity and reduced the risk of a disruptive, painful strike for recognition of comparable worth.

Benefits. Talk with Jane to find out her past experiences. If you agree that there's a good chance nothing will come of your current work, raise that issue with the entire task force. With Jane, or in the task force, brainstorm strategies for overcoming that likelihood. Play an active part, behind the scenes or visibly, to act on those strategies.

Stress. Work with Jane to identify the time and resource problems that are increasing her stress. Once again, develop strategies to overcome the problems, including a proposal to Jane's boss which outlines the problems and asks for additional resources. Offer to do what you can to ease the burden of her responsibilities. Follow through on those commitments.   [1985]

Note

1. EEO: Equal Employment Opportunity.

Understanding the Reading

1. Explain the difference between visible resistance and hidden resistance.
2. Explain the twelve reasons for resistance.
3. How do information, feelings, and influence affect resistance?

Suggestions for Responding

1. Describe a time when someone tried to impose a change on you that you didn't like. In what ways did you resist? How was the conflict finally resolved?
2. Explain what kinds of resistance to your plan of action you anticipate and how you plan to handle them. ◆

96

Psychologists Find Ways to Break Racism's Hold

DANIEL GOLEMAN

As racial violence continues to roil communities like Bensonhurst and more subtle prejudice permeates many American institutions, psycholo-

gists are refining their understanding of how bigotry develops and devising new ways to fight and prevent it.

Some of the most promising techniques are aimed at grade-school children, whose biases have not had time to harden. But research has also led to a range of principles that can be used by any organization, whether university or corporation or city government or armed service, to change the atmosphere that leads to racial incidents.

"There is no single cure for racism," said Dr. Robert Slavin, a psychologist at Johns Hopkins University. But he and other psychologists have used data from experiments to identify techniques and principles for reducing the hold of racism.

INTERRACIAL LEARNING TEAMS

One of the most successful methods is dividing students into interracial learning teams, which, like sports teams, knit members together in common purpose that can lead to friendship.

Such learning groups are widespread in the United States, especially in school districts with potential or actual racial problems. In Israel, they have been used to defuse tensions between Jewish students of Middle Eastern and European descent; in Canada between Canadians and immigrants; and in California between Hispanic and non-Hispanic students.

Such cooperative groups reduce prejudice by undercutting the categories that lead to stereotyped thinking, according to research published in the August issue of *The Journal of Personality and Social Psychology*.

"Once you categorize people into groups in any way, you tend to like people in your own group more than those in others," said Dr. Samuel Gaertner, a psychologist at the University of Delaware who conducted the research.

"It happens in many situations apart from race relations," he added. "You see it often, for instance, in a corporate merger, when people in the acquiring company continue to stereotype people from the acquired company with disdain, and those from the acquired company resent what they see as a favored status for those with the acquiring firm."

In Dr. Gaertner's experiment, volunteers were formed into arbitrary groups to work on a hypothetical problem about surviving after a crash landing. Once they had become a unified group, they began to like each other more than they liked people who were put in other groups, a simulation of the process that can lead to prejudice in other circumstances.

When the working groups were then mixed with others into a single unified group to work on another problem, their preferences shifted again.

"Cooperation widens your sense of who's in your group," Dr. Gaertner said. "It changes your thinking from 'us and them' to 'we.' People you once saw as part of some other group now are part of your own. That's why team learning groups can reduce bias."

The need for such efforts is as great as ever, psychologists say. Incidents like the killing of Yusuf K. Hawkins, the black teen-ager shot during an attack by whites in the Bensonhurst section of Brooklyn on Aug. 23, are only the most visible and public reminders.

SUBTLE PREJUDICE PERSISTS

Although surveys show a decline over the last 40 years in the number of people who openly express bigotry, prejudice persists in more subtle forms. Dr. Howard Gadlin, a psychologist at the University of Massachusetts in Amherst, says the behavior of college students is a telling indication of racial attitudes. Campuses were in the forefront of the civil-rights movement in the 1960's; yet in the past two years, he notes, "racial incidents have been on the rise on campuses across the country."

In devising ways to combat racism, psychologists can turn to a strong body of research into the mental processes that lead to bigotry. Dr. Janet Schofield, a psychologist at the University of Pittsburgh, has demonstrated ways in which social barriers between racial groups can create suspicion and mistrust.

In one junior high school she observed, the students were split into hostile racial cliques. "A socially active black kid was more likely to be seen as aggressive than was a white kid doing exactly the same thing," Dr. Schofield said. "For in-

stance, if he asked someone in the cafeteria, 'Can I have your cake?' or even if he happened to bump someone in the hall, that was interpreted as an aggressive act if it was done by a black kid, but not by a white."

That perception was part of a cycle in which the social distance between blacks and whites fostered stereotypes that could not be broken down even by positive experiences.

"Whites and blacks avoided each other," Dr. Schofield said. "Because the whites were prone to interpret even normal social activity by blacks as hostile and aggressive, they felt afraid of social contact. That made the blacks see the whites as stuck-up, which tended to actually make them hostile in response."

PIGEONHOLES OF THE MIND

The most widely used technique for promoting racial harmony, mixing racial or ethnic groups into teams where they cooperate for a common goal, is intended to break down just such barriers to understanding.

The growing consensus from psychological experiments is that racial and ethnic prejudices are an unfortunate byproduct of the way the mind categorizes all experience. Essentially, the mind seeks to simplify the chaos of the world by fitting all perceptions into categories. Thus it fits different kinds of people into pigeonholes, just as it does with restaurants or television programs.

That is where the problem begins, psychologists say. Too often people see the category and not the individual. Once these categories are formed, the beliefs and assumptions that underlie them are confirmed at every possible opportunity, even at the cost of disregarding evidence to the contrary.

David Hamilton, a psychologist at the University of California at Santa Barbara, has found in the series of experiments that people tend to forget facts that would change their assumptions about categories, while seeking and remembering information that would confirm those assumptions. When they meet someone who does not fit the stereotype, they tell themselves the individual is an exception.

The strength of stereotypes—both innocent and hostile—is attributed to the mind's natural bent to seek to confirm its beliefs. While several experiences to the contrary can challenge those beliefs, an isolated experience is unlikely to do so.

The Power of Teamwork

Such self-confirmation of stereotypes is especially likely when members of different groups have little contact with each other. Merely integrating a school, business or neighborhood may fail to change old stereotypes if the groups keep to themselves.

The learning-team approach was based on pioneering work on intergroup harmony in the 1950's by psychologists like Dr. Gordon Allport and Dr. Muzafer Sherif. It was given added scientific impetus by research on prejudice among high school students in the 1970's. That work, by Dr. Slavin and others, found that in mixed-race schools, students with the least prejudice and most friends from other races were members of sports teams or bands in which they had to work together.

The most widespread approach puts students together in four- or five-member "learning teams." The racial or ethnic makeup of each team reflects the overall makeup of the school. While members study together and are encouraged to teach each other, they are tested individually. But the team gets a score or other recognition of its work as a unit. Teams work together for about six weeks, and then students are reassigned to a new team to promote as many contacts as possible among students.

"No point is made of the fact that these are mixed racial groups," Dr. Slavin said. "The kids see nothing unusual; it seems random. The effects are very positive, especially in junior and senior high school, where the problem is greatest."

After the students work together in teams, Dr. Slavin and other researchers have found a significant increase in the number who say their friends are from other races or ethnic groups.

'Zero Tolerance' for Bias

"Even in cooperative groups, students may still carry biases into the sessions," Dr. Schofield said. "Blacks may expect that the whites will dominate, for instance. Sometimes you can combat these attitudes by giving minority kids a head start on a lesson, and having them teach it to the white kids."

Apart from engineering mixed-race working groups, psychologists say the overall social climate is also important in fighting racism. They say those in charge can establish a clear norm that racism will not be tolerated.

"Administrators and managers can show that they have zero tolerance for racial putdowns," Dr. Slavin said.

The psychologists say a sense of fairness is also important. If one group is perceived to be treated better or to have higher status than another, the situation is ripe for tensions. For that reason, psychologists stress the importance of openly acknowledging differences in the ways groups are treated.

"My research shows that when people try to act colorblind, as though there were no racial or ethnic differences, it backfires," Dr. Schofield said.

Dr. Slavin says school officials need to recognize and address such differences.

"If 90 percent of the kids suspended are black or Hispanic, or all the kids on the student council are Oriental or white, you need to bring that fact into the open before you can deal with it," he said. "The worst thing is for members of some group to feel, 'People like me have no chance here.'

"You need to pay careful attention to issues of equity. If it's a school, for instance, you need to be sure the cheerleading squad and student council are racially mixed in a way that represents the student body, even if that means a certain proportion are appointed."

Many universities are now appointing ombudsmen to deal impartially with complaints of racial, ethnic or sexual bias, among other grievances.

"It may seem obvious, but it's often overlooked," said Dr. Gadlin, who is the ombudsman at the University of Massachusetts. "You must have a system in place where those who feel racially harassed can lodge a complaint that will be acted on, not covered up.

"We need ways of dealing openly with the fears and resentments that breed racial tensions," he added. "We have no forums where you can do much more than talk around the problems in ways that are proper and polite but avoid the real issues. If you have to pretend that racial problems don't exist, the tensions will escalate until they explode." [1989]

Understanding the Reading

1. Explain why interracial learning teams reduce prejudice.
2. What are the effects of social distance between racial groups?
3. Why do people categorize others, and what effect does such categorization have?
4. Why don't people change their assumptions about people when experience contradicts the stereotype?
5. What can administrators and managers do to combat racism?

Suggestion for Responding

Describe a different strategy to combat racism in schoolchildren, and explain why it might be effective. ✦

97

Battered Women

CYNTHIA DIEHM AND
MARGO ROSS

Any examination of the status of American women cannot ignore the plight of the estimated three to four million or more women who are beaten by their intimate partners each year. The home, once seen as a sanctuary for women, is increasingly being recognized as a place where females may be at risk of psychological and physical abuse.

Abusive and violent behavior among people who are married, living together, or have an ongoing or prior intimate relationship is referred to as spouse abuse, battering, or domestic violence. It occurs among people of all races, age groups, religions, lifestyles, and income and educational levels. Approximately 95 percent of the victims of such violence are women.

A battering incident is rarely an isolated occurrence. It usually recurs frequently and esca-

lates in severity over time. It can involve threats, pushing, slapping, punching, choking, sexual assault, and assault with weapons. Each year, more than one million women seek medical assistance for injuries caused by battering. Battering may result in more injuries that require medical treatment than rape, auto accidents, and muggings combined.

A typical response to domestic violence is to question why women remain in abusive relationships. Actually, many women do leave their abusers. In one study of 205 battered women, 53 percent had left the relationship. Moreover, there is no way to know how many women have chosen not to identify abuse as the reason they ended their marriages.

Divorce proceedings can be particularly difficult for battered women, especially when child custody litigation is involved. If a battered woman has left the home without her children, she may lose custody of them because her action may be perceived as desertion. If the batterer is established in the community, the court may see him as a better custodial parent, regardless of his wife's accusations of violence, because she may appear to be in transition and unstable. If the woman is granted custody, the abuser usually is given child visitation rights—a situation that continually places the woman at risk of abuse. Some states have passed legislation that mandates consideration of spouse abuse as evidence in custody litigation.

Battered women, in general, do not passively endure physical abuse, but actively seek assistance in ending the violence from a variety of sources, including police, lawyers, family members, and the clergy. Frequently, it is the failure of these individuals and systems to provide adequate support that traps women in violent relationships. A study of more than 6,000 battered women in Texas found that, on average, the women had contacted five different sources of help prior to leaving the home and becoming residents of battered women's shelters.

Certainly, many battered women suffer in silence. These women endure physical abuse for a variety of reasons:

- A woman may feel that it is her duty to keep the marriage together at all costs because of religious, cultural, or socially learned beliefs.

- A woman may endure physical and emotional abuse to keep the family together for the children's sake.
- A woman may be financially dependent on her husband and thus would probably face severe economic hardship if she chose to support herself and her children on her own.
- A battered woman frequently faces the most physical danger when she attempts to leave. She may be threatened with violence or attacked if she tries to flee. She fears for her safety, her children's safety, and the safety of those who help her.

THE LEGACY OF INDIFFERENCE

Despite the severity of domestic violence, it is a problem that, until quite recently, has been cloaked in secrecy. Up to the early 1970s, battered women had few options but to suffer in silence or to attempt single-handedly to leave controlling and violent men. To understand why society is just beginning to confront domestic violence, it is essential to view the problem within its historical context.

Domestic violence is not a new phenomenon; historically, husbands had the legal right to chastise their wives to maintain authority. In the United States, wife beating was legal until the end of the nineteenth century. Alabama and Massachusetts were on record as rescinding the "ancient privilege" of wife beating in 1871, but most states merely ignored old laws.

While battering was no longer legally sanctioned by the early part of the twentieth century, the spirit of the law remained and abuse was still common. Social and justice systems have viewed domestic violence as a private family matter and have been reluctant to intervene.

CHANGE THROUGH GRASSROOTS ACTIVISM

The legacy of society's indifference to violence in the home fueled a grassroots "battered women's movement," which gained nationwide momentum in the mid-1970s. Inspired by the feminist anti-rape movement's analysis of male violence against women as a social and political issue, battered women began to speak out about the

physical abuse they were suffering in their marriages and intimate relationships.

At first, battered women helped one another individually by setting up informal safe homes and apartments. In such an environment—free from intimidation by their abusers—battered women could speak openly and thus soon discovered the commonality of their experiences. As the issue was publicized, women of all races, cultures, ages, abilities, and walks of life began to expose the violence they suffered. It quickly became clear that woman battering was a pervasive problem, and a nationwide movement started to take shape.

The early experience of the movement revealed the acute need of safe shelter for battered women and their children. Unless a woman could feel truly safe, she could not effectively evaluate her situation and make clear decisions about her future. Operating on shoestring budgets, battered women's advocates began to establish formal programs around the country. Only a handful of such programs existed in the mid-1970s; today, there are more than 1,200 shelters, hot-lines, and safe-home networks nationwide. Grassroots lobbying efforts at the federal level led to congressional passage of the 1984 Family Violence Prevention and Services Act, which earmarked federal funding for programs serving victims of domestic violence.

Creating and expanding a network of shelters and services for battered women and their children, while essential, was not the only goal of the grassroots movement. Equally important was the task of promoting changes in the criminal justice system that would hold abusers accountable for their violence and uphold the rights of battered women.

In 1984, the report of the Attorney General's Task Force on Family Violence reaffirmed the need for an improved criminal justice response to domestic violence, stating: "The legal response to family violence must be guided primarily by the nature of the abusive act, not the relationship between the victim and the abuser." The report focused on the role of the criminal justice system and recommended actions for each of its components that would increase the effectiveness of its response and better ensure the victim's safety. Across the country advocates continue to work with law enforcement personnel, prosecutors, judges, and legislators to implement new policies and enact legislation.

THE CRIMINAL JUSTICE RESPONSE

Domestic violence is now a crime in all 50 states and the District of Columbia, either under existing assault and battery laws or under special legislation. However, the true extent of crimes involving domestic violence remains largely unknown, since no accurate statistics on the number of battered women exist. Neither of the two sources of national crime statistics—the Federal Bureau of Investigation's Uniform Crime Report (UCR) and the federal Bureau of Justice Statistics' National Crime Survey (NCS)—is specifically designed to measure the incidence of crime in the domestic setting.

The UCR, which is based on police department reports, only collects information on the victim-offender relationship in the homicide category. Despite the UCR's limitations, it does provide a chilling picture of the potential lethality of domestic violence. According to the latest report, 30 percent of female homicide victims were killed by their husbands or boyfriends.

To supplement the UCR, the Bureau of Justice Statistics conducts an ongoing national telephone survey of some 60,000 American households to glean information on crimes not reported to police. Originally designed to collect data on such crimes as burglary and aggravated assault, the NCS also asks respondents about their relationships to offenders and thus inadvertently obtains information on domestic violence. Results of the 1978–82 NCS led analysts to estimate that 2.1 million women were victims of domestic violence at least once during an average 12-month period. This estimate is not intended to portray the true extent of the problem; rather, it is an indication of the number of women who believed domestic violence to be criminal and who felt free to disclose such information over the telephone to an unknown interviewer.

National crime statistics are based primarily on local police department reports, which traditionally have not included a discrete category for domestic violence. Police departments in a number of jurisdictions are just beginning to develop methods to report domestic violence crimes

separately. It will be many years before this practice becomes universal and a more accurate picture of the nature and incidence of domestic crimes is available.

Law enforcement has traditionally operated from a philosophy of nonintervention in cases of domestic violence. Unless severe injury or death was involved, police rarely arrested offenders. Expert police opinion was that there was little law enforcement could do to prevent such crimes. Moreover, it was believed that even if an offender were arrested, cases would never go to trial because of the victim's fear of testifying against her abuser.

The police response to domestic violence has been altered significantly in the last few years. In 1982, a study in Minneapolis found that arrest was more effective than two nonarrest alternatives in reducing the likelihood of repeat violence over a six-month follow-up period. Interestingly, only two percent of abusers who were arrested in the study went before a judge to receive court punishment. Thus, the Minneapolis study showed that arrest appears to reduce recidivism, even if it does not lead to conviction. The results of the study were widely publicized and have contributed to a more aggressive law enforcement response to domestic violence.

Research results, however, have been only partially responsible for changes in police policies. Class action lawsuits brought by victims against police departments for lack of protection also have effected policy change. In 1985, for example, a battered woman in Torrington, Connecticut, won a multimillion dollar settlement from the city for the failure of the police department to protect her from her husband's violence. *Thurman v. Torrington* was a catalyst for the state's passage of the 1986 Family Violence and Response Act, which mandates arrest in domestic violence cases when probable cause exists.

For the past several years, the Crime Control Institute has conducted a telephone survey of police departments serving jurisdictions with populations of 100,000 or more. In 1986, 46 percent of these departments indicated they had a pro-arrest policy in cases of domestic violence, as compared with 31 percent in 1985 and 10 percent in 1984. In addition, the percent of urban police departments reporting more actual domestic violence arrests appears to have risen from

24 percent in 1984 to 47 percent in 1986.

Other components of the criminal justice system have also begun to take a tougher stance on domestic violence. Many district attorneys' offices have established separate domestic violence units to encourage more vigorous prosecution of offenders. Judicial training on domestic violence has been promoted so that stronger court sanctions are imposed against abusive men.

The changes in the criminal justice system's response to domestic violence are quite new, however, and have not occurred universally. Although states have enacted various types of statutes to promote more aggressive treatment of domestic violence as a crime, whether this approach is upheld by individual actors within the system varies from jurisdiction to jurisdiction.

In many jurisdictions, courts can order batterers to attend special counseling programs either before the case is adjudicated or as a condition of probation. Frequently, criminal charges are dismissed if the defendant "successfully" completes the program. Unfortunately, the effectiveness of special programs for abusive men is hard to measure, and little information exists on the effectiveness of intervention.

LEGAL PROTECTION FOR THE VICTIM

In the early 1970s, few legal remedies existed for the battered woman seeking protection from abuse. If married, she could file for divorce, separation, or custody, and in some states obtain an injunction ordering her husband not to abuse her while domestic relations proceedings were pending.

Since that time, 47 states and the District of Columbia have enacted legislation allowing battered women to obtain civil protection or restraining orders. Depending on the state, through such legislation the court can order the abuser to move out of the residence, refrain from abuse of or contact with the victim, enter a batterers' treatment program, or pay support, restitution, or attorney's fees. However, "a protection or restraining order is meaningful only if violation of the order constitutes a crime and police are able to verify the existence of an order when a violation is alleged."

The ability of such orders to protect all do-mestic violence victims is inconsistent across jurisdictions. Some areas require the victim to be married to and currently cohabitating with the abuser. Abuse may be narrowly defined as an attempt or infliction of bodily injury or serious bodily injury, providing no protection from threats of violence or destruction of property. The duration of protection orders can range from 15 days to no more than one year, thereby forcing many women to relocate to avoid abuse. Moreover, it is believed that protection orders are poorly implemented and enforced. It may be quite difficult for low-income women, women of color, and women who have defended themselves against physical abuse to obtain this type of protection. The use and enforcement of civil protection orders is now under study through funding from the Justice Department.

THE IMPORTANCE OF PREVENTION

Clearly, just responding to domestic violence is not sufficient. An improved criminal justice response and the development of court-ordered programs for abusive men are not panaceas for the problem. Battered women's advocates believe that to bring an end to domestic violence, it is necessary to examine how the culture teaches young men and women to play roles that lead to such violent behavior, and how restricted access to economic resources can trap women in the potentially lethal cycle of violence.

If the cycle of violence is to be broken, advocates on behalf of battered women stress that young women must be encouraged to go beyond traditionally passive, dependent roles, while young men must be taught that abusive, violent, and controlling behavior is never acceptable. To this end, battered women's advocates have established children's programs in many shelters, as well as curricula on domestic violence for use in elementary, middle, and high schools.

Finally, equal access to employment, housing, and economic resources must be available to all women. This situation is particularly acute for battered women, who frequently remain in abusive relationships simply because of economics. Thus, a critical determinant of whether a battered woman will live without violence or be forced to return to an abusive partner often is the availability of decent affordable housing, adequate pay, and other forms of economic assistance.

Violence in the home is a problem with serious repercussions for the battered woman, her children, and the entire community. Breaking the cycle of violence requires financial support for services to battered women, a strong criminal justice response that holds abusive men accountable for their violence, and, most important, ongoing social activism that focuses on improving the status of all women.   [1988]

Understanding the Reading

1. Why do women stay in abusive relationships?
2. What actions have battered women undertaken to combat domestic violence?
3. What legal action has been taken to respond to the problem of domestic violence?
4. What can be done to *prevent* domestic violence?

Suggestion for Responding

How would you respond to someone you know who is in an abusive relationship? Be sure you take into account the resistance that the person may express. ✦

98

Freedom for the Thought We Hate

GERALD GUNTHER

I am deeply troubled by current efforts—however well-intentioned—to place new limits on freedom of expression at this and other campuses. Such limits are not only incompatible with the mission and meaning of a university; they also send exactly the wrong message from academia to society as a whole. University campuses should exhibit greater, not less, freedom of expression than prevails in society at large.

Proponents of new limits argue that historic First Amendment rights must be balanced against the university's commitment to the diversity of ideas and persons. Clearly, there is ample room

and need for vigorous university action to combat racial and other discrimination. But curbing freedom of speech is the wrong way to do so. The proper answer to bad speech is usually more and better speech—not new laws, litigation, and repression.

Lest it be thought that I am insensitive to the pain imposed by expressions of racial or religious hatred, let me say that I have suffered that pain and empathize with others under similar verbal assault. My deep belief in the principles of the First Amendment arises in part from my own experiences. I received my elementary education in a public school in a very small town in Nazi Germany. There I was subjected to vehement anti-Semitic remarks from my teacher, classmates, and others—"Judensau" (Jew pig) was far from the harshest. I can assure you that they hurt.

More generally, I lived in a country where ideological orthodoxy reigned and where the opportunity for dissent was severely limited.

The lesson I have drawn from my childhood in Nazi Germany and my happier adult life in this country is the need to walk the sometimes difficult path of denouncing the bigots' hateful ideas with all my power, yet at the same time challenging any community's attempt to suppress hateful ideas by force of law.

Obviously, given my own experience, I do *not* quarrel with the claim that *words* can do harm. But I firmly deny that a showing of harm suffices to deny First Amendment protection, and I insist on the elementary First Amendment principle that our Constitution usually protects even offensive, harmful expression.

That is why—at the risk of being thought callous or doctrinaire—I recently opposed attempts by some members of my university community to enlarge the area of forbidden speech to prohibit not only "personal abuse" but also "defamation of groups"—expression "that by accepted community standards . . . pejoratively characterizes persons or groups on the basis of personal or cultural differences." Such proposals, in my view, seriously undervalue the First Amendment and far too readily endanger its precious content. Limitations on free expression beyond those established by law should be eschewed in an institution committed to diversity and the First Amendment.

In explaining my position, I will avoid extensive legal arguments. Instead, I want to speak from the heart, on the basis of my own background and of my understanding of First Amendment principles—principles supported by an ever larger number of scholars and Supreme Court justices, especially since the days of the Warren Court.[1]

Among the core principles is that any official effort to suppress expression must be viewed with the greatest skepticism and suspicion. Only in very narrow, urgent circumstances should government or similar institutions be permitted to inhibit speech. True, there are certain categories of speech that may be prohibited; but the number and scope of these categories has steadily shrunk over the last fifty years. Face-to-face insults are one such category; incitement to immediate illegal action is another. But opinions expressed in debates and arguments about a wide range of political and social issues should not be suppressed simply because of disagreement with those views, with the content of the expression.

Similarly, speech should not and cannot be banned simply because it is "offensive" to substantial parts of a majority of the community. The refusal to suppress offensive speech is one of the most difficult obligations the free speech principle imposes upon all of us; yet it is also one of the First Amendment's greatest glories—indeed it is a central test of a community's commitment to free speech.

The Supreme Court's 1989 decision to allow flag-burning as a form of political protest, in *Texas v. Johnson,* warrants careful pondering by all those who continue to advocate campus restraints on "racist speech." As Justice Brennan's majority opinion in *Johnson* reminded, "If there is a bedrock principle underlying the First Amendment, it is that the Government may not prohibit the expression of an idea itself offensive or disagreeable." In refusing to place flag-burning outside the First Amendment, moreover, the *Johnson* majority insisted (in words especially apt for the "racist speech" debate): "The First Amendment does not guarantee that other concepts virtually sacred to our Nation as a whole—*such as the principle that discrimination on the basis of race is odious and destructive*—will go unquestioned in the marketplace of ideas. We decline, therefore, to create for the flag an exception to the joust of principles protected by the First Amendment." (Italics added.)

Campus proponents of restricting offensive speech are currently relying for justification on the Supreme Court's allegedly repeated reiteration that "fighting words" constitute an exception to the First Amendment. Such an exception has indeed been recognized in a number of lower court cases. However, there has only been *one* case in the history of the Supreme Court in which a majority of the justices has ever found a statement to be a punishable resort to "fighting words." That was *Chaplinsky v. New Hampshire,* a nearly fifty-year-old case involving words which would very likely not be found punishable today.

More significant is what has happened in the nearly half-century since: Despite repeated appeals to the Supreme Court to recognize the applicability of the "fighting words" exception by affirming challenged convictions, the court has in every instance refused. One must wonder about the strength of an exception that, while theoretically recognized, has for so long not been found apt in practice.

The phenomenon of racist and other offensive speech is not a new one in the history of the First Amendment. In recent decades, for example, well-meaning (but in my view misguided) majorities have sought to suppress not only racist speech but also anti-war and anti-draft speech, civil rights demonstrators, the Nazis and Ku Klux Klan, and left-wing groups.

Typically, it is people on the extremes of the political spectrum (including those who advocate overthrow of our constitutional system and those who would not protect their opponents' right to dissent were they the majority) who feel the brunt of repression and have found protection in the First Amendment; typically, it is well-meaning people in the majority who believe their sensibilities, their sense of outrage, justify restraints.

Those in power in a community recurrently seek to repress speech they find abhorrent, and their efforts are understandable human impulses. Yet freedom of expression—and especially the protection of dissident speech, the most important function of the First Amendment—is an anti-majoritarian principle. Is it too much to hope that, especially on a university campus, a majority can be persuaded of the value of freedom of expression and of the resultant need to curb our impulses to repress dissident views?

The principles to which I appeal are not new. They have been expressed, for example, by the most distinguished Supreme Court justices ever since the beginning of the court's confrontations with First Amendment issues nearly seventy years ago. These principles are reflected in the words of so imperfect a First Amendment defender as Justice Oliver Wendell Holmes: "If there is any principle of the Constitution that more imperatively calls for attachment than any other it is the principle of free thought—not free thought for those who agree with us but freedom for the thought that we hate." This is the principle most elaborately and eloquently addressed by Justice Louis D. Brandeis, who reminded us that the First Amendment rests on a belief "in the power of reason as applied through public discussion" and therefore bars "silence coerced by law—the argument of force in its worst form."

This theme, first articulated in dissents, has repeatedly been voiced in majority opinions in more recent decades. It underlies Justice Douglas's remark in striking down a conviction under a law banning speech that "stirs the public to anger": "A function of free speech [is] to invite dispute. . . . Speech is often provocative and challenging. That is why freedom of speech [is ordinarily] protected against censorship or punishment."

It also underlies Justice William J. Brennan's comment about our "profound national commitment to the principle that debate on public issues should be uninhibited, robust and wide-open, and that it may well include vehement, caustic and sometimes unpleasantly sharp attacks"—a comment he followed with a reminder that constitutional protection "does not turn upon the truth, popularity or social utility of the ideas and beliefs which are offered."

These principles underlie as well the repeated insistence by Justice John Marshall Harlan, again in majority opinions, that the mere "inutility or immorality" of a message cannot justify its repression, and that the state may not punish because of "the underlying content of the message." Moreover, Justice Harlan, in one of the finest First Amendment opinions on the books, noted, in words that we would ignore at peril at this time:

"The constitutional right of free expression is powerful medicine in a society as diverse and populous as ours. . . . To many, the immediate consequence of this freedom may often appear to be only verbal tumult, discord and even offensive utterance. These are, however, within established limits, in truth necessary side effects of the broader enduring values which the process of open debate permits us to achieve. That the air may at times seem filled with verbal cacophony is, in this sense, not a sign of weakness but of strength."

In this same passage, Justice Harlan warned that a power to ban speech merely because it is offensive is an "inherently boundless" notion, and added that "we think it is largely because governmental officials cannot make principled distinctions in this area that the Constitution leaves matters of taste and style so largely to the individual." (The Justice made these comments while overturning the conviction of an antiwar protestor for "offensive conduct." The defendant had worn, in a courthouse corridor, a jacket bearing the words "Fuck the draft."

I restate these principles and repeat these words for reasons going far beyond the fact that they are familiar to me as a First Amendment scholar. I believe—in my heart as well as my mind—that these principles and ideals are not only established but right. I hope that the entire academic community will seriously reflect upon the risks to free expression, lest we weaken hard-won liberties at our universities and, by example, in this nation. [1990]

Note

1. WARREN COURT: The Supreme Court under Chief Justice Earl Warren, which passed down such decisions as the prohibition of school segregation.

Understanding the Reading

1. Why does Gunther describe his childhood in Germany?
2. Why does he argue that speech should not "be banned simply because it is 'offensive'"?

3. What connection does Gunther make between flag-burning and racist speech?
4. Why does he object to the use of the concept of "fighting words" to prohibit racist speech?
5. Explain each of the quotations of the five Supreme Court Justices.

Suggestion for Responding

Gunther presents a persuasive advocacy of freedom of speech. Develop an argument in favor of some restrictions. ◆

99

Acknowledging the Victims' Cry

CHARLES R. LAWRENCE III

I have spent the better part of my life as a dissenter. As a high-school student, I was threatened with suspension for my refusal to participate in a civil-defense drill, and I have been a conspicuous consumer of my First Amendment liberties[1] ever since. There are very strong reasons for protecting even speech that is racist. Perhaps the most important is that such protection reinforces our society's commitment to tolerance as a value. By protecting bad speech from government regulation, we will be forced to combat it as a community.

I have, however, a deeply felt apprehension about the resurgence of racial violence and the corresponding increase in the incidence of verbal and symbolic assault and harassment to which African-Americans and other traditionally excluded groups are subjected. I am troubled by the way the debate has been framed in response to the recent surge of racist incidents on college and university campuses and in response to some universities' attempts to regulate harassing speech. The problem has been framed as one in which the liberty of free speech is in conflict with the elimination of racism. I believe this has placed the bigot on the moral high ground and fanned the rising flames of racism.

Above all, I am troubled that we have not listened to the real victims—that we have shown so little understanding of their injury, and that we have abandoned those whose race, gender, or sexual orientation continues to make them second-class citizens. It seems to me a very sad irony that the first instinct of civil libertarians has been to challenge even the smallest, most narrowly framed efforts by universities to provide African-Americans and other minority students with the protection the Constitution, in my opinion, guarantees them.

The landmark case of *Brown v. Board of Education*[2] is not a case that we normally think of as a case about speech. But *Brown* can be broadly read as articulating the principle of equal citizenship. *Brown* held that segregated schools were inherently unequal because of the message that segregation conveyed: that African-American children were an untouchable caste, unfit to go to school with white children. If we understand the necessity of eliminating the system of signs and symbols that signal the inferiority of African-Americans, then we should hesitate before proclaiming that all racist speech that stops short of physical violence must be defended.

University officials who have formulated policies to respond to incidents of racial harassment have been characterized in the press as "thought police," even though such policies generally do nothing more than impose sanctions against intentional face-to-face insults. Racist speech that takes the form of face-to-face insults, catcalls, or other assaultive speech aimed at an individual or small group of persons falls directly within the "fighting words" exception to First Amendment protection. The Supreme Court has held in *Chaplinsky v. New Hampshire* that words which "by their very utterance inflict injury or tend to incite an immediate breach of the peace" are not protected by the First Amendment.

If the purpose of the First Amendment is to foster the greatest amount of speech, racial insults disserve that purpose. Assaultive racist speech functions as a preemptive strike. The invective is experienced as a blow, not as a proffered idea. And once the blow is struck, a dialogue is unlikely to follow. Racial insults are particularly undeserving of First Amendment protection, because the perpetrator's intention is not to discover truth or initiate dialogue but to injure the victim. In most situations, members of minority groups realize that they are likely to lose if they fight back, and are forced to remain silent and submissive.

Courts have held that offensive speech may not be regulated in public forums (such as streets, where the listener may avoid the speech by moving on). But the regulation of otherwise protected speech has been permitted when the speech invades the privacy of the unwilling listener's home, or when the unwilling listener is a "captive audience" and cannot avoid the speech. Racist posters, fliers, and graffiti in dormitories, bathrooms, and other common living spaces would seem to fall within the reasoning of these cases. Minority students should not be required to remain in their rooms in order to avoid racial insult. Minimally, they should find a safe haven in their dorms and in all other common rooms that are a part of their daily routine.

I would also argue that the university's responsibility for ensuring that these students receive an equal educational opportunity provides a compelling justification for regulations that ensure them safe passage in all common areas. A minority student should not have to risk becoming the target of racially assaulting speech every time he or she chooses to walk across campus. Regulating vilifying speech that cannot be anticipated or avoided need not preclude announced speeches and rallies—situations that would give minority-group members and their allies the opportunity to organize counterdemonstrations or avoid the speech altogether.

The most commonly advanced argument against the regulation of racist speech proceeds something like this: We recognize that minority groups suffer pain and injury as the result of racist speech, but we must allow this hate-mongering for the benefit of society as a whole. Freedom of speech is the lifeblood of our democratic system. It is especially important for minorities, because often it is their only vehicle for rallying support for the redress of their grievances. It will be impossible to formulate a prohibition so precise that it will prevent the racist speech you want to suppress without catching in the same net all kinds of speech that it would be unconscionable for a democratic society to suppress.

Such arguments seek to strike a balance between our concern, on the one hand, for the continued free flow of ideas and the democratic process dependent on that flow, and, on the other, our desire to further the cause of equality. There can, however, be no meaningful discussion of how we should reconcile our commitment to equality with our commitment to free speech until it is acknowledged that racist speech inflicts real harm, and that this harm is far from trivial.

To engage in a debate about the First Amendment and racist speech without a full understanding of the nature and extent of that harm is to risk making the First Amendment an instrument of domination rather [than] a vehicle of liberation. We have not all known the experience of victimization by racist, misogynist, and homophobic speech, nor do we equally share the burden of the harm it inflicts. We are often quick to say that we have heard the cry of the victims when we have not.

The *Brown* case is again instructive, because it speaks directly to the psychic injury inflicted by racist speech by noting that the symbolic message of segregation affected "the hearts and minds" of African-American children "in a way unlikely ever to be undone." Racial epithets and harassment often cause deep emotional scarring and feelings of anxiety and fear that pervade every aspect of a victim's life.

Brown also recognized that African-American children did not have an equal opportunity to learn and participate in the school's community when they bore the additional burden of being subjected to the humiliation and psychic assault contained in the message of segregation. University students bear an analogous burden when they are forced to live and work in an environment where at any moment they may be subject to denigrating verbal harassment and assault. The same injury was addressed by the Supreme Court when it held that, under Title VII of the Civil Rights Act of 1964, sexual harassment which creates a hostile or abusive work environment violates the ban on sex discrimination in employment.

Carefully drafted university regulations could bar the use of words as assault weapons while at the same time leaving unregulated even the most heinous of ideas provided those ideas are presented at times and places and in manners that provide an opportunity for reasoned rebuttal or escape from immediate insult. The history of the development of the right to free speech has been one of carefully evaluating the importance of free expression and its effects on other important societal interests. We have drawn the line between protected and unprotected speech before without dire results. (Courts have, for example, exempted from the protection of the First Amendment obscene speech and speech that disseminates official secrets, defames or libels another person, or is used to form a conspiracy or monopoly.)

African-Americans and other people of color are skeptical about the argument that even the most injurious speech must remain unregulated because, in an unregulated marketplace of ideas, the best ones will rise to the top and gain acceptance. Experience tells quite the opposite. People of color have seen too many demagogues elected by appealing to American's racism, and too many sympathetic politicians shy away from issues that might brand them as being too closely allied with disparaged groups.

Whenever we decide that racist speech must be tolerated because of the importance of maintaining societal tolerance for all unpopular speech, we are asking African-Americans and other subordinated groups to bear the burden for the good of all. We must be careful that the ease with which we strike the balance against the regulation of racist speech is in no way influenced by the fact that the cost will be borne by others. We must be certain that those who will pay that price are fairly represented in our deliberations and that they are heard.

At the core of the argument that we should resist all government regulation of speech is the idea that the best cure for bad speech is good— that ideas that affirm equality and the worth of all individuals will ultimately prevail. This is an empty ideal unless those of us who would fight racism are vigilant and unequivocal in that fight. We must look for ways to offer assistance and support to students whose speech and political participation are chilled in a climate of racial harassment.

Civil rights lawyers might consider suing on behalf of African-Americans whose right to an equal education is denied by a university's failure to ensure a nondiscriminatory education climate or conditions of employment. We must embark upon the development of a First Amendment jurisprudence grounded in the reality of our history and our contemporary experience. We must think hard about how best to launch legal attacks against the most indefensible forms of hate speech. Good lawyers can create exceptions and narrow interpretations that limit the harm of hate speech without opening the floodgates of censorship.

Everyone concerned with these issues must find ways to engage actively in actions that resist and counter the racist ideas that we would have the First Amendment protect. If we fail in this, the victims of hate speech must rightly assume that we are on the bigots' side.   [1990]

Notes

1. FIRST AMENDMENT LIBERTIES: Freedom of worship, speech, press, and assembly.
2. *BROWN V. BOARD OF EDUCATION:* A case in which the U.S. Supreme Court declared segregated schools unconstitutional.

Understanding the Reading

1. What are "fighting words"?
2. Why does Lawrence feel that universities should regulate racist speech?
3. How does he answer opponents of regulation?
4. What connection does he see between *Brown v. Board of Education* and current policies on racist speech?

Suggestions for Responding

1. Lawrence presents a persuasive advocacy of some restrictions on "racist speech." Develop an argument against such restrictions.
2. Explain how you will evaluate your plan of action after you have implemented it. If you already have undertaken the action, write an evaluation of it. ◆

SUGGESTION FOR RESPONDING TO PART IX

ACTION PROJECT FOR SOCIAL CHANGE

The readings in Part IX have tried to show that you can actually do something to effect social change. Now it's time to put what you have learned into practice. Simply follow the steps described in the introduction to Part IX, commit yourself, and take action.

First identify something as a problem, such as becoming aware of sexism on MTV. You then have to have a desire to do something about the problem, and you need to figure out specifically what it is that you find offensive and what you want to achieve. Then, alone or together with whoever else is going to join you in your action, brainstorm about possible actions you could realistically take. With the MTV example, you could write to the producers of the videos or to the network; you could try to organize a boycott; you could undertake other different actions. Then plan your action project, considering what you will do, when you will do it, and how you will evaluate the success of your project. Then do it and become a change maker yourself.

X
Change Makers

WE USUALLY THINK OF CHANGE MAKERS AS THE movers and shakers of the world, those larger-than-life people who "really make a difference." On everyone's list would be major figures like George Washington, Abraham Lincoln, General Dwight Eisenhower, Andrew Carnegie, Henry Ford, and just maybe social worker Jane Addams. Part X is not about people of such heroic proportions, however. Instead it is about people pretty much like ourselves; not necessarily wealthy, privileged, or from influential families. This is not to imply that all those listed above had these advantages; it is just that their achievements are so embedded in our understanding of American history that they no longer seem to be "real" people like us.

The people we will read about here are young and old. Mother Jones was a 50-year-old widow when she first became a union organizer of coal miners, and César Chávez, founder of the United Farm Workers Union, was a young man when he began work as a labor organizer. The third union organizer, Carmen Domingues, only recently began to organize garment workers in El Paso, Texas. Louise Palmer tells how Domingues's group, La Mujer Obrera, has moved beyond the workplace to address other problems of women workers and of the community.

The next two selections give some insight into the civil rights movement, the most envel-oping and dynamic social movement of the twentieth century, one that has transformed U.S. society. Martin Luther King, Jr.'s nonviolent protest strategy encouraged mass involvement by many students, one of whom was Anne Moody. A destitute student from an impoverished southern black family, Moody suddenly became a central actor in the desegregation of the business district of Jackson, Mississippi. G., only a high school student when James Baldwin met him, didn't see himself as transforming the world, but when he registered at a previously all-white school, that role was thrust upon him, and he and his family had to cope as well as they could.

The next two pieces introduce change makers from the most impoverished group in the United States, Native American women. Despite their lack of resources, they are improving life on their reservations. Michael Ryan tells how, despite obstructive government regulations and lack of funds, three women created on their Yakima, Washington, reservation a college that in eight years has graduated over 400 students. Ann Davis introduces us to the indefatigable Cecilia Fire Thunder, who has organized her tribal sisters to transform life and politics on their Lakota reservation.

Middle-class people are also effective change makers. Renée La Couture Tulloch waged a single-handed battle to get passage and gubernatorial approval of a sexual battery bill in California. Michele N-K Collison reports on student efforts to eliminate sexist language, specifically the exclusionary term "freshman."

All of us can learn important lessons from the change makers who speak in these pages. The closing selection optimistically describes American society today. Richard Rodriguez sees America as a society where people from all over the world have learned to live side by side, influencing and being influenced by one another and creating our multicultural, pluralistic, uniquely American culture, a vision many of us have learned to share.

100

Victory at Arnot

Mary Harris "Mother" Jones[1]

Before 1899 the coal fields of Pennsylvania were not organized. Immigrants poured into the country and they worked cheap. There was always a surplus of immigrant labor, solicited in Europe by the coal companies, so as to keep wages down to barest living. Hours of work down under ground were cruelly long. Fourteen hours a day was not uncommon, thirteen, twelve. The life or limb of the miner was unprotected by any laws. Families lived in company owned shacks that were not fit for their pigs. Children died by the hundreds due to the ignorance and poverty of their parents.

Often I have helped lay out for burial the babies of the miners, and the mothers could scarce conceal their relief at the little ones' deaths. Another was already on its way, destined, if a boy, for the breakers; if a girl, for the silk mills where the other brothers and sisters already worked.

The United Mine Workers decided to organize these fields and work for human conditions for human beings. Organizers were put to work. Whenever the spirit of the men in the mines grew strong enough a strike was called.

In Arnot, Pennsylvania, a strike had been going on four or five months. The men were becoming discouraged. The coal company sent the doctors, the school teachers, the preachers and their wives to the homes of the miners to get them to sign a document that they would go back to work.

The president of the district, Mr. Wilson, and an organizer, Tom Haggerty, got despondent. The signatures were overwhelmingly in favor of returning on Monday.

Haggerty suggested that they send for me. Saturday morning they telephoned to Barnesboro, where I was organizing, for me to come at once or they would lose the strike.

"Oh Mother," Haggerty said, "Come over quick and help us! The boys are that despondent! They are going back Monday."

I told him that I was holding a meeting that night but that I would leave early Sunday morning.

I started at daybreak. At Roaring Branch, the nearest train connection with Arnot, the secretary of the Arnot Union, a young boy, William Bouncer, met me with a horse and buggy. We drove sixteen miles over rough mountain roads. It was biting cold. We got into Arnot Sunday noon and I was placed in the coal company's hotel, the only hotel in town. I made some objections but Bouncer said, "Mother, we have engaged this room for you and if it is not occupied, they will never rent us another."

Sunday afternoon I held a meeting. It was not as large a gathering as those we had later but I stirred up the poor wretches that did come.

"You've got to take the pledge," I said. "Rise and pledge to stick to your brothers and the union till the strike's won!"

The men shuffled their feet but the women rose, their babies in their arms, and pledged themselves to see that no one went to work in the morning.

"The meeting stands adjourned till ten o'clock tomorrow morning," I said. "Everyone come and see that the slaves that think to go back to their masters come along with you."

I returned to my room at the hotel. I wasn't called down to supper but after the general manager of the mines and all of the other guests had gone to church, the housekeeper stole up to my room and asked me to come down and get a cup of tea.

At eleven o'clock that night the housekeeper again knocked at my door and told me that I had to give up my room; that she was told it belonged to a teacher. "It's a shame, mother," she whispered, as she helped me into my coat.

I found little Bouncer sitting on guard down in the lobby. He took me up the mountain to a miner's house. A cold wind almost blew the bonnet from my head. At the miner's shack I knocked.

A man's voice shouted, "Who is there?"

"Mother Jones," said I.

A light came in the tiny window. The door opened.

"And did they put you out, Mother?"

"They did that."

"I told Mary they might do that," said the miner. He held the oil lamp with the thumb and his little finger and I could see that the others were off. His face was young but his body was bent over.

He insisted on my sleeping in the only bed, with his wife. He slept with his head on his arms on the kitchen table. Early in the morning his wife rose to keep the children quiet, so that I might sleep a little later as I was very tired.

At eight o'clock she came into my room, crying.

"Mother, are you awake?"

"Yes, I am awake."

"Well, you must get up. The sheriff is here to put us out for keeping you. This house belongs to the Company."

The family gathered up all their earthly belongings, which weren't much, took down all the holy pictures, and put them in a wagon, and they with all their neighbors went to the meeting. The sight of that wagon with the sticks of furniture and the holy pictures and the children, with the father and mother and myself walking along through the streets turned the tide. It made the men so angry that they decided not to go back that morning to the mines. Instead they came to the meeting where they determined not to give up the strike until they had won the victory.

Then the company tried to bring in scabs.[2] I told the men to stay home with the children for a change and let the women attend to the scabs. I organized an army of women housekeepers. On a given day they were to bring their mops and brooms and "the army" would charge the scabs up at the mines. The general manager, the sheriff and the corporation hirelings heard of our plans and were on hand. The day came and the women came with the mops and brooms and pails of water.

I decided not to go up to the Drip Mouth myself, for I knew they would arrest me and that might rout the army. I selected as leader an Irish woman who had a most picturesque appearance. She had slept late and her husband had told her to hurry up and get into the army. She had grabbed a red petticoat and slipped it over a thick cotton night gown. She wore a black stocking and a white one. She had tied a little red fringed shawl over her wild red hair. Her face was red and her eyes were mad. I looked at her and felt that she could raise a rumpus.

I said, "You lead the army up to the Drip Mouth. Take that tin dishpan you have with you and your hammer, and when the scabs and the mules come up, begin to hammer and howl. Then all of you hammer and howl and be ready to chase the scabs with your mops and brooms. Don't be afraid of anyone."

Up the mountain side, yelling and hollering, she led the women, and when the mules came up with the scabs and the coal, she began beating on the dishpan and hollering and all the army joined in with her. The sheriff tapped her on the shoulder.

"My dear lady," said he, "remember the mules. Don't frighten them."

She took the old tin pan and she hit him with it and she hollered, "To hell with you and the mules!"

He fell over and dropped into the creek. Then the mules began to rebel against scabbing. They bucked and kicked the scab drivers and started off for the barn. The scabs started running down hill, followed by the army of women with their mops and pails and brooms.

A poll parrot in a near by shack screamed at the superintendent, "Got hell, did you? Got hell?"

There was a great big doctor in the crowd, a company lap dog. He had a little satchel in his hand and he said to me, impudent like, "Mrs. Jones, I have a warrant for you."

"All right," said I. "Keep it in your pill bag until I come for it. I am going to hold a meeting now."

From that day on the women kept continual watch of the mines to see that the company did not bring in scabs. Every day women with brooms or mops in one hand and babies in the other arm wrapped in little blankets, went to the mines and watched that no one went in. And all night long they kept watch. They were heroic women. In the long years to come the nation will pay them high tribute for they were fighting for the advancement of a great country.

I held meetings throughout the surrounding country. The company was spending money among the farmers, urging them not to do anything for the miners. I went out with an old wagon and a union mule that had gone on strike, and a miner's little boy for a driver. I held meetings among the farmers and won them to the side of the strikers.

Sometimes it was twelve or one o'clock in the

morning when I would get home, the little boy asleep on my arm and I driving the mule. Sometimes it was several degrees below zero. The winds whistled down the mountains and drove the snow and sleet in our faces. My hands and feet were often numb. We were all living on dry bread and black coffee. I slept in a room that never had a fire in it, and I often woke up in the morning to find snow covering the outside covers of the bed.

There was a place near Arnot called Sweedy Town, and the company's agents went there to get the Swedes to break the strike. I was holding a meeting among the farmers when I heard of the company's efforts. I got the young farmers to get on their horses and go over to Sweedy Town and see that no Swede left town. They took clotheslines for lassos and any Swede seen moving in the direction of Arnot was brought back quick enough.

After months of terrible hardships the strike was about won. The mines were not working. The spirit of the men was splendid. President Wilson had come home from the western part of the state. I was staying at his home. The family had gone to bed. We sat up late talking over matters when there came a knock at the door. A very cautious knock.

"Come in," said Mr. Wilson.

Three men entered. They looked at me uneasily and Mr. Wilson asked me to step in an adjoining room. They talked the strike over and called President Wilson's attention to the fact that there were mortgages on his little home, held by the bank which was owned by the coal company, and they said, "We will take the mortgage off your home and give you $25,000 in cash if you will just leave and let the strike die out."

I shall never forget his reply:

"Gentlemen, if you come to visit my family, the hospitality of the whole house is yours. But if you come to bribe me with dollars to betray my manhood and my brothers who trust me, I want you to leave this door and never come here again."

The strike lasted a few weeks longer. Meantime President Wilson, when strikers were evicted, cleaned out his barn and took care of the evicted miners until homes could be provided. One by one he killed his chickens and his hogs. Everything that he had he shared. He ate dry bread and drank chicory. He knew every hardship that the rank and file of the organization knew. We do not have such leaders now.

The last of February the company put up a notice that all demands were conceded.

"Did you get the use of the hall for us to hold meetings?" said the women.

"No, we didn't ask for that."

"Then the strike is on again," said they.

They got the hall, and when the President, Mr. Wilson, returned from the convention in Cincinnati he shed tears of joy and gratitude.

I was going to leave for the central fields, and before I left, the union held a victory meeting in Bloosburg. The women came for miles in a raging snow storm for that meeting, little children trailing on their skirts, and babies under their shawls. Many of the miners had walked miles. It was one night of real joy and a great celebration. I bade them all good bye. A little boy called out, "Don't leave us, Mother. Don't leave us!" The dear little children kissed my hands. We spent the whole night in Bloosburg rejoicing. The men opened a few of the freight cars out on a siding and helped themselves to boxes of beer. Old and young talked and sang all night long and to the credit of the company no one was interfered with.

Those were the days before the extensive use of gun men, of military, of jails, of police clubs. There had been no bloodshed. There had been no riots. And the victory was due to the army of women with their mops and brooms.

A year afterward they celebrated the anniversary of the victory. They presented me with a gold watch but I declined to accept it, for I felt it was the price of the bread of the little children. I have not been in Arnot since but in my travels over the country I often meet the men and boys who carried through the strike so heroically.

[1972]

Notes

1. MARY HARRIS "MOTHER" JONES: After the loss of her four children and her husband in a yellow-fever epidemic and the destruction of her dressmaking shop in the Chicago fire, "Mother" Jones became a legendary labor union organizer.

2. SCABS: Strike breakers.

Understanding the Reading

1. What were the miners' lives like?
2. Why was Mother Jones not called down to supper, and what was the real reason that she had to give up her room at the hotel?
3. What was the effect of the sheriff's putting the family who sheltered her out of their house?
4. Why did Mother Jones organize an "army of women" rather than men to face the scabs?
5. Why did the miners finally win the strike?

Suggestion for Responding

Describe a time when you joined with others to organize for change. ◆

101

The Organizer's Tale

CÉSAR CHÁVEZ

It really started for me 16 years ago in San Jose, California, when I was working on an apricot farm. We figured he was just another social worker doing a study of farm conditions, and I kept refusing to meet with him. But he was persistent. Finally, I got together some of the rough element in San Jose. We were going to have a little reception for him to teach the *gringo*[1] a little bit of how we felt. There were about 30 of us in the house, young guys mostly. I was supposed to give them a signal—change my cigarette from my right hand to my left, and then we were going to give him a lot of hell. But he started talking and the more he talked, the more wide-eyed I became and the less inclined I was to give the signal. A couple of guys who were pretty drunk at the time still wanted to give the *gringo* the business, but we got rid of them. This fellow was making a lot of sense, and I wanted to hear what he had to say.

His name was Fred Ross, and he was an organizer for the Community Service Organization (CSO) which was working with Mexican-Americans in the cities. I became immediately really involved. Before long I was heading a voter registration drive. All the time I was observing the things Fred did, secretly, because I wanted to learn how to organize, to see how it was done. I was impressed with his patience and understanding of people. I thought this was a tool, one of the greatest things he had.

It was pretty rough for me at first. I was changing and had to take a lot of ridicule from the kids my age, the rough characters I worked with in the fields. They would say, "Hey big shot. Now that you're a *politico,* why are you working here for 65 cents an hour?" I might add that our neighborhood had the highest percentage of San Quentin graduates. It was a game among the *pachucos*[2] in the sense that we defended ourselves from outsiders, although inside the neighborhood there was not a lot of fighting.

After six months of working every night in San Jose, Fred assigned me to take over the CSO chapter in Decoto. It was a tough spot to fill. I would suggest something, and people would say, "No, let's wait till Fred gets back," or "Fred wouldn't do it that way." This is pretty much a pattern with people, I discovered, whether I was put in Fred's position, or later, when someone else was put in my position. After the Decoto assignment I was sent to start a new chapter in Oakland. Before I left, Fred came to a place in San Jose called the Hole-in-the-Wall and we talked for half an hour over coffee. He was in a rush to leave, but I wanted to keep him talking; I was scared of my assignment.

There were hard times in Oakland. First of all, it was a big city and I'd get lost every time I went anywhere. Then I arranged a series of house meetings. I would get to the meeting early and drive back and forth past the house, too nervous to go in and face the people. Finally I would force myself to go inside and sit in a corner. I was quite thin then, and young, and most of the people were middle-aged. Someone would say, "Where's the organizer?" And I would pipe up, "Here I am." Then they would say in Spanish—these were very poor people and we hardly spoke anything but Spanish—"Ha! This *kid?*" Most of them said they were interested, but the hardest part was to get them to start pushing themselves, on their own initiative.

The idea was to set up a meeting and then get each attending person to call his own house meeting, inviting new people—a sort of chain letter effect. After a house meeting, I would lie awake going over the whole thing, playing the tape back, trying to see why people laughed at one point, or why they were for one thing and against another. I was also learning to read and write, those late evenings. I had left school in the 7th grade after attending 67 different schools, and my reading wasn't the best.

At our first organizing meeting we had 368 people: I'll never forget it because it was very important to me. You eat your heart out; the meeting is called for 7 o'clock and you start to worry about 4. You wait. Will they show up? Then the first one arrives. By 7 there are only 20 people, you have everything in order, you have to look calm. But little by little they filter in and at a certain point you know it will be a success.

After four months in Oakland, I was transferred. The chapter was beginning to move on its own, so Fred assigned me to organize the San Joaquin Valley. Over the months I developed what I used to call schemes or tricks—now I call them techniques—of making initial contacts. The main thing in convincing someone is to spend time with him. It doesn't matter if he can read, write or even speak well. What is important is that he is a man and second, that he has shown some initial interest. One good way to develop leadership is to take a man with you in your car. And it works a lot better if you're doing the driving; that way you are in charge. You drive, he sits there, and you talk. These little things were very important to me; I was caught in a big game by then, figuring out what makes people work. I found that if you work hard enough you can usually shake people into working too, those who are concerned. You work harder and they work harder still, up to a point and then they pass you. Then, of course, they're on their own.

I also learned to keep away from the established groups and so-called leaders, and to guard against philosophizing. Working with low-income people is very different from working with the professionals who like to sit around talking about how to play politics. When you're trying to recruit a farmworker, you have to paint a little picture, and then you have to color the picture in. We found out that the harder a guy is to convince, the better leader or member he becomes. When you exert yourself to convince him, you have his confidence and he has good

motivation. A lot of people who say OK right away wind up hanging around the office, taking up the workers' time.

During the McCarthy era[3] in one Valley town, I was subjected to a lot of redbaiting. We had been recruiting people for citizenship classes at the high school when we got into a quarrel with the naturalization examiner. He was rejecting people on the grounds that they were just parroting what they learned in citizenship class. One day we had a meeting about it in Fresno, and I took along some of the leaders of our local chapter. Some redbaiting official gave us a hard time, and the people got scared and took his side. They did it because it seemed easy at the moment, even though they knew that sticking with me was the right thing to do. It was disgusting. When we left the building they walked by themselves ahead of me as if I had some kind of communicable disease. I had been working with these people for three months and I was very sad to see that. It taught me a great lesson.

That night I learned that the chapter officers were holding a meeting to review my letters and printed materials to see if I really was a Communist. So I drove out there and walked right in on their meeting. I said, "I hear you've been discussing me, and I thought it would be nice if I was here to defend myself. Not that it matters that much to you or even to me, because as far as I'm concerned you are a bunch of cowards." At that they began to apologize. "Let's forget it," they said. "You're a nice guy." But I didn't want apologies. I wanted a full discussion. I told them I didn't give a damn, but that they had to learn to distinguish fact from what appeared to be a fact because of fear. I kept them there till two in the morning. Some of the women cried. I don't know if they investigated me any further, but I stayed on another few months and things worked out.

This was not an isolated case. Often when we'd leave people to themselves they would get frightened and draw back into their shells where they had been all the years. And I learned quickly that there is no real appreciation. Whatever you do, and no matter what reasons you may give to others, you do it because you want to see it done, or maybe because you want power. And there shouldn't be any appreciation, understandably. I know good organizers who were destroyed, washed out, because they expected people to appreciate what they'd done. Anyone who comes in with the idea that farmworkers are free of sin and that the growers are all bastards, either has never dealt with the situation or is an idealist of the first order. Things don't work that way.

[1966]

Notes

1. *GRINGO:* A disparaging term used in Mexico and elsewhere in Latin America for North Americans.
2. *PACHUCOS:* A nickname for Mexican-American youth, especially delinquents and gang members.
3. MCCARTHY ERA: Senator Joseph McCarthy used his office to crusade against internal subversion and to charge high governmental and military officials, including several Presidents, with being Communists or "fellow travelers" of Communism.

Understanding the Reading

1. What made Chávez interested in organizing the Mexican-Americans?
2. What steps did he take to organize the new CSO chapter in Oakland?
3. What techniques did he use to make initial contacts?
4. What tactics were used to discredit Chávez?

Suggestion for Responding

What leadership qualities does Chávez display? ✦

102

Workers Demand Rights

LOUISE PALMER

On a hot, dusty afternoon last August, someone turned out the lights in the El Paso CMT garment factory. With eight years experience in the industry behind her, Carmen Domingues saw the potential for protest in the darkness of the warehouse building. Angry workers earlier had abandoned the production lines when their demands for promised Labor Day pay fell on deaf ears. So Domingues led them, one hundred weary immigrant women, out the door.

The next day the garment workers returned to CMT with the media, a lawyer, and members of the labor rights group La Mujer Obrera (Working Woman). The walk-out worked: the owner agreed to some concessions, including holiday pay. Although the concessions were hardly groundbreaking, the incident spurred on Mujer Obrera's high-profile crusade to improve working conditions in El Paso's hundred-plus garment factories. For a poor grassroots organization with 700 members, the results have been remarkable. By picketing, marching, and hunger striking, Mujer Obrera has demanded—and received—the attention of city, state, and federal officials.

The group's ability to organize is all the more notable in an industry that has historically relied upon an immigrant workforce cowed into submission by the fear of job loss. Most El Paso garment workers are recent female immigrants from Mexico who speak no English, have few skills and little education. For many, sewing or cutting cloth for $3.80 an hour is the only job they know, a job that may be the lifeline for a family of four, five, or six.

As members of the underclass, they have long been forced to withstand slavish conditions, working in delapidated buildings with broken toilets and no toilet paper, no heating or ventilation systems, and little or no light. Many clock long hours on dangerous, out-dated machinery without worker's compensation, benefits or vacation time. Worse still are those employers who, on occasion, simply do not pay their workers.

For more than a decade, Mujer Obrera waged a low-key battle with local authorities, who all but ignored these sweat shops. With little to show for their efforts, Obrera opted for a more dramatic approach in June when Diana Fashions shut down, owing its workers weeks of pay. As a last-ditch effort to retrieve their wages, six women, including Mujer Obrera's executive director Cecilia Rodriguez, chained themselves to sewing machines located in a new factory—opened by the former owner of Diana's.

"We were desperate because we had bills to pay," said Felipa Perez, a mother of four who was dragged from the factory site by the police. "We thought it would help to go directly to him (the owner). But the only reaction we got was his silent stare and the cops, who came to throw us in jail."

Although the workers spent three nights in jail and never received their wages, the incident captured the attention of the Department of Labor, who ordered a strike force after meeting with Mujer Obrera. The inspection of fewer than half of El Paso's small factories revealed that more than 300 workers were owed $87,000 in back pay.

Such egregious violations, says DOL regional director Bill Belt, are perpetrated by unscrupulous, fly-by-night operators who exploit the weak enforcement of laws that are, in any case, filled with loopholes. Belt says government agencies do not have the power to shut down these shops or arrest their owners who owe both workers and the IRS[1] money.

"Because only a small amount of capital is needed to go into business in the garment industry," explains Belt, "you have these marginal operators who keep closing down and opening up under new names, with different partners and different capital in another part of town. Some of these people haven't paid taxes in years. Often, you can't trace the original owner back to an operation once it has closed." For a worker, that can mean writing off hundreds of desperately needed dollars.

"These conditions amount to slavery," says Mujer Obrera's development specialist, Cindy Arnold. "This lawlessness exists because these workers are women and they are immigrants." While the DOL points a finger at factory operators, Arnold and Democratic Congressman Ronald Coleman blame government agencies—including the DOL—that have not vigorously enforced the law. They say violations have mushroomed during the eighties precisely because there was no commitment to protecting worker rights in the Reagan/Bush Administration. Although the DOL and the Occupational Safety and Health Agency deny these allegations, Arnold says the agencies committed strike forces into El Paso's garment factories only when Mujer Obrera garnered the media's attention.

While six women fasted under the shade of a tent set up in the middle of a downtown El Paso park, Mujer Obrera galvanized the support of labor, Hispanic and feminist organizations through activities emphasizing worker solidarity. The strike was a radical call to action, aimed at educating the entire community about the oppression damaging the lives of women workers in the garment industry. But it also provided an opportunity for women to exercise their leadership qualities, an essential activity for Mujer Obrera members. The organization's education, social and economic programs—food and bread co-operatives, classes, youth outreach—emphasize building self-confidence, developing individual capabilities, and promoting self-sufficiency. "The women begin to see value in themselves, and not just as objects," says Carmen Domingues, an eight year veteran of garment factories who participated in the strike. "They see that we have our rights and our struggles and they carry that attitude home, where they have been told, 'you're dumb.'"

DYING A SLOW DEATH

The odds of winning this fight are not good for Mujer Obrera. Deteriorating conditions in the factories are inextricably linked to a force beyond the group's control: the creeping paralysis in the garment industry. Over the last decade, El Paso lost almost five thousand jobs. Across the nation, the figure reads half a million. Big employers—corporate manufacturer's such as Billy the Kid and Farah Inc.—moved their El Paso factories off-shore to Mexico or the Caribbean where labor is even more pliant. Industry experts view the offshore trend as yet another example of this nation's collapsing industrial base, its inability to persevere in the face of a low-rent Third World labor force.

Because cheap sewing machines are always available, shops run by subcontractors pop up overnight, existing month-to-month depending on the availability of contracts. Unlike the large manufacturing corporations, these undercapitalized shops have no money for investments in technology and upgrading, says Trish Winstead, director of El Paso Manufacturer's Association. This means that some shops are not capable of satisfying the demands of manufacturers. As a result, clothing orders are returned without pay, leaving the subcontractor—and the workers—out of pocket.

"I just had a batch of jeans come back last week," says Alejandro Ruiz, operator of Christian Fashions. "But I've also had checks from manufacturers bounce repeatedly. When something like that happens, it creates cash flow problems for subcontractors. Some can't pay their workers because they don't have the money."

Mujer Obrera maintains that the manufacturers should shoulder at least partial responsibility for wage theft and working conditions in subcontractors shops because they benefit most. "The industry is structured so that five or six levels of people are taking cuts of profit from a single garment, with the manufacturer at the top of the pile," explains Arnold. "That dictates the kind of exploitation and enslavement that exists at the subcontractor level. Everyone wants to maintain their level of profit regardless of how much costs rise. So the lower levels of this structure are squeezed to keep prices down."

The drive to lower production costs has intensified as manufacturers move south, leaving shop operators to compete for a shrinking pool of contracts, and workers to fight for fewer and fewer jobs. Subcontractors may be struggling, but ultimately it is the workers, clinging to the lowest rung on the ladder, who bear the brunt of cost-cutting measures in the workplace.

Ironically, Mujer Obrera's efforts to secure pay and better working conditions may speed the departure of manufacturers from El Paso—and this country. Apparel manufacturers like Mark Mainwaring, Vice President of El Paso's OMSA,[2] believe Mujer Obrera may cause irreparable damage to factories in the area. "Although Mujer Obrera is obtaining short term goals, the long term effect will be to cast aspersions on the whole industry and prevent people from sending work to El Paso. They may decide it's not worth it and just move their operation across the border." For Mujer Obrera, it's a risk worth taking, says executive director Cecilia Rodriguez. "To the industry we say, 'If it's going to come down to a choice between exploiting us or leaving, we say go.'"

But Rodriguez is hopeful that El Paso's garment industry can be revived with some innovative thinking.

Through the commission, Mujer Obrera hopes to encourage manufacturers to reinvest in and upgrade shops they buy from. Mujer Obrera believes this can happen if the city commits resources to promoting and nurturing the garment industry. They say the Chamber of Commerce, for example, should lobby to attract manufacturers by advertising the advantages the city offers: skilled workers in shops that work small orders with quick turn-around time. Manufacturers can avoid red tape, quotas, delays and freight costs if the work is done in the U.S.

Mujer Obrera knows it's a long shot. But they also know the survival of the industry is not a measure of their success. Mujer Obrera has already created a dynamic group of leaders, who are prompting members of this community to reconsider their position in the ongoing struggle for equal rights in the workplace. "Our protests are meant to force you to take a moral stance," said Mujer Obrera's executive director, Cecilia Rodriguez, exhorting a crowd gathered for the hunger strike vigil. "Is this indeed what women deserve?"   [1991]

Notes

1. IRS: Internal Revenue Service.
2. OMSA: Overseas Manufacturing Systems of America.

Understanding the Reading

1. What tactics did Carmen Domingues and La Mujer Obrera employ to improve their working conditions?
2. What obstacles did they face?
3. Why are these garment factories able to operate under these conditions?
4. How has La Mujer Obrera become more than simply a labor union?
5. What future problems does the El Paso garment industry face?
6. What response to them does La Mujer Obrera propose?

Suggestion for Responding

Compare the experiences of these women with those of the miners Mother Jones helped organize. ✦

103

The Movement

ANNE MOODY

I had counted on graduating in the spring of 1963, but as it turned out, I couldn't because some of my credits still had to be cleared with Natchez College. A year before, this would have seemed like a terrible disaster, but now I hardly even felt disappointed. I had a good excuse to stay on campus for the summer and work with the Movement, and this was what I really wanted to do. I couldn't go home again anyway, and I couldn't go to New Orleans—I didn't have money enough for bus fare.

During my senior year at Tougaloo, my family hadn't sent me one penny. I had only the small amount of money I had earned at Maple Hill. I couldn't afford to eat at school or live in the dorms, so I had gotten permission to move off campus. I had to prove that I could finish school, even if I had to go hungry every day. I knew Raymond and Miss Pearl were just waiting to see me drop out. But something happened to me as I got more and more involved in the Movement. It no longer seemed important to prove anything. I had found something outside myself that gave meaning to my life.

I had become very friendly with my social science professor, John Salter, who was in charge of NAACP[1] activities on campus. All during the year, while the NAACP conducted a boycott of the downtown stores in Jackson, I had been one of Salter's most faithful canvassers and church speakers. During the last week of school, he told me that sit-in demonstrations were about to start in Jackson and that he wanted me to be the spokesman for a team that would sit-in at Woolworth's lunch counter. The two other demonstrators would be classmates of mine, Memphis and Pearlena. Pearlena was a dedicated NAACP worker, but Memphis had not been very involved in the Movement on campus. It seemed that the organization had had a rough time finding students who were in a position to go to jail. I had nothing to lose one way or the other. Around ten o'clock the morning of the demonstrations,

NAACP headquarters alerted the news services. As a result, the police department was also informed, but neither the policemen nor the newsmen knew exactly where or when the demonstrations would start. They stationed themselves along Capitol Street and waited.

To divert attention from the sit-in at Woolworth's, the picketing started at J. C. Penney's a good fifteen minutes before. The pickets were allowed to walk up and down in front of the store three or four times before they were arrested. At exactly 11 A.M., Pearlena, Memphis, and I entered Woolworth's from the rear entrance. We separated as soon as we stepped into the store, and made small purchases from various counters. Pearlena had given Memphis her watch. He was to let us know when it was 11:14. At 11:14 we were to join him near the lunch counter and at exactly 11:15 we were to take seats at it.

Seconds before 11:15 we were occupying three seats at the previously segregated Woolworth's lunch counter. In the beginning the waitresses seemed to ignore us, as if they really didn't know what was going on. Our waitress walked past us a couple of times before she noticed we had started to write our own orders down and realized we wanted service. She asked us what we wanted. We began to read to her from our order slips. She told us that we would be served at the back counter, which was for Negroes.

"We would like to be served here," I said.

The waitress started to repeat what she had said, then stopped in the middle of the sentence. She turned the lights out behind the counter, and she and the other waitresses almost ran to the back of the store, deserting all their white customers. I guess they thought that violence would start immediately after the whites at the counter realized what was going on. There were five or six other people at the counter. A couple of them just got up and walked away. A girl sitting next to me finished her banana split before leaving. A middle-aged white woman who had not yet been served rose from her seat and came over to us. "I'd like to stay here with you," she said, "but my husband is waiting."

The newsmen came in just as she was leaving. They must have discovered what was going on shortly after some of the people began to leave the store. One of the newsmen ran behind the woman who spoke to us and asked her to identify herself. She refused to give her name, but said she was a native of Vicksburg and a former resident of California. When asked why she had said what she had said to us, she replied, "I am in sympathy with the Negro movement." By this time a crowd of cameramen and reporters had gathered around us taking pictures and asking questions, such as Where were we from? Why did we sit-in? What organization sponsored it? Were we students? From what school? How were we classified?

I told them that we were all students at Tougaloo College, that we were represented by no particular organization, and that we planned to stay there even after the store closed. "All we want is service," was my reply to one of them. After they had finished probing for about twenty minutes, they were almost ready to leave.

At noon, students from a nearby white high school started pouring in to Woolworth's. When they first saw us they were sort of surprised. They didn't know how to react. A few started to heckle and the newsmen became interested again. Then the white students started chanting all kinds of anti-Negro slogans. We were called a little bit of everything. The rest of the seats except the three we were occupying had been roped off to prevent others from sitting down. A couple of the boys took one end of the rope and made it into a hangman's noose. Several attempts were made to put it around our necks. The crowds grew as more students and adults came in for lunch.

We kept our eyes straight forward and did not look at the crowd except for occasional glances to see what was going on. All of a sudden I saw a face I remembered—the drunkard from the bus station sit-in. My eyes lingered on him just long enough for us to recognize each other. Today he was drunk too, so I don't think he remembered where he had seen me before. He took out a knife, opened it, put it in his pocket, and then began to pace the floor. At this point, I told Memphis and Pearlena what was going on. Memphis suggested that we pray. We bowed our heads, and all hell broke loose. A man rushed forward, threw Memphis from his seat, and slapped my face. Then another man who worked in the store threw me against an adjoining counter.

Down on my knees on the floor, I saw Memphis lying near the lunch counter with blood run-ning out of the corners of his mouth. As he tried to protect his face, the man who'd thrown him down kept kicking him against the head. If he had worn hard-soled shoes instead of sneakers, the first kick probably would have killed Memphis. Finally a man dressed in plain clothes iden-tified himself as a police officer and arrested Memphis and his attacker.

Pearlena had been thrown to the floor. She and I got back on our stools after Memphis was arrested. There were some white Tougaloo teachers in the crowd. They asked Pearlena and me if we wanted to leave. They said that things were getting too rough. We didn't know what to do. While we were trying to make up our minds, we were joined by Joan Trumpauer. Now there were three of us and we were integrated. The crowd began to chant, "Communists, Commu-nists, Communists." Some old man in the crowd ordered the students to take us off the stools.

"Which one should I get first?" a big husky boy said.

"That white nigger," the old man said.

The boy lifted Joan from the counter by her waist and carried her out of the store. Simultane-ously, I was snatched from my stool by two high school students. I was dragged about thirty feet toward the door by my hair when someone made them turn me loose. As I was getting up off the floor, I saw Joan coming back inside. We started back to the center of the counter to join Pearlena. Lois Chaffee, a white Tougaloo faculty member, was now sitting next to her. So Joan and I just climbed across the rope at the front end of the counter and sat down. There were now four of us, two whites and two Negroes, all women. The mob started smearing us with ketchup, mustard, sugar, pies, and everything on the counter. Soon Joan and I were joined by John Salter, but the moment he sat down he was hit on the jaw with what appeared to be brass knuckles. Blood gushed from his face and someone threw salt into the open wound. Ed King, Tougaloo's chap-lain, rushed to him.

At the other end of the counter, Lois and Pear-lena were joined by George Raymond, a CORE[2] field worker and a student from Jackson State College. Then a Negro high school boy sat down next to me. The mob took spray paint from the counter and sprayed it on the new demonstra-tors. The high school student had on a white shirt; the word "nigger" was written on his back with red spray paint.

We sat there for three hours taking a beating when the manager decided to close the store because the mob had begun to go wild with stuff from other counters. He begged and begged everyone to leave. But even after fifteen minutes of begging, no one budged. They would not leave until we did. Then Dr. Beittel, the president of Tougaloo College, came running in. He said he had just heard what was happening.

About ninety policemen were standing outside the store; they had been watching the whole thing through the windows, but had not come in to stop the mob or do anything. President Beittel went outside and asked Captain Ray to come and escort us out. The captain refused, stating the manager had to invite him in before he could enter the premises, so Dr. Beittel himself brought us out. He had told the police that they had better protect us after we were outside the store. When we got outside, the policemen formed a single line that blocked the mob from us. However, they were allowed to throw at us everything they had collected. Within ten minutes, we were picked up by Reverend King in his station wagon and taken to the NAACP headquarters on Lynch Street.

After the sit-in, all I could think of was how sick Mississippi whites were. They believed so much in the segregated Southern way of life, they would kill to preserve it. I sat there in the NAACP office and thought of how many times they had killed when this way of life was threatened. I knew that the killing had just begun. "Many more will die before it is over with," I thought. Before the sit-in, I had always hated the whites in Mississippi. Now I knew it was impossible for me to hate sickness. The whites had a disease, an incurable disease in its final stage. What were our chances against such a disease? I thought of the students, the young Negroes who had just begun to protest, as young interns. When these young interns got older, I thought, they would be the best doctors in the world for social problems.

Before we were taken back to campus, I wanted to get my hair washed. It was stiff with dried mustard, ketchup and sugar. I stopped in at a beauty shop across the street from the NAACP office. I didn't have on any shoes because I had lost them when I was dragged across the floor at Woolworth's. My stockings were sticking to my legs from the mustard that had dried on them. The hairdresser took one look at me and said, "My land, you were in the sit-in, huh?"

"Yes," I answered. "Do you have time to wash my hair and style it?"

"Right away," she said, and she meant right away. There were three other ladies already waiting, but they seemed glad to let me go ahead of them. The hairdresser was real nice. She even took my stockings off and washed my legs while my hair was drying.

There was a mass rally that night at the Pearl Street Church in Jackson, and the place was packed. People were standing two abreast in the aisles. Before the speakers began, all the sit-inners walked out on the stage and were introduced by Medgar Evers.[3] People stood and applauded for what seemed like thirty minutes or more. Medgar told the audience that this was just the beginning of such demonstrations. He asked them to pledge themselves to unite in a massive offensive against segregation in Jackson, and throughout the state. The rally ended with "We Shall Overcome" and sent home hundreds of determined people. It seemed as though Mississippi Negroes were about to get together at last. [1968]

Notes

1. NAACP: National Association for the Advancement of Colored People.
2. CORE: Congress of Racial Equality.
3. MEDGAR EVERS: The NAACP field secretary in Mississippi who was assassinated a few weeks after this event.

Understanding the Reading

1. How do you account for the various reactions of the whites at the lunch counter when the demonstrators sat down?
2. Why did the high school students respond differently than these people?
3. Explain the reaction of the women in the beauty shop.

Suggestion for Responding

Explain how Moody's experience illustrates the various features of nonviolent resistance. ◆

104

A Fly in Buttermilk

JAMES BALDWIN

"You can take the child out of the country," my elders were fond of saying, "but you can't take the country out of the child." They were speaking of their own antecedents, I supposed; it didn't, anyway, seem possible that they could be warning me; I took myself out of the country and went to Paris. It was there I discovered that the old folks knew what they had been talking about: I found myself, willy-nilly, alchemized into an American the moment I touched French soil.

Now, back again after nearly nine years, it was ironical to reflect that if I had not lived in France for so long I would never have found it necessary—or possible—to visit the American South. The South had always frightened me. How deeply it had frightened me—though I had never seen it—and how soon, was one of the things my dreams revealed to me while I was there. And this made me think of the privacy and mystery of childhood all over again, in a new way. I wondered where children got their strength—the strength, in this case, to walk through mobs to get to school

"You've got to remember," said an older Negro friend to me in Washington, "that no matter what you see or how it makes you feel, it can't be compared to twenty-five, thirty years ago—you remember those photographs of Negroes hanging from trees?" I looked at him differently. *I* had seen the photographs—but *he* might have been one of them. "I remember," he said, "when conductors on streetcars wore pistols and had police powers." And he remembered a great deal more. He remembered, for example, hearing Booker T. Washington[1] speak, and the day-to-day progress of the Scottsboro case,[2] and the rise and bloody fall of Bessie Smith.[3] These had been books and headlines and music for me but it now developed that they were also a part of my identity.

"You're just one generation away from the South, you know. You'll find," he added, kindly, "that people will be willing to talk to you . . . if they don't feel that you look down on them just because you're from the North."

The first Negro I encountered, an educator, didn't give me any opportunity to look down. He forced me to admit, at once, that I had never been to college; that northern Negroes lived herded together, like pigs in a pen; that the campus on which we met was a tribute to the industry and determination of southern Negroes. "Negroes in the South form a *community*." My humiliation was complete with his discovery that I couldn't even drive a car. I couldn't ask him anything. He made me feel so hopeless an example of the general northern spinelessness that it would have seemed a spiteful counterattack to have asked him to discuss the integration problem which had placed his city in the headlines.

At the same time, I felt that there was nothing which bothered him more; but perhaps he did not really know what he thought about it; or thought too many things at once. His campus risked being very different twenty years from now. Its special function would be gone—and so would his position, arrived at with such pain. The new day a-coming was not for him. I don't think this fact made him bitter but I think it frightened him and made him sad; for the future is like heaven—everyone exalts it but no one wants to go there now. And I imagine that he shared the attitude, which I was to encounter so often later, toward the children who were helping to bring this future about: admiration before the general spectacle and a skepticism before the individual case.

That evening I went to visit G., one of the "integrated" children, a boy of about fifteen. I had already heard something of his first day in school, the peculiar problems his presence caused, and his own extraordinary bearing.

He seemed extraordinary at first mainly by his silence. He was tall for his age and, typically, seemed to be constructed mainly of sharp angles, such as elbows and knees. Dark gingerbread sort of coloring, with ordinary hair, and a face disquietingly impassive, save for his very dark, very large eyes. I got the impression, each time that he raised them, not so much that they spoke but that they registered volumes; each time he dropped them it was as though he had retired into the library.

We sat in the living room, his mother,

younger brother and sister, and I, while G. sat on the sofa, doing his homework. The father was at work and the older sister had not yet come home. The boy had looked up once, as I came in, to say, "Good evening, sir," and then left all the rest to his mother.

Mrs. R. was a very strong-willed woman, handsome, quiet-looking, dressed in black. Nothing, she told me, beyond name-calling, had marked G.'s first day at school; but on the second day she received the last of several threatening phone calls. She was told that if she didn't want her son "cut to ribbons" she had better keep him at home. She heeded this warning to the extent of calling the chief of police.

"He told me to go on and send him. He said he'd be there when the cutting started. So I sent him." Even more remarkably, perhaps, G. went.

No one cut him, in fact no one touched him. The students formed a wall between G. and the entrances, saying only enough, apparently, to make their intention clearly understood, watching him, and keeping him outside. (I asked him, "What did you feel when they blocked your way?" G. Looked up at me, very briefly, with no expression on his face, and told me, "Nothing, sir.") At last the principal appeared and took him by the hand and they entered the school, while the children shouted behind them, "Nigger-lover!"

G. was alone all day at school.

"But I thought you already knew some of the kids there," I said. I had been told that he had friends among the white students because of their previous competition in a Soapbox Derby.

"Well, none of them are in his classes," his mother told me—a shade too quickly, as though she did not want to dwell on the idea of G.'s daily isolation.

"We don't have the same schedule," G. said. It was as though he were coming to his mother's rescue. Then, unwillingly, with a kind of interior shrug, "Some of the guys had lunch with me but then the other kids called them names." He went back to his homework.

I began to realize that there were not only a great many things G. would not tell me, there was much that he would never tell his mother.

"But nobody bothers you, anyway?"

"No," he said. "They just—call names. I don't let it bother me."

Nevertheless, the principal frequently escorts him through the halls. One day, when G. was alone, a boy tripped him and knocked him down and G. reported this to the principal. The white boy denied it but a few days later, while G. and the principal were together, he came over and said, "I'm sorry I tripped you; I won't do it again," and they shook hands. But it doesn't seem that this boy has as yet developed into a friend. And it is clear that G. will not allow himself to expect this.

I asked Mrs. R. what had prompted her to have her son reassigned to a previously all-white high school. She sighed, paused; then, sharply, "Well, it's not because I'm so anxious to have him around white people." Then she laughed. "I really don't know how I'd feel if I was to carry a white baby around who was calling me Grandma." G. laughed, too, for the first time. "White people say," the mother went on, "that that's all a Negro wants. I don't think they believe that themselves."

Then we switched from the mysterious question of what white folks believe to the relatively solid ground of what she, herself, knows and fears.

"You see that boy? Well, he's always been a straight-A student. He didn't hardly have to work at it. You see the way he's so quiet now on the sofa, with his books? Well, when he was going to————High School, he didn't have no homework or if he did, he could get it done in five minutes. Then, there he was, out in the streets, getting into mischief, and all he did all day in school was just keep clowning to make the other boys laugh. He wasn't learning nothing and didn't nobody care if he *never* learned nothing and I could just see what was going to happen to him if he kept on like that."

The boy was very quiet.

"What were you learning in————High?" I asked him.

"Nothing!" he exploded, with a very un-boyish laugh. I asked him to tell me about it.

"Well, the teacher comes in," he said, "and she gives you something to read and she goes out. She leaves some other student in charge. . . ." ("You can just imagine how much reading gets done," Mrs. R. interposed.) "At the end of the period," G. continued, "she comes back and tells you something to read for the next day."

So, having nothing else to do, G. began amusing his classmates and his mother began to be afraid. G. is just about at the age when boys begin dropping out of school. Perhaps they get a girl into trouble; she also drops out; the boy gets work for a time or gets into trouble for a long time. I was told that forty-five girls had left school for the maternity ward the year before. A week or ten days before I arrived in the city eighteen boys from G.'s former high school had been sentenced to the chain gang.

"My boy's a good boy," said Mrs. R., "and I wanted to see him have a chance."

"Don't the teachers care about the students?" I asked. This brought forth more laughter. How could they care? How much could they do if they *did* care? There were too many children, from shaky homes and worn-out parents, in aging, inadequate plants. They could be considered, most of them, as already doomed. Besides, the teachers' jobs were safe. They were responsible only to the principal, an appointed official, whose judgment, apparently, was never questioned by his (white) superiors or confreres.

The principal of G.'s former high school was about seventy-five when he was finally retired and his idea of discipline was to have two boys beat each other—"under his supervision"—with leather belts. This once happened with G., with no other results than that his parents gave the principal a tongue-lashing. It happened with two boys of G.'s acquaintance with the result that, after school, one boy beat the other so badly that he had to be sent to the hospital. The teachers have themselves arrived at a dead end, for in a segregated school system they cannot rise any higher, and the students are aware of this. Both students and teachers soon cease to struggle.

"If a boy can wash a blackboard," a teacher was heard to say, "I'll promote him."

I asked Mrs. R. how other Negroes felt about her having had G. reassigned.

"Well, a lot of them didn't like it," she said—though I gathered that they did not say so to her. As school time approached, more and more people asked her, "Are you going to send him?" "Well," she told them, "the man says the door is open and I feel like, yes, I'm going to go on and send him."

Out of a population of some fifty thousand Negroes, there had been only forty-five applications. People had said that they would send their children, had talked about it, had made plans; but, as the time drew near, when the application blanks were actually in their hands, they said, "I don't believe I'll sign this right now. I'll sign it later." Or, "I been thinking about this. I don't believe I'll send him right now."

"Why?" I asked. But to this she couldn't, or wouldn't, give me any answer.

I asked if there had been any reprisals taken against herself or her husband, if she was worried while G. was at school all day. She said that, no, there had been no reprisals, though some white people, under the pretext of giving her good advice, had expressed disapproval of her action. But she herself doesn't have a job and so doesn't risk losing one. Nor, she told me, had anyone said anything to her husband, who, however, by her own proud suggestion, is extremely close-mouthed. And it developed later that he was not working at his regular trade but at something else.

As to whether she was worried, "No," she told me; in much the same way that G., when asked about the blockade, had said, "Nothing, sir." In her case it was easier to see what she meant: she hoped for the best and would not allow herself, in the meantime, to lose her head. "I don't feel like nothing's going to happen," she said, soberly. "I *hope* not. But I know if anybody tries to harm me or any of my children, I'm going to strike back with all my strength. I'm going to strike them in God's name."

G., in the meantime, on the sofa with his books, was preparing himself for the next school day. His face was as impassive as ever and I found myself wondering—again—how he managed to face what must surely have been the worst moment of his day—the morning, when he opened his eyes and realized that it was all to be gone through again. Insults, and incipient violence, teachers, and—exams.

"One among so many," his mother said, "that's kind of rough."

"Do you think you'll make it?" I asked him. "Would you rather go back to———High?"

"No," he said, "I'll make it. I ain't going back."

"He ain't thinking about going back," said his mother—proudly and sadly. I began to suspect that the boy managed to support the extreme tension of his situation by means of a nearly fanatical concentration on his schoolwork; by holding in the center of his mind the issue on which, when the deal went down, others would be *forced* to judge him. Pride and silence were his weapons. Pride comes naturally, and soon, to a Negro, but even his mother, I felt, was worried about G.'s silence, though she was too wise to break it. For what was all this doing to him really?

"It's hard enough," the boy said later, still in control but with flashing eyes, "to keep quiet and keep walking when they call you nigger. But if anybody ever spits on me, I *know* I'll have to fight."

His mother laughs, laughs to ease them both, then looks at me and says, "I wonder sometimes what makes white folks so mean."

This is a recurring question among Negroes, even among the most "liberated"—which epithet is meant, of course, to describe the writer. The next day, with this question (more elegantly phrased) still beating in my mind, I visited the principal of G.'s new high school. But he didn't look "mean" and he wasn't "mean": he was a thin, young man of about my age, bewildered and in trouble. I asked him how things were working out, what he thought about it, what he thought would happen—in the long run, or the short.

"Well, I've got a job to do," he told me, "and I'm going to do it." He said that there hadn't been any trouble and that he didn't expect any. "Many students, after all, never see G. at all." None of the children have harmed him and the teachers are, apparently, carrying out their rather tall orders, which are to be kind to G. and, at the same time, to treat him like any other student.

I asked him to describe to me the incident, on the second day of school, when G.'s entrance had been blocked by the students. He told me that it was nothing at all— "It was a gesture more than anything else." He had simply walked out and spoken to the students and brought G. inside. "I've seen them do the same thing to other kids when they were kidding," he said. I imagine that he would like to be able to place this incident in the same cheerful if rowdy category, despite the shouts (which he does not mention) of "nigger-lover!"

Which epithet does not, in any case, describe him at all.

"Why," I asked, "is G. the only Negro student here?" According to this city's pupil-assignment plan, a plan designed to allow the least possible integration over the longest period of time, G. was the only Negro student who qualified.

"And, anyway," he said, "I don't think it's right for colored children to come to white schools just *because* they're white."

"Well," I began, "even if you don't like it . . ."

"Oh," he said quickly, raising his head and looking at me sideways, "I never said I didn't like it."

And then he explained to me, with difficulty, that it was simply contrary to everything he'd ever seen or believed. He'd never dreamed of a mingling of the races; had never lived that way himself and didn't suppose that he ever would; in the same way, he added, perhaps a trifle defensively, that he only associated with a certain stratum of white people. But, "I've never seen a colored person toward whom I had any hatred or ill-will."

His eyes searched mine as he said this and I knew that he was wondering if I believed him.

I certainly did believe him; he impressed me as being a very gentle and honorable man. But I could not avoid wondering if he had ever really *looked* at a Negro and wondered about the life, the aspirations, the universal humanity hidden behind the dark skin. As I wondered, when he told me that race relations in his city were "excellent" and had not been strained by recent developments, how on earth he managed to hold on to this delusion.

I later got back to my interrupted questions, which I phrased more tactfully.

"Even though it's very difficult for all concerned—this situation—doesn't it occur to you that the reason colored children wish to come to white schools isn't because they want to be with white people but simply because they want a better education?"

"Oh, I don't know," he replied, "it seems to me that colored schools are just as good as white schools." I wanted to ask him on what evidence he had arrived at this conclusion and also how they could possibly be "as good" in view of the kind of life they came out of, and perpetuated, and the dim prospects faced by all but the most exceptional or ruthless Negro students. But I only suggested that G. and his family, who certainly should have known, so thoroughly disagreed with him that they had been willing to risk G.'s present well-being and his future psychological and mental health in order to bring about a change in his environment. Nor did I mention the lack of enthusiasm evinced by G.'s mother when musing on the prospect of a fair grandchild. There seemed no point in making this man any more a victim of his heritage than he so gallantly was already.

"Still," I said at last, after a rather painful pause, "I should think that the trouble in this situation is that it's very hard for *you* to face a child and treat him unjustly because of something for which he is no more responsible than—than *you* are."

The eyes came to life then, or a veil fell, and I found myself staring at a man in anguish. The eyes were full of pain and bewilderment and he nodded his head. This was the impossibility which he faced every day. And I imagined that his tribe would increase, in sudden leaps and bounds was already increasing.

For segregation has worked brilliantly in the South, and, in fact, in the nation, to this extent: it has allowed white people, with scarcely any pangs of conscience whatever, to *create,* in every generation, only the Negro they wished to see. As the walls come down they will be forced to take another, harder look at the shiftless and the menial and will be forced into a wonder concerning them which cannot fail to be agonizing. It is not an easy thing to be forced to reexamine a way of life and to speculate, in a personal way, on the general injustice.

"What do you think," I asked him, "will happen? What do you think the future holds?"

He gave a strained laugh and said he didn't know. "I don't want to think about it." Then, "I'm a religious man," he said, "and I believe the Creator will always help us find a way to solve our problems. If a man loses that, he's lost everything he had." I agreed, struck by the look in his eyes.

"You're from the North?" he asked me, abruptly.

"Yes," I said.

"Well," he said, "you've got your troubles too."

"Ah, yes, we certainly do," I admitted and shook hands and left him. I did not say what I was thinking, that our troubles were the same

trouble and that, unless we were very swift and honest, what is happening in the South today will be happening in the North tomorrow.   [1961]

Notes

1. BOOKER T. WASHINGTON: A Negro educator and the founder of Tuskegee Institute.
2. SCOTTSBORO CASE: A celebrated case in which eight Negro teenagers were sentenced to death for the alleged rape of two white women; four were later acquitted on appeal.
3. BESSIE SMITH: A black American blues singer.

Understanding the Reading

1. What does Baldwin learn from the Negroes he met before he visited G.?
2. What tactics were used to intimidate G. and discourage him from attending the previously all-white school?
3. Why do you think G. is so silent and impassive?
4. Describe the problems of the all-Negro school.
5. Why does Baldwin say that the principal is not a "nigger lover"? How is he "a victim of his heritage"?

Suggestion for Responding

Baldwin says that G. and his family had been willing to risk G.'s "future psychological and mental health" by having him reassigned. What effects do you think his experience in an otherwise all-white school will have on his future? What kind of adult do you think he will become? ✦

105

"Don't Tell Us It Can't Be Done"

MICHAEL RYAN

Martha Yallup, Sister Kathleen Ross and their colleagues made something wonderful happen on the Yakima Indian Reservation in Washington State a decade ago. In a poor area where higher education was almost inaccessible, they began to train Head Start[1] teachers from the Indian communities. It was hard work, but it was doubly rewarding. Not only did the program give adults new skills, but it also helped provide a leg up for the children born into the grueling poverty of the reservation. For Martha, the tribe's Head Start director, and Sister Kathleen, the academic vice president of Fort Wright College in Spokane, the program was a splendid example of how a private college and a community group could work together to change lives.

Then disaster struck.

"In 1980, the board of Fort Wright decided to close the college," Sister Kathleen recalls. "I had the job of coming down here and telling Martha that we were going to have to end the program because the home campus was closing. I gave her the bad news, and I remember she just looked at me and said: 'No, it's not closing.'"

Instead of sitting by and watching their dream die, Martha Yallup got together with a colleague, Violet Rau, and Sister Kathleen and decided on a plan of incredible daring: They would start a college on their own.

The idea seemed as doomed as it was courageous. The reservation was no place to raise the funds needed to start a college from scratch. And Fort Wright was in no position to help much. A small liberal-arts school run by the Catholic Sisters of the Holy Names of Jesus and Mary, it had been driven out of business by competition from larger, better-financed schools. And, although Martha and Violet were confident, virtually nobody believed in them—except Sister Kathleen. "People on the reservation said, 'You're crazy. It's going to fail,'" Martha recalls.

But Martha and Violet went to work on the reservation, lining up community leaders, public officials and business people to form a board of directors for the new college—and to start raising money for it. Back in Spokane, Sister Kathleen persuaded college officials to keep Fort Wright open through the spring of 1982. Then the hard work began.

First, the new college needed recognition from the IRS[2] so that it could accept donations. Sister Kathleen fought her way through the agency's bureaucracy and emerged with official recognition. Then the women tried to persuade the authorities to transfer Fort Wright's accreditation to their new school. "Our philosophy had always been, 'If you don't ask, you don't get,'" Martha says with a laugh. They failed, but they made a strong enough case that they were granted candidate status—the last step before full accreditation. That meant that their new school's courses could be recognized for full credit by other institutions.

But they had one more obstacle to clear: A college designed for some of the poorest people in the country would have to be able to offer financial aid. And the federal government's rule held that a school must be in business two years before its students qualify for federal loans. "We went to the top person in the Seattle office," Sister Kathleen says, "and he said, 'There's got to be a way,' so I asked him if I could see the book of regulations." She found a section that allowed the government to authorize financial aid when a school is sold to a new owner. It was clearly intended to cover vocational schools, but the rule didn't say that explicitly. "The guy looked at me like I was crazy," Sister Kathleen recalls. "Then he said, 'Why not?'" Sister Kathleen and her board of directors purchased their education program from Fort Wright for $1, and a new college was born.

The day I went to visit, Heritage College had been in business for eight years. It is a nondenominational institution—although a small group of nuns still holds key administrative positions at the school. Sister Kathleen Ross has been the president since before the college opened its doors. Martha Yallup, now the deputy director of the Yakima tribe's Department of Human Services, was the board's first chair and still serves as its secretary.

But the story that began with the determination of a handful of courageous women has become a story of courage and determination on the part of hundreds. This year, Heritage College will confer 199 degrees and certificates. The average Heritage student is 35 and, as the faculty likes to say, "place-bound"—inhibited by family and work commitments from traveling the 90 minutes it takes to get to the nearest college off the reservation. For most of the students, college is a dream which could never have come true without Heritage.

If you want to know how great the accomplishment of Sister Kathleen, Martha Yallup and the others is, meet Hipolito Mendez. He may be the typical Heritage student—an industrious, outgoing man who works part-time to pay his tuition and speaks eagerly of his planned career as a high school teacher. He is also a 47-year-old father of five. "My wife and I had a business, and it went down the tubes," he says. "We decided, 'Now's the time to back to school and do something with our lives.' But we discovered we just couldn't afford to go to the state university. There wasn't much hope for us. Then we heard about Heritage."

Admittedly, he says, it felt strange for a man in middle age to become a college student, but Mendez found that Heritage's emphasis on personalized education eased his transition. "The first week, I was apprehensive," he says. "After that, I fit right in." Next fall, he will begin a new life as an educator—and his wife, Paula, will start teaching elementary school as well.

Or look at how Heritage has changed the life of Edith Walsey, 32. "If this college wasn't here, I wouldn't have gone to college, because of my family and my tradition and my husband," she confides. "I'm from the Warm Springs reservation in Oregon. The teachers here understand my customs. At first, it was kind of hard for me. My husband wasn't for me going to school. We have three children. Now he takes care of them while I'm in class and working part-time. I'm a junior studying computers. When I graduate, I hope to go home and work with my tribe."

In its eight years of existence, Heritage has grown from a three-room cottage to a set of buildings on the campus of a former elementary school in the reservation town of Toppenish. It now has 25 full-time faculty, an additional 70 or so part-time, and more than 400 degree-holding alumni. These are impressive statistics, but not as impressive as the testimonial one recent graduate gave Sister Kathleen last year. A native of the reservation, she had gone away to college but dropped out, feeling uncomfortable in an alien culture. Then she heard about Heritage. She enrolled and finished her degree. In one sentence, she summed up the magic of the school. As she told Sister Kathleen: "You allowed me not to be a failure."   [1991]

Notes

1. HEAD START: A federal program for disadvantaged preschoolers.
2. IRS: Internal Revenue Service.

Understanding the Reading

1. What problems did Yallup, Rau, and Sister Kathleen face in starting Heritage College?
2. How did they overcome each of them?
3. Evaluate the effectiveness of the project.

Suggestion for Responding

Describe a time when you faced what seemed to be impossible obstacles and explain how you tackled them, alone or with the help of others. ✦

106

Cecilia Fire Thunder: She Inspires Her People

ANN DAVIS

Cecilia Fire Thunder hunches over a doll she's making, clamping one more silver buckle on the belt before she fastens it to a dark blue, shell-decorated dress. The kitchen table where she works is a cluttered stage of tall, elegant Plains Indian women, hands outstretched with an eagle wing fan or holding a fringed shawl close in to their waists.

Her small trailer home on the Pine Ridge reservation in South Dakota is a Frankenstein's[1] laboratory—plastic bags full of arms, legs, and torsos bulge beneath the planter, overflow behind the TV. Corpses waiting for heads line the sofa.

Fire Thunder sits back and studies the doll, reading glasses perched at the end of her nose. "Some of that old stuff is ugly," she mutters, attaching a small buckskin bag to the belt. "I like my bodies to resemble bodies—they don't have to look like stuffed tamales."

When Fire Thunder started making dolls a few years ago, her original impetus was simple: to reflect contemporary Plains Indian women, the friends she dances with at pow-wows around the Midwest. When her foot-high dolls won her awards and trips to Washington, D.C., to demonstrate dollmaking techniques at the Smithsonian, she took it in stride. Making art is part of her life, and speaking in public goes with the territory.

You might think dollmaking an utterly apolitical activity. Not for Fire Thunder. Even her dolls are lessons in history and cultural values. The cowrie shells on her traditional dolls reveal the extensive trade routes existing between tribes on the West Coast and the Great Plains. The tanned hides are a vehicle to talk about the Lakota's relation to other life forms and their philosophy of natural harmony.

When she talks to non-Indian audiences, Fire Thunder uses the dolls to clear away misconceptions about Native Americans. When she speaks in local schools, she uses her dolls to talk about traditional values and the problems of drugs and alcohol.

"I talk to high school kids, not about how it should be, but about how it is," Fire Thunder said. Instead of lecturing about the evils of substance abuse, Fire Thunder asks them point-blank how many still do drugs, even after years of being preached at in the schools. Most raise their hands, Then they tell her about growing up in alcoholic homes, about nights of no sleep, worrying whether they'll get beat up by a drunk adult.

Even though students understand that drugs and alcohol are bad for them, Fire Thunder believes they will not change their behavior until adult problem drinkers admit it and share their experiences with younger people.

Fire Thunder says that part of the reason she can reach Indian people at a gut level is because she is one of them. She can tell jokes that non-Indians could never get away with, jokes that in a humorous way reveal people's dysfunctional behavior to themselves. For instance, What is Indian love? Answer: a black eye and a hickie.

"The gift I have is my humor, my gift to communicate," Fire Thunder said. "No white person can say what I say." She believes it is up to Indian people to solve their own problems.

When asked if she ever gets overwhelmed by all the work, Fire Thunder says no. "My passion is what I do. The most important thing I have is that I know who I am," she says. "I still have a lot of quirks, but my identity is pretty strong. And I know when to play."

Out on the dance floor in the Rapid City Civic Center, Fire Thunder wears her traditional women's dress, decorated with cowrie shells and a handsome silver belt. Like the Pied Piper,[2] she breaks away from the movement of the group and leads a long snakeline of women in and out around a kaleidoscope of feathers and swirling fringe. She bends her head to hear a joke, laughs and continues her swinging walk, head tilted back elegantly, like one of her dolls. She's easy to pick out among hundreds of dancers. "If you feel good about yourself, you're just going to shine," says Cecilia Fire Thunder, and she does.

Fire Thunder goes non-stop. A dazzling public speaker, organizer in her home community of the Pine Ridge reservation, a founder of the Oglala Lakota Women's Society, registered nurse, mother, political lobbyist, pow-wow enthusiast, traditional dollmaker, KILI radio personality: you might think this enough for a lifetime or two. But this summer, Fire Thunder, who ran for tribal president—and lost—was also appointed tribal health planner for the Pine Ridge reservation and charged with building the first comprehensive plan to fight alcoholism.

Many community groups approved when Fire Thunder was appointed to the sensitive political post. "If anyone can do it, she can," was the comment heard frequently around the tribal office, according to Taylor Little White Man, executive director of the Oglala Sioux Tribe.

Like her dolls, she is tall and captivating with deep brown eyes, a brilliant smile and abundant energy. And some internal switch seems to have locked in the "on" position when Fire Thunder was born. It's an intensity that delights some and frustrates others. Her rebelliousness infuriated the nuns at Red Cloud Indian School, a Catholic boarding school she attended until tenth grade. The nuns tried to convince the head priest not to let her come back; she was too influential with the other girls.

She rebelled most against the violence: How the religious brothers beat boys with thick belt-straps outside the girls' classroom windows. How the nuns humiliated "bad" girls by forcing them to bend over a big piano in front of the class, pulling down their panties and smacking them with rulers. How they did things so bad that Fire Thunder won't tell me about them.

"They hurt us to make us cry because once you cried, they'd defeated you," she said.

It took Fire Thunder years to undo the emotional damage caused by the boarding school, an internalized violence she feels she carried into her relationship with her children. "In order to do what I do, you have to confront your own devils, because something or someone will remind you of your past," Fire Thunder said. Fire Thunder's attempts at easing children's suffering is a constant in her work as community organizer, health planner, speaker, even dollmaker.

Inspired by her meeting with organizer Eileen Iron Cloud at a pow-wow in Colorado, and their discussions about empowering women and influencing state legislation at Pine Ridge, Fire Thunder, along with Iron Cloud, formed the Oglala Lakota Women's Society in 1987.

Fire Thunder recounts Lakota spiritual tradition, saying that thousands of years ago a woman gave her people a pipe and told them how to pray with it in ceremonies. This woman who came among the people was the inspiration for the women's society, says Fire Thunder. Through the society, women are able to air their concerns about community and tribal affairs.

Repeatedly, the number one issue on the nine reservations was alcohol. Not a surprising statistic, since some nine out of ten people on Pine Ridge are alcoholic.

"Part of community organizing is getting people to tell you what you already know," Fire Thunder said.

Now that women had identified their major focus, the group decided to take on the candidates for tribal election. Fire Thunder talked about sober leadership on her radio show; the women's society sent out 1,000 mailings urging voters to support sober leaders. At stump speeches, women badgered the candidates to state whether they still drank. "We didn't care who you were, what you did, what kind of past you had," Fire Thunder said. "If you were sober, we were gonna vote for you."

Though their criteria were crude, their results were impressive: after the smoke cleared on election night, 11 of the 16 new tribal council members were declared non-drinkers.

The domestic violence was next. Tribal law had required that women sign a complaint against abusive partners before the police would act. In 1988, the women's society lobbied for and won a mandatory arrest law for domestic violence. Since fall of last year, whenever there is probable cause of domestic abuse, the perpetrator automatically spends the night in jail. The complaint is signed by the arresting officer. At first, a lot of "men in shock" were sitting in jail cells, Fire Thunder said. The women's society was criticized as "manhaters" and the trial court briefly tried to overturn the law. But most have now come to accept mandatory arrest as reality.

Part of the women's focus was on helping abusive men to change. Through their efforts, they won a grant to provide counseling to men who batter. "We did this because we also love our men," Fire Thunder said. "We want them to understand their rage and anger."

The Society's other main concern was child sexual abuse. In 1988, the group staged a candlelight march in support of National Child Abuse Prevention Month. Last year, they went one step further by letting abused children speak out about their experience. In a two-hour show broadcast live on radio station KILI, six children talked about how it felt to be beaten, raped, ridiculed and neglected. "In those two hours, we reached more people in the listening audience than with anything else we ever did," Fire Thunder said.

Such confrontational tactics have not always made her a popular figure. She and others in the women's society have been accused of butting into other people's business. Some reservation people have complained that women's groups are not "traditional."

But Fire Thunder brushes off the criticism, saying she is motivated more by the pain of children than the fear of criticism. "When oppression is so great, there's no nice way to get to the heart of the people," she said. "The only way was 'shock treatment'—hit 'em hard and shake 'em up. Now that they've accomplished an awareness of issues on Pine Ridge, their tactics can change," she said.

The fierce pace of the women's society has slowed in the past year. Iron Cloud says the group lost its focus. She has been studying organizing models and believes that women's society needs to reorient itself to keep all women involved, rather than having a few do all the work.

Fire Thunder believes everyone just got worn out. "We pulled back because we had to. For three years, we gave 150 percent of everything in our lives" to the women's society, she said. Fire Thunder agrees the group needs to restructure itself for the next phase of work.

Some say Fire Thunder sold out when she accepted a position with the tribal government this summer. "They say, 'Oh, they're gonna shut her up,'" Fire Thunder says. "But I took the position with the understanding that I could do more."

Though Iron Cloud counseled her not to take the new job, she believes Fire Thunder has the strength to hang in there and not sell out to political interests.

Perhaps she will. Fire Thunder has already written grants for half a million dollars and taken charge of the committee overseeing a new plan to house all alcohol programs under one roof. She says the tribe has a lot of catching up to do to enable people to face the pain of their addictions. [1991]

Notes

1. FRANKENSTEIN: A fictional scientist who created a monster that destroyed its maker.
2. PIED PIPER: A legendary piper whose music charmed first the rats and then the village children into following him out of town forever.

Understanding the Reading

1. What tactics does Fire Thunder use in her work with high school students?
2. What is the purpose of the Oglala Lakota Women's Society?
3. What tactics did Fire Thunder employ to combat alcoholism on the Lakota reservation?
4. How did she address the problem of domestic violence?
5. What did she do about the problem of child abuse?

Suggestion for Responding

The article reports that the Women's Society has lost its earlier momentum. Using your knowledge about the change process, what advice would you give them (or a similar group working on some community problem) about the one specific outcome that you feel is most necessary? Explain its priority and the strategies you would recommend to realize that outcome. ♦

107

How I Changed the Governor's Mind

RENÉE LA COUTURE TULLOCH

A young woman is attacked by a stranger who holds her in a viselike grip as he licks and bites her breasts through her clothes. He was caught in the act, but not sent to prison or forced to register as a sex offender. In fact, he could, if he wished, be licensed as a child care worker.

There was no law in California (or most other states) that could adequately address this insidious crime, because the victim was attacked through her clothing. Illegal touching was defined by sexual assault laws as skin-to-skin contact, or through the clothing of the attacker. It did not include touching through the victim's clothing. The only charge that applied was battery, which carries a light maximum prison sentence and therefore is rarely prosecuted.

I am the young woman who was mentioned in the beginning of this article. I was the one who was attacked. The police watch commander told me that this crime is reported every day in his precinct, and many officers—including the one who investigated my case—even underline that portion of the sexual battery law in their penal code books. They do it, he said, to show victims that there is really nothing to be done.

I could not contain my outrage, and vowed the law would change. I knew I had to get the full attention of my assemblyman (now a state senator), Patrick Johnston. But I had no idea how to, until I was at a fund-raiser for the local battered women's shelter. One of the items up for auction was a private lunch and state capitol tour with him. I made the highest bid—$125—using my travel money for Christmas.

When I met with Johnston, I came prepared. I presented him with a package of information that he said looked better than those of most lobbyists. He also told me that another assemblyman, Bill Filante, had drafted a bill, AB 674, calling for a similar legal change. He said it had been voted on once before and failed.

I found out why after I talked with a staffer for

another representative. He said assemblymen were afraid that young men in college would be with a date, fondle her, and then be charged with sexual battery. They felt that a boy shouldn't be put away for "miscommunication" with a date. He told me that most of the state assemblymen had been college boys once themselves.

I contacted Filante's office. As it turned out, a staffer said that the bill had the votes to pass this time. The big problem was that the governor at the time, George Deukmejian, had privately said that he'd veto it.

I asked what I could do. She said I could launch an all-out effort to change the governor's mind—if enough people got involved, maybe, just maybe, he'd sign it.

I wrote a paper explaining the loophole in sexual assault laws that hurt me and so many other women. I wrote sample letters to the governor and made copies of them for distribution. I told every friend to contact their friends. I gave out the pack to all my coworkers, and asked them to spread the word.

I spoke at the Women's Center of San Joaquin County and disclosed that I was a survivor. The speech generated tremendous support, especially at the sexual assault center. Women there contacted other centers around the state. I called the leaders of major women's organizations and racial equality groups. Calls, letters, and even telegrams poured into the governor's office calling for passage of AB 674, the "Sexual Battery" bill.

The day slated for the governor's veto came. I called his office with apprehension. His staffer told me that the bill was postponed for further consideration. I contacted everybody I could to keep up the pace for justice. Time was running out. The governor had to make the decision about this and a thousand other bills before midnight. He had three choices. He could either sign the bill, not sign it (in which case it would automatically become law), or veto it.

The waiting became its own hell. I could not sleep. I cried. I prayed. The next morning, September 30, 1989, I called the governor's office at 8 A.M. I asked the staffer for the status of AB 674. When I was on hold waiting, tears streamed down my face. Finally, this disembodied voice said, "It became law."

The man added, "The governor even chose to sign it. That shows he now supports the bill."

I found that one determined individual has the power to change an unjust system. Somebody asked me, "Does this mitigate your attack?" Absolutely not. I still have the scars. But no woman in California need ever again endure what I did. Still, I do worry about the other states that have this loophole. I want to inspire others (that means you) to change these terrible laws. I have found that when women, along with men who share our vision, band together we can make a difference. We can change the world!

[1991]

Understanding the Reading

1. What steps did Tulloch take to get the law that protected her attacker changed?
2. How does she evaluate her success?

Suggestion for Responding

What law would you like to see changed? Why is the change needed, and how would you go about getting the change? ✦

108

Many Students Press Colleges to Substitute 'First-Year Student' for the Term 'Freshman'

MICHELE N-K COLLISON

Forget the conflict over the canon.

Across the country, wordsmiths have stirred up a controversy by attacking one of the last bastions of collegiate tradition—the freshman. Indeed, it looks as though "freshman" could soon join the list of words judged to be politically incorrect.

Many students say the word excludes women. The students are pushing colleges to substitute a gender-neutral term, like "first-year student" or "freshperson." Some students have even suggested "freshmore."

Students say their efforts are part of a larger push to improve the status of women on the nation's campuses.

"The changing of the term doesn't necessarily change attitudes," says Thomas H. Goldstein, executive director of the American Association of University Students. "It's a small step in the fight to alleviate gripes about the way women are treated in higher education."

Mr. Goldstein's group is among those leading the charge. He says he is urging students at the 270 institutions that belong to his organization to adopt "first-year student." The association, whose members are research universities and liberal-arts colleges, promotes discussion of a variety of topics on campuses.

Students who are advocating the change say they have run into opposition. "A lot of people roll their eyes and say, 'Oh, it's just your generation,'" says Terri Ferinde, a senior at American University and president of A.A.U.S. "But women are tired of professors' calling them 'freshmen.' The term 'freshman' doesn't include everyone." Ms. Ferinde is pushing the university to adopt "first year" for entering students.

The faculty senate at Trinity University in Texas voted four years ago to use "first year" rather than "freshman" in all official university publications. "In conversations, you almost never hear the word 'freshman,'" says Coleen Grissom, vice-president for student affairs.

Some student newspapers have begun adopting the new language. Starting this fall, DePauw University's student newspaper, *The DePauw,* will use "first year" instead of "freshman." "For too long, we just took it for granted that 'freshmen' included women," says Gail Reddemann, editor of *The DePauw.* "It's an underlying current in American language. But the press affects people's ideas and opinions, and we can help remove the bias from language."

Faculty members are also grappling with the name change. "It's an archaic term," says Richard Guarasci, director of the First Year Program at Macalester College. "It doesn't make sense to call entering students 'freshmen' anymore."

Mr. Guarasci says faculty members voted to use "first year" to describe the university's seminar for incoming students when professors realized that calling it a "freshman program" was inconsistent with the seminar's curriculum. The program examines gender, race, and class issues.

Changes at some colleges and universities regarding "first year" have been made informally. At Brown University, many students and faculty members began using "first year" about three years ago. "It's very informal," says Tara J. Levine, president of the undergraduate council of students. "It's enforced by general sentiment. If you call someone a 'freshman,' you will be chastised. It's like calling a woman a 'girl.'"

Fern Johnson, provost and professor of English at Clark University, says "first year" was introduced on campuses about 10 years ago. "There is an overall trend to reduce the gender bias in language," Ms. Johnson says. She says the word "freshman" "carries a lot of sexist baggage."

"It's an artifact of a bygone era. You can't talk about eliminating sex bias while using sexist language."

Some in higher education, however, are reluctant to fiddle with tradition. The trustees of Miami University defeated a proposal two years ago to refer to entering students as "first-year students" in the university's publications. The trustees said they "didn't believe that 'freshman' was a sexist term," says Arlene M. Meyer, director of publications at the university.

Others are equally reluctant to abandon "freshman." For 10 years, John N. Gardner has spearheaded an effort to improve students' first year in college. He has held a variety of conferences entitled "The Freshman Year."

Mr. Gardner, who is a vice-chancellor for university campuses and continuing education at the University of South Carolina, says he'll continue to use "freshman" here in the United States. But when he held a conference in England in 1986, he called it "The First-Year Experience"—because, he said, in other countries almost everyone uses "first year."   [1990]

Understanding the Reading

1. Why do some people want to change the term "freshman"?
2. What strategies for change are described in the article?

Describe your plan of action either for changing usage of the word "freshman" or for supporting its continuing use on your campus. ✦

109

Does America Still Exist?

RICHARD RODRIGUEZ

For the children of immigrant parents the knowledge comes easier. America exists everywhere in the city—on billboards, frankly in the smell of French fries and popcorn. It exists in the pace: traffic lights, the assertions of neon, the mysterious bong-bong-bong through the atriums of department stores. America exists as the voice of the crowd, a menacing sound—the high nasal accent of American English.

When I was a boy in Sacramento (California, the fifties), people would ask me, "Where you from?" I was born in this country, but I knew the question meant to decipher my darkness, my looks.

My mother once instructed me to say, "I am an American of Mexican descent." By the time I was nine or ten, I wanted to say, but dared not reply, "I am an American."

Immigrants come to America and, against hostility or mere loneliness, they recreate a homeland in the parlor, tacking up postcards or calendars of some impossible blue—lake or sea or sky. Children of immigrant parents are supposed to perch on a hyphen between two countries. Relatives assume the achievement as much as anyone. Relatives are, in any case, surprised when the child begins losing old ways. One day at the family picnic the boy wanders away from their spiced food and faceless stories to watch other boys play baseball in the distance.

There is sorrow in the American memory, guilty sorrow for having left something behind—Portugal, China, Norway. The American story is the story of immigrant children and of their children—children no longer able to speak to grandparents. The memory of exile becomes inarticulate as it passes from generation to generation, along with wedding rings and pocket watches—like some mute stone in a wad of old lace. Europe. Asia. Eden.

But, it needs to be said, if this is a country where one stops being Vietnamese or Italian, this is a country where one begins to be an American. America exists as a culture and a grin, a faith and a shrug. It is clasped in a handshake, called by a first name.

As much as the country is joined in a common culture, however, Americans are reluctant to celebrate the process of assimilation. We pledge allegiance to diversity. America was born Protestant and bred Puritan, and the notion of community we share is derived from a seventeenth-century faith. Presidents and the pages of ninth-grade civics readings yet proclaim the orthodoxy: We are gathered together—but as individuals, with separate pasts, distinct destinies. Our society is as paradoxical as a Puritan congregation: We stand together, alone.

Americans have traditionally defined themselves by what they refused to include. As often, however, Americans have struggled, turned in good conscience at last to assert the great Protestant virtue of tolerance. Despite outbreaks of nativist frenzy, America has remained an immigrant country, open and true to itself.

Against pious emblems of rural America—soda fountain, Elks hall, Protestant church, and now shopping mall—stands the cold-hearted city, crowded with races and ambitions, curious laughter, much that is odd. Nevertheless, it is the city that has most truly represented America. In the city, however, the millions of singular lives have had no richer notion of wholeness to describe them than the idea of pluralism.

"Where you from?" the American asks the immigrant child. "Mexico," the boy learns to say.

Mexico, the country of my blood ancestors, offers formal contrast to the American achievement. If the United States was formed by Protestant individualism, Mexico was shaped by a medieval Catholic dream of one world. The Spanish journeyed to Mexico to plunder, and they may have gone, in God's name, with an arrogance peculiar to those who intend to convert.

But through the conversion, the Indian converted the Spaniard. A new race was born, the *mestizo,* wedding European to Indian. José Vasconcelos, the Mexican philosopher, has celebrated this New World creation, proclaiming it the "cosmic race."

Centuries later, in a San Francisco restaurant, a Mexican-American lawyer of my acquaintance says, in English, over *salade niçoise,* that he does not intend to assimilate into gringo society. His claim is echoed by a chorus of others (Italian-Americans, Greeks, Asians) in this era of ethnic pride. The melting pot has been retired, clanking, into the museum of quaint disgrace, alongside Aunt Jemima and the Katzenjammer Kids.[1] But resistance to assimilation is characteristically American. It only makes clear how inevitable the process of assimilation actually is.

For generations, this has been the pattern. Immigrant parents have sent their children to school (simply, they thought) to acquire the "skills" to survive in the city. The child returned home with a voice his parents barely recognized or understood, couldn't trust, and didn't like.

In Eastern cities—Philadelphia, New York, Boston, Baltimore—class after class gathered immigrant children to women (usually women) who stood in front of rooms full of children, changing children. So also for me in the 1950s. Irish-Catholic nuns. California. The old story. The hyphen tipped to the right, away from Mexico and toward a confusing but true American identity.

I speak now in the chromium American accent of my grammar school classmates—Billy Reckers, Mike Bradley, Carol Schmidt, Kathy O'Grady. . . . I believe I became like my classmates, became German, Polish, and (like my teachers) Irish. And because assimilation is always reciprocal, my classmates got something of me. (I mean sad eyes; belief in the Indian Virgin;[2] a taste for sugar skulls on the Feast of the Dead.) In the blending, we became what our parents could never have been, and we carried America one revolution further.

"Does America still exist?" Americans have been asking the question for so long that to ask it again only proves our continuous link. But perhaps the question deserves to be asked with urgency now. Since the black civil rights movement of the 1960s, our tenuous notion of a shared public life has deteriorated notably.

The struggle of black men and women did not eradicate racism, but it became the great moment in the life of America's conscience. Water hoses, bulldogs, blood—the images, rendered black, white, rectangular, passed into living rooms.

It is hard to look at a photograph of a crowd taken, say, in 1890 or in 1930 and not notice the absence of blacks. (It becomes an impertinence to wonder if America *still* exists.)

In the sixties, other groups of Americans learned to champion their rights by analogy to the black civil rights movement. But the heroic vision faded. Dr. Martin Luther King, Jr. had spoken with Pauline eloquence of a nation that would unite Christian and Jew, old and young, rich and poor. Within a decade, the struggles of the 1960s were reduced to a bureaucratic competition for little more than pieces of a representational pie. The quest for a portion of power became an end in itself. The metaphor for the American city of the 1970s was a committee: one black, one woman, one person under thirty. . . .

If the small town had sinned against America by too neatly defining who could be an American, the city's sin was a romantic secession. One noticed the romanticism in the antiwar movement—certain demonstrators who demonstrated a lack of tact or desire to persuade and seemed content to play secular protestants. One noticed the romanticism in the competition among members of "minority groups" to claim the status of Primary Victim. To Americans unconfident of their common identity, minority standing became a way of asserting individuality. Middle-class Americans—men and women clearly not the primary victims of social oppression— brandished their suffering with exuberance.

The reality of America persists. Teenagers pass through big-city high schools banded in racial groups, their collars turned up to a uniform shrug. But then they graduate to jobs at the phone company or in banks, where they end up working alongside people unlike themselves. Typists and tellers walk out together at lunchtime.

It is easier for us as Americans to believe the

obvious fact of our separateness—easier to imagine the black and white Americas prophesied by the Kerner report[3] (broken glass, street fires)—than to recognize the reality of a city street at lunchtime. Americans are wedded by proximity to a common culture. The panhandler at one corner is related to the pamphleteer at the next who is related to the banker who is kin to the Chinese old man wearing an MIT sweatshirt. In any true national history, Thomas Jefferson begets Martin Luther King, Jr., who begets the Gray Panthers.[4] It is because we lack a vision of ourselves entire—the city street is crowded and we are each preoccupied with finding our own way home—that we lack an appropriate hymn.

Under my window now passes a little white girl softly rehearsing to herself a Motown[5] obbligato.   [1984]

Notes

1. AUNT JEMIMA AND THE KATZENJAMMER KIDS: A stereotypic black mammy and stereotypic immigrant "brats," respectively.
2. INDIAN VIRGIN: The Virgin of Guadalupe, the patron saint of Mexico. The Feast of the Dead is the Mexican celebration of All Souls' Day, November 2, when sweets shaped like skulls are eaten.
3. THE KERNER REPORT: The report of the Commission on Civil Disorders, appointed by President Lyndon Johnson, headed by Ohio Governor Otto Kerner, and charged with investigating the racial outbreaks in the mid-1960s.
4. GRAY PANTHERS: An activist organization for the improvement of the lives of older people, especially women.
5. MOTOWN: The nickname for Detroit, Michigan (Motor City), where rhythm and blues music originated in the 1960s.

Understanding the Reading

1. What does Rodriguez mean by "the memory of exile"?
2. What does he mean when he says "we stand together, alone"?
3. According to Rodriguez, how have Mexico's Catholic history and the United States' Protestant history shaped each culture?
4. What does Rodriguez think "the reality of America" is?

Suggestion for Responding

How do you answer Rodriguez's title question, "Does America Still Exist?" ◆

SUGGESTIONS FOR RESPONDING TO PART X

1. Write a personal essay describing yourself as a change maker. Make clear what problem you decided to work on, how you chose to attack it, what happened, and how successful (or unsuccessful) your effort was.
2. Make an oral presentation to the class about your action project, briefly covering the points raised in question 1.
3. Research a civil rights activist or organization, focusing on one particular action she, he, or they undertook. Write an essay describing and evaluating the project.
4. Investigate a group on your campus or in your community that is working to implement a change you consider desirable. Write an article for your local newspaper publicizing the group's efforts.
5. Explain how you are personally affected by our diverse, multicultural American society.

SUGGESTIONS FOR RESPONDING TO CHANGE

Important social and economic change has historically been the result of organized movements. The following assignments are intended to give you a better understanding of organized non-governmental forces that have changed life in America.

1. Research the origins of a specific labor union, such as the American Federation of Labor; Congress of Industrial Organizations; AFL-CIO; Actors' Equity Association; Knights of Labor; National Women's Trade Union League; National Consumers League; International Workers of the World; National Education Association; Longshoremen's and Warehousemen's Union; United Farm Workers of America; 9–5; Teamsters; Association of Federal, State, County and Municipal Employees; International Ladies' Garment Workers Union; and so on. Write a report on the forces that led to the initial organizing and the obstacles the organizers faced.

2. Research and report on the strategies employed by the abolition movement, and analyze their effectiveness.

3. Research and report on the strategies employed by the National Woman Suffrage Association, the American Woman Suffrage Association, or the National American Woman Suffrage Association, and analyze the effectiveness of the organization.

4. In the post–Civil War years, women organized for a number of different purposes. Research one of these, such as the women's club movement, the temperance movement, settlement houses, or the National Consumer League, and report on their short-term and long-term achievements.

5. Write a biography of a major historical change maker, focusing on her or his contributions to the larger movement of which she or he was a part. Consider such activists as Lucretia Mott, Sarah and Angelina Grimke, William Lloyd Garrison, Frederick Douglass, Elizabeth Cady Stanton, Susan B. Anthony, Carrie Chapman Catt, Mary McLeod Bethune, Frances Willard, Mary Church Terrell, Jane Addams, Florence Kelley, Lillian Wald, Louis Brandeis, Sophie Loeb, Emma Goldman, Elizabeth Gurley Flynn, Rose Schneiderman, Mary Anderson, Abigail Scott Duniway, Thurgood Marshall, or Morris Deese.

6. Research and report on the goals and strategies employed by one of the civil rights organizations of the 1950s and 1960s, for example, the Student Non-Violent Coordinating Committee, Southern Christian Leadership Conference, National Association for the Advancement of Colored People, Congress of Racial Equality, Black Panthers, American Indian Movement, La Raza Unita, National Organization for Women, National Abortion Rights Action League, or National Association for the Legalization of Marijuana.

7. Identify someone in your community who has effected a change that has had a direct impact on you, your family, or your friends or neighbors. Go to your local library or newspaper morgue and review the clipping file on this person; arrange for an interview if you can. Report on what motivated the person, what resources she or he had to make this effort effective, what obstacles she or he had to overcome, and evaluate the value of this person's efforts.

CREDITS

Index